D1617167

Arms races, arms control, and conflict analysis

Arms races, arms control, and conflict analysis

Contributions from Peace Science
and Peace Economics

WALTER ISARD
Cornell University

Written with the assistance of
CHRISTINE SMITH
and

CHARLES H. ANDERTON
YASUSHI ASAMI
JAMES P. BENNETT
BRUCE BURTON
WILLIAM DEAN

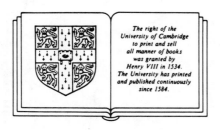

The right of the
University of Cambridge
to print and sell
all manner of books
was granted by
Henry VIII in 1534.
The University has printed
and published continuously
since 1584.

CAMBRIDGE UNIVERSITY PRESS
New York   New Rochelle   Melbourne   Sydney

Published by the Press Syndicate of the University of Cambridge
The Pitt Building, Trumpington Street, Cambridge CB2 1RP
32 East 57th Street, New York, NY 10022, USA
10 Stamford Road, Oakleigh, Melbourne 3166, Australia

First published 1988

Printed in the United States of America

Library of Congress Cataloging-in-Publication Data

Isard, Walter.
Arms races, arms control, and conflict analysis.
Bibliography: p.
Includes index.
1. Nuclear arms control – United States.
2. Nuclear arms control – Soviet Union.   3. Peace – Research.
I. Smith, Christine, 1956–   .   II. Anderton, Charles H.
III. Peace Science Society (International)   IV. Title.
JX1974.7.I74   1989   327.1'74   88–25833

ISBN 0-521-36297-0
ISBN 0-521-36842-1 (pbk).

British Library Cataloguing-in-Publication Data
Isard, Walter
Arms races, arms control, and conflict
analysis: contributions from Peace Science
and Peace Economics.
1. Peace. Maintenance
I. Title   II. Smith, Christine, *1956–*
327.1'72

ISBN 0-521-36297-0
ISBN 0-521-36842-1 (pbk).

To my grandchildren,
whose grandchildren will, I hope,
have grandchildren to whom
they can dedicate their books

Contents

xiv   **Contents**

List of illustrations

List of tables

Preface

Born shortly after World War I, I has seen immense changes during my life – changes whose immensity has been no greater perhaps than in the destructive capability of military weaponry. It is still unimaginable to me how mankind could have allowed technology to develop from a simple airplane that could drop a bomb that on average would result in a few casualties to a modern bomber that can launch missiles capable of annihilating probably hundreds of thousands if not millions with horrible after-effects upon many more millions. If such an increase in destructive capability is possible in one's lifetime, I shudder to think what this capability will be when the grandchildren of my grandchildren write their books. Yet, I remain optimistic and hope that this book will make a contribution, however limited, to the most pressing problem of mankind – arms control – and that the grandchildren of my grandchildren also will be able to make their contributions to the solution of critical social problems.

It is difficult to say exactly when the ideas contained in this book began to take form in my mind. Certainly a desire to say something hopefully of value for averting wars and controlling international conflicts was well advanced when colleagues and I founded the Peace Research Society (International) in 1963 in Malmo, Sweden, later renamed the Peace Science Society (International). The Peace Science Society (International) is an international association for the advancement of peace research and related studies. The society operates as an objective, scientific organization without political, social, financial, or nationalistic bias. Its main objectives are to foster exchange of ideas and promote studies focusing on peace analysis and utilizing tools, methods, and theoretical frameworks specifically designed for peace research as well as concepts, procedures, and analytical techniques of the various social and natural sciences, law, engineering, and other disciplines and professions. The society supports these objectives by promoting acquaintance and discussion among its members and with scholars from all fields and regions of the world, by stimulating research, by encouraging the publication of scholarly studies, and by performing services to aid the advancement of its members and peace research.

Since the formation of the society I have been exposed to the thinking on conflict management, arms control, disarmament, and so on, of various scholars from various disciplines. To all of them I am indebted, for almost unavoidably over the last quarter of a century or so I have been absorbing their ideas. Thus this book is primarily a presentation of their ideas, hopefully ordered in a fairly systematic fashion, and not a potpourri of ideas. Many of their ideas are contained in the 29 volumes of *Papers* published by the Peace Science Society (International), later replaced by the *Journal of Peace Science,* now renamed *Conflict Management and Peace Science.* There were, too, many other unpublished contributions made and presented by scholars at Peace Science and other conferences that have influenced my thinking.

This book has two aims. One is to provide some basic background on international conflicts – particularly the U.S.–Soviet arms control conflict – which hopefully will be of value in some way or other (perhaps provide one or two new insights) to scholars, active negotiators, political leaders, primarily by covering the relevant contributions of scholars in many disciplines. After all, no one knows all there is to know about the interplay of forces governing a major conflict, say, the U.S.–Soviet arms control conflict; and the broad coverage of forces contained in this book can serve an educational purpose for each of us. For example, consider two of the major figures deeply involved in the U.S.–Soviet negotiations on arms control (1986–7) while this book was being written: U.S. Secretary of State George Shultz, whom I got to know when both of us taught elementary economics at MIT using the Samuelson textbook in its first mimeographed form, and Ambassador Max Kampleman (Head, U.S. Delegation to Negotiations on Nuclear and Space Arms), who engaged in extensive discussions when we were fellow conscientious objectors at the Big Flats campsite during World War II. Both have brilliant minds, tremendous intellectual capacities, and enormous stocks of knowledge. Yet each could learn much about the U.S.–Soviet arms control problem from writings of scholars reported upon in this book.

The other aim, equally important, has been to help lay a sound foundation for the interdisciplinary field of Peace Science. I do not profess to cover all the relevant topics that should come under the umbrella of this discipline, only some of the key areas. There are undoubtedly several that have not been dealt with properly, for example, game theory and historical analysis. Some of these are noted and suggested in Chapters 14 and 15 of the book *Conflict Analysis and Practical Conflict Management Procedures* (Ballinger, Cambridge, Mass., 1982), written with Christine Smith, where a first attempt was made to define the field of Peace Science. I trust that younger scholars will come along to treat these topics adequately and handle better those covered in this manuscript.

At this point, it may be useful to suggest how different scholars and students might read this book most effectively. The present sequence of chapters is perhaps best for the nonmathematical reader. In Chapter 2, the difficult mathematics has by and large been confined to footnotes, and the more advanced chapters come in Part II of the book. The more advanced student and scholar might read the technical footnotes along with the text. He or she may also choose to read Chapter 13, on the synthesis of arms race models, immediately after Chapter 2, a survey of arms race models. The student may also want to read Chapter 14 (on learning by a group and its individual members), Chapter 15 (on information research and development from a dynamical systems viewpoint), and Chapter 16 (on invention and innovation in information research and development for problem solving) immediately after Chapter 6, on learning, problem solving, and information research and development. There are of course readers who may be interested in only one of the several basic topics covered by the book. Those interested in arms races only should find interesting materials in Chapters 2 and 13. Those interested in individual and group behavior and decision making should find relevant materials in Chapters 3–5. Those interested in learning, problem solving, and information development should read Chapters 6 and 14–16. Those interested in policy formulation and argumentation and the development of supporting data should read Chapters 7–9. Those interested in negotiations and mediation should read Chapter 10 and perhaps Chapter 11.

Acknowledgments

In writing this book, I am most indebted to Christine Smith. She not only wrote several chapters (7, 10, and 15) with me but spent many hours reading and rereading the manuscript; her exacting mind forced me to order consistently and state more precisely materials in a number of the chapters. To Charles H. Anderton I am indebted for writing Chapter 2 with me, which draws heavily upon his impressive doctoral dissertation at Cornell University, for developing an extensive and organized bibliography on arms race models, and for advice in writing Chapter 13. To James Bennett I am indebted for writing Chapter 8 with me, which draws upon much of Bennett's unpublished materials, which Blane Lewis helped me to organize. Yasushi Asami wrote Sections 7.6 and 7.7 and Appendixes 7.B and 7.C with me. William Dean coauthored Appendixes 9.A–9.D, Bruce Burton was extremely helpful in the development of materials in Chapter 16. Kai Michaelis helped develop the Appendix to Chapter 14, and Paul Kiwort assisted in writing Section 5.4. Helpful financial support was provided by the Peace Studies Program at Cornell University.

At the risk of failing to mention the many scholars whose analyses have influenced my thought, let me mention Norman Alcock, Heyward Alker, Kenneth Boulding, Nazli Choucri, Claudio Cioffi-Revista, Karl Deutsch, Roger Fisher, Bruce Fitzerald, Thomas Fogarty, Ralph Gentile, Douglas Johnson, Herbert Kelman, Lawrence Klein, Harold Lasswell, Wassily Leontief, Nancy Meiners, Richard Merritt, Robert North, Bruce Russett, Thomas Saaty, David Singer, Jan Tinbergen, Julian Wolpert, and Dina Zinnes.

To Priscilla Edsall and Helena Wood I am deeply indebted for their unending patience and excellent secretarial and art work in the preparation of the manuscript. I am grateful to Scott Keith Duncan for constructing with me the indexes. And once again, I must acknowledge the constant support, encouragement, and assistance from my wife, Caroline, in the writing of yet another long book.

Permission to reproduce materials from the articles "Arms Race Models: A Survey and Synthesis," "Social System Framework and Causal History: Part II, Behavior Under Stress and Cognition," "James P. Bennett on Subjunctive Reasoning, Policy Analysis and Political Argument," and "Social System Framework and Causal History: Part I, Learning Processes" in *Conflict Management and Peace Science,* Vol. 8, No. 2, Spring 1985, pp. 27–98; Vol. 6, No. 2, Spring 1982–3, pp. 59–93; Vol. 8, No. 1, Fall 1984, pp. 71–112; and Vol. 6, No. 1, Fall 1981, pp. 63–94, respectively, in Chapters 2, 4, 5, 8, and 14 is gratefully acknowledged.

Permission to reproduce material from "Elementary Locational Analysis in Policy Space," *Papers,* Regional Science Association, Vol. 45, 1980, pp. 17–44, and from *International and Regional Conflict: Analytic Approaches* (W. Isard and Y. Nagao), 1983, in Chapters 7 and 15, respectively, has been granted by the Regional Science Association and Ballinger Publishing Company, respectively.

CHAPTER 1

Introduction and overview

1.1   The structure of the book

As noted in the Preface, we aim with this book to provide a sound structure for study in the Peace Science field – a highly interdisciplinary field.
We wish to do so, however, in a way that ensures that the diverse analyses
we draw upon from the several relevant disciplines will be problem oriented and not just abstract in character. Hence we concentrate in the first
major chapter of this book (Chapter 2) on what is the most central and
most important problem area of Peace Science. This is the escalation and
deescalation of military expenditures, weapon accumulation and development, and arms control in general. We do so by a survey of arms race
models and the factors considered key in these models. Toward the end
of Part I, in Chapter 11, we attempt to indicate several important ways
in which the materials covered in the preceding chapters apply to the
U.S.–Soviet arms control conflict problem.

 We start in Chapter 2 with the classic Richardson model. Key extensions are taken up, including more satisfactory ways to link a nation's
arms expenditures to resource constraints (costs), the domestic economy
as a whole, forces for optimization and optimal control, diverse strategies
and different types of (needs for) weapons development (conventional,
nuclear, etc.), policies to reduce unemployment and utilize idle productive capacity in general, deficit and balance-of-payments problems, and
the impact of military expenditures on inflation and interest rates. The
effects of public opinion (negative and positive), the political party in
office, the grievances against and hostility toward its rivals, its ambition
and distrust of its opponents, as well as the extent of trade with them and
other factors are examined. The influence of the military expenditures
and weaponry stocks of a nation's allies and the allies of its rival upon its

own weapons development (for both attack and deterrence purposes) are considered as well as the possibilities of waging economic warfare – through forcing disinvestment upon its rival and the decline of its rival's productive capacity for weapon development. Uncertainty with respect to future weapons technology, psychological elements, the stocks and capability of its rival's weapons, the international climate, and the structure and functioning of the international system are among many other factors looked into as well as the play of organizational politics in determining the military budget for any given year.

Once Chapter 2 lays out in a systematic way the many factors that are considered significant in the extensive literature on arms races, we begin to probe still more deeply in Chapter 3 by examining the setting and forces that affect decision making by behaving units – say, by a Gorbachev, a Reagan, a legislative body, or any other of numerous units that may be involved. Such decision making accounts for specific levels of military expenditures, commands and orders that are issued, particular policies that are in effect, specific appropriations that have been approved, and so forth. The effect upon decision making of different attitudes – pessimistic, optimistic, conservative, mixed, that involving rational expectations – is examined with the use of a payoff matrix – as an economist or operations researcher might view the problem. Particular attention is given to situations when one or more other behaving units are involved so that *interdependent* decision making necessarily takes place. A preliminary look at how specific guiding principles and a particular conflict management procedure may be employed is taken. Decision making, however, is also related to diverse elements that cognitive scientists emphasize – mental representations including scripts, schema, stories, and the like; mental retrieval structures; the existence and persistence of decision-making pathologies; and the limitations of the brain as an information-processing mechanism.

The approaches of economics, operations research, cognitive science, and other disciplines are brought together in a more formal manner in Chapter 4. There the effect upon the selection of an action or decision is related to a behaving unit's action space, restrictions imposed upon it, its perceptions of these (and various magnitudes and other elements), its expectations, the number and kinds of things it is attending to (and can attend to), summary cues, its relevant beliefs, its active and total memory, its aspirations, its utility (welfare) function, its learning *(ex post)* from experience (when, e.g., comparing perceived outcomes with those expected), and learning *(ex ante)* from search activity. When the behaving unit is a group, interpretive packages are extremely important.

Chapter 4 deals with decision making in noncrisis situations. In crisis situations such typically takes place under conditions of much greater stress and anxiety. As discussed in Chapter 5, when under psychological stress, a behaving unit frequently fails to conduct vigilant information processing. Instead it may adopt a stress-coping strategy, such as unconflicted adherence to a policy, defensive avoidance, and hypervigilance (associated with a state of panic). It is subject to cognitive closure, or cognitive constriction (failing to recognize all available options), selective forgetting, and procrastination and may shift responsibility, distort the meaning of warning messages, and the like. When the behaving unit is a group, it is subject to "groupthink," involving such elements as illusions of invulnerability, unquestioned belief in the group's inherent morality and rectitude, and the like.

Against this background of ways in which individuals and groups behave, we proceed in Chapter 6 to examine the matter of problem solving. Whether or not behaving units are aware of at least some of the shortcomings in their thinking, they frequently recognize the need for creative problem solving. Clearly, this need exists in the U.S.–Soviet arms control conflict situation. What can various disciplines tell us about creative problem solving? A cognitive scientist might consider a need for creative problem solving as a need to go from an ill-defined mental model to one that is well-defined with a solution and to do so by exploiting (developing) intradomain analogies as well as interdomain ones (from other fields than that of the current problem). An artificial intelligence (AI) scholar might employ a means–end approach, fully exploiting the computational and memory capabilities of the computer and exploring all kinds of heuristics in a search for a solution. The economist would conduct information R&D (research and development) using a broadly defined benefit–cost approach. Information (taken as a commodity) from sample surveys and other signals would be considered as investment, since such information adds to the *stock* of knowledge. All these approaches and others are discussed in some detail, and evaluations are made regarding their applicability – with a view for their use in creative conflict management to be discussed in a later chapter.

Whereas the materials of Chapters 3–6 relate to behavior of individuals and other units, when we focus upon the major conflicts that arise in the international arena – as for example the U.S.–Soviet arms control conflict – we need to have more specific information and understanding about how political leaders, as key figures, behave. Hence in Chapter 7 we undertake this task where we view each type of policy as measurable along a dimension. So, when a leader needs to confront a number of policies, he or she may be regarded as choosing a position in policy space. Using basic concepts of location theory and regional science, we analyze how a leader finds (or hopes to find) a position in policy space that maximizes the probability that he or she will be in power. We view the leader in competition with other political leaders and being both affected by and affecting public opinion. We also consider the possibility that via sample surveys and other measures he or she may be motivated to acquire information, taking into account all costs and benefits.

Having found what he or she considers to be an optimal position in policy space (optimal set of policies), a key political leader (or group) still has the problem of setting forth an effective political argument. A constituency, at times a world constituency, needs to be convinced of the soundness of one or more of the proposed policies. Thus in Chapter 8 we investigate the basic elements of a political argument – claims, grounds, warrants, backing, qualifiers, and counterrebuttals – and the problems of developing them and putting them together in an effective way, especially in complex political situations. We illustrate by examining arguments for the "'no first use' of nuclear weapons in the European theater" policy.

Basic to grounds for a political argument are data. In complex economic and political situations much data exists but also a great deal must be estimated (forecast, projected). Consequently, a sound political argument must have such data generated and must have models to do this. Hence, in Chapter 9, we examine the use of models for this purpose; and since we largely focus on international conflicts, we examine such world models as the Leontief–United Nations World Input–Output model, the Computable General Equilibrium model (once strongly supported by the World Bank), the Klein–LINK econometric model (Wharton School origin), and the GLOBUS model (Western German support). We evaluate their potentials (currently and when improved in the future) for generating data that negotiators might like to have on outcomes of different scenarios that they might like to consider – for example the outcomes of a "reduced military expenditures scenario." That is, we examine as best we can what models can say and what they cannot say.

With our understanding of behavior of individuals and groups (developed in Chapters 3–5), of approaches to problem solving that behaving units may adopt (Chapter 6), of forces that affect the position that key behaving units – political leaders and groups – take on different policy issues (Chapter 7), and of arguments they may develop (Chapter 8) supported by data generated by models (Chapter 9), we come to what some analysts may consider the last step – namely, the use of principles of negotiation and mediation when political leaders (such as Reagan and Gorbachev) and more generally behaving units come together to iron out differences, to manage a conflict. In the first part of Chapter 10 we set down diverse principles that have been put forward, and we examine them in the context of possible key characteristics of conflict situations. In the second part, we launch into the problem of identifying appropriate conflict management procedures given the key characteristics of a conflict situation and the principles of negotiation and mediation that participants have adopted or are prone to. We take into account the properties they have and the properties required of them. The use of each conflict management procedure may also be viewed as a scenario to be inputted into world system and other models – especially in the case of conflict among advanced, industralized nations with sophisticated, research-oriented negotiators. These models then yield data on outcomes that together with a scenario as input data can be examined for political and economic feasibility of that scenario and for comparing the relative desirability of different scenarios and their associated conflict management procedures.

Against the background of all the findings and analyses of the preceding chapters we attempt in Chapter 11 to see what we can say about the current U.S.–Soviet arms control conflict problem. As we note, the INF treaty constitutes just a very small step in the right direction. Not being specialists on this problem, we only attempt to identify some basic properties of an effective conflict management procedure for this problem. We do not have any illusions as to the value of what we discuss. Clearly, this problem requires the creative development of a basic new conflict management procedure. What we say may provide some insight useful for the design of such a procedure. The contents of this chapter may perhaps be considered "obvious" to some of those actively engaged in the negotiations on this problem or in scholarly writing about it. However, there is no question whatsoever that *for all* there is some value to the study and reading of the materials in the previous chapters upon which the contents of Chapter 11 are based. To reiterate what was said in the Preface, anyone professing to speak on this subject as an informed policy analyst, negotiator, or scholar would be remiss in not checking with the analytical thinking of the distinguished scholars from diverse disciplines reported upon in this book – thereby to search for new insights.

Chapter 12 is a summary chapter, where we pull together the findings and analyses of the several chapters in a way that may be useful to the reader. For us, it closes the circle in that we start with a survey of arms race models and end with exploring properties for use in the design of an effective conflict management procedure to treat the U.S.–Soviet arms control conflict problem arising from the arms race between these two nations.

Chapters 13–16 are on more technical materials as indicated in the Preface. In order, they cover (13) a synthesis of arms race models, (14) a model of learning by a group and its members, (15) a model of information production (and investment in information) by protagonists and a mediator to effect the management of a conflict, and (16) an exploratory model relating the demand and supply of creative ideas and information for invention and innovation of new conflict management procedures. They illustrate the depth Peace Science as a discipline must seek on many relevant subjects (topics), and for the time being these chapters must be considered as relevant for advanced scholars who may be specialized in or deeply interested in the topics covered.

Before concluding this section, we should note that the conflict related to arms races and arms control is not the only conflict to whose analysis and management the field of Peace Science can contribute. We take up this conflict in order to ensure, as indicated earlier, that the diverse analyses we draw upon will be problem oriented and not just abstract in character; and we concentrate on it in order to achieve as much analytical depth as we are able to. However, there are innumerable international conflicts in whose management Peace Science can contribute. There has been and will continue to be conflicts over the use of ocean resources (the Law of the Sea problem). There are and will continue to be the age-old conflicts over possession of territory: the current Soviet–Mainland China border disputes, the India–Pakistan dispute over Kashmir, the Middle East conflict regarding a homeland for the Palestine Liberation Organization (PLO), the recent Falkland Island war, and many, many more. There are and will continue to be major conflicts over the environment, restrictions on its pollution, regulations of its exploitation and use, and other policies aimed at maintaining and enhancing its quality; for example, the conflicts associated with the current acid rain problem between the United States and Canada and among European nations. There are and will continue to be major conflicts relating to the areas of trade among nations – over tariff policies, dumping, quotas, and the like – and to the monetary and fiscal policy of key nations since via capital flows and trade such policy can have a major effect on the economy of other nations.

It is unnecessary to list the many other international problems that give rise to conflicts to whose management the analyses of Peace Science can contribute. Likewise, we can list unendingly noninternational problems where Peace Science analyses can contribute. Within a nation, there are constantly conflicts over different policies (growth, environmental quality, energy, housing, resource development, taxes, education, etc.) that its several regions demand, that interest groups representing different economic sectors lobby for, that different ethnic and religious groups advocate, and so forth. The problems examined by different social science fields, law, engineering, and other professions frequently relate to these kinds of conflicts for which peace science tools, approaches, and methods are relevant.

Clearly, the interactive behavior that takes place in the conflict situations just noted and in numerous others is quite similar to the interactive behavior among nations involved in the arms race and arms control conflict. The organizational politics model we succinctly present in Chapter 2 with respect to reaching a decision on the level of military expenditures applies to decisions pertaining to the expenditures level on diverse governmental programs, as will become evident in Chapter 13. The approaches to decision-making analyses in Chapters 3 and 4 are generally applicable to those in other conflict situations as are also the problem-solving approaches, the policy space analyses, and the political argument discussion of Chapters 6, 7, and 8, respectively. The discussion pertaining to world models presented in Chapter 9 as relevant to major disarmament as a shock to the world economy is also relevant for other types of shocks – such as a major change in tariff policies (structure), or a major effort at ocean resource development, or major regulation of the environment, or even a moratorium on third world debt. Likewise, the discussion of Chapter 10 on principles of negotiation and mediation is generally applicable to diverse conflict situations, and so are the discussions on information research and development and learning in Chapters 14–16.

1.2   The nature of Peace Science

As the title of this book suggests, the analyses to be developed represent contributions from the field of Peace Science. For those scholars and practitioners who may be interested, we briefly sketch here the nature and scope of this field.

Peace Science is by and large an interdisciplinary field. It aims to develop a balanced combination of theory and methods (tools, models, and the like) and a record of significant applications. As an interdisciplinary field it draws heavily upon the theories and methods of existing disciplines – political science, sociology, economics, regional science and geography, psychology and the newly emerging cognitive sciences, operations research and applied mathematics, law, and other scientific and professional areas. Being a fledgling field, it has not yet had a chance to develop a full array of its own basic theories and a well-rounded kit of tools. However, as will be shortly pointed out, it has a unique core, and we can point to solid development of theories and tools at and about this core. Also, because of its youth, we cannot point to a number of significant applications. But the need for its theories and methods is crystal clear. Witness the major international conflicts – for example, the Middle East conflicts or the U.S.–Soviet ones to which we often refer in this book. The existence of these conflicts and the hitherto inadequate ability of society to cope with them clearly points up the failure of the existing disciplines and professions – those already mentioned and others – to manage, let alone resolve, these conflicts. Thus the need for the interdisciplinary field of Peace Science – the need to draw upon the many strengths of the theories and methods of existing disciplines and professions, to fuse these strengths in compatible and feasible ways, and to develop from careful probing and dissection of the existing fields and disciplines the elements to provide scaffolding for new and more effective theory and method.

Elsewhere (Isard and Smith 1982, Chaps. 14 and 15; Isard 1979, 1980) we have defined the field of Peace Science. The core was envisioned as orthogonal (perpendicular) to many existing fields such as economics, regional science and geography, political science, psychology, and sociology, having much in common with at least some of these in the area of intersections. Succinctly we may present the Peace Science field as a knowledge system comprising three major intimately interrelated (interconnected, interdependent) subsystems. There is first the Economic (Production–Consumption–Trade) subsystem designated P (see Figure 1.1a,b). This subsystem links relevant variables and the theories and methods pertaining to them that come from the disciplines of economics, regional science and geography, operations research and applied mathematics, and, of course, closely related parts of other disciplines and professions. Thus if we are concerned with a major conflict among nations, we construct for nation J a P^J box and a corresponding box for every other nation. The P^J box in Figure 1.1a is concerned with key variables such as nation J's arms production, foregone consumption, capacity to produce both civilian and military goods based on human and natural resources as well as plant and equipment, inflationary tendencies from deficit spending caused by heavy military expenditures, the basic material needs of its population, and the like. (More generally, the items that might appear in the P^J box would be production, consumption, income generation and distribution, investment, price formation, etc.) Each nation's production system (the P^J, P^K, P^L, $\cdots$ boxes) is interconnected with the $\mathcal{R}$ box of Figure 1.1a as indicated by arrows, providing inputs to and receiving feedback from it. The $\mathcal{R}$ box is concerned with key variables such as military assistance, trade, exchange rates, development aid, capital flows, and the like – selected magnitudes that charac-

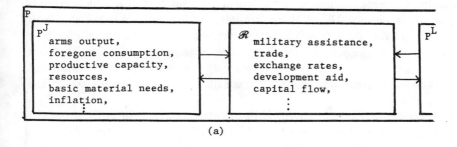

(a)

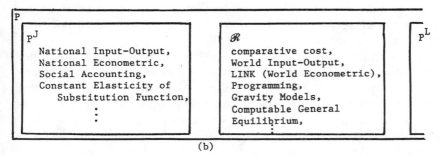

(b)

Figure 1.1. (a) Selected variables of the national and world economic (Production–Consumption–Trade) subsystem P. (b) Selected methods (models) for the analysis of the behavior of the P subsystem variables and for the projection of their magnitude.

terize a global economy, its spatial distribution and location patterns, world markets, and related structure. All these boxes together with their interconnections comprise the P subsystem.

Whereas Peace Science is concerned with these selected and other key variables of the global system, the focus of Peace Science is on theories and methods (tools and models) that allow us to understand the interrelations of these variables, their levels, and changes in these levels resulting from changes in policies, joint actions, and in general minor or major shocks. Hence in Figure 1.1b we list selected relevant methods of analysis, all of which will be discussed in what follows, at least to some extent. Thus in the P^J box we note National Input–Output, National Econometric, and Social Accounting models and methods, the use of constant elasticity of substitution functions, and the like. And in the $\mathcal{R}$ box, we note Comparative Cost (as governing arms and other trade), World Input–Output, LINK (world Econometric), Programming, Gravity, and Computable General Equilibrium models and methods and the like. Under-lying most, if not all, of these models and methods are theories and hypotheses that have found general acceptance or have been validated or both. Since we wish to ensure that this book is problem oriented and not just abstract in character, we shall largely discuss models and methods and the associated analyses rather than their theoretical bases and tested hypotheses.

A second major subsystem of the Peace Science field is the C or, in general, the Cognitive (Decision-Making, Policy Formation) subsystem. The C^J box for nation J, and the corresponding box for every other nation, is concerned with key sociological, psychological, and political variables and elements such as attitudes (hostility, competitiveness, etc.), perceptions and misperceptions, stress-coping strategies and decision-making pathologies, scripts, schema and stories, perspectives, expecta-tions, aspirations, interpretive packages (groupthink), public opinion, and the like (see Figure 1.2a). Each nation's cognitive system is intercon-nected, as indicated by arrows with the J box, providing inputs to and receiving feedback from it. The J box refers to the international arena wherein key variables and elements are arms control policies, interna-tional tension, tariff and other trade policies, international monetary sta-bility and exchange rate fluctuation, World Bank policy, ocean resource development, United Nations operations, and the like. Again, see Figure 1.2a. For the analysis of (1) the level and changes in the level of the pre-ceding cognitive-type variables, (2) existing policies and changes in them as well as the emergence of new policies, and (3) other elements, we record selected methods in Figure 1.2b. Thus in the C^J box we record policy space analyses, learning models, AI and other problem-solving techniques (such as intradomain analogies), information research and development, organizational politics models, negotiation principles, and the like. In the J box we list arms race models, conflict management pro-cedures, GLOBUS (and other world models such as FUGI, internation simulation) where the emphasis is more on noneconomic rather than eco-nomic variables, coalition analyses, bargaining (game) theory, mediation principles, and the like, although some of the items in the J box are also relevant for the C^J box and vice versa.

The third basic subsystem of Peace Science is the information subsys-tem M. This contains all knowledge – historical events and interpreta-tions, all data sets (such as that of the Correlates of War Project), all the-ories, all hypotheses, validated or not, all know-how or methods, and so on. We could list here all these items and others and also indicate the more limited (filtered) knowledge base possessed by and accessible by nation J and every nation with boxes M^J, M^K, $\cdots$, but such is unnec-

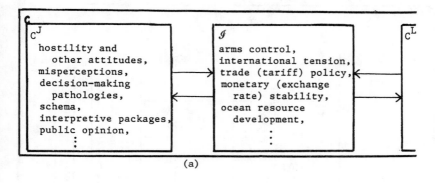

(a)

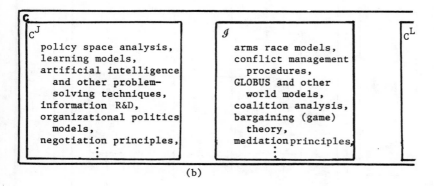

(b)

Figure 1.2. (a) Selected variables and elements of the national and international cognitive, decision-making, policy formation subsystem C. (b) Selected methods (models) for the analysis of (1) the behavior of variables, (2) policies and their changes, and (3) other elements within the C subsystem.

essary. However in Figure 1.3 we present an overall sketch of the Peace Science field, indicating the interconnections (via inputs and feedbacks) of the diverse boxes and their elements. As detailed elsewhere (Isard and Smith 1982, Chaps. 14, 15; Isard 1979, 1980), we view the core of Peace Science as comprising the elements in the $\mathcal{M}$, $\mathcal{J}$, and $\mathcal{R}$ boxes and the connections with elements in other boxes. The $\mathcal{M}$, $\mathcal{J}$, $\mathcal{R}$ boxes form a vertical set orthogonal to (1) the P subsystem wherein by and large lie economics and regional science and economic geography and (2) the C subsystem wherein by and large lie sociology, political science, and psychology and the cognitive sciences.

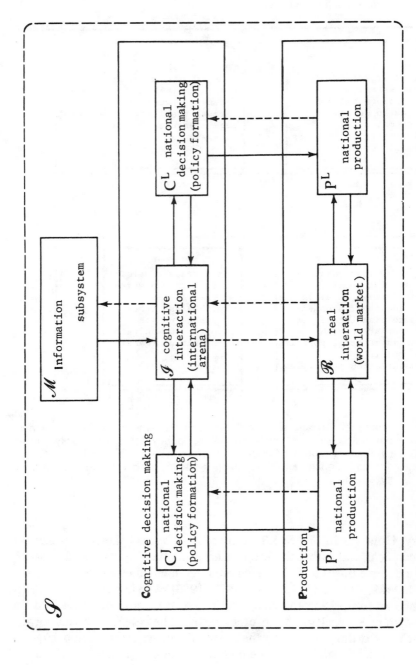

Figure 1.3. A system's structure.

The preceding represents one sketch of the Peace Science field. Doubtless, other scholars have other conceptions. More significantly, given experience with applications, the field will take on a more highly focused and recognizable structure and define for itself its future directions.

References

Isard, W. (1979) "A Definition of Peace Science, the Queen of the Social Sciences, Part I." *Journal of Peace Science* 4:1–47.

Isard, W. (1980) "A Definition of Peace Science, the Queen of the Social Sciences, Part II." *Journal of Peace Science* 4:97–132.

Isard, W., and C. Smith (1982) *Conflict Analysis and Practical Conflict Management Procedures.* Cambridge, MA: Ballinger.

Basic framework and set of analyses

CHAPTER 2

A survey of arms race models

Written with Charles H. Anderton

2.1   Introduction

As noted previously, we focus in this chapter on a survey of arms race models. Escalation and deescalation of military expenditures, weapon accumulation and development, and arms control in general are the most central and most important problem areas of Peace Science. We choose to concentrate on these problem areas in the first major chapter of this book in order to ensure that the diverse analyses we draw upon from the several relevant disciplines and professions will be problem oriented and not just abstract in character.

There exists a wealth of arms race models, and in this chapter we shall discuss key elements of many of them. However, it is desirable first to consider the definition of an arms race since many factors have been set forth as relevant for the analysis and understanding of past and current arms races.

As can be expected, there is no common, accepted definition of an arms race. One definition (Anderton 1986) takes an arms race to be "a situation where two or more parties change the quantity or quality of their armed forces in response to perceived past, current or anticipated future increases in the quantity or quality of armed forces of the other party(ies)" (p. 9). This definition includes situations wherein each nation reacts positively to the other and in particular increases its military expenditures when the other does. Each may do so in order to

1. reduce insecurity (reflecting a balance-of-power motivation);
2. retaliate for the insecurity caused it by the other's increased military expenditures, thereby increasing the insecurity of the other nation (reflecting a balance-of-terror motivation);
3. counteract the ambition of the other [e.g., when the other is led

by a power-driven élite or when there exists system competition (as has been the case with the United States and USSR) based on ideology, religion, or other factors; here, one nation may be the aggressor (initiator) and the other a follower (imitator), or both may be aggressors with propensity to initiate]; and/or

4. be in a position of strength (greater strength) when negotiations on arms control are expected in the future (as characterized the position of Reagan in many of the years of his administration).

This definition also includes situations wherein misperceptions regarding the aggressive (or cooperative) intentions of nations result when cultural differences, distorted and technical breakdown of communications, and other structural factors cause

1. mutual perceptions of threat from the mere existence of military capabilities; or
2. misperceptions regarding the intentions of one or more nations; or
3. extreme attitudes (e.g., excessive conservatism) leading to worst case analysis or unbounded and unfounded optimism (e.g., associated with religious fanaticism).

However, the preceding definition does exclude from arms races those situations where one or more parties incur military expenditures to affect the internal social–political–economic state of a nation [as was the case when President Kennedy, in keeping with the analysis of the brilliant economist Paul Samuelson, proposed to increase military expenditures to buoy up the U.S. economy (Matusow 1984, p. 42) or when Hitler, coming into power in Germany's extremely severe depression period of the thirties, embarked on a major military buildup in order to shock the economy out of its doldrums (Toland 1976)]. This definition also excludes situations where increases in military expenditures result from pressures to maintain or increase the political and economic power base of the existing military–industrial complex – that is, from bureaucratic-type forces aimed at both survival and growth, including situations where the military–industrial complexes of two adversaries collude and via mutually directed misinformation generate increased insecurity in each other's nation to achieve thereby their requests for enlarged budgets.

Whereas one expects in an arms race that an adversary's arms expenditure will increase as a given nation increases its military effort, the reaction may in fact be negative – that is, lead to decreases, as will be noted in the submissiveness models to be sketched. Also, whereas two nations may both be increasing their arms budgets, this may simply reflect a complementary effort and not an arms race phenomenon, for example, when one nation specializes in bomber production and its ally specializes in small-fighter production (as was the case with the United States and Britain in the post–World War II years in order to *maintain* their defensive or attack capability under conditions of technological change).

Further, one may distinguish among arms races that reflect policies for

1. preparation for war (or some form of aggression),
2. prevention of war (as is claimed for current deterrence efforts), and
3. conduct of a surrogate war [as in the supposed economic warfare that some claim the United States is currently (1987) conducting vis-à-vis the Soviet Union].

The preceding discussion at best represents some initial considerations relevant for the development of a proper definition of the concept of arms race and the many distinctions and classifications that must be made (e.g., see Gantzel 1973; and Fogarty 1987). We do not attempt such in this book since this itself would involve a book-length manuscript. Rather we proceed in this chapter to undertake a survey of arms race models, partly chronological and partly in order of analytical depth. Of course, in examining specific arms race situations of reality (wherein the hostility element has been formally established), one finds many complexities. One finds that *real* arms race elements reflective of military policy are mixed up with other elements reflective of other policy issues so that the analysis and understanding of a specific so-called arms race situation is simply not achievable by a pure arms race model. This will be evident as we conduct the survey and as we go through the analyses pertaining to conflict situations in general in the succeeding chapters.

In the next section, we present the classic Richardson model, the first basic analysis of an arms race, and some extensions of this model. In section 2.3 we consider in more detail the play of scarce resources, the ties to the domestic economy, and the possibility of a disequilibrium and partial adjustment process in the realization of a desired stock of weaponry. Section 2.4 introduces utility optimization behavior for a nation. It is first examined in terms of a static trade-off between civilian goods and security based on both a deterrence and an attack capability with the rival's weapons stock taken as given. Next, an optimal time path of resources to be allocated to the military is considered when (1) the rival's time path in weaponry stocks is given and (2) the rival's time path of resources allocated to the military is strategically managed, which then poses a differential game problem.

Strategy is more closely examined in models sketched in section 2.5. Deterrence and attack capabilities are more precisely defined, zones of mutual deterrence and of attack initiation are established, and numbers of casualties, decision rules, and a hypothetical missile war and its payoff are introduced. Economic warfare based on resource exhaustion and the impact on deescalation of nonthreatening weapons that reduce the negative externalities imposed on a rival are examined. In section 2.6, models with races in both conventional and strategic weapons are reviewed.

Section 2.7 takes up a number of diverse elements. Asymmetries in the possible behavior of nations, the effect of uncertainty on military expenditures, the issue of secrecy and intelligence efforts, and the play of technology are considered. Different treatments of international tension and hostility and their impact are reviewed as well as the significance of the closely related variables of diplomatic climate and diplomatic time and psychological factors such as insecurity, distrust, and suspicion.

Section 2.8 takes up the short-run reality of organizational politics, one study for the United States involving the Defense Services Agencies, the Office of the President, Congress, and the Department of Defense. Although each of these units (interest groups) has a most desired level of military spending, each is realistic and arrives at a budget request or a demand for only a partial attainment of that level based on rules, expectations, and/or the preceding year's realization.

In section 2.9 we review briefly models that cover a number of domestic political economy factors considered significant for arms expenditures, such as unemployment rate, distribution of income, balance of payments, deficits, rate of inflation, level of private consumption and investment, economic planning cycle, public opinion and concern, domestic violence, and foreign aid.

Section 2.10 reviews the literature on n-nation systems and alliances. Its framework permits better analysis of collective security and a "balancing-of-power" position that a nation might take. Also, the impact of the military–industrial complex as a coalition is examined.

In section 2.11 we broaden the scope of our survey of arms races to cover those models that view military expenditures as one of a set of basic political and economic variables of a nation that are interconnected with similar basic variables of other nations within the world system, thereby yielding a world system model.

We do not attempt synthesis in this chapter. Because of the need for more advanced analyses, that task is undertaken in Chapter 13.

2.2   The classic Richardson model and key extensions

The classic Richardson model for two opposing nations, say J and L, states in words that the change in J's military expenditures is equal to J's reaction coefficient times the military expenditures M^L of L reduced by an amount obtained by multiplying a cost-type coefficient c^J times J's military expenditures M^J and increased by an amount g^J reflecting a grievance-type factor. When empirical studies are conducted to test this model, this relationship often takes a measure of a change in J's military expenditures for a given year (or other time period) t, namely $\Delta M^J(t)$, and relates it to the level in the previous year (or other time period) designated $t - 1$ of L's military expenditures, namely $M^L(t - 1)$. So in equation form we have

$$\Delta M^J(t) = \rho^J M^L(t - 1) - c^J M^J + g^J \qquad (2.2.1)$$

In this equation, the reaction coefficient ρ^J of a nation J reflects its need for security, its distrust of the other, its need to be aggressive (to have effective attack capability), all per unit level of the other's military expenditures (sometimes called defenses or armaments). Necessarily the units of ρ^J is military expenditures of J per unit of L's expenditures. The second term on the right side of Eq. (2.2.1) typically represents the drag (a negative effect) on the time rate of change in a nation's military expenditures that the level of those expenditures has. The coefficients c^J represent a cost (expense) or a fatigue (or an equivalent burden or restraint factor of some sociopoliticoeconomic character) measured in dollars (or equivalent) per unit of M^J, respectively. The third term g^J represents the effect on ΔM^J of grievance that nation has regarding its opponent, its ambition, or the state of international tension (Richardson 1960; Zinnes 1976; Zinnes, Gillespie, and Rubison 1976a; Hamblin et al. 1977; Hollist 1977a,b; Cusack and Ward 1981; Stoll 1982), all measured in terms of dollars (or equivalent).

Whereas Eq. (2.2.1) may be used in empirical studies and does reflect a time lag in reaction of one nation's behavior to another's behavior, which very often typifies reality, it does not permit the use of calculus to obtain certain insights relevant to arms race phenomena. Accordingly, Richardson and others adept in the use of mathematics have found it convenient and helpful to reduce the time periods involved to time points (more accurately to infinitesimally small units of time) so that they can substitute the time rate of change $\dot{M}^J(t)$ of J's military expenditures for $\Delta M^J(t)$ and replace $M^L(t - 1)$ with $M^L(t)$. Thus, Eq. (2.2.1) for J and the corresponding equation for L in reaction to J become in the Richardson arms race model

$$\dot{M}^J(t) = \rho^J M^L(t) - c^J M^J(t) + g^J(t) \qquad (2.2.2a)$$
$$\dot{M}^L(t) = \rho^L M^J(t) - c^L M^L(t) + g^L(t) \qquad (2.2.2b)$$

The reader should keep in mind the instantaneous-reaction assumption of this Richardson model, which is unrealistic for many arms race situations.

At times we may replace Eq. (2.2.2a) with Eq. (2.2.3), where we may conveniently suppress the t symbol since all the magnitudes refer to the same point of time:

$$\dot{M}^J = \rho^J(M^L - M^J) - c^J M^J + g^J \tag{2.2.3}$$

where the reaction embodied in the ρ^J coefficient is to the difference $M^L - M^J$ in military expenditures (Richardson 1960; Hollist 1977a,b). When the equations of both nations are of this form, they have been taken to describe a *rivalry* model. When

$$\dot{M}^J = \rho^J M^L[1 - \omega(M^L - M^J)] - c^J M^J + g^J \tag{2.2.4}$$

is taken to replace Eq. (2.2.2a) with a similar type of equation replacing Eq. (2.2.2b), we have the *submissiveness* model. The larger is M^L relative to M^J, the greater the negative effect on $\dot{M}^J$, ceteris paribus; also the larger the value of ω, the greater this effect, again ceteris paribus (Richardson 1960; Smoker 1964, 1967; Zinnes, Gillespie, and Schrodt 1976b; Hollist 1977a,b; Hollist and Guetzkow 1978).

Another variant of the Richardson model considers the sum $M^J + M^L$ and the time rate of change of this sum (see Richardson 1960; Smoker 1966, 1967a,b). This variant has been sharply criticized (e.g., see Schrodt and Rubison 1973; Zinnes and Gillespie 1973; Wagner, Perkins, and Taagepera 1975).

It has been clearly recognized that the reaction factor may apply not only to the level of military expenditures but also to the level of military stocks of weaponry (military capability), hitherto designated S^J and S^L (Lambelet 1975; Rattinger 1976b; Taagepera 1979–80; Ward 1984a,b). Where the reaction is to stocks, we may substitute S^J for M^J and S^L for M^L in Eqs. (2.2.2a) and (2.2.2b), respectively. In this case, the reaction coefficients ρ^J and ρ^L are military expenditures per unit of military stocks. The $\dot{M}^J$ and $\dot{M}^L$ in the new equations then need to be translated into $\dot{S}^J$ and $\dot{S}^L$ in order to reflect the change in stocks from one point of time to the next; accordingly, two "definitional"-type equations are required. Often these have not been presented. Moreover, when stocks are involved, necessarily the question of depreciation and replacement of obsolete weaponry must be faced (Brito 1972; Taagepera 1979–80; Ward 1984a,b). Accordingly, we have

$$\dot{S}^Q(t) = M^Q(t)/p^Q - \alpha S^Q(t) \qquad Q = J, L \tag{2.2.5}$$

where p^Q is in terms of dollars per unit stock. It translates dollar expenditures M^Q into military stock and may be viewed as the price or cost of a "composite" unit of stock. The coefficient α is a depreciation (obsolescence) rate. Note that the change in stocks is related to total military expenditure at time t.[1] Hence, in the basic behavioral equation, say, for nation J, M^J may be taken to replace $\dot{M}^J$:

$$M^J = \bar{\rho}^J S^L - c^J M^J + g^J \tag{2.2.6}$$

which states that the level of military expenditures (rather than its time rate of change) is related to the opponent's stock, costs, and grievance. But, in other situations, a model with $\dot{M}^J$ as the relevant dependent variable may be justified (also see Taagepera 1979–80; Ward 1984a,b).[2]

Whereas the reaction, fatigue, and grievance parameters in the preceding equations are typically taken to be positive, they can indeed be negative and be associated with theoretically meaningful behavior (Zinnes et al. 1976a; Siljack 1976, 1977a; Schrodt 1978a; Taagepera 1979–80; Liossatos 1980). For example, when g^J is negative, it is often viewed as a measure of cooperation or friendliness (Wagner et al. 1975; Zinnes et al. 1976a; Stoll 1982).

Additionally, levels of military expenditures or stocks in ratio form (i.e., M^J/M^L or S^J/S^L) and their inverses may be used to establish goals and thus lead to a ratio goal model (Huntington 1958; Moll 1974; Chatterjee 1975a; Lambelet 1975; Wallace 1976, 1978; Wallace and Wilson 1978).[3] This model can be related to the rivalry model of Eq. (2.2.3) when the fatigue and grievance elements can be omitted or considered negligible.

Finally, time lags can be recognized where one nation reacts to the magnitudes depicting the state (military expenditures or stocks) of a second nation in one or more previous time periods. When the reaction is to past military expenditures and the weaponry produced by these expenditures are properly depreciated, this reaction may be viewed as a reaction to the accumulated stock of the second nation. See, among others, Gillespie, Zinnes and Rubison (1978) and Majeski and Jones (1981). Hill (1978) discusses such time lags and their implications for stability.

2.3   The effects of resource constraints and linkage to the domestic economy

In the Richardson model, the term $-c^J M^J$ relates the arms race to the economy, sometimes stated in terms of (1) dollar costs, (2) the use of

---

[1] Alternatively, we could let the change in stock be related to the amount of military expenditures in previous years which result in new weaponry during the current year.
[2] Note that by substitution of the value for M^J from Eq. (2.2.6) into Eq. (2.2.5), we obtain

$$\dot{S}^J(t) = [(\bar{\rho}^J S^L(t) - c^J M^J(t) + g^J(t))/p^J] - \alpha S^J(t) \tag{2.2.7}$$

[3] In this connection, also see Zinnes and Gillespie (1973) and Zinnes, Gillespie, and Schrodt (1976a) for diverse threat terms.

scarce resources, or (3) GNP that is absorbed (taken away from "civilian peace time" uses). Also, as already mentioned, c^J may have a negative value so that the term $-c^J M^J$ leads to an increase in $\dot{M}^J$, ceteris paribus, as may obtain in an economy with extensive unemployed resources.

To an economist or a policy maker extremely sensitive to employment implications, regional economic impacts, social welfare effects, and the like, such a treatment of the linkage to the economy is too simplistic. An early extension by Caspary (1967) introduces a ceiling value $\overline{\overline{R}}^J$ on resources (in dollars) available for military purposes and $\bar{c}^J$ as the cost of maintaining a unit of stock. Therefore,

$$\overline{\overline{R}}^J - \bar{c}^J S^J = \overline{R}^J \qquad (2.3.1)$$

are the resources (in dollars) available for building new stock (procurement of new weapons). Hence, where the cost of desired new procurement (in the simple action–reaction Richardson model) exceeds the resources available for such, only part of that desired procurement is realizable, and a reformulation of the Richardson model is required.

In response to L's stock S^L of weapons, let S^{J*} represent J's desired level of military stocks (existing stocks plus addition to stocks from new procurement after replacement of obsolete, or "depreciated," stock). Thus we define the desired increase $\dot{S}^{J*}$ in stock by

$$\dot{S}^{J*} \equiv S^{J*} - S^J \qquad (2.3.2)$$

Using the rivalry type of model suggested by Eq. (2.2.3), we may also write

$$\dot{S}^{J*} = \tilde{\rho}^J(S^L - S^J) + \tilde{g}^J \qquad (2.3.3)$$

where the tilde over the parameters indicates that they are of the same nature but somewhat different from those in Eq. (2.2.2a).

Since the realized $\dot{S}^J$ is less than $\dot{S}^{J*}$ when the resource constraint is binding, we have for $0 < \lambda < 1$

$$\dot{S}^J = \lambda \dot{S}^{J*} = \lambda[\tilde{\rho}^J(S^L - S^J) + \tilde{g}^J] \qquad (2.3.4)$$

that is, the constraint precludes the realization of the full myopic Richardson-type reaction. Only the fraction λ is realized. However, as S^J increases from period to period (assuming S^L constant), a point is reached when the available resources $\overline{R}^J$ per period are no longer binding, and the full reaction can be realized.[4]

---

[4] To depict the operation of the constraint, Caspary has suggested the function

$$p^J \dot{S}^J = \lambda \overline{R}^J [1 - \exp(-p^J \dot{S}^{J*}/\overline{R}^J)] \qquad (2.3.5)$$

Clearly, where p^J, λ, and $\overline{R}^J$ are fixed, as stock increases from year to year, $\dot{S}^{J*}$ decreases by Eq. (2.3.2) for *fixed S^L and $\tilde{g}^J$*. Ultimately, then, the power to which e is raised approaches

We do not wish here to comment upon the validity of the functions [such as Eq. (2.3.5) used by Caspary, Squires (1976), and others to embody fully the resource constraint. We simply observe that these functions do make explicit this constraint and introduce the economic system in a more probing manner than the use of the simple fatigue, cost, or expense term $-c^J M^J$ in Eq. (2.2.2a).[5]

A resource-constrained model for each nation immediately converts the myopic, equilibrium response Richardson-type model into a myopic disequilibrium, partial-adjustment model. Each nation can only partially adjust in any period to the other's magnitudes. The escalation process still takes place, although at a slower rate per period.

In later sections we shall explore more systematically and in much greater detail the role of economic variables. Suffice it to mention here that Luterbacher (1976) introduces a resource constraint by defining the resource ceiling as a fraction of GNP (as does Gregory 1974), recognizing that GNP normally grows over time. Wolfson (1985) introduces the resource constraint by explicitly treating the trade-off in the use of a nation's total resources (production potential) between military and non-military expenditures, as does Fischer (1984) and as was done earlier by R. Smith (1980), Brito (1972), McGuire (1965), Ferejohn (1976), and others, some of whose models will be discussed later. In Lambelet, Luterbacher, and Allan (1979) the desired level of military expenditures is related directly to GNP. (See section 2.7.) Liossatos (1980) formally incorporates the positive impact of military expenditures upon an economy afflicted with heavy unemployment and large amounts of idle physical capital and equipment (see section 2.7), an effect previously well recognized by Zinnes et al. (1976a).

2.4   Arms, security, and the maximization of national welfare

Implicit in the Richardson-type models and those that introduce resource constraints is a best response, a goal representing a best possible outcome, or other aspect reflecting a motivation to optimize. Such a factor is made explicit in the optimization and control theory type of models developed extensively in the 1970s, an excellent early probe being by McGuire in 1965.

---

zero and accordingly $\dot{S}^J$ does, consistent with attaining a myopic Richardson-type equilibrium reaction. Note that if $\overline{\overline{R}}^J$ is fixed, $\overline{R}^J$ also decreases with an increase in S^J but typically not as rapidly as $\dot{S}^{J*}$.

An obvious variation of Eq. (2.3.5) that then leads to a slightly different model substitutes $\overline{R}^J$ for R^J in Eq. (2.3.5) and $p^J S^{J*} + \overline{c}^J S^J$ for $p^J \dot{S}^{J*}$. See Caspary (1967).

[5] Also note that Caspary and others use the exponential function of Eq. (2.3.5) to depict what they call a "diminishing returns" effect.

We note here that although McGuire and others write about the maximization of national utility, or national welfare, or social welfare, no one as yet has developed an adequate measure of these concepts or an appropriate way of proceeding from individual preferences to social preferences. However, public opinion polls can be and are used extensively, and they do yield some indication of society's preferences and social (national) utility and welfare.

In the McGuire study each nation, for example, J, is motivated to maximize its utility u^J, which is taken to depend on (is a function of) an implied variable security S_e^J and resources R_c^J allocated to the production of civilian (nonmilitary) goods and services – and thus is often written as $u^J = u^J(S_e^J, R_c^J)$. The variable security, however, cannot be specified unless the attitude of J is also specified. For example, security would be defined quite differently by a pessimist than by an optimist.[6] McGuire implicitly assumes that J has the attitude of a highly conservative (pessimistic) behaving unit. He specifically takes security S_e^J to be a function of both:

$\mathcal{S}^J$:   minimum number of J's surviving missiles from its stock S^J that can be achieved with high assurance (say, 90 percent), assuming an attack by L (thus $\mathcal{S}^J$ relates to J's deterrence potential), and

$\mathcal{S}^L$:   maximum number of L's surviving missiles from its stock S^L (with assurance of, say, 90 percent), assuming an attack by J (thus $\mathcal{S}^L$ relates to L's retaliatory attack potential should J attack).

Clearly, $\mathcal{S}^J$ and $\mathcal{S}^L$ are functions (respectively, ϕ and ψ) of L's stock S^L of missiles, of J's stock S^J, and other factors.

Replacing S_e^J in J's utility function with $\mathcal{S}^J$ and $\mathcal{S}^L$, McGuire defines J's problem in maximizing its utility as

$$\max u^J(\mathcal{S}^J, \mathcal{S}^L, R_c^J) \tag{2.4.1}$$
$$\text{subject to:} \quad \mathcal{S}^J = \phi(S^J, S^L, \ldots) \tag{2.4.2}$$
$$\mathcal{S}^L = \psi(S^J, S^L, \ldots) \tag{2.4.3}$$
$$\overline{R}^J = R^J - R_c^J \tag{2.4.4}$$

where $S^L, \ldots$ refers to the given stock of L's missiles and other parameters and, as defined previously, R^J is J's total stock of resources (in dollars) and $\overline{R}^J$ is the amount of resources (in dollars) allocated to maintaining and increasing S^J.[7]

McGuire then derives and interprets the conditions that need to be sat-

---

[6] As elsewhere indicated, the specific attitude characterizing a nation J significantly affects its definition of $\mathcal{S}^J$ and $\mathcal{S}^L$ (Isard et al. 1969, chap. 4; Isard and C. Smith 1982, pp. 21–4).

[7] Note that by Eq. (2.2.5) and previous discussion,

$$\overline{R}^J = p^J S^J + \bar{c}^J S^J \tag{2.4.5}$$

isfied if utility is to be maximized. For example, he examines the traditional trade-off between resources R_c^J devoted to the production of civilian goods (inclusive of investment and other peace time uses) and resources $\overline{R}^J$ devoted to increasing S^J and thus both to increasing the number $\mathscr{S}^J$ of J's surviving missiles (with 90 percent assurance) should L attack and to decreasing the number of L's surviving missiles $\mathscr{S}^L$ should J attack. Assuming a specific separable and additive utility function, one such condition for J's use of resources is

$$mu \text{ of resources (money)} = \frac{mu \text{ of } \mathscr{S}^J}{mc \text{ of } \mathscr{S}^J} + \frac{mu \text{ of } \mathscr{S}^L}{mc \text{ of } \mathscr{S}^L} \qquad (2.4.6)$$

where mu is marginal utility and mc is marginal cost. In this statement, the marginal utility of resources (money) is taken to be the utility generated by the last dollar spent on civilian goods. The marginal cost for both $\mathscr{S}^J$ and $\mathscr{S}^L$ is the cost of the last unit of S^J (strictly speaking fractional part of a missile), which by Eqs. (2.4.2) and (2.4.3) leads to changes in both $\mathscr{S}^J$ (an increase) and $\mathscr{S}^L$ (a decrease) and thereby to two additive increments of utility, as indicated by the right side of Eq. (2.4.6).

Extensions of McGuire's study obviously obtain when dynamic models are constructed but at a sacrifice in richness of interpretation. In Brito (1972) and Intriligator and Brito (1976) a dynamic optimization model is presented. There they take resources for military purposes $\overline{R}^J$ as their control variable. They then take J's utility u^J to be a function of R_c^J (the resources available for civilian goods production) and the index of defense D^J (which is a function of S^J and S^L, where S^L is assumed as given). Further, they take welfare to be the summation of discounted utility generated over a time span from time point (or initial year) t_0, which is convenient to set equal to 0, to time point (or terminal year) t_1. For empirical studies for which annual data are available and for a positive discount factor r, the summation Σ of discounted utility would be

$$\sum_{t=t_0=0}^{t=t_1} (1 + r)^{-t} u(t)$$

However, some analysts seek to gain insights from the use of calculus, once again at the expense of assuming behavior that undertakes utility calculations over an infinite number of infinitesimally small time periods, as represented by the integral expression $\int_{t_0}^{t_1} \ldots dt$. To do so, Intriligator and Brito state the problem of maximizing welfare (W^J) using the variable $\overline{R}^J$ as the control variable:

$$\max W^J(\overline{R}^J) = \int_{t_0}^{t_1} e^{-rt} u^J(R_c^J, D^J) \, dt \qquad (2.4.7)$$

where

e^{-rt} = discount factor applied to utility at time t, r being appropriate rate of discount

The objective of Eq. (2.4.7) is subject to the constraints

$$\dot{S}^J = \frac{\overline{R}^J}{p^J} - \alpha^J S^J \tag{2.4.8}$$

$$R_c^J = R^J - \overline{R}^J \tag{2.4.9}$$

discussed in connection with Eqs. (2.2.5) and (2.4.4), where R^J is given. Equilibrium conditions (existence of equilibrium) are then discussed in traditional ways, and under certain assumptions, Richardson's basic model is derived.

The dynamic optimization model naturally leads to a differential game model [as, e.g., in Simaan and Cruz (1975a)]. There, in a two-nation model for, say, J and L, the welfare of J is dependent on not only the resources $\overline{R}^J$ it devotes to military purposes but also the resources $\overline{R}^L$ its opponent L devotes to military purposes. As a consequence, J's defense index D^J is affected by changes in S^L resulting from changes in $\overline{R}^L$ as L reacts to J. Each nation is, of course, subject to a net missile investment constraint such as Eq. (2.4.8). [However, few if any differential game models have introduced a resource constraint for each nation such as Eq. (2.4.9).] Using a quadratic objective function, Simaan and Cruz examine traditional questions such as the existence of a solution; they too are able to derive the Richardson equations, however with time-varying parameters.

Variations of this differential game model are provided by Gillespie, Zinnes, and Tahim (1977a) and Zinnes et al. (1978b) wherein a quadratic objective function is based on diverse goals regarding deterrence, international tension, arms balance, aid balance, minimization of war probability (ceteris paribus), minimization of foreign aid expenditures (ceteris paribus), and the like. The goals enter the objective function of each nation in an additive fashion, as is described in section 2.9.

At this point we should note an important distinction. Previous to our discussion of differential games, it could be said that most if not all the models (except McGuire's theoretical analysis) can be characterized as treating myopic behavior. Whereas the presence of an opponent with a position was frequently made explicit, it was assumed by and large that its position was fixed or at least not subject to major change as a consequence of the behavior of the nation being analyzed. Implicitly, however, most of the model builders, in particular Brito (1972),[8] were fully aware of the possibility that the opponent would change its position. However, they did not incorporate it (for various understandable reasons) in their models.[9] The differential game models do incorporate the opponent's behavior as a variable, and in this respect we consider them truly (fully) nonmyopic.

Once nonmyopic behavior is explicitly treated, we come into the realm of game theory. Brams's game-theoretic analysis (1977, 1981 with Wittman), for instance, deals with nonmyopic behavior to its fullest extent. However, when we treat, say, nonmyopic behavior at n levels of depth (i.e., n rounds), we are forced to aggregate excessively, that is, to aggregate a number of key factors governing behavior, losing thereby a number of relationships critical for understanding arms race phenomena. Hence, except for differential games, we only touch upon game-theoretic studies in this chapter; but in Appendix B to Chapter 3 we do examine insights regarding strategic behavior that game theory can provide. For a systematic and comprehensive study of the potential of game theory in the social sciences inclusive of international conflict, see Shubik (1982, 1984).

2.5   Concepts and types of strategy in arms race models

Differential game models typically involve strategies of a general type. They consider general measures of defense or military capability of two or more actors. Typically they tend not to focus on the specific potentials of arms use and its effect on arms production. This effect, however, has been considered in a set of other models. These latter have dealt with relationships that were earlier embodied in McGuire's theoretical and graphic analysis. An important model in this set is that by Intriligator and Brito (1976, 1984), which focuses upon the use of arms for both (1) attack and (2) deterrence purposes. There are two basic terms in determining

[8] Brito, for example, states "the assumption that both countries behave in a myopic manner makes it very easy to analyze the stability of the equilibrium. The assumption, however, is very unrealistic. It is obvious to anyone who reads a newspaper that military expenditures are based not only on the current arms level of the potential enemy, but also on projected arms level" (p. 366).

[9] Lambelet (1971) justifies models involving myopic behavior on the grounds that leaders frequently confront such noncalculable, complex uncertainties regarding their current and future environments and have no reasonable way of behaving other than myopically.

Note that in their model Milstein and Mitchell (1969) specify a second-order differential equation with military expenditures as the dependent variable. Their model allows each nation to look ahead to where its rival will be in the future. But Milstein and Mitchell have each nation assume a constant rate of increase of its rival's military expenditures. In this sense, the Milstein and Mitchell model cannot be categorized as truly nonmyopic, given the rival's current level of expenditures.

the level of missiles necessary for deterrence for, say, nation J. One term specifies the number of J's missiles that L can destroy with its stock S^L. In oversimplified fashion, this number is derived by multiplying S^L by a factor f^L (indicating the destructive effectiveness of one L missile) yielding the term $f^L S^L$. The second term specifies the number of J's missiles that must remain intact (after L in an attack has used up its entire stock S^L) in order for J to inflict what it estimates to be an unacceptable number, at least $\overline{C}^L$, of civilian casualties on L. In oversimplified fashion, if each of J's missiles can cause v^J of such casualties, then $\overline{C}^L/v^J$ must be the number of J's missiles that must remain intact. Thus, in oversimplified fashion the amount S^J of missiles that J must have for deterrence purposes is given by

$$S^J \geq f^L S^L + \overline{C}^L/v^J \tag{2.5.1}$$

A proper statement of this relationship recognizes that there is a time delay before J can retaliate after a missile attack and that there would be a time period during which retaliation would occur.[10]

On the other hand, J may contemplate the use of arms for a potential attack. Where f^J is the effectiveness of one of J's missiles in destroying L's missiles, $f^J S^J$ is the number of L's missiles J can destroy with its stock S^J. Then J must consider the number of L's missiles, $S^L - f^J S^J$, left intact after its (J's) attack. Nation J must find acceptable the number of civilian casualties in J's country that this left-over number can inflict. If v^L is the number of J's casualties an L missile can inflict, then oversimplifying it must be for J to attack that

$$v^L(S^L - f^J S^J) \leq \hat{C}^J \tag{2.5.3}$$

where $\hat{C}^J$ is the maximum number of civilian casualties that J considers acceptable. By reordering terms in Eq. (2.5.3), we obtain[11]

$$S^J \geq \frac{1}{f^J}\left(S^L - \frac{\hat{C}^J}{v^L}\right) \tag{2.5.4}$$

---

[10] Where $0, \ldots, \Theta^L$ is the time interval during which L attacks and $\Theta^L, \ldots, \Theta^L + \Psi^J$ is the time interval during which J retaliates, Eq. (2.5.1) is properly stated as

$$S^J \geq f^L[1 - \exp(-\overline{\beta}\Theta^L)]S^L + \frac{\overline{C}^L}{v^J[1 - \exp(-\overline{\alpha}\Psi^J)]} \tag{2.5.2}$$

where $\overline{\beta}$ is the rate at which L fires its missiles in the first-strike strategy and $\overline{\alpha}$ is J's rate of retaliation. There have been other refinements; for example, in Brito and Intriligator (1973, 1974), account is taken of the response lag and uncertainty about whether a missile site is empty.

[11] The equation should be properly stated as

$$S^J \geq \frac{1}{f^J[1 - \exp(-\overline{\alpha}'\Theta^J)]}\left(S^L - \frac{\hat{C}^J}{v^L[1 - \exp(-\overline{\beta}\Psi^L)]}\right) \tag{2.5.5}$$

using the definitions for Eq. (2.5.2).

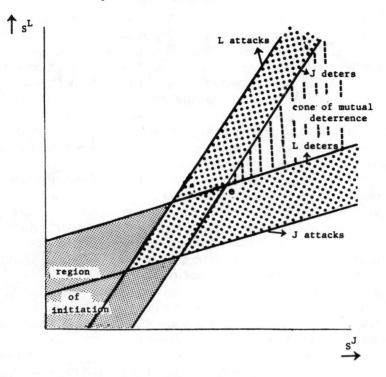

Figure 2.1. Deterrence and attack lines.

Assuming L's reactions are similar in nature to those of J, we have two similar equations for L. When the equality sign holds and when we graph these four relations, we obtain the familiar Intriligator–Brito figure presented here as Figure 2.1. Those combinations of S^J and S^L that lie on the line "J deters" and in the area to its right are combinations where the stock S^J is sufficient to deter L from attacking. Likewise, combinations of S^J and S^L on and above the line "L deters" are combinations where the stock S^L is large enough to deter J from attacking. The dashed area in the upper right can then be clearly designated the *cone of mutual deterrence*.

Those combinations of S^J and S^L lying on and below the line "J attacks" are combinations where J can effectively attack. None of these combinations give L deterrence capability. Those combinations of S^J and S^L lying on and to the left of line "L attacks" are combinations where L can effectively attack. We have also indicated in Figure 2.1 a dotted area comprising those combinations where neither J nor L attacks or deters – where possible casualties that the surviving missiles of an opponent can inflict prevents a nation from attacking. Finally we have indicated with the sawtoothed shaded area at the lower left of the figure the combinations where one or both nations are motivated to attack.

The Intriligator–Brito framework can be used to undertake a comparative statics analysis of the impact of changes in arms race factors on the regions of Figure 2.1. For example, as the maximum acceptable levels of casualties decrease in size, the intersections of the lines of attack with the respective axes shift toward the zero point, and as the estimated minimum unacceptable levels of casualties decrease, the lines of deterrence move closer to the parallel lines of attack.[12]

We do not have the time and space to present other significant aspects of this model. Mayer (1986) points out that the weapons plane topology of Figure 2.1 is highly sensitive to assumptions about the nature of nuclear war and about the conditions that prompt or deter a nuclear attack. Mayer presents a number of alternative weapons plane topologies to illustrate his point. Other analysts such as Kupperman and Smith (1976) question the linearity assumption of the model.

The preceding model does not make explicit any utility maximization objective that might motivate one or both nations. In other works, Intriligator and Brito (1985a) do embed this model into a utility maximization framework such as given by Eq. (2.4.7) and the associated discussion. This is done for, say, J by replacing D^J in Eq. (2.4.7) with the term $[S^{J*}(S^L) - S^J]$ where S^{J*} indicates J's desired stock as a function of S^L and where the term may be viewed as defining a missile gap. This term in turn can be related to different decision rules. Brito and Intriligator speak of the following rules:

1. The desired stock of missiles S^{J*} is that required to deter the opponent, in which case it is defined by the equality relation of Eq. (2.5.2).
2. The desired stock of missiles S^{J*} is that required to attack the opponent, in which case it is defined by the equality relation of Eq. (2.5.5).
3. Parity:
    $$S^{J*} = S^L \tag{2.5.6}$$
4. Superiority:
    $$S^{J*} = \epsilon S^L, \qquad \epsilon > 1 \tag{2.5.7}$$

In the use of rules 1 and 2, they conduct a hypothetical missile war that for terminal year t_1 has, say, for nation J, a payoff Π^J defined by the

---

[12] They ultimately start at the zero point when these levels become zero and coincide with the respective lines of deterrence such that the cone of mutual deterrence begins at the origin, with the origin (zero levels of missiles) as the equilibrium point.

remaining weapon stocks at t_1 and the resulting casualties to both J and L.[13] Nation J's military selects rates of fire and counterforce proportions so as to maximize its payoff subject to the missile war equations[14]; and the results, Brito and Intriligator claim, may be relevant for a defense agency in justifying its budget request.

In an earlier work, Brito and Intriligator (1972) allowed a trade-off between R_c^J and D^J in Eq. (2.4.7). To do so, it is then necessary that the defense D^J for any given S^L always correspond to the optimum utilization of J's weaponry by J's military and hence correspond to the optimization of Π^J (or of the expected payoff from a combination of relevant Π^J functions).

The Intriligator–Brito strategic deterrence–attack model implies that when a nation attacks, it is motivated to do so because of an anticipated increase in *net* utility – the sum of utility gains from moving to the expected post attack state of affairs less the disutilities (utility costs) from casualties and other negative outcomes from so moving. However, the attack–deterrence model of Figure 2.1 does not look at gains and resource costs explicitly. In a very simplified example Nalebuff (1984) introduces gains and resource costs. He too is able to identify a Nash equilibrium point. At this point, each party makes the other's attack cost so high that the other's gains do not exceed the cost; thus each deters and is deterred.

While Nalebuff's simple example provides much insight on the effect of resource costs, a fuller treatment of this effect and trade-offs between missile and civilian goods production is developed by Wolfson (1985). Wolfson introduces the trade-off aspect with the use of the traditional transformation function of economics, taking into account scale economies, externalities, and other nonlinearities.

In developing his analysis, Wolfson supplements the mathematical formulation just presented with graphic analyses. Letting Figure 2.1 be the fourth quadrant of Figure 2.2 and retaining only the "L deters" line,

---

[13] That is,

$$\Pi^J = \Pi^J[S^J(t_1), S^L(t_1), \tilde{C}^J(t_1), \tilde{C}^L(t_1)] \tag{2.5.8}$$

where $\tilde{C}^J(t_1)$ and $\tilde{C}^L(t_1)$ are resulting casualties.

[14] The missile war model has the following variables: (1) missile stocks at time t, $S^J(t)$ and $S^L(t)$; (2) rates $\tilde{\alpha}^J(t)$ and $\tilde{\alpha}^L(t)$ at which J and L, respectively, launch their missiles at time t; (3) respective proportions $\tilde{\beta}^J(t)$ and $\tilde{\beta}^L(t)$ of total missiles launched at the opponent's missiles (counterforce use), the proportions $1 - \tilde{\beta}^J(t)$ and $1 - \tilde{\beta}^L(t)$ of total missiles being launched at the opponent's cities (countervalue use); (4) effectiveness of missiles f^J, f^L, v^J, and v^L as defined; and (5) the initial missile stocks $S^J(t_0)$ and $S^L(t_0)$. The four equations that summarize the evolution of the war are (suppressing the time symbol t)

$$\dot{S}^J = -\tilde{\alpha}^J S^J - \tilde{\beta}^L \tilde{\alpha}^L S^L f^L, \quad S^J(t_0) = S_0^J \tag{2.5.9}$$
$$\dot{S}^L = -\tilde{\alpha}^L S^L - \tilde{\beta}^J \tilde{\alpha}^J S^J f^J, \quad S^L(t_0) = S_0^L \tag{2.5.10}$$
$$\dot{\tilde{C}}^J = (1 - \tilde{\beta}^L)\tilde{\alpha}^L S^L v^L, \quad \tilde{C}^J(t_0) = 0 \tag{2.5.11}$$
$$\dot{\tilde{C}}^L = (1 - \tilde{\beta}^J)\tilde{\alpha}^J S^J v^J, \quad \tilde{C}^L(t_0) = 0 \tag{2.5.12}$$

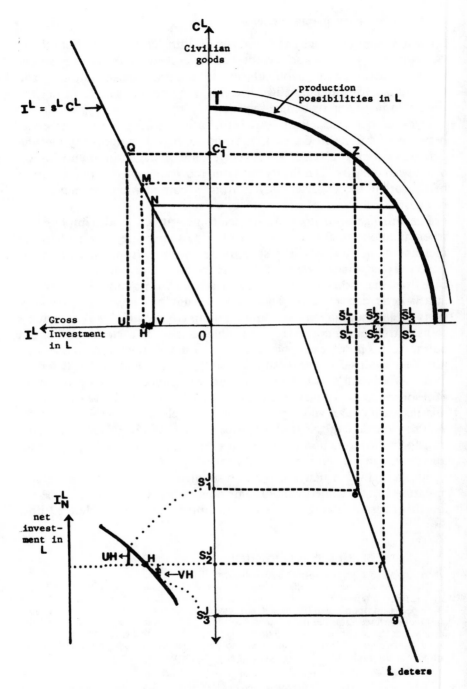

Figure 2.2. Nation J waging economic warfare.

Wolfson constructs in the first quadrant a typical transformation function between military and civilian goods production. For a given GNP of country L that function is represented by the bold curve TT, a function that depicts everywhere decreasing rates of transformation (substitution) of one type of good into another. To understand the links between the several relationships embodied in this figure, take point Z as representing a current situation of optimal resource allocation by L between military goods measured along the horizontal axis and civilian goods production measured along the vertical. This point defines amounts $\bar{S}_1^L$ and C_1^L of these goods, respectively. The specific amount $\bar{S}_1^L$ of military goods production is required in order that L have a stock S_1^L of missiles, also measured along the horizontal. (By taking both $\bar{S}_1^L$ and S_1^L to be measured along the horizontal, we are oversimplifying by assuming a fixed relationship between the two. This oversimplification does not interfere with the basic analysis that Wolfson employs.) The stock S_1^L is what is required to deter J, whose missiles are taken to be given at level S_1^J. See point e in the fourth quadrant, where we measure J's stock of missiles S^J vertically downward from 0, the zero point.

As already noted, the production point Z indicates civilian goods production of C_1^L measured along the vertical in the first quadrant. In the second quadrant, a linear relationship is depicted between gross investment I^L (in real terms) and civilian goods production C^L, where we take gross investment to equal savings and where we take savings to equal a fixed percentage of civilian goods production, a constant savings ratio s^L times C^L. We see by point Q that the level of gross investment in L (measured along the horizontal to the left of the zero point is $0U$. However, the amount $0H$ is required to maintain L's productive capacity (to replace its used-up plant and equipment), leaving UH as net investment. If we now go to the lower left of the third quadrant, we can measure along the vertical net investment (in real terms and for constant $0H$), where we continue to measure gross investment along the horizontal. Thus, corresponding to the level S_1^J of J's missile stock, there is net investment of UH. Pursuing comparative statics analysis, for each given level of S^J we can thus associate a net level of investment by L. For S_2^J, this level is zero (as depicted by the dot-dash lines); for S_3^J, it is the negative amount VH (as depicted by the nondashed lines).

Note that this curve can be said to represent a myopic optimal response by L to J, given the various linear relationships and parameters assumed, when L's military concern is with deterrence. If S_1^J is the level of J's missile stock, then L needs a stock S_1^L for effective deterrence, but no more. So clearly point Z is a point of tangency between an indifference curve of L's preference structure and the transformation curve TT. Any point lying on the TT curve below and to the right of Z indicates an allocation of resources to the attainment and maintenance of a missile stock by L greater than is necessary for deterrence purposes and thus precludes some production of desirable consumer goods. Any point lying on the TT curve above and to the left of Z means that insufficient resources are devoted to military goods production to allow L to have a missile stock sufficiently large to deter.

Returning to the initially assumed situation, we note that J's missile stock S_1^J gives rise to net investment of UH by L. This then increases L's productive capacity (i.e., its stock of resources available for allocation), which gives rise to a higher transformation curve (the nonbold curve in the first quadrant). When L needs to have only S_1^L stock of missiles, this means that more resources can be devoted to civilian goods production and thus to still greater net investment. And so forth. Thus we have the typical situation of a growth economy when resources devoted to production of military goods is not excessive and is constant or does not grow at an excessive rate.

Note, however, that if there is a significant increase of S^J and S^L over time, as characterizes arms races,[15] the increase in S^J, say, from S_1^J to S_2^J, can lead to a situation where there is zero net investment in L, and if S^J goes to S_3^J, there results negative net investment in L. The transformation curve of L then contracts and moves toward the origin and increasingly L cannot achieve (have) a stock S^L sufficient to deter without increasingly eating up its production capacity. This process, if continued long enough, reduces L's productive capacity to a level insufficient to maintain a stock of missiles large enough to deter J if J has a stock equal to S_3^J or greater. In this situation, Wolfson suggests that J is in effect conducting economic warfare on L and that L, recognizing its ultimate fate, will be compelled to attack before it is economically forced into submission (defeat). Wolfson further notes that if J has access (via the world economy) to other nations that can furnish J with capital (loans) and goods via exports to J (and even more so, when the capital provided J can be used to purchase these goods) – as was the case in the United States (especially with regard to its NATO partners) – and if L does not have such access, then the ability of J to wage economic warfare on L is thereby enhanced.

[15] Wolfson provides certain economic rationale for escalation based on the different technologies used by opposing nations when they have different resource endowments. He demonstrates how an economy with a resource endowment able to build and use high-technology weapons may overestimate, using its internal prices, the military expenditures of an economy with a resource endowment more suited to low-technology weapons. Likewise, the latter, using its internal prices, may overestimate the military expenditures of the former. Clearly, for a situation where both may be said to have and seek to maintain approximately equal military capability (assuming such can be measured with sufficient accuracy), escalation can result.

Table 2.1. *Inputs and outputs for civilian and military industries*

Industries operated by nation J	Inputs from nation J		Outputs to nation J		Inputs from nation L		Outputs to nation L	
	Civilian	Security	Civilian	Security	Civilain	Security	Civilian	Security
1. Civilian	1	0	b	0	0	0	0	0
2. Military	1	0	0	c	0	d	0	0

Thus far we have taken L to be concerned with deterrence alone. However, if L views security as a function of both ability to deter and ability to attack and where security is a basic argument in L's preference function, the optimal reaction in this model to any stock, say, S_1^J, will not be S_1^L but a larger magnitude, reflecting a point of tangency of the transformation curve TT with an indifference curve of a different preference structure.

A still more involved motive for weapon accumulation has been examined by Brito and Intriligator (1977a,b). Not only does weapon accumulation affect deterrence and attack capability, but by permitting a nation to make a more credible threat of war, it also may enable that nation to be in a better bargaining position with regard to various issues and in fact to control a larger fraction of the world's resources. Such could lead to an increase in its GNP and thus to a larger capability for weapon production.

While the preceding models recognize the influence (in essence, the externality) of one nation's weapons upon the welfare of a second, they fail to probe as deeply into this externality as is possible. Here, Fischer (1984) makes a significant contribution. First he sets up a very simple framework for analytic purposes. Let there be two nations, J and L, with identical technology and resources, each producing two goods, one being civilian goods, the other being security. Let each engage in two processes. One, the civilian industry, produces civilian (consumption and investment) goods, requiring a unit input of civilian goods to produce b units of civilian goods, $b > 1$. The second, the military industry, produces security, requiring as inputs one unit of civilian goods from the nation of production and d units of security goods from the rival nation and yielding c units of security for the nation of production. The requirement of d units of security goods from the rival nation represents an externality (negative) imposed on that nation. It can be viewed as a negative output (a reduction of stock for the rival nation). Then, to be able to use a von Neumann–type model, Fischer summarizes the situation, say, for nation J, in the form of Table 2.1.

A similar table may be set up for nation L, where to produce c units of security, L requires one unit of civilian goods (which it produces) *plus d units of security good from J*. The operation of its civilian sector would not impose any externality on J.

Fischer then considers a von Neumann growth model as appropriate for his analysis, wherein both the civilian and military sector of each nation come to grow at the same rate. If the fraction v^J of J's resources is allocated to its military sector with $1 - v^J$ being allocated to its civilian sector, it follows that the growth factor of the civilian sector in J is

$$\gamma_{civ}^J = (1 - v^J)b \tag{2.5.13}$$

If we take into account the input $v^L d$ that is required from J for the operation of L's security sector if that sector is operated at a level of v^L, then according to Fischer, the growth factor for the security sector in J is

$$\gamma_{sec}^J = \frac{v^J c}{v^L d} \tag{2.5.14}$$

If now the growth factor of both J's civilian and military sectors are taken to be the same, as Fischer does, we have

$$(1 - v^J)b = v^J c / v^L d \tag{2.5.15}$$

or

$$v^J = v^L/(v^L + e) \quad \text{where} \quad e = c/db \tag{2.5.16}$$

This relation yields curve $0ANB$ when plotted in Figure 2.3 when the value of e is taken to be ½. The curve is J's reaction curve, indicating how J responds to every possible value of v^L.

Simplifying by taking both economies to be alike in all respects in order to gain maximum insight into the underlying processes, Fischer obtains a reaction curve for L similar to Eq. (2.5.16) except that v^L replaces v^J wherever the latter occurs and v^J replaces v^L. Plotting this relation in Figure 2.3 yields curve $0A'NB'$. As can be easily seen, each of the intersections of the two curves is a Nash equilibrium point corresponding to the two solutions

$$v^J = 1 - e = 1 - c/db = v^L \tag{2.5.17}$$
$$v^J = v^L = 0 \tag{2.5.18}$$

Point N represents a stable Nash equilibrium whereas the point $v^J = v^L = 0$ represents an unstable equilibrium.

In this model, the critical parameters are b, c, and d. Fischer in particular is concerned with the ratio c/d. The greater this ratio, the greater the *nonthreatening* character of the nation's military activities to its rival.

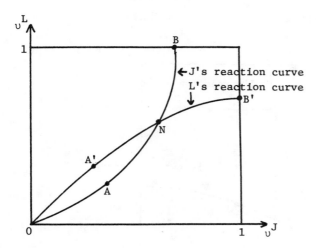

Figure 2.3. Reaction curves of nations J and L and Nash equilibrium points N and 0.

The smaller the ratio, the more threatening a nation's security sector is to its rival. That is, per unit of security output of J, the smaller c/d, the greater is the required input (reduction) of security of L. The implications of these statements are most clearly seen if we plot the two nations' reactions curves when $e = 2$ – a situation when for constant b the ratio c/d is much larger than when $e = ½$. We obtain Figure 2.4. When we compare Figure 2.4 with Figure 2.3, we see how the point N has receded to the origin, thereby making the origin a stable Nash equilibrium point – a point where both nations allocate no resources to their security sectors. This solution always obtains when $c/db \geq 1$.

As with most models, there are serious questions concerning the relevance of Fischer's von Neumann–type model, which can be extended to n nations and m sectors. Nonetheless, it does point up the significance of different types of military technology.[16] A highly nonthreatening defense system (such as one comprising purely retaliatory second-strike weapons and lines of antitank, antiaircraft missiles backed up by reservists that could defend their own territory) by itself does not reduce the security of a rival and can deescalate an arms race. For a given nation that has no desire for conquest, Fischer even goes so far as to suggest that a unilateral shift by it from a threatening to a nonthreatening weapons system can

[16] Fischer, of course, examines the effects of different ratios c/d on the growth of the civilian sector (e.g., the higher the ratio c/d, the faster its economic growth) and the converse.

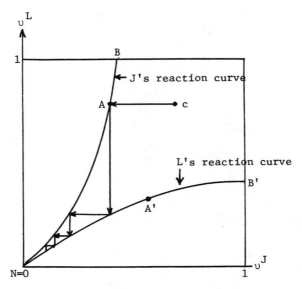

Figure 2.4. Optimal response curves for nations J and L that lead to a stable Nash equilibrium at $N = 0$.

lead to disarmament (primarily because its rival's reaction curve in Figure 2.3 would shift closer to the axis measuring the given nation's armaments). Hence the intersection point N would recede to the origin.[17]

It is interesting to examine how a shift from a threatening to a nonthreatening security strategy (designated *transarmament* by Fischer) can be depicted in an Intriligator–Brito figure such as Figure 2.1. A shift by nation J may be viewed as, on the average,

1. decreasing f^J since J's stock S^J will have more nonthreatening and less threatening weapons;
2. decreasing v^J since the same is likely to hold for J's surviving stock after an attack by L;[18]
3. decreasing f^L because more of J's weapons will be aimed at defense against L's attack, thereby decreasing the effectiveness of any L missile; and
4. leaving v^L unchanged were all of J's weapons completely used up in a J attack on L but in all likelihood decreasing v^L somewhat

[17] Fischer also suggests that it may be in one nation's interest to make available to an opponent the former's breakthroughs in nonthreatening weapons technology.
[18] That is, we assume that L's attack has focused as much, if not more, on J's attack weapons.

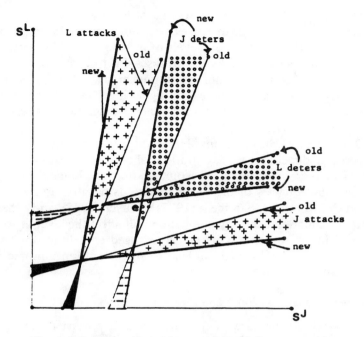

Figure 2.5. Old and new deter and attack lines: area of increased deterrence, O; decreased deterrence, −; increased attack potential, ■; decreased attack potential, +.

since a shift toward nonthreatening weapons by J would leave J holding some purely defensive weapons that could not be employed in an attack and so would be in place and intact for a more effective defense against L's missiles that did survive.

If we put these changes into J's deterrence and attack Eqs. (2.5.1) and (2.5.4) and the two equations for L's deterrence and attack, we obtain the bold lines of Figure 2.5. We have also reproduced in this figure the four corresponding lines (based on purely threatening weapons) before J's unilateral shift toward nonthreatening weapons. Note that the abscissa for the "J deters" and "L attacks" lines shift toward the right because of a decrease in v^J, the shift of the latter being somewhat lesser. Also, both their slopes significantly increase because of a decrease in f^L. Further, the intercepts of the "J attacks" and "L deters" lines increase somewhat because of the small decrease in v^L, the increase being slightly greater for the latter. More important, their slopes significantly decrease because of a decrease in f^J.

A careful study of this figure suggests that at large weapon stocks the area of deterrence increases, the increase being indicated by the areas containing the circles. However, at low levels of missile stocks, the areas of deterrence decrease as indicated by the minuses. Further, at low levels of missile stocks, the area where either can initiate attack increases as indicated by the solid black areas, whereas at higher levels of missile stocks, the areas where singly J and L can initiate attack are significantly reduced as indicated by the pluses.

Figure 2.5 just illustrates one possible set of impacts. Other possible sets could emerge depending on assumptions about the changes in f^J, f^L, v^J, and v^L. Moreover, interpretation becomes extremely clouded when we recognize the inadequacies of the linear model, as pointed up by Kupperman and Smith (1976), Sandberg (1977a), Mayer (1985), and others. Surely, too, the unilateral shift by one nation will affect the level of security perceived by the other and its perceived need and desire for both deterrence and attack and hence can lead to significant (and unpredictable) changes in its behavior.

2.6   Races with conventional and strategic weapons

Whereas an accurate measure of military capability must examine in detail the many categories of weapons and defensive measures that one nation has relative to its rival [see Rattinger (1976b) regarding the Middle East arms race], we are not able to cope with much disaggregation in an arms race model. However, it is instructive to distinguish between conventional and strategic weapons, as does Lambelet (1973) and Luterbacher (1976). Luterbacher aims to fuse the action–reaction Richardson process with strategic thinking on first-strike and second-strike capability. In one model, he considers the second-strike capabilities SSC^J and SSC^L of J and L, respectively, and their respective total strategic potentials, namely, ST^J and ST^L. He also considers the destructive effectiveness of a strategic potential of a given nation, say L, it being dependent not only on the destructive power of L's weapons stock, but also on the size, hardness, and density of the targets. Thus Luterbacher considers the *probability* of destruction of J's strategic potential when L strikes first, namely, $^J q^L$. But since L desires to have a second-strike capability after it attacks, this limiting factor on the use of its strategic potential ST^L is depicted by the coefficient $\eta = (ST^L - SSC^L)/ST^J$, that is, the ratio of L's strategic potential available for first strike to J's full strategic potential. Thus, in this model Luterbacher considers second-strike capability for, say, J as

$$SSC^J = ST^J(1 - {}^J q^L)^\eta \qquad (2.6.1)$$

Luterbacher then adopts a disaggregated Richardson-type approach, where he has two equations for each nation, one for a time rate of change of its strategic potential (weaponry) and one for a time rate of change of its conventional weaponry, with linkage between the two.[19]

2.7 The effects on races of asymmetry, uncertainty, technology, international tensions, and key psychological factors

As can be expected, there are numerous variations of the basic relations contained in the preceding models. For example, consider the general element of *asymmetry*. Liossatos (1980), a scholar sensitive to neo-Marxian doctrine, would recognize the asymmetry in reaction propensities between the United States and the USSR. He would use a Richardson-type model (if forced to use a model) such as that in Eq. (2.2.2a) to depict Soviet behavior, with proper modification to achieve more sophisticated analysis.

However, for the United States, he would make explicit an upper bound B below which arms expenditure just uses idle resources and is not at the expense of civilian production. He would replace the fatigue term $-c^J M^J$ with another term that would be positive when $M^J < B$, zero when $M^J = B$, and negative when $M^J > B$.[20]

When specific models are designed to treat a prespecified arms race,

[19] Thus for J we have

$$dST^J/dt = (SSC^{J*} - SSC^J) - \bar{c}^J ST^J + \phi(CV^J, CV^L) \tag{2.6.2}$$
$$dCV^J/dt = \rho^J CV^L - \bar{c}^J CV^J + \psi(ST^J, ST^L) + g^J \tag{2.6.3}$$

where SSC^{J*} is the desired second-strike capability such that the term $SSC^{J*} - SSC^J$ replaces $\bar{\rho}^J ST^L$ in the conventional Richardson-type model; CV^J and CV^L are conventional forces of J and L, respectively; $\phi(CV^J, CV^L)$ and $\psi(ST^J, ST^L)$ are functions that link strategic and conventional forces; and $\bar{c}^J$, $\bar{c}^J$ are cost parameters, ρ^J a reaction rate, and g^J the grievance. Note that this formulation begins to raise the problem of equivalence classes of weapons.

Limitations of data forces Luterbacher's model to be greatly simplified for testing purposes. Further, resource and other constraints need to be added, as Luterbacher and others (e.g., Lambelet 1973; Squires 1976) have recognized.

Anderton (1986) also casts light on nuclear–conventional weapons substitutability and in particular analyzes cross-dimensional action–reactions – for example, an increase in conventional weapons due to an adversary's increase in nuclear weapons. In his two-nation arms race model, security is a function of the nuclear weapons of each nation, the conventional weapons of each nation, and the qualities of these weapons. His model, however, is static, involving the maximization of utility (a function of civilian goods and national security) subject to a total resource constraint.

[20] That is, he would replace $-c^J M^J$ with the general function $f^J(M^J)$:

$$f^J(M^J) \gtreqless 0 \qquad \text{where} \quad 0 < M^J \lesseqgtr B \tag{2.7.1}$$

As one possible specific form of $f^J(M^J)$, he suggests

$$f^J(M^J) = \rho^J M^J(1 - M^J/B) \tag{2.7.2}$$

We note that Liossatos's asymmetrical equations are in keeping with Hunter (1980), who emphasizes that differences in econometrically derived or hypothesized parameters for the same Richardson-type equation for two adversaries might reflect major differences in the structure of their behavioral processes and so should be made explicit.

clearly asymmetries must be made explicit. Among others, Wolfson (1968) has the Soviets reacting to their own successes with the United States also reacting to Soviet successes, while later (1985) he examines the escalation potential of the different resource mixes of nations. Lambelet (1975) recognizes asymmetry in his model of the World War I naval race between Britain and Germany. Chatterji (1969) explicitly sets up significantly different equations for explaining the behavior of Pakistan and India in their arms race. Hunter (1980) examines the behavior of alliances in symmetric and asymmetric situations in a three-nation arms race. Cusack and Ward (1981) do the same as Chatterji except that they examine military spending of the United States, the USSR, and Mainland China.

Uncertainty (and/or risk) is another critical factor affecting arms races. Among others, see Burns (1959), Saaty (1968), Pitman (1969), Midgaard (1970), Schrodt (1976), and Taagepera (1979–80). With regard to this factor, McGuire (1965) has done sterling analysis. Suppose J can only estimate M^L as the expected value μ^L with standard deviation σ^L, as indicated by $E^J(\mu^L, \sigma^L)$. Hence replacing M^L with $E^J(\mu^L, \sigma^L)$ in a simple Richardson model, we have for J (and symmetrically for L)

$$\dot{M}^J = \rho^J[E^J(\mu^L, \sigma^L)] - c^J M^J + g^J \tag{2.7.3}$$

Assuming a very conservative attitude (safety-first policy) by both J and L, so that each acts on the assumption that the level of the rival's stock is that beyond which there is only a low statistical chance that the rival's stock lies, we may state[21]

$$E(\mu, \sigma) = \mu + h\sigma \tag{2.7.4}$$

Thus Eq. (2.7.3) becomes

$$\dot{M}^J = \rho^J[\mu^L + h\sigma^L] - c^J M^J + g^J \tag{2.7.6}$$

From Eq. (2.7.6), it is clear that J's reaction function is now partly controlled by L since the information that L lets out affects J's estimate of both μ^L and σ^L. Moreover, J must take into account the fact that L also behaves in accord with a reaction function such as Eq. (2.7.6) and thus that L reacts to its own (L's) estimates of μ^J and σ^J, which J in part controls. To illustrate one way in which uncertainty can affect reaction functions and armament stocks, McGuire assumes that

1. L can only influence μ^L by changing M^L;

---

[21] McGuire defines h such that in the case of J

$$\mathrm{pr}(M^L > M^{L*}) = \mathrm{pr}[\,|(M^{L*} - \mu^L)/\sigma^L| > h] \le 1/h^2 \tag{2.7.5}$$

2. μ^L will in fact always be identical with M^L; and
3. σ^L is determined by the secrecy precautions taken by L and the intelligence effort by J (with symmetric assumptions for J, μ^J, and σ^J).

Then he shows for a given (say, 95 percent confidence interpretation) how the reaction curves shift relative to the certainty case. For example, in a figure on reaction curves such as Figure 2.3, L's reaction curve would start from the origin and rise more steeply than, and everywhere lie above, L's reaction curve as depicted there for the certainty case. In contrast, J's reaction curve would rise more slowly than, and everywhere lie below, J's reaction curve as depicted there for the certainty case. As a consequence, the reaction curves would intersect at a point (a stable equilibrium) involving higher armament stocks for both J and L.

Introducing secrecy and intelligence effort into an arms race model adds another basic variable. As McGuire has effectively demonstrated, investment in intelligence effort can reduce uncertainty sufficiently so that the cost of this effort is more than offset by the savings in armaments production. For example, the smaller the uncertainty about the rival's armament effort, the smaller σ and thus $E(\mu, \sigma)$ that enters Eq. (2.7.3).[22]

Moreover, recognizing that efforts at secrecy may be "profitable," J may put resources into increasing secrecy regarding the number of its missiles and their hardness and location. Secrecy regarding weapons location alone has the effect to increase $\mathcal{S}^J$, the number of J's surviving missiles from an L attack, and we may then enter resources devoted to obtaining secrecy as another variable in the welfare optimization problem. However, secrecy in general may lead a rival to

1. increase its intelligence effort;
2. increase its missiles stock (because of uncertainty) or possibly decrease it (because of resource constraint);
3. decrease investment in its economic system and thus the rate of growth of its production potential; or
4. pursue some combination of these.

---

[22] Accordingly, in Eq. (2.4.7) we would replace $W^J(\overline{R}^J)$ with $W^J(\overline{R}^J, N^J)$, where N^J is expenditures on intelligence effort, where D^J is now taken to be functionally related to both S^J and the expected value $E^J(S^L, \bar{\sigma}^L)$, that is,

$$D^J = D^J(\bar{\mu}^J, E^J(\bar{\mu}^L, \bar{\sigma}^L)) \tag{2.7.7}$$

and where the constraint in Eq. (2.4.9) is changed to read

$$R_c^J = R^J - \overline{R}^J - N^J \tag{2.7.8}$$

and where

$$E^J(S^L, \bar{\sigma}^L) = f(N^J, \dots) \tag{2.7.9}$$

Accounting for such effects would require the objective (welfare) function of J to be reformulated in a game-theoretic framework (Simaan and Cruz 1975a), but even so it is not clear how such should be done.[23]

Whereas McGuire takes a major step forward in treating intelligence effort and secrecy as variables, his framework still needs to be further extended, as he fully recognizes. This is so because information, when produced, not only serves as input into any current index of defense D^J, but also remains as an increase in the information stock (with an appropriate rate of decay) and so as an input into any index of defense at all future time points. Hence, any set of indifference curves representing current preference structure must embody both current and future use of produced information. The complexities of such embodiment are touched upon in Isard and Smith (1982).

However, as Allison (1974) most forcefully points out, for modern-day arms races, the situation is even more complex. Not only does nation J need to cope with uncertainty regarding S^L, or M^L under conditions where M^L can be taken to be a proxy for S^L, but also it needs to cope with the uncertainty associated with the magnitude and direction of its rival's R&D efforts and thus the types of weapons that will be included in its rival's stocks in future years. Thus the reaction coefficient ρ^J of J's decision makers is not the simple Richardson type of Eq. (2.2.1) but is one oriented to unbelievable complexities. It must be sensitive to the forces of momentum embodied in organizational politics compounded by the uncertainties regarding the types and effectiveness of weapons that its own R&D efforts will yield. Though this type of down-to-earth statement has a disparaging effect on any attempt at modeling, this effect is nonetheless offset by the need in policy and decision making to grapple with a handful or so of major factors and thus to have a model that can check for consistency in any hypothesized interplay of these factors. In this regard, the use (coupled with sound judgment) of a simple Richardson-type reaction coefficient as a proxy for the much more complex one of reality is to be desired rather than the use of none at all. So we continue.

Technology as a parameter and variable has been discussed extensively in the arms race literature. In fact, hardly any scholar fails to recognize that at least the reaction coefficient, costs, grievance, asymmetry, uncertainty, or some other key factor is directly related to the state of technology and that this relation changes with time as technological development takes place. For example, Sorenson (1980) has discussed at length technology development as both a real and perceived variable. He emphasizes the point that since a major technological advance by one's

[23] With regard to inspection as a variable, see Saaty (1968).

rival is always possible, this leads each nation to weapon levels beyond those dictated by the actual level of its rival, a factor that can lead to major instability. For example, in one variation of a Richardson-type model, he would restate Eq. (2.2.1) as

$$\dot{Q}^J = \bar{\rho}^J Q^L - \bar{c}^J Q^J + \bar{g}^J \qquad (2.7.10)$$

where Q^L represents some function of (1) numbers of L's weapons (missiles), (2) their capacity, and (3) possible or anticipated technological change (defined, e.g., as improvement in the accuracy) of L's weapons.[24]

Moreover, when Sorenson introduces resource constraints, he takes into account not only the marginal rate of substitution (trade-off) between defense and nondefense expenditures, but also between expenditures on current-technology weapons and expenditures on new-technology weapons. He holds that uncertainty regarding the costs of new-technology weapons and the experience of cost overruns typically raises the true dollar value of one dollar of estimated expenditures on new-technology weapons.

Many others have dug into technology as a basic variable through its obvious impact upon such parameters as f^J, f^L, v^J, and v^L in Eqs. (2.5.1)–(2.5.5), as has been discussed by Intriligator and Brito (1976, 1984), and Wolfson (1985).

International tension is another basic variable. Rattinger (1975) introduces it into a Richardson-type equation, measuring it by the type of verbal statements made by relevant nations and subsystems. Choucri and North (1975) and Ashley (1980) speak of intensity of intersections, as briefly discussed in section 2.11. Into his Iraqi–Iranian arms race, Abolfathi (1978) introduces international tensions, as particularly linked to the Soviet–U.S. world rivalry. Zinnes et al. (1978b) refer to international tension (measured by the sum of military expenditures), which they associate with war probability in a differential game model (see section 2.9). Ward (1984a,b) explicitly introduces into his Richardson-type equations perceived levels of international tension existing between the United States and the Soviets as measured by flows of event–interaction data.

---

[24] Equation (2.2.1) may be restated as

$$\dot{M}^J = \bar{\rho}^J \gamma^L S^L - \bar{c}^J S^J + \bar{g}^J \qquad (2.7.11)$$

where γ^L is the "overall probability of reliability" as Sorenson defines it and S^J and S^L represent numbers of weapons (in standardized units). Here we replace the M^J in Sorenson with the stock-type variable S^J to reflect the cost of maintaining and operating a stock of weapons. Equation (2.2.1) may also be rewritten as

$$\dot{Q}^J = \bar{\rho}^J Q^L + \bar{\rho}^J S^L - \bar{c}^J Q^J + \bar{g}^J \qquad (2.7.12)$$

where J reacts not only to Q^L as a combined quantitative–qualitative index, but also to S^L.

Typically, the international tension variable has been introduced as a variable to be added to several other basic ones in a model. However, another approach – a macrosystem approach – might center on international hostility as the single basic variable. For example, in a "pure" hostility model Muncaster and Zinnes (1982–3) set the time rate of change in the rate of increase (or decrease) of hostility, namely, $\ddot{H}(t)$, equal to the sum of four independent factors:

1. the level of arms of each nation as representing *directed hostilities*, which is captured in a combined way by a term $\alpha \dot{H}(t)$;
2. the Richardson grievance variables captured by a second term $\beta / H(t)$;
3. the rapidly mounting fear of war as the level of H approaches some relatively high level H^* represented by the term $\gamma / (\epsilon + [H^* - H(t)]^2)$, ϵ being a very small positive constant included to avoid discontinuities when $H = H^*$; and
4. the acceleration of hostilities that takes place immediately preceding the outbreak of war (which occurs when $H = H^{**}$) represented by the term $\xi / [H^{**} - H(t)]$.

In this model, each of the four terms has a parameter whose value must be set (estimated).

The Muncaster and Zinnes approach suppresses information on the behavior of individual nations and other key behaving units and therefore by itself cannot be categorized as an arms race model. A race by definition has at least two participants. However, this approach points up system effects beyond the control of individual behaving units. These effects do forcefully enter arms races and therefore must be incorporated into arms race models as well as other behaviorally oriented models. We shall discuss this point further in section 2.10.

Closely related to the international tension variable is the variable *diplomatic time* developed by Allan (1983). He holds that (1) diplomatic time T increases more rapidly than normal time t when interactions (as measured by relevant events *weighted by their intensities*) occur more than usual and (2) interactions themselves increase (decrease) with an increase (decrease) of diplomatic time. Thus, more change can be packed into a given real-time interval when the frequency of events causes diplomatic time to run faster than normal time.

To point up the significance of diplomatic time, Allan extends the two-nation basic arms race model of Lambelet et al. (1979). Writing the equation for nation J only, he obtains

$$\dot{M}^J = \alpha^J [\exp(a^J - b^J / DC^J - c^J / M^L - h^J / GNP^J) - M^J] \qquad (2.7.13)$$

Here a^J, b^J, c^J and h^J are constants and α^J (as in Strauss 1972, 1978) is the speed of adjustment between the desired (the first term in the brackets on the right side) and actual level M^J of power capability as measured by military expenditures. In this equation, e^{-c^J/M^L} is a mutual stimulation force (the larger is M^L, the larger is this term), e^{-h^J/GNP^J} is a self-stimulation force reflecting change in military expenditures resulting simply from change in GNP (an economic growth-bureaucratic momentum factor), and e^{-b^J/DC^J} is the escalation (deescalation) force stemming from increase (decrease) in diplomatic climate DC^J as perceived by J. The diplomatic climate for J is defined as the cumulation of all past conflictual behavior by L up to and including the present time t (where each item of behavior is discounted by a time rate of forgetting r^J).[25]

Although the Allan model is conceptually complex, it represents one of the most comprehensive treatments of general variables for an arms race model that is tested against available data. In effect, Allan fuses into one an arms race submodel and a conflict submodel.

Finally, in this section we want to say a few words about *psychological factors*. There are many: insecurity, fear, suspicion and distrust, anxiety, and so on. Many of these factors have been examined. For example, Abelson (1963) shows how the concepts of provocation and counterprovocation, sensitivity, and forgiveness can be employed to generate a Richardson-type arms race model. Further, Squires (1976) explicitly introduces trust in a Richardson model disaggregated by conventional and strategic weapons but does so by relating it to perceived probabilities of "hostilities breaking out." Moreover, Pilisuk (1984) is exploring the effects of personality, unilateral initiatives, and the nature of communication between parties (as it affects their suspicions and fears) upon the outcome of two-party conflicts. And so forth. We do not have the space

---

[25] Specifically, where $\tau = t_0, \ldots, t$, diplomatic time is given by

$$DC^J = \beta^J \int_{t_0}^{t} E^L(\tau) r^J \exp[-r^J(t - \tau)] d\tau \qquad (2.7.14)$$

where β^J is a constant. Conflictual behavior by L, namely, E^L, at a point of time τ is equal to such behavior at the start of the previous point of time $\tau - 1$ plus the change $\dot{E}^L$ (increase or decrease) during that time where

$$\dot{E}^L = \frac{dE^L}{dT} \frac{dT}{dt} \qquad (2.7.15)$$

In Eq. (2.7.15) the expression dT/dt represents change in diplomatic time and is defined as

$$dT/dt = \mu \log(E^J + E^L + 1) \qquad (2.7.16)$$

where E^J and E^L are indices of the number of events associated with J and L, respectively, weighted by their conflict intensity and μ is a scaling factor that should be chosen so that $T = t$ in the long run. Then Allan further introduces relative bargaining power and resolve.

to go into detail. However, it is perhaps useful to cite the model of Hamblin et al. (1977), which also can be related in part to a Richardson model. In Hamblin, the key psychological variable is insecurity, and the two basic relations involved are psychological sensation and adaption. Following Stevens (1966, 1972), Hamblin et al. state that change in *psychological sensation dp/p* is proportionate to change in stimulus *ds/s*. That is,

$$dp/p = \bar{h}\, ds/s \qquad (2.7.17)$$

where $\bar{h}$ is a constant of proportionality. This relation yields a power function that has been shown to describe the behavior of a wide range of perceptual attitudinal interactions, including negative factors such as *insecurity* accumulating in time in "low-stakes" conflict. The process of sensory *adaption* is assumed to take place when decision makers in a nation, say, J, feel threatened by their relative weakness. Here, psychophysical experiments by Ekman (1970) suggest not a Stevens's power function but an exponential, where the change in J's insecurity $d\tilde{I}^J/\tilde{I}^J$ is proportionate to the increment dM^L in L's armament effort. That is,

$$d\tilde{I}^J/\tilde{I}^J = \omega\, dM^L \qquad (2.7.18)$$

where ω is a constant. If the response to the cumulative insecurity is as per Stevens [Eq. (2.7.17)], then the relative increase dM^J/M^J in J's armaments (J's response) at time t should be proportionate to the relative increase in J's insecurity (the stimulus). That is,

$$dM^J/M^J = h\, d\tilde{I}^J/\tilde{I}^J \qquad (2.7.19)$$

where h is a constant of proportionality. Putting Eq. (2.7.18) into (2.7.19), dividing both sides by dt, and integrating to solve for M^J yields

$$M^J(t) = b\, \exp[\sigma M^L(t)] \qquad (2.7.20)$$

where $\sigma = hc$ and where, according to Hamblin, b is part scaling constant and part grievance parameter.

Since Hamblin assumes an asymmetrical situation where nation L is substantially ahead of J in armaments, he assumes L does not act under duress and thus does not adapt. Rather, L behaves according to a Stevens's power function as in Eq. (2.7.17) where M^J replaces s and where, as with J, the percentage change in $\tilde{I}^L$ and thus g^L is directly related to the percentage change in the rival's military expenditures.

Hence, after integration and allowance for a time lag in L's response to J's action, we obtain

$$M^L(t) = \theta M^J(t - 1)^q \qquad (2.7.21)$$

where θ is partly a scaling constant and partly an aggression parameter and where q is a product of constants of proportionality. Thus Hamblin suggests the preceding asymmetrical nonlinear model as a replacement of the Richardson model, and he puts forth empirical materials to support this replacement.

Although Hamblin makes a contribution in recognizing the asymmetry and nonlinear character of the arms race, his major contribution lies in his emphasis on basic psychological processes that underlie the arms race. By providing a purely psychological behavioral interpretation, the physical manufacture of weapons being simply the outcome of the decisions made (orders or commands issued), he makes clear that an arms race model, linear or nonlinear, symmetrical or asymmetrical, cannot be interpreted as reflecting system effects alone. However, he fails to bring in the problem of allocation of scarce resources between military goods and civilian goods production – the central problem as perceived by the economist. Nor does he give adequate attention to the optimizing behavior characterizing each of several interest groups with conflicting objectives and the resulting balance-of-power outcomes – a central problem as perceived by the political scientist.

2.8   Organizational politics and the determination of the arms budget

The last point, namely, the struggle for power among interest groups and the accompanying competition wherein each tries to optimize (or satisfice) on its objective has significant bearing on the level of military expenditures and the resulting weaponry stock of a nation. Such struggle and competition has led certain scholars to develop "organizational politics" models. These models are basic for the short-run determination of the level of military expenditures and types and scope of weapon development. Drawing heavily upon work by Davis, Dempster, and Wildavsky (1966), Allison (1971), Gist (1974), Ostrom (1977a, 1978b), and others, Majeski (1983b) constructs the following organizational politics model for the United States involving four policy-making groups:

1. the Defense Services Agencies with a request for a budget for military expenditures;
2. the president, who follows with his/her request;
3. the Congress, which then makes an appropriation; and, finally,
4. the Department of Defense, which then spends the appropriation and when necessary requests a supplementary appropriation.

In his disaggregated decision-making model, Majeski assumes that

1. each behaving unit can effectively organize its set of objectives (goals) so that it can state its desired level of military expenditures;
2. a partial adjustment mechanism (disequilibrium-type process) characterizes the reaching of a decision by each behaving unit; and
3. adaptive expectations prevail.

Adaptive expectations means that the expectation of the magnitude of military expenditures at time t is equal to the expectation at the previous time $t - 1$ plus typically some fraction of the difference between the actual magnitude realized then and the expectation.

With regard to the budget for military expenditures, Majeski defines:

M_1 = Defense Services Agencies' request
M_2 = president's budget request
M_3 = congressional appropriation
M_4 = actual military expenditures by the Department of Defense
DE = expected federal deficit
AP = supplementary military appropriations

He indicates *expected magnitude* by the "hat" ($\hat{\ }$) placed *over* the relevant symbol and *desired magnitude* by the asterisk (*) placed *after* the symbol. Then, according to Majeski:

(a) *For the Defense Services Agencies:*

$$M_1^j(t) = a_1 \hat{M}_2^j(t) + \bar{z}\dot{M}^L(t - 1)$$
$$\text{where} \quad a_1 > 1.0 \text{ and } \bar{z} \geq 0 \quad (2.8.1)$$
$$\hat{M}_2^j(t) = \hat{M}_2^j(t - 1) + \beta_1[M_2^j(t - 1) - \hat{M}_2^j(t - 1)]$$
$$\text{where} \quad \beta_1 > 0.5 \quad (2.8.2)$$

where we have added to Majeski's Eq. (2.8.1) the variable $\dot{M}^L(t - 1)$, namely, change in military expenditures of the Soviet Union, in order to link Majeski's model more effectively to models already discussed.

(b) *For the president:*

$$M_2^{j*}(t) = a_2 M_1^j(t) + q\mathrm{DE}(t)$$
$$\text{where} \quad a_2 < 1.0, q < 0.0 \quad (2.8.3)$$
$$M_2^j(t) = M_2^j(t - 1) + \beta_2[M_2^{j*}(t) - M_2^j(t - 1)]$$
$$\text{where} \quad 0 < \beta_2 < 1 \quad (2.8.4)$$

(c) *For the congressional appropriation:*
$$M_3^{J*}(t) = a_3 M_2^J(t) + \gamma DE(t)$$
$$\text{where} \quad a_3 < 1.0, \gamma < 0.0 \quad (2.8.5)$$
$$M_3^J(t) = M_3^J(t-1) + \beta_3[M_3^{J*}(t) - M_3^J(t-1)]$$
$$\text{where} \quad \beta_3 < 1.0 \quad (2.8.6)$$
(d) *For the Department of Defense:*
$$M_4^{J*}(t) = a_4[M_3^J(t) + AP(t)]$$
$$\text{where} \quad a_4 > 1.0 \quad (2.8.7)$$
$$M_4^J(t) = M_4^J(t-1) + \beta_4[M_4^{J*}(t) - M_4^J(t-1)]$$
$$\text{where} \quad 0 < \beta_4 < 1 \quad (2.8.8)$$

This model is designed to capture some of the basic politics that enter into the determination of the military expenditures in the United States. Clearly, it has significance for the short run, in particular for the level of military expenditures for a given year t or the following year. Whereas some may claim that for the long run the factors involved in an organizational politics model may be much less significant, yet the long run is after all a sequence of short runs, and the cumulation of what happens in each of the short runs can have a major impact on the long run. Hence, the short run and organizational politics cannot be set aside.

We can only cite a few other organizational politics models of significance. Crecine and Fischer (1973) introduce a budget cut equation having casualties and political party in power as two of its variables and introduce standard budget-cutting rules. Rattinger (1975), influenced by incrementalist thinking, digs into bureaucratic momentum as a variable (which to some scholars places a constraint on the play of organizational politics) and adds international tensions as another major factor. Ostrom (1978b) develops an important reaction linkage model, covering many of the preceding relations but considering also the number of U.S. servicemen killed in wars and the congressional mood while introducing as shocks presence of war, change in presidential party, and change in public opinion. Lucier (1979) examines parametric changes in organizational politics models resulting from dramatic changes (e.g., the election of Roosevelt). Brito and Intriligator (1980) cast additional light on organizational politics with their game theory model of the allocative process.

Ostrom and Marra (1986) offer a model based upon a synthesis of the organizational process and bureaucratic politics perspectives. In this model, Ostrom and Marra recognize both the multistage character of the U.S. budgetary process and the fact that Soviet defense expenditures and U.S. public opinion are potentially relevant causative factors in U.S. defense spending.

2.9   The import of domestic political economy factors

In the Majeski organizational politics model, the deficit in the federal budget is an important variable in influencing the request and actual and supplementary appropriations for military expenditures. A number of other variables of a political–economic character have been put forward by scholars as significant in determining levels of military expenditures. For example, Hartley and McLean (1978) have introduced the following into explanatory equations: per capita income, unemployment rate, balance of payments, political party in office, and planned military expenditures as a percentage of total government expenditures. Nincic and Cusack (1979) have added private consumption and investment and electoral cycle to their war mobilization variable. Saris and Middendorp (1980), like Wolfson (1985), have stressed productive capacity; they have pointed up the negative impact of excessive military expenditures upon productive capacity (as may be modified by technology) and thus the future ability of a nation to generate high levels of military expenditures. Cusack and Ward (1981) have added the economic planning cycle to the variables economic performance (related to GNP), electoral cycle (leadership tenure), war mobilization, and domestic violence. Griffin, Wallace, and Devine (1982) and later Mintz and Hicks (1984) have added to the list percentage change in monopoly profits, percentage change in industrial concentration, control for inflation, and government revenue.

Another basic variable is *public opinion* and the associated variable *internal unrest*. Abolfathi (1980) has examined at some depth its significance. Replacing the term *public opinion* with *public concern* for international problems, he has designed the following three-equation model for the United States (where all magnitudes are for time t except when indicated otherwise):

$$PC = a_1 + a_2 Z - a_3 MP(t - 1) + a_4 H \qquad (2.9.1)$$
$$PS = b_1 - b_2[M(t - 1)/G(t - 1)] + b_3 PC \qquad (2.9.2)$$
$$r_R = c_1 + c_2 PS(t - 1) + c_3 Z + c_4 H \qquad (2.9.3)$$

where

PC = public concern for international problems, taken to be equivalent to public perception of threat as measured by the annual average percentage of respondents in national opinion surveys singling out international and foreign policy issues as the most important problems facing the United States;

Z = a dummy variable (ranging from 0 to 3) representing the extent of U.S. war involvement, which together with H represents actual external threats;

MP = number of active military personnel in U.S. armed forces, to reflect perception by the public of the adequacy of defense capability;

H = a second dummy variable (ranging from 0 to 3) representing the level of international tension affecting U.S. interests as based on coded materials;

PS = public support for increased defense outlays as measured by the annual average percentage of respondents in national opinion surveys supporting increases in such spending;

M/G = defense spending M as a percentage of total U.S. federal spending G as reflecting the public's perception of the adequacy of government concern for defense;

r_R = real change in defense spending as measured by annual percentage compound growth rate of defense consumption in 1957 prices;

and where a_1, a_2, a_3, a_4, b_1, b_2, b_3, c_1, c_2, c_3, and c_4 are constants. Ostrom (1978b), in a less sophisticated manner, handles large changes in public opinion as shocks, which he then introduces as dummy variables in his estimating equation.

Closely associated with the public opinion variable is internal unrest. Here Cusack and Ward (1981) point up domestic violence (internal unrest) and the associated need for its control as a major variable in their explanatory equation for military expenditures in Mainland China. Also Abolfathi (1978) has explored domestic violence within Iran and Iraq as significant variables affecting their respective military expenditures.

Foreign aid is another significant political economy variable. Here Ferejohn (1976) starts with a static utility optimization model wherein the utility of each nation is dependent on (1) its civilian goods expenditures, (2) its military expenditures, and (3) its forecast of its rival's military expenditures, subject to a resource constraint and a military expenditures constraint based on its reaction to its forecast of its rival's expenditures. He next examines how a one-shot dose of military aid from a third source has continuing effects on both nations' arms expenditures. He does so under several kinds of situations and tests his model with empirical materials on the India–Pakistan arms race. A more sophisticated differential game analysis with foreign aid as a basic variable is performed by Zinnes et al. (1978b), who state:

> Nations have a variety of ways of handling potential conflicts. Another approach is to win friends and influence nations through foreign aid pro-

grams. Both for the purpose of establishing allies who might give direct assistance in a future conflict and to neutralize potential enemies, the "aid race," while more indirect than an "arms race," would appear to be an equally important part of any model of international confrontation. (p. 17)

In their differential game, Zinnes et al. take v^J and v^L, the respective expenditures on foreign aid of nations J and L, as their control variables. They assume that M^J and M^L (military expenditures of J and L, respectively) are mechanistically determined as per a bureaucratic politics model and so are state variables that nations can affect only indirectly through manipulating foreign aid decisions. They suggest that this is a reasonable assumption when there are stormy battles over foreign aid allocations. Considering that each nation finds it desirable to have as much as possible of its limited resources available for civilian goods production, each nation is taken to choose its foreign aid expenditures so that a quadratic expression representing the sum of several goals regarding international confrontation is minimized. For example, for J the goals are

1. *arms balance,* reflected in the term $\omega_1^J(M^J - \lambda_1^J M^L)^2$, indicating that J would like to be λ_1^J times as strong as L;
2. *aid balance,* reflected in the term $\omega_2^J(v^J - \lambda_2^J v^L)^2$, indicating that J would like to provide λ_2^J times as much aid as L;
3. *minimization of war probabilities* (ceteris paribus), reflected in the term $\omega_3^J(M^J + M^L)^2$, where war probability is considered proportional to the square of the sum of armament expenditures of the two rivals; and
4. *minimization of foreign aid expenditures* (ceteris paribus), reflected in the term $\omega_4^J(v^J + v^L)^2, \ldots$.

Accordingly, J's objective function, which is to be minimized taking into account that L (with a similar type of objective function) is also optimizing, is (omitting the t symbol when obvious)

$$J(v^J, v^L) = \int_{t_0}^{t_1} [\omega_1^J(M^J - \lambda_1^J M^L)^2 + \omega_2^J(v^J - \lambda_2^J v^L)^2$$
$$+ \omega_3^J(M^J + M^L)^2 + \omega_4^J(v^J + v^L)^2 + \cdots] \, dt \qquad (2.9.4)$$

Next, Zinnes et al. set up a Richardson-type equation for each nation, the equation for J being

$$\dot{M}^J = \rho_1^J M^L + \rho_2^J v^L - c_3^J[M^J + \xi^J v^J] + g^J \qquad (2.9.5)$$

where the first two terms on the right side represent J's reactions to L's military and foreign aid expenditures, respectively, and where the third term represents the burden on J's economy.

Following standard procedures in the analysis of differential games, Zinnes et al. derive optimal strategy and trajectories for each nation regarding foreign aid expenditures for various assignments of values to their parameters, each representing a particular scenario.

Abolfathi (1978) has constructed a related econometric model of the Iraq–Iran arms race (1945–70) involving the variables military aid and exports by the United States and the Soviet Union to Iran and Iraq, respectively. McGuire (1982) constructs an econometric model, pointing up how U.S. assistance affects and is affected by Israel's allocation of resources between defense, public nondefense, and private consumption goods and how Arab allocations are influenced. Also McGuire (1987) develops an econometric method for the study of competitive or complementary relations among capital formation, national defense, and foreign assistance in developing and other aid-receiving countries, applying the method to Israel.

2.10   Defense spending and alliances in an *n*-nation system

Two-nation arms race models have dominated the field not only because of their much greater mathematical tractability, but also because the world has been dominated by two major powers (and their respective blocs) at odds with each other ever since World War II. Nonetheless, the world is a U-nation (*n*-nation) system, and this system has major impact upon each of the two big powers, via macrosystem effects and via dyadic relationships. Moreover, alliance behavior, which has dominated so much of past history, still plays an important role today and undoubtedly will play a dominating role in decades to come as Mainland China asserts itself in the world system as an emerging power.

The linear Richardson model has been concisely stated for a U-nation system by Siljak (1977a). The change in each nation's military expenditures is taken as a linear function of the military expenditures of every other nation in the system. In matrix form,

$$\dot{M} = \rho M + g \qquad\qquad (2.10.1)$$

where

$M =$ a $U \times 1$ column vector of the U military expenditures, one for each nation, $\dot{M}$ being a corresponding column vector;

$\rho =$ a matrix of coefficients, the principal diagonal coefficients being fatigue coefficients, one for each nation, with the other coefficients $\rho^{JL}(J \neq L)$ indicating the reaction of nation J to the military expenditures of nation L;

$g =$ a $U \times 1$ column vector of U grievance coefficients, one for each nation.

This model can be reformulated:

1. to allow alliances among nations such that the reaction coefficients ρ^{JL} between any two allied nations J and L may be negative, as previously suggested by Zinnes et al. (1976a);
2. to allow for a linear model with time-varying coefficients $\rho^{JL}(t)$ for which $\pmb{\rho}(t)$ replaces $\pmb{\rho}$;
3. to allow for a model with nonlinear time-varying elements $\rho^{JL}(t, M)$ for which $\pmb{\rho}(t, M)$ replaces $\pmb{\rho}$, including the competitive species (Lotka-Volterra) model; and
4. where stochastic elements (random variables) are introduced leading to the equations

$$dM = \pmb{\rho}(t, M)\, dt + \Gamma(t, M)\, dz \qquad (2.10.2)$$

wherein questions of stability and the impact of alliances upon stability are examined.

A still more general conceptual framework (nonstochastic and non-lagged) is developed by Sandberg (1977a, 1978) wherein a U-nation arms race is regarded as one special case of a general dynamic process. In this framework there is communication of a pertinent type among behaving units, and reactions tend to be reciprocated in a certain weak sense. For the special case of an arms race, a model might take the general form

$$pp^J = \rho^J(M^A, \ldots, M^J, \ldots, M^U; g^\alpha, \ldots, g^\eta), \qquad (2.10.3)$$
$$J = A, B, \ldots, U$$

where

pp^J = propensity of nation J to change its level of military expenditures and ordinarily is taken to be $\dot{M}^J$;

$g^\alpha, \ldots, g^\eta$ = grievance constants (which will be $U^2 - U$ in number when there is a grievance for each nation toward every other).

Here again existence of an equilibrium, stability, and other properties of an abstract U-nation system can be examined. For example, Siljak (1977a) shows that if each of three pairs of nations is separately stable in a three-nation arms race, there remains the possibility that the triplet of nations may be unstable, which is an argument advanced by Richardson. Conversely, if the triplet is stable, the pairwise arms races are also stable, confirming a similar argument by Richardson. Also see Isard and Liossatos (1972a,b, 1979, chaps. 12, 13) for U-nation analyses and relativistic effects.

On a less abstract level, Schrodt (1978a) examines the U-nation model described by Eq. (2.10.1). When coefficients ρ^{JL}, $\rho^{LJ} > 0$, nations J and L

are mutually antagonistic; when ρ^{JL}, $\rho^{LJ} < 0$, J and L are in a mutual defense alliance; when both these coefficients are zero, J and L are mutually neutral; and so forth. Schrodt then can effectively employ the coefficient matrix ρ to characterize an alliance structure. He examines under what values of the coefficients ρ^{JL} and the g^J, J, $L = A, \ldots, U$, collective security (a state of affairs where the coalition of $U - 1$ nations against one offender is sufficient to ensure the defeat of that offender) is preserved by the Richardson model of Eq. (2.10.1). He also examines the conditions under which a single nation can operate as a "balancer" in the sense that by changing its own reaction coefficients, it can stabilize the entire arms race, ceteris paribus.

Many other scholars have studied alliance structures and models. For example, Milstein (1970) analyzes Soviet–American influences on the Arab–Israeli arms race, which race Lambelet (1971) also analyzes. Squires (1976) considers defense alliances in his conceptual framework that involves trust and resource constraints and differentiates between conventional and strategic weapons. By adding a mechanism for the incremental change of alliances, he makes the alliance structure of the U-nation system a dynamic part of the arms race model. Choucri and North (1975) consider alliances in their study (see section 2.11). Baugh (1978) examines cases where minor powers are allied to major powers. Hunter (1980) examines three-nation arms races, with no alliances, with two nations allied against a third, and with one nation having a secret alliance with each of the other two.

Before leaving this topic, note the possibility of coalitions among interest groups. Intriligator and Brito (1985d) model a six-person game in which each of two rival nations (or blocs) has an arms industry, an arms bureaucracy, and a civilian sector. The arms industries in both nations maximize a payoff function that depends on both profit levels and employment; these are related to the level of military contracts, which in turn is governed by the budget of the arms bureaucracy. The arms bureaucracy in each nation maximizes a payoff function that depends on its budget (the percentage of national resources allocated to the military) and the perceived levels of weaponry of the adversary and allies. Thus, because the payoff of both the arms industry and the arms bureaucracy in each nation in general increases with an increase in the military budget, the well-known emergence of the military–industrial complex as a coalition of the arms industry and the arms bureaucracy is to be expected. However, because the civilian sector in both nations has a payoff function that, when optimized, assigns more resources to the military and less to civilian goods production as the perceived level of security decreases, it is to the interest of the arms bureaucracies of the two rival nations to collude. In this model they do so by disseminating to the public misinformation that exaggerates their actual perceptions of the rival's military capability.

2.11   Arms races and the operation and functioning of the world system

Any arms race necessarily operates within the world system, however that system may be defined.[26] Inevitably, the current state of that system, its past, and its dynamics directly and indirectly have influence on that race. Choucri and North (1975) have delved into these effects in their study of the dynamics of international violence. In their study, the key endogenous variables in addition to military expenditures $M^J(J = A, B, \ldots, U)$ are *alliances* (AL), *violence behavior* toward other nations (VB), *intensity of intersections* (II), and *colonial area* (CA), the last variable being of significance for the pre–World War I period they studied. In Figure 2.6, the basic relationships of their model for any one nation are presented. Military expenditures are taken as a linear function of

1. previous year expenditures,
2. military expenditures of nonallies,
3. intensity of intersections (II),
4. colonial area (CA), and
5. the product of population (POP) and national income (NI).

That is, for nation J,

$$M^J(t) = \lambda_0 + \lambda_1 M^J(t - 1) + \lambda_2 \sum_L M^L(t) + \lambda_3 II^J(t)$$
$$+ \lambda_4 CA^J(t) + \lambda_5 [POP^J(t) \times NI^J(t)] \quad (2.11.1)$$

where L is a nonally and $\lambda_0, \ldots, \lambda_5$ are coefficients. We do not have the space to spell out the details of this explanatory equation nor of the others that Choucri and North put forth, such as

$$II^J(t) = \omega_0 + \omega_1 CA^J(t) + \omega_2 M^J(t) + \omega_3 \sum_L CA^L(t)$$
$$+ \omega_4 VB^J + \omega_5 \sum_L VB^L \quad (2.11.2)$$

where VB is violence behavior toward others and $\omega_0, \ldots, \omega_5$ are coefficients. Rather, we note the major step forward they take in explicitly introducing system effects and constructing an exploratory testable model – a model seriously questioned by Zuk (1985) and others.

Choucri and North studied the pre–World War I period (1871–1914)

---

[26] Although a discussion of international data sets is beyond the scope of this book, we should mention here the invaluable collection of the Correlates of War Project by Singer and his associates. See Chapter 8, footnote 7.

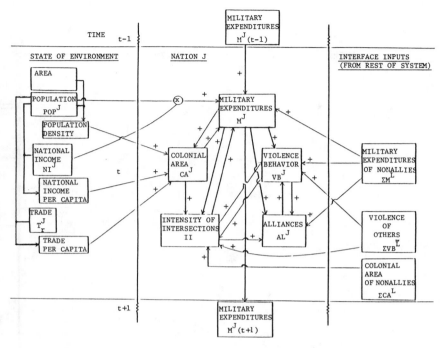

Figure 2.6. The Choucri–North model of international violence.

with a simultaneous-equations approach, testing their framework against empirical materials for Britain, France, Germany, Italy, Russia, and Austria–Hungary. One of their students, Ashley (1980), studied the post–World War II period, 1951–72. He was able to dig at greater depth, however only for three nations: the United States, the Soviet Union, and Mainland China. His main contribution lies in the introduction of some dynamics into the Choucri–North framework by allowing for time lags in a block-recursive model.

The most complete and balanced system framework has been and continues to be developed by Deutsch, Bremer, and their associates in the GLOBUS model (Bremer 1987).[27] Results of various simulations have been and are being examined and evaluated. In Figure 2.7 we present a sketch of the GLOBUS model within Isard's conceptual framework of Peace Science as a discipline. This framework is presented in Figure 1.3 and summarily discussed in section 1.2.[28]

---

[27] Note, among other frameworks, Mesarovic and Pestel (1974), Barney (1980), Leontief et al. (1977), Klein (1977), and Onishi (1983). Also see Chapter 9 of this volume, wherein we discuss how military expenditures enter into world economy models.

[28] See Isard and Smith (1982, chaps. 14 and 15) for a full discussion of this framework.

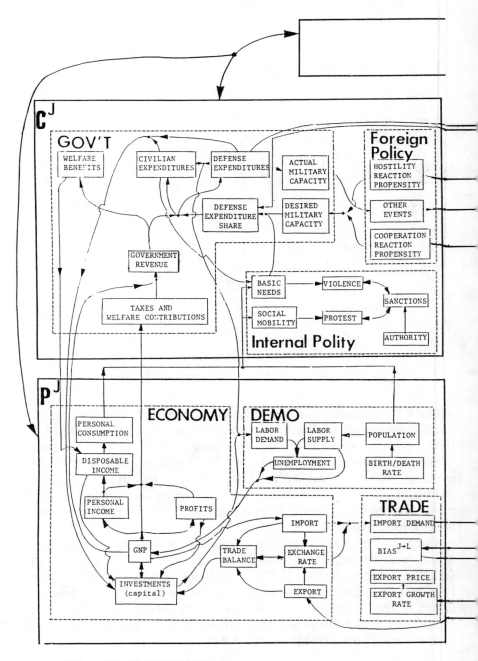

Figure 2.7. The GLOBUS framework.

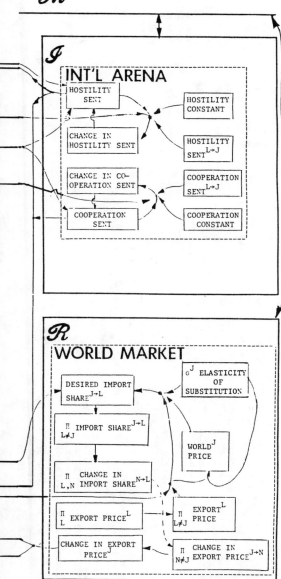

$\mathcal{I}$

INT'L ARENA

HOSTILITY SENT

HOSTILITY CONSTANT

CHANGE IN HOSTILITY SENT

$\text{HOSTILITY SENT}^{L \rightarrow J}$

CHANGE IN CO-OPERATION SENT

$\text{COOPERATION SENT}^{L \rightarrow J}$

COOPERATION SENT

COOPERATION CONSTANT

$\mathcal{R}$

WORLD MARKET

$\text{DESIRED IMPORT SHARE}^{J \rightarrow L}$

$\prod_{L \neq J} \text{IMPORT SHARE}^{J \rightarrow L}$

σ^{J} ELASTICITY OF SUBSTITUTION

WORLD^{J} PRICE

$\prod_{L,N} \text{CHANGE IN IMPORT SHARE}^{N \rightarrow L}$

$\prod_{L} \text{EXPORT PRICE}^{L}$

$\prod_{L \neq J} \text{EXPORT}^{L}$ PRICE

$\text{CHANGE IN EXPORT PRICE}^{J}$

$\prod_{N \neq J} \text{CHANGE IN EXPORT PRICE}^{J \rightarrow N}$

US-USSR

├─ Expenditures

├─ Capabilities
　　├─ Aggregated
　　└─ Disaggregated

Expenditures

Smoker 1963a (1948-52 g)	Smoker 1963b (1948-60 g)	Gillespie 1980* et al (1948-75 e)	Wallace 1980 (1950-76 e)
Smoker 1964 (1948-60 g)	Smoker 1966* (1948-61 g)	Majeski & 1981* Jones (1949-75 e)	Hollist & 1982 Johnson (1948-76 e)
Zinnes & 1973* Gillespie (1949-72 e)	Gregory 1974 (1950-67 e)	Griffen 1982 (1949-76 e)	Freeman 1983* (1949-75 e)
Taagepera 1975* et al (1945-72 g)	Luterbacher 1974* (1947-65 s,e)	Allan 1983 (1946-63 s)	Majeski 1983a,b (1953-79 e)
Hollist 1977a* (1948-73 e)	Gillespie 1977c* et al (1947-72 e)	Ward 1984a*,b* (1951-79 s)	Nincic 1983 (1955-78 e)
Ostrom 1977a (1954-69 e)	Hollist 1977b (1948-70 e)	Marra 1985* (1947-80 e)	Majeski 1985* (1949-81 e)
Ostrom 1978a (1954-69 e)	Gillespie 1978* et al (1950-71 e)	Zuk & 1986 Woodbury (1948-82 e)	Ostrom & 1986 Marra (1967-84 e)
Hollist & 1978 Guetzkow (1958-70 e)	Ostrom 1978b (1955-73 e)		
Gillespie 1979* et al (1947-72 e)	Strauss 1978 (1951-69 e)		
	Lambelet 1979 et al (1959-75 s)		

Capabilities

Aggregated	Disaggregated
Lambelet 1973 (1951-71 e)	Luterbacher 1976 (1960-70 s)
McGuire 1977* (1960-73 e)	McGuire 1977* (1960-73 e)
Ward 1984a*,b* (1951-79 s)	Hamblin 1977* et al (1949-73 e)
Mayer 1985 (1951-78 s)	Saris & 1980 Middendorp (1960-77 e)
Ayanian 1986* (1965-84 e)	McCubbins 1983 (1964-76 e)
	Marra 1985* (1947-80 e)
	Ayanian 1986* (1965-84 e)

64

65

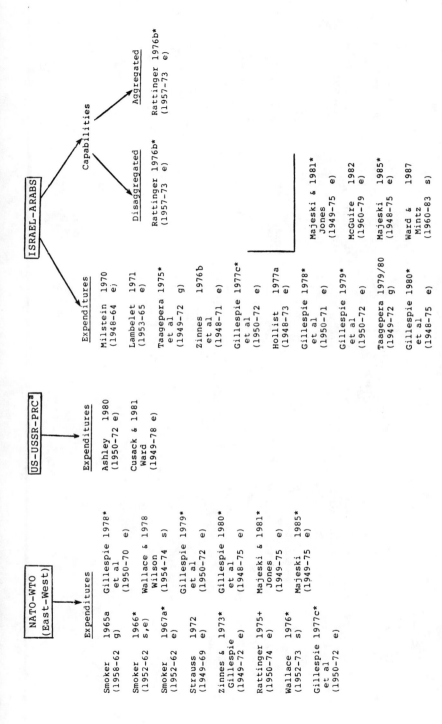

Figure 2.8. Arms races empirically analyzed (see key and notes on p. 67).

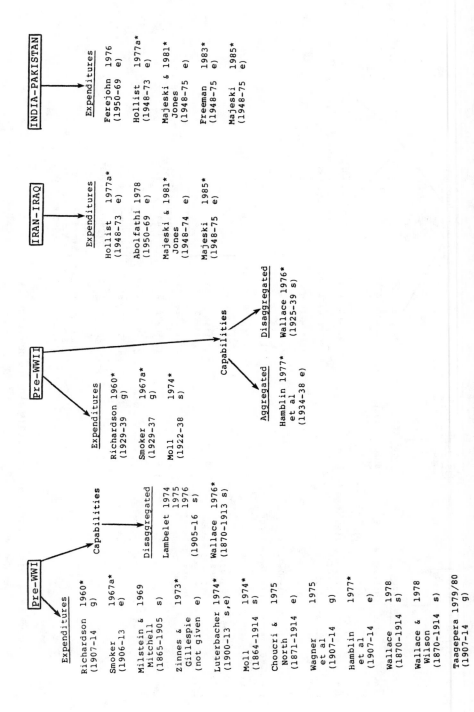

66

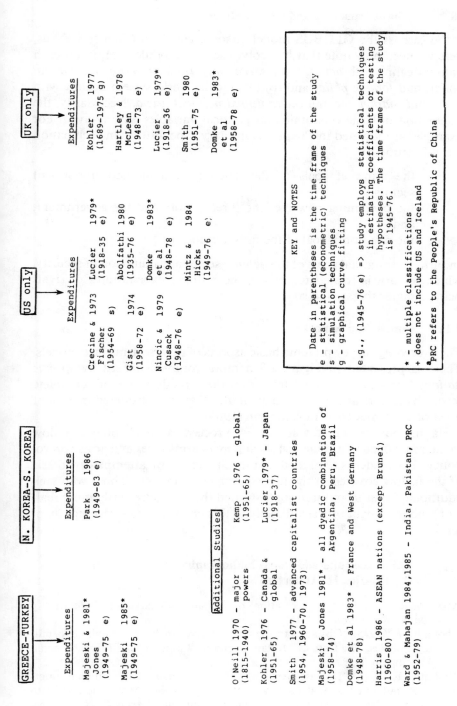

GREECE-TURKEY

Expenditures

Majeski & 1981*
Jones
(1949-75 e)

Majeski 1985*
(1949-75 e)

N. KOREA-S. KOREA

Expenditures

Park 1986
(1949-83 e)

Additional Studies

O'Neill 1970 - major
(1815-1940)   powers

Kohler 1976 - Canada &
(1951-65)   global

Smith 1977 - advanced capitalist countries
(1954, 1960-70, 1973)

Majeski & Jones 1981* - all dyadic combinations of
(1958-74)   Argentina, Peru, Brazil

Domke et al 1983* - France and West Germany
(1948-78)

Harris 1986 - ASEAN nations (except Brunei)
(1960-80)

Ward & Mahajan 1984,1985 - India, Pakistan, PRC
(1952-79)

Kemp 1976 - global
(1951-65)

Lucier 1979* - Japan
(1918-37)

US only

Expenditures

Crecine & 1973   Lucier   1979*
Fischer   (1918-35   e)
(1954-69 s)

Gist   1974   Abolfathi 1980
(1958-72 e)   (1935-76 e)

Nincic & 1979   Domke   1983*
Cusack   et al
(1948-76 e)   (1948-78   e)

                 Mintz &   1984
                 Hicks
                 (1949-76   e)

UK only

Expenditures

Kohler 1977
(1689-1975 g)

Hartley & 1978
McLean
(1948-73 e)

Lucier   1979*
(1918-36 e)

Smith   1980
(1951-75 e)

Domke   1983*
et al
(1958-78 e)

KEY and NOTES

Date in parentheses is the time frame of the study
e - statistical (econometric) techniques
s - simulation techniques
g - graphical curve fitting

e.g., (1945-76 e) => study employs statistical techniques
in estimating coefficients or testing
hypotheses. The time frame of the study
is 1945-76.

* - multiple classifications
+ - does not include US and Iceland
[a]PRC refers to the People's Republic of China

Figure 2.8 (cont.)

We discuss the GLOBUS model at some length in Chapter 9. Thus, here we need only note that it involves several modules: (a) six for each nation dealing with *demographics, economy, trade, government, internal policy,* and *foreign policy* and (b) two for the world system dealing with the *world market* and the *international political arena*. Necessarily, the interaction of basic economic and political variables are involved. For example, as indicated in Chapter 9, military expenditures in each nation *J* is a function of

1. the minimal goals of the defense, civilian, and investment sectors,
2. the bargaining power of the three sectors and the government, and
3. the maximum goal of the fiscal authorities.

In turn, the minimal goals of the defense sector are a function of security, which in turn is related to threats, the military expenditures of rivals being a major threat, and so on.

2.12   Concluding remarks

The preceding survey presents basic aspects of diverse arms race models. There is presented in Figure 2.8 a more complete record by *specific nations* (arms race theaters) treated in these models. A more complete record by factors and associated attributes that are considered in each of most of these models is in Anderton (1986).

Having now presented a survey, we proceed in the chapters to follow to dig more deeply into the factors at play in arms races and arms control policy. The reader is reminded that in Chapter 13 we attempt a synthesis of the factors covered in the diverse arms race models. Those who seek additional input from more sophisticated (but not necessarily more realistic) models might proceed directly to this chapter before reading Chapter 3.

References and additional bibliography
(by Charles H. Anderton)

Abelson, R. P. (1963) "A 'Derivation' of Richardson's Equations." *Journal of Conflict Resolution* 7:13–15.

Abolfathi, F. (1975) "Obstacles to the Quantitative Analysis of Public Expenditure Policies: The Case of Military Spending," mimeo. CACI, Inc., Federal: Washington, D.C.

Abolfathi, F. (1978) "Defense Expenditures in the Persian Gulf: Internal, Interstate, and International Factors in the Iraqi–Iranian Arms Race, 1950 to 1969." In W. L. Hollist (ed.), *Exploring Competitive Arms Processes.* New York: Marcel Dekker, pp. 99–129.

Abolfathi, F. (1980) "Threat, Public Opinion, and Military Spending in the United States, 1930–1990." In P. McGowan and C. W. Kegley, Jr. (eds.), *Threats, Weapons, and Foreign Policy. Sage International Yearbook of Foreign Policy Studies* 5:83–133.

Afheldt, H., and P. Sonntag (1973) "Stability and Deterrence Through Strategic Nuclear Arms." *Journal of Peace Research* 10:245–50.

Allan, P. (1983) *Crisis Bargaining and the Arms Race.* Cambridge, MA: Ballinger Publishing.

Allison, G. (1971) *The Essence of Decision.* Boston: Little, Brown.

Allison, G. (1974) "Questions About the Arms Race: Who's Racing Whom? A Bureaucratic Perspective." In R. L. Pfaltzgraff (ed.), *Contrasting Approaches to Strategic Arms Control.* Lexington, MA: D.C. Heath, pp. 31–72.

Altfeld, M. F. (1983) "Arms Races – and Escalation? A Comment on Wallace." *International Studies Quarterly* 27:225–31.

Anderton, C. (1986) "Arms Race Modeling: Systematic Analysis and Synthesis." Ph.D. diss., Cornell University.

Ash, M. A. (1951) "An Analysis of Power with Special Reference to International Politics." *World Politics* 3:218–37.

Ashley, R. K. (1980) *The Political Economy of War and Peace.* London: Frances Pinter.

Ayanian, R. (1986) "Nuclear Consequences of the Welfare State." *Public Choice* 49:201–22.

Banks, F. E. (1975) "The Equilibrium Theory of Arms Races: A Comment." *Journal of Peace Research* 12:235–7.

Barney, G. O. (1980) (Study director) *The Global 2000 Report to the President: Entering the Twenty-first Century.* Vol. 3. U.S. Council on Environmental Quality and Department of State, U.S. Government Printing Office: Washington, D.C.

Baugh, W. H. (1976) "An Operations Analysis Model for the Study of Nuclear Missile System Policies." In D. A. Zinnes and J. V. Gillespie (eds.), *Mathematical Models in International Relations.* New York: Praeger, pp. 274–305.

Baugh, W. H. (1977a) "Transient-Response Analysis of Richardson-Type Arms Race Models." In J. V. Gillespie and D. A. Zinnes (eds.), *Mathematical Systems in International Relations Research.* New York: Praeger, pp. 241–8.

Baugh, W. H. (1977b) "Rejoinder." In J. V. Gillespie and D. A. Zinnes (eds.), *Mathematical Systems in International Relations Research.* New York: Praeger, pp. 256–63.

Baugh, W. H. (1977c) "Is There an Arms Race: Alternative Models of Slow Growth Processes." *Proceedings of the Society for General Systems Research* 22:445–50.

Baugh, W. H. (1978) "Major Powers and Their Weak Allies: Stability and Structure in Arms Race Models." *Journal of Peace Science* 3:45–54.

Bishop, W. J., and D. S. Sorenson (1982) "Superpower Defense Expenditures and Foreign Policy." In C. W. Kegley, Jr., and P. McGowan (eds.), *Foreign Policy USA/USSR. Sage International Yearbook of Foreign Policy Studies* 7:163–82.

Blumberg, A. A. (1971) "Model for a Two-Adversary Arms Race." *Nature* 234:158.

Bobrow, D. B. (1977a) "Comment." In J. V. Gillespie and D. A. Zinnes (eds.),

Mathematical Systems in International Relations Research. New York: Praeger, pp. 297–8.

Bobrow, D. B. (1977b) "Comment." In J. V. Gillespie and D. A. Zinnes (eds.), *Mathematical Systems in International Relations Research.* New York: Praeger, pp. 386–8.

Boserup, A. (1965) "On a Theory of Nuclear War." *Journal of Peace Research* 2:92–3.

Boulding, K. E. (1962) *Conflict and Defense.* New York: Harper & Row.

Brams, S. J. (1975) *Game Theory and Politics.* New York: Free Press.

Brams, S. J. (1977) "Deception in 2 × 2 Games." *Journal of Peace Science* 2:171–203.

Brams, S. J. (1985) *Superpower Games.* New Haven, CT: Yale University Press.

Brams, S. J., M. D. Davis, and P. D. Straffin, Jr. (1979a) "The Geometry of the Arms Race." *International Studies Quarterly* 23:567–88.

Brams, S. J., M. D. Davis, and P. D. Straffin, Jr. (1979b) "A Reply to Detection and Disarmament." *International Studies Quarterly* 23:599–600.

Brams, S. J., and D. M. Kilgour (1987) "The Path to Stable Deterrence." In J. Kugler and F. Zagare (eds.), *Exploring the Stability of Deterrence.* Boulder: Lynne Rienner, pp. 107–22.

Brams, S. J., and D. M. Kilgour (1988) *Game Theory and National Security.* New York: Basil Blackwell.

Brams, S. J., and D. Wittman (1981) "Nonmyopic Equilibria in 2 × 2 Games." *Conflict Management and Peace Science* 6:39–62.

Bremer, S. A. (ed.) (1987) *The GLOBUS Model.* Boulder: Westview.

Brito, D. L. (1972) "A Dynamic Model of an Armaments Race." *International Economic Review* 13:359–75.

Brito, D. L., and M. D. Intriligator (1972) "A General Equilibrium Model of the Stability of an Armaments Race." In *Proceedings of the Sixth Asilomar Conference on Circuits and Systems,* pp. 355–60.

Brito, D. L., and M. D. Intriligator (1973) "Some Applications of the Maximum Principle to the Problem of an Armaments Race." *Modeling and Simulation* 4:140–4.

Brito, D. L., and M. D. Intriligator (1974) "Uncertainty and the Stability of the Armaments Race." *Annals of Economic and Social Measurement* 3:279–92.

Brito, D. L., and M. D. Intriligator (1977a) "Nuclear Proliferation and the Armaments Race." *Journal of Peace Science* 2:213–18.

Brito, D. L., and M. D. Intriligator (1977b) "Strategic Weapons and the Allocation of International Rights." In J. V. Gillespie and D. A. Zinnes (eds.), *Mathematical Systems in International Relations Research.* New York: Praeger, pp. 199–215.

Brito, D. L., and M. D. Intriligator (1977c) "Rejoinder." In J. V. Gillespie and D. A. Zinnes (eds.), *Mathematical Systems in International Relations Research.* New York: Praeger, p. 220.

Brito, D. L., and M. D. Intriligator (1980) "A Game Theoretic Approach to Bureaucratic Behavior." In P. T. Liu (ed.), *Dynamic Optimization and Mathematical Economics.* New York: Plenum, pp. 223–36.

Brito, D. L., and M. D. Intriligator (1982) "Arms Races: Behavioral and Economic Dimensions." In J. A. Gillespie and D. A. Zinnes (eds.), *Missing Ele-*

ments in Political Inquiry: Logic and Levels of Analysis. Beverly Hills: Sage Publications, pp. 93–116.

Brito, D. L., and M. D. Intriligator (1985) "Conflict, War and Redistribution." *American Pol. Sci. Review* 79:943–57.

Brito, D. L., A. M. Buonristiani, and M. D. Intriligator (1977) "A New Approach to the Nash Bargaining Problem." *Econometrica* 45:1163–72.

Brubaker, E. (1973) "Economic Models of Arms Races." *Journal of Conflict Resolution* 17:187–205.

Brun-Hansen, E., and J. W. Ulrich (1964) "Some Problems of Nuclear Power Dynamics." *Journal of Peace Research* 1:137–49.

Brun-Hansen, E., and J. W. Ulrich (1965) "A Rejoinder to a Comment to 'Some Problems of Nuclear Power Dynamics'." *Journal of Peace Research* 2:192–5.

Burns, A. L. (1959) "A Graphical Approach to Some Problems of the Arms Race." *Journal of Conflict Resolution* 3:326–42.

Busch, P. E. (1970) "Mathematical Models of Arms Races." In B. M. Russett (ed.), *What Price Vigilance?* New Haven, CT: Yale University Press, pp. 193–233, 251–6.

Cady, R. (1966) "Some Notes on the Theory of Arms Races." Bendix Systems Res. Memor. No. 2063, Ann Arbor, Bendix Systems Division.

Caspary, W. R. (1967) "Richardson's Model of Arms Races: Description Critique and an Alternative Model." *International Studies Quarterly* 11:63–88.

Chase, P. E. (1969) "Feedback Control Theory and Arms Races." *General Systems* 14:137–49.

Chatterjee, P. (1974) "The Equilibrium Theory of Arms Races: Some Extensions." *Journal of Peace Research* 11:203–11.

Chatterjee, P. (1975a) *Arms, Alliances, and Stability.* New York: Halsted.

Chatterjee, P. (1975b) "The Equilibrium Theory of Arms Races: Reply to the Comments by F. E. Banks." *Journal of Peace Research* 12:239–41.

Chatterji, M. (1969) "A Model of Resolution of Conflict Between India and Pakistan." *Peace Research Society (International) Papers* 12:87–102.

Chester, E. (1978) "Military Spending and Capitalist Stability." *Cambridge Journal of Economics* 2:293–8.

Choucri, N., and R. C. North (1969) "The Determinants of International Violence." *Peace Research Society (International) Papers* 12:35–7.

Choucri, N., and R. C. North (1975) *Nations in Conflict.* San Francisco: W. H. Freeman.

Cioffi-Revilla, C. A. (1979) "Mathematical Models in International Relations: A Bibliography." IRSS Technical Papers Number 4, University of North Carolina at Chapel Hill.

Clark, R., and A. A. Pisani (1985) "Defense Resource Dynamics." *Proceedings of the 1985 International Conference of the System Dynamics Society* 1:150–60. Keystone, CO., July 2–5, 1985.

Crecine, J. P., and G. W. Fischer (1973) "On Resource Allocation in the U.S. Department of Defense." In C. P. Cotter (ed.), *Political Science Annual,* Vol. 4. Indianapolis: Bobbs-Merrill, pp. 181–236.

Cusack, T. R. (1985) "Contention and Compromise: A Comparative Analysis of Budgetary Politics." International Institute for Comparative Social Research and Global Development, West Berlin.

Cusack, T. R., and M. D. Ward (1981) "Military Spending in the United States, Soviet Union, and the People's Republic of China." *Journal of Conflict Resolution* 25:429–69.

Dacey, R. (1979) "Detection and Disarmament." *International Studies Quarterly* 23:589–98.

Dacey, R. (1985) "Ambiguous Information and the Arms Race and the Mutual Deterrence Games." In C. Cioffi-Revilla, R. L. Merritt, and D. A. Zinnes (eds.), *Interaction and Communication in Global Politics.* Beverly Hills: Sage Publications, pp. 163–79.

Dash, J. F. (1967) "Comments on the Paper by Smoker 'The Arms Race as an Open and Closed System.'" *Peace Research Society (International) Papers* 7:63–5.

Davis, D. A., M. A. H. Dempster, and A. Wildavsky (1966) "A Theory of the Budgetary Process." *American Political Science Review* 60:529–47.

Deagle, E. A. (1967) "The Politics of Missilemaking: A Dynamic Model." *Public Policy* 16:181–207.

Deger, S., and S. Sen (1983) "Military Expenditure, Spin-off and Economic Development." *Journal of Development Economics* 13:67–83.

DeRivera, J. (1967) *The Psychological Dimension of Foreign Policy.* Columbus: Merrill.

Diehl, P. F. (1983) "Arms Races and Escalation: A Closer Look." *Journal of Peace Research* 20:205–12.

Domke, W. K., R. C. Eichenberg, and C. M. Kelleher (1983) "The Illusion of Choice: Defense and Welfare in Advanced Industrial Democracies, 1948–1978." *American Political Science Review* 77:19–35.

Donovan, J. C. (1974) *The Cold Warriors.* Lexington, MA: D.C. Health.

Ekman, G. (1970) "Quantitative Approaches to Psychological Problems." In P. Lindblom (ed.), *Theory and Methods in Behavioral Science.* Stockholm: Scandinavia University Books, pp. 53–72.

Ermarth, F. W. (1978) "Contrasts in American and Soviet Strategic Thought" *International Security* 3:138–55.

Ferejohn, J. (1976) "On the Effects of Aid to Nations in an Arms Race." In D. A. Zinnes and J. V. Gillespie (eds.), *Mathematical Models in International Relations Research.* New York: Praeger, pp. 218–51.

Fischer, D. (1984) "Weapons Technology and the Intensity of Arms Races." *Conflict Management and Peace Science* 8(1):49–70.

Fogarty, T. (1987) "Thoughts on Arms Races" unpublished manuscript, Department of Geography, Colgate University, Hamilton, N.Y.

Freeman, J. R. (1983) "Granger Causality and the Time Series Analysis of Political Relationships." *American Journal of Political Science* 27:327–58.

Friberg, M., and D. Jonsson (1968) "A Simple War and Armament Game." *Journal of Peace Research* 5:233–47.

Galbraith, J. K. (1971) *The New Industrial State.* Boston: Houghton Mifflin.

Gantzel, K. J. (1973) "Armament Dynamics in the East–West Conflict: An Arms Race?" *Peace Science Society (International) Papers* 20:1–24.

Gillespie, J. V. (1976) "Why Mathematical Models?" In D. A. Zinnes and J. V. Gillespie (eds.), *Mathematical Models in International Relations.* New York: Praeger, pp. 37–61.

Gillespie, J. V., and D. A. Zinnes (1982) *Missing Elements in Political Inquiry: Logic and Levels of Analysis.* Beverly Hills: Sage Publications.

Gillespie, J. V., and D. A. Zinnes (1975) "Progressions in Mathematical Models of International Conflict." *Synthèse* 31:289–321.

Gillespie, J. V., D. A. Zinnes, and R. M. Rubison (1978) "Accumulation in Arms Race Models: A Geometric Lag Perspective." *Comparative Political Studies* 10:475–94.

Gillespie, J. V., D. A. Zinnes, P. A. Schrodt, and G. S. Tahim (1980) "Sensitivity Analysis of an Armaments Race Model." In P. McGowan and C. W. Kegley, Jr. (eds.), *Threats, Weapons, and Foreign Policy. Sage International Yearbook of Foreign Policy Studies* 7:275–310.

Gillespie, J. V., D. A. Zinnes, and G. S. Tahim (1975) "Foreign Military Assistance and the Armaments Race: A Differential Game Model with Control." *Peace Research Society (International) Papers* 25:35–51.

Gillespie, J. V., D. A. Zinnes, and G. S. Tahim (1977a) "Deterrence as Second Attack Capability: An Optimal Control Model and Differential Game." In J. V. Gillespie and D. A. Zinnes (eds.), *Mathematical Systems in International Relations Research.* New York: Praeger, pp. 367–85.

Gillespie, J. V., D. A. Zinnes, and G. S. Tahim (1977b) "Rejoinder." In J. V. Gillespie and D. A. Zinnes (eds.), *Mathematical Systems in International Relations Research.* New York: Praeger, pp. 391–5.

Gillespie, J. V., D. A. Zinnes, G. S. Tahim, P. A. Schrodt, and R. M. Rubison (1977c) "An Optimal Control Model of Arms Races." *American Political Science Review* 71:226–44.

Gillespie, J. V., D. A. Zinnes, G. S. Tahim, M. W. Sampson III, P. A. Schrodt, and R. M. Rubison (1979) "Deterrence and Arms Races: An Optimal Control Systems Models." *Behavioral Science* 24:250–62.

Gist, J. R. (1974) "Mandatory Expenditures and the Defense Sector: Theory of Budgetary Incrementalism." In R. B. Ripley (ed.), *American Politics Series.* Series Number 04-020, Vol. 2. Beverly Hills: Sage Publications, pp. 5–39.

Gray, C. (1971) "The Arms Race Phenomenon." *World Politics* 24:39–79.

Gregory, P. (1974) "Economic Growth, U.S. Defense Expenditures and the Soviet Budget." *Soviet Studies* 24:72–80.

Griffin, L. J., M. Wallace, and J. Devine (1982) "The Political Economy of Military Spending and Evidence from the United States." *Cambridge Journal of Economics* 6:1–14.

Hamblin, R. L., M. Hout, J. L. L. Miller, and B. L. Pitcher (1977) "Arms Races: A Test of Two Models." *American Sociological Review* 71:338–54.

Harris, G. (1986) "The Determinants of Defense Expenditure in the ASEAN Region." *Journal of Peace Research* 23:41–9.

Harsanyi, J. C. (1962) "Mathematical Models for the Genesis of War." *World Politics* 14:687–99.

Harsanyi, J. C. (1965) "Game Theory and the Analysis of International Conflicts." *Australian Journal of Politics and History* 11:292–304.

Hartley, K., and P. McLean (1978) "Military Expenditure and Capitalism: A Comment." *Cambridge Journal of Economics* 2:287–92.

Hill, W. W. (1978) "A Time-Lagged Richardson Arms Race Model." *Journal of Peace Science* 3:55–62.

Hilton, G. (1977a) "Comment." In J. V. Gillespie and D. A. Zinnes (eds.), *Mathematical Systems in International Relations Research*. New York: Praeger, pp. 190–3.

Hilton, G. (1977b) "Comment." In J. V. Gillespie and D. A. Zinnes (eds.), *Mathematical Systems in International Relations Research*. New York: Praeger, pp. 389–90.

Hollist, W. L. (1977a) "Alternative Explanations of Competitive Arms Processes: Tests on Four Pairs of Nations." *American Journal of Political Science* 21:313–40.

Hollist, W. L. (1977b) "An Analysis of Arms Processes in the United States and the Soviet Union." *International Studies Quarterly* 21:503–28.

Hollist, W. L., and H. Guetzkow (1978) "Cumulative Research in International Relations: Empirical Analysis and Computer Simulation of Competitive Arms Processes." In W. L. Hollist (ed.), *Exploring Competitive Arms Processes*. New York: Marcel Dekker, pp. 165–95.

Hollist, W. L., and T. H. Johnson (1982) "Political-Economic Competition: Three Alternative Simulations." In C. W. Kegley, Jr. and P. McGowan (eds.), *Foreign Policy USA/USSR. Sage International Yearbook of Foreign Policy Studies* 7:65–88.

Huisken, R. (1974) "The Dynamics of World Military Expenditure." *SIPRI Yearbook 1974*. Stockholm: Almqvist and Wiksell, Chapter 7.

Hunter, J. E. (1980) "Mathematical Models of a Three-Nation Arms Race." *Journal of Conflict Resolution* 24:241–52.

Huntington, S. (1958) "Arms Races: Prerequisites and Results." *Public Policy* 8:41–86.

Hutchings, R. (1973) "Fluctuations and Interaction in Estimates of Soviet Budget Expenditure." *Osteuropa Wirtschaft,* June. pp. 55–79.

Intriligator, M. D. (1964) "Some Simple Models of Arms Races." *General Systems* 9:143–7.

Intriligator, M. D. (1967) "Strategy in a Missile War: Targets and Rates of Fire." Security Studies Paper 10. University of California, Los Angeles, Security Studies Project.

Intriligator, M. D. (1968) "The Debate Over Missile Strategy: Targets and Rates of Fire." *Orbis* 11:1138–59.

Intriligator, M. D. (1975) "Strategic Considerations in the Richardson Model of Arms Races." *Journal of Political Economy* 83:339–53.

Intriligator, M. D. (1978) *Econometric Models, Techniques, and Applications*. Englewood Cliffs: Prentice Hall.

Intriligator, M. D. (1982) "Research on Conflict Theory." *Journal of Conflict Resolution* 26:307–27.

Intriligator, M. D., and D. L. Brito (1976) "Formal Models of Arms Races." *Journal of Peace Science* 2:77–88.

Intriligator, M. D., and D. L. Brito (1977a) "Strategy, Arms Races, and Arms Control." In J. V. Gillespie and D. A. Zinnes (eds.), *Mathematical Systems in International Relations Research*. New York: Praeger, pp. 173–89.

Intriligator, M. D., and D. L. Brito (1977b) "Rejoinder." In J. V. Gillespie and D. A. Zinnes (eds.), *Mathematical Systems in International Relations Research.* New York: Praeger, pp. 196–8.

Intriligator, M. D., and D. L. Brito (1978) "Nuclear Proliferation and Stability." *Journal of Peace Science* 3:173–83.

Intriligator, M. D., and D. L. Brito (1981) "Nuclear Proliferation and the Probability of Nuclear War." *Public Choice* 37:247–60.

Intriligator, M. D., and D. L. Brito (1983) "Nuclear Proliferation and the Probability of Nuclear War." In B. Brodie, M. D. Intriligator, and R. Kolkowicz (eds.), *National Security and International Stability,* Cambridge, MA: Delgeschlager, Gunn and Hain, pp. 251–71.

Intriligator, M. D., and D. L. Brito (1984) "Can Arms Races Lead to the Outbreak of War?" *Journal of Conflict Resolution* 28:63–84.

Intriligator, M. D., and D. L. Brito (1985a) "Heuristic Decision Rules, the Dynamics of the Arms Race, and War Initiation." In U. Luterbacher and M. Ward (eds.), *Dynamic Models of International Conflict.* Boulder: Lynne Rienner, pp. 133–60.

Intriligator, M. D., and D. L. Brito (1985b) "Non-Armageddon Solutions to the Arms Race." *Arms Control* 6:41–57.

Intriligator, M. D., and D. L. Brito (1985c) "Wolfson on Economic Warfare." *Conflict Management and Peace Science* 8(2):21–6.

Intriligator, M. D., and D. L. Brito (1985d) "A Game Theoretic Analysis of the Arms Industry in the International Security System." In D. C. Hague (ed.), *Structural Change, Economic Interdependence, and World Development.* London: Macmillan, pp. 219–31.

Intriligator, M. D., and D. L. Brito (1986) "Mayer's Alternative to the I-B Model." *Journal of Conflict Resolution* 30(1):29–31.

Intriligator, M. D., and D. L. Brito (1987) "The Stability of Mutual Deterrence." In J. Kugler and F. Zagare (eds.), *Exploring the Stability of Deterrence.* Boulder: Lynne Rienner, pp. 13–19.

Isard, W. (1979) "A Definition of Peace Science, the Queen of the Social Sciences, Part I." *Journal of Peace Science* 4:1–47.

Isard, W. (1980) "A Definition of Peace Science, the Queen of the Social Sciences, Part II." *Journal of Peace Science* 4:97–132.

Isard, W., and C. Anderton (1985) "Arms Race Models: A Survey and Synthesis." *Conflict Management and Peace Science* 8(2):27–98.

Isard, W., and P. Liossatos (1972a) "A Small Nation-Two Big Powers Model." *Peace Research Society (International) Papers* 18:1–21.

Isard, W., and P. Liossatos (1972b) "A General Equilibrium System for Nations: The Case of Many Small Nations and One Big Power." *Peace Research Society (International) Papers* 19:1–28.

Isard, W., and P. Liossatos (1978) "A Formal Model of Big Step Disarmament and Domino Effects." *Journal of Peace Science* 3:131–46.

Isard, W., and P. Liossatos (1979) *Spatial Dynamics and Optimal Space-Time Development.* New York: North-Holland.

Isard, W., and C. Smith (1982) *Conflict Analysis and Practical Conflict Management Procedures.* Cambridge, MA: Ballinger Publishing.

Isard, W., T. E. Smith, P. Isard, T. H. Tung, and M. Dacey (1969) *General Theory: Social, Political, Economic, and Regional with Particular Reference to Decision-Making Analysis.* Cambridge, MA: MIT Press.

Janis, I. (1972) *Victims of Groupthink.* New York: Houghton Mifflin.

Job, B. L. (1977) "Comment." In J. V. Gillespie and D. A. Zinnes (eds.), *Mathematical Systems in International Relations Research.* New York: Praeger, pp. 249–53.

Job, B. L. (1982a) "Introduction: Two Types of Dynamic Models." In J. A. Gillespie and D. A. Zinnes (eds.), *Missing Elements in Political Inquiry: Logic and Levels of Analysis.* Beverly Hills: Sage Publications, pp. 89–92.

Job, B. L. (1982b) "Synthesis: Problems and Prospects in Dynamic Modeling." In J. A. Gillespie and D. A. Zinnes (eds.), *Missing Elements in Political Inquiry: Logic and Levels of Analysis.* Beverly Hills: Sage Publications, pp. 141–9.

Karmeshu (1980) "Statistical Study of the Richardson's Arms Race Model With Time Lag." *Conflict Management and Peace Science* 4:69–78.

Kemp, A. (1976) "A Diachronic Model of International Violence." *Peace Research* 8:75–86.

Keohane, R. O., and J. S. Nye (1977) *Power and Interdependence: World Politics in Transition.* Boston: Little, Brown.

Klein, L. R. (1977) *Project Link.* Center of Planning and Economic Research, Lecture Series 30. Athens, Greece.

Knorr, K. (1975) *The Power of Nations.* New York: Basic Books.

Kohler, G. (1976) "Une Theorie Structuro-Dynamique des Armaments." *Etudes Internationales* (Canada) 7:25–50.

Kohler, G. (1977) "Exponential Military Growth." *Peace Research* 9:165–75.

Kohler, G. (1979) "Toward A General Theory of Armaments." *Journal of Peace Research* 16:117–35.

Kreutzer, D. P. (1985) "A Microcomputer Workshop Exploring the Dynamics of Arms Races." *Proceedings of the 1985 International Conference of the System Dynamics Society* 1:463–76. Keystone, CO, July 2–5, 1985.

Kugler, J., and F. Zagare (eds.) (1987) *Exploring the Stability of Deterrence.* Boulder: Lynne Rienner.

Kupperman, R. H., and H. A. Smith (1971) "On Achieving Stable Mutual Deterrence." *Journal of Cybernetics* 1:5–28.

Kupperman, R. H., and H. A. Smith (1972) "Strategies of Mutual Deterrence." *Science* 176:18–23.

Kupperman, R. H., and H. A. Smith (1976) "Formal Models of Arms Races: Discussion." *Journal of Peace Science* 2:8–96.

Kupperman, R. H., and H. A. Smith (1977) "Deterrent Stability and Strategic Warfare." In J. V. Gillespie and D. A. Zinnes (eds.), *Mathematical Systems in International Relations Research.* New York: Praeger, pp. 139–66.

Kupperman, R. H., H. A. Smith, and L. R. Abramson (1972) "On Strategic Intelligence in Deterrence." *Journal of Cybernetics* 2:3–20.

Lagerstrom, R. P. (1968) "An Anticipated-Gap, Mathematical Model of International Dynamics." Institute of Political Studies, Stanford University.

Lambelet, J. C. (1971) "A Dynamic Model of the Arms Race in the Middle East 1953–1967." *General Systems* 16:145–167.

Lambelet, J. C. (1973) "Towards a Dynamic Two-Theater Model of the East–West Arms Race." *Journal of Peace Science* 1:1–38.

Lambelet, J. C. (1974) "The Anglo-German Dreadnought Race 1905–1914." *Peace Research Society (International) Papers* 22:1–45.

Lambelet, J. C. (1975) "A Numerical Model of the Anglo-German Dreadnought Race." *Peace Research Society (International) Papers* 24:29–48.

Lambelet, J. C. (1976) "A Complementary Analysis of the Anglo-German Dreadnought Race, 1905–1916." *Peace Research Society (International) Papers* 26:219–66.

Lambelet, J. C. (1985) "Arms Races as Good Things?" In U. Luterbacher and M. Ward (eds.), *Dynamic Models of International Conflict.* Boulder: Lynne Rienner, pp. 161–74.

Lambelet, J. C., and U. Luterbacher with P. Allan (1979) "Dynamics of Arms Races: Mutual Stimulation vs. Self-Stimulation." *Journal of Peace Science* 4:49–66.

Leidy, M. P., and R. W. Staiger (1985) "Economic Issues and Methodology in Arms Race Analysis." *Journal of Conflict Resolution* 29:503–30.

LeLoup, L. T. (1978) "The Myth of Incrementalism: Analytical Choices in Budgetary Theory." *Polity* 10:488–509.

Leontief, W., and F. Duchin (1977) *The Future of the World Economy.* New York: Oxford University Press.

Levine, M. (1977a) "Comment." In J. V. Gillespie and D. A. Zinnes (eds.), *Mathematical Systems in International Relations Research.* New York: Praeger, pp. 216–17.

Levine, M. (1977b) "Comment." In J. V. Gillespie and D. A. Zinnes (eds.), *Mathematical Systems in International Relations Research.* New York: Praeger, pp. 357–61.

Liossatos, P. (1980) "Modeling the Nuclear Arms Race: A Search for Stability." *Journal of Peace Science* 4:169–85.

Lovell, J. P. (1970) *Foreign Policy in Perspective: Strategy, Adaption, and Decision-Making.* New York: Holt, Rinehart, and Winston.

Lucier, C. E. (1979) "Changes in the Values of Arms Race Parameters." *Journal of Conflict Resolution* 23:17–39.

Luterbacher, U. (1974) *Dimensions Historiques de Modeles Dynamiques de Conflict.* Genève: Institut Universitarie des Hautes Etudes Internationales.

Luterbacher, U. (1975) "Arms Race Models: Where Do We Stand?" *European Journal of Political Research* 3:199–217.

Luterbacher, U. (1976) "Towards a Convergence of Behavioral and Strategic Conceptions of the Arms Race: The Case of American and Soviet ICBM Buildup." *Peace Research Society (International) Papers* 26:1–21.

McCubbins, M. (1979) "A Decision-Theoretic Approach to Arms Competition." Social Science Working Paper Number 194, California Institute of Technology.

McCubbins, M. D. (1983) "The Policy Components of Arms Competition." *American Journal of Political Science* 27:485–514.

McGuire, M. C. (1965) *Secrecy and the Arms Race.* Cambridge, MA: Harvard University Press.

McGuire, M. C. (1977) "A Quantitative Study of the Strategic-Arms Race in the Missile Age." *Review of Economics and Statistics* 59:328–39.

McGuire, M. C. (1982) "U.S. Assistance, Israeli Allocation, and the Arms Race in the Middle East: An Analysis of Three Interdependent Resource Allocation Processes." *Journal of Conflict Resolution* 26:199–235.

McGuire, M. C. (1987) "Foreign Assistance, Investment, and Defense: A Methodological Study with an Application to Israel, 1960–1979." *Economic Development and Cultural Change* 35(4):847–73.

McNamara, R. S. (1968) *The Essence of Security*. New York: Harper & Row.

Majeski, S. J. (1983a) "Mathematical Models of the U.S. Military Expenditure Decision-Making Process." *American Journal of Political Science* 27:485–514.

Majeski, S. J. (1983b) "Dynamic Properties of the U.S. Military Expenditure Decision-Making Process." *Conflict Management and Peace Science* 7:65–86.

Majeski, S. J. (1984) "Arms Races as Iterated Prisoner's Dilemma Games." *Mathematical Social Sciences* 7:253–66.

Majeski, S. J. (1985) "Expectations and Arms Races." *American Journal of Political Science* 29:217–245.

Majeski, S. J. (1986) "Technological Innovation and Cooperation in Arms Races." *International Studies Quarterly* 30:175–91.

Majeski, S. J., and D. L. Jones (1981) "Arms Race Modeling: Causality Analysis and Model Specification." *Journal of Conflict Resolution* 25:259–88.

Maki, D. (1977) "Comment." In J. V. Gillespie and D. A. Zinnes (eds.), *Mathematical Systems in International Relations Research*. New York: Praeger, pp. 330–2.

Malinvaud, E. (1970) *Statistical Methods of Econometrics*. Amsterdam: North-Holland.

Marra, R. F. (1985) "A Cybernetic Model of the U.S. Defense Expenditure Policymaking Process." *International Studies Quarterly* 29:357–84.

Matusow, A. J. (1984) *The Unraveling of America*. New York: Harper & Row.

Mayer, T. F. (1985) "Transform Methods and Dynamic Models." In U. Luterbacher and M. Ward (eds.), *Dynamic Models of International Conflict*. Boulder: Lynne Rienner, pp. 175–219.

Mayer, T. F. (1986) "Arms Races and War Initiation: Some Alternatives to the Intriligator-Brito Model." *Journal of Conflict Resolution* 30(1):3–28.

Mehay, S. L., and R. A. Gonzalez (1987) "An Economic Model of the Supply of Military Output." Working Paper No. 87-08, Naval Postgraduate School, Monterey, CA.

Mesarovic, M. D., and E. C. Pestel (1974) *Mankind at the Turning Point*. New York: E. P. Dutton.

Midgaard, K. (1970) "Arms Races, Arms Control, and Disarmament." *Cooperation and Conflict* 1:20–51.

Midlarsky, M. I. (1977a) "Comment." In J. V. Gillespie and D. A. Zinnes (eds.), *Mathematical Systems in International Relations Research*. New York: Praeger, pp. 194–5.

Midlarsky, M. I. (1977b) "Comment." In J. V. Gillespie and D. A. Zinnes (eds.), *Mathematical Systems in International Relations Research*. New York: Praeger, pp. 218–19.

Milstein, J. (1970) "Soviet and American Influences on the Arab–Israeli Arms Race: A Quantitative Analysis." *Peace Research Society (International) Papers* 15:6–27.

Milstein, J. S., and W. C. Mitchell (1969) "The Vietnam War and the Pre-World War I Naval Race." *Peace Research Society (International) Papers* 12:117–36.

Mintz, A., and A. Hicks (1984) "Military Keynesianism in the United States, 1949–76: Disaggregating Military Expenditures and Their Determination." *American Journal of Sociology* 90:411–17.

Moberg, E. (1966) "Models of International Conflicts and Arms Races." *Conflict and Cooperation* 1:80–93.

Moll, K. (1974) "International Conflict as a Decision System." *Journal of Conflict Resolution* 18:555–77.

Moll, K. D., and G. M. Luebbert (1980) "Arms Race and Military Expenditure Models." *Journal of Conflict Resolution* 24:153–85.

Montroll, E. W., and L. W. Badger (1974) *Introduction to Quantitative Aspects of Social Phenomena.* New York: Gordon and Breach.

Morgenthau, H. J. (1965) *Politics Among Nations: The Struggle for Power and Peace.* New York: Knopf.

Moses, L. E. (1961) "A Review: Lewis F. Richardson's Arms and Insecurity and Statistics of Deadly Quarrels." *Journal of Conflict Resolution* 5:390–4.

Muncaster, R. G., and D. A. Zinnes (1982–3) "A Model of Inter-Nation Hostility Dynamics and War." *Conflict Management and Peace Science* 6:19–38.

Nalebuff, B. J. (1984) "A Question of Balance." Discussion Paper Number 1046. Harvard Institute of Economic Research, Cambridge, MA.

Nicolis, G., and I. Prigogine (1977) *Self-Organization in Nonequilibrium Systems.* New York: Wiley.

Nincic, M. (1983) "Fluctuations in Soviet Defense Spending." *Journal of Conflict Resolution* 27:648–60.

Nincic, M., and T. R. Cusack (1979) "The Political Economy of U.S. Military Spending." *Journal of Peace Research* 16:101–15.

Olinick, M. (1978) *An Introduction to Mathematical Models in the Social and Life Sciences.* Reading, MA: Addison-Wesley.

Olvey, L. D., J. R. Golden, and R. C. Kelly (1984) *The Economics of National Security.* Wayne, NJ: Avery Publishing.

O'Neill, B. (1970) "The Pattern of Instability Among Nations: A Test of Richardson's Theory." *General Systems* 15:175–81.

Onishi, A. (1983) "World Development Conflicts and FUGI Global Macroeconomic Model – Simulation Analyses on Arms Race and Global Disarmament for World Development." The Institute of Applied Economic Research, Soka University. Tokyo, Japan.

Organski, A. F. K. (1958) *World Politics.* New York: Knopf.

Ostrom, C. W., Jr. (1977a) "Evaluating Alternative Foreign Policy Models: An Empirical Test Between an Arms Race Model and an Organizational Politics Model." *Journal of Conflict Resolution* 21:235–65.

Ostrom, C. W., Jr. (1977b) "Comment." In J. V. Gillespie and D. A. Zinnes (eds.), *Mathematical Systems in International Relations Research.* New York: Praeger, pp. 333–8.

Ostrom, C. W., Jr. (1978a) "An Empirical Evaluation of a Richardson-Type Arms

Race Model." In W. L. Hollist (ed.), *Exploring Competitive Arms Processes.* New York: Marcel Dekker, pp. 65–97.

Ostrom, C. W., Jr. (1978b) "A Reactive Linkage Model of the U.S. Defense Expenditure Policy Making Process." *American Political Science Review* 72:941–57.

Ostrom, C. W., Jr., and R. F. Marra (1986) "U.S. Defense Spending and the Soviet Estimate." *American Political Science Review* 80:819–42.

Park, T. W. (1986) "Political Economy of the Arms Race in Korea." *Asian Survey* 26:839–50.

Patchen, M. (1970) "Models of Cooperation and Conflict: A Critical Review." *Journal of Conflict Resolution* 14:389–407.

Patchen, M. (1984) "When Do Arms Buildups Lead to Deterrence and When to War?" Paper presented at the Second World Peace Science Congress, Rotterdam, The Netherlands, June 8, 1984.

Phillips, W. R. (1974) "Where Have All the Theories Gone?" *World Politics* 26:155–88.

Pilisuk, M. (1984) "Experimenting with the Arms Race." *Journal of Conflict Resolution* 28:296–315.

Pitman, G. R., Jr. (1969) *Arms Races and Stable Deterrence.* Security Studies Paper 18. University of California, Los Angeles. Security Studies Project.

Plous, S. (1987) "Perceptual Illusions and Military Realities: Results from a Computer-Simulated Arms Race." *Journal of Conflict Resolution* 31:5–33.

Pruitt, D. G. (1969) "Stability and Sudden Change in Interpersonal and International Affairs." In J. N. Rosenau (ed.), *International Politics and Foreign Policy.* New York: Free Press, pp. 392–408.

Rajan, V. (1974) "Variations on a Theme by Richardson." In P. J. McGowan (ed.), *Sage International Yearbook of Foreign Policy Studies.* 2:15–45.

Rapoport, A. (1957) "Lewis F. Richardson's Mathematical Theory of War." *Journal of Conflict Resolution* 1:249–304.

Rapoport, A. (1961) *Fights, Games, and Debates.* Ann Arbor: University of Michigan Press.

Rapoport, A. (1969) "The Mathematics of Arms Races." In J. Rosenau (ed.), *International Politics and Foreign Policy.* New York: Free Press, pp. 492–7.

Rapoport, A. (1976) "Mathematical Methods in Theories of International Relations: Expectations, Caveats, and Opportunities." In D. A. Zinnes and J. V. Gillespie (eds.), *Mathematical Models in International Relations.* New York: Praeger, pp. 10–36.

Rapoport, A. (1983) *Mathematical Models in the Social and Behavioral Sciences.* New York: Wiley.

Rattinger, H. (1975) "Armaments, Detente and Bureaucracy: The Case of the Arms Race in Europe." *Journal of Conflict Resolution* 19:571–95.

Rattinger, H. (1976a) "Econometrics and Arms Races: A Critical Review and Some Extensions." *European Journal of Political Research* 4:421–59.

Rattinger, H. (1976b) "From War to War to War." *Journal of Conflict Resolution* 20:501–31.

Richardson, L. F. (1951) "Could an Arms Race End Without Fighting?" *Nature,* September 19, 1951, 567–8.

Richardson, L. F. (1960) *Arms and Insecurity.* Pittsburgh: Homewood.

Rosenau, J. N. (1976) "Intellectual Identity and Their Study of International Relations, or Coming to Terms with Mathematics as a Tool of Inquiry." In D. A. Zinnes and J. V. Gillespie (eds.), *Mathematical Models in International Relations.* New York: Praeger, pp. 3–9.

Rubison, R. M. (1977) "Comment." In J. V. Gillespie and D. A. Zinnes (eds.), *Mathematical Systems in International Relations Research.* New York: Praeger, pp. 299–301.

Ruloff, D. (1975) "The Dynamics of Conflict and Cooperation Between Nations: A Computer Simulation and Some Results." *Journal of Peace Research* 12:109–21.

Russett, B. (1974) "The Revolt of the Masses: Public Opinion of Military Expenditures." In J. P. Lovell and P. S. Kronenberg (eds.), *New Civil–Military Relations: The Agonies of Adjustment to Post-Vietnam Relations.* New Brunswick, NJ: Transaction Books, pp. 57–88.

Russett, B. (1983) "International Interactions and Processes: The Internal vs. External Debate Revisited." In A. W. Finifter (ed.), *Political Sciences: The State of the Discipline.* Washington, D.C.: The American Political Science Association, pp. 541–68.

Saaty, T. L. (1968) *Mathematical Models of Arms Control and Disarmament.* New York: Wiley.

Sandberg, I. W. (1974) "On Mathematical Theory of Interactions in Social Groups." *IEEE Transactions: Systems, Man and Cybernetics* 4(5):432–45.

Sandberg, I. W. (1977a) "Some Qualitative Properties of Nonlinear Richardson-Type Arms Race Models." In J. V. Gillespie and D. A. Zinnes (eds.), *Mathematical Systems in International Relations Research.* New York: Praeger, pp. 305–29.

Sandberg, I. W. (1977b) "Rejoinder." In J. V. Gillespie and D. A. Zinnes (eds.), *Mathematical Systems in International Relations Research.* New York: Praeger, pp. 339–41.

Sandberg, I. W. (1977c) "Comment." In J. V. Gillespie and D. A. Zinnes (eds.), *Mathematical Systems in International Relations Research.* New York: Praeger, pp. 302–3.

Sandberg, I. W. (1978) "On the Mathematical Theory of Social Process Characterized by Weak Reciprocity." *Journal of Peace Science* 3:1–30.

Saris, W., and C. Middendorp (1980) "Arms Races: External Security or Domestic Pressure?" *British Journal of Political Science* 10:121–8.

Schelling, T. C. (1960) *The Strategy of Conflict.* Cambridge, MA: Harvard University Press.

Schelling, T. C. (1966) *Arms and Influence.* New Haven, CT: Yale University Press.

Schmidt, C. (1985) "Semantic Variations on Richardson's Armament Dynamics," mimeo. Université de Paris IX Dauphine, CASCI.

Schrodt, P. A. (1976) "Richardson's Model as a Markov Process." In D. A. Zinnes and J. V. Gillespie (eds.), *Mathematical Models in International Relations.* New York: Praeger, pp. 156–75.

Schrodt, P. A. (1977) "Comment." In J. V. Gillespie and D. A. Zinnes (eds.), *Mathematical Systems in International Relations Research.* New York: Praeger, pp. 254–5.

Schrodt, P. A. (1978a) "The Richardson *N*-Nation Model and the Balance of Power." *American Journal of Political Science* 22:364–90.

Schrodt, P. A. (1978b) "Statistical Problems Associated with the Richardson Arms Race Model." *Journal of Peace Science* 3:159–172.

Schrodt, P. A. (1982) "Microcomputers in the Study of Politics: Predicting Wars with the Richardson Arms Race Model." *Byte,* 7(7):108–34.

Schrodt, P. A. (1985) "Adaptive Precedent-Based Logic and Rational Choice: A Comparison of Two Approaches to the Modeling of International Behavior." In U. Luterbacher and M. Ward (eds.), *Dynamic Models of International Conflict.* Boulder: Lynne Rienner, pp. 373–400.

Schrodt, P. A., and M. Rubison (1973) "Analysis of Richardson Data," mimeo. Indiana University.

Shubik, M. (1982) *Game Theory in the Social Sciences.* Cambridge, MA: MIT Press.

Shubik, M. (1984) *A Game-Theoretic Approach to Political Economy.* Cambridge, MA: MIT Press.

Siljak, D. D. (1976) "A Competitive Analysis of the Arms Race." *Annals of Economic and Social Measurement* 5:283–95.

Siljak, D. D. (1977a) "On the Stability of the Arms Race." In J. V. Gillespie and D. A. Zinnes (eds.), *Mathematical Systems in International Relations Research.* New York: Praeger, pp. 264–96.

Siljak, D. D. (1977b) "Rejoinder." In J. V. Gillespie and D. A. Zinnes (eds.), *Mathematical Systems in International Relations Research.* New York: Praeger, p. 304.

Simaan, M., and J. B. Cruz, Jr. (1973) "A Multistage Game Formulation of Arms Race and Control and Its Relationship to Richardson's Model." *Modeling and Simulation* 4:149–53.

Simaan, M., and J. B. Cruz, Jr. (1975a) "Formulation of Richardson's Model of the Arms Race from a Differential Game Viewpoint." *Review of Economic Studies* 42:67–77.

Simaan, M., and J. B. Cruz, Jr. (1975b) "Nash Equilibrium Strategies for the Problem of Armament Race and Control." *Management Science* 22:96–105.

Simaan, M., and J. Cruz, Jr. (1977a) "Equilibrium Concepts for Arms Race Problems." In J. V. Gillespie and D. A. Zinnes (eds.), *Mathematical Systems in International Relations Research.* New York: Praeger, pp. 342–56.

Simaan, M., and J. B. Cruz, Jr. (1977b) "Rejoinder." In J. V. Gillespie and D. A. Zinnes (eds.), *Mathematical Systems in International Relations Research.* New York: Praeger, pp. 363–6.

Singer, J. D. (1981) "Accounting for International War: The State of the Discipline." *Journal of Peace Research* 19:1–18.

Smale, S. (1980) "The Prisoner's Dilemma and Dynamical Systems Associated to Non-Cooperative Games." *Econometrica* 48:1617–34.

Smith, R. (1977) "Military Expenditure and Capitalism." *Cambridge Journal of Economics* 1:61–76.

Smith, R. (1978) "Military Expenditure and Capitalism: A Reply." *Cambridge Journal of Economics* 2:299–304.

Smith, R. (1980) "The Demand for Military Expenditure." *Economic Journal* 90:811–820.

Smith, T. C. (1980) "Arms Race Instability and War." *Journal of Conflict Resolution* 24:253–84.

Smoker, P. (1963a) "A Mathematical Study of the Present Arms Race." *General Systems* 8:51–60.

Smoker, P. (1963b) "A Pilot Study of the Present Arms Race." *General Systems* 8:61–76.

Smoker, P. (1964) "Fear in the Arms Races: A Mathematical Study." *Journal of Peace Research* 1:55–64.

Smoker, P. (1965a) "Trade, Defense and the Richardson Theory of Arms Races: A Seven Nation Study." *Journal of Peace Research* 2:161–76.

Smoker, P. (1965b) "On Mathematical Models in Arms Races." *Journal of Peace Research* 2:94–5.

Smoker, P. (1966) "The Arms Race: A Wave Model." *Peace Research Society (International) Papers* 4:151–92.

Smoker, P. (1967a) "Nation State Escalation and International Integration." *Journal of Peace Research* 4:61–75.

Smoker, P. (1967b) "The Arms Race as an Open and Closed System." *Peace Research Society (International) Papers* 7:41–62.

Sorenson, D. S. (1980) "Modeling the Nuclear Arms Race: A Search for Stability." *Journal of Peace Science* 4:169–85.

Squires, M. L. (1976) "Three Models of Arms Races." In D. A. Zinnes and J. V. Gillespie (eds.), *Mathematical Models in International Relations*. New York: Praeger, pp. 252–73.

Stevens, S. S. (1957) "On the Psychophysical Law." *Psychological Review* 64:153–81.

Stevens, S. S. (1961) "To Honor Fechner and Repeal His Law." *Science* 133:80–6.

Stevens, S. S. (1962) "The Surprising Simplicity of Sensory Metrics." *American Psychologist* 17:29–39.

Stevens, S. S. (1966) "A Metric for the Social Consensus." *Science* 151:530–41.

Stevens, S. S. (1971) "Issues in Psychophysical Measurement." *Psychological Review* 170:426–50.

Stevens, S. S. (1972) *Psychophysics and Social Scaling*. Morristown, NJ: General Learning Press.

Stevens, S. S. (1975) *Psychophysics*. New York: Wiley-Interscience.

Stoll, R. J. (1982) "Let the Researcher Beware: The Use of the Richardson Equations to Estimate the Parameters of a Dyadic Arms Acquisition Process." *American Journal of Political Science* 26:77–89.

Strauss, R. P. (1972) "An Adaptive Expectations Model of the East–West Arms Race." *Peace Research Society (International) Papers* 19:29–34.

Strauss, R. (1978) "Interdependent National Budgets: A Model of U.S.–U.S.S.R. Defense Expenditures." In W. L. Hollist (ed.), *Exploring Competitive Arms Processes*. New York: Marcel Dekker, pp. 89–97.

Taagepera, R. (1979–80) "Stockpile-Budget and Ratio Interaction Models for Arms Races." *Peace Science Society (International) Papers* 29:67–78.

Taagepera, R., G. M. Shiffler, R. T. Perkins, and D. L. Wagner (1975) "Soviet–American and Israeli–Arab Arms Races and the Richardson Model." *General Systems* 20:151–8.

Tanter, R. (1972) "The Policy Relevance of Models in World Politics." *Journal of Conflict Resolution* 16:555–83.

Thompson, M. (1977) "Comment." In J. V. Gillespie and D. A. Zinnes (eds.), *Mathematical Systems in International Relations Research*. New York: Praeger, p. 362.

Toland, J. (1976) *Adolf Hitler*. Garden City, NY: Doubleday.

Treddenick, J. (1985) "The Arms Race and Military Keynesianism." *Canadian Public Policy* 11:77–92.

Wagner, D. L., R. T. Perkins, and R. Taagepera (1975) "Complete Solution to Richardson's Arms Race Equations." *Journal of Peace Science* 1:159–72.

Wallace, M. D. (1976) "Arms Races and the Balance of Power: A Mathematical Model." *Applied Mathematical Modeling* 1:83–92.

Wallace, M. D. (1978) "Fueling the Arms Race: A Mathematical Model of Nonlinear and Discontinuous Influences on Great Power Arms Expenditures, 1870–1914." In W. L. Hollist (ed.), *Exploring Competitive Arms Processes*. New York: Marcel Dekker, pp. 133–64.

Wallace, M. D. (1979) "Arms Races and Escalation: Some New Evidence." *Journal of Conflict Resolution* 23:3–16.

Wallace, M. D. (1980) "Accounting for Superpower Arms Spending." In P. McGowan and C. W. Kegley, Jr. (eds.), *Threats, Weapons, and Foreign Policy. Sage International Yearbook of Foreign Policy Studies* 5:259–73.

Wallace, M. D. (1982) "Armaments and Escalation: Two Competing Hypotheses." *International Studies Quarterly* 26:37–56.

Wallace, M. D., and J. M. Wilson (1978) "Nonlinear Arms Race Models." *Journal of Peace Research* 15:175–92.

Ward, D. M. (1984a) "Differential Paths to Parity: A Study of the Contemporary Arms Race." *American Political Science Review* 78:297–317.

Ward, D. M. (1984b) "The Political Economy of Arms Races and International Tension." *Conflict Management and Peace Science* 7:1–23.

Ward, M. D. (1985) "Simulating the Arms Race." *Byte* 10(10):213–22.

Ward, M. D., and A. K. Mahajan (1984) "Defense Expenditures, Security Threats, and Government Deficits: A Case Study of India, 1952–1979." *Journal of Conflict Resolution* 28:382–419.

Ward, M. D., and A. K. Mahajan (1985) "A Simulation Study of Indian Defense Expenditures, 1952–1979." *Simulation and Games* 16:371–98.

Ward, M. D., and A. Mintz (1987) "Dynamics of Military Spending in Israel." *Journal of Conflict Resolution* 31:86–105.

Weede, E. (1983) "Extended Deterrence by Superpower Alliance." *Journal of Conflict Resolution* 27:231–54.

Wohlstetter, A. (1974a) "Is There a Strategic Arms Race?" *Foreign Policy* 15:3–20.

Wohlstetter, A. (1974b) "Rivals, But No Race." *Foreign Policy* 16:48–81.

Wolfson, M. (1968) "A Mathematical Model of the Cold War." *Peace Research Society (International) Papers* 9:107–23.

Wolfson, M. (1985) "Notes on Economic Warfare." *Conflict Management and Peace Science* 8:1–20.

Zinnes, D. A. (1976) *Contemporary Research in International Relations*. New York: Macmillan.

Zinnes, D. A. (1980) "Three Puzzles in Search of a Researcher." *International Studies Quarterly* 24:315–42.

Zinnes, D. A., and J. V. Gillespie (1973) "Analysis of Arms Race Models: USA vs USSR and NATO vs WTO." *Modeling and Simulation* 4:145–8.

Zinnes, D. A., and J. V. Gillespie (eds.) (1976) *Mathematical Models in International Relations.* New York: Praeger.

Zinnes, D. A., J. V. Gillespie, and R. M. Rubison (1976a) "A Reinterpretation of the Richardson Arms Race Model." In D. A. Zinnes and J. V. Gillespie (eds.), *Mathematical Models in International Relations Research.* New York: Praeger, pp. 189–217.

Zinnes, D. A., J. V. Gillespie, and P. A. Schrodt (1976b) "The Arab–Israeli Arms Race: An Empirical Examination." *Jerusalem Journal of Int. Relations* 2:28–62.

Zinnes, D. A., J. V. Gillespie, and G. S. Tahim (1978a) "Modeling a Chimera: Balance of Power Revisited." *Journal of Peace Science* 3:31–44.

Zinnes, D. A., J. V. Gillespie, P. A. Schrodt, G. S. Tahim, and R. M. Rubison (1978b) "Arms and Aid: A Differential Game Analysis." In W. L. Hollist (ed.), *Exploring Competitive Arms Processes.* New York: Marcel Dekker, pp. 17–38.

Zuk, G. (1985) "National Growth and International Conflict: A Reevaluation of Choucri and North's Thesis." *Journal of Politics* 47:269–81.

Zuk, G., and N. R. Woodbury (1986) "U.S. Defense Spending, Electoral Cycles, and Soviet American Relations." *Journal of Conflict Resolution* 30:445–68.

CHAPTER 3

Individual and group behavior: noncrisis situation

3.1   Introduction and the general setting

In this chapter we probe more deeply into decisions that are made, for example, actions that are taken, commands and orders that are issued, and proposals that are put forth, especially with regard to military expenditures. It is after all these decisions that establish the level of military expenditures, the M^J or $\dot{M}^J$ for each country J, in the arms race models. It is also these decisions that reflect, for example, in the Richardson model:

1.   the reactions to the military expenditures of other nations that are embodied in the ρ^J coefficients and the $\rho^J M^L$ terms;
2.   the diverse costs that are embodied in the c^J coefficient and the $c^J M^J$ term; and
3.   the grievance factors that are embodied in the g^J term.

We want to inquire why these and other decisions are made in order (1) to understand better the terms and levels of the parameters in arms race models and models of other conflict phenomena and (2) to suggest avenues by which the parameters may be changed by deliberate action and policy. In this chapter we have in mind that such decisions are made by individuals as behaving units – for example, political leaders (say, a president, prime minister, or dictator), business people, administrators, and religious personages – and by groups of diverse types and size (say, a ruling élite or political party), especially whenever a group can be taken to act as an entity.

In the following section we shall consider the effect of the attitude variable upon the individual's choice of an action using the traditional approach of economics, operations research, and regional science. In section 3.3 we consider interdependent decision making, wherein one or more behaving units employ guiding principles or conflict management procedures to resolve the conflict that would arise were each to act independently out of pure and narrow self-interest. In section 3.4 we approach behavior of the individual from the much different standpoint of cognitive science, emphasizing mental representations and the associated schema and stories, retrieval structures, and the functioning of the brain. In section 3.5 we make some concluding remarks.

3.2   Attitude as a basic variable

Consider a hypothetical behaving unit Z confronting a decision situation.[1] To be concrete, let Z be a political leader, say, in nation J in 1985. He or she must propose a level of military expenditures. The action (proposal) space of Z comprises four alternatives: a_1, a_2, a_3, and a_4. Specifically, where the political leader's staff has specified (estimated) the time path of increase of military expenditures of rival nation L, these might be

$a_1 =$ increase military expenditures at a rate sufficiently greater than that of nation L so that J has assurance of adequate attack and deterrence potential in all relevant theaters;

$a_2 =$ increase military expenditures at the same rate as L;

$a_3 =$ do not change the level of military expenditures;

$a_4 =$ decrease the level of military expenditures by a fair amount.

(To facilitate understanding, some readers may wish to associate the Soviet Union with nation J, the United States with nation L, and Mainland China with the new, potentially major power mentioned in what follows.) Also let Z consider that four (and only four) states of the environment are pertinent for the relevant future:

i. L maintains its alliance structure with other countries and furthermore establishes an effective alliance with a new, potentially major power.

ii. L maintains its alliance structure but does not establish an effective alliance with any other nation.

---

[1] The general setting for this decision situation is formally stated in Isard et al. (1969, chap. 4), which develops at much greater depth the discussion of this section. For a rigorous, systematic, and much more thorough treatment of many of the concepts and processes discussed in this and subsequent chapters, the reader is referred to the excellent works by Shubik (1982, 1984). These works also discuss the general applicability of the game theory approach to diverse social, economic, and political behavioral processes.

Table 3.1. *A hypothetical outcome (payoff) matrix for Z*

Z's possible actions	States of the environment			
(proposals)	i	ii	iii	iv
a_1	225	81	0	169
a_2	64	100	64	81
a_3	0	36	169	25
a_4	16	81	144	49

  iii. *L*'s existing alliance structure disintegrates, but *L* establishes an effective alliance with a new, potentially major power.

  iv. *L*'s alliance structure disintegrates, and *L* does not establish an effective alliance with a new, potentially major power.

Assume for the moment that the actions of other nations, groups, and individuals can have no influence whatsoever on the outcomes or payoff associated with each action of *Z*. (We shall use the words "outcome" and "payoff" interchangeably unless otherwise specified.) Then we may conceive of an outcome (payoff) function for *Z* that associates a unique number to every combination of an action by *Z* and a state of the environment. The operation of this function yields the outcomes of Table 3.1, which we designate an outcome (payoff) matrix.

A first question is: What are these ouctomes? If we consider *Z* to be an industrialist, where a_1, a_2, a_3, and a_4 represent four possible investment actions, and i, ii, iii, and iv correspond to states of the environment relevant for the industrialist, then the numbers in the table might represent dollars (in millions) of profits. In the case of a political figure, in one type of situation they may represent the number of voters in a body whose support is forthcoming for each of the four states of the environment. Or they may represent a qualitative score or position, where, for example,

    0 may represent political suicide
  50 may represent major deterioration in political standing
  75 may represent noticeable deterioration
  90 may represent slight deterioration
100 may represent no change
125 may represent noticeable improvement
200 may represent major improvement
350 may represent drastic improvement

Alternatively, the figures may represent the number of people in a group who speak favorably of the subject, or the number of favorable responses in a public opinion poll of limited size, or an index of public regard, or a measure of a leader's political acumen or relative rank in a superior body.

For example, if a political figure in nation J were to put forth proposal a_1 (increase military expenditures to assure adequate attack and deterrence potential in *all* theaters), he (or she) would receive, say, 225 votes were there realized the state of environment i (L's alliance structure maintained and in addition L effects an alliance with a new, potentially major power); this outcome would reflect the "fact" that he properly anticipated a state of the environment for which the proposal would have nation J properly prepared. He would have received 81 votes were there realized state ii (L's alliance structure maintained, and no new alliance); this would reflect the fact that his proposal would have put nation J in an overly armed situation at the expense of meeting pressing civilian demands. He would receive zero votes were there realized state iii (L's alliance structure disintegrated, with no new alliance); this would reflect the fact that J's proposal would have been way out of line with what materialized and would have nation J excessively overarmed, leading to popular dissatisfaction and unrest; and so forth.

We do not wish to attribute any significance as such to the numbers of Table 3.1. We use them only to evaluate the outcome (payoff) matrix as a tool for analysis. Clearly, a first basic question in this approach is the actual identification of the outcomes. In certain situations, these can be precise numbers as dollar profits, votes, winnings in games of chance, and so on. They may be given (predetermined) or estimated, involving perhaps at one extreme many computations of a complex nature. But in many other situations including most political situations, outcomes are not clearly identifiable and not stable as numerical magnitudes; they involve social–psychological and other subjective and qualitative elements to be discussed later.

A second basic question concerns the extent to which the individual perceives his or her action space and the states of the environment, a phenomenon related to the person's knowledge and the information available. This question becomes increasingly important as the outcome matrix becomes larger. For example, there may be more than four alternatives in Z's action space or there may be more than four possible states of the environment. Also, contrary to the assumption of the previous paragraph, outcomes to Z may not be independent of the action of the second behaving unit – individual, group, or nation; in this instance there would be an outcome matrix similar to that of Table 3.1 for each possible action of the second behaving unit or the outcome matrix may be viewed as three dimensional. Outcomes to Z also may not be independent of actions by third, fourth, . . . , nth behaving units. Clearly, as Z's outcome function is extended to include more and more of the "relevant" variables at play, the likelihood is less and less that Z has complete information and perceives the outcomes of all possible combinations of the alternatives that the variables may present. Hence, it is essential to have an assumption concerning the extent to which the individual perceives all these possible combinations. Hence, too, the processes of searching and becoming better informed (acquiring additional information) become extremely relevant for understanding and projecting behavior. Although we keep these processes in mind, we put off their full consideration until Chapters 6 and 13. For the present, we assume that the individual has reached the end of his or her learning process.

A third basic question concerns the way in which the individual attaches a significance to any outcome in terms of his (or her) own internal accounting system. How does he transform the one or more quantities representing an outcome into a utility, an "internal" payoff, or other subjective account? We examine this question in part in sections 3.4 and 3.5.

A fourth basic question concerns the motivation and attitude the individual possesses while viewing one or a set of outcome matrices. The choice of an alternative within the individual's action space is not independent of the objective function and the view of the external world that govern his or her thinking and response pattern. We now turn to this question.

First, a preliminary remark. One assumption often made by the classical economist is that of perfect information. In this case, there may be no uncertainty about the relevant aspects of the state of the environment, for example, what the market is, or what the demand or supply schedule (curve) is, or what the actions of competitors are or will be. In effect, there may be only one possible state of this environment, not two or more. Hence there is only one column in Table 3.1 or other outcome matrix. All the individual needs to do to optimize profits is to select that action that corresponds to the highest magnitude in the single column, no matter how many actions (rows) there are. In fact, there may theoretically be an infinite number of actions when an action involves a variable that is continuous, such as military expenditures.[2]

Unfortunately, in arms races and many other situations, there is considerable uncertainty and lack of information regarding the state of the environment that will be realized, and several must be considered as possible. Hence, when Z selects an action (proposal, or later strategy), in gen-

---

[2] See Isard et al. (1969 chap. 4) for a full discussion of these points wherein the formal analysis is presented for the cases of the Pure Monopolist in One-Point Space, the Locating Monopolist under Simple Conditions, and others.

eral, he or she cannot be sure of the outcome (payoff). At most, all one may be sure of is that this outcome (when it can be defined) will be one of the elements in the row corresponding to the alternative chosen. The state that the environment takes on determines the element.

Clearly an individual can assign a value to an action in various ways. Probably the simplest procedures are those in which the individual assigns to an action the value of a single element in the row corresponding to that action. This type of assignment is relevant for several kinds of individual behavior involving different attitudes and implied objectives and thus different interpretations of an optimal state of affairs.

3.2.1   The 100 percent conservative

Consider the individual whose attitude is so conservative as to consider only "sure things." For this individual the concept of an optimal state of affairs is the achievement of the maximum of the sure things that are possible. This individual's objective is to maximize the level of outcome (payoff) that certainly must be achieved. We shall designate this objective as one of the class of "max–min" objectives.[3] He or she will choose that action (row) that has the largest minimum among all rows.[4] Given Table 3.1, action a_2 is chosen.

Whereas this simple type of value assignment to actions may be relevant for some individuals, others may wish to consider explicitly all the elements of a row. In order to assign a single value to any action based on all of its possible outcomes, some rule for combining outcome elements must be used. Further, in many instances, the individual may wish to weight or discount, say, with a probability, each outcome element of the row associated with any given action, in accord with his or her attitude as to the possible realization of that element. One procedure for modifying an outcome element is multiplication by its "probability weight."[5]

---

[3] Other types of attitudes may also give rise to a max–min objective. Some of these will be considered in what follows.

[4] Assigning to each action the value of a single element in the row corresponding to that action can also lead to such other interpretations of an optimal state as (a) the individual's objective is to maximize the level of payoff for that state of nature having the highest probability of occurrence (a statement that has meaning when significance attaches to the modal probability of occurrence in each row) or (b) the individual's objective is to maximize the level of "centrally located" payoff (a statement that has meaning when significance attaches to the median value in each row).

[5] As with "payoffs" and "outcomes," in this chapter we do not ask how these "probability" numbers are obtained. Frequently, individuals may assign subjective probabilities or "probability type" weights that do not sum to unity. See Isard et al. (1969, p. 132n).

3.2.2   The expected payoff calculator

For an individual who makes calculations solely on the basis of probabilities, the concept of an optimal state of affairs is the achievement of
the maximum expected payoff. From among the actions (rows) he or she
will choose that action (row) having the highest expected payoff. That is,
let the probability that Z attaches to the jth state of the environment be
pr_j ($j = 1, 2, \ldots, n$ and in the case of Table 3.1, $j = $ i, ii, iii, and iv). Also
let the payoff element in the ith row and jth column of a payoff table be
o_{ij} (where $i = 1, 2, \ldots, m$ and in the case of Table 3.1, $i = a_1, a_2, a_3, a_4$).
For the example in Table 3.1, $o_{23} = 64$, being the payoff element in the
cell corresponding to the second row and third column. (Alternatively,
o_{23} might be designated $o_{a2,\mathrm{iii}}$.) Then $\mathrm{pr}_j o_{ij}$ is a probabilistic payoff element;
and the value of any action a_i is

$$\sum_{j=1}^{n} \mathrm{pr}_j o_{ij} \quad \text{where} \quad \sum_{j=1}^{n} \mathrm{pr}_j = 1 \tag{3.2.1}$$

If the probabilities for the states of Table 3.1 are $\mathrm{pr}_i = 0.4$ and $\mathrm{pr}_{ii} = \mathrm{pr}_{iii}$
$= \mathrm{pr}_{iv} = 0.2$, the individual chooses action a_1.

3.2.3   The 100 percent pessimist, the 100 percent optimist, and the
middle-of-the-road individual

Corresponding to the 100 percent conservative, we have the *100 percent
pessimist.* He (or she) is certain that whatever action he takes, the worst
will occur, that is, he will be left with the least possible payoff. Hence, as
for the 100 percent conservative, he assigns to any action the lowest value
in its row and selects that action that has the largest minimum, a *max–
min* strategy. Given Table 3.1, he chooses action a_2. In contrast, *the 100
percent optimist,* perhaps one with the belief that "God is always with
me," is certain that for any given action, he (or she) will receive the highest possible payoff. Hence, he assigns to any action the highest value in
its row and chooses that action with which is associated the maximum of
these highest values, a *max–max* strategy. Given Table 3.1, he chooses
action a_1.

   In between is the more sober individual, partly pessimistic and partly
optimistic. Either because this individual has limited capabilities or is
extremely critical of sophisticated, highly refined analysis, the best and
worst outcomes that can be associated with any action are considered and
a weight (probability) assigned to each of these outcomes to obtain a
value for the given action, ignoring intermediate outcomes. In the sim-

plest case this may be just an average of the two. Then that action associated with the highest weighted payoff is chosen.

3.2.4 The equiprobable expected payoff calculator

Consider a more general case of an individual who is motivated to maximize expected payoff and who knows that each state of the environment has an equal chance of occurring. Or, no information may be available about the occurrence of the several states of the environment, and it is simply assumed that they will occur with equal probability. Or the individual may be so overloaded with information and have no hope of processing it, or face so many states of the environment, or confront so many complications in any attempt at "rational" analysis, that he or she may despair and assume that the states of the environment will occur with equal probability. In this case the optimizing individual selects that action that corresponds to the row with the highest sum of outcome elements. Given Table 3.1, he or she chooses action a_1.

3.2.5 The utility maximizer

As indicated in the previous chapter, the decision-making unit may implicitly or explicitly think in terms of a level of satisfaction or utility or the welfare of a constituency or society. In doing this, he (or she) converts an outcome or payoff element (or vector as a set of elements) into a single index, which we shall henceforth designate utility, although sometimes we shall speak of welfare. As generally used in the previous chapter, the utility associated with a utility function was of a cardinal nature; it could be precisely measured or stated in terms of a precise number by the behaving unit. However, economists and psychologists view utility still more broadly by relating it to preferences. When a behaving unit's preferences among outcomes is such that he can attach a precise number to the utility of each outcome, then he may be said to have *cardinal* utility. When the behaving unit can only state how many times he prefers one outcome to another, then he may be said to have *relative* utility. Finally, when his preferences among outcomes is such that he can only order outcomes in term of desirability, he may be said to have *ordinal* utility.

With these distinctions, we now consider the behaving unit as maximizing his (or her) level of utility. Where he is a 100 percent pessimist, or a 100 percent conservative, or a 100 percent optimist and attaches importance to only one outcome along any given row, then all he needs to be able to do is to rank the single outcome for each row in order of preference to identify the one that maximizes his utility. When, however, he attaches probabilities to the state of the environment, he must deal with *expected utility;* and in order to identify the action that maximizes his expected utility, he must be able to multiply precise numbers by these probabilities. To do this, he then must have cardinal utility. For example, if the utility of an outcome is given by the square root of that outcome (a crude calculation often used), then (1) taking the square roots of the outcomes in Table 3.1 and (2) assuming equal probabilities for the states of the environment yields a_1 as the optimal action.

The individual may have any one of other attitudes. He (or she) may be a person who always regrets that he did not choose another action in light of the state of affairs that evolved, provided that it would have resulted in a more desirable outcome for him. He may then behave as a 100 percent pessimistic regretter, or an expected regret calculator, or a 100 percent conservative regretter. Or he may be a satisficer or a constrained satisficer, à la Simon. Some of these cases are discussed in the Appendix to this chapter.

Finally, turning back to Table 3.1, we note how the use of a payoff matrix enables us to see more clearly how we can influence a decision maker. For example, take the case of a 100 percent conservative leader (a banker) who favors action a_2 but would select action a_1 (say, the one we most prefer) if it were not for the possibility that states of the environment i and iv might be realized. If the outcomes of Table 3.1 are votes (dollar profits) and 64 is a satisfactory outcome, but nothing less, we need only guarantee him before-hand an outcome of at least 64 votes (or dollar profits) regardless of what state of the environment is realized. The expected cost is then the cost of delivering 64 votes (or of ensuring $64 profit) times the probability of state iii occurring, although in situations where votes must be delivered before an action is chosen, the cost would be the full costs of delivering those votes.

In concluding this section, we wish to stress the attitude of the decision maker as a basic factor that governs the action he or she chooses even when the rational approaches of economics, operations research, and regional science are followed. In actuality, as will become evident later, this type of rational approach to political decision making is of limited applicability for the analysis of arms race and arms control phenomena.

3.3   Interdependent decision making

Having considered a set of cases with just one unit behaving, we now proceed to examine interdependent decision-making cases involving more than one behaving unit. Increasing the number of behaving units from one to just two enormously complicates the decision situation and reduces considerably what we can say about the outcome. Formally speaking, an interdependent decision situation involves for an individual at a particular point of time and space a choice problem with the five following aspects:

1. The individual perceives certain alternative courses of *action.*
2. He (or she) perceives certain *outcomes* that may result from the choice of any of his alternative courses of action, these outcomes depending upon the actions of other active participants as well as certain aspects of his environment that are independent of the behavior of these participants.
3. He values these outcomes differently, that is, he exhibits *preferences* among them.
4. He is constrained in his choice of an action by *guiding principles* that eliminate the consideration of outcomes inconsistent with these principles.
5. He has certain *objectives* that embody his concept of an "optimal" action and in the light of his preferences motivate him to choose that action whose outcomes, consistent with his guiding principles, characterizes the action as optimal.

These five aspects are discussed in detail in Isard et al. (1969, chap. 5, 5A). We shall discuss them only as required when we examine different types of decision situations and actions taken therein.

To facilitate analysis, we present a simple hypothetical setting for two behaving units J and L; to provide concreteness, the reader may characterize them as the Soviet Union and the United States, respectively. Let both be concerned with deescalation of an arms race. Each has a utility or social welfare function where, for example, J's utility is dependent on its security, civilian goods produced, and the rate of growth of its productive capacity, its security in turn being a function of its stock of weapons and that of L's, and so forth. (Such a function is implied in the previous chapter in the discussion of Wolfson's analysis and in the formal analysis of section 13.3.) Likewise for L. Now let us assume the political leaders of both J and L concentrate on the short run, each considering levels of deescalation that involve reductions ($0, $2, $4, $6, and $8 billion) of military expenditures at an agreed upon exchange rate (or the equivalent in terms of weaponry). In Table 3.2 these levels are indicated along the horizontal for J (constituting its actions a^J) and the vertical for L (constituting its actions a^L). In the body of the table we record the utilities or social welfare of J and L that would result for each combination

Table 3.2. *Utility outcomes from deescalation in military expenditures*

	Deescalation by J (Soviet) in billions of equivalent dollars									
	$0		$2		$4		$6		$8	
	(1) J	(2) L	(3) J	(4) L	(5) J	(6) L	(7) J	(8) L	(9) J	(10) L
Deescalation by L (USA) in billions of dollars										
$8	160,	40	208,	50	216,	60	184,	70	122,	80
6	120,	90	176,	110	192,	130	168,	150	114,	170
4	80,	95	144,	125	168,	155	152,	185	106,	215
2	40,	70	112,	110	144,	150	136,	190	98,	230
0	0,	0	80,	50	120,	100	120,	150	90,	200

of a deescalation level by J and one by L. The first element of each pair corresponds to J's utility u^J, the second to L's utility u^L. Thus J's utilities are always recorded in the odd-numbered columns of Table 3.2, and L's are in the even-numbered columns. These utilities may be perceived utilities, or utilities calculated by experts, or the equivalent, but they are cardinal. They are taken to be known objective information and to be the same by both parties, admittedly a very strong assumption but one that is frequently employed by economists, regional scientists, and operation researchers in game-theoretic, interdependent decision situations. Very crudely speaking, if J were to choose $0 billion as its deescalation level and L were to choose $0, $2, $4, $6, or $8 billion, the resulting utility for J would be 0, 40, 80, 120, or 160 respectively. Note that these utilities are taken to increase for J by constant amounts for each additional $2 billion deescalation by L. We would expect increasing utility for J given that J's security can be generally taken to increase steadily with every decrease in L's stock of weaponry (as projected by J), which is associated with every $2 billion deescalation by L but not by constant amounts. However, not knowing whether these increases in utility would grow or diminish in size or behave irregularly, it is convenient for us to look upon them as constant increases, thereby also to establish firmly the hypothetical character of Table 3.2.

Nation J, too, might consider several levels of deescalation. Suppose L were not to deescalate at all. Then, J may reason that a situation of overkill clearly exists and that much of the current military expenditures just increases its overkill capability. Hence, it may consider favorably a $2 billion deescalation since (1) such would obtain from the world community much favorable reaction embodied in the commodity c-respect[6] it would receive and (2) such would allow greater production of civilian goods for diverse social programs (investments, resource development, and household consumption). Its utility would thereby increase by 80 as indicated at the bottom of the third column. If it were to consider a still higher level of deescalation, namely, $4 billion, it would receive still more c-respect from the world community and be able to pursue still larger social programs but perhaps at the expense of some security. Hence, its utility increase on net would be, say, 120 (indicated at the bottom of column 5) and not twice 80. If it were to increase its level of deescalation to $6 billion, the gain from additional c-respect and larger social programs would be balanced out by a decrease in security so that its increase in utility would remain at 120 (see the bottom of column 7). Finally, if it were to deescalate by $8 billion, the increase in its utility would drop to 90 (see the bottom of column 9).

Consider the third column of Table 3.2. Suppose J's level of deescalation is $2 billion. As already mentioned, if L were not to deescalate, J's increase in utility would be 80. However, if L were to deescalate by $2 billion, then J's increase in utility would move up to 112; and for every $2 billion additional deescalation by L, J's increase in utility goes up by 32. These increases in J's utility over the increase from c-respect bestowed on J by the world community are associated with the greater security J obtains as L deescalates more and more. Note, however, that J's increase from every $2 billion dose of L's deescalation is only 32, in contrast to 40 in column 1. This is because J's increase in utility starts from the 80 level in column 3 rather than the zero level in column 1; it also reflects the fact that the c-respect it receives from the world community from its $2 billion deescalation is less and less (partly reflected in the difference between columns 3 and 1) as L steadily increases its deescalation and competes more and more effectively for third-world allegiance (via foreign aid made possible by reductions in its military expenditures). For the same reasons, the increments in the increase in utility for J are taken to be 24 in column 5, 16 in column 7, and 8 in column 9.

Now consider L's utility. Similar factors are at play. If J were not to deescalate and likewise L, then the increase in L's utility is zero, as indi-

---

[6] We use the symbol "c-" as a prefix here and elsewhere to indicate that we have in mind treating the value element that follows as a noneconomic commodity.

cated at the bottom of column 2, which records L's increases in utilities. However, if L were to deescalate by $2 billion, it would receive an increment in utility of 70, reflecting the c-respect received from the world community and the possibility of supporting larger social programs (including foreign aid). This increase would rise to 95 if L were to deescalate by $4 billion, reflecting still greater c-respect received from the world community and the possibility of still larger social programs but at the same time a small decrease in its level of security. The utility increment would drop to 90 and 40 if L were to deescalate by $6 and $8 billion, respectively, reflecting the fact that the decrements in security come to dominate increasingly.

As we did for J, we explain the pattern of utility increments for L in each of the columns 4, 6, 8, and 10. For example, for a given level of J's deescalation the utility increment to L from the gain from c-respect and larger social programs come to be dominated by security losses at high levels of deescalation by L.

Note the steady increase in increments in L's utility from column to column (for any given row). This reflects the increase in L's security from increasing deescalation by J. Thus from the bottom row these increments in utility are 50, 100, 150, and 200 for deescalation levels by J of $2, $4, $6, and $8 billion, respectively.

We have said enough about the simple hypothetical situation of Table 3.2. Both its simplicity and hypothetical character should now be obvious to the reader. We are not interested in the numbers of the table per se. Rather we are interested in the reasoning that lies behind the choice of an action (a decision); and we use the numbers in the table to help point up the logical thinking that an economist, regional scientist, or operations researcher might pursue.

First examine the impasse that results when no guiding principle, or conflict management procedure, or use of some form of arbitration, mediation, or the equivalent is involved. From Table 3.2, J clearly prefers the joint action ($8, $4), where the first figure in the parentheses refers to L's level of deescalation and the second figure to J's, in billions of dollars. Nation J would obtain the utility of 216 thereby. Nation L most prefers joint action ($2, $8) and would thereby obtain the utility of 230. (From here on shall refer to the numbers in Table 3.2 as utilities rather than the more precise but more awkward term "increases in utilities.") An impasse exists. To break the impasse, many ways have been proposed by diverse scholars. Each involves changing the structure of the interdependent decision situation or the rules (the constitution) of the game when the situation is viewed as a game. The new structure may involve a change in the restricted action space of one or both participants, or a change in their outcome space, or both. The former type of change may be effected by explicitly adding to (increasing) or subtracting from (reducing) the set of a participant's action space – for example, by adding or subtracting rows, columns, or both to the initially perceived or specified payoff matrix. It may also be effected by introducing a guiding principle or conflict management procedure into the situation, which restricts the available options of one participant in view of what the outcome or impact would be on the other. Such a principle or procedure may be imposed by an arbitrator, suggested by a mediator, or simply adopted by both parties when they are sufficiently cooperative.

Let us illustrate each type of change. Suppose there is a wise mediator who persuades the participants that beyond (1) c-respect from the world at large, (2) the magnitude of civilian goods production, and (3) one's security, there are other important values involved. Along with the c-respect that comes from the reduction in armaments, there would also be an increase in the feeling of security throughout the world. Entrepreneurs would be less hesitant to engage in risky enterprises. International trade would increase. International terrorism might subside and in turn internal violence. Such would be a gain to all nations, including both J and L. Taking such indirect outcome factors into account could mean that the value of outcomes for J along each row consistently increases and likewise for L along each column. If so, then J and L would each find that the joint action (8, 8) would be optimal. A harmony point would have come to exist, and the impasse would have disappeared. The conflict would thus become managed through the introduction of common, universal values as per Burton (1969, 1972), that is, through change in (in this case, extension of) the outcome space to cover other relevant elements.

Next consider change in action spaces. A third party, foreseeing the impasse that would result from the use of the outcome matrix of Table 3.2 and knowing the obstinate, inflexible (uncompromising) attitudes of each party, might persuade each party that for diverse reasons it would be unwise to consider more than a \$4 billion deescalation. In effect, it would have persuaded each participant independently to change its action space; as a consequence, a harmony point (\$4, \$4) would have come to exist. The impasse would have been avoided.

Another simple procedure involves the use of a split-the-difference operation as a guiding principle in reaching a compromise in the joint action space. To illustrate, suppose \$8 billion deescalation by L was not politically feasible. Then the first row of Table 3.2 would not exist. In this situation J would most prefer the joint action (6, 4) whereas L would most prefer (2, 8). In this case, the use of a *split-the-difference principle* in the joint action space, involving an operation that might be judged fair by both J and L, would break the impasse and yield (4, 6) as the compromise joint action.

A split-the-difference principle may be replaced in some situations by a weighted-average principle where for some reason one participant's optimal proposal is given the greater weight than that of the other in reaching a compromise. Or a principle involving a sequence of compromises in the joint action space may be acceptable to the participants. Or the participants may be willing to accept a principle that involves simple compromises over their outcomes, weighted or unweighted, or a sequence of such compromises, and so on.

There are other procedures that might have appeal:

1. Select the joint action that maximizes the lower of the two outcomes, a *max–min principle,* but one that assumes that the payoffs (utilities) of the two participants are comparable (an assumption of intercardinal utility).
2. Pursue a series of small concessions whereby on any move that participant who has least to lose percentagewise should concede (a *Zeuthen concession principle* when participants can only compare percentage losses from their best outcome or goal).
3. Select that joint action that maximizes the product of their utilities [when participants have von Neumann–Morgenstern utility (linear) functions, a *Nash principle*].

And so forth.

Elsewhere, Isard and Smith (1982) have set forth 100 or so of the less technical guiding principles and conflict management procedures available in the literature. They consider

1. whether the joint action space is continuous;
2. the type of information on their preferences that participants can provide;
3. the ability of participants to focus nonemotionally on outcomes; and
4. whether concessions need to be taken or improvements effected.

Elsewhere, too, a number of these procedures have been stated in axiomatic form (Isard et al. 1969) and have been rigorously formalized by game theorists. We do not wish to review this literature; in Appendix B of this chapter and in Chapter 10 we shall have more reference to it. However, we do wish at this point to restate the veto–incremax procedure in order to lay bare a number of critical (unrealistic) assumptions made by the economist, regional scientist, and operations researcher and to provide the background for contributions by psychologists and cognitive and other social scientists.

First, let us state informally the appealing features of veto–incremax procedures:

1. Each can be presented in a relatively simple form for a given situation and can be rigorously defined mathematically.
2. Each clearly points up the inefficiency of the existing position (deadlock, threat point, current-stand point, or prominent reference point) and identifies a common goal [the achievement of a compromise position (solution) on the efficiency frontier].
3. Each requires the assumption of ordinal utility only; that is, *only a preference ranking of outcomes is required from each participant,* and thus each depends on no intercomparisons of utility.
4. Each assures that no participant will ever be made worse off by any move.
5. Each allows each participant to be as conservative and cautious as it desires with respect to amount of change in a proposed joint action on any one of a sequence of moves; that is, it allows within extreme limits each participant to make as small a commitment on change as it desires.
6. Each ensures that an efficient outcome will be reached but that no participant is able beforehand to identify this outcome.
7. Each suggests a "fair compromise" or "equitable" procedure by which all participants may share in the gains from the gradual advancement to a mutually more efficient state of affairs.
8. Each allows the participants considerable flexibility in combining its appealing features with the appealing features of several other incremax procedures into a single synthesized incremax procedure.
9. Each allows each participant to exercise a veto power a predetermined fixed number of times.

Each of these points will become apparent in the more formal discussion that follows.

Now let us specify the required assumptions using figures to illustrate.

i. Each participant (J and L) has a continuous action space that is bounded and representable by a straight line. This requirement

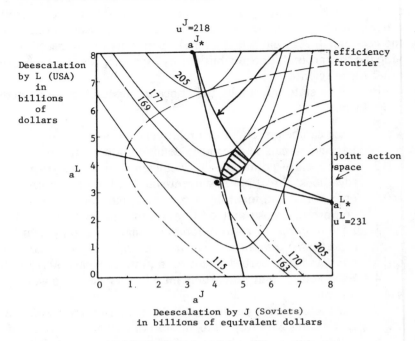

Figure 3.1. The indifference curves of J and L.

is fulfilled when in Figure 3.1 we (1) measure the decrease in military expenditures of J along the horizontal axis and in military expenditures of L along the vertical and (2) specify the maximum decrease in military expenditures of each to be \$8 billion.[7]

ii.   Each participant has an ordinal utility function (i.e., can only state whether it prefers one outcome to another or is indifferent to both) that is representable by a set of well-behaved indifference curves[8] as in Figure 3.1. Nation J's indifference curves are nondashed; L's are dashed curves. Note that we have "smoothed out" the matrix Table 3.2 to contain the box of Figure 3.1, which indicates J's and L's outcomes for all fractional as well as whole

---

[7] Strictly speaking, the joint action space must be compact (closed and bounded) and convex. First, observe that each of the action spaces is continuous, as typically perceived by a human behaving unit since a decrease in military expenditures can be specified in terms of units as small as pennies, or even mills, or tenths of mills, etc. Further, as already noted, each is bounded. Therefore each is closed. Each is also convex since a straight line (such as an axis) is convex. Since the actions of the two behaving units are independent, it then follows that the joint action space is compact and convex.

[8] Strictly speaking, the preference structure of each must be quasi-concave.

billions of dollars. These outcomes are represented by the numbers on the indifference curves, the particular numbers used being only one of many possible arbitrary sets that retain the order of these indifference curves.

iii. Each participant is fully informed of the outcomes of all possible joint actions and of the properties of any outcome that are relevant for it.

iv. Each assumes that the other is identical to itself in all relevant aspects other than preferences and action spaces.

v. Each nation's objective is to maximize its utility.

Now consider the conflict regarding a cooperative joint action, as depicted by Figure 3.1. There, J most prefers joint action a^{J*} whereas L most prefers a^{L*}. Presently, because of short-sighted myopic independent behavior, we take them to be at the stable equilibrium point e.[9] That is, neither is willing to take a *unilateral* action to move away from this point since such would put them on a lower indifference curve (a less preferred position). Together, however, they are now able to resolve their conflict if they adopt the following rules, which are consistent with the appealing features noted in the preceding.

Rule 1: In a manner consistent with appealing feature 4, in considering a move from the current position e or from any compromise joint action in later moves, each participant shall propose a move to some joint action in the *improvement* set. The striped area in Figure 3.2,[10] which is a detail of the striped area of Figure 3.1,[11] is the improvement set for the first move.

Rule 2: In a manner consistent with appealing feature 5, on each move each participant may wish to establish limits on the maximum amount of change in its action (or the joint action) that it will consider on that move – the change being from the current standpoint or any other reference point. The lesser of the maxima determines the commitment set that for the first move we have depicted as a small box with e as center in Figure 3.2. The heavily shaded area in Figure 3.2 is the intersection of the commitment

[9] See Isard et al. (1969, chap. 7) for a discussion of the rationale of the Nash equilibrium point as the current standpoint for J and L.
[10] Figure 3.2 was first developed in a paper delivered September 4, 1985, at a Peace Science conference in Cracow, Poland, and subsequently published (Isard and Smith, 1966).
[11] We designate this striped area as an improvement set since any interior point lies on a higher indifference curve for each participant than point e and thus represents an outcome it prefers to the outcome it would receive at point e. For full discussion see Isard et al. (1969, chap. 7).

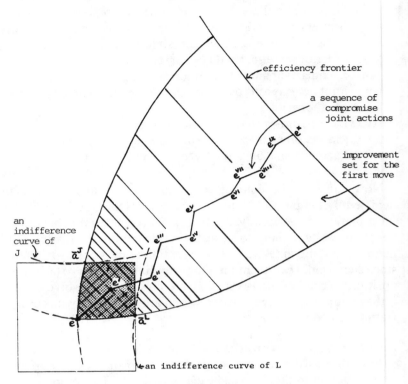

Figure 3.2. A sequence of split-the difference compromises.

set and improvement set. Therefore, on the first move, each participant is to propose a joint action in the area of intersection.

Rule 3: If on any move the proposed joint actions are not identical, the
participants shall adopt as the compromise joint action that joint
action defined by the midpoint of the line segment joining the
two proposed joint actions – a split-the-difference operation. In
Figure 3.2, J and L, each maximizing, respectively propose $\bar{a}^J$
and $\bar{a}^L$ as joint actions, e' then being the midpoint of the line
connecting the two and thus the compromise joint action (the
reference point) for the next move.

Rule 4: Each participant can exercise the veto power no more than k
(some finite number of) times. Each time a veto power is exer-
cised, the participants return to point e or some joint action
reached previously as a compromise point on a move, according
to the wishes of the vetoer.

If the two participants are motivated to adopt rules 1–4, we say that each is guided by the *split-the-difference veto–incremax principle*. Moreover, as demonstrated in Isard et al. (1969, chap. 7), the preceding assumptions lead via a sequence of steps (as illustrated in Figure 3.2) to a preindeterminate solution on the efficiency frontier having all the desirable properties listed in the foregoing. It is interesting to note the similarity of this figure to that in Raiffa (1982, p. 212), where the successful use of a Single Negotiating Text (as in the 1978 Camp David talks) is graphically depicted. As already noted, the veto–incremax procedure may be said to provide a theoretical basis for the use of a Single Negotiating Text in mediation (see also section 10.5.2).

We have briefly sketched a conflict management procedure typical of the analysis pursued by economists, operation researchers, and regional scientists, and we have explicitly stated some of their key assumptions. This analysis represents one of the extreme types, being based on a set of strong, unrealistic assumptions – for example, no uncertainty; well-informed if not fully informed participants who have no misperceptions and who become long-sighted and do not let emotions, past grievances, and so on, interfere with the choice of their actions; where there is no need for negotiations; and so forth. It may be pertinent for behaving units in some conflict situations in the real world, but such situations would be relatively few. We now wish to proceed toward an analysis at the other extreme by examining the behavioral problem as seen by cognitive scientists, who would maintain that their behavioral analysis pertains to a much larger fraction of the world's conflict situations, that is, is more realistic.

3.4 A cognitive science approach to decision making

In one sense the analysis presented in the previous two sections may be viewed as falling within the traditional frame of a stimulus–response situation. The stimulus might be, for example, assassination of one's political leader, and the response might be the action to mobilize one's troops – a last pair of an action and reaction that might have led the two nations to a point such as point *e* in Figure 3.1. In between one could place a black box, as was done many years ago by psychologists employing the stimulus–response paradigm. However, as peace scientists, we are concerned with what is contained in the black box of a behaving unit – not only for understanding the sequence of operations that occur, but also in order to be able to influence, at least in part, responses in subsequent stimulus – response situations of like character. Hence, we shall begin to present some of the concepts and analytic frameworks of cognitive psychology and other cognitive sciences; these concepts and frameworks will be further developed in subsequent chapters.

First, if à la psychology there is a stimulus, its recognition must take place. That is, the stimulus must be sensed as a neurophysiological phenomenon involving chemical and electrical processes within the brain with messages transmitted along interconnected cells. The point at which we social scientists become interested is when the stimulus is *recognized (perceived) by the mind*. What is important to us in defining a stimulus (which may be symbolized by a simple word such as parade or a single physical phenomenon such as lightning) depends on what a behaving unit *attends to, encodes, and comprehends*. That is, it depends on the one or more mental representations existing within the mind that the stimulus evokes (retrieves).

The mind contains a tremendous number of mental representations. These mental representations pertain to specific problem areas such as language understanding, reasoning, planning, problem solving, and image understanding and in general constitute part of a behaving unit's stock of knowledge.

But what is a mental representation? Since cognitive science is not yet at the stage where it possesses well-defined and generally accepted concepts, we do not attempt a rigorous definition of a mental representation. At the core, however, is the concept of schema, broadly defined. To Thorndyke (1984),

> [a] schema comprises a cluster (bundle) of knowledge representing a particular generic procedure, object, precept, event, sequence of events, or social situation. This cluster provides a skeleton structure for a concept that can be "instantiated," or filled out, with detailed properties of the particular instance being represented. (p. 167)

For example, a schema for the annual European meetings of the Peace Science Society (International) would encode the standard properties (a pattern map) of a scientific conference, such as its location, date, session types, length of presentations, business meeting, and social events. As with Thorndyke, we shall use the term "schema" to cover frames, scripts,[12] images, units, and objects when these are or have been taken to be knowledge structures encoding prototypical properties of concepts.

Schemata as knowledge clusters (i.e., organized collections of facts and relations) regarding a concept are then used to comprehend (via memory

---

[12] As Black (1984, p. 240) notes, "a *script* is a knowledge structure that contains causally related conceptualizations, which represent what we know about the standard actions, objects and actors in conventional situations."

retrieval) and store new instances of the concept. A schema guides comprehension of new instances by providing expectations for and constraints on the related properties associated with that concept, that is, a structure (scaffolding) on which to encode (attach) the information generated by the new instances, whether simple or complex world events. For example, take the forthcoming 1989 North American meetings of the Peace Science Society (International). As already noted, it would call forth information based on knowledge of the generic North American PSS(I) meeting. The time would be from Monday to Wednesday noon during the first or second week of November. It would take place at a city close by a major international airport, with papers of 25 minutes in length centered around a few major themes. There would be no plenary session and no concurrent sessions. Meetings would begin at 9:30 A.M. each morning and 2:30 P.M each afternoon.

In a most general form, a schema encodes knowledge of how events are structured, how event sequences combine and form episodes, and how entire stories (such as the attack on Pearl Harbor, the Bay of Pigs crisis, U.S. involvement in Vietnam, and USSR interjection in Afghanistan) are constructed from sequences of episodes. (Each of the stories, of course, embodies lessons that are learned.) Schemata, and in particular stories, represent information organized and indexed in the mind in ways that allow one to access the information when needed.

A current (1985) story in oversimplified form might be as follows:

1. President Reagan wanted to have the United States 100 percent protected against nuclear attack and superior in attack capability (the *goal*).
2. He therefore consulted with his close associates and his advisors on security policy (part of an *attempt*).
3. Finally, his close associates and advisors, after studying and listening to reports by expert scientists and strategists, came up with a four-star recommendation (another part of the *attempt*).
4. He then examined the recommendation and declared the proposed *Strategic Defense Initiative* (Star Wars) most appropriate for achieving his goal (the *outcome*).

Actually, this episode represents a tremendous understatement of what must have gone on in Reagan's adoption of the Strategic Defense Initiative policy. The full story would be long and complex. According to Black (p. 247), it would have involved three kinds of memory retrieval structures:

1. *reference hierarchies,* that is, hierarchies of statements organized in such a way that, for example, a first statement containing a

concept (or referent) – for example, "100% protection" – is superordinate to any later statement that contains the concept, explicitly or implicitly;

2. *episode hierarchies*, where a hierarchy of goals exist such that attempts to attain the main (overall) goal evokes other subgoals that must be achieved, and consequently the episodes for the subgoals are embedded in the episode for the overall goal; and

3. *plot unit networks*, which interconnect several plot units, where each plot unit consists of a particular goal–outcome event (e.g., Reagan won the election), and thus the network permits a coherent summarization.[13]

It is not necessary to delve any deeper into these concepts, especially since they are subject to drastic change and replacement as the rapidly developing field of cognitive science matures. For our purposes they point up the existence of several memory retrieval structures, each frequently playing a key role in complex international decision making. Moreover, the extent to which these several memory retrieval structures become available for use is affected by the extent to which a crisis is present in a decision situation.

Of particular interest to us is the use of stories and other schemata in conflict situations where problem solving (rather than routine action or decision making) is required. As already noted, schemata provide a framework for the organization and encoding of incoming information. Thus they provide a sophisticated type of advanced information organization that an individual uses to make sense of and efficiently encode new facts. In this respect, a schema is invaluable in situation assessment, especially where contingency planning may be involved. Such, for example, was involved in a study by the Rand Corporation that defined each of a variety of world situations in terms of 15 attributes, each situation being depicted by a point in fifteen-dimensional space. Using actual historical data and hypothetical situation–response sets based on their perception of Soviet doctrine and schemata, the study assessed Soviet intentions and projected likely Soviet behavior for each situation.

At this point, consider a characteristic phenomenon of behaving units critical for understanding decision making in the international arena. As stressed by Jervis (1976) and others, when confronted with exceedingly complex situations that generate information beyond the capacity of the

---

[13] According to Black (1984), plot units are composed of causally linked mental states (goals), positive events (a positive outcome for one plan), and negative events (a negative outcome for another plan), as in a competitive plot unit, and a network that links together patterns of specific episode content (p. 245).

mind to process, the behaving unit is compelled to oversimplify – often
to a major extent. An economic way for a behaving unit to do so is to
seek *cognitive consistency,* that is, to try to keep beliefs, feelings, and
actions mutually consistent. Such facilitates (1) the interpretations of old
and new information and (2) the retention and recall of information; and
this in turn avoids the expenditure of an excessive or economically
infeasible amount of effort and time in making a specific decision. However, such also leads to systematic bias in favor of information that is
consistent with what we have already acquired and absorbed, that is, in
favor of images that policy makers have come to possess about the world
and the motives of actors in it. Since schemata are cumulatively developed and reconstructed, the events experienced early in life and the schemata (images) to which they lead have disproportionate impact upon
decision making at a much later point in life, ceteris paribus.

As developed and documented by Lebow (1981), cognitive consistency
must lead to

1.   persistent denial of new information (ignoring, twisting, or
     explaining it away) and diminished ability to learn from the envi-
     ronment, or
2.   premature cognitive closure, perceptual satisficing, or masking
     effects of preexisting beliefs, or
3.   inadequate sensitivity (desensitivity) to trade-off among values
     and objectives, or
4.   postdecisional rationalizations, or
5.   combinations of these.

In the Rand study of Soviet behavior noted in the preceding, undoubtedly the images of the Rand analysts about Soviet behavior were at play.
Yet in general, projecting likely behavior in a variety of world situations
wherein conflict is involved is of course key to Peace Science studies. In
a number of ways, it is close to identifying the payoff or utility matrix
that a behaving unit implicitly or explicitly confronts. In the Soviet study,
each of the world situations represented a state of affairs that could be
said to correspond to a column of a payoff matrix. Each of the different
likely behaviors projected for the Soviet represented a row of the matrix.
Implicit, if not explicit, would be an assumed attitude of the Soviet; and
if the outcomes of the payoff matrix were not specified, it is implied that
for any column the outcome associated with the row of the projected
likely Soviet behavior was the likely maximum for that column.

In general, associated with the use of a schema or set of schema for
situation assessment is an implicit payoff matrix. Frequently, if not typically, one is considering at least two actions, one being "do nothing" and

another being "do something." Moreover, in assessing the situation, especially when a second behaving unit is involved whose behavior, motivation, preferences, and so on, are not fully known, one confronts at least two possible states of the environment: the most likely state and at least one alternative. Thus, at least explicitly, a minimal 2×2 payoff (utility) matrix is being considered.

Note also that projecting likely behavior of a behaving unit (whether Soviet or not) in a variety of world situations – thus hypothesizing implicit, if not explicit, contingency planning by that unit – in turn may imply advocacy of or actual contingency planning by those units (such as the Rand Corporation and its client) who undertake the projecting.

Equally important for Peace Science is projecting likely behavior, not under a variety of assumed world situations, but rather when the world situation actually changes. Here, problem solving must be confronted. Since in problem solving, mental representations such as stories and other schemata play a fundamental role, one should be aware of how the brain's information-processing mechanism copes with change. According to Kosslyn (1984, p. 98), there are three sublevels in the information processing of the brain, each differing in part in the degree of abstraction:

1.   *The level of computation* (the most abstract) specifies the nature (and purpose) of a computation, that is, the transformation of information (the input) into new information (the output). It specifies *what* is computed without regard to how it is computed.

2.   *The level of the functional architecture* specifies *how* the processing is actually performed. It pertains to the structures and processes available in the "black box" into which goes an information input and out of which comes the information output.

3.   *The level of the algorithm* (the most particular) specifies a set of steps that are so precisely defined that they can be carried out automatically without the use of human understanding or intuition. Provided the correct information input is provided, an algorithm guarantees the production of a specific output.

Clearly, then, when a decision maker must solve a problem, that is, find an appropriate action, there are several ways in which new information may influence his (or her) choice of an action. First, his choice of action can be influenced through becoming informed of (a) outcomes other than those he currently perceives as possible from a given set of inputs, or (b) sets of inputs other than those he currently perceives as required to achieve a given set of outputs, or (c) input–output functions involving both sets of inputs and sets of outcomes beyond those he is currently aware of. In short, his action can be influenced by information that enlarges or corrects his perceived input–output functions given the functional architecture of his brain and the algorithms with which he is familiar and capable of employing.

Second, his (or her) action can be influenced by changes in the functional architecture of his brain. For example, becoming aware of an interregional input–output model and its capabilities, which adds to the media (know-how) of his brain may enable him to compute with reasonable accuracy outcomes of whose importance he was well aware (such as jobs and economic security of his opponent) but were up to now impossible for him to estimate.

Third, his (or her) action can be influenced by change in the set of algorithms available to him. He may have been fully informed of all relevant input–output schema and have had the requisite functional architecture (know-how in the form of ability to understand and use linear systems), but he may have lacked an algorithm (an automatic series of steps or a computer program) by which to realize the potential outcome in a reasonable amount of time. (The use of a simple substitution procedure taught us in our ninth-grade algebra course would require an amount of time in calculating a solution to a large linear system well beyond that which may be available; but not so with the use of an inverse of a coefficient matrix generated in seconds by a computer.)

Lastly, his or her action may be influenced, if we follow Kosslyn's conceptual framework, by any combination of the preceding three types of changes.

Against this background, we now briefly focus on problem-solving activity, which we shall discuss at length in Chapter 6 (section 6.2). Problem-solving activity, in contrast to the routine use of knowledge to reach a solution (as currently in the use of an inverse to solve an input–output problem), typically involves a combination of memory (a passive storehouse of facts, relations, schemata, etc.) and at least some imagination. Whereas the solution to a problem at times comes about suddenly and autonomously, typically a solution based on new ideas is the product of intelligent, goal-directed transformations of existing knowledge. Behind the genesis of new ideas exists a mental model (the core element) that is a psychological representation of the environment and its expected behavior. When problems are *well defined* – that is, when the initial situation, allowable actions, and desired state of affairs or goal are clearly specified – one can often tackle them successfully with a minimum of imagination and appropriate solution methods (as in using an inverse to solve a properly stated linear system). In such cases, problem solving is not creative. However, when problems are ill-defined, the exercises of imagination and creativity come to the fore. Here, problem solving involves recognizing in full that a problem exists, forming some initial mental model of it, transforming an initially vague model into one that is better specified, and eventually, if all goes well, using the model to plan and execute a concrete solution. See Holyoak (1984). In model construction, there is of course tremendous simplification of reality wherein only relevant features and relations are retained and where the correspondences of these features and relations between the model and the real world are preserved under state changes.

When creative problem solving is required of a behaving unit, several basic components of its mental activity are subject to influence. First, the unit must recognize (perceive) a problematic situation. Here the unit may need to be educated with regard to the existence of the problem and its diverse elements, with corrections of its misperceptions. Second, its construction of an initial problem model (which may involve an incompatibility or contradiction) may be improved. Its statement of the goal may be made less vague; inefficient and conflicting subgoals may be eliminated; and its concern for community welfare may be explicitly introduced. Relevant objects may be more accurately identified and their relations better specified. Too abstract or ill-defined or misperceived actions or operators may be eliminated from consideration. Constraints, either totally or partially unrecognized, may be pointed up.

Such education as the preceding that fills out and corrects the behaving unit's stock of information does not ensure that a solution procedure automatically comes to the fore. It may be necessary to search for some analogy, ideally an isomorphism, to help suggest a feasible solution. It may be either an intradomain analogy (an analogy within the same domain of problems) or an interdomain analogy (an analogy from a different domain of problems, perhaps one far afield where the surface differences with the analogy are major but the hidden structural properties similar). Or it may be that no analogy can be found, and the search for a solution, no matter how much imagination is resorted to or appeal to the random or irrational is made, stays unsuccessful (such as the search for a solution to the Northern Ireland crisis or the Middle East problem). Then the response may be a "do nothing" action or at most inadequate action with little scientific basis or none, though perhaps associated with much superficial rationalization.

To recapitulate, the black box that lies between the stimulus and response is the object of discussion. We see how, according to the cognitive scientist, a stimulus, when recognized, calls forth one or more mental representations. These representations can be complex in character and typically involve elaborate and intricate stories or schemata for the international conflict situations with which we are concerned. These schemata

are clusters of knowledge about objects, events, relationships, and the like
that provide a skeleton structure that can be "instantiated" or filled out
with detailed properties of the particular instance being represented. A
complex schema, particularly when it functions as a story taken to teach
a lesson, involves reference hierarchies, episode hierarchies, and plot unit
networks stored in the memory. Because schemata encode knowledge of
how events are structured and how event sequences combine and form
episodes from which lessons are learned, they provide a basic framework
within the memory for the organization and encoding of incoming information that is associated with a stimulus. They thus are exploited for
assessing the new situation associated with that stimulus; however, they
almost invariably lead to at least some irrationality from denial of information, misperceptions, and the like because of the need for cognitive
consistency owing to limited mental resources. Equally, if not more
important, schemata serve as a framework for constructing new mental
models for nonroutine (creative) problem solving – the key requirement
for the management of most if not all major international conflicts.
Looked at in one way, such mental models involve

1. a level of computation that proposes what is to be computed;
2. a level of functional architecture, which specifies how things can
    be computed; and
3. a level of algorithm, which specifies precisely the steps by which
    an input is transformed into an output.

Looked at in another way, the mental model for problem solving requires

1. a well-defined goal (which nonetheless can be abstract in char-
    acter) associated with the specification of what is to be computed;
2. the specification of relevant objects, which serve as both inputs
    and outputs and again is associated with what is to be computed;
3. actions (or operations) that can effect the desired transformation,
    which is associated with functional architecture, that is, the exis-
    tence of potential know-how within the memory; and
4. constraints that limit or prohibit the use of certain classes of
    objects or operators, which are essentially imposed by the envi-
    ronment, the functional architecture of a behaving unit's mem-
    ory, and the algorithms it possesses or has access to.

The foregoing background, although it covers only a part of the basic
knowledge stemming from the surging field of cognitive science, provides
us with sufficient direction and insight to take the next step – a more
adequate, even though diffuse, symbolic representation of the decision-
making process characteristic of international conflict situations.

3.5   Concluding remarks

We have examined the choice of actions of behaving units from several different standpoints. First we considered the attitude variable in a situation where a behaving unit confronted several states of the environment, each one covering a given (or presumed or prespecified) joint action of others. With the standard approach of economics, operations research, and regional science as background, we indicated how its particular attitude (pessimistic, optimistic, conservative, etc.) affected its definition of an optimal action. Next we considered conflict situations involving interdependent decision making by two behaving units, say, the United States and the Soviet Union, with regard to deescalation. With the use of guiding principles and associated conflict management procedures, we suggested some ways in which conflicts can be managed – an area of study that will be more deeply probed in Chapter 10 along with the negotiating process. Obviously, where possible, any third party to a conflict should – through observation of past behavior or other means including the use of experts on attitude formation and change – identify the attitudes of the parties in conflict and take these into consideration in suggesting any guiding principles and associated conflict management procedures.

The alternative, much different cognitive approach toward understanding and projecting behavior and decision making was then discussed. The role of schemata and other mental representations for instantiation, for encoding new information, and for assessing a situation was developed. The information-processing mechanism and functional architecture of the brain was then examined as well as the brain's construction of mental models by analogy for problem solving. The informal discussion of behavior, decision making, and problem solving of this chapter serves as background for the more formal analysis in subsequent chapters.

Appendixes

3.A   Behavior associated with other types of attitude

The 100 percent conservative regretter and other regretters

As noted in the text there are individuals who wish (strongly) to avoid feelings of regret, that is, the unhappiness that results when they observe that they could have chosen another action than the one they did choose, which in the light of the environmental state that materialized would have made them better off. Such an individual may then implicitly think in terms of a regret matrix, or actually construct one, such as Table 3.A.1. Table 3.A.1 is based on Table 3.1. In any cell, say, row *i* and column *j,* the number recorded is the regret r_{ij} derived by subtract-

Table 3.A.1. *A regret matrix*

	States of the environment			
	i	ii	iii	iv
Z's possible actions (proposals)				
a_1	0	19	169	0
a_2	161	0	105	88
a_3	225	64	0	144
a_4	209	19	25	120

ing the outcome o_{ij} in that row and column in Table 3.1 from the maximum outcome o_j^* in that column. Accordingly, we obtain the regret matrix in Table 3.A.1. If the behaving unit is 100 percent conservative, he (or she) will select action a_2, which ensures that his regret will not exceed 161, the minimum of the maximum of the several rows. (The 100 percent pessimist regretter would also use a minmax strategy.) If we were to want him to select action a_4, we would need to guarantee him that he would receive at least 65 votes were environmental state i realized, in which case the regret of 209 would fall to 160. The expected cost to us would be 65 − 16 (see Table 3.1) times the probability that environment state i is realized.

The expected regret calculator, given the probabilities of occurrence of the several states of the environment, would select that action for which the total of expected regret would be a minimum. Theoretically (but hardly realistically), there might be a 100 percent optimistic regretter. He or she would use a min–min strategy, selecting that action whose minimum regret was the least of all minima.

The satisficer

Another type of attitude is associated with the satisficer – a behaving unit that is satisficed and does not search farther once an action leading to an acceptable (satisfactory) outcome is found. He (or she) may thereby be viewed as maximizing his leisure and family time, minimizing the strain of making a decision, and so on. Often each of his set of acceptable outcomes are labeled +1, or win, and the unacceptable outcomes, 0 or lose. Thus, if in Table 3.1 the state of the environment iii is the one and only one realizable and if outcomes of 60 or more are the acceptable ones, the satisficer would keep on searching if the first examined action were a_1 (which may be assigned the number 0) and would stop searching as soon as he examined action a_2, a_3, or a_4 (each of which may be assigned the number +1). On the other hand, if he estimated a positive probability for each of the states in Table 3.1, only action a_2 would generate an acceptable outcome for every possible state.

For other more rigorous analysis of the satisficer, see Isard et al. (1969, Chap. 5).

Table 3.B.1. *The payoff matrix*

	L's actions	
	a_1	a_2
J's actions		
a_1	3, 3	$-13,\ 9$
a_2	$9,\ -13$	$-6,\ -6$

3.B   The relevance of game theory

An important area of knowledge essential for understanding many conflict situations and potentials for their control and resolution is game theory, an area also of major significance for the application of the principles of negotiation and mediation associated with *understanding enhancement,* to be discussed in Chapter 10. [For application of game theory to conflict situations, see, among others, Luce and Raiffa (1957), Rapaport (1966), Brams (1977, 1980), Raiffa (1982), Shubik (1982, 1984), Brams and Kilgour (1988), and the literature contained and cited in the journal *Game Theory.*] Since the literature is so extensive, we can only make brief illustrative reference to it and suggest that the reader consult the preceding publications and Isard and Smith (1982). For games specifically designed to characterize national security problems, see Brams and Kilgour (1988) and Shubik (1988). Whereas game theory itself is rather formal and in many ways abstracts from reality when one examines such complex problems as national security, it can help to eliminate the mushiness of much inductive thinking on this problem and can make significant contributions to systematic strategic analysis. But as Shubik (1988, p. 54) has noted, "Paradoxically the precision of the mathematical methods of game theory have helped to illustrate the imprecision and the elusiveness of many of the concepts at the basis of the science, art and social process of war."

One major part of the game theory literature refers to two-person games. Whereas two-person zero-sum game theory has found many significant applications, we in Peace Science are concerned with two-person games that are not zero sum. Of these the Prisoner's Dilemma and Chicken are among the most useful to examine. The basic ideas of a Prisoner's Dilemma game can be illustrated in a 2 × 2 table, Table 3.B.1. There are two players: J and L. Each may choose one of the two actions a_1 and a_2. Action a_1 represents cooperation, and a_2 represents noncooperation, or defection, or some action of similar character. Player J's actions correspond to rows a_1 and a_2, and L's actions correspond to columns a_1 and a_2. The numbers in any cell of the table are the payoffs to each player when J takes the action corresponding to the row of that cell and L the action corresonding to the column of that cell. The first number in each cell is J's payoff, and the second number is L's payoff.

Each player is 100 percent self-interested. He (or she) is motivated to maximize his payoff. Thus, given the action of the other participant, it is always best strategy for a player to choose a_2. For instance, suppose J has taken action a_1. Then L finds it better to choose a_2 than a_1, for if he chooses a_2, he gets a payoff of 9; if he were to choose a_1, he would get a payoff of only 3. Or suppose J takes action a_2. Then L still finds it better to choose a_2 than a_1, for if he chooses a_1, his payoff is -13, whereas if he chooses a_2, his payoff is -6. Since this payoff matrix is symmetrical, it also always pays J to choose a_2 for any given action that L takes. Hence, in this game, each chooses a_2, and the equilibrium payoff to each is -6. Neither is motivated to change his action unilaterally.

If by chance both players had started off by taking action a_1, so that their payoffs were (3, 3), such would not represent an equilibrium, for where actions are independent and retractable and where this game is played only once, each participant would, out of pure self-interest, find it profitable to change his or her action to a_2. Thus, the joint action (a_2, a_2) results. It corresponds to a stable but undesirable equilibrium.

We should note that the undesirable joint action (a_2, a_2) results for any set of payoffs for which for each party the most desirable payoff replaces 9 in Table 3.B.1, the second most desirable replaces 3, the least desirable replaces -13, and the next to least desirable replaces -6.

There has been extensive discussion of the Prisoner's Dilemma game, which has often been used to characterize in a highly oversimplified manner arms race situations (such as the current Soviet–U.S. race) and other basic conflicts (such as when strikes or any number of kinds of deadlocks exist). Many different procedures have been proposed to lead the two parties from the joint, noncooperative action (a_2, a_2) to the joint cooperative one (a_1, a_1). For example, there is the procedure associated with the Howard metagame (see Isard and Smith 1982, pp. 43–8, 53–7). Moreover, scholars such as Brams would contend that the two parties are not likely to be as myopic as assumed in the preceding. They are likely to recognize that their opponent will react to whatever action they take and may anticipate a sequence of actions and reactions. Hence, if they are initially at a cooperative joint action (a_1, a_1), each may not defect from a cooperative action since each knows that such would lead his (or her) opponent to do likewise in order to minimize his loss and thus would lead them both into a situation that yields each a smaller payoff. And other lines of reasoning of this sort have been considered. None, however, satisfactorily attack the problem, especially when initially the players are involved in an (a_2, a_2) joint action. However, it should be noted that Brams and Kilgour (1988) have recently extended Prisoner's Dilemma, allowing each player (1) *initially* to choose any level of provocation (a probability of escalation) along a disarm–arm dimension and (2) *subsequently* to choose any level of response to a provocation (a probability of retaliation) if it is viewed as escalatory or noncooperative provided the player's own initial choice was considered cooperative. They claim this new game, designated the "Deescalation Game," as a model, offers a more realistic representation of the superpowers' arms race than do others; and they demonstrate how the players in this game can travel from their current noncooperative equilibrium to the deescalation equilibrium.

Another two-person game frequently discussed in the literature and that also can be extended to a national security game of significant interest currently (see Brams and Kilgour 1988) is Chicken. This game takes the form shown in Table

Table 3.B.2. *The game of Chicken*

	L's actions	
	a_1	a_2
J's actions		
a_1	3, 3	2, 4
a_2	4, 2	1, 1

3.B.2. The myopic equilibria in this game are (4, 2) and (2, 4). To see this, suppose the players are initially at (3, 3). Player J could change his (or her) action from a_1 to a_2, thereby increasing his payoff to 4. Player L could do the same, thereby increasing his payoff to 4. However, if both were simultaneously to change from a_1 to a_2, they would both receive their worst outcome (1, 1). Whoever is the more aggressive, say, L, changes his action first and obtains his most preferred outcome. The other, J, must then accept a lower payoff, for once (2, 4) is reached, neither L nor J has an incentive to change his action. The less aggressive, J, is in effect a "chicken." Although at the start he could have increased his payoff by changing his action from a_1 to a_2 provided he did so before L, he hesitated to do so for fear that his opponent would do the same concomitantly and that as a result they would end up at (a_2, a_2) with a payoff of (1, 1).

Brams and Kilgour (1988) have extended this game, too, by introducing for each player a probability of preemption and a probability of retaliation if preempted, thereby converting Chicken into a "Deterrence Game." They are motivated to do so in their concern for the central problem of the superpowers' deterrence policies, namely, that the threat of retaliation via a second strike may not be credible if the second strike leads to a much worse outcome – a nuclear holocaust – than a superpower would experience from tolerating a limited first strike and not retaliating. They are able to identify a deterrence equilibrium that is "Pareto-superior, dynamically stable," and when supported by robust threats, as "invulnerable as possible to misperceptions or miscalculations by the players" (Brams and Kilgour 1988, p. 51).

Whereas by the preceding analyses and other contributions, Brams and Kilgour and many others have provided many fruitful advances and insights in particular contexts (such as defined by the explicit and implicit assumptions of Brams and Kilgour), in the words of Shubik, "it must be stressed without qualification that for dynamic non-constant-sum games in general there is no generally agreed upon solution concept" (1988, pp. 58–9).

Another major part of the game theory literature pertains to situations in which there are three or more players and where coalitions are possible. This case will be specifically illustrated in the discussion of the example in section 7.4 on *compromise points in policy space*. There we consider four political actors each of whom could gain from reaching agreement (a compromise) on one or more policies (joint actions) – that is, by agglomerating at a common position in policy space by forming an *all-player coalition*. Thus in Figure 7.7 we label the four participants (e.g., nations) *A, B, C,* and *D* with their respective initial position on some issues (matters) represented by points *A, B, C,* and *D.* There we construct for each participant a set of isolines (isodapanes) where an isoline connects positions involving for the participant the same total patronage cost; and we identify for each participant the *critical* isoline beyond which the total costs from agglomerating (compromising) begin to exceed gains. The set of agglomeration points (i.e., compromise positions) for the four participants thus lies within their critical isolines, each point being efficient in the sense that each participant would be better off if the compromise corresponding to that point were realized than if it were to remain at its initial position. But the four participants have different preferences for the many possible compromises, each preferring those compromises corresponding to those points lying closest to their initial positions. Furthermore, there are possible gains for each participant if it were to join up with one other participant in just a two-participant compromise; but even in considering a two-participant compromise, there are a number of possible compromises, each of the two participants preferring those corresponding to points lying closest to their initial positions.

One can proceed to define the *core* of this four-player game, that is, the set of allocations of games that allow no individual acting alone to do any better or any two-players (or set of individuals) to do any better. Unhappily, there is no unique solution to this conflict situation. See, for example, the lucid discussion in Raiffa (1982, chap. 17). One could attempt to construct Shapley values for the participants and use these as the solution or derive a Raiffa-type solution. Or one could attempt to have the participants employ other criteria using diverse principles of negotiation and mediation or both or a conflict management procedure, as will be discussed in Chapter 10. Still, no solution of general acceptability has as yet been identified. Thus coalition analysis has little to say for real-life situations.

In general, one must conclude that, aside from two-person zero-sum game theory, there is a wide gap between formal game theory and application. As will be increasingly apparent, the specific state of affairs, the sociocultural, psychological, and organizational factors economists, regional scientists, operational researchers, and others carefully exclude (explicitly or implicitly) from their game theory models do in reality play important roles.

References

Black, J. B. (1984) "Understanding and Remembering Stories." In J. R. Anderson and S. M. Kosslyn (eds.), *Tutorials in Learning and Memory.* New York: W. H. Freeman, pp. 235–56.

Brams, S. J. (1977) "Deception in 2 × 2 Games." *Journal of Peace Science* (2):171–203.

Brams, S. J. (1980) *Biblical Games: Strategic Analyses of Stories in the Old Testament,* Cambridge, MA: MIT Press.

Brams, S. J., and D. M. Kilgour (1988) *Game Theory and National Security.* New York: Basil Blackwell.

Burton, J. W. (1969) *Conflict and Communication: The Use of Controlled Communication in International Relations.* London: Macmillan.

Burton, J. W. (1972) "Resolution and Conflict." *International Studies Quarterly* 16(1):5–30.

Holyoak, K. J. (1984) "Mental Models in Problem Solving." In J. R. Anderson and S. M. Kosslyn (eds.), *Tutorials in Learning and Memory.* New York: W. H. Freeman, pp. 193–218.

Isard, W., and T. E. Smith (1966) "A Practical Application of Game Theoretical Approaches to Arms Reduction." *Papers,* Peace Research Society (International), Vol. IV, pp. 85–98.

Isard, W., T. E. Smith, P. Isard, T. H. Tung, and M. Dacey (1969) *General Theory: Social, Political, Economic and Regional.* Cambridge, MA: MIT Press.

Isard, W., and C. Smith (1982) *Conflict Analysis and Practical Conflict Management Procedures: An Introduction to Peace Science.* Cambridge, MA: Ballinger.

Jervis, R. (1976) *Perception and Misperception in International Politics.* Princeton: Princeton University Press.

Kosslyn, S. M. (1984) "Mental Representation." In J. R. Anderson and S. M. Kosslyn (eds.), *Tutorial in Learning and Memory.* New York: W. H. Freeman, pp. 91–118.

Lebow, R. N. (1981) *Between War and Peace.* Baltimore: Johns Hopkins Press.

Luce, R. D., and H. Raiffa (1957) *Games and Decisions: Introduction and Survey.* New York: Wiley.

Raiffa, H. (1982) *The Art and Science of Negotiation.* Cambridge, MA: Harvard University Press.

Rapaport, A. (1966) *Two-Person Game Theory: The Essential Ideas.* Ann Arbor, MI: University of Michigan Press.

Shubik, M. (1982) *Game Theory in the Social Sciences.* Cambridge, MA: MIT Press.

Shubik, M. (1984) *A Game-Theoretic Approach to Political Economy.* Cambridge, MA: MIT Press.

Shubik, M. (1988) "The Uses, Value and Limitations of Game Theoretic Methods in Defence Analysis." In C. Schmidt and F. Blackaby (eds.), *Peace, Defence and Economic Analysis.* London: MacMillan, pp. 53–84.

Thorndyke, P. W. (1984) "Applications of Schema Theory in Cognitive Research." In J. R. Anderson and S. M. Kosslyn (eds.), *Tutorials in Learning and Memory.* New York: W. H. Freeman, pp. 167–92.

CHAPTER 4

A more formal cognitive framework for individual and group behavior

4.1   Introduction

In section 3.3 on interdependent decision making, we presented a typical economics, operations research, and regional science approach to decision making by an individual *i* wherein the environment contains other behaving units whose characteristics and actions must be considered by *i* in making a decision. It was a framework for decision making by an *economic* person. In section 3.4 we presented a cognitive approach to decision making, wherein an individual *i* takes an action or makes a conscious and deliberate response to a stimulus from the environment (including other behaving units) guided by his or her mental representations. It was a framework for decision making by a *cognitive sci* person. Now we shall try to pull together the strengths of both frameworks, admittedly through loose formalizing. In section 4.2 we concentrate on individual behavior. In section 4.3 we pursue parallel discussion on group behavior. Section 4.4 offers some concluding remarks. Again, note that we are motivated to inquire into behavior and why decisions are made in order (1) to understand better the terms and levels of the parameters in arms race models and models of other conflict phenomena and (2) to suggest avenues by which the parameters may be changed by deliberate action and policy.

In this chapter we do use many mathematical symbols but only as a shorthand. Except for addition, subtraction, multiplication, and division, no mathematical operations are carried out. Thus, although the presentation of this chapter could be entirely verbal, we find that the use of

I am heavily indebted to Douglas Johnson and James Bennett, upon whose ideas I have drawn extensively in writing this chapter, and to Christine Smith for clarifying many points. The author is alone responsible for all shortcomings of the analysis.

121

mathematical symbols enables us to state many relationships succinctly so that the reader can perceive at any moment of time a much larger set of relationships than would otherwise be the case. All the relationships noted are simple, straightforward, and general. We wish to stress this point, not only (1) to indicate to the nonmathematical reader that there is no relationship in this chapter that he or she cannot restate in words, but also and equally important, (2) to avoid misleading the technical reader familiar with mathematics. The literature in the several social sciences has not reached the point where for the purposes of this chapter we can set down specific functions. When, for example, we write the relationship $o = o(a, e)$, we wish to imply no specific function but only what the symbols stand for, namely, that an *outcome* (designated o) *is* (designated by the equal sign) *a function* [designated on the right-hand side of the equation by $o(\ )$] of two variables, one being *the set of actions* (one taken by each behaving unit, designated by a) and the second being *the state of the environment* (designated by e). Or we simply read the relationship $o = o(a, e)$ as the outcome o depends on the set of actions a taken and the state e of the environment. Also, when we use more complicated patterns of symbols, we intend again nothing more than the statement of a very general relationship.

4.2   Behavior of the individual as a decision-making unit

4.2.1   The action space of the individual

Start with the economist's concept of action space. Let there be n individuals where the general symbol i can represent any of these individuals, that is, $i = 1, 2, \ldots, n$. He or she views the individual i as having at any point of time t a set of possible actions, which set comprises his or her action space $A_i(t)$. For each possible state e of the environment E, each action a_i may consist of the inputs he or she associates with an input–output relation where we define such a relation broadly to cover inputs and outputs of noneconomic as well as economic goods. One of the technical (physical) constraints imposed by the environment is that each i has available for use no more than 24 man-hours of labor per day.

Through interaction with other individuals, additional constraints are imposed on the set of actions $A_i(t)$ that i can take. A common one is the budget constraint. This constraint states that i's expenditures must not exceed his or her income (or does not exceed it by some allowable debt set by society and its institutions); but i's income and thus expenditures are affected in a major way by the prices that prevail on the market, such prices being determined by the actions of innumerable other behaving units. Laws on allowable behavior (including production processes) represent another set of constraints imposed by the actions of others.

Let each individual but i take an action. Thus we have a_1 (the action of the first), a_2 (the action by the second), a_{i-1} [the action of the $(i-1)$th], and so on. For short, let this set be represented by $\{a_k\}$. That is, $\{a_k\} = (a_1, \ldots, a_{i-1}, a_{i+1}, \ldots, a_n)$. This set of actions then places constraints on what actions i can take, and we define i's restricted action space at time t, namely, $\tilde{A}_i(t)$, as dependent on both A_i and $\{a_k\}$, that is, $\tilde{A}_i = \tilde{A}_i(A_i, \{a_k\})$, where here and elsewhere we suppress the symbol t when implied by the discussion. See the dependency relation 1 in the upper (right-hand side) of Figure 4.1, where the solid lines indicated by the number 1 and coming from the A_i and the $\{a_k\}$ boxes come together at a point and lead (as indicated by the arrowhead) to the $\tilde{A}_i$ box. Strictly speaking, we should introduce the actions of groups and social institutions together with the actions $\{a_k\}$ of other individuals as setting the constraints, but we do not do so to avoid complicated expressions. Later we shall consider effects of groups and their behavior.

4.2.2 The individual as a perceiver

It is one thing to talk about technical action and restricted action spaces. It is another thing to talk about the set of actions that i perceives as available in any given decision-making situation. From infancy through childhood up to his (or her) current adult status he has had experiences that are stored in his memory as schemata and the like, very simple at first and increasingly complex as he attains maturity and finally becomes perhaps a wise old man (distinguished political leader). Thus, the action space that he perceives is by and large a learned action space. Moreover, it includes actions consistent with the "fixes," "packages," biases, and ways of his culture, about which we shall say more later. Moreover, when he is under high stress and panics, his perceived actions may not include a number of actions that under normal conditions in a previous time he had been aware of or could retrieve from long-term and even short-term memory.

We therefore speak of $\mathcal{P}_i(A_i)$ and $\mathcal{P}_i(\tilde{A}_i)$, that is, i's perceptions of his action and restricted action spaces, respectively. [$\mathcal{P}_i(\tilde{A}_i)$ is noted in the upper right corner of Figure 4.1.] These perceived spaces will typically be of significantly smaller size than what is actually possible. Moreover, i may perceive options as available within the set $\mathcal{P}_i(\tilde{A}_i)$ that in fact are not available to him because he is not aware of their technical infeasibility or of restrictions imposed by the actions of others. He thus may choose to effect an action $a_i \in \mathcal{P}_i(\tilde{A}_i)$, (where $\in$ stands for element of) which at times

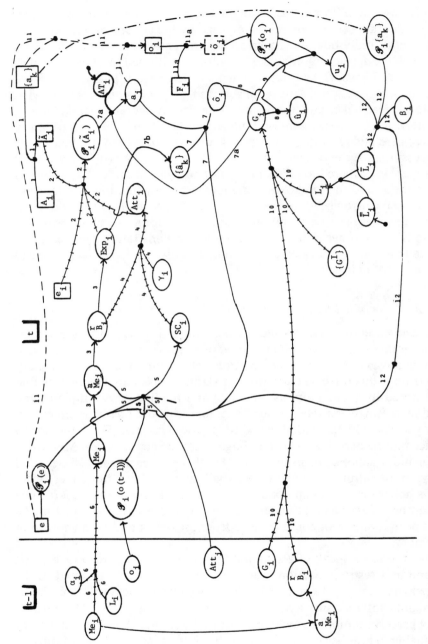

Figure 4.1. A formal cognitive science frame.

may be unrealizable (blocked). If it is unrealizable, frustration or other outcome elements may result, and learning L_i may take place; i is then required to select another action (presumably at the next point of time) even if it is to "do nothing."

Perceptions of i enter into his decision-making problem at many other places. As already indicated, at any point of time there exists a state of the environment $e \in E$. Although an analyst may be able to describe fully the state e, or at least its relevant properties, what is important in i's decision-making process is his perception $\mathcal{P}_i(e)$ of that state. It is possible that i may often misperceive the state's properties and, in fact, may perceive properties of e that actually do not exist.

Similarly, when we speak later of outcome o, action a_k of participant k, goals G_k of k, time duration τ, and so on, what i acts upon is his perceptions $\mathcal{P}_i(o)$, $\mathcal{P}_i(a_k)$, $\mathcal{P}_i(G_k)$, $\mathcal{P}_i(\tau)$, . . ., of these items, respectively. Likewise, when we talk of relations (say, an input–output production relation or an alliance between nations), what i acts upon is his perceptions of these relations.

It is not enough to talk about perceptions. We need to know at least something about what determines perceptions. One definition of perception (Webster 1961) is "physical sensation as interpreted in the light of experience: the integration of sensory impressions of events in the external world by a conscious organism, especially as a function of nonconscious expectations derived from past experience and serving as a basis either for or as verified by further meaningful motivated action." Another definition of perception (Funk and Wagnalls 1961) is "the faculty, process, or product of cognition in general, whether in the more immediate and seemingly intuitive way of the senses, or by activity of thinking, bringing, or holding before, the conscious mind." Funk and Wagnalls go on to state:

> While psychologists differ as to the details involved in perception . . . there is nearly universal agreement on the following points: completed perception involves (1) a fusion of complex sensations, chiefly of the kinesthetic and visual sort; (2) a variety of ideational elements, or mental images derived from past experiences; (3) mental activity in discriminating and recognizing; and (4) a certain process of externalizing and localizing the object, with an accompanying faith or belief in its reality. These distinctions are, however, all matters of degree, so that no hard and fast line can be drawn between *perceptions* and *ideas* or *imaginations*.

More recently, some cognitive scientists would define perceptions to be transformations of so-called objective information – transformations in part designed to simplify a reality that is too complex for the mind to grasp as a whole. Frequently, we know a misperception occurs when a behaving unit thinks that the other side (whether another behaving unit or group) sees him (or her) (the behaving unit) and his group as he himself does; basically, he takes his perception of causal and other relationships as correct and fails to perceive (is insensitive to) the possibility of alternative explanations. And so forth. Misperception may also be defined broadly enough to cover *distortion,* in which one manipulates facts and relations to make them more acceptable, and *denial,* to ignore discomforting facts and relations especially when threatened.

The preceding definitions of perceptions enable us to work only loosely with the perception variable. For our conceptual framework we need a tighter definition. We take the perception $P_i(z)$ of any actual object or relation or item z to be functionally related (here indicated by the symbol f) to other variables. In particular, we take

$$P_i(z) = f(\tilde{z}_i, \text{Exp}_i, \text{Att}_i, e_i) \qquad (4.2.1)$$

where

$\tilde{z}_i$ = information about z that has passed through the filtering operations of i and groups to which he or she belongs;

Exp_i = i's expectations about z;

Att_i = objects, issues, relationships, beliefs, and other items to which i is attending;

e_i = environmental setting as it impinges on i.

Now at this point we are concerned with i's restricted action space $\tilde{A}_i$ and his or her perception of it, $P_i(\tilde{A}_i)$. So, if we substitute $\tilde{A}_i$ for z in Eq. (4.2.1), we obtain relation 2 in the upper right of Figure 4.1, where hatched lines with numbers 2 from the $\tilde{A}_i$, Exp_i, Att_i, and e_i boxes converge at a point and lead to the $P_i(\tilde{A}_i)$ box.

The relationship of Eq. (4.2.1) requires further discussion. The variable $\tilde{z}$ represents information about z that has passed through *filtering activity* F_i by i, the groups including nations and their media to which he (or she) belongs, and by the general social environment that surrounds him. Although, in part, such filtering keeps him from being overwhelmed by too much information, he still needs to detail this information further and process it, as will be noted in what follows. We may simply represent the result of this filtering operation by

$$\tilde{z}_i = \tilde{z}_i(z, F_i) \qquad (4.2.2)$$

When we take z to be the variable o, the filtering operation is depicted by relation 11a at the extreme right of Figure 4.1.[1]

---

[1] The filtering activity itself may be related to various variables such as Att_i, but we have not indicated such in Figure 4.1.

Cognitive scientists frequently note that what an individual perceives depends in part on his (or her) *expectations,* the Exp_i in Eq. (4.2.1). Aspects of the environment, properties of an outcome, characteristics of the actions of others, and their goals that are perceived tend to be those that are expected. That is, i tends to seek, identify, recognize, or desire to process information that confirms his expectations; and he tends not to do so with regard to information that disconfirms his expectations, although this relationship is not as simple as just stated. Hence, what i perceives of item z depends on his expectations about z, the recognition of, say, an object or pattern being made much easier when that item is expected.

Because any individual i has limited information-processing capacity and a limited short-run, or active, memory (to be discussed in what follows), he or she can focus upon and attend to (pay attention to) only a limited number of things – objects, issues, relationships, beliefs, schemata, and other items. What is perceived by i clearly draws upon knowledge relevant to this limited number of things – hence the *attention variable* Att_i in Eq. (4.2.1).

Finally, the environmental setting itself affects what individual i can perceive. His (or her) visual perceptions may depend in a major way upon whether there is a heavy fog or a clear atmosphere. His ability to pay attention to detail may depend to a significant extent upon whether the setting is noisy. His mood or attitude may be greatly influenced by whether he is at the center of a world capital or at a rural retreat or whether there is a high or low level of international tension around him; it is also influenced by the types of actor with whom he is interacting and his preconceptions about them. Kahneman and Tversky (1979) have clearly shown how perceptions of i's decision problems vary when these problems are put in different frames. Shubik (1988) fruitfully talks about "context rational behavior." Thus, we include the variable e_i in Eq. (4.2.1).

4.2.3   The individual as a believer and knower

What determines i's expectations Exp_i about a given object or relation? These may be taken to come from that part $\acute{B}_i$ of i's belief system B_i that is relevant for the given decision-making situation. These beliefs are broadly defined to incorporate so-called objective information as well as ideas on (1) objects that are valuable (relevant) to i as well as to other participants, (2) relations that govern the interaction of i with others, and (3) other causal relations.

Using the symbol $\subset$ to mean "contained in," we may write

$$\text{Exp}_i \subset \acute{B}_i \qquad\qquad (4.2.3)$$

and obviously

$$\overset{r}{B}_i \subset B_i \tag{4.2.4}$$

The set of beliefs B_i that i holds obviously comes from stories, other schemata, and packages of groups (to be discussed later) and other information in his or her stock, which we characterize as memory Me_i. (Note that beliefs of i, especially those associated with stories and other schemata, encompass what i holds to be the beliefs of his or her opponents and others and how these latter beliefs determine the strategies, tactics, and other behavior of opponents and others.) Hence we may write

$$B_i \subset Me_i \tag{4.2.5}$$

Similarly, the $\overset{r}{B}_i$ part of the belief system will draw upon (contain) parts of i's memory necessary to support the beliefs it covers.

On the other hand, some brain theorists and others have distinguished between active memory $\overset{a}{Me}_i$ and that which is nonactive, the latter being part of long-run memory. Hence, we may restate Eq. (4.2.5) as

$$B_i \subset \overset{a}{Me}_i \subset Me_i \tag{4.2.6}$$

However, given Eqs. (4.2.1) and (4.2.2), we may write

$$Exp_i \subset \overset{r}{B}_i \subset \overset{a}{Me}_i \subset Me_i \tag{4.2.7}$$

See relation 3 in the upper part of Figure 4.1.

Now consider the factors determining the *attention variable* Att_i. In particular, we take this variable to be a function of not only active beliefs $\overset{b}{B}_i$ but also of *summary cues* SC_i and i's ability $\overline{\gamma}$ to handle (concentrate on) a multiplicity of variables. That is,[2]

$$Att_i = Att_i(\overset{b}{B}_i, SC_i, \overline{\gamma}_i) \tag{4.2.8}$$

See relation 4 above and to the right of the center of Figure 4.1.

Summary cues act to spring specific encodings of information from all those encodings that have been stored. Thus, when they are limited in number, summary cues confine i's relevant beliefs about a situation to a few key objects and relations among them. These cues in turn may be taken to relate to: past attention $Att_i(t-1)$, that is, things attended to in the past, in particular in the previous time period $t-1$; active memory $\overset{a}{Me}_i$; and the perception of the state of the environment $P_i(e)$, of the outcome at the previous time period $P_i(o(t-1))$, of the actions of others $P_i[a_k]$, and at times other random things $P_i(\ldots)$. For example, a cue might be a piece of information on the physical background or other set-

---

[2] Alternatively, because $\overset{b}{B}_i \subset \overset{a}{Me}_i$, we may take

$$Att_i = Att_i(\overset{a}{Me}_i, SC_i, \overline{\gamma}_i)$$

ting associated with the experience of the encoding in the past or it may be a piece of information contained in that encoding. Thus, suppressing again the symbol t when we refer to values of the variables for the current time period, we have

$$SC_i = SC_i(Att_i(t - 1), \overset{a}{M}e_i, \mathcal{P}_i(e), \mathcal{P}_i(o(t - 1)), \mathcal{P}_i\{a_k\}, \mathcal{P}_i(\ldots)) \tag{4.2.9}$$

See relation 5 above the center of Figure 4.1.[3]

As indicated in Eq. (4.2.9), summary cues are dependent on active memory $\overset{a}{M}e_i$, which by Eq. (4.2.6) is part of total memory Me_i. The current stock of knowledge in i's total memory is what is handed down from the previous time period $Me_i(t-1)$ subject to i's rate of forgetting α_i *plus* learning $L_i(t-1)$ during the previous time period.[4] That is,

$$Me_i = (1 - \alpha_i)Me_i(t - 1) + L_i(t - 1) \tag{4.2.10}$$

See relation 6 in the upper left corner of Figure 4.1. Learning is broadly defined to include mere sensing of new information, for example, the association of thunder with lightning. Strictly speaking, the rate of forgetting should perhaps be taken to mount increasingly with both the age Q_i of i and the level of his or her stock of information, although more rigorously α_i should be related to the vintage of i's stock of information and other factors as well.[5]

Having discussed expectations in general, let us be specific about certain key expectations. For example, take i's expected outcome $\hat{o}_i$ from an action a_i that he (or she) is contemplating adopting. We may state

---

[3] Note that with SC_i so defined, we may rewrite Eq. (4.2.4) and part of Eq. (4.2.7) respectively as

$$\overset{r}{B}_i = \overset{r}{B}_i(B_i, SC_i)$$
$$\overset{a}{M}e_i = \overset{a}{M}e_i(Me_i, SC_i)$$

[4] Other specific functional relations that might replace the equations in the previous footnote are respectively

$$\overset{r}{B}_i = \overset{r}{B}_i(\overset{a}{M}e_i, SC_i)$$

and

$$\overset{a}{M}e_i(t) = \overset{a}{M}e_i(\overset{a}{M}e_i(t-1), L_i(t-1))$$

Clearly, i's relevant belief system as well as the rest of his or her active (and inactive) memory are intimately (inextricably) linked to past episodes, scripts, schemata, packages, data stories, and the like, which are part of the active memory and belief systems of the groups to which he or she does belong (and has belonged in the past).

[5] That is,

$$\alpha_i = \alpha_i(Q_i, Me_i)$$

with the first and second partial derivatives all positive.

$$\hat{o}_i = \hat{o}_i(a_i, \{\hat{a}_k\}, \mathcal{P}_i(e))$$ (4.2.11)

where $\{\hat{a}_k\}$ is the expected joint action of all other behaving units k ($k =$ 1, 2, . . . ; $k \neq i$), an expected proposal $\hat{a}_k$ by k being one of his actions perceived as possible by i. See relation 7 to the right of the center of Figure 4.1. The highly sophisticated i may proceed further and relate his expectations of k's action to his (i's) estimate, $\hat{B}_{k(i)}$, of k's relevant belief system.[6]

Note that when we speak here of an expected magnitude, we do so in a way different than in our discussion of an expected magnitude based on objective (or minimally subjective) probabilities of different states of the environment (or states of affairs), as discussed in section 3.2.2. There the expected magnitude was a "prospect" as precisely defined by an economist. Here the expected magnitude can be the same but is much more likely to be a magnitude much more subjectively determined.

Another important magnitude is i's *expected utility* $\hat{u}_i$, from any given action a_i. We take it to be a function of his (or her) expected outcome $\hat{o}_i$ [from Eq. (4.2.11)] and his goals G_i (to be discussed later). That is,

$$\hat{u}_i = \hat{u}_i(\hat{o}_i, G_i)$$ (4.2.12)

See relation 8 to the right of the center of Figure 4.1.

Finally, i has (or knows) his preference structure, which, although highly complex in reality, we write as a simple utility function

$$u_i = u_i(\mathcal{P}_i(o_i), G_i)$$ (4.2.13)

where

o_i = elements (properties) relevant to i of a realized outcome o;
$\mathcal{P}_i(o_i)$ = i's perception of these outcome elements;
G_i = i's goals.

See relation 9 at the lower right of Figure 4.1.

Note that we distinguish between the realized outcome elements o_i and how i perceives them, that is, $\mathcal{P}_i(o_i)$. This is very important. Whereas o_i are what an analyst can observe, subject to certain subjective elements that he (or she) cannot eliminate when he makes an observation, it is the perceived outcome elements $\mathcal{P}_i(o_i)$ that are significant to i at a given time t and to his learning and subsequent behavior. We also include i's goals G_i in his utility function since for many, if not most, important situations

---

[6] Where G_i are i's goals (associated with his objective function) to be discussed in what follows and AT_i his attitude, we take $a_i = a_i(\mathcal{P}_i(A_i), G_i, AT_i)$ and $\{\hat{a}_k\} = f(\text{Exp}_i)$. See relations 7a and 7b, respectively, of Figure 4.1.

the utility derived is dependent upon the extent to which goals (inclusive of aspirations) are realized, again as perceived by i. As will be discussed later, these goals change with experience (learning) and time.

We usually implicitly assume that i's preference structure is at least ordinal, consistent, and transitive; but in fact, it may be inconsistent, intransitive, and in other ways not "well behaved." Moreover, with complex personalities, i's utility function may be related to the utility that he or she perceives other participants to receive, that is, to $P_i\{u_k\}$, $k = 1, 2, \ldots ; k \neq i$. Hence we may need to rewrite (4.2.13) as[7]

$$u_i = u_i (P_i(o_i), \{P_i(u_k)\}, G_i) \qquad (4.2.14)$$

4.2.4   The individual as goal setter (aspirer)

The individual frequently aspires for certain outcomes, sets targets, goals (both abstract and concrete), and the like, which relate to his (or her) basic values and life purposes. His current goals G_i may be taken to relate to (1) his goals $G_i(t-1)$ in the previous period; (2) his relevant belief system $\overset{i}{B_i}(t-1)$ at that time; (3) his learning $L_i(t-1)$ from the previous time period, which allows him to reevaluate what is possible, what his needs are, and so on, and so to reset his goals as a result of experience; and (4) the current goals $\{G^I\}$ of the groups $I = A, B, \ldots$ to which he belongs. That is, we may write

$$G_i = G_i(G_i(t - 1), \overset{i}{B_i}(t - 1), L_i(t - 1), \{G^I\}) \qquad (4.2.15)$$

See relation 10 at the lower right of Figure 4.1. For some situations, $\overset{a}{Me_i}(t - 1)$ may be taken to replace $\overset{i}{B_i}(t - 1)$ since a change in i's goals may draw upon more than his belief system at time $t-1$. Also, in setting his goals, i may be affected by the goals of other behaving units and of groups other than those to which he belongs.[8]

4.2.5   The individual as a decision maker (chooser of an action or strategy)

(a) In a noncrisis (low-stress) situation: We take i to be motivated to choose some best action a_i^* or strategy from his (or her) perceived

---

[7] See Isard et al. (1969, pp. 258–60, 289–90) for a discussion of such a complex, interdependent utility function.

[8] Recall that goals may imply a set of subgoals. Thus for period $t - 1$ we may have such a set. Since subgoals often become valued in and of themselves, even though the original rationale for them no longer exists, this phenomenon then comes to interfere with the proper resetting of the primary goals G_i for year t.

restricted action space $P_i(\tilde{A}_i)$. As in section 3.2, what is his best action is dependent on his attitude AT_i. As already indicated, typically each schema or set of schemata or other mental representation that is actively present in his thinking at his decision point of time involves either implicitly or explicitly a payoff or utility matrix or the like with more than one column and more than one row. Thus, as discussed in section 3.2, the optimal action a_i^* or strategy is conditioned by his attitude AT_i, that is, whether he is a pessimist, optimist, risk averter, satisficer, and so on. This variable together with $P_i(\tilde{A}_i)$ enters into relation 7a in Figure 4.1 governing his choice of action a_i.

Relation 7a in Figure 4.1 also suggests that i's goals G_i may be relevant in his (or her) choice. He may view his best action as one that minimizes the discrepancy $G_i - \hat{o}_i$, where G_i is a goal that cannot be exceeded, $\hat{o}_i$ is an expected outcome, and $G_i - \hat{o}_i$ may be taken to be the objective function. Traditionally, in economics and regional science, the observed outcome o (which consists of o_i, the set of outcome elements directly relevant to i, and of other elements of no or negligible relevance to him) is given by

$$o = o(a, e) \tag{4.2.16}$$

where $a = (a_1, \ldots, a_i, a_j, a_k, \ldots)$ is the joint action of all behaving units (inclusive of groups) and e is the state of the environment. See relation 11 in Figure 4.1. As already suggested, the outcome o that an analyst observes is not what is significant to i. Rather what is important to i is his or her estimate $\hat{o}_i$ of relevant outcome elements defined by Eq. (4.2.11). Thus it is the discrepancy between G_i and $\hat{o}_i$ that guides i's choice of an action.

Where G_i can be exceeded and where it is undesirable to exceed as well as to fall short of a goal, i's objective may be to minimize the absolute difference $|G_i - \hat{o}_i|$.[9] Or i's objective may be to maximize his or her expected outcome $\hat{o}_i$ or expected utility $\hat{u}_i$. Also recall that i may select $a_1^* \in P(\tilde{A}_i)$ where $a_1^* \notin \tilde{A}_i$ – that is, i may seek to adopt an a_1^* that is perceived as available but is unrealizable (technically, economically, or otherwise). Hence i must by default select (be content with) another action or strategy (even the "do nothing" strategy).

Note also that $\hat{o}_i$ is dependent upon each $\hat{a}_k$, more accurately designated $\hat{a}_{k(i)}$, that is, i's expectation of the action that each k will take. See Eq. (4.2.11). As noted, i may relate $\hat{a}_{k(i)}$ to i's estimate $\hat{B}_{k(i)}$ of k's relevant belief system, that is,

---

[9] To avoid negative numbers, analysts often set up the objective $\min(G_i - \hat{o}_i)^2$, an objective that may be entirely foreign to the participants in a conflict situation.

$$\hat{a}_{k(i)} = \hat{a}_{k(i)}(\tilde{B}_{k(i)}, \ldots) \qquad (4.2.17)$$

and in certain situations $\hat{a}_{k(i)}$ may be viewed as threats to i's goals.[10]

If i were to adopt satisficing rather than optimizing behavior, then he or she would select the first $a_i \in \mathcal{P}_i(\tilde{A}_i)$ for which

$$\hat{o}_i \geqq h_i \qquad (4.2.18)$$

where h_i represents the prespecified satisficing level. If it happens that his or her perceptions of the realized outcome is less than h_i, that is,

$$\mathcal{P}_i(o_i) < h_i \qquad (4.2.19)$$

then i necessarily has experience that makes possible a choice of an action at the next point of time, which presumably, but not necessarily, is more efficient.[11]

Note that when decision making is exceedingly complex, the behaving unit may act in a way that some characterize as "cybernetic." That is, he (or she) may avoid any involved outcome calculation or reference to utility. Rather he may rely on a small set of responses or decision rules to determine the course of action to take once he has received information to which he is sensitive – typically on only a few critical feedback variables of the environment. He screens out information that his established set of responses is not programmed to accept. His concern may be more with survival than anything else and only seeks change in his set of responses when all responses are unacceptable given an environmental change.

Needless to say, in selecting an action, the decision maker may be influenced by a hypothesis he or she wishes to verify and therefore overlooks (or tends to downplay) empirical evidence that does not support his or her theory, especially if it supports a theory of an opponent. This is consistent, of course, with the strong tendency to view what one's group does

---

[10] Individual i may also believe that like himself or herself each k will choose an optimal action $a_{k(i)}^* \in (\mathcal{P}_k(\tilde{A}_k))_i$ that minimizes $|G_{k(i)} - \hat{o}_{k(i)}|$, or simply maximizes $\hat{o}_{k(i)}$ when G_k is not relevant, or optimizes a magnitude defined by some other specific utility (payoff) function that i believes k employs. Here $\hat{o}_{k(i)}$, i's estimate of the outcome k expects, is given by

$$\hat{o}_{k(i)} = \hat{o}_{k(i)}(\hat{a}_{1(k)i}, \ldots, \hat{a}_{i(k)i}, \ldots, \hat{a}_{k(i)}, \ldots, \mathcal{P}_{k(i)}(e))$$

where $a_{k(i)}^*$, $\mathcal{P}_k(\tilde{A}_k)_i$, $G_{k(i)}$, $\hat{a}_{1(k)i}$, $\ldots$, and $\mathcal{P}_{k(i)}(e)$ are i's estimates and/or beliefs of scalars, vectors, sets, and relationships relevant for k.

Although here and in the discussion of the text, we have looked upon the action as directly related to diverse variables, the relationship may be indeed quite indirect. As per Axelrod (1976), we might view the expected outcome (or utility) of i as the last element in a cognitive mapping that involves the consideration of a sequence of (causal) relationships among relevant variables and concepts. The cognitive map that is developed may be a simple linear one but may be complex as well.

[11] It is only presumably more efficient, for in the meantime the structure of the situation may have changed.

as "good" (perhaps consistent with some kind of welfare theory) and what one's adversary's group does as "bad" [see Jervis (1976) and Lebow (1981)].

(b) In a crisis situation: Here the reader is referred to the discussion in Chapter 5.

4.2.6   *The individual as a learner*

We take the learning L_i of i to consist of two parts:

$$L_i = \underline{L}_i + \overline{L}_i \tag{4.2.20}$$

The first part $\underline{L}_i$ derives from experience, from his (or her) taking his perceptions at time t (of the outcomes, the actions, the state of the environment, his utility, and in general, the state of affairs) and contrasting them with what he had expected. In addition, he examines these contrasts in relation to (against the background of) other elements (e.g., schemata) in his active memory $\overset{a}{M}e_i(t)$; and the learning that results reflects his ability β_i at information processing in general. The learning that results can of course be with regard to any one or more of the changes in mental representations discussed in the previous section. Hence, if we let

$$\mathcal{P}_i(\cdot) = (\mathcal{P}_i(o_i), \mathcal{P}_i\{a_k\}, \mathcal{P}_i(e), \ldots) \tag{4.2.21}$$

and

$$\mathrm{Exp}_i(\cdot) = (\hat{o}_i, \{\hat{a}_k\}, \hat{u}_i, \ldots) \tag{4.2.22}$$

then we may write

$$\underline{L}_i = \underline{L}_i(\mathcal{P}_i(\cdot), \mathrm{Exp}_i(\cdot), \overset{a}{M}e_i, \beta_i) \tag{4.2.23}$$

See the relation 12 depicted in the lower right of Figure 4.1.

The second part $\overline{L}_i$ of i's learning derives from active search, often in connection with an effort to solve major problems where inadequate information is at hand. The current state of affairs (outcomes, utility, etc.) as perceived by him (or her) may be unsatisfactory given his aspirations, goals, sense of equity, and the like. Thus, he actively goes out to learn about (identify) new possible actions and strategies. His search activity, however, is modified by the cost c_i involved, his estimate of the probability pr_i that he will find useful new information, taking into account his own ability ξ_i at finding new information. Thus we may write

$$\overline{L}_i = \overline{L}_i(|G_i - \mathcal{P}_i(o_i)|, c_i, \mathrm{pr}_i, \xi_i) \tag{4.2.24}$$

The term $|G_i - \mathcal{P}_i(o_i)|$ may be viewed as a measure of frustration[12] rather than dissatisfaction. When it is large (small), presumably i undertakes much (little) search activity, ceteris paribus, and consequently much (little) learning is to be anticipated. Note also that c_i reflects the cost of capital (including the availability of slack capital) and other resources required to successfully carry out search activity. Hence obstacles θ_s to search set up by society are clearly a major factor determining c_i. That is

$$c_i = c_i (\theta_s, \ldots) \tag{4.2.25}$$

The obstacles θ_s are a function of how well society (its groups, the establishment) is performing. If it is performing poorly (well), then obstacles are small (great). For further discussion, see Kaniss (1978).

In Chapters 6, 15, and 16 we shall go into much greater detail regarding information search, information investment, and information research and development. For the moment, however, note that $\bar{L}_i$ may be claimed to be learning "after the action." This is *ex post* learning. It is learning from i's perception of the actual state of affairs when contrasted to the expected. By contrast, $\bar{\bar{L}}_i$ may often be claimed to be learning "before the action." This is *ex ante* learning, or learning that takes place before an action (strategy) is chosen.

4.2.7 *The individual as a relocator (mover)*

Individual i typically belongs to a number of groups, his or her belonging to a group sometimes being only implicit. Almost invariably, an individual has the opportunity to move from one group to another or to exit from a group and become a "one-person" group or to abandon the status of "not belonging" to a specific type of group. In certain respects such movement resembles movement of a good from one position (location) in physical space to another. The condition for such a movement of commodity h from an originating position (region) J to a terminating position (region) N is:

$$p_h^N \geq p_h^J + \text{t.c.} \tag{4.2.26}$$

where p_h^N, p_h^J represent prices of commodity h at J and N, respectively, and t.c. represents transport cost. In effect, $p_h^N - p_h^J$ represents a gross

---

[12] Other measures of frustration may be employed – e.g., we may choose a term such as $|u_i^d - u_i|$, where u_i^d represents i's desired utility and u_i his realized utility.

benefit (advantage) from movement; t.c. a cost (disadvantage); and $p_h^N -$
$(p_h^I + \text{t.c.})$ the net benefit. When a net benefit is positive, the shipment of
the commodity takes place, and that shipment tends to increase until the
net benefit disappears.[13]

In like manner, we may hypothesize that i calculates the net advantage
of shifting from group I, providing a service, to another group N, providing the same service. If the net advantage is positive (after taking into
account all relocation costs), he or she will shift to group N.[14]

To state the problem generally and in a form usable for most kinds of
movement, we adopt an Alonso-type framework. Let w^N be an index of
all attractive (pull-in) features of group N (such as the level of c-prestige,
social status, and friendliness). Let v^I be an index of the unattractive
(push-out) features of group I (such as religious intolerance and imper-
sonality). Let d^{IN} be an index of the distances (physical, ideological, psychological, social, economic, etc.) separating groups I and N. Further, let
C^N be a measure of congestion at N (or system competition to join N or
resistance at N to entry by an individual) and D^I be a measure of the ease
of exit from group I or the elasticity of response at group I to attractive
forces elsewhere (which varies inversely with average inertia at I and
directly with availability of knowledge at I). Then the probability
$\text{pr}(M_i^{I \rightarrow N})$ that an individual i in group I would shift to group N might be
written

$$\text{pr}(M_i^{I \rightarrow N}) = \frac{w^N}{C^N} \frac{v^I}{D^I} \frac{1}{d^{IN}} \tag{4.2.27}$$

That is, the probability would vary proportionately with (i) w^N/C^N, the
attractive features w^N at N adjusted for the difficulty of getting into N
because of congestion, competition, resistance, and other factors; (ii) $v^I/$
D^I, the unattractive features v^I at group I adjusted for the lack of respon-
siveness (the inertia, the lack of knowledge) at I; and (iii) inversely with
d^{IN}, namely, the index of separation (distance) between groups I and N.
A fuller and more refined exposition of this model is available in Anselin
and Isard (1979).[15]

---

[13] See Isard et al. (1969, pp. 528–31) for relevant discussion.

[14] More generally, each group may be considered as providing a vector of services, and the
calculation is made over all services, where the amount of one or more of these services
provided by a group may be zero.

[15] Also see Orbell, Schwartz-Shea, and Summers (1984), Smith (1985), Hansen (1985), and
the literature cited therein for extensive discussion of why individuals belong and do not
belong to groups.

4.3   A formal cognitive framework for understanding the group's behavior

We now proceed to the analysis of group behavior. As already indicated, a behaving unit may involve an aggregate of two or more individuals, that is, a group. Moreover, the behaving unit may itself be a group composed of several groups each behaving as a subgroup within a hierarchy (regular or irregular) of subgroups. We could discuss at length the functioning of a hierarchical structure of several levels composed of subgroups within a group, subsubgroups within each subgroup, and so on, each group, subgroup, and subsubgroup being a behaving unit with individuals as behaving units at the grass-roots level. See Isard and Liossatos (1979, chap. 12) for some relevant discussion. However, we do not have the space to discuss hierarchical theory and its relevance for Peace Science. We must by and large limit ourselves to the behavior of a group in a nonhierarchical setting. In doing so, we shall in large part parallel the analysis presented in the previous section for understanding the individual's behavior.

Briefly put, the framework for group behavior is as follows:

1.   The group has an action space.
2.   It perceives things, its perceptions being greatly conditioned by its social–cultural senses (sensitivities).
3.   It has a set of beliefs, each major active belief corresponding to an interpretive package to be discussed in what follows.
4.   It desires (aspires for) things; that is, it has goals, representing, in part at least, the resolution of the desires of its component interest groups and individual members.
5.   It takes decisions, that is, selects actions (strategies) from its perceived restricted action space in both noncrisis and crisis situations.
6.   It learns from experience and, when appropriate, searches for new information and strategies.
7.   It relocates, that is, shifts positions in policy and other spaces when such is desirable.

Just as individual i has schemata and other mental representations that generate expectations and guide his or her behavior, so does the group I have packages and other internal (social) representations. As Gamson (1981) and Gamson and Lasch (1983) have set forth, a political culture consists of a set of idea elements rooted in time and space that are organized and clustered in various ways. Events such as a nominee's acceptance speech at a presidential convention provide an occasion for the display of a culture; so do the newspapers, television, and other media in their reporting and commentaries. Idea elements do not exist in isolation. Rather they are grouped into meaningful clusters and interpretive packages as knowledge structures. To the group, interpretive packages play a similar role as schemata to the individual. Frequently, a package as a whole can be indicated by a single prominent element, such as the concept of David and Goliath in the Israeli–Arab conflict. Essentially, the interpretive package is (1) a core consisting of an overall frame that organizes the sense data of politics and provides meaning to political events and (2) a mix of reasoning and justification that breaks down a complex whole into discrete causes and consequences in temporal sequence. Both the overall frame and reasoning can relate to either a single episode or a sequence of episodes, each with or without a basic causal process.

Pursuing the analogy further, we view the group as receiving stimuli to which it responds as a behaving unit. We wish to understand the processes that take place during the interim period, which processes admittedly are at least in part a black box. As just indicated, the group has a set of interpretive packages. Each of the stimuli typically retrieves from group memory (often corresponding to the memory of a few or even one of its leading figures) one or more particular packages. What is retrieved depends of course on what the group or these figures are able to attend to and the particular way events of the past have been "encoded" and "comprehended" as interpretive packages. The interpretive package that is employed, such as *David and Goliath* (as described in Table 4.1) is the skeleton structure (scaffolding). It can be instantiated or filled out with detailed properties of the particular instance being represented, often encompassing lessons learned. It guides comprehension and interpretation of the new instance provided by the stimulus and may involve, just as schemata do, reference hierarchies, episode hierarchies, and plot unit networks. However, as noted in the column heads of Table 4.1, Gamson speaks instead of *framing devices* such as *metaphors, exemplars* (real events of the past and present), *catchphrases* (attempted summary statements about the principal subject, such as "invasion from the north" in the 1965 Vietnam War), and *depictions* (such as Huns), and *visual images* (the American flag). In speaking of reasoning and justification devices, he emphasizes *roots* (causal dynamics underlying the strip of events), *consequences* (outcomes), and *appeals to principle* (morality).

A concrete representation of the approach of Gamson is given in Table 4.1, a signature matrix of the Arab–Israeli conflict. The rows refer to six interpretive packages, each package being labeled (given a signature) in the first column and each being succinctly summarized by statements in each row. For example, the David and Goliath package (second row) involves as its *frame* the issue of the unwillingness of the Arab world to accept Israel's right to exist. The *position* of the United States is its moral obligation to help Israel to survive. The *metaphor* is David against Goliath. An *example* is the Holocaust. A *catchphrase* illustrating Arab emnity is "push the Jews into the sea." A *depiction* is Israel as one small country against 20 Arab countries. A *visual image* is Arabs as fanatic extremists. And so on.

As with a schema and other mental representation, a set of interpretive packages can be invaluable in situation assessment and contingency planning. Each interpretive package may be represented by a payoff matrix specifying the possible actions the group may take and the likely consequences (outcomes) under one or more states of (stimuli from) the environment, each state representing a column of the matrix. Then the choice of an action depends upon the group's objective function, implicit or not, and if explicit, however loosely defined or perceived. This function is, of course, closely related to its attitude.

As Gamson has noted, interpretive packages are rooted in time and space. Just as schemata change with experiences and over time, so do interpretive packages. Part of problem solving that groups (and organizations) confront involves such change. The group, whether as a cybernetic person or not, may find that its set of responses (take a tough stand against terrorism, be soft to anticommunistic dictatorships, denounce communistic governments) need to change; and further it may be motivated to search for new responses (as the Nixon foray with Mainland China). Here, again, we may think of changes as embodying

1. new input–output transformations involving the recognition of new kinds of inputs, outputs, or both;
2. new methods of analysis and new ways of thinking that change its know-how for digesting stimuli and determining appropriate responses; and
3. new algorithms, namely, specific sets of steps for actually generating (effecting) the response.

In a political culture an interpretive package of a group, which in one way or another is necessarily an interest group, is often associated with one or more counterpackages held by other groups (necessarily interest groups). Except for rare instances, a culture is composed of two or more groups: an incumbent political party and its one or more adversaries; an in-group and one or more out-groups; an élite and the nonélitists; and so

Table 4.1. *Signature matrix: Arab–Israeli conflict*

Label	Core					Depictions	Visual images	Roots	Consequences	Appeals to principle
	Frame	Position	Metaphor	Exemplars	Catchphrases					
Strategic interest	The issue is how to best pursue America's strategic interests in the Middle East in the context of our larger conflict with the Soviet Union.	The United States should support and encourage countries that share our opposition to Soviet penetration of the Free Middle East and will help to secure the Free World's oil lifeline.	A board game in which the countries of the Middle East are pieces that can change hands, and the United States and the Soviet Union are the competing players.	Attempted Soviet takeover of Iran in 1946; Soviet invasion of Afghanistan; Soviet military aid and advisors in various Arab countries; *Lesson:* the Soviet Union is actively seeking to expand its influence in the Middle East.	—	Russia as having imperial designs on the region. The Middle East as a major cold war arena. Israel or pro-Western Arab countries as buffers against Soviet influence.	A grizzly bear with a hammer and sickle hovering over the Middle East.	Indigenous conflict exacerbated greatly by Soviet exploitation of the conflict for its own imperial aims.	Effect on American security and access to resources is emphasized.	Defense of the free world.
David and Goliath	The issue is the unwillingness of the Arab world to accept Israel's right to exist.	The United States has a moral obligation to help Israel to survive in a hostile environment and to	David against Goliath.	The Holocaust. *Lesson:* the vulnerability of a stateless people, unable to organize their own means of self-defense.	Illustrating Arab enmity: "Only a sword in their side." "Push the Jews into the sea."	Israel as one small country against 20 Arab countries with a population more than 20 times its	Arabs as violence-prone, fanatic extremists.	Arab unwillingness to recognize Israel's right to exist.	Effect on Israel's security is emphasized.	The right of any people to live in peace and security, especially a people that has been the victim of a long

	—	encourage the Arab countries to accept Israel's right to exist.	Hitler's pronouncements against the Jews: *Lesson*, one cannot ignore or treat as mere rhetoric verbal threats of annihilation. The beginning of World War I: *Lesson*, a local conflict can spread into a world war.	—	size. Arabs as fanatics and zealots, unwilling to make peace with Israel.	Middle East as a tinderbox or time bomb ready to go off.		history of oppression.
Feuding neighbors	The issue is whether the fight that is going on over there will end up engulfing all of us in another world war.	The United States should try to mediate the dispute as best it can but should not take major risks that would involve America directly in the fighting in the Middle East.	The Hatfields and the McCoys.	A plague on both your houses.	Both sides as unreasonable, fanatic. Innocent bystanders (the world) as the real victim.	A destructive cycle of hostile acts that stimulate hostile responses. An unwillingness by both sides to forget the injuries of the past and make peace.	Effects on the probability of a larger war emphasized.	Live and let live; let bygones be bygones.
Dual liberation	The issue is a conflict between two national liberation movements both of which have a legitimate	The United States should support a compromise in which Israel's right to exist in secure,	The Benelux countries: *Lesson,* Belgium and the Netherlands did not work as a unitary state, but the two peoples,	Israel *and* Palestine. A new partition.	The Palestinian issue as more than a refugee problem since a legitimate Palestinian national	Two people and two national movements each with a valid historical claim to the same land.	Effects on the legitimate rights of both sides emphasized.	Self-determination for all people.

Table 4.1 (*cont.*)

Label	Core		Metaphor	Exemplars	Catchphrases	Depictions	Visual images	Roots	Consequences	Appeals to principle
	Frame	Position								
Dual liberation (*cont.*)	historical claim to the same piece of land.	recognized borders is accepted and some sort of Palestinian state is created.		living in separate states, maintain good stable relations and close economic ties.		movement exists.				
Western imperialism	The issue is the use of Israel as an instrument to maintain Western control over the resources of the Middle East and the Arab people.	The United States should abandon the economic and political structure that requires the maintenance of world empire. Short of that, the United States should abandon its support for Israel.	Israel as an attack dog of its American master.	South Africa, Rhodesia: *Lesson*, Israel is like European settler states that try to maintain dominance over the indigenous population of a region.	Zionism is racism. The Zionist entity.	PLO as freedom fighters. Arab violence as a symptom and response to injustice. Israel as an American tool. Camp David accord as betrayal of Arab cause.	Israeli aggression against weak and helpless Arabs.	Efforts to maintain Western domination of the region, which leads to support of Israel and Israeli intransigence.	Effects on spread of socialism in Arab world emphasized.	National liberation and justice for the Palestinian people.

Jewish conspiracy (variation)	Strategic interest core plus American Jews use their great influence to divert U.S. policy from its strategic interests in the Arab world. Feuding neighbors core plus American Jews use their great influence to get the United States unnecessarily involved on the side of Israel. Western imperialism core plus American Jews use their great influence to support U.S. imperialism.	Fifth columnists in World War II: *Lesson*, American Jews place loyalty to Israel above loyalty to the United States	The Israeli lobby. The Zionist lobby.	Jews as controlling media and banks. Jews as powerful, behind-the-scenes force.	Jews as manipulative villians.	The root from the core package plus undue influence by American Jews.	Effects on Jewish influence emphasized.	Keeping the United States free of foreign influence.

143

on. Consequently, even the most general themes and their associated interpretive packages, as pontificated by those in authority, confront and are influenced by counterthemes and packages.

In U.S. society, for example, (a) the technological development–national security–economic growth theme of the military–industrial complex is opposed by the conservation–environmental protection–small is beautiful–disarmament countertheme of the antinuclear groups; (b) the self-reliance, striving, achieving, risk-taking, independence (Horatio Alger) theme of the entrepreneurial élite is opposed by the poverty elimination–civil rights protection–equality countertheme of the social welfarists; and so forth. In brief, themes and their associated goals (objectives) of any one group almost invariably go hand in hand with counterthemes and different (conflicting) objectives of one or more other groups; and their understanding and potential for change are interconnected with the latter.

As is now evident, in many ways the terms of Gamson and other sociologists when they study groups are paralleled by terms with similar coverage as used by cognitive scientists when they study individual behavior. In both cases much remains to be developed, theoretically and in terms of empirically tested hypotheses. Both, however, greatly enrich or complement the approach of the economist, operations researcher, and regional scientist in understanding behavior and in suggesting hypotheses on ways to influence that behavior.

4.3.1   The action space of the group

Just as with the individual, group I $(I = A, B, \ldots, U)$ has an unrestricted action space A^I. It confronts constraints imposed by its limited resources and knowledge and by the environmental setting, including the behavior of diverse individuals and other groups. These constraints define I's restricted action space $\tilde{A}^I$. See the discussion in section 4.2.1. Group I acts on its perceptions of these spaces, namely, $\mathcal{P}^I(A^I)$ and $\mathcal{P}^I(\tilde{A}^I)$, respectively.

4.3.2   The group as a perceiver

The group's perceptions are obviously related to the packages and other mental representations inherited from the past and subject to change as events are sensed and experience (learning) is acquired. We need not repeat the discussion in section 4.2.2, which pertains to group I as well as individual i. We note, for emphasis, that some if not many of the group's perceptions may be misperceptions, that is, inaccurate, often highly inaccurate, transformations of so-called objective information. Also, we may hypothesize that the group typically reacts less to changes in physical phenomena than the individual. Yet it perceives just as much. It has social and cultural sensitivities, or feelers that "sense" the environment, the outcome, the actions taken by other groups and individuals, and so on. Perhaps it is more attuned to noneconomic goods than the individual or more responsive to the friendliness or hostility of the actions of other groups. But, by and large, the discussion of section 4.2.2 on individual behavior also pertains here.

Thus, when we consider the group's perception $\mathcal{P}^I(z)$ of an item z, we must relate it to the filtered information $\tilde{z}^I$ about z, the expectations Exp^I of I, the things to which it attends Att^I, and the state of the environment e^I as it impinges on I. Hence, we may write

$$\mathcal{P}^I(z) = f(\tilde{z}^I, \text{Exp}^I, \text{Att}^I, e^I) \tag{4.3.1}$$

where

$$\tilde{z}^I = \tilde{z}^I(z, F^I)$$

and where z may be o^I (the outcome to group I), a^N and G^N (respectively, the action chosen by and goals of group N, $N = A, \ldots, U, N \neq I$), or other relevant object or relation.

In general, the discussion of the variables in Eq. (4.3.1) for group I is similar to that in section 4.2.2 of the variables for individual i in Eq. (4.2.1). We must, of course, (a) replace the term individual i by group I; (b) bear in mind that there can be higher order groups of which group I is a constituent in a hierarchical sense; and (c) effect substitutions of parallel concepts such as packages for schemata.

4.3.3 The group as a believer and knower

We let Exp^I, $\overset{r}{B}{}^I$, $\overset{a}{Me}{}^I$, and Me^I represent, respectively, the expectations, set of relevant beliefs (packages), active memory, and total memory of group I. As in the discussion of individual behavior in section 4.2.3, we may write

$$\text{Exp}^I \subset \overset{r}{B}{}^I \subset \overset{a}{Me}{}^I \subset Me^I \tag{4.3.2}$$

Regarding group I's attention Att^I, relevant beliefs $\overset{r}{B}{}^I$, summary cues SC^I, and ability to handle a multiplicity of variables γ^I, we may write

$$\text{Att}^I = \text{Att}^I(\overset{r}{B}{}^I, \text{SC}^I, \gamma^I) \tag{4.3.3}$$

Also considering other variables pertaining to group I, namely, its perception of the state of the environment $\mathcal{P}^I(e)$, its relevant outcome $\mathcal{P}^I(o^I)$, the set of actions of other groups $\mathcal{P}^I\{a^N\}$, and other factors $\mathcal{P}^I(\ldots)$, we may state

$$\text{SC}^I = \text{SC}^I(\text{Att}^I(t-1), \overset{a}{M}e^I, \mathcal{P}^I(e), \mathcal{P}^I(o^I), \mathcal{P}^I\{a^N\}, \mathcal{P}^I(\ldots)) \qquad (4.3.4)$$

Further, considering still other variables pertaining to group I, namely, its beliefs B^I, its memory Me^I, its rate of forgetting α^I, its learning L^I, its expected outcome $\hat{o}^I$, the expected actions of other groups $\{\hat{a}^N\}$, and its action a^I, we may write

$$\overset{r}{B}{}^I = \overset{r}{B}{}^I(B^I, \text{SC}^I) \qquad (4.3.5)$$
$$\overset{a}{M}e^I = \overset{a}{M}e^I(Me^I, \text{SC}^I) \qquad (4.3.6)$$
$$Me^I = (1 - \alpha^I)Me^I(t-1) + L^I(t-1) \qquad (4.3.7)$$

and

$$\hat{o}^I = \hat{o}^I(a^I, \{\hat{a}^N\}, \mathcal{P}^I(e))$$

These symbols and relations parallel those discussed in connection with individual behavior in section 4.2.3.

Compared to the individual, the group is less likely to change its beliefs suddenly since the group is an average of individuals. If one member of the group suddenly changes his or her beliefs in a particular way, it is unlikely that other individuals will do so in the same way – although this can happen when that individual is a very strong leader.

The notion that a group is an average of individuals also suggests, as previously noted, that there may be subgroups within a group, especially when the group is medium or large in size. Each subgroup possesses or adheres to some variant of the set of basic packages that may be said to characterize the group, particularly as seen by an outsider who views the group (say, the Japanese society) as rather homogeneous.[16] At times, the variant that dominates a group is that variant of the subgroup a constituency votes into power by a majority or perhaps two-thirds rule. In effect, the weight of each i in determining that variant is unity when he or she has the right to vote and zero otherwise, with each i having the option of using his or her weight (voting) or not (abstaining). Thus in addition to the incumbent variant there is the opposition variant and perhaps variants of dissident and other groups. Thus at any point of time, the belief structure of a group is a set of variants of the set of basic packages, each having different weight in the choice of an action or strategy.

In parallel fashion, there exists no simple relation between the memory

---

[16] In fact, even with each individual i there may be several packages (schemata), each associated with one of his or her subpersonalities, e.g., as a warm family member, a cold-blooded competitor, and a practicing Catholic.

Me^I of group I and the memory of its members. In one sense, we may state

$$Me^I = \bigcup_i Me_i \tag{4.3.8}$$

that is, the memory of the group is the union $\bigcup_i$ of the memories of its members. (It is not the sum since such would involve duplication.) But this concept implies that all the memory of any member i, however unimportant, which does not intersect with the memory of any other member, constitutes part of Me^I – a rather strong assumption, as would be a statement that $\mathring{M}e^I = \bigcup_i \mathring{M}e_i$.

Moreover, when we consider the variables, expectations Exp^I of the group (or any component, e.g., the expected outcome $\hat{o}^I$), and its attention Att^I, there is no simple relation between those of the group and that of its members. Often, however, we take a group variable to be a weighted average or union of the corresponding variable for its members.

Associated with the expected outcome $\hat{o}^I$ is the group's notion of its welfare W^I (which substitutes for the concept of utility as a measure of individual welfare). In parallel with i's expected utility and letting G^I represent I's goals, we may write I's expected welfare as

$$\hat{W}^I = \hat{W}^I(\hat{o}^I, G^I) \tag{4.3.9}$$

However, since the group's welfare is some function of the welfare of its members and since comparability of the welfare (utility) of its members is typically not possible, usually some macromagnitude such as GNP or percentage of favorable reaction to (or estimation of approval of) the group as it functions must be employed.

The magnitude $\hat{W}^I$ is an estimated *(ex ante)* magnitude based on expected outcome $\hat{o}^I$ (which is related to the choice of an action a^I by I), expected action by others, and so on. When an outcome o^I is realized, the welfare that results is a perceived welfare $\mathcal{P}^I(W^I)$ of group I, which we may write as

$$\mathcal{P}^I(W^I) = \hat{f}(\mathcal{P}^I(o^I), G^I) \tag{4.3.10}$$

Again, we make the important distinction between expected outcome $\hat{o}^I$ and perception of realized outcome $\mathcal{P}^I(o^I)$, which give rise to expected welfare $\hat{W}^I$ and perceived welfare $\mathcal{P}^I(W^I)$, respectively. We also observe that the group I may have a more complex perceived welfare function that relates its perceived welfare to the perceived welfare of other groups, $\{\mathcal{P}^I(W^N)\}$. Such an interdependent welfare function may be written

$$\mathcal{P}^I(\overline{W}^I) = \overline{g}(\mathcal{P}^I(o^I), G^I, \{\mathcal{P}^I(\overline{W}^N)\}) \tag{4.3.11}$$

4.3.4   The group as an aspirer or a target (goal) setter

In parallel with our discussion of the individual i as an aspirer, we may write for group I's goals

$$G^I = G^I(G^I(t-1), \overset{a}{M}e^I(t-1), L^I(t-1), \{G^N\}) \qquad (4.3.12)$$

or the same with $\overset{a}{M}e^I(t-1)$ replaced by $\overset{r}{B}^I(t-1)$. Here $\{G^N\}$ represents the goals of higher order groups of which I is a constituent.

The goals of a group are likely to change less often and by smaller amounts than for the average individual. This is so since the group's goals may be viewed in an oversimplified manner as a weighted average of its members' goals. As the changes in members' goals usually are not all in the same direction, they offset each other to some extent at least and lead to changes in the group's goals, which are smaller than for the individual member on average, even in the presence of dominating personalities. Moreover, individuals can move from one group to another. Those individuals whose goals have changed greatly are more likely to leave a given group for another, ceteris paribus. This tends to leave in any group those individuals whose changes in goals are of smaller magnitude; hence there results less pressure to change the group's goals.

Group I's goals are also affected by learning. Learning supplements the group's active memory $\overset{a}{M}e^I$ or its set of relevant beliefs $\overset{r}{B}^I$ leading to a change in the stock of such for future use. Learning may pertain to (a) the question of the feasibility, technically or politically, of different actions or strategies that the group may take or (b) the needs of its members.

Although not indicated in Eq. (4.3.12), the goals of group I may also be related to the estimates of goals of other groups with which I interacts. For example, political parties at each level of government (federal, state, local) look to see what goals the opposition is setting before setting (finalizing) their own because of competition for membership. In that case we add $\{G^N\}$, where $N = $ A, B, . . . and refers to groups of the same order as I. Finally, G^I should somehow be related to the goals G_i of its members as well as to the weights that reflect the importance (influence, power) of the several members and their goals. Such, however, is not indicated in Eq. (4.3.12).

4.3.5   The group as a decision maker (chooser of an action or strategy)

Similar to the individual, the group is motivated to select some best action, a^{I*}, or strategy from its perceived restricted action space $\mathcal{P}^I(\tilde{A}^I)$, or to choose the first action or strategy that is satisficing. As one model of choice where the group's leader is very strong, we may follow closely the optimizing model presented for the individual i. The leader takes the objective function that pertains to the group (a function that may have been reached as a result of group action or simply set up by the leader) and chooses an optimal action. Thus the optimal action a^{I*} might be the one that minimizes $|G^I - \hat{o}^I|$, or maximizes $\hat{o}^I$, or some other operational representation of I's welfare function consistent with the leader's or group's attitude. Accordingly, the discussion of section 4.2.5 largely pertains here.

Another model of group choice involves active participation by all its members. Here, where a_i^I represents the proposal of member i in group I, we may take the group's action as the weighted average of members' proposals, that is,

$$a^I = \sum w_i a_i^I \quad \text{where} \quad \sum w_i = 1 \quad (4.3.13)$$

or it may be the weighted average of members of the dominant coalition $\mathcal{C}$,

$$a^I = \sum_{i \in \mathcal{C}} w_i a_i^I \quad (4.3.14)$$

or of the majority, and so on.

Or the group may reach a decision after interaction of members and its leaders in accord with the learning process (in microtime) extensively discussed in Chapter 14.

The group may also behave as a satisficer, select the first action for which

$$\hat{o}^I \geq h^I \quad (4.3.15)$$

and confront frustration when

$$\mathcal{P}^I(o^I) < h^I \quad (4.3.16)$$

See the related discussion in section 5.4. Also, the group in certain situations may behave as a cybernetic organization, concerned primarily with survival and relying on only a small set of responses or decision rules in the choice of an action (a response) to a stimulus (or feedback from the environment).

4.3.6 The group as a learner

As with the individual, we may take the learning L^I of group I to consist of two parts:

$$L^I = \overline{L}^I + \overline{\overline{L}}^I \quad (4.3.17)$$

Letting $\mathcal{P}^I(\cdot)$ and $\mathrm{Exp}^I(\cdot)$ represent I's perceptions and expectations, we may write

$$\mathcal{P}^I(\cdot) = (\mathcal{P}^I(o^I), \mathcal{P}^I\{\overline{a}^N\}, \mathcal{P}^I(e, \ldots)) \tag{4.3.18}$$

and

$$\mathrm{Exp}^I(\cdot) = (\hat{o}^I, \{\hat{a}^N\}, \hat{W}^I, \ldots) \tag{4.3.19}$$

Accordingly, we can define $\overline{L}^I$ by

$$\overline{L}^I = \overline{L}^I(\mathcal{P}^I(\cdot), \mathrm{Exp}^I(\cdot), \overset{a}{M}e^I, \beta^I) \tag{4.3.20}$$

where β^I is I's ability at information processing. Also we can define $\overline{\overline{L}}^I$ by

$$\overline{\overline{L}}^I = \overline{\overline{L}}^I(|G^I - \mathcal{P}^I(o^I)|, c^I, \mathrm{pr}^I, \xi^I) \tag{4.3.21}$$

where c^I, pr^I, and ξ^I are costs of search activity, probability that group I will find useful new information, and ability at finding new information, respectively. We also may write

$$c^I = c^I(\overline{\theta}_s, \ldots) \tag{4.3.22}$$

where $\overline{\theta}_s$ are obstacles to group I's search set up by the larger society. However, in the case of the group we must recognize the greater complexity of learning than with the individual. Necessarily, group learning, being for an entity composed of individuals, embodies all the complexities of the individual's learning process and more whether the group is dominated by one or more individuals. Hence, additional processes such as those discussed in Chapter 14 are relevant.

Finally, where the group tends to be a cybernetic-type organization and when the stimulus or feedback on critical variables lies outside the range for which it possesses an adequate response in its limited repertory of action patterns, it copes (learns) by adding personnel possessing the new required response capability (with new specialized and adequate mental representations). In such an organization, the decision making by each of the several individuals (subunits) is likely to be hierarchically arranged. There may be a rigid, ordered sequence in which individuals (subunits) make decisions within their particular problem area with little if any integration across individuals (subunits). See Steinbruner (1976).

4.3.7   The group as a relocator

Although the movement of a typical group is much less frequent and extensive than that of an individual, such movement can occur and have significant implications. We mention the possibility of movement in physical space. However, the predominant aspect of movement we have in mind is relocation in policy, psychological, sociological, ideological, and other spaces. The motive for such may be to maximize the probability of survival or members' profits; or to minimize costs, losses, and other negative outcomes; or to achieve some combination of these and others. Or, it may be that the relocation occurs because the group, currently at an unsatisfactory position, desires a satisficing one.[17]

There are several ways we can model group relocation. One simple way is to recognize that many groups are often concerned with members, supporters, or some other set of associated individuals. Each may wish to maximize the number of these persons belonging to it. Therefore, if individuals who qualify have most preferred positions that are distributed over some space (policy, psychological, ideological, etc.) and if there is a cost to overcome the distance between the location of the group in that space and that most preferred by given individuals,[18] the group will want to locate as close as it can to these individuals' most preferred positions given the total cost of overcoming distance that it can incur. Alternatively, if the group seeks a specific number of members or supporters or, say, a majority of a population as constituents, it will want to find that location that minimizes the total cost of overcoming distance in the relevant policy spaces to achieve that goal. In other contexts, the group may, for example, seek a location and choose the first one that provides it with a satisfactory number of members given the total cost that it can incur.

A more sophisticated analysis recognizes that there can only be a probability that an individual will be a member, supporter, or constituent of (be associated with) a specified group for any given distance of his or her most preferred location from that of the group no matter how small that distance. Moreover, there may exist other groups similar to it so that the competition and "support areas" of these other groups must be considered by the specified group in any relocation decision.

Moreover, there is a cost of relocation. In that respect Eq. (4.2.26) concerning conditions for commodity shipment may be said to have some application here. If a group is to relocate from position x to position z, the net gains of a location at z (advantages and disadvantages, taking into account all types of "locational revenues" and "locational costs") sym-

---

[17] A group's position may be represented by a nonfixed point in n-dimensional space. The group generally has a leader, part of whose income comes from the c-respect and c-power accruing to him (or her) from growth in his group's numbers, prestige, power, rectitude, etc. So he may want and actually be able to persuade other members to allow the group to relocate in the above spaces because such would increase its numbers (via net immigration), permit realization of more welfare for the group, increase its probability of survival, etc. Or, all members may actively desire to see the group shift its position because that would increase the group's profit, money, or (implicit) income, etc., and thus the absolute amount each i receives when he receives a fixed share of the total.

[18] See Isard and Smith (1980) for a discussion of the location problem in such a space.

bolized by p^z must exceed the same symbolized by p^x by at least the cost that the group would incur in relocation. Alternatively, the "locational revenue differentials" and "locational cost differentials"[19] symbolized by $p^z - p^x$ must *on net* be in favor of location z by at least the cost of relocation. Included in these differentials would be those relating to c-power, c-respect, c-sanctions, patronage cost, and the typical economic revenues and costs.[20]

Still more sophisticated analysis recognizes that the cost of relocation may be regarded as an investment cost since the new location may be estimated to be desirable not only for the current unit of time (say, a year) but for many units of time, say, the period τ, where $\tau = t_1 - t$. In that case appropriate investment conditions must be met.

There are other ways to model group relocation. The membership of a group may be fixed, but a relocation may increase the probability that that membership will stay in power, maintain the status quo (when that group is the leading "power"), or ensure ascendancy in the power structure.[21]

Finally, we may model group location with an Alonso-type framework. Here we would need to construct a model of the form

$$\text{pr}(M^{x\to z}) = \frac{w^z}{C^z} \frac{v^x}{D^x} \frac{1}{d^{xz}} \tag{4.3.23}$$

with interpretations of the variables and the relationships somewhat similar and parallel to those associated with the discussion of Eq. (4.2.27). Here locations x and z replace groups I and N in the statements interpreting Eq. (4.2.27).[22]

4.4   Concluding remarks

This chapter has presented a more formal representation of decision making by a behaving individual. In any action that he or she takes we view him or her as a perceiver, as a believer and knower, as a goal setter, as a learner, and as a relocator. In parallel fashion we presented one pos-

[19] See Isard (1956) for a discussion of such differentials.
[20] Also included should be the cost (negative elements) associated with the irresponsibility (nondependability) and opportunism element when a group relocates too often in the eyes of its constituency.
[21] Or, the group may relocate in such a way that in shifting it loses members who are highly dissident and gains an equal number of much less dissident members, thereby maximizing internal cohesion (or minimizing internal dissonance). In doing so, it may be in effect moving to a more "modal" position.
[22] We may, however, associate with the locations x and z the positions taken by higher order groups $\bar{J}$ and $\bar{N}$ (and thus allegiance to groups $\bar{J}$ and $\bar{N}$).

sible representation of behavior by the group. In both cases we attempted to employ from economics and regional science some of their strengths in the formal and consistent presentation of relationships, adopting the notion of the payoff matrix of section 3.2 and the influence of the attitude variable. However, the question may be asked: Have we or have we not effectively fused the concepts of *cognitive sci* person and *economic* person? Have we synthesized the precedent-based, analogical reasoning associated with cognitive processes with the rational-choice approach of economics and regional science? We can only answer, "to some limited extent." This qualified answer is largely a reflection of the fact that neither the cognitive science approach nor that of economics and regional science captures the *full reality* of the behaving unit. Each has been abstracted from important features. Somehow or other, the behaving individual integrates his or her cognitive processes and psychological tendencies with a certain amount of rationality – the drive to survive among competing species compels (or has compelled) this to be so. Hence, what we have attempted in this chapter is to depict and understand the behaving individual (not *cognitive sci* person and not *economic* person) by putting side by side some of the strengths of the two approaches. We have not attempted to fuse these two approaches since each has serious deficiencies; rather we have tried to force their strong points to lie within a single frame as, for example, represented by Figure 4.1.

We conclude by observing that in this chapter we did not consider decision making under conditions of high stress and crisis, to which we shall turn in the next chapter. Moreover, we only scratched the surface when we discussed *ex ante* learning for problem solving via search and information R&D, which will be pursued in Chapters 6, 15, and 16.

References

Anselin, L., and W. Isard (1979) "On Alonso's General Theory of Movement." *Man, Environment, Space and Time* 1(1):52–63.

Axelrod, R. M. (ed.)(1976) *Structure of Decision: The Cognitive Maps of Political Elites.* Princeton: Princeton University Press.

Funk and Wagnalls (1961) *New "Standard" Dictionary of the English Language.* New York: Funk and Wagnalls.

Gamson, W. (1981) "The Political Culture of the Arab-Israeli Conflict." *Conflict Management and Peace Science* 5(2):79–94.

Gamson, W. A., and K. E. Lasch (1983) "The Political Culture of Social Welfare Policy." In H. J. Spiro (ed.), *Evaluating the Welfare State: Social and Political Perspectives.* New York: Academic Press.

Hansen, J. M. (1985) "The Political Economy of Group Membership." *American Political Science Review* 79:79–96.

Isard, W. (1956) *Location and Space Economy.* New York: M.I.T. Press and Wiley.

Isard, W., and P. Liossatos (1979) *Spatial Dynamics and Optimal Space-Time Development.* New York: Elsevier-North Holland.

Isard, W., and C. Smith (1980). "Elementary Locational Analysis in Policy Space." *Papers of the Regional Science Association* 45:17–44.

Isard, W., T. E. Smith, P. Isard, T. H. Tung, and M. Dacey (1969) *General Theory: Social, Political, Economic and Regional.* Cambridge, MA: M.I.T. Press.

Jervis, R. (1976) *Perception and Misperception in International Politics.* Princeton: Princeton University Press.

Kahneman, D., and A. Tversky (1979) "Prospect Theory: An Analysis of Decision Under Risk." *Econometrica* 47:263–90.

Kaniss, P. C. (1978) "Evolutionary Change in Hierarchical Systems: A General Theory," *Regional Science Dissertation & Monograph Series #9.* Department of City Planning. Ithaca: Cornell University.

Lebow, R. N. (1981) *Between Peace and War.* Baltimore: Johns Hopkins University Press.

Orbell, J. M., P. Schwartz-Shea, and R. T. Summers (1984) "Do Cooperators Exist More Readily than Defectors?" *American Political Science Review* 78:147–62.

Shubik, M. (1988) "The Uses, Value and Limitations of Game Theoretic Methods in Defense Analysis." In C. Schmidt and F. Blackaby (eds.), *Peace, Defence and Economic Analysis.* London: MacMillan, pp. 53–84.

Smith, V. K. (1985) "A Theoretical Analysis of the 'Green Lobby'." *American Political Science Review* 79:132–47.

Steinbruner, J. (1976) "Beyond Rational Deterrence: The Struggle for New Conceptions." *World Politics* 18(January):223–42.

Webster's Third New International Dictionary (1961) Springfield, MA: Merriam.

CHAPTER 5

Decision-making behavior under major psychological stress and crisis conditions

5.1 Introductory remarks

In the previous chapter we examined the behavior of the individual, group, and in general of a decision-making unit, which was routine or nonroutine but by and large did not require the solution of any major problem. We assumed nonstressful situations wherein the unit had limited information and perhaps many misperceptions and responded to stimuli in accord with schemata (patterns), interpretive packages, and other mental representations accumulated from experience; at times the unit even responded mechanistically (cybernetically). We assumed that the unit had at least some rough knowledge of (1) its restricted action space, (2) perhaps some crudely derived probabilities about possible states of the environment and joint actions of others, and (3) some components of the outcome function. In a sense, the unit was partially rational, partially precedent oriented, partially impulsive (playing hunches without any real reason), and so on, and for the rest unexplainable in its behavior. We now examine behavior under major stress and crisis conditions – as is often the case in the international arena. We do so more formally than is done in the existing literature extending thereby the framework developed in the previous chapter. We draw heavily upon the work of Janis and Mann (1977) and Lebow (1981). We shall continue to use some mathematical symbols as shorthand to permit a more precise and more comprehensive grasp of relationships. No mathematical operations beyond addition, subtraction, and comparison of magnitudes is involved.

Before discussing the Janis and Mann framework, we note that it would be desirable to define a crisis and crisis conditions. Unfortunately, there

The author is grateful to Paul Kiwort for assistance in writing section 5.4.

do not exist generally acceptable definitions in the literature (Hopple and Rossa 1981, p. 70; Hermann and Mason 1980; Robinson 1972); and we are not able to provide such. However, after the discussion of this chapter, some elements of a possible definition may be apparent. It will also be apparent then that decision making under crisis conditions has certain key features not normally present in the usual frameworks (such as those covered in Chapter 4) of decision making in general.

5.2   Some preliminary remarks on Janis and Mann

Janis and Mann view humans as reluctant decision makers. They are emotional beings, beset by doubts and uncertainties and having incongruous longings, antipathies, and loyalties that generate conflict and psychological stress. As reluctant decision makers, they continue along their chosen course of action until a stress-producing threat to their important goals cause them to (1) seek a better solution from vigilance and diligent search, (2) rationalize their present course of action, particularly if too much stress is present and too little time is available to search for new alternatives, or (3) panic from very high stress.

Janis and Mann fully recognize that (1) the limited cognitive capability of humans to digest information and (2) the restrictions imposed by powerful persons or groups (whose wishes have to be respected) confine their ability and freedom to engage in "vigilant information processing." But so also does the anxiety generated by psychological stress.

What is vigilant information processing? Janis and Mann consider such processing as met when in arriving at a choice the decision maker (to the best of his or her ability)

1. thoroughly canvasses a wide range of alternative courses of action;
2. surveys the full range of objectives to be fulfilled and the values implicated by the choice;
3. carefully weighs whatever he knows about the costs and risks of negative consequences, as well as positive consequences, that could flow from each alternative;
4. intensively searches for new information relevant to further evaluation of the alternatives;
5. correctly assimilates and takes account of any new information or expert judgment to which he is exposed, even when the information or judgment does not support the course of action he initially prefers;
6. reexamines the positive and negative consequences of all known alter-

natives, including those originally regarded as unacceptable, before making a final choice;
7. makes detailed provisions for implementing or executing the chosen course of action, with special attention to contingency plans that might be required if various known risks were to materialize.
(Janis and Mann 1977, p. 11)

Rarely does the decision maker conduct vigilant information processing when making "consequential" decisions. This is so because all such decisions cause him (or her) some concern or anxiety. Possibly he may not be able to achieve his objectives. Or he may need to incur costs (money, time, effort, emotional involvement, reputation, morale, etc.) greater than he can afford. Or he may not be able to cope with the uncertainties, let alone risk. Or he may lack sufficient time to identify and implement a best decision. Or he may confront some combination of all of these items. As a consequence, his decision making falls short of vigilant information processing. Janis and Mann identify four stress-coping patterns that reflect his failure to achieve such processing – that is, that characterize inadequate or poor decision making. They are unconflicted adherence, unconflicted change, defensive avoidance, and hypervigilance, which we now discuss. But first note that although the Janis and Mann framework is of major import for understanding crisis decision making, some analysts would claim that it has lesser and lesser significance for situations involving, respectively, less and less psychological stress even though Janis and Mann assert that it is pertinent for all consequential decisions.

5.3   Some preliminary formal structure

Janis and Mann base their frame upon extensive experience and evidence accumulated over time. They do not use mathematical symbols and functions to depict this frame, being satisfied with verbal discussion and illustrative figures such as Figure 5.1. In order to facilitate linkage of their frame with others both in this book and elsewhere,[1] we formulate it mathematically as far as we are able to, thereby partly extending it. Also, we have in mind (1) a decision maker motivated to acquire the gains from a stress-producing opportunity as well as (2) Janis and Mann's decision maker, who by and large is motivated to avoid losses from a stress-producing threat.

[1] For example, see Isard et al. (1969) and Isard and Smith (1982).

To start, let the payoff matrix symbol $\#_i(t-1)$ crudely represent the "perspective" at time $t-1$ of a typical decision maker i who is involved in routine decision making. As discussed in section 3.2, each row represents one of the restricted number of options (actions) he (or she) has in mind. Each column represents one of the restricted number of combinations he perceives of a realizable state of the environment and joint action of all other participants. Each cell records the outcomes (which can be a sequence of events over a relevant period of time) that he crudely estimates if he takes the option (action) of that row and if the combination of the corresponding column is realized.

Against this background, we envisage a decision maker with an unchanging perspective selecting an option in routine fashion – his (or her) action choice being determined by the combination of e, the state of the environment, and $\{a_k\}$, the joint action (actions) of others that is realized or that he expects. We now let a change at $t-1$ take place – that is, a change in e, $\{a_k\}$, or the outcome o or some combination of changes such that his perspective at the time $t-1$, namely $\#_i(t-1)$, is different from that at the next point of time t, namely, $\#_i(t)$.[2] This change represents a challenge $\mathcal{C}(t)$ at time t. It could be a positive feedback (opportunity) or a negative feedback (threat) as per Janis and Mann. We proceed to stage I of Figure 5.1.

5.3.1   Stage I: appraising the challenge

Here the first question (in box 1) is:

Q1: Are the risks serious if I do not change at the next point of time $t+1$ what would be currently (at time t) my best action given the expected combination (or set of combinations) of a state of the environment and joint action of others that might be realized at $t+1$?

This is equivalent to asking whether there exists a nonnegligible probability that a new alternative $\bar{a}_i(t+1)$ not in the current perspective $\#_i(t)$ might be revealed – this new alternative being one that might be expected to yield a significantly greater utility than the optimal action $a_i^*(t)$ of the current perspective. That is, is there a significant probability ($\text{pr} \overset{s}{>} 0$) that there exists $\bar{a}_i(t+1)$ for which

$$[\hat{u}_i(\bar{a}_i(t+1); \ldots) \overset{s}{>} \hat{u}_i(a_i^*(t); \ldots)] \overset{s}{>} 0 \qquad (5.3.1)$$

---

[2] This perspective now incorporates the change occurring at $t-1$, but its dimensions are not altered in the light of the challenge that this change generates.

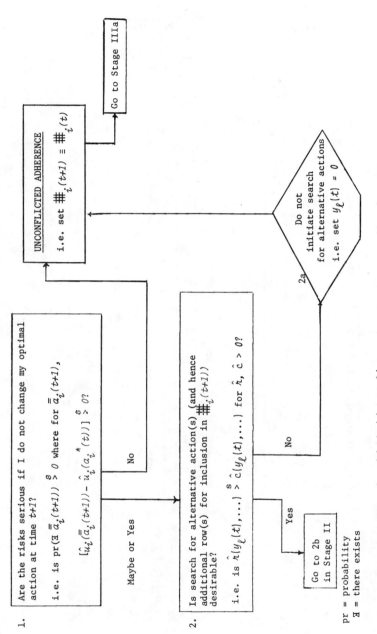

STAGE I: Appraising the Challenge $\mathscr{C}$ at Time t

1.

| Are the risks serious if I do not change my optimal action at time $t+1$?

i.e. is $\mathrm{pr}(\exists \ \overline{\overline{a}}_i(t+1)) \overset{s}{>} 0$ where for $\overline{\overline{a}}_i(t+1)$,

$$[\hat{u}_i(\overline{\overline{a}}_i(t+1)) - \hat{u}_i(a_i^*(t))] \overset{s}{>} 0?$$

Maybe or Yes

No

UNCONFLICTED ADHERENCE

i.e. set $\#_i(t+1) = \#_i(t)$

Go to Stage IIIa

2.

Is search for alternative action(s) (and hence additional row(s) for inclusion in $\#_i(t+1)$) desirable?

i.e. is $\hat{h}(y_\ell(t), \ldots) \overset{s}{>} \hat{c}(y_\ell(t), \ldots)$ for $\hat{h}, \hat{c} > 0$?

Yes

No

Go to 2b in Stage II

2a

Do not initiate search for alternative actions

i.e. set $y_\ell(t) = 0$

pr = probability

$\exists$ = there exists

Figure 5.1. Stages in crisis decision making.

159

STAGE II. Surveying the Alternative Actions Available Given $\mathscr{C}(t)$

2b (Initiate search for alternative actions i.e. set $y_{\ell h}(t) > 0$)

3. Has an alternative action been identified?

i.e. is $[\mathscr{P}_i(\tilde{A}_i(t+1)) \neq \mathscr{P}_i(\tilde{A}_i(t))]$

where $\mathscr{P}_i(\tilde{A}_i(t+1)) = f(y_i(t); \mathscr{P}_i(\tilde{A}_i(t)), \mathscr{C}(t))$

Yes — No

No → Return to 2

4. Is this alternative acceptable?

i.e. does there exist an $\bar{\bar{a}}_i \in \mathscr{P}_i(\tilde{A}_i(t+1)); \bar{\bar{a}}_i \notin \mathscr{P}_i(\tilde{A}_i(t))$

for which $\hat{u}_i(\hat{o}_i[\bar{\bar{a}}_i(t+1); \{\hat{a}_k(t+1)\}, \hat{e}(t+1)]) \geq \overset{o}{u}_i$

Maybe or Yes — No

No → Discard alternative $\bar{\bar{a}}_i$ and return to 2

5. If Maybe or Yes and not simple satisficer, are the risks serious if I do not consider other alternatives?

i.e., is the $\mathrm{pr}(\exists\; \bar{\bar{a}}_i(t+1))^s > 0$ where for $\bar{\bar{a}}_i(t+1)$

$[\hat{u}_i(\hat{o}_i[\bar{\bar{a}}_i(t+1); \{\hat{a}_k(t+1)\}, \hat{e}(t+1)]) - u_i(\hat{o}_i[\bar{\bar{a}}_i(t+1); \{\hat{a}_K(t+1)\}, \hat{e}(t+1)])]^s > 0?$

If yes and if simple satisficer, then adopt $\bar{\bar{a}}_i$, thereby going to Stage Va without considering negative feedback from others

Maybe or Yes

No → UNCONFLICTED CHANGE
i.e. set $\#_i(t+1)$ up including only a limited set of new alternatives

Go to Stage IIIa

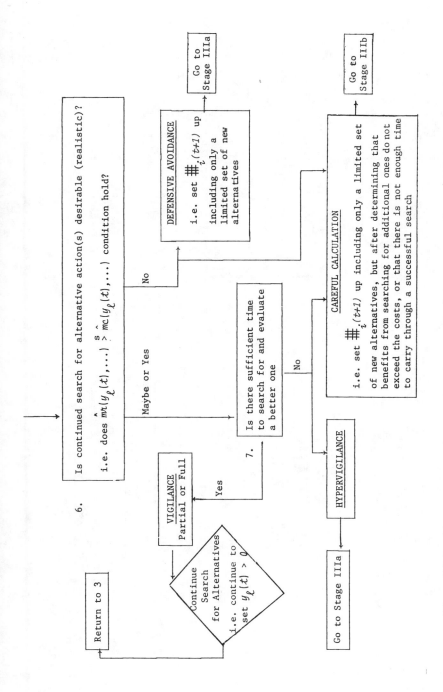

6. Is continued search for alternative action(s) desirable (realistic)?

i.e. does $\overset{\wedge}{mt}(y_\ell(t),\dots) \overset{s}{>} \overset{\wedge}{mc}(y_\ell(t),\dots)$ condition hold?

No

Maybe or Yes

DEFENSIVE AVOIDANCE

i.e. set $\#_i(t+1)$ up including only a limited set of new alternatives

Go to Stage IIIa

7. Is there sufficient time to search for and evaluate a better one

No

VIGILANCE Partial or Full

Yes

Continue Search for Alternatives

i.e. continue to set $y_\ell(t) > 0$

CAREFUL CALCULATION

i.e. set $\#_i(t+1)$ up including only a limited set of new alternatives, but after determining that benefits from searching for additional ones do not exceed the costs, or that there is not enough time to carry through a successful search

Go to Stage IIIb

HYPERVIGILANCE

Return to 3

Go to Stage IIIa

Figure 5.1 (cont.)

161

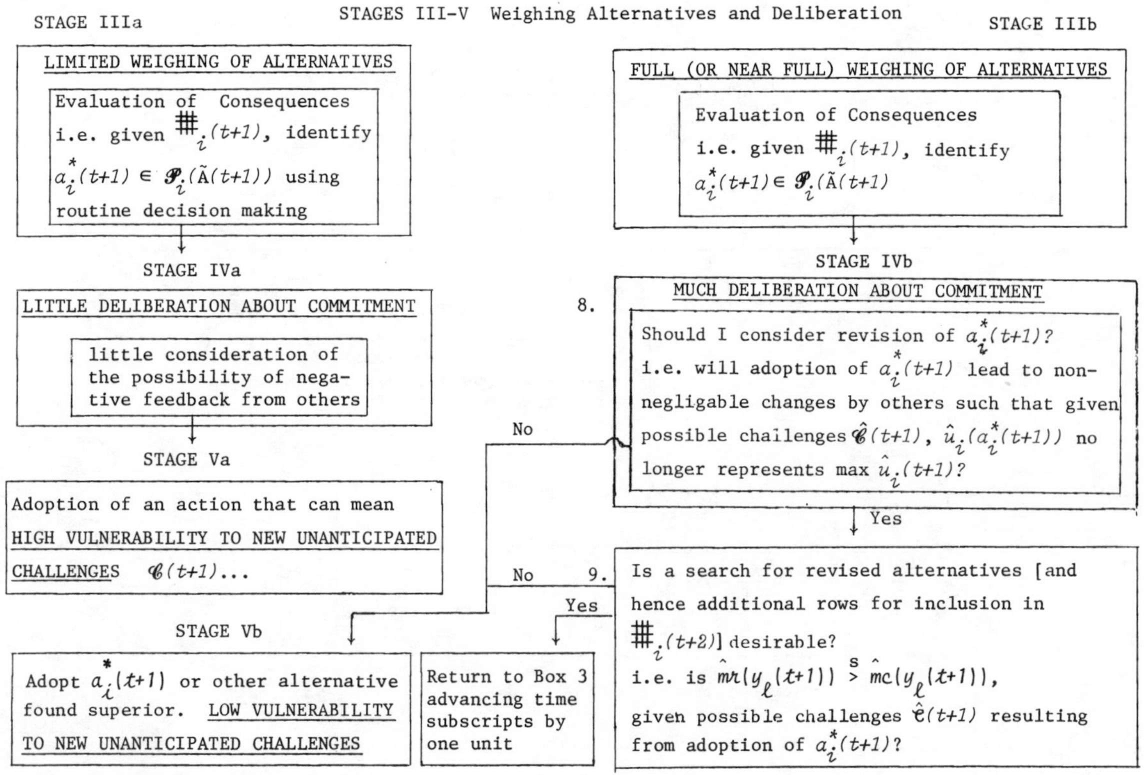

STAGES III-V   Weighing Alternatives and Deliberation

STAGE IIIa

STAGE IIIb

LIMITED WEIGHING OF ALTERNATIVES

FULL (OR NEAR FULL) WEIGHING OF ALTERNATIVES

Evaluation of Consequences
i.e. given $\#_{.i}(t+1)$, identify
$a_{i}^{*}(t+1) \in \mathscr{P}_{i}(\tilde{A}(t+1))$ using
routine decision making

Evaluation of Consequences
i.e. given $\#_{.i}(t+1)$, identify
$a_{i}^{*}(t+1) \in \mathscr{P}_{i}(\tilde{A}(t+1))$

STAGE IVa

STAGE IVb

LITTLE DELIBERATION ABOUT COMMITMENT

MUCH DELIBERATION ABOUT COMMITMENT

little consideration of
the possibility of nega-
tive feedback from others

8. Should I consider revision of $a_{.i}^{*}(t+1)$?
i.e. will adoption of $a_{.i}^{*}(t+1)$ lead to non-
negligable changes by others such that given
possible challenges $\hat{\mathscr{C}}(t+1)$, $\hat{u}_{.i}(a_{.i}^{*}(t+1))$ no
longer represents max $\hat{u}_{i}(t+1)$?

Yes

No

STAGE Va

Adoption of an action that can mean
HIGH VULNERABILITY TO NEW UNANTICIPATED
CHALLENGES $\mathscr{C}(t+1)$...

9. Is a search for revised alternatives [and
hence additional rows for inclusion in
$\#_{.i}(t+2)$] desirable?
i.e. is $\hat{ms}_{i}(y_{\ell}(t+1)) > \hat{mc}(y_{\ell}(t+1))$,
given possible challenges $\hat{\mathscr{C}}(t+1)$ resulting
from adoption of $a_{.i}^{*}(t+1)$?

Yes

No

Return to Box 3
advancing time
subscripts by
one unit

STAGE Vb

Adopt $a_{.i}^{*}(t+1)$ or other alternative
found superior. LOW VULNERABILITY
TO NEW UNANTICIPATED CHALLENGES

162

Figure 5.1 (cont.)

where

$\overset{s}{>}$ = significantly greater than;

$\bar{a}_i(t + 1)$ = element of $\mathcal{P}_i(\tilde{A}_i(t + 1)$, the restricted action space that might be perceived at time $t + 1$ should the behaving unit change his (or her) perspective to $\#_i(t + 1)$; where the latter is taken to be a function of his current perspective $\#_i(t)$, the challenge $\mathcal{C}(t)$, and the labor inputs (time and effort) that he might put forth to meet the challenge;

$a_i^*(t)$ = action by i that maximizes his expected utility $\hat{u}_i(t)$ given his current perspective $\#_i(t)$.

There are two possible answers to this question:

1. If the answer is no, then i goes into a state of *unconflicted adherence* to the current perspective, that is, he (or she) considers the perspective $\#_i(t + 1)$ to be the same as his current one. The individual is under no stress; he continues to make the same kind of decisions, in the same routine way, with low-level interest in messages and new information. In effect, the individual proceeds directly to state IIIa, *limited weighing of alternatives,* of Figure 5.1.
2. If the answer is maybe or yes, then i needs to pose a second more specific question involving costs and benefits.

This question (in box 2) is:

Q2: Is the search for an alternative action(s) and additional row(s) for inclusion in my perspective $\#_i(t + 1)$ desirable?

This is equivalent to asking:

$$\text{Is } \hat{r}(y_i(t), \dots) \overset{s}{>} \hat{c}(y_i(t), \dots) \quad \text{for } \hat{r}, \hat{c} > 0 \tag{5.3.2}$$

where

y_l = labor inputs required for production (generation) of relevant information;

$\hat{r}$ = expected gains from information produced by anticipated amounts of inputs $y_i(t)$;

$\hat{c}$ = expected costs of those inputs.

There are two possible answers to this question:

1. If the answer is no, then i does not initiate any search. Rather, he or she adopts a stance of unconflicted adherence and hence proceeds directly to stage IIIa of Figure 5.1.
2. If the answer is yes, then i proceeds to stage II of Figure 5.1.

5.3.2   Stage II: surveying the alternative actions available given the challenge

In particular, i decides to expend labor at a search for an alternative action during time t – that is, he or she sets $y_i(t) > 0$ and then, at time $t + 1$, asks the question (in box 3):

$Q3$: Has an alternative action $\bar{a}_i$ been identified as a result of my search?

Presumably this alternative would be a new one that does not appear in his or her perspective $\#_i(t)$ at time t. That is,

$$\bar{a}_i \in \mathcal{P}_i(\tilde{A}_i(t + 1))$$

where[3]

$$\mathcal{P}_i(\tilde{A}_i(t + 1)) \neq \mathcal{P}_i(\tilde{A}_i(t)) \tag{5.3.3}$$

There are two possible answers to this question:

1. If the answer is no, then i should return to question 2 and ask whether he or she should engage in further search.
2. If the answer is yes, then i needs to pose a fourth more specific question concerning the identified alternative.

This question (in box 4) is:

$Q4$: Is the alternative $\bar{a}_i$ an acceptable one?

This is equivalent to asking

$$\text{Is } \hat{u}_i(\hat{o}_i(t + 1)) > \mathring{u}_i \tag{5.3.4}$$

where

$\hat{u}_i$ = expected utility as function of expected outcome;
$\hat{o}(t + 1)$ = expected outcome as function of (1) his (or her) adopting $\bar{a}_i$ at $t + 1$ and (2) what he considers to be the likely action $\{\hat{a}_k\}$ of others and the likely state $\hat{e}$ of the environment;
$\mathring{u}_i$ = lower bound on utility level that i considers acceptable.[4]

There are three types of response to this question:

1. If the answer is no, then i discards the alternative $\bar{a}_i$ and returns to question 2.

---

[3] Although the search may reveal more than one alternative given $y_i(t)$, to facilitate the description of the process, we assume that only one alternative is identified. The reader can easily extend the analysis when more than one alternative is exposed.
[4] Here the lower bound $\mathring{u}_i$ is taken as fixed. Alternatively, as the decision maker accumulates more information and reassesses what it is realistic to hold out for, this bound may vary from one round of search to another.

2. If the answer is yes and if i is a *simple satisficer*, he or she stops the search[5] (i.e., sets $y_l = 0$) and adopts $\overline{a}_i$, thereby going directly to stage Va[6] – a stage characterized by *high vulnerability to unanticipated challenges*.
3. If the answer is maybe or yes and if i is not a simple satisficer, then i needs to engage in a more detailed evaluation of the identified alternative.

That is, he or she asks the question (in box 5):

Q5: Are the risks serious if I change to this alternative and do not consider others that might possibly be found with further search?

This is equivalent to asking whether there is a nonnegligible probability that there exists still another alternative $\overline{\overline{a}}_i$ as yet unidentified that could be expected to yield a utility significantly greater than that expected from the best current alternative. That is, is there pr $\overset{s}{>}$ 0 that there exists $\overline{\overline{a}}_i(t + 1)$ for which

$$\hat{u}_i[\hat{o}(\overline{\overline{a}}_i(t + 1), \dots)] \overset{s}{>} \hat{u}[\hat{o}_i(\overline{a}_i(t + 1), \dots)] \tag{5.3.5}$$

There are two possible answers to this question:

1. If the answer is no, then i moves into a state of *unconflicted change*, that is, stops the search (i.e., sets $y_l = 0$) and adopts the new perspective $\#_i(t + 1)$, including only one additional alternative – namely, $\overline{a}_i$. He or she then proceeds to stage IIIa.[7]
2. If the answer is maybe or yes, then i needs to pose a sixth more specific question concerning costs and benefits.

This question (in box 6) is:

Q6: Is it realistic to hope to find a better alternative from continued search considering the labor inputs required for this search?

This is equivalent to asking whether the following holds:

$$\hat{m}r(y_l(t), \dots) \overset{s}{>} \hat{m}c(y_l(t), \dots) \quad \text{for } \hat{m}r, \hat{m}c > 0 \tag{5.3.6}$$

---

[5] A careful calculator may also stop here if he or she judges that there does not exist a state of the environment e_λ and a set of actions $\{a_k\}$ with nonnegligible probability such that $\hat{u}_i(\hat{o}_i(\overline{a}_i(t + 1), \dots)) \overset{s}{>} \hat{u}_i(t + 1)$ when $\hat{u}_i(t + 1)$ pertains to the perspective $\#_i(t)$ that does not contain $\overline{a}_i$.

[6] We assume here that none of the alternatives faced in stage 1 meet this lower bound requirement.

[7] Note that such does not allow the unconflicted changer to consider the possibility of feedback from others. If it is felt that such a decision maker does indeed take into account possible changes in others' actions $\{\hat{a}_k\}$ as a consequence of his (or her) own action choice, then he should be rerouted to stage IIIb.

where $\dot{m}r$ and $\dot{m}c$ are expected marginal gains and marginal costs, respectively, of labor and other inputs at collecting information. There are three types of response to this question:

1. First, the answer may be no because *careful calculation* and evaluation of all information available, and in particular the probability of finding a superior alternative $\bar{\bar{a}}_i$, does not lead the decision maker to conclude that the expected gains from further search would exceed the expected costs. Where this is the case, i proceeds to stage IIIb, *full (or near full) weighing of alternatives* via the careful calculation box.

2. Second, the answer may be no because of another reason. Being under stress, risk averse, and subject to considerable anxiety, the decision maker is unable to carry through careful calculation and evaluation of information pertaining to risky alternatives.[8] To paraphrase Janis and Mann, under severe (decisional) conflict because each alternative poses a serious risk of not exploiting the opportunity, the decision maker loses hope about finding a solution better than the least objectionable one. He or she adopts a stance of *defensive avoidance*. This stance is characterized by "lack of vigilant search, selective inattention, selective forgetting, distortion of the meaning of warning messages," procrastination, the shifting of the responsibility for the decision, and construction of wishful rationalizations that minimize negative consequences of an existing action and exaggerate its positive aspects (Janis and Mann 1977, 50).[9] When the answer to question 6 is *no* as a result of adopting a stance of defensive avoidance, then i proceeds to stage IIIa, *limited weighing of alternatives*. Note that under crisis conditions, especially when there is an extreme shortage of time for decision making, i may have adopted a stance of defensive avoidance earlier in the no answer to questions 1, 2, 3, 4, or 5. If so, the arrow from box 6 to the defense avoidance box should be replaced by an arrow from a previous box.

3. Finally, the answer to question 6 could be maybe or yes. Where this is the case, the decision maker must ask still another question.

[8] For example, the political leader of a nation who may be under considerable pressure to exploit the opportunity may nonetheless be highly sensitive to the complicated dynamics and instability of the international system and may be fearful that he or she cannot do anything other than mess things up.
[9] In effect, he or she avoids cues that stimulate anxiety or other discomfort from trying to cope with complexity. Closely related to this evasive form of defense avoidance is "buck passing" – that is, depending upon someone else to make a decision.

This question (in box 7) is:

Q7: Is there sufficient time to search for and evaluate a better alternative?

There are three types of response to this question:

1. First, after quick and careful calculation and thought, the answer may be no. Where this is the case, *i* stops the search at this point and proceeds to stage IIIb.

2. Second, the answer may be no for another reason. The decision maker may be in a state of *hypervigilance.* According to Janis and Mann, this state is one of severe conflict because time is short to meet a deadline or respond to the challenge: "A person in this state experiences so much cognitive constriction and perseveration that his thought processes are disrupted. The person's immediate memory span is reduced and his thinking becomes more simplistic in that he cannot deal conceptually with as many categories as when he is in a less aroused state" (Janis and Mann 1977, p. 51). Expecting that he (or she) will not be able to exploit the opportunity unless he acts quickly, the person in the hypervigilant (panic) state "fails to recognize all the alternatives open to him and fails to use whatever time is available to evaluate adequately those alternatives of which he is aware. He is likely to search frantically for a solution, persevere in his thinking about a limited number of alternatives, and then latch onto a hastily contrived solution that seems to promise immediate relief, often at the cost of considerable postdecisional regret" (Janis and Mann 1977, p. 51). When the answer to question 7 is no as a result of adopting a stance of hypervigilance, then we view the decision maker as proceeding to state IIIa. Note, that as with defense avoidance a state of hypervigilance may have been reached at an earlier stage because of an extreme shortage of time.

3. Finally, if the answer to question 7 is yes, then the decision maker is viewed as entering a state of *vigilance.*[10] That is, he continues his search for new alternatives – once again setting $y_i > 0$ for additional search and returning to box 3. He keeps on going from box 3 to box 7 over successive rounds until a no response to question 7 is reached at some point. When a no response is reached after such vigilant search, *i* proceeds to stage IIIb.

This completes our discussion of stage II.

---

[10] According to Janis and Mann (1977, p. 51), a state of vigilance involves a moderate degree of stress in response to a challenge; absence of stress results in too little motivation to search for information and work out a good solution (i.e., a high-quality decision). Also see Herek, Janis, and Huth (1987).

5.3.3   Stages III–V: weighing alternatives and deliberation

When a decision maker has adopted a stance of unconflicted adherence, unconflicted change, or defensive avoidance, he (or she) proceeds to stage IIIa. In effect, he conducts a limited weighing of alternatives and a limited evaluation of their consequences. This is followed in stage IVa with *little deliberation about commitment* and with little consideration of the possibility of negative (or positive) feedbacks from others. This then leads to stage Va when he adopts, say, $\bar{a}_i$, generating a state of high vulnerability to new unanticipated challenges. (The decision maker, as already noted, will also reach stage Va if he behaves as a simple satisficer after adopting a limited search for new alternatives.)

Alternatively, where a decision maker has engaged in careful calculation – after one or more rounds of search – he (or she) proceeds to stage IIIb. Here he conducts a full (or near full) weighing of alternatives and evaluation of their consequences; that is, given $\#_i(t + 1)$, he identifies the optimal action $a_i^*(t + 1) \in \mathcal{P}_i(\tilde{A}_i(t + 1))$. He then proceeds to stage IVb, where according to Janis and Mann, he deliberates much about his commitment. In particular, he asks yet another question (in box 8):

Q8: Should I reconsider the choice of $a_i^*(t + 1)$ in light of the possible nonnegligible reactions (changes in the actions) of others such that this choice can no longer be said to represent an optimal outcome?

This is equivalent to asking: Will $\hat{u}_i(a_i^*(t + 1))$ still maximize $\hat{u}_i(t + 1)$? Here, of course, is where we encounter the action–reaction responses that resemble those of participants in a conflict and those in other situations of real life in which learning takes place. Here then is a point of synthesis with both interdependent decision-making theory and learning theory. There are two possible responses to this question:

1. If after careful deliberation the answer is no, he adopts a_i^*, thereby entering stage Vb, wherein there is *low vulnerability to new unanticipated challenges;*
2. If the answer is yes, then another question concerning costs and benefits is asked.

This question (in box 9) is:

Q9: Is a search for revised alternatives, and hence additional rows for inclusion in a new perspective at time $t + 2$ desirable?

This is equivalent to asking: Is $\acute{m}r(y_i(t + 1), \dots) \overset{s}{>} \acute{m}c(y_i(t + 1), \dots)$ given possible new challenges, $\mathcal{C}(t + 1)$, resulting from i's adopting $a_i^*(t + 1)$? If the answer to question 9 is no, then i adopts $a_i^*(t + 1)$, thereby entering stage Vb. On the other hand, if the answer is yes, then he returns to box 3 and conducts a new search for alternatives – advancing the reference time point by one unit at all stages.

The preceding sketch presents some of the basic elements of the Janis and Mann approach. It differs significantly from the rational approach of game theory, economics, and regional science. The latter would have the decision maker informed fully (or as fully as possible) about the payoff matrix and then have him (or her) choose that action that, for example, maximized his payoff as defined by some objective function. That is, he would know the outcome function $o = o(a, e)$, the probability distribution over the several states of the environment, and so on.

5.4   Evaluation and further extensions of the framework

In the previous section we attempted to reformulate and extend the Janis and Mann framework to facilitate the fusion of its strong points with valid aspects of other decision-making frameworks. There are several points at which improvement is possible. One concerns time pressure and its escalation, which we can designate escalatory time pressure, or simply *e-time pressure*. As a number of scholars have stated (e.g., Bronner 1982), time pressure is indicated by a shorter interval than normal before a decision must be made and where, in particular, decision makers are sensitive to the decrease in the time interval. As per Janis and Mann, psychological stress is present as well. However, more penetrating thinking on the time pressure concept is possible. For example, as already noted in section 2.7, Allan (1983) uses a concept of diplomatic time. He holds that (1) diplomatic time increases more rapidly than normal time when interactions (as measured by relevant events *weighted by their intensities*) occur more frequently than usual and (2) interactions themselves increase (decrease) with an increase (decrease) of diplomatic time. That is, more change can be packed into a given real-time interval when the frequency of events causes diplomatic time to run faster than normal time. Allan then proceeds to develop a model incorporating this concept into an arms race type of crisis, obviously relating diplomatic time (time pressure) to decisions on military expenditures and thus to actual realization of weapons production. We find this aspect of decision making under crisis conditions to be key; we prefer to talk about time pressure and its escalation, or *e*-time pressure, instead of diplomatic time since Allan's thinking applies to crisis situations beyond those in which diplomacy is involved.

At a still deeper level within this more "dynamic" framework, one needs to explain how a decision is reached and how *e*-time pressure affects the choice of an action. When we consider *e*-time pressure at any decision point of time, we may have in mind some initial sequence of events that increases somewhat the time pressure at that point followed by successive sequences of events, each sequence tending to increase the time pressure at any later decision point of time. Clearly, if at any decision point of time there is intense time pressure and less time (actual or perceived) in which to reach a decision, the payoff matrix becomes truncated. It may be truncated in terms of (1) the number of options (rows), or (2) the number of combinations of state of the environment and joint action of others (columns), or (3) the number of elements in the outcome in any cell (the cell magnitudes), or some combination of these. Thus as time pressure mounts, we may reach a situation where the payoff matrix becomes severely restricted to, say, just two rows [e.g., (1) be tough or (2) be willing to concede], or to just two columns (where the opponent is perceived to have two options, to cooperate or not to cooperate), or to just two magnitudes in each cell (e.g., one being win or lose the disputed territory and the other being number of casualties), or to some combination of these. In such a highly truncated payoff matrix situation there may be realization of possible trade-offs of the very limited type that Snyder (1978) has discussed, a type that he suggests Khrushchev may have made in the Cuban crisis (p. 365). The eliminated factors (and thus rows, columns, and outcome criteria corresponding to those factors) may be those that have been dropped because they fail to meet the "representativeness" criteria of Kahneman, Slovic, and Tversky (1982). Put another way, these eliminated factors may be those that do not appear in or are inconsistent with, for example, the immediate concerns in the evoked set of Jervis (1976) or the beliefs concerning political actions in the operational code of George (1969) and Holsti (1970). Such elimination may also be associated with the cognitive closure that occurs when a leader, in his (or her) emotion-free policy analysis, is tied (as per Gamson 1981) to an interpretive package of his political culture (also see Holsti 1986). For example, the option "friendly cooperation with the Soviet Union" was not permitted to enter the minds of U.S. political leaders in their decision making in many situations during that part of the interwar period when a strong anticommunism doctrine prevailed. Such would have denied the existing mental representations.

It is also the case that e-time pressure may become so severe that entrapment as per Brockner and Rubin (1985) occurs. That is, because of past investment of his (or her) time, effort, and other resources with respect to a given action and because of the extreme shortage of time to conduct a reappraisal of alternatives, the decision maker may feel compelled to continue with the given action (one row in a payoff matrix). Or the behaving unit may find himself in a *compellence*-type situation as per

Schelling (1966); that is, he may be put into a situation by his adversary that he has or perceives no choice if he wishes to avert disaster. Or he may be driven to behave according to rules and, as *cybernetic person* (Steinbruner, 1974), consider that single action that corresponds to the rule applicable in the given situation.

Or severe time pressure may lead the decision maker to perceive only one possible action by an opponent (i.e., only one possible combination of a state of the environment and joint action of other behaving units). For example, in studying 13 cases of brinkmanship in international crisis, Lebow (1981) finds that "in every instance brinkmanship was predicated upon the belief that the adversary in question would back down when challenged" (pp. 270–1). Specifically, this was the case, Lebow claims, when in July 1914 German leaders ignored the possibility of significant British resolve to support Russia and Serbia. In this case and the 12 others, one might claim that the "brinkman" perceived one and only one column in a payoff matrix that was explicitly in his or her mind.

Or severe time pressure may force the decision maker to consider or lead him or her to perceive one and only one relevant item in the possible set of outcomes. This type of situation may be said to characterize certain terrorist situations – such as that confronted by Carter in the 1980 hostage rescue attempt. There it may be said that at a particular point of time previous to the attempt, severe time pressure had forced Carter to focus entirely, or almost entirely, on a single outcome element, "bring the hostages home." He may have evaluated the outcome of any action he might take, except for one, as zero, whatever the several states of the environment and actions of others he may have considered realizable. That single exception was a rescue attempt, and even then he had to recognize that the outcome would be zero unless there was perfect coordination of efforts of those directly and indirectly involved in the rescue effort *and* a favorable physical environment (e.g., weather).

Or severe time pressure may force the decision maker to consider or lead him or her to perceive any combination of the preceding and thus knowingly or unknowingly truncate the payoff matrix, implicitly or explicitly.

At this point we may note how the foregoing discussion easily relates to the different kinds of deviations from rational decision making in crisis performance that Lebow (1981, p. 112) characterizes as *decision-making pathologies*. The pathology – *overvaluation of past performance as against present reality* – is simply perception of outcome values (greater when they give rise to positive utility, smaller when they give rise to disutility) that are significantly different from what the best analysis (models) would "objectively" establish for the action that corresponds to past performance. The second and third pathologies – *overconfidence in policies to which decision makers are committed* and *insensitivity to information critical of those policies* – often involve the same kind of perception, although there may also be misperceptions of the number and kinds of combinations of a state of the environment and joint actions of other behaving units that might correspond to the columns of a payoff matrix.

Obviously, the *cognitive consistency* principle of Jervis can also be related to the preceding discussion, in particular to insensitivity to new information inconsistent with a behaving unit's existing set of perceptions. However, we must recognize that cognitive consistency seeking is in certain respects desirable; it is an economic way by which to encode new information. In actuality, human beings and organizations extensively employ this principle.

We should also bear in mind the failure to perceive all the relevant elements (rows, columns, and outcome criteria of an explicit or implicit payoff matrix) when a decision-making unit is affected by "groupthink," a concept set forth by Janis (1972). There are eight major symptoms of groupthink (concurrence seeking tendency) that emerge from the study of historic fiascos by Janis and Mann (1977, pp. 130–1):

1. illusion of invulnerability leading to excessive optimism and greater willingness to take extreme risks;
2. collective rationalization and discounting of warnings about dangers and misinformation;
3. unquestioned belief in the group's inherent morality and rectitude;
4. stereotyped views of adversaries as too evil, weak, or stupid;
5. pressures and sanctions against members of the group who deviate or dissent;
6. self-censorship of such deviation or discussion;
7. a resulting shared illusion of unanimity; and
8. self-appointed mindguards who protect the group from questioning any adverse information regarding the effectiveness and morality of their decisions.

As these symptoms imply, groupthink is also responsible for

1. limiting the perceived range of alternative actions in emotion-laden situations (rows in a payoff matrix), as was indeed the case with the Johnson administration's decision to bomb North Vietnam (Janis 1971, p. 102ff.) or when fanatic religious leaders (Ayatollah Khomeini, a case in point) dominate politics; and
2. distorted estimation of outcomes (magnitudes in certain key cells), as was indeed the case when the Kennedy administration

was so wrong regarding its assumptions and expectations in the Bay of Pigs fiasco.

Further, we should bear in mind, as Janis and Mann emphasize, the effects of emotional elements. When such elements are present, they tend to reduce even more the rows, columns, and outcome criteria of any pay-off matrix that is perceived implicitly or explicitly by a behaving unit. An extreme case occurs where uncontrolled anger and extreme frustration take over when certain of an individual's actions are restricted, that is, when certain freedoms are eliminated and lead the decision maker to be reckless in assessment and inattentive to relevant outcomes – the *reactance* concept of Brehm and Brehm (1981). Also typical, emotion-laden organizational politics within an adversary's political community can lead to the completely irrational act of preemption causing mass destruction of all parties involved, a combination of a state of the environment and joint action of others that a nation's nuclear deterrence advocates may often fail to perceive.

5.5 Concluding remarks

In this chapter we have attempted to formalize the important contributions of Janis and Mann to decision making under psychological stress and crisis conditions. At least for some types of analysts the formalization undertaken permits a deeper appreciation of this contribution and the way it can be fused with the broad concepts of cognitive consistency, cognitive closure, decision-making pathologies, and the like. We introduced the concept of e-time pressure (a broadening of Allan's diplomatic time); and it is the presence of e-time pressure (a cumulating force) as a key factor that distinguishes decision making under crisis conditions from "ordinary" decision making. We view this "dynamic-type" concept as basic to any full definition of crisis. In particular, when we incorporate the concept of a payoff matrix and its elements into our framework, we generally conceive a crisis situation as one in which there has occurred and is occurring a continuous contraction of rows, or columns, or outcome criteria, or some combination of these in a payoff matrix, explicit or implicit in the mind(s) of one or more decision makers.

We have extensively introduced the concept of a payoff matrix as a further development of the Janis and Mann framework. The consideration of the elements of a payoff matrix permits significant disaggregation of the factors at play and thus, for some kinds of minds, deeper insight into the decision-making problem. When combined with the concept of e-time pressure, it enables one to see better how the concepts of highly limited trade-offs, representativeness, evoked set, operational code, interpretive package, entrapment, compellence, cybernetic person, hyper-vigilance, and reactance fit in with the broader concepts such as cognitive consistency seeking and decision-making pathologies. Moreover, the concept of the payoff matrix together with its elements will allow us in later chapters to incorporate, via fusion,

1. the analysis of political leaders selecting (supporting) platforms, sets of programs, and the like in policy space;
2. the structuring and presentation of political arguments to support one or more policies (programs); and
3. information search and research and development for major problem solving, with some attention to dynamical forces and learning that alters perceived payoff matrices.

References

Allan, P. (1983) *Crisis Bargaining and the Arms Race: A Theoretical Model.* Cambridge, MA: Ballinger.

Brehm, S. S., and J. W. Brehm (1981) *Psychological Reactance: A Theory of Freedom and Control.* New York: Academic Press.

Brockner, J., and J. Z. Rubin (1985) *Entrapment in Escalating Conflicts: A Social Psychological Analysis.* New York: Springer-Verlag.

Bronner, R. (1982) *Decision Making under Time Pressure.* Lexington, MA: D. C. Heath.

Gamson, W. (1981) "The Political Culture of the Arab–Israeli Conflict." *Conflict Management and Peace Science* 5(2):79–94.

George, A. (1969) "The 'Operational Code': A Neglected Approach to the Study of Political Leaders and Decision-Making." *International Studies Quarterly* 13(June):190–222.

Herek, G., I. Janis, and P. Huth (1987) "Decision Making During International Crisis." *Journal of Conflict Resolution* 31(2, June):203–26.

Hermann, C. F., and R. E. Mason (1980) "Identifying Attributes of Events that Trigger International Crises." In O. R. Holsti, R. M. Siverson, and A. George (eds.), *Change in the International System.* Boulder: Westview Press.

Holsti, O. R. (1970) "The 'Operational Code' Approach to the Study of Political Leaders." *Canadian Journal of Political Science* 32:123–55.

Holsti, O. R. (1986) "Crises, and Ways to Keep Them from Escalating." In R. K. White (ed.), *Psychology and the Prevention of Nuclear War.* New York: New York University Press, pp. 419–31.

Hopple, G. W., and P. J. Rossa (1981) "International Crisis Analysis: Recent Developments and Future Directions." In P. T. Hopmann, D. A. Zinnes, and J. D. Singer (eds.), *Cumulation in International Relations Research.* Monograph Series in World Affairs, Vol. 18. Denver: University of Denver, pp. 65–97.

Isard, W., T. E. Smith, P. Isard, T. H. Tung, and M. Dacey (1969) *General Theory: Social, Political, Economic and Regional.* Cambridge, MA: MIT Press.

Isard, W., and C. Smith (1982) *Conflict Analysis and Practical Conflict Management Procedures: An Introduction to Peace Science.* Cambridge, MA: Ballinger.

Janis, I. (1972) *Victims of Group Think.* Boston: Houghton Mifflin.

Janis, I., and L. Mann (1977) *Decision Making: A Psychological Analysis of Conflict, Choice, and Commitment.* New York: Free Press.

Jervis, R. (1976) *Perception and Misperception in International Politics.* Princeton: Princeton University Press.

Kahneman, D., P. Slovic, and A. Tversky (1982) *Judgement under Uncertainty: Heuristics and Biases.* Cambridge: Cambridge University Press.

Lebow, R. N. (1981) *Between Peace and War: The Nature of International Crisis.* Baltimore: Johns Hopkins.

Robinson, J. A. (1972) "Crisis: An Appraisal of Concepts and Theories." In C. F. Hermann (ed.), *International Crises: Insights from Behavioral Research.* New York: Free Press, pp. 3–17, 20–38.

Schelling, T. C. (1966) *Arms and Influence.* New Haven: Yale University Press.

Snyder, J. L. (1978) "Rationality at the Brink: The Role of Cognitive Processes in Failures of Deterrence." *World Politics* 30:345–65.

Steinbruner, J. (1974) *The Cybernetic Theory of Decision.* Princeton: Princeton University Press.

CHAPTER 6

Learning, problem solving, and information research and development

6.1 Introduction

In section 4.2 we dealt in part with the process of learning. There we considered learning as a result of experience. A behaving unit chose an action a_i from his (or her) perceived restricted action space $P_i(\tilde{A}_i)$, expecting a state of affairs covering a set of actions $\{\hat{a}_k\}$ of all other behaving units and his perception $P_i(e)$ of the state of the environment. He expected an outcome $\hat{o}_i$ as given by

$$\hat{o}_i = \hat{o}_i(a_i, \{\hat{a}_k\}, P_i(e)) \tag{6.1.1}$$

The choice of action a_i was consistent with optimizing on some set of objectives.

In actuality, at the next point in time, an outcome o_i occurred as a result of the actual state of the environment, e, that was realized and the joint action $\{a_k\}$ of other participants that took place, the outcome being determined by the *real* objective outcome function:

$$o = o(a, e) \tag{6.1.2}$$

At this point of time, his (or her) perceiving (1) the elements of the actual outcome relevant to him, $P_i(o_i)$, (2) the realized joint action of other behaving units, $P_i(a_k)$, and (3) the realized state of the environment $P_i(e)$ and his making implicitly or explicitly comparisons with what was expected constitutes learning from experience. Such learning was characterized as *ex post* learning (learning after the action). The next time he takes an action, he has this learning in his memory, to the extent that it has been recorded (if not ignored) and then not forgotten; and such may be pertinent in the choice of the action.[1]

---

[1] As will be discussed in section 6.4 this behaving unit's perception of $o_i(t)$, $\{a_k(t)\}$, and $e(t)$ may be said to constitute an observation (a vector of signals) from an "experiment." Thus

In this chapter we are concerned with another aspect of learning, namely, that learning that involves major problem solving (touched upon in section 4.2). Such requires additional knowledge before an action can be selected, at least in the judgment of the behaving unit. Such was characterized as *ex ante* learning (learning before the action). Here is where *search* is required and where we can speak of the need for *information research and development*. Of course, no clear line of demarcation exists between learning from experience and learning from information research and development. In learning from experience, the behaving unit may pause, look up in the dictionary the meaning of a word, consult a handbook for the proper formula to use in calculating interest income, call up a friend or professional associate to obtain advice, and the like, thus involving research, albeit minimal. In Chapter 5, we did consider stages in stressful situations where there is search for alternatives, especially when the decision making involves vigilant information processing. But what we wish to emphasize here is information and research development in problem solving where psychological stress and time constraints are not pressing and where the behaving unit conducts vigilant information processing but acutely needs to go beyond such.

In the cognitive sciences, much has been written on problem solving. Typically, however, this literature has related to well-defined problems such as the "missionaries–cannibals"[2] problem or game playing such as chess, where the initial situation, allowable actions, and goals are clearly set forth. In reviewing the problem-solving approaches of this literature, Anderson (1985) notes among others:

1. the *difference reduction method* where one solves a problem by setting subgoals to be achieved where the achievement of each reduces the differences between the current state and the goal state;
2. the *working-backward method* where one breaks a goal into a set of subgoals whose solutions logically lead to solution of the original goal;
3. the *analogy method* where one uses the structure of the solution to one problem to guide the solution to another problem; and
4. the *means–end method* where one selects actions (operators) to

one may view *ex post* learning as resulting from one or more observations in a sequence of experiments. For example, see Kihlstrom, Mirman, and Postlewaite (1984) on experimental consumption and the learning that takes place.

[2] Three missionaries and three cannibals are on one side of a river. They have a boat that can carry two people at a time across the river. If at any time there are more cannibals than missionaries on one side of the river, the missionaries will be eaten. How can all six persons be carried safely across to the other side of the river?

reduce the differences between current state and the goal state but *where one also transforms the current state* so that the needed actions can apply.

In the next section, we discuss the analogy method as one way of problem solving via mental model construction. In section 6.3, we discuss the means–end method as one of the artificial intelligence approaches to problem solving. Then, in section 6.4 we view problem solving from an economist's angle as investment in information research and development. Some evaluative and concluding remarks are made in section 6.5; and in Chapters 14–16 on advanced analysis we present much more technical materials relating to *ex ante* learning and information research and development.

The current chapter relates, of course, to the learning that is essential for political leaders in arms control and other international negotiations and foreign policy formation. Although we have little to say substantively, the discussion should make us aware of and provide some insight into the difficulties for political leaders to acquire such learning. In crisis situations where there is insufficient time for problem-solving learning, the thinking in this chapter is not particularly relevant.

6.2   Problem solving as mental model construction

When we come to the problem solving faced by behaving units in international conflict situations, we find that typically problems are ill-defined. Thus, to repeat, most of the discussion in the cognitive sciences on methods and experimental findings does not directly apply, although extremely useful insights are provided. Usually, it becomes necessary first to construct initial mental models of the current situation, often unclear and uncertain as to relevant variables and environmental characteristics, and proceed from there with newly conceived *creative* actions to a goal that itself can be only vaguely stated. In this connection, the work of Holyoak (1983; also Gick and Holyoak 1980, 1983) is enlightening.

Holyoak claims that (as noted in section 4.2) new ideas do not arise out of nothing. Rather, they are the result of intelligent, goal-directed transformations of existing knowledge. The core for the genesis of ideas is the concept of a mental model (a scheme, or mental representation) – a psychological depiction of the environment and its expected behavior. A mental model is, however, not a complete depiction. Rather, as we all know, it is an abstraction that preserves in its frame correspondences between elements (components) that are relevant (causally and otherwise) in the real world. Also, the model preserves both static relationships and, to the extent that we can indicate, the dynamics of relationships – that is, transition functions, to use Holyoak's terminology. A model thus ignores nonessential elements of the modeled domain.

Before a behaving unit undertakes to solve a problem – for example, how to cope with maintaining national security or with famine from a sudden crop failure – the unit must be aware that (1) something is amiss, contradictory, and the like and (2) it (the unit) is unable to take an immediate action to cope with (resolve) the difficulty. Next, the unit must begin to analyze the situation and construct an initial *problem model*. In general, a problem model, whether initial or not, parallels the utility-maximizing framework of section 4.2, a framework that has four central components:

1. *The goal,* or more generally, the *maximum (or minimum) value to be obtained for a set of objectives embraced in an objective function.* Initially, the goal, or objective function, may be vague, too general, or otherwise inadequately specified and may be adequately specified (if at all) only after much struggle and effort in coping with the problem.
2. *Objects,* that is, relevant *inputs* (e.g., resources), *outputs* (tanks), and the like. Again, these objects may not be well specified initially and only become so as attempts are made to cope with the problem.
3. *Operators,* that is, *actions,* that can potentially transform the object elements, there being the possibility of a zero operator (do nothing). Initially, the operators may be inappropriate. Holyoak indicates that a behaving unit can also posit an abstract operator (as transform lead into gold), which by definition is not technically feasible and therefore is not included in the economist's action space A_i. However, although an abstract operator is technically infeasible, the recognition of its infeasibility may help lead to the specification of new, creative, technically feasible actions.
4. *Constraints,* such as resource constraints, technical know-how, laws, and actions of other behaving units, briefly discussed in section 4.2 but that also include noneconomic and other sociopolitical constraints not indicated there; some of these relevant constraints may not be initially recognized by the behaving unit or may not be properly appreciated.

As already indicated, once the behaving unit is aware that something is amiss with which it cannot cope, it examines this initial problem model (which it constructs or had already constructed) – a model that in one or more aspects is too vague, inadequate, and thus inapplicable. To transform the initial-problem model (based upon schemata, mental representations, and the like, which the behaving unit has in mind or immediately retrieves from memory), the behaving unit may search for information. Such requires actions (the use of operators) and involves time and effort whether the information is (a) generated internally, or (b) secured from the external world, or, in the usual case, (c) both. (In section 6.4, we shall examine the question of how much time and effort to invest in the acquisition of information.)

The task of transforming an initial-problem model that is ill-defined into an effective model and ultimately a satisfactory one is set forth by Holyoak using the concepts of morphism, homomorphism, and isomorphism. He takes a morphism to be a mapping of the elements (states and actions) of one set of such into the elements (states and actions) of a second set of such. This correspondence is maintained when the actions lead to transformed elements, that is, the mapping is preserved under corresponding state changes. However, Holyoak has in mind valid models of the real world wherein the relationship between the external world and a model is a homomorphism – a morphism[3] in which the mapping is many-to-one. Specifically, to him, a good problem model captures the core (basic) structure of the real world and can depict many world problem situations that differ from one another in noncausal and otherwise irrelevant detail.[4]

Holyoak uses a figure such as Figure 6.1 to depict a good problem model. The top of the figure is constructed to represent the real world, namely, (1) the problem situation (initial state) $S(t)$, (2) goal-satisfying states of $S(t + \theta)$ to be reached after time period θ, and (3) potential sequences of actions $\{a(t), a(t + 1), \ldots, a(t + \theta)\}$ (or sets of actions)[5] that yield corresponding sequences of state changes in reaching these goal-satisfying states. This real world is, however, not completely known, not

---

[3] In what follows, we shall not use the terms "morphism" and "homomorphism" since we prefer to reserve them for use according to their strict, rigorous mathematical definitions, as in group theory. With regard to a morphism, e.g., Gilbert (1976) states: "Let $(S, *)$ and $(T, \circ)$ be two algebraic structures consisting of the sets S and T, together with binary operators $*$ on S and $\circ$ on T. Then a function $f: S \to T$ is said to be a morphism from $(S, *)$ to $(T, \circ)$ if for every $x, y \in S$

$$f(x*y) = f(x) \circ f(y)$$

If these structures contain more than one operation, the morphism must preserve all these operations. Furthermore, if the structures have identities, these must be preserved too" (pp. 5–6).

[4] For example, a model of the dynamics of airplane operation applies to the many airplanes differing only in the color of seats; hence Holyoak would consider it a homomorphism.

[5] That is, $\{a_1(\eta), a_2(\eta), \ldots, a_n(\eta)\}; \eta = t, t + 1, t + 2, \ldots, t + \theta\}$.

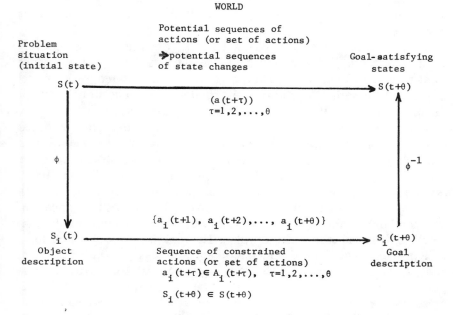

Figure 6.1. A problem model as a homomorphism.

only at current time t, but especially at time points $t + 1, \ldots, t + \theta$. The behaving unit must then identify

1. an initial set of relevant objects $S_i(t)$, the *object description*, which in Figure 6.1 involves a mapping ϕ of $S(t)$ into $S_i(t)$);
2. an initial conception of one or more states that would be satisfactory corresponding to the goal description $S_i(t + \theta)$ in Figure 6.1; and
3. a sequence of constrained actions, $\{a_i(t), a_i(t + 1), \ldots, a_i(t + \theta)\}$, a *transition function*, that will lead to a satisfying state, that is, a *solution plan*.[6]

If a proper problem-solving model has been developed, as represented by the bottom of Figure 6.1, then the inverse mapping ϕ^{-1}, when applied to the satisfactory goal state identified by that model, should yield a set

---

[6] In many ways this view of problem solving resembles that of the economist and regional scientist. The task, in their words, is to construct a model that is a replica of the real world, which similar to a mental model preserves in its frame correspondences between elements that are relevant (causally and otherwise) in the real world and preserves static relationships and, where possible, dynamic ones.

$S(t + \theta)$ of possible goal-satisfying states of the real world, and one of these states should be realized in the real world when the solution plan is implemented.

What happens if the problem model thus constructed is not entirely valid, if the homomorphism is incomplete? This may be so either because some causally relevant aspects of the world are not captured by the model or because the series of actions in the model does not accurately mirror the relevant parts of the transition function of the world.

Another attempt may then be made to acquire information to be added to or to replace existing information. Often, however, a well-defined problem model is not attained; the problem-solving process becomes stuck. Existing schemata, mental representations, and the like, plus information, do not work. At this point Holyoak introduces modeling with analogies.[7] To elucidate this process, Holyoak introduces the concept of a *base* model. Defining a *target* model to be the well-defined model that identifies a satisfactory solution plan, Holyoak introduces search for a base problem – one that is understood and similar to the target problem and perhaps suggested by cues from the target problem. A useful base problem "will be one that (1) can itself be successfully modeled and (2) preserves the critical causal features relevant to an adequate solution to the target problem" (p. 206). The base problem may or may not have fewer elements and may or may not be simpler than the target.

Holyoak uses a figure such as Figure 6.2 to illustrate the relation between a base problem model and the target problem, the relation of the latter to the real world remaining the same. Essentially, Holyoak maps (Ψ) the causally relevant elements of the base model into the target model, thereby identifying a well-defined target problem having a workable solution plan. Ideally, the mapping should be isomorphic – that is, one-to-one regarding objects, sequence of actions (transition function), and goal description. In practice, this second-order modeling will fall short of this ideal, and the resulting target model, if adequate, may be obtained only after several stages of improvement wherein the elements of the target modeled may be reviewed and redefined to avoid structure-violating differences with the base problem.

In his studies, Holyoak distinguishes between intradomain and interdomain analogies, the latter involving different domains of knowledge, where the analogy "is in effect a kind of metaphor, based on the percep-

---

[7] Strictly speaking, Holyoak develops his analogy approach having in mind the use of a behaving unit's internal information alone. We extend his frame to include analogies using external information alone or in combination with internal information. For other related literature, see Wicklegren (1974), Wallsten (1980), Polson and Jeffries (1982), Sternberg (1982), Estes (1982), and Gardner (1983).

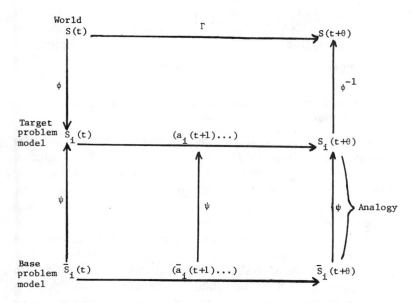

Figure 6.2. An analogy with the model for a base problem can be used to construct a model for a target problem.

tion of structural similarities hidden beneath a veneer of surface differences" (p. 208). He also notes how the use of a specific base analogy to develop a target model may also lead to the construction of a more general model (an abstract problem schema) applicable to a broader range of problems.

To illustrate the fruitful use of an interdomain analogy, we may refer to the gravity model now used extensively in economics, regional science, Peace Science, and other social science areas. Here gravitational force, mutual energy, and other concepts of Newtonian physics have been reformulated to help to understand and project trade flows among nations and regions, communication levels, the spread of conflict among nations, and other spatial phenomena. For example, see O'Loughlin (1986).

The use of analogies is one line of attack in problem solving that may be effective. So is the addition of information – which allows the deepening of analysis and theoretical development at different points in the problem-solving activity and is consistent with vigilant information processing as per Janis and Mann and the critical need to go beyond. So may the elimination of information and accepted theories that stand in the way of new creative thinking. So may the sharpening (perhaps step by step) of old concepts and the development of new ones (perhaps by intuitive leaps) to facilitate interdomain transfers of analytical methods. So may the use of artificial intelligence (AI) and computer simulation, to which we now turn.

6.3   The use of artificial intelligence (AI) and other problem-solving methods oriented to external information

As already noted, the use of analogies for problem solving may at times not require external information, that is, can be based solely on internal knowledge and mental inputs. When we come to the use of AI methods, external knowledge and labor and capital inputs (in the regular economic sense) are necessarily involved. Information investment questions arise, the economies of which we shall address in the next section.

Artificial intelligence as a problem-solving method when conflicts, in particular international conflicts, are of concern is a computer-based process. It has often taken the form of a means–end approach. It starts from a given state (situation) that can be defined as the set of initial objects. It then searches for a path – a set of relevant subgoals – for reaching one or more goals – the set of desired objects – as an end (a desired state). Once appropriate subgoals have been identified and judged effective in terms of goal achievement, it applies means, that is, relevant heuristics, to reach these subgoals; in essence, it operates on the set of initial objects and transforms them. If a subgoal is not reached by following a given heuristic, then another is tried and then another until the subgoal is attained. If a subgoal cannot be attained after all heuristics have been applied, then a new set of relevant subgoals must be identified and evaluated and heuristics applied to attain them. And so forth, until the set of desired objects is achieved or the search for a solution to the problem abandoned.

Paraphrasing Newell and Simon (1972, p. 416), we note:

1. If a given object is not one that is desired, differences will be detected between the given object and the desired one.
2. Operators (serving as means) affect some features of the objects operated on and leave others unchanged. Hence operators can be characterized by the changes they produce and used to try to eliminate or narrow down differences between the objects on which they operate and desired objects.
3. If a selected operator is not applicable, it may be useful to change its inputs so that it does become applicable.
4. Some differences will prove more difficult to affect than others. Hence it is desirable to eliminate "difficult" differences even at

the cost of introducing new differences of lesser difficulty. This process can be continued as long as progress is being made toward eliminating the more difficult differences.

The AI model based on the use of computers as an information-processing system is designed by some of its ambitious proponents to simulate the entire range of human problem solving. It has large storage capacity that holds complex strategies (programs) that may be evoked by stimuli. The stimulus that occurs determines which one or more strategies will be put into operation; the content of these strategies is already determined by previous experience and know-how. Thus the system is able to respond to a simple stimulus in complex and highly selective ways.

The technique *general problem solver (GPS)* as set forth by Newell and Simon (1972) has been applied to many problem-solving situations to solve on the one hand simple, well-defined problems such as the missionaries–cannibals problem and on the other hand an exceedingly complex problem such as playing chess, which as yet is not well defined. For example, in the missionaries–cannibals problem (see footnote 2, this chapter), it turns out that to achieve the goal where all three missionaries and all three cannibals have crossed from one side to the second side of the river, the subgoal SG_1 of three missionaries and two cannibals on the second side must be achieved so that the operation having one cannibal return to the first side to pick up the remaining cannibal on that side can be applied. But to achieve subgoal SG_1, a previous subgoal SG_2 must have been achieved, namely, three missionaries and one cannibal on the second side so that the operation having one cannibal return to the first side to pick up a second cannibal on the side can be applied. But to achieve subgoal SG_2, a previous subgoal SG_3 must have been achieved, namely, two missionaries and two cannibals on the second side,[8] and so on.

When we consider the ill-defined complicated problem of winning at chess (when playing against a grand master), the GPS and other AI models fail. This is because the number of possible pathways for an entire

[8] So that the operation having one missionary and one cannibal return to the first side so that two missionaries can travel to the second side can be applied. But to achieve subgoal SG_3, a previous subgoal SG_4 must have been achieved, namely, three cannibals on the second side so that the operation having one cannibal return to the first side so that two missionaries can travel to the second side can be applied. But to achieve subgoal SG_4, a previous subgoal SG_5 must have been achieved, namely, two cannibals on the second side so that the operation having one cannibal return to the first side so that he or she can return to the second side with the third cannibal can be applied. But to achieve subgoal SG_5, the operation, which is the very first operation, having two cannibals row from the first side to the second side is to be applied. [See Solso (1979, p. 400) for a pictorial representation.]

game, namely, about 10^{120}, cannot be stored and examined by even the most sophisticated computers imaginable. Hence, an AI approach cannot be built upon an algorithm (a procedure that guarantees a solution) but upon heuristics (sets of empirical rules or strategies that operate as a rule of thumb). But when it comes to heuristics in chess, which essentially involves "chunk" information about the situation of specific pieces and the concentrated attention on developing a strategy around sensitive pieces and moves, a machine as yet cannot outdo a grand master. A machine just cannot account for the diversity, complexity, and economy of the human mind to recognize patterns within a brief exposure.

In brief, for problems where rapid and voluminous mathematical search-and-match activity can be applied, an AI approach has great potential for finding solutions in an efficient manner. Where the need is to extract meaningful cues from an enormously complex world of sensory information, to call forth first-round mental models and representations of relationships of features and variables from those cues and in turn still more involved (higher order) relationships and associations, and to develop well-articulated cognitive plans while at the same time keeping these internal operations consistent with the external reality, the AI computer-based approach can only crudely approximate the capacities of the human being. Yet there is great promise in having computer models simulate the way human subjects solve problems. This is so (1) in terms of facilitating new effective solutions by humans and (2) through efforts at modeling human memory systems (active and passive), memory elements, central processors, coding techniques, retrieval pathways, and so on, in understanding how in fact human cognitive processes proceed.[9] In these two ways AI models have great potential and are eligible objects for investment purposes.

There are still other models of problem solving. Another one of interest but overlapping those discussed is that of Greeno (1972, 1978). With him, attended-to information enters *short-term memory,* which has a very limited capacity and from which information is easily retrieved. Here the problem is perceived and passes on to *working memory.* Working memory constructs an organized and coded cognitive tree where, for example, for a mathematical problem there would be an organized and coded list

---

[9] There are, of course, limits to the ability of computers to simulate problem solving by humans. One limit follows from the fact that computers are single minded and not subject to distraction (as when the doorbell rings, or a fire engine passes by, or a thunderstorm suddenly occurs) or to random mistakes and slips of memory as the human does when solving a problem – sometimes having in mind other problems and switching back and forth between them in an unpredictable fashion.

For other related discussion see Simon (1978a,b) and Dehn and Shank (1982).

of variables. It then constructs a network of connections between the given variables and the specification of the elements and relationships that could comprise a solution together with the required operators on the variables. Such are developed from information rules, relationships, and theory held in *long-term memory,* which information in turn may make it necessary to revise the network structure held in working memory.

As the strict version of the Holyoak model, the Greeno model and others in their concentration on cognitive processes still do not depict the task of problem solving with sufficient breadth. They fail to capture the decision (a cognitive process) to search for new information – why, when, and how it is made or not made. This decision, whether conscious or not, is an inextricable part of problem solving, a question however that may not be able to be properly addressed until the cognitive sciences have achieved considerably more progress. Nonetheless, it is useful to consider the question from the external standpoint of economics, operations research, regional science, and (external) conflict management.

6.4   Investment in information research and development for problem solving

In the previous two sections we presented the best available thinking on problem solving by humans, particularly on the type of ill-defined problems that are associated with the making of foreign policy by a nation and in decision making regarding international conflicts. These approaches are more realistic than the so-called rational approaches of economics, regional science, and operations research, which we briefly covered in sections 3.2 and 3.3. Yet the rational approaches are of great value. They are able to suggest directions for improvement of the current ways in which humans solve problems and in particular to suggest fruitful areas for further information collection, processing (external), and evaluation. The basic notion from game theory of a payoff matrix serves a fundamental need in this regard.

At this point, let us set down systematically the various reasons already discussed why a behaving unit may have needs and demands for information research and development – needs and demands because a behaving unit's store of information is incorrect, inadequate, improperly organized, poorly processed, and insufficiently exposed to the flow of currently generated information. These needs and demands exist for several reasons:

(1) The behaving unit has limited capacity to store knowledge – whether relating to facts, concepts, relationships, schemata, other mental

models and representations, stories, and theories. Hence, a problem to be solved may create a demand for new items of information of any of the types just listed. Such new information may replace rather than simply add to the stock of information, especially when that stock contains obsolete or irrelevant information. Hence we may imagine that with regard to the unit's implicit or explicit payoff matrix there may be

(a) new rows added to or replacing existing rows indicating the reality of possible actions previously not known to the unit;

(b) new columns each representing a combination of actions of others and a state of the environment that had not been known; or

(c) new expected outcome items for both the unit and others in one or more cells (such as one of Burton's universal values, of which the behaving unit was not aware) and which may have resulted from discarding an old theory and adopting a new one in its place, thereby leading to changed expectations.

(2) The behaving unit has limited ability at perception. Hence what he (or she) has perceived in any given situation during his past life may not have encompassed all the relevant information of the types cited in the preceding. Hence a problem to be solved may require that his perception of relevant situations in the past be supplemented by information about pertinent things he failed to perceive. Further, because of limited experiences, travel, associations with diverse groups and like activity, his store of perceptions lacks the breadth required for solving a problem. He may have made inadequate "investment" in such activity in the past because he (and society) may not have foreseen that he would need to confront the current problem at the present point of time or he may simply have misjudged the benefits from such activity.

(3) The behaving unit may have incorrect information in stock, misperceptions, wrong images, and the like. Part of this may have been due to his (or her) use, consciously or unconsciously, of a cognitive consistency principle. In effect, he may have interpreted events, relationships, and situations in such a way as to fit them into schemata, other mental models, and theories that he was taught by society and accumulated from experience and that allowed him to see what he wanted to see. Thus he would have discarded nonconfirming information inconsistent with the preceding and perceptions that did not jibe and left him uncomfortable, and so forth.

(4) The behaving unit may have limited know-how to process information, his (or her) brain's functional architecture may be insufficiently developed, and his tool kit of rules of thumb, standard operating procedures, algorithms, AI procedures, programming methods, and other ana-

lytical devices may be exceedingly small. Consequently, his ability to reason based upon stored strategies and planning techniques may not be up to the level required by the problem he confronts.

(5) The behaving unit's thinking may be strongly conditioned by the views, interpretive packages, and political culture of his (or her) group (nation). He may not be sufficiently aware of those of an out-group and other groups (nations) and their members (constituents). He may have refrained from thinking dissonantly or seeking information that might have weakened the raison d'être and thus the cohesiveness and morale of his group. He may also have had a strong need to identify with a group and thus not to question the correctness of its statements, the validity of its objectives, the means it employed to achieve them, and so on.

(6) The behaving unit may be subject to emotional states that preclude a proper use of his (or her) stock of knowledge, his store of perceptions, and his brain's functional architecture. Socialization processes may have ingrained within him a need for achievement, power, identity, and affiliation, as already mentioned, as well as a constant and persistent need to "save face." Thus when making consequential decisions under conditions of stress and uncertainty, let alone crisis, he may be subject to one of more of Lebow's decision-making pathologies:

(a) overvaluation of past performance;
(b) overconfidence in policies or ways of using information and rules in decision making to which he has recently subscribed and has been committed; and
(c) insensitivity to information critical of these policies, ways, and rules.

(7) As a result of all these factors, which overlap with one another, he (or she) may have surrounded himself with an inadequate network of communication channels. He may currently receive newspapers and magazines and be exposed to other media that provide information and analyses that support his beliefs, whereas he is not exposed to, or even aware of, information media generating conflicting information and analyses. Or he may have failed to be up to date and expose himself to new media and new channels (as in establishing contact with new political regimes). Or he may have allowed certain of his communication channels to be congested and clogged up. Or he may even have closed some (as when nations break off diplomatic relations). And so forth. As a consequence of all these factors and others, the behaving unit may have need for information and for research and development and other activities that produce information.

From the standpoint of an analytical economist, information is in many respects a good. Hence, the demand for it should be matched by a supply of it. In the usual case this will be so if the demander is willing to pay a high enough price (therewith to provide the incentive for production) and if from a technical standpoint the information can be produced. Sources of supply yield information at different costs, some important sources being

1. a unit's own observations over time and own research;
2. general news services such as publications and radio;
3. findings of formal research organizations;
4. findings through contracts with professional consultants and research centers; and
5. social associations with individuals (friends, relatives, and colleagues).

However, the supply of information almost invariably represents an investment since the very use of information, unlike the consumption of, say, a typical economic good such as bread, does not reduce its magnitude. Hence new information that is produced and considered relevant and thus recorded (encoded) in the mind of a behaving unit remains as part of the stock (memory) of that unit even though immediately used and even though it may be transmitted to other behaving units.

What is information? To a modern economic theorist, each bit of information is a signal. A price is a signal emanating from a market. The estimated magnitude of GNP is another. A nation's iron and steel production is still another, and so forth.[10] Theoretically, in the economist's mind there should be one or more signals associated with the value or other pertinent attribute of all relevant variables that should be at all moments under consideration. This is so whether or not the behaving unit is aware

[10] Note, however, that the economist does not attempt to define a "unit" of information. Although he or she recognizes that according to engineering theory of the Shannon type, two bits of information may be equal as units, he or she emphasizes that there may be large differences in the economic costs and benefits associated with these two bits (Marshak and Radner 1972). Yet, the economist does compare in an ordinal sense the information conveyed by two different experiments, i.e., by two different pieces of statistical evidence. For example, one experiment may be considered more informative than another if all behaving units with an interest in a parameter about which the two experiments provide evidence prefer to base an action on the evidence provided by the former rather than that provided by the latter. Or, one experiment may be considered more informative than a second if the first is sufficient for the second in a statistical sense. Or, where an uncertainty function is taken as a measure of the uncertainty associated with a probability distribution, one experiment is more informative than a second if, where an a priori distribution is given, for all uncertainty functions the expected uncertainty of the a posteriori distribution resulting from the first experiment is lower than the expected uncertainty of the posteriors resulting from the second experiment. Or one experiment is more informative than a second if the standard measure of the first experiment is more risky than the standard measure of the latter. See Kihlstrom (1984), who discusses the equivalence of these four ordinal statements and the current inability to derive a cardinal measure of the amount of information.

of all these variables.[11] Though the economist typically finds it convenient to assume that the unit is fully aware of these variables, in actuality the behaving unit is most (if not all) of the time unaware of the relevance of certain variables and is inadequately informed about others. In particular, he (or she) may not have received or been alert to signals recording past and present values and attributes of some of the relevant variables. Moreover, he lacks future values essential for proper decision making even were he to focus on just critical variables – for example, future prices when an investment decision is to be made or future missile stocks of his adversary when a decision on new weapon development is to be taken. In short, he confronts great uncertainty about the past and present and particularly about the future and thus is motivated to search for information, certainly in the sphere of problem solving with which we are concerned.

Frequently, the economist views the behaving unit, whether an individual or organization, as starting off with an a priori probability distribution over the space of all possible signals that he (or she) or anyone else might conceivably receive now and in the future. These signals must be viewed broadly. Some might relate to the actions and action spaces of other units (especially his competitors and supporters), some might relate to the attributes of the environment (physical, social, and political), and some might relate to the likely outcomes of his actions – all contributing to the basic background for decision making. A signal (when observed and encoded) may then be viewed as any event capable of altering the prior probability distribution and yielding thereby a posterior distribution. This transformation (or reaffirmation) of probabilities is precisely what constitutes the acquisition of information.

We may depict this view in terms of our basic concept of an actual or perceived payoff matrix. At any moment, with respect to all variables involved, a perfectly informed behaving unit would confront a payoff matrix with innumerable columns and rows. Each column would represent some combination of actions of other units and a state of the environment. Each row would represent a possible action (strategy) of the unit. Each cell would record the estimated outcome or prospect (a probability distribution over outcomes). All the attributes of each action, state, and estimated outcome would be fully specified. However, in actuality, for reasons already stated, the unit perceives (correctly or incor-

---

[11] These types of statements are consistent with the general equilibrium frameworks of the economist. See Arrow and Debreu (1954) and Debreu (1959). They also can be extended to cover a general interregional economic and political equilibrium framework. See Isard et al. (1969, chaps. 13, 14), where political behaving units are incorporated. However, both these frameworks are still inadequate in the sense that they cannot deal effectively with the uncertainty of the future. See Arrow (1984, chap. 11).

192   I. Basic framework and set of analyses

rectly) a limited number of columns, rows, and outcomes and a limited set of their attributes. Moreover, when a major problem is to be solved by the unit, the unit, say, individual *i,* may reflect the fact that he or she (1) is not aware of or does not have access to information (signals) that exists about which he or she needs to be educated or (2) requires basic information that does not exist and needs to be developed. In reality, then, *i* implicitly or explicitly perceives a limited number of columns and assigns to each a zero or nonzero probability and a limited number of outcome attributes in each cell.[12]

subset of critical signals, partly because of the knowledge assumption that the economist makes and the resulting narrower set of problem-solving actions that he (or she) considers. Typically, the information-theorist economist takes as given the action space (the set of alternatives) of the behaving unit – partly because his actions frequently relate to a given (known) stock of resources and more important the *current state of technology.* But in general, a unit confronting a major problem – as when none of his actions lead to an expected outcome that is satisfactory (when he perceives, e.g., that each of his actions implies warfare) – may be motivated to (1) search for new actions (payoff matrix rows) of which he is currently unaware and may involve new technology and organization and thus lie outside the current socioeconomic structure as well as (2) investigate more carefully the possibility of *outcome attributes* from other combinations of actions of other units and environmental states (payoff matrix columns).[13]

Despite the restriction on the class of problems which the economist treats, it is useful to set down certain insights that he has acquired given his framework.[14] First, because of the limited capabilities of the behaving

[12] At the risk of repetition, we note that he (or she) becomes conscious of the existence of a problem when, given the way he uses his subjective probabilities (if he does employ them), he perceives that none of his actions leads to an expected outcome that is satisfactory. (He may perceive, e.g., that each of his actions implies warfare.) In reality, then, the unit does have a prior distribution of probabilities, in line with thinking characteristics of the modern economic theorist, and it may be thought of as extending over the space of all possible signals that *i* or anyone else might conceivably receive now and in the future. Only, because of *i*'s limited capability and stock of knowledge, many of these probabilities may be implicitly set at zero. Hence, when a signal (as defined by an economist) is received by him that he considers relevant in his problem situation, that signal changes or reaffirms his probability distribution.
[13] In this regard, see Langlois (1984), who points out how the neoclassical economic literature on information and uncertainty fails to give proper attention to what he designates imperfect structural information.
[14] Further development of many of the points in the following discussion is contained in Arrow (1984, vol. 4); Marschak and Radner (1972); Lamberton (1974); Spence (1974); Grossman, Kihlstrom, and Mirman (1977); Dasgupta, Gilbert, and Stiglitz (1982, 1983); Killingsworth (1982); Fixler (1983); Machlup and Mansfield (1983); Wright (1983); Gallini and Kotowicz (1985); and Morgan and Manning (1985).

unit and related factors, often described in organization theory as the *limited span of control,* one may expect a type of diminishing returns to steady, constant doses of new information (signals), particularly during any unit of time. Moreover, even if exposure to signals is costless, still to encode it in the mind (or otherwise record it) involves a use of a scarce resource and diminishing returns in such a case. Second, information is not only an investment – since once a relevant signal (including signals on possible new alternatives or actions) is received, it is recorded in one's memory and stays there as an addition to stock – but also an irreversible investment. That information cannot be exchanged back for the time, effort, and other inputs that may have gone into its production. For example, the inputs that go into learning to reason consistently, developing a new strategy, or understanding mathematics cannot be reclaimed.[15]

Again, note that acquisition of information may not be a result of directed time, effort, and other inputs. A sudden solution may be stumbled upon in an unexpected direction; a random event of history may occur. These can come to shape the subsequent structure of the stock of information and associated communication channels as well as deliberate, directed search. This effect upon structure follows because of the investment character of information. Once a new technology becomes available, whether randomly or nonrandomly, and has been encoded by the behaving unit, a language has been learned, an interpretation of history has been accepted, and so on, it is often cheaper to use this technology, learning, interpretation, and the like rather than to replace it with another, ceteris paribus. One thus avoids a replacement cost, which might involve new time, labor, and other inputs. In fact, whether we treat an individual, whose memory in some respects at least may be viewed as operating as a filing system, or an organization, which has evolved a regular or irregular structure (hierarchical or nonhierarchical) in decision making, the behaving unit may continue for at least some time to employ knowingly an inefficient and obsolete structure in order to avoid significant restructuring costs.

The deliberate and directed acquisition of information involves cost. Information costs, however, are not the same in all directions; hence to achieve a given objective, say, the solution to a problem, one tends to direct information acquisition in that direction that is least costly, ceteris paribus. Usually, these are directions that explore known territory or territory easily accessible. For example, one searches for new employment opportunities requiring skills and know-how that one currently possesses

---

[15] On the other hand, a unit may be able to affect the rate of forgetting (depreciation) of information or the rate at which information becomes obsolete and is replaced by new signals.

or can easily refashion. Also, one tends to acquire information that can be by-products of one's work or other activities, an aspect of "learning by doing."[16] On the other hand, the *value* of information along different directions, even with a given objective in mind, may also differ and must be taken into consideration. After all, information primarily reduces uncertainty; and thus information along different directions may reduce uncertainty in different amounts and thus have different value when acquired, ceteris paribus. Also, information may have value since it can be transmitted (sold) to other users (behaving units); thus to the extent that information along different directions incurs different transmission costs by the producer, its value will vary.[17]

Associated with value and cost are all kinds of resource allocation problems. In taking a sample, a statistician typically must decide at some point that the cost of an additional observation is not equal to the expected increment to the value of the sample. Or at some point, the costs of development of new models and of new methods of computation (i.e., an increase in the stock of computational information) will exceed the

---

[16] Moreover, the cost of an item of information to a behaving unit may vary with the scale of operation of that unit whether the scale relates to output (as in a firm) or some other magnitude (as population in a nation). Since an item of information typically is indivisible in its use, a large-scale operation finds the cost of that information per unit of operations much less than a small-scale operator, a factor that leads to major-scale economies in economic production.

[17] For example, it is easier to transmit information to users who speak the same language or employ the same code and analytic methods than to others who do not. In this sense a market for information exists (including the submarket that the behaving unit comprises); and transmission costs affects sales in each sector (part) of that market.

Moreover, the question of transmission is related to the question of "appropriation" of information. Information is inappropriable in the sense that an individual can transmit and sell it without ever losing it. The ease (cost) of transmission, however, does affect its production. If there are legal, political, and technical conditions that ensure low-cost transmission of or easy access to new information (as is the case within the NATO alliance), then each potential user is motivated to refrain from any high-cost production, leaving it to others to incur such high costs. Or where most units in a group cannot afford the production of such high-cost information, even though of great value to each in reducing uncertainty, the one with adequate resources may do so with or without contributions by others. [The collection of arms expenditures and arms trade data by the Stockholm International Peace Research Institute (SIPRI) is a case in point. Another is a leader in an industry who conducts the necessary market and other analysis for the industry as a whole and sets the price and pricing system that is simply followed by (implicitly complied with) other firms in the industry.] On the other hand, if transmission cost is high (or if secrecy is desired and can be effected as is the case among adversaries regarding technology of potential value for weapons production), then there is excessive production from a social standpoint because each competing unit is forced to produce the desired information.

Note also that a unit may find it advantageous to incur transmission cost to others, as where a firm advertises the particular qualities of its product or when a nuclear power proclaims to the world (or its adversary) that it has acquired a second-strike capability.

We should also note that in a strict, rigorous manner, Radner and Stiglitz (1984) have shown for an important class of decision problems that whenever the marginal cost of information is strictly positive, a small amount of information has a negative marginal net value. This implies that (1) there must be *increasing returns to information* over some range of the

expected value of such.[18] And at some point resources devoted to information acquisition in total as well as among different types of information must be balanced against the use of such resources for producing other civilian and military goods.

The effects of limited mental capacity, limited time, and other scarce resources together with tendencies after a point toward diminishing returns and thus limited capability at information acquisition and processing is, of course, to limit the number of issues that can be addressed, or actions that can be taken, or commands that can be issued, or in general, decisions that can be made. This is so because each one of these items requires information acquisition and/or processing. Put otherwise, the agenda of any decision-making unit must necessarily be limited, non-agenda items being those for which information tends not to be collected and/or processed. However, in considering decision areas, we should distinguish between those leading to (1) decisions to act and (2) decisions to collect information, which according to statistical decision theory are *terminal acts* and *experiments*, respectively. These two are intricately connected since it is from experiments in areas that are monitored but in which terminal acts are not taken that actions to add new decision areas to the agenda derive (and also actions to drop less important decision areas in which experiments are currently taking place).[19] For instance, accumulation of information on internal unrest in a nation hitherto considered too small to bother with may in time lead a world power to decide

---

relevant parameter if there is some amount of information that has positive net value (a nonconcavity in the value function for this information) which in turn means that the demand for information on this parameter will not be a continuous function of its price and thus suggests one rationale for specialization. Stiglitz (1984) has also rigorously demonstrated, under a set of strong assumptions typical of traditional economics, that more information (or cheaper information) may result in making everyone worse off (and so decrease social welfare) in many basic markets (such as in the labor, agriculture, and stock markets). His analysis is consistent with the same point made by Boulding (1984), who maintains that knowledge is often gained by the orderly loss (filtering) of information and by restructuring it.

[18] Note, in keeping with previous comments, that the value of a model (say, one involving an optimization procedure) may mostly derive not from the results of its operation (e.g., the identification of a most efficient action) but rather from its calling attention to new data and other information that should be collected and processed. This is so especially for theoretically oversimplified models designed to start the process of accumulating relevant data and identifying additional variables to be included. Such allows a behaving unit to construct better and better models and to narrow down the range of what might be designated "acceptable and feasible actions" if not to yield successively better approximations to a good or best action.

[19] Based on this distinction, Arrow (1984, chap. 13) distinguishes among (i) *active decision areas* (in which experiments are performed, signals received, and terminal acts then taken), (ii) *monitored decision areas* (where some experiments are being performed but where the resulting signals convey too little information to justify taking terminal acts but possibly enough information to justify continuing experimentation), and (iii) *passive decision areas* (in which no experiments are being conducted and for which no terminal acts are on the agenda).

to intervene in one way or another. Or, accumulation of information leading to a change in military technology may change the set of nations in which military bases are desirable and thus those on the list of foreign assistance. And so forth.

One final point. Within a behaving unit, especially an organization, there is the complicated problem of the optimal investment between (1) information collection and processing, (2) communication channels, and (3) regulatory activities. As already mentioned, it is desirable within an organization to have individuals specialize on experiments they are conducting, thereby exploiting the gains that are possible from specialization. Such, however, requires that these individuals transmit over communication channels relevant information they collect and information summaries to nodes where such can be coordinated and terminal acts taken. The need to economize on communication channels may therefore lead to the collection of less information than would otherwise be the case. Moreover, the change in agenda deriving from the outcome of continuing experiments may lead to the conduct of new kinds of experiments as well as a change in the network of communication channels, thereby running into resistance of vested interest groups and problems and costs of disinvestment. Such resistance and problems are well known within agencies of government concerned with foreign policy in the dynamic international setting. Further, specialization within an organization, say, in a foreign policy agency, where information is collected by specialists on different parts of the world, means that information released (via reports, policy recommendations, and the like) by one node may have negative effects (externalities) upon the usefulness of information and policy regarding other parts of the world. This then necessitates investment in and operation of another activity, namely, *regulation* (monitoring of reports, censorship, and controls on the dissemination of information). The regulatory process, however, is itself subject to obsolescence and inflexibility and as a consequence can generate inefficiencies. (For example, the inflexibilities in the structure of the United Nations impose severe constraints on its peace-keeping and other world welfare functions.) In short, proper functioning of an organization requires several levels (strata) at which information is collected and processed, at which a network of communication channels exists, and at which regulation takes place within a changing, evolutionary frame (Nelson 1980; Nelson and Winter 1982; Arrow 1984).[20]

---

[20] In one sense this is a problem within the much larger (worldwide) problem of information integration. In noting the increasing fragmentation and specialization of information generation, Kochen (1974a) effectively argues that "we need systems that help reintegrate the fragmented literatures more than we need systems to help us gain access to the frag-

6.5   Concluding remarks

This chapter has treated learning from the standpoint of search and information research and development for reaching solutions to problems that cannot be attacked in routine fashion. We have considered this question from the standpoint of three approaches – that of cognitive science, AI, and economics – often using the concept of a payoff matrix and its elements to help define the problem. In each case the literature on this subject is very recent, in the case of economics less than two decades old despite the fact that economics as a discipline has existed for two centuries or more. Hence, what we have reported as knowledge in this area must be considered as very tentative. There will be major advances in such knowledge as these three approaches develop along the lines we mentioned or along lines we failed to mention and as other approaches effectively probe this extremely difficult but extremely challenging subject area. In this chapter we have avoided the use of any technical materials and mathematical formulation of relationships. The reader is reminded that some possibly relevant mathematical formulations and models are presented in Chapters 14–16 on advanced analyses. These chapters treat, respectively, learning by a group and its individual members, information research and development from a dynamical systems viewpoint, and invention and innovation in research and development for problem solving: an exploratory view. The advanced reader may turn to these chapters before proceeding to Chapter 7 on policy space analysis and policy proposals. Such proposals, we shall see, are in a major way related to (1) what a political leader has learned about the wishes of his (or her) constituencies and objectives of diverse interest groups, (2) what information he has acquired (developed) from research reports, surveys, and similar activities, and (3) what ways he judges that key problems can be attacked.

References

Anderson J. R. (1985) *Cognitive Psychology.* New York: W.H. Freeman.
Arrow, K. J. (1984) *The Economics of Information.* Cambridge, MA: Harvard University Press.
Arrow, K. J., and G. Debreu (1954) "Existence of an Equilibrium for a Competitive Economy." *Econometrica* 22(3, July):265–90.
Boulding, K. (1984) "Foreword: A Note on Information, Knowledge, and Pro-

ments" (p. xiii). With a better understanding of factors that lead to literature disintegration, he proposes a "growing encyclopedia system" (GES) to summarize, organize, and reintegrate knowledge. This is a task for the emerging field of information science. Also see Kochen (1974b).

duction." In M. Jussawalla and H. Ebenfield (eds.) (1984), *Communication and Information Perspectives*. Amsterdam: Elsevier, pp. vii–ix.

Dasgupta, P., R. Gilbert, and J. Stiglitz (1982) "Invention and Innovation under Alternative Market Structures: The Case of Natural Resources." *Review of Economic Studies* 49:567–82.

Dasgupta, P., R. Gilbert, and J. Stiglitz (1983) "Strategic Considerations in Invention and Innovation: The Case of Natural Resources." *Econometrica* 51(5, September):1439–48.

Debreu, G. (1959) *Theory of Value*. New York: Wiley.

Dehn, N., and R. Schank (1982) "Artificial and Human Intelligence." In R. J. Sternberg (ed.), *Handbook of Human Intelligence*. London: Cambridge University Press, pp. 352–91.

Estes, W. K. (1982) "Learning, Memory and Intelligence." In R. J. Sternberg (ed.), *Handbook of Human Intelligence*. London: Cambridge University Press, pp. 170–224.

Fixler, D. J. (1983). "Uncertainty, Market Structure and the Incentive to Invent." *Economica* 50(200, November):407–24.

Gallini, N. T., and Y. Kotowitz (1985) "Optimal R and D Processes and Competition." *Economica* 52(207, August):321–34.

Gardner, H. (1983) *Frames of Mind, the Theory of Multiple Intelligences*. New York: Basic Books.

Gick, M. L., and K. J. Holyoak (1980) "Analogical Problem Solving." *Cognitive Psychology* 12:306–55.

Gick, M. L., and K. J. Holyoak (1983) "Schema Induction and Analogical Transfer." *Cognitive Psychology*. 15:1–38.

Gilbert, W. J. (1976) *Modern Algebra with Applications*. New York: Wiley.

Greeno, J. G. (1972) "The Structure of Memory and the Process of Solving Problems." In R. L. Solso (ed.), *Contemporary Issues in Cognitive Psychology*. New York: Wiley.

Greeno, J. G. (1978) "Nature of Problem Solving Abilities." In W. K. Estes, (ed.), *Handbook of Learning and Cognitive Processes*. New York: Wiley, pp. 239–270.

Grossman, S. J., R. E. Kihlstrom, and L. J. Mirman (1977) "A Bayesian Approach to the Production of Information and Learning by Doing." *Review of Economic Studies* 44:533–48.

Holyoak, K. (1984) "Mental Models in Problem Solving." In J. R. Anderson and S. M. Kosslyn (eds.), *Tutorials in Learning and Memory*. New York: W. H. Freeman, pp. 193–218.

Isard, W., T. E. Smith, P. Isard, T. H. Tung, and M. Dacey (1969) *General Theory: Social, Political, Economic and Regional*. Cambridge, MA: MIT Press.

Kihlstrom, R. E. (1984) "A Bayesian Exposition of Blackwell's Theorem on the Comparison of Experiments." In M. Boyer and R. E. Kihlstrom (eds.), *Bayesian Models in Economic Theory*. Amsterdam: Elsevier, pp. 13–32.

Kihlstrom, R. E., L. G. Mirman, and A. Postlewaite (1984) "Experimental Consumption and the 'Rothschild' Effect." In M. Boyer and R. E. Kihlstrom (eds.), *Bayesian Models in Economic Theory*. Amsterdam: Elsevier, pp. 279–302.

Killingsworth, M. R. (1982) "'Learning by Doing' and 'Investment in Training' Synthesis of Two 'Rival' Models of the Life Cycle." *Review of Economic Studies* 49:263–71.

Kochen, M. (1974a) *Integrative Mechanisms in Literature Growth.* Westport, CT: Greenwood Press.

Kochen, M. (1974b) *Principles of Information Retrieval.* New York: Wiley.

Lamberton, D. M. (1984) "The Emergence of Information Economics." In M. Jussawalla and H. Ebenfield (eds.), *Communication and Information Perspectives.* Amsterdam: Elsevier, pp. 7–22.

Langlois, R. N. (1984) "Internal Organization in a Dynamic Context: Some Theoretical Considerations." In M. Jussawalla and H. Ebenfield (eds.), *Communication and Information Perspectives.* Amsterdam: Elsevier, pp. 23–49.

Machlup, F., and U. Mansfield (eds.) (1983) *The Study of Information: Interdisciplinary Messages.* New York: Wiley.

Marschak, J., and R. Radner (1972) *Economic Theory of Teams.* New Haven: Yale University Press.

Morgan, P., and R. Manning (1985) "Optimal Search." *Econometrica* 53(4, July):923–44.

Nelson, R. R. (1980) "Production Sets, Technological Knowledge and R & D: Fragile and Overworked Constructs for Analysis of Productivity Growth?" *American Economic Review* 70(May):62–7.

Nelson, R. R., and S. G. Winter (1982) *An Evolutionary Theory of Economic Change.* Cambridge, MA: Harvard University Press.

Newell, A., and H. A. Simon (1972) *Human Problem Solving.* Englewood Cliffs, NJ: Prentice-Hall.

O'Loughlin, J. (1986) "Spatial Models of International Conflicts: Extending Current Theories of War Behavior." *Annals of the Association of American Geographers* 76:63–80.

Polson, P., and R. Jeffries (1982) "Problem Solving as Search and Understanding." In R. J. Sternberg (ed.), *Advances in the Psychology of Human Intelligence,* Vol. I. Hillsdale, NJ: Lawrence Erlbaum Associates, pp. 367–411.

Radner, R., and J. Stiglitz (1984) "Nonconcavity in the Value of Information." In M. Boyer and R. E. Kihlstrom (eds.), *Bayesian Models in Economic Theory.* Amsterdam: Elsevier, pp. 33–52.

Simon, H. A. (1978a) "On How to Decide What to Do." *Bell Journal of Economics* 9(2, Autumn):494–507.

Simon, H. A. (1978b) "Information-Processing Theory of Human Problem Solving" In W. K. Estes (ed.), *Handbook of Learning and Cognitive Processes,* Vol. 5. New York: Wiley, pp. 271–95.

Solso, R. L. (1979) *Cognitive Psychology.* New York: Harcourt, Brace, Jovanovitch.

Spence, A. M. (1974) *Market Signalling: Informational Transfer in Hiring and Related Screening Processes.* Cambridge, MA: Harvard University Press.

Sternberg, R. J. (1982) "Reasoning, Problem Solving and Intelligence." In R. J. Sternberg (ed.), *Handbook of Human Intelligence.* New York: Cambridge University Press, pp. 225–307.

Stiglitz, J. E. (1984) "Information, Screening, and Welfare." In M. Boyer and R.

E. Kihlstrom (eds.), *Bayesian Models in Economic Theory*. Amsterdam: Elsevier, pp. 209–39.

Wallsten, T. S. (ed.) (1980) *Cognitive Processes in Choice and Decision Behavior*. Hillsdale, NJ: Lawrence Erlbaum Associates.

Wickelgren, W. A. (1974) *How to Solve Problems*. San Francisco: Freeman.

Wright, B. D. (1983) "The Economics of Invention Incentives: Patents, Prizes and Research Contracts." *American Economic Review*. 73(4, September):691–707.

CHAPTER 7

Policy space analysis: the choice of policies regarding arms expenditures and other issues and the value of information development

Written with Christine Smith and Yasushi Asami

7.1   Introduction

As early as section 2.3 and frequently thereafter we raised the question of allocation of scarce (fixed) resources among military programs and civilian programs as a whole or among a number of relevant civilian programs. Such allocation was difficult because of the conflicting objectives and hence pressing demands of different interest groups. On other occasions, we have alluded to the drive or desire of political leaders or groups to stay in power if they are incumbents, or if not, to acquire such. They consequently require a majority of votes or whatever vote is necessary to win in a basic relevant election wherein, say, military expenditures is a key policy issue. Hence, we now must pursue analysis of the behavior of a political unit with regard to proposals and actions on the level of military programs (expenditures) and others. This brings us into the area of policy space analysis where we can pursue such analysis with a graph of two dimensions when we are dealing with only two issues but need to consider three- or more dimensional space when we treat three or more issues. Here the behavior of a political leader or group constitutes the choice of a position (location) in two- or more dimensional space, the position being depicted by a point indicating along each dimension the level of program (expenditures) on the issue represented by that dimension.

In this chapter we aim to probe into the behavior of political leaders and groups (key decision makers behind arms races and the arms control actions of chapter 2) in a way that is still more deep and focused than in

Sections 7.2–7.5 and Appendix 7.A were written jointly with Christine Smith and draw very heavily upon Isard and Smith (1980). Sections 7.6 and 7.7 and Appendixes 7.B and 7.C were written jointly with Yasushi Asami.

the behavioral, problem-solving, and learning analyses in Chapters 3–6. For example, if we return to Figure 4.1 of Chapter 4 and the associated discussion, we may imagine a political leader about to take an action at time $t + 1$ having learned *(ex post)* from his (or her) experience (actions and perceptions of outcomes and other variables) at time t. He would like the outcome to be "a win in an election." What set of policy proposals does he set forth in his platform; that is, what location in policy space does he consider as best?

Note that in the preceding context this question largely focuses on the short run or at most the intermediate run. The long-run perspective – that of the individual concerned with the wise use of resources, the possibility of economic warfare, or the conduct of research and development – enters in a miniscule way if at all, as will be the case for most of the policy space analysis that we consider in this chapter. Some scholars, such as the political analyst, will say that it is the short run that is all important. Others, such as the evolutionary theorist, will say the long run. To us both are important, the long run in certain respects being a sequence of short runs and thus unavoidably significantly affected by the short run. Yet the long run is just as significant in shaping the short run and affects the psychology, emotional, and other characteristics of even the 100 percent self-interested myopic behaving unit and his or her environment.

In what follows, we can treat the policy space as continuous [which is possible since levels (in dollars) of military expenditures and expenditures on various nonmilitary programs are for all practical purposes continuous] or as a discrete set of points (e.g., in terms of billions of dollars on each specific program such as Star Wars). In either case we can think of each possible location that a behaving unit considers as a row of a payoff matrix whose outcomes under different states of the environment are 0 and 1 (lose and win), or range from 0 to 100 (in terms of percentage of voter support), or otherwise.

There has been recently a considerable literature on policy space analysis. We shall not attempt here to cover all the aspects, which would lead to a book in itself. Rather we shall aim to examine the interplay of the most important factors that have been considered, with particular emphasis on policy that relates to the international system and military expenditures. Our procedure will be to begin at a very simplified level of analysis, building it up step by step and thereby approaching more and more the reality of the political world. We draw heavily upon the extensive spatial analysis in the location theory literature of regional science and economics that has developed over the last century and a half.

In section 7.2 we begin with an analysis of a highly oversimplified situation in two-dimensional policy space wherein a political leader is moti-

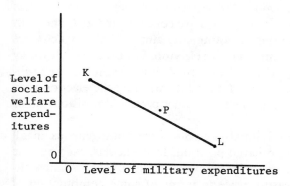

Figure 7.1. Clusters in a two-dimensional policy space.

vated to find that position (location) on issues that will minimize his (or her) total patronage costs (promises, jobs, money payments, and the like) for attaining 51 percent of the vote from two or more clusters of voters, the most preferred positions of the members of any given cluster being approximately the same. In section 7.3, we examine the effects upon the issues position of that leader when lobbyists and related groups of individuals offer money and other support to induce him to take a position that they desire. Section 7.4 then examines the possible gains and costs from forming coalitions with other leaders – that is, from agglomerating in policy space at a compromise location. In section 7.5 and Appendix 7.A a support area analysis is conducted when the most preferred positions of voters are distributed uniformly and/or irregularly and in clusters. Here we introduce competition by other political leaders. Section 7.6 and Appendixes 7.B and 7.C take up the problem of reducing uncertainty and in particular examine the costs and benefits from adopting an optimal sampling procedure aimed at information development.

7.2   Some basic aspects of policy space analysis

7.2.1   The traditional line case in two-dimensional policy space

To begin analysis,[1] take a highly oversimplified case where there are two and only two issues characterizing a political situation. Measure different positions on one issue (e.g., level of military expenditures) along one axis of Figure 7.1 and the different positions on another issue (e.g., level of

[1] See Stokes (1963) for a verbal discussion in an n-dimensional context.

social welfare expenditures) along the second.[2] Let there be two clusters of voters whose most preferred positions are concentrated at K and L in Figure 7.1. Assume the combined voting strengths of these two clusters are sufficient and just sufficient to ensure election. For example, they may constitute 51 percent of the voters. In its most simplified form, the problem for a political leader concerned only with winning the election is to determine where in relation to these two most preferred positions he or she should locate.[3]

Initially, assume that individuals as voters are homogeneous in all respects except their most preferred position. In particular, each has the same reservation or abstinence price below which he (or she) would withhold his support. [We measure price in terms of some combination of patronage by a political leader, obligation to look after a constituent's welfare, dollars (when paid for a vote), promises, and other relevant items.] This abstinence price then represents the minimum price the potential constituent will accept from a political leader were the leader to choose a position corresponding to his (the constituent's) most preferred position.[4] When the leader's position is not the potential constituent's most preferred position, then in order to be certain of receiving this individual's vote, the leader must offer him a support price equal to his abstinence price[5] plus an additional amount (a cost to the leader) in order to offset the distance between the two positions.

This additional amount (an additional incentive payment) is what is required to ensure that the individual will support the leader despite the distance between the leader's position and the individual's most preferred position. This additional amount (cost) is taken to increase with an increase in the distance.[6]

[2] Here we follow the classical Hotelling model wherein specific well-defined issues are involved. Where issues are dispositional, our analysis is of much less relevance. See Stokes (1963) and Rabinowitz (1978) for a discussion of the concept of dispositional issues. On the other hand, see Poole and Daniels (1985), who apply metric multidimensional unfolding to interest group ratings of Congress. Their empirical analysis suggests that a single liberal-conservative dimension accounts for more than 80% of the variance in the ratings and a second dimension associated with party unity accounts for another 7%. Also see the literature cited therein. However, see the broader structural realignment analysis in MacDonald and Rabinowitz (1987).
[3] In this chapter, the analysis is primarily concerned with winning an election. For a discussion of the relevance of this simplified framework where the outcome per se is downplayed, see Wittman (1983) and the literature cited therein.
[4] See Davis et al. (1970) for an extensive discussion relating to abstinence and the meaning of an abstinence price. Also see Palfrey and Rosenthal (1985), Foster (1984), and the literature cited therein for more recent discussion of factors affecting abstinence.
[5] From the political leader's standpoint, we can substitute for the abstinence price a family of abstinence prices pertinent for different probabilities of support by the (average) individual.
[6] This is consistent with the findings of Zipp (1985). He found in his election studies (1968–80) that increased distance of a voter's most preferred position from that taken by a leader

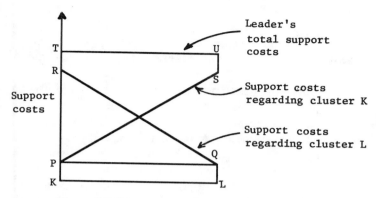

Figure 7.2. Support costs for different positions of a political leader.

First, it is clear that the cost-minimizing political leader will not locate at any position off the straight line connecting K and L. For were he or she to do so, it can be shown that there always exists some point on the straight line less costly than the chosen location.[7]

To facilitate exposition, let the straight line KL correspond to the horizontal axis in Figure 7.2. Different levels of support costs facing the political leader at different locations are measured along the vertical axis.

For the moment, take the size of the clusters at K and L to be the same. Then KP, the part of total cost to the leader of meeting the abstinence price of all the constituents at K, equals QL, the part of total cost to the leader of meeting the abstinence price of all constituents at L. We then construct PS and QR, which represent support cost gradients relating to voting clusters K and L, respectively. The *gradient* of line PS indicates how the part (a second part) of total cost to the leader, which consists of the *additional* amounts he (or she) must pay to retain the support of all constituents at K, increases absolutely as he shifts his position away from K. The sum of these two costs then yields line PS, which defines the total costs to the leader to obtain the full support of constituents at K for different positions along the line KL. Similarly, the line QR defines the total cost to the leader to obtain the full support of constituents at L for different positions along the line KL. Adding the two lines yields overall

significantly decreases the probability of the voter's voting. He qualifies this finding by the many factors employed to explain participation. Also see the literature cited by Zipp.
[7] For example, imagine the political leader to consider a location at some point P above the line. Construct a perpendicular from P to KL intersecting KL at point M, a point that is also not indicated on the figure. Then $KM < KP$ and $LM < PL$. This will be so regardless of how many units relating to one issue are considered equivalent in *terms of support costs* to one unit of the second issue.

total costs, given by line TU for all positions along KL. (Note that RT and SU are constructed equal to KP and LQ, respectively, and thus to each other.) In this oversimplified case the cost-minimizing leader incurs the same total cost at all locations along KL and thus is free to locate at any of them.

Even when the average abstinence price of the individuals comprising one voting cluster differs from that of the individuals comprising the other voting cluster, the location of the political leader still remains indeterminate if the support cost gradients are of equal slope and proportional to distance. This is immediately apparent when one makes the appropriate adjustments to Figure 7.2.

However, generally speaking, the support cost gradients cannot be expected to be proportional to distance. Rather, as the distance between the political leader's chosen position and the most perferred position of a given individual increases, the support costs required to ensure the support of that individual may increase either more or less than proportionately. Support cost gradients reflecting cost structures more than proportional to distance encourage the adoption of a midpoint location, such as in Figure 7.3. By way of contrast, cost structures less than proportional to distance lead to support cost gradients that encourage adoption of the most preferred position of one of the clusters of voters. This result is consistent with endpoint location of firms in traditional Weberian location theory and practice.

In addition, the slopes of the support cost gradients relating to the two voting clusters may differ. At one extreme, the voters at one cluster may hold to their most preferred position so strongly that they will not consider any compromise from this position.[8] If the support of this cluster is essential for election, the leader must locate at the cluster's position, just as a firm using an immobile resource must locate at the site of that resource. At the other extreme, the voters at one cluster may be completely swept away by the charisma of the political leader; they support the leader no matter where his or her chosen location should lie in relation to their most preferred position.[9] Accordingly, the leader will locate at the position of the other cluster (just as the firm locates at the market when the single resource required in production is ubiquitous).

[8] This parallels the concept of an immobile resource or a raw material involving infinite weight loss in traditional Weberian location analysis. In this case, the support cost gradient relating to the affected cluster would have infinite slope.

[9] This parallels the concept of an absolute ubiquity in traditional Weberian location analysis. In this case, the support cost gradient relating to the affected cluster would have zero slope.

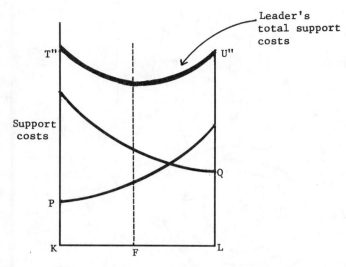

Figure 7.3. Total support costs with support cost gradients more than proportional to distance.

More realistically, however, the individuals comprising one voting cluster, say, K, may have a stronger intensity of feelings toward their most preferred position (or be less influenced by charisma for the political leader) than the individuals comprising voting cluster L. In this situation, the support cost gradient regarding cluster K *is greater than that* regarding cluster L. The political leader's support-cost-minimizing location is pulled toward the cluster whose members are least willing to move away from their most preferred position (e.g., away from the midpoint F in Figure 7.3 and toward cluster K when support cost gradients are more than proportional to distance).

7.2.2 Isotims and isodapanes in two-dimensional policy space

In location theory, when a production process in physical space involves many raw materials/markets and/or discontinuous transport cost structures, we leave behind transport gradient lines and concentrate on the use of isotims and isodapanes. We can do this in policy space.[10]

---

[10] Note that we do not develop in policy space parallels to the locational and weight triangles of Weber. From a behavioral standpoint, the geometric solutions developed with the use of these triangles are less meaningful than solutions based on the use of isotims and isodapanes. Further, geometric solutions involve difficulties with the choice of a metric and the appropriate definition of ideal weights.

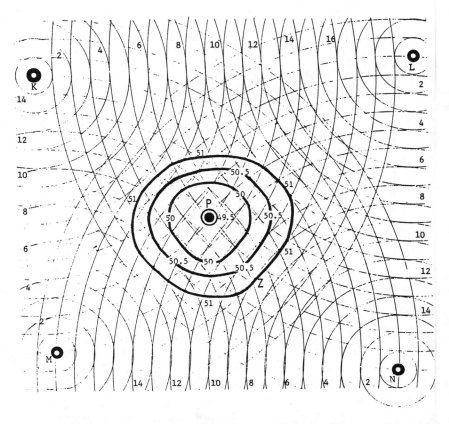

Figure 7.4. Isotims and isodapanes in policy space (in terms of thousands of dollars).

To illustrate, consider Figure 7.4, which represents a two-dimensional policy space with clusters of voters (corresponding to localized resources) whose most preferred positions are given by points *K, L, M,* and *N.* In order to determine where the point of minimum total support costs lies, one pursues the following steps:

1. Construct a set of isotims around each cluster. An isotim labeled 2, for example, represents the locus of positions each of which would cost the leader $2,000 more than if he or she chose the position at *N* to obtain the support of individuals at *N.* (This figure is obtained by multiplying the number of individuals at *N* by the amount above the abstinence price required to induce each to support the leader when he chooses a position on the 2 isotim.) An isotim labeled 4 corresponds to an additional cost of $4,000.

2.   Construct a set of isodapanes (such as 50 and 51 in Figure 7.4 representing costs of \$50,000 and \$51,000, respectively). Each isodapane is obtained by connecting all points that, as a choice of location for the political leader, would incur the same total costs (after each individual has been paid his abstinence price) in obtaining the support of all individuals clustered at K, L, M, and N. For example, at point Z, additional costs of \$16,000, \$15,000, \$11,000 and \$9,000 are involved for obtaining support of individuals at K, L, M, and N, respectively, or a total of \$51,000. Likewise, the same total costs are obtained for every point on the 51 isodapane.

3.   Identify the point P that minimizes these total support costs. As in traditional location theory, this point lies within the innermost isodapane when support cost functions are well behaved, that is, increase regularly with an increase in distance in policy space.

Note that we avoid the problem of defining appropriate metrics. We assume as Lösch, Christaller, and many others in regional science and economics that all voters including the political leader are alike, except for their most preferred position, and so have the same trade-off functions pertaining to a change in position on one issue as that on a second.[11] In this case, the political leader can from introspection construct relevant isotims for the several clusters. Or we may be more realistic and require that the political leader estimate the different trade-off functions for the several clusters, as he or she must do implicitly (if not explicitly) in reality.

The preceding type of analysis can be extended to incorporate as many clusters of voters as the leader requires to ensure election. It can also be generalized to n-dimensional policy space.

7.3   Particular advantageous policy positions: lobby and related effects

Now let us add another element of reality. In physical space, we consider particularly advantageous sites such as cheap labor points, cheap power points, cheap land cost points, and others reflecting savings as *irregularities* imposed on the regular transport cost structure and examine their locational impact by use of the concept of critical isodapanes. So too with

---

[11] This is, of course, an unrealistic assumption. Weights are attached to different issues according to their perceived degree of importance, and the weights are not common for all voters/leaders. See, e.g., the extensive discussion in Davis et al. (1970). However, as Lösch's simplifying assumptions, it does provide some useful insights.

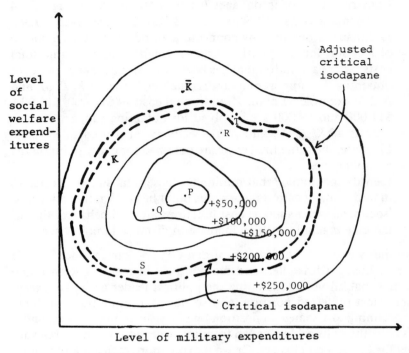

Figure 7.5. Particular advantageous policy positions: critical isodapanes in policy space.

respect to a position that yields to a political leader a particular type of benefit from taking that position, the particular type of benefit being irregularly available in policy space.

For example, the adoption of a specific position on a particular issue may lead to "cost savings" in the form of

1. an award to the political leader of a certain number of jobs by a higher level political leader to be used for patronage purposes;
2. an offer of a certain level of contributions to campaign funds by a corporation, an industrial cartel, or a business lobby; and
3. a pledge of political support from a social group (such as the Roman Catholic church, a labor union, or a feminist organization).

Given the "provisionally optimum" location P (see Figure 7.5) determined on the basis of the criterion of minimization of support costs alone, a series of isodapanes can be constructed showing how total support costs increase as one moves away from P (Figure 7.5 depicts a more asymmetrical but more realistic situation than Figure 7.4). One such isodapane connects all points at which the total support costs exceed the minimum incurred at P by an amount equal to the cost savings offered by the alternative advantageous policy position. This one is termed the "critical isodapane." For example, if a contribution of $200,000 were available were the political leader to shift from position P to position R (indicating, e.g., a 50 percent increase in the size of the army), then the critical isodapane is the one that involves $200,000 support cost above those at P.

If the advantageous policy position were to lie on the critical isodapane (e.g., if it were S), then the political leader is indifferent to location at either P or S. If the advantageous policy position were to lie inside the critical isodapane, as it would if it were R, then the dollar or dollar equivalent advantage that can be gained at this position is greater than the additional support cost incurred, and it is worthwhile for the political leader to shift his or her position from P to that point.

If there are a number of irregular positions in policy space, each offering a different advantage to the political leader, then one constructs the critical isodapane corresponding to each of these positions and determines which, if any, yields the highest *net* gain, that is, which is the "best" alternative policy position. Approximately, it is the position that lies farthest within its critical isodapane. In Figure 7.5, for example, it would be preferable for the political leader to transfer to policy position Q rather than R when Q's critical isodapane is the $150,000 line.

The preceding analysis needs to be extended. For example, if the advantageous policy position lies outside its critical isodapane (as T does), then the political leader should not automatically reject it in favor of the minimum support cost point. Rather he or she calculates the additional support cost savings that might accrue from seeking the support of one or more clusters of voters – such as at $\overline{K}$ closer to point T than, say, K (i.e., from the use of "replacement deposits" in Weberian terms) – and, although not necessarily involving the same number of constituents, would still permit the leader to have at least 51 percent of the vote. The leader's critical isodapane is then adjusted by the amount of such savings from "replacement clusters." If upon reexamination, T now lies within this *adjusted critical isodapane,* then it is worthwhile for the political leader to transfer to this point from the minimum support cost point P,[12] assuming no other options exist.

[12] If one is prepared to accept the notion of a "production function" or the equivalent facing a political leader, he or she may make adjustments for factor substitution options as well. For example, if a particular advantageous policy position offers extremely low-cost labor for campaigning purposes (as a feminist organization might offer), then this could enable a substitution of labor outlays for television and other media outlays, thereby tending to reduce total campaign costs.

After adjustments for replacement clusters, one can use this technique for comparing positions offering different levels of the same type of advantages, for example, $100,000 in campaign contributions from corporation X to $250,000 from corporation Y. Equally important, one can compare positions offering different types of advantages, for example, $100,000 in campaign contributions from corporation X to a pledge of political support from the Roman Catholic church. However, recognizing another type of advantage irregularly distributed over policy space requires consideration of the possibility that a particular position in policy space may be associated with two or more different types of special advantages or *disadvantages*. For example, a particular position that yields $100,000 campaign contributions from corporation X might at the same time generate opposition from a feminist organization or the National Council of Churches. In sum, each position having a special advantage must be examined for the occurrence of special disadvantages as well as other types of special advantages, again as we do in traditional Weberian theory.

7.4   Compromise points in policy space

Next consider another element of reality, namely, *agglomeration,* defined to be coalition formation with one common set of policies in policy space to which each leader strictly adheres. In policy space, an agglomeration economy may represent the benefits that can be expected to accrue from being or increasing the probability of being a member of a winning coalition, or from the associated factor of being able to have a stronger influence or exercise greater control over a legislative process, or from other related factors. Among the variables influencing the size of a leader's expected agglomeration economy are

1. the probability (1.00 or less) of being a member of a winning coalition, which is a function of the size of the coalition's combined voting strength and the degree of conflict with the policy positions of excluded leaders; and
2. the benefits to be derived from being a member of a winning coalition, which is a function of the importance of the issue(s) to a leader's constituents or to his or her own power position and welfare or a combination of both.

As in traditional location theory, we begin with the possibility of one and only one level of agglomeration (coalition formation). Let there be two political leaders whose present policy positions are given by A and B in Figure 7.6. They consider forming a coalition. Together, they com-

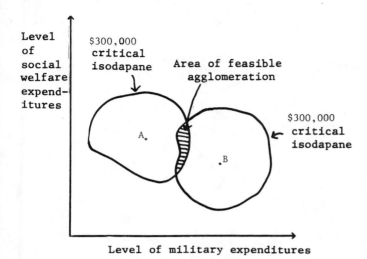

Figure 7.6. Area of feasible agglomeration: one level of agglomeration.

mand 20 percent of the vote and estimate that this would give them a 50 percent probability of becoming a winning coalition. The benefits to be gained from being successful in getting desired legislation passed are estimated by both leaders to be equivalent to a reduction in support costs of $300,000 for each leader. So $300,000 is the expected agglomeration economy for each.

Next construct critical isodapanes[13] around each leader's previously determined optimal positions. If these two critical isodapanes intersect, then joint location anywhere within the area of intersection (the agglomeration set) is beneficial to each political leader. (As in the previous section, further refinement of the analysis requires adjustment of the critical isodapanes to embody additional support cost savings from replacement clusters and other elements.) If the critical isodapanes after adjustments do not intersect, then agglomeration is not feasible.

Next, consider the possibility of two levels of agglomeration, that is, two sizes of coalition. Let four political leaders whose present policy positions are given by A, B, C, and D in Figure 7.7 consider agglomeration at a common position. The benefits to be gained by each from being successful in getting desired legislation passed are estimated by all leaders to

[13] Here a "critical isodapane" is defined as the locus of positions that would force the leader to incur additional support costs just equal to the benefits he or she expects to gain (in terms of reduction in other costs) from agglomeration.

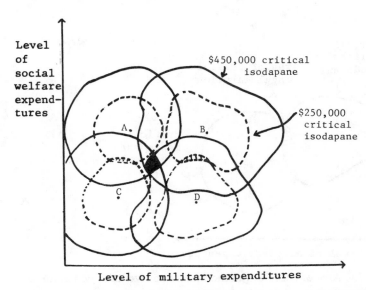

Figure 7.7. Areas of feasible agglomeration: two levels of agglomeration.

be equivalent to $500,000.[14] If all four leaders were to form a coalition, then they would command 40 percent of the vote. They estimate that this would give them a 90 percent probability of being a winning coalition and an expected agglomeration economy for each of $450,000. Alternatively, *A* and *B* together command 20 percent of the vote, as do *C* and *D* together. They estimate that this lower level of agglomeration would reduce their chances of being a member of a winning coalition to 50 percent and their expected gains from agglomeration to $250,000. Each political leader's $250,000 and $450,000 critical isodapanes have been identified in Figure 7.7. As the $450,000 critical isodapanes intersect, a four-leader coalition is possible anywhere within the blacked-in area in the center. However, both sets of $250,000 critical isodapanes intersect as well. Therefore, the two-leader coalition of *A* and *C* would find it feasible to agglomerate anywhere within their common area (dotted) and that of *B* and *D* can agglomerate anywhere within their common area (dashed).

To determine which of the two possible levels of agglomeration will materialize is not possible given the information on behavior already

[14] Here, as previously and in what follows, we assume similar costs and outcomes for each political leader simply to facilitate exposition. The analysis remains unchanged when leaders face different costs and outcomes.

provided. Figure 7.7 clearly indicates that a four-leader agglomeration can make possible an allocation of gains that would leave each political leader better off than if he or she were not to agglomerate at any level or if he were to agglomerate at a two-level agglomeration. Whether such agglomeration would occur in reality depends upon the negotiating behavior and numerous other factors that have been intensively examined in the literature of coalition theory but have not yielded any general solutions. In Weberian location theory literature, this game theory type of problem and indeterminacy of solution, as noted in Appendix B of Chapter 3, is well recognized.

Figure 7.7 illustrates just one type of result in a situation where the possibility of two levels of agglomeration can be considered. Others might involve larger areas of intersection at the two-leader level, or no area of intersection at all, or a much smaller intersection area at the four-leader level, or none at all. Moreover, analysis might be extended to incorporate the possibility of three or more levels of agglomeration and carried on to the point where a smooth function of agglomeration economy might be developed as an approximation when the possibility of numerous levels of agglomeration is posited.[15]

7.5 Support (supply and market) area analysis in policy space

Before introducing additional reality into the framework, let us consider another extreme unrealistic analysis in order to enrich our thinking. In the previous section and in traditional Weberian location theory, the leader and the firm are allowed to move continuously from location to location while the clusters of constituents (voters) they serve and the sources of raw materials used and markets served, respectively, are posited to be concentrated at relatively few points. We now may drop this last assumption and in keeping with traditional market and supply area analysis assume *at the other extreme* that the potential constituents and markets are continuously distributed in space.[16] This approach will allow us to examine more effectively problems of competition among leaders. Whereas to facilitate exposition we shall consider a distribution of constituents along a straight line measuring a position on a single issue, in

[15] For further analysis, refer to the literature on game theory applied to location theory. For example, see Isard et al. (1969, chaps. 7–9). Also see Enelow (1984), who develops a model of congressional compromise that supports "the expectation of compromises close to a 50–50 split under a broad range of conditions" (p. 708), and Wright and Goldberg (1985) and the literature cited therein on the effect of risk and uncertainty on coalition maintenance and rationale.
[16] See among others Hotelling (1952), Fetter (1970), Lösch (1954), Isard (1956), Christaller (1966), and Hyson and Hyson (1970).

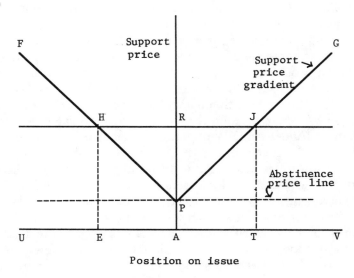

Figure 7.8. The support price gradient.

large part the analysis holds for constituents where (1) their distribution in two-dimensional policy space approximates a straight line (such as *KL* in Figure 7.1) that does not need to be horizontal but can be treated as such or (2) the most preferred position of each constituent in two-dimensional policy space can be viewed as equivalent to some location on a straight line such as *KL* in Figure 7.1.

7.5.1   The support price gradient

(a) One political leader: In Figure 7.8, different positions on a single issue (e.g., levels of military expenditures) are measured on the horizontal axis. The political leader's chosen position is given by point A.[17] Individuals as potential constituents are assumed, for the moment, to be uniformly distributed along line *UV*. The position of each individual on this line corresponds to his (or her) most preferred level of military expenditures. Initially, it is assumed that all individuals are homogeneous in all respects except their most preferred position. In particular, each has the same abstinence price below which he would withhold his support. As before, when the leader's chosen position is not the individual's most pre-

---

[17] Note that such a clear and unambiguous position is frequently not characteristic of political reality. See Page (1976) for a good statement on political ambiguity.

ferred position, then in order to be certain of support, the leader must offer the individual a support price equal to his abstinence price plus the costs involved in overcoming the distance between the two positions.

Different levels of support price offered by the political leader are measured on the vertical axis of Figure 7.8. Here AP represents the abstinence price that must be paid to all constituents regardless of their position in policy space, whereas FPG represents the support price gradient. This line measures the costs to the political leader, whose position is fixed at A, of obtaining the support of each individual on the assumption that the individual is to receive a net price equal to his or her abstinence price.[18] It parallels the transport cost gradient in traditional market area analysis.

The objective of the political leader is to maximize his or her support area; however, this area cannot extend beyond the point(s) where the leader's political resources are exhausted. We thus may posit that this point is reached when the leader's support area is ET (see Figure 7.8) where at the margin the leader offers a support price of AR ($= EH = TJ$).

(b) Competition between political leaders: Introduce a second political leader. Consider the case when each leader has adequate political resources to meet the abstinence price of all individuals distributed uniformly along line AB in Figure 7.9, plus support costs necessary to offset the effect of the distance separating each individual's most preferred position from the leader's chosen position. Both leaders are taken to be spatially immobile, that is, they are committed to their initial positions, represented by A and B.

Let the leader A be the first to enter the arena. He (or she) offers to all constituents the net support price AP, his corresponding support price gradient being PG. Then leader B enters. To bid the support of individuals away from A, he offers a somewhat higher net price (say, BQ), B's corresponding support price gradient being QF; hence he captures the support of all individuals. In turn, A may be expected to respond by offering a still higher net price, say, AR. And so, a price escalation takes place reminiscent of a price-cutting war among producers.

There is an absolute limit to this process. Eventually one of the political leaders reaches the limit of his (or her) political resources (faces bankruptcy) and is forced to withdraw from the arena. However, it could be

---

[18] In Figure 7.8, the support price gradient is constructed as a straight line. This would be appropriate only under circumstances where support price varied at a rate proportional to distance in policy space. However, in reality the support price gradient could be concave (reflecting a rate structure less than proportional to distance) or convex (reflecting a rate structure more than proportional to distance).

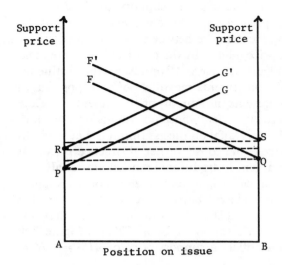

Figure 7.9. Two competing political leaders.

expected that before, and perhaps well before, this absolute limit is reached, one of the leaders would voluntarily temper his attempt to capture the entire set of supporters from his competitor. Instead, he would recognize that for the same volume of resource expenditure he could relinquish his most distant potential constituent to his competitor and raise the net price offered to all others. In turn, the second leader might do the same with regard to his most distant potential constituent. The nature of the competitive process then becomes more complicated. In general, however, the individuals whose most preferred positions lie close to either political leader receive a net price only somewhat or moderately above their abstinence price, whereas intense competition ensues for the support of the individuals whose most preferred positions are in the center area of line *AB*.

At this point we may drop the assumption of continuous distribution of political constituents along *UV*. They may be discretely distributed. To obtain the support of any constituent at a location along *UV*, it is necessary for a leader to offer a price at least as high as that specified by the support price gradient of Figure 7.8 and at least as high as that offered by any competitor (according to his or her support price gradient of Figure 7.9). Further, when constituents are sensitive to two or more issues and thus are distributed continuously or discontinuously in two- or more dimensional policy space, we still are able to construct critical isodapanes

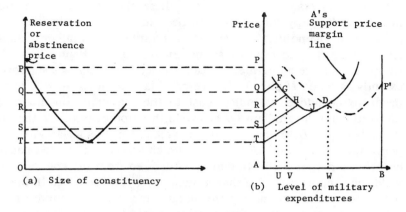

Figure 7.10. (a) Variation of abstinence price with constituency size: a cost curve to the leader. (b) Support price margin line for political leader.

(or isosurfaces) and identify support areas for leaders according to their price behavior.

7.5.2   Scale effects: the support price margin line

(a) One political leader: Dropping the assumption of constant abstinence price, we recognize the existence for the political leader of bandwagon and congestion effects. These are comparable to the scale economies and diseconomies facing the industrial producer. Initially, the abstinence price required to ensure the support of an individual may fall as more and more individuals align themselves with the leader. In fact, if a very large bandwagon effect operates, this fall could continue for the entire set of individuals.[19] Typically, however, after some point the individual as a constituent becomes increasingly lost in the mass of supporters. Congestion–pollution-type effects appear, and the abstinence price begins to rise. Thus, were a leader's support cost to be identical to the required abstinence price (as would be the case if all constituents were concentrated at *A*), a U-shaped support cost curve similar to that shown in Figure 7.10a emerges.[20] This curve shows how the abstinence price (as a required cost) falls at a fast rate as the bandwagon effect is realized and then rises at an increasing rate as the congestion–pollution effect materializes.

[19] Assuming that there is a well-defined set of individuals eligible to vote on the issue and that no other leader competes for the support of this constituency.
[20] Regarding bandwagon phenomena, see the interesting empirical study by Bartels (1985).

In order to examine the impact of these phenomena on the support price regarding any constituent, we need to add to the abstinence price (as a cost to the political leader and as it varies with number of supporters) the patronage cost to each supporter. We do so in Figure 7.10b. There we measure price along the vertical. We see that when A's support area extends as far as U, the abstinence price falls from AP to AQ, to which needs to be added patronage cost to the marginal constituent at U (derived from the gradient QF) to yield the support price UF that leader A needs to pay U. When A's support area extends as far as V, the abstinence price falls from AP to AR, to which needs to be added patronage cost to the marginal constituent at V (derived from the gradient RG) to yield the support price VG that A must pay V, and so forth. In this manner we derive A's support price margin line, the bold curve of Figure 7.10b, showing how the support price varies at the margin of leader A's support area as the support area increases from A to the right.[21]

(b) Competition between political leaders: Introduce a second political leader who as the first is assumed to be spatially immobile, that is, committed to his or her initial position B. He, too, has a margin line that begins at a point such as P' on a vertical axis at B measuring B's support price. We have indicated B's support price margin line as the dashed line beginning at P', which intersects A's support price margin line at point D. Were A and B not to engage in competition, their respective support areas would be AW and BW. However, as in Figure 7.9, this situation is unstable. Spatial discrimination regarding net support price can be expected to occur as well as competition and perhaps an intense support price war between the leaders for the individuals whose most preferred positions lie intermediate between the fixed positions of the two leaders.

Once again we can allow constituents to be continuously or discretely distributed in a policy space of one or more dimensions and conduct an analysis, although not graphically when more than two dimensions are involved.

7.5.3   The constituent's net price line

In the previous two sections, we have assumed that the political leader was responsible for bearing the patronage costs involved in overcoming the distance between each constituent's most preferred position and his

---

[21] Isard (1956) contains a detailed description of the method of construction of margin lines.

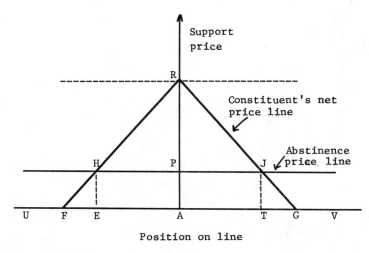

Figure 7.11. The constituent's net price line.

or her (the leader's) chosen position. We now examine the other extreme when the individual constituents are assumed to be indirectly and implicitly responsible for bearing these patronage costs, that is, where the incentive of an individual constituent to vote for the leader becomes smaller and smaller as the leader's position is more and more distant from the constituent's most preferred position.

(a) One political leader: In Figure 7.11, we assume the political leader's position is fixed at the point *A* and his or her potential constituents are uniformly distributed along the line *UV*. Let there be a fixed political budget that permits the leader to offer a uniform support price *AR* to all. We can then derive a constituent's net price line such as *FRG*. This line measures the net price received by the individual after deducting from *AR* the implicit costs involved in offsetting the distance separating the leader's chosen position and the individual's most preferred position,[22] that is, after adjusting *AR* to take into account the disincentive of the individual to support the leader because the leader's position is at a distance from the individual's most preferred position.

Assuming all individuals have the same abstinence price *AP* and that there is no competition from other leaders, the leader's support area can-

[22] This constituent's net price line may be taken to reflect a loss function. See Davis et al. (1970).

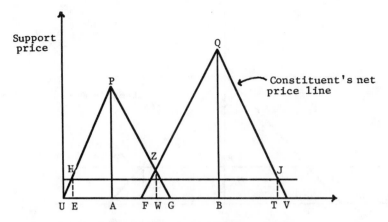

Figure 7.12. The constituent's net price lines: two political leaders with different budget constraints.

not extend beyond the points E and T where the net price received by an individual is equal to his (or her) abstinence price. Note, also, that each constituent lying within the stretch ET receives a surplus (that parallels consumer surplus in economics) equal to the difference between the net price at his location and the abstinence price. In contrast, in Figure 7.8 the leader does not permit (retains for himself) such potential surplus.

If the number of individuals whose most preferred positions lie somewhere between E and T constitute less than 51 percent of the voting strength, then the leader cannot be successful in a bid to be elected (reelected) while maintaining the position A. On the other hand, if more than 51 percent of the voting strength is captured, then the leader can afford to reduce the support price offered to constituents and retain some political resources in stock for another campaign.

(b) Competition between political leaders: Introduce a second political leader B who is committed to his (or her) initial position as is A; see Figure 7.12. Let A be the first leader to enter the arena. His fixed political budget permits him to offer all individuals the support price AP; his constituent's net price line is then given by UPG. Next B enters. Let B have a larger political budget. This permits him to offer a higher support price BQ, and the corresponding constituent's net price line is given by FQV.

Those individuals whose most preferred position lies to the right of point W will then support the leader at B (if they support anyone) because they obtain a higher net price from him; whereas those to the left of W will consider supporting only A. Assuming a uniform abstinence price represented by EH ($= TJ$), those individuals whose most preferred positions lie to the left of E and to the right of T will support neither the leader at A nor the leader at B – for the net price received is less than their abstinence price.[23] Each leader now has a well-defined support area and can estimate what proportion of the constituents' most preferred positions lie within this support area.

Figure 7.12 was constructed assuming the same slope for each political leader's constituent's net price line and for all sets of constituents. We can let the slopes vary regularly or irregularly to reflect different degrees of charisma and willingness of individuals to compromise from their most preferred positions. The results are obvious. Moreover, we can easily generalize the analysis to handle discrete distributions of the most preferred positions of constituents in policy space of one or more dimensions.

7.5.4   Scale effects and marginal productivity: the net price margin line

(a) One political leader: In this section we recognize that the support price a leader is prepared to offer an individual may reflect the potential effect of that individual's support on the leader's political power base. Specifically, the leader may focus on the marginal product he or she obtains from an individual's support. When the level of support for a leader comes from a relatively few individuals, we may hypothesize that the marginal product of an additional unit of support increases as more and more individuals are attracted to the leader. In fact, it could be possible for this increase to continue (although at a decreasing rate) until the entire set of individuals supports the leader. However, following traditional economic production theory, one may hypothesize that after some point the support of additional individuals adds less and less to the political leader's power base (e.g., there may be diminishing productivity in the production of power per se) and hence that marginal product falls. The result is that the leader confronts an inverted U-shaped marginal productivity

---

[23] If the abstinence price of individuals is so high that the net constituent's price lines intersect the abstinence price line before they intersect each other, then the leaders do not effectively compete.

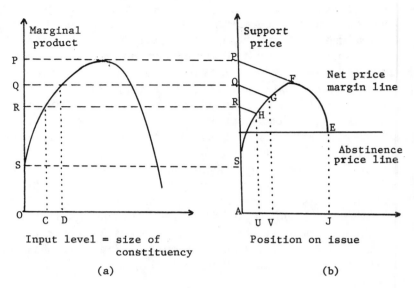

Figure 7.13. (a) A marginal productivity curve. (b) A net constituent margin line.

curve, such as in Figure 7.13a, showing how the marginal product of an additional unit of support rises sharply at first, falls off, and then declines at an increasing rate as the number of supporters steadily increases.

In order to examine the effect of the phenomena of varying marginal productivity upon the constituent's net price line, we need to subtract from the marginal product price the patronage costs that constituents indirectly or implicitly bear when their most preferred position does not coincide with the leader's position. We do so in Figure 7.13b. There we measure along the vertical axis the support price defined by marginal product. Thus, if the size of the constituency is $0C$, by Figure 7.13a the marginal product is $0R$; and as a result leader A's support price for all constituents that he or she pays is AR, as depicted on Figure 7.13b. But if a size $0C$ of constituency corresponds to a support area in which U is a marginal constituent (on the boundary), then U indirectly or implicitly bears a patronage cost defined by the gradient RH so that his or her net price is only UH. If the size of the leader's constituency is $0D$, by Figure 7.13a the marginal product is $0Q$. But if a size $0D$ of constituency corresponds to a support area in which V is a marginal constituent, then V indirectly or implicitly bears a patronage cost defined by the gradient QG so that his or her net price is only VG. And so forth. In this manner we

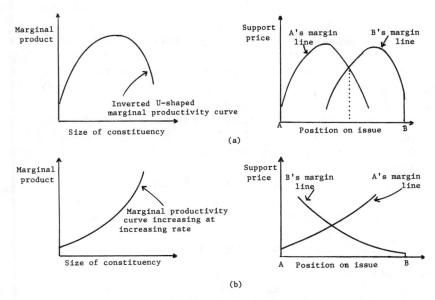

Figure 7.14. Scale effects: two competing political leaders: (a) stable situation; (b) unstable situation.

derive the curve of Figure 7.13b, showing how the constituent's net price at the margin varies with the change in the size of the constituency within the political leader's support area.

Assuming no competition from other political leaders, once the constituent's abstinence price is given (e.g., line *JE* in Figure 7.13b), the boundary of the leader's support area can be found; it is that point (*J* in Figure 7.13b) where the net price received by the constituent at the margin is equal to his or her abstinence price.

(b) Competition between political leaders: Introduce a second leader *B* with his or her net price margin line (see Figure 7.14a, b). Figure 7.14a indicates a stable situation. The net price margin lines of the two political leaders are declining when they intersect, and the point of intersection forms the boundary between the support areas of the two leaders. Figure 7.14b indicates an unstable situation. The net price margin lines of the two political leaders are increasing when they intersect. However, whichever leader enters the arena first can set a support price high enough so that the second leader would have little incentive to enter. This case is comparable to the case of instability that arises in physical (economic)

space when two firms are subject to continuously decreasing marginal costs in production.[24]

There are two other cases involving symmetry that are of interest. One would involve the intersection of margin lines when both are declining, as in Figure 7.14a, but where marginal productivity for each political leader is increasing throughout, though at a decreasing rate. This case, as the one depicted in Figure 7.14a, is stable. The second would involve the intersection of margin lines when both are increasing at a decreasing rate, in contrast to the case in Figure 7.14b where the margin lines are increasing at an increasing rate. This case, as the one depicted in Figure 7.14b, is unstable.

Once again, we can extend the analysis to cover cases where potential constituents are discretely distributed over space; in such cases the margin lines may lose their regularity.

7.6   Relocation of potential leaders: Hotelling-type analysis

In the discussion of the previous section on support areas for two political leaders, we assumed that each leader's choice of a location was fixed beforehand. However, in reality, political leaders, as mobile hotdog stands along a beach, do relocate. We may begin to conduct an analysis by assuming, as before, an even distribution of individuals' most preferred positions along a line, say, line AB. However, we now allow the political leaders at A and B to shift location at zero cost.[25] Posit the following:

1. Conditions of constant marginal productivity obtain and marginal product pricing is in effect.
2. The support prices AP and BQ are the same and fixed for all individuals (see Figure 7.15a, b).
3. The gradients of the net constituent price lines are the same in both directions and equal for each political leader such that all individuals can always receive a net price at least equal to their abstinence price.
4. Complete information (no uncertainty) exists,[26] an assumption we shall later drop.

---

[24] In Figure 7.14a, b the marginal productivity curves are such as to yield only one equilibrium point. When their shape is such as to yield more than one equilibrium point, modification of the statements in the text is required.

[25] Note that we move from one extreme assumption (complete spatial immobility) to another extreme assumption (complete spatial mobility). However, political leaders may often be restricted by historical and cultural factors, party lines, previous commitments, etc., in their set of permissible locations.

[26] We are also assuming a simple action–reaction situation with each leader taking the other's actions as fixed. Of course, more sophisticated strategies are possible, e.g., see Hinich et al. (1973) and McKelvey and Ordeshook (1976), which consider game-theoretic approaches.

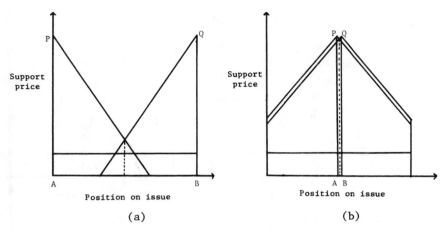

Figure 7.15. (a) A set of "unstable" separated positions. (b) A set of "stable" central location positions.

Then, as per Hotelling, the two leaders A and B will converge to positions next to each other at (or very close to) the center of the line (see Figure 7.15b). This is so because if such were not the case, then that leader who was serving the smaller side of the area (line) would (1) relocate next to the second leader if the second were already at the center point or (2) leapfrog over the second leader in order to serve the larger side of the area (line), in turn causing the second leader to leapfrog over the first and generating a sequence of leapfrogs until they both converge to the center. The resulting equilibrium is stable in a well-behaved situation.[27]

If convergence at a central location results in some individuals receiving a net price less than their abstinence price, then the political leaders in seeking to maximize their support areas will reach a stable equilibrium situation with separated locations[28] (see Figure 7.16a, b). This is so since by shifting away from each other, each gains more constituents than he or she loses.

Maintain all assumptions in the first paragraph of this section but allow the support price offered by each political leader to increase above $AP = BQ$. Also let the leaders have resources to effect such an increase. Price escalation will result. The absolute limit to this escalation is reached

---

[27] This result, based here on constituent's net price lines, has also been reached and further elaborated in Downs (1957) and Smithies (1941).

[28] If separated locations still leave some potential constituents with a net support price less than their abstinence price from either leader, then the nature of the final noncompetitive equilibrium is indeterminate. A number of sets of separate locations yield identical support areas for each political leader.

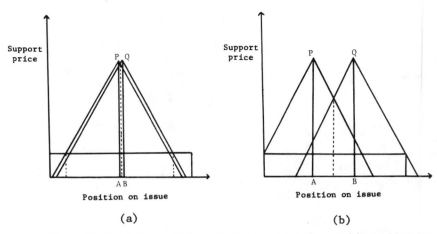

Figure 7.16. (a) A set of "unstable" central location positions. (b) A set of "stable" separated positions.

when one of the leaders exhausts his (or her) political resources (i.e., faces "bankruptcy") and is forced to leave the arena.[29] Before this limit is reached, however, one of the leaders may voluntarily cease bidding up his support price offer when he judges that the marginal costs of doing so would exceed his expected marginal gains.[30] In effect, he leaves the arena.

Maintain all the assumptions initially stated but allow the gradients of the constituent's net price lines of the two leaders to be different, the gradient for a given political leader being the same in both directions. This might reflect different levels of charismatic appeal. A support area enclave for the leader with the steepest gradient, say, B, temporarily appears and disappears as political leader A constantly reacts to B's location choice by locating adjacent to B and B reacts to A by locating away from A. Figure 7.17 depicts a temporary support area enclave for B. If we drop the assumption of short-sighted political leaders, A can adopt the strategy of announcing that he or she will always take the same policy position as B. This yields a stable equilibrium with B eliminated.

Maintain all initial assumptions but allow the support prices offered by the two leaders to differ (reflecting, e.g., different marginal productivity). As in the discussion associated with Figure 7.17, a support area enclave

[29] Even if the leaders start off with or reach positions identical to the "stable" separated locations, either competitive or noncompetitive, associated with Figure 7.16b, the fact that they have access to political resources results in this price escalation.

[30] However, if we permit spatial discrimination in the support price offered individuals, each political leader will recognize that the practice of such discrimination could result in an increase in his support area given the volume of his resources and the action of the other leader. Consequently, a more complicated price escalation results.

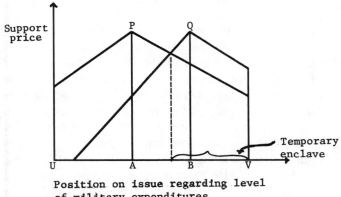

Figure 7.17. A temporary support area enclave: leaders with different gradients of constituent's net price line.

for the leader with the lower price, say, *B*, temporarily appears and disappears as political leader *A* constantly reacts to *B*'s location position choice by locating adjacent to *B* and *B* reacts to *A* by locating away from *A*. As before, if we allow *A* to adopt the strategy of announcing that he or she will always take the same policy position as *B*, a stable equilibrium results with *B* eliminated.

The discussion thus far has assumed a uniform distribution of individuals' most preferred positions. However, if the distribution were symmetric and single peaked at the center, it would appear that all the preceding conclusions hold. To see this, conceive the axis *UV* in Figure 7.17 as an elastic rubber band. Then, bearing in mind that no two individuals can occupy the exact same position in space, redefine distance so that every two neighboring individuals are a unit apart. The constituent's net price lines of the preceding figures are no longer of constant slope, but still they always slope down from the center (when the slope is not zero), though irregularly.

Examination of the consequences of relaxing any of the other assumptions (e.g., allowing constituent's net price lines to have different gradients in the two directions or to be nonproportional to distance or allowing unequal abstinence prices, multiple-peak and nonsymmetric distributions of constituents, etc.) is beyond the scope of this book.

7.7   Effects and value of information development

Now we drop a major unrealistic assumption. We take the leader to have incomplete information. He (or she) has just some imprecise ideas about the distribution of the most preferred positions of the voting population. He may not know too much about their abstinence prices, the patronage costs required to obtain support from different clusters of voters, his charismatic appeal as well as that of his opponent, and so on. In brief, he is uncertain about many factors that affect voter support, the c-power obtainable, and the like. However, he does have the option of collecting and processing information to increase his stock of information. Thereby he can reduce his uncertainties and, in accord with the discussion in Chapter 6, be better able to attack his problem of finding that position in policy space (a set of policies) that would be best for him.

There are innumerable ways in which the leader may collect, process, and/or disseminate information. Also, there are innumerable background situations (psychological, social, economic, etc.) from which his efforts might stem. For our purposes, limited space forces us to consider only a few; and we consider simple ones that can help in pulling together the diverse analytical frames thus far discussed.

7.7.1   A search for the mode: gains and costs

Consider a leader facing a political opponent in a simple Hotelling-type situation such as depicted in Figure 7.15b. However, let us be more realistic and recognize incomplete information and, in particular, incomplete information regarding the distribution of the most preferred positions of the voting population. This situation may obtain because there has recently been a major shift in public opinion.[31] Let the leader be motivated to obtain information on this distribution. He (or she) accepts the view that the most preferred positions of the voting population are symmetrically distributed about a single mode, which then must be, ex definitione, the mean position. He assumes that neither he nor his opponent currently is offering a platform consistent with the modal position. Therefore, to win an election, he needs only to shift his current position to the modal one, ceteris paribus.[32]

More specifically, the leader, as is currently (1985–6) the case, considers the level of military expenditures the key issue around which a platform must be built. Since the voting population thinks only in terms of a whole number of billions of dollars, he or she wants to estimate the

---

[31] See the interesting, related discussion by Brady (1985), who analyzes how the impact of change in preferences and views of the electorate leads to a strong and unified policy in Congress and hence to the necessary power to effect appropriate major shifts in policy. See also Page and Shapiro (1983).

[32] He also assumes that his opponent is or will be at a sufficient distance from the modal position so that if he (the leader) were to locate there, his and his opponent's positions would be clearly distinguishable.

mean of a random sample of the positions of the voting population that is no more than $1.5MMM different than the true mean (true mode). From observing past public opinion polls, the leader is convinced that 95% of the positions taken by the voting population (one position per voter) are always within a 10 percent range of the existing level of expenditures.[33]

To ease computations, in what follows we use round numbers. We take $300MMM to be the existing level (roughly the U.S. level in 1986) and $300 ± 30MMM to define the preceding 95 percent range. Hence, using standard statistics for a normal distribution, the leader's assumption may be taken to be equivalent to $1.96\sigma = \$30$MMM, where σ is the standard deviation of the positions of the voting population. For his or her decision making regarding information production, the leader requires (wants from us) a function indicating how his or her level of confidence in a sample mean will rise with an increase in the sample. This can be provided using the standard statistical z tables for

$$z = \frac{\bar{x} - \mu}{\sigma/\sqrt{n}} \tag{7.7.1}$$

where $\bar{x}$ is the mean of the sample, μ is the true mean (mode) of the population, σ is the standard deviation of the population, and n is the size of the sample. Since the leader requires that

$$|\bar{x} - \mu| \leq 1.5\text{MMM} \tag{7.7.2}$$

and since he or she proceeds on the assumption that $1.96\sigma = \$30$MMM, we obtain

$$z = \frac{\$1.5\text{MMM}\sqrt{n}}{\$30\text{MMM}/1.96} = \frac{1.96}{20}\sqrt{n} \quad \text{or} \quad 0.098\sqrt{n} \tag{7.7.3}$$

Using the standard z table, we derive that to achieve, for example, 92 percent probability that the sample mean will be the true mean requires a sample of 320 observations, and to achieve 99 percent probability, a sample of 681 observations is needed.

In deciding whether he (or she) will undertake the sample and incur its cost, the leader has in mind the value V of winning the election. He also has in mind a probability τ of his winning should he not obtain the information that the sample would generate and the probability of winning if

---

[33] Of course, the same type of analysis as undertaken in this section can be repeated for alternative assumptions by the political leader. The numerical values within each table and for the examples given in what follows and in the Appendixes will change, but the method for constructing such tables remains the same.

Table 7.1. *Size of optimal sample and profits for selected costs per unit sample*

Cost of a sample (1)	α = 0.0		α = 0.4	
	Size of optimal sample (2)	Profits (3)	Size of optimal sample (4)	Profits (5)
$1.00	1,003	$98,806	907	98,903
2.00	873	97,876	779	98,068
5.00	705	95,548	613	96,020
10.00	580	92,373	491	93,296
20.00	460	87,244	376	89,031
50.00	310	76,057	240	80,167
100.00	208	63,445	157	70,570
200.00	120	47,697	97	58,391

he selects a platform consistent with the mean value of the sample. Finally, he has estimated the cost c per voter sampled.

If the leader were 100 percent confident that the mean value of the sample was the true mean, he (or she) would estimate the net gain Π from sampling as

$$\bar{E}(\Pi) = V - nc - \tau V \tag{7.7.4}$$

However, he knows after talking with an expert pollster that he cannot have such confidence; hence he estimates his net gain as

$$E(\Pi) = qV - nc - \tau V \tag{7.7.5}$$

where q is the probability that the sample mean will be within $1.5MMM of the true mean given his assumptions regarding symmetry and distribution. That is,

$$q = \mathrm{pr}(|\mu - \bar{x}_n| \le \nu) \tag{7.7.6}$$

where $\nu = \$1.5MMM$ and pr means probability.

The pollster, however, might point out to the leader that he (or she) is understating his expected gains from the sample since even if $|\bar{\mu} - x_n| > \$1.5MMM$, say, by a little bit, his opponent (given the state of incomplete information) can never be certain of where the true mean lies even if he, the opponent, conducts an extensive sample after the leader has taken a position. Hence, he might advise the leader to add a term $\alpha\bar{q}$ to Eq. (7.7.5). In this term (1)

$$\bar{q} = \mathrm{pr}(\nu \le |\mu - \bar{x}_n| \le a) \tag{7.7.7}$$

Table 7.2. *Effects of variation in α*

Degree of optimism, α	Optimal size of sample, n*	Expected profits, E (Π)
0.0	460	$87,244
0.1	442	87,617
0.2	423	88,031
0.3	401	88,498
0.4	376	89,031
0.5	348	89,651
0.6	315	90,391
0.7	279	91,296
0.8	240	92,429
0.9	204	93,843
1.0	176	95,548

where a is an amount (say, $3MMM) by which if the mean sample were to differ from the true mode, the leader judges for sure (although statistically such cannot be the case) that the opponent will propose a level of expenditures closer to the true mean; and (2) α is a probability reflecting the leader's attitude (pessimistic–optimistic) about whether his opponent will be closer to the true mean than he if $\nu < |\mu - \bar{x}_n| \leq a$.

In any case we know that with Eq. (7.7.5), with or without the conditions of the term $\alpha\bar{q}$, the pollster can tell the leader what the leader's optimal size n of the sample should be. [In section 7.C.1 we present the relevant mathematical statement lying behind the determination of an optimal n that is unique for each possible c (cost per unit sample)]. For example, the pollster might present the leader with Table 7.1 (for $V = $100,000$, $\nu = $1.5MMM$, $a = $3MMM$, and $\tau = 0.0$). (This example, as well as all others to follow, refer to a 95 percent confidence level.)

As can be expected, as the cost per unit sample increases, the size of the optimal sample decreases, as does profit, for $\alpha = 0.0$ and $\alpha = 0.4$. Also, when $\alpha = 0.4$, profits are always greater, ceteris paribus, and the optimal sample smaller. Note that as long as $\tau < 0.47697$, it is profitable to conduct a sample even at the high cost of $200 per unit.

It may be of interest to note how total profits and the optimal size of the sample vary as α varies. In Table 7.2 we show this for $c = 20.00 and $\tau = 0.0$.

7.7.2 *Determining the investment value of information*

As suggested in the previous chapter, a neglected area of research in social science in general is the analysis of the role of information as a stock and

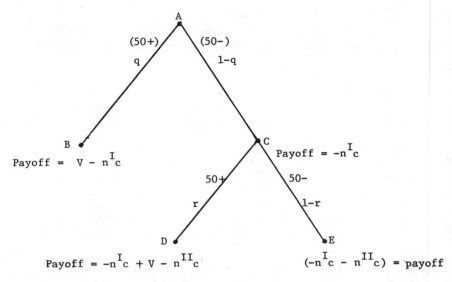

Figure 7.18. A two-election tree.

thus as a capital investment.[34] In particular, not too much attention has been given to the operational use of information in a realistic setting. We therefore wish to provide a simple illustration of such and thus to help begin more sophisticated and extensive investigation of this possibility for policy analysis and Peace Science.

Within the framework of the election problem just examined, we may ask: What is the value of the information gathered by the political leader for later use? For example, suppose the political leader contemplates running for a second election if he or she is unsuccessful – as may be the case when an election for senator in a state takes place two years after the preceding one. The leader thus has a second opportunity to obtain $50+$ percent of the vote. Assuming both elections are alike and the political situation has the same characteristics, his or her problem may be described by the tree of Figure 7.18.

He (or she) starts at node A. He collects n^I observations regarding the first election, which generates the probability q that he will receive $50+$ percent of the votes. If he does receive $50+$ percent of the votes, he reaches node B. He is elected and hence receives payoff $V - n^I c$. However, if he receives only $50-$ percent of the votes, which consequence has

---

[34] However, in economics this role has been receiving an increasing amount of attention. For example, see Arrow (1984) and Stiglitz (1984) and others cited in the previous chapter.

the probability $1 - q$, he arrives at point C, incurring the cost of $-n^l c$. At point C a second election opportunity arises. He takes n^{ll} observations, which together with the previous n^l observations generates the probability r that he will receive 50+ percent of the votes. If so, he arrives at node D and receives from this second election a payoff of $V - n^{ll}c$. If not, he arrives at point E, where the expected additional costs are $-n^{ll}c$.

Looked at as a whole, the expected net payoff $E(\Pi)$ for $\tau = 0.0$ is

$$E(\Pi) = (qV - n^l c) + (1 - q)(rV - n^{ll}c) \tag{7.7.8}$$

His or her expected costs are

$$E(\text{costs}) = n^l c + (1 - q)n^{ll}c = E(c) \tag{7.7.9}$$

The problem is to select an optimal combination of n^l and n^{ll}. The optimal values for these numbers together with the resulting q, r, $E(c)$, $E(\Pi)$, and s (s being the probability of election for two tries) have been derived (see Appendix 7.C) and are given in Table 7.3 for selected values of c and α. For the moment ignore column 16 of that table. As can be expected, Table 7.3 reveals that as the cost of a unit sample rises, both n^{l*} and n^{ll*} decrease (columns 2, 3, 9, and 10). This is associated with a decrease in expected profits $E(\Pi)$ (columns 7 and 14) and, up to $c = \$500$, an increase in expected costs (columns 8 and 15). When c rises to $\$1,000$, the decrease in the size of the sample is large enough to reduce total expected costs in the case of $\alpha = 0.0$ even though c rises. As can also be expected, q, r, and s also steadily decrease. See section 7.B.1 for further discussion.

In reality, it is often the case that the information n^l cannot be expected to have full use for the second stage. In these cases we can apply a "depreciation" factor γ, where $0 \le \gamma \le 1$, so that the number of usable samples in the second try is $\gamma n^l + n^{ll}$. Such an adjustment tends to reduce the expected value of election. Also, we may often expect a second type of adjustment. This adjustment discounts the worth of the addition to expected gain accruing from the second try primarily because it occurs at a later time. See section 7.B.2 for a relevant example and discussion.

With Table 7.3, we can now proceed to answer our basic question, namely, what is the investment value (IV) of the first sample n^l, in particular, the value of the use of n^l for the second election try? In Table 7.3, we observe that when $c = \$500$ or more, the size of the second sample is zero for $\alpha = 0.0$. Taking the case where $c = 500$, we note that overall expected profits are $\$51,400$, or approximately $\$12.0$ per unit of n^{l*} for $\tau = 0.0$. However, if the second try was not taken, the expected profits after the first try would be $qV - n^{l*}c = \$48,000 - \$21,500 = \$36,500$, or approximately $\$8.5$ per unit of n^{l*}. The difference, namely, $\$3.5$, may

Table 7.3. Outcomes for selected values of c and α

| α = 0.0 | | | | | | | | α = 0.4 | | | | | | | |
c (1)	n^{I*} (2)	n^{II*} (3)	q (4)	r (5)	s (6)	E(II) (7)	E(c) (8)	n^{I*} (9)	n^{II*} (10)	q (11)	r (12)	s (13)	E(II) (14)	E(c) (15)	IV (16)
$5	187	518	82.0	99.1	99.8	98,400	1,402	134	479	83.7	99.08	99.85	98,800	1,061	0.82
10	169	411	79.7	98.2	99.6	97,100	2,523	120	371	81.7	98.2	99.7	97,800	1,877	1.83
20	149	311	76.8	96.4	99.2	94,700	4,421	105	271	79.3	96.6	99.3	96,100	3,222	4.01
50	120	190	71.7	91.6	97.6	88,900	8,689	84	156	75.0	92.2	98.0	91,900	6,153	12.50
100	97	111	66.6	84.2	94.7	81,300	13,412	67	90	70.3	86.3	96.0	86,600	9,372	29.70
200	74	46	60.1	71.7	88.7	70,200	18,473	52	45	64.9	77.8	92.2	78,600	13,558	70.20
500	43	0	48.0	48.0	72.9	51,400	21,500	33	10	55.2	60.8	82.4	63,700	18,741	224.40
1,000	21	0	34.6	34.6	57.3	36,300	21,000	21	0	46.0	46.0	70.9	49,900	21,000	460.00
2,000	8	0	21.8	21.8	38.9	22,900	16,000	10	0	33.2	33.2	55.4	35,400	20,000	1,336.00
5,000	2	0	11.0	11.0	20.8	10,800	10,000	3	0	18.7	18.7	33.9	18,900	15,000	4,065.00

Note: s = probability of election for two tries.

then be viewed as one type of investment value. Where, however, n^{II*} is not zero, we may take the *addition* to the expected value of the first try resulting from the second try with sample n^{I*} (rather than $n^{I*} + n^{II*}$) as the investment value of n^{I*}. Dividing this addition by $n^{I}*$ yields one type of investment value for a unit of n^{I*}.

Still another procedure derives the investment value by focusing on the margin. It involves the following argument:

1. The *mc* (marginal cost) of the sample n^{II} in the second election problem is c.
2. Hence the *mr* (marginal gain) from the sample n^{II} in the second problem is c.
3. Thus the *mr* (marginal gain) from the sample n^{I} in the second problem is c since a unit of n^{I} makes the same contribution to the second election problem as a unit of n^{II}.
4. Since at the time of the sampling for the first election problem, the probability is $1 - q$ that the first sample will be used for the second election problem, the *mr* at that time of the first sample for its use in the second election problem is therefore only $(1 - q)c$, the *investment value* (at the margin) of a unit of n^{I}.[35]

In column 16 of Table 7.3, we have recorded the investment values (at the margin) of sample n^{I} for the different unit sample costs and for $\alpha = 0.4$. As can be expected, these values rise significantly as c increases and the associated value of q decreases.[36]

With the preceding reasoning, we can determine the investment value (at the margin) of a unit of n^{I} when there are more than two election possibilities of the character noted. For example, it is

$$(1 - q^{I})(1 - q^{II})c + (1 - q^{I})q^{II}c = (1 - q^{I})c$$

when there are three such probabilities,[37] and where q^{I} and q^{II} are the probabilities of receiving 50+ percent of the votes in the first election and second election, respectively.

This discussion indicates in one way how the dynamical systems

---

[35] Of course, since the *mc* of n^{I} is c and since the *mr* of n^{I} must equal the *mc* of n^{I}, it follows that $c - (1 - q)c = qc$, the *mr* of n^{I} for the first election problem. That is, qc is the marginal value of n^{I} for the current use.

[36] If we recognize in the undiscounted case that only $(1 - \gamma)n^{I}$ of n^{I} is useful for the second election problem $(0 \leq \gamma \leq 1)$, where γ is the rate of depreciation (obsolescence), then the *mr* of $1/(1 - \gamma)$ units of n^{I} is equal to the marginal revenue of one unit of sample n^{II}, which is equal to c. Hence, the *investment value* of a unit of $n^{I} = (1 - \gamma)(1 - q)c$.

[37] When there are n such possibilities, it is

$$(1 - q^{I})q^{II}c + (1 - q^{I})(1 - q^{II})q^{III}c + \cdots$$
$$+ (1 - q^{I})(1 - q^{II}) \cdots (1 - q^{n-1})c = (1 - q^{I})c \qquad (7.7.10)$$

approach to information as an investment (discussed in Chapter 15) can be operationalized. In that chapter we speak about inputs, in particular labor inputs, that a participant and a mediator, might employ in information production – which of course results when new information is collected and preserved. This phenomenon can be viewed as occurring when in the example of this section we take the variable c to comprise the cost of the labor input of the leader, when he himself conducts the survey, by telephone or in person.

However, the variable c can be taken to comprise labor inputs of other individuals in taking the sample and also other resource inputs; and the dynamical systems analysis of Chapter 15 can be easily broadened to consider such inputs. Hence, when the procedures of this section are considered to be among the set of ways that may be deemed by a political leader to be valid for determining the investment value of sample information, the examples of this section can be considered to represent one kind of operationalization of dynamical systems analysis.

7.7.3   Some complicating factors

Admittedly, the previous simple example abstracts too much from reality to be taken to have general significance. However, it does enable us to consider a host of other factors that impinge upon the question of whether or not to collect, process, and/or disseminate information and if so what kinds of information, how, and for whom.

For example, after a survey of the population eligible to vote, the leader may expect with a probability of 99 percent that the sample mean and thus the position he (or she) is motivated to take is within $1.5MMM of the true mean of the most preferred positions of the voting population. Such, however, does not mean that all the voting population will in effect vote and that 50+ percent (with 99 percent probability) may vote for him. On one side of the distribution the tendency to abstain from voting may be greater than on the other, ceteris paribus; and/or his opponent may have more charisma than he does so that the opponent's supporters are less likely to abstain when there is bad weather or other extenuating circumstances for voting. Hence, to preclude differential abstinence that is unfavorable to him, he may need to incur a patronage cost per voter. In one situation it may be a constant amount over all voters (as depicted in Figure 7.11), and so its effectiveness may decline with the distance a voter's most preferred position is from that chosen by the leader. In another situation patronage cost may rise with the distance of the voter's most preferred position from the position chosen by the leader when the leader wishes its effectiveness to be the same among all voters (see Figure

7.8). When combined with the cost of the sample required to yield a certain level of assurance of victory, such patronage cost may in the mind of the leader exceed the expected gross profit of the sample itself. Hence this may cause the leader to forgo a sample. Or the sum of the two costs (patronage and sample) may exceed the total resources at his command; thus he may set a constraint on the cost of the sample, which in turn would affect its size as well as expected gross profits. Perhaps, too, he may need to consider a cost of relocation from his present position.

In the even simpler situation where the leader confronts a fixed set of voters with no opponent present, he (or she) may judge *ex ante* that the cost of the sample would be more than offset by the savings in total patronage cost that would result were he to take a position at the sample mean rather than the position he would take without the sample information.

The problem of estimating patronage cost, that is, of setting a patronage price to be paid each voter, raises the question of what is the proper price. This problem has aspects parallel to the traditional "inventory" problem of business. The leader may set too low a price and thus receive too little support and thereby fail to win the election (or decrease the probability of winning); such corresponds to the loss of profits from having an inventory inadequate for the actual demand that materializes. Or he or she may set too high a price and thus receive more "positive" support than required to have a given confidence level for winning – and thus to have incurred too high a cost – although as with excess inventory such may have some future "investment" value, a value again to be estimated, and one that may fall sharply over time.

Consideration of both patronage costs and sampling costs can be even more involved. It may be that a major money contribution or other support is offered by a lobby or similar group provided the leader locates at a position desired by that lobby or group. Thus the expected patronage cost at the sample mean may be greater than the *net* of (1) a larger patronage cost less (2) a major contribution were he or she to locate at the position that would call forth such support. Here, then, it becomes necessary to construct critical isodapanes – critical with reference to the sample mean position – and even more so when there are several points at which different money contributions and support might be forthcoming. A still more involved problem arises when the distribution of voters is not unimodal and regular, when, for example, there are several modes. At one extreme the frequency of the most preferred positions may fall off very sharply on each side of a mode to yield clear-cut clusters; at the other, the frequency may fall off very slowly, merging with another at a point intermediate between that mode and a neighboring mode.

Information regarding multimodal distributions becomes essential when we consider the problem of agglomeration in the sense of coalition formation. As was clearly pointed out in the discussion associated with Figures 7.6 and 7.7, there are usually many possible positions for agglomeration (compromise points in the agglomeration set), each an equilibrium point but each having a different value for each participant. Information about the distribution of one's own constituency as well as that of each other participant (obtained by additional samples) can be of great value to a participant in the bargaining over where to locate (which compromise to adopt). Moreover, such information may also be useful in the decision as to which level of agglomeration to propose or which coalition to strive for.

Pursuing the analysis further, we run into the question of "reaction-type" effects (positive and negative) – for example, the extent to which the very location of a leader at the sample mean position comes to change the most preferred position of some of the voters and affect the true mean μ and the true standard deviation σ. This effect cannot be identified by a sample, for on one account alone we never know how close the sample mean is actually to the true mean. But of course, in making his (or her) estimate of patronage cost, say, with location at the sample mean, the leader should adjust his calculations for these positive and negative reaction effects. Moreover, as in the discussion associated with Figure 7.10, he should consider these effects, too, with regard to the support of his opponent.

Where constituents' reactions lead to an irregular (and even a multimodal) distribution of most preferred positions, the analysis becomes still more complicated when the leader and his (or her) opponents find it expedient to relocate as per Hotelling (as discussed in section 7.6). In one case, the leader may behave as a Stackelberg leader (see Isard et al. 1969) and take a position to which the expected optimal response of his opponent (as a follower) results in an equilibrium joint action. In another case, there may be a series of reactions of the opponent and the leader to each other, leading perhaps to a stable myopic equilibrium position. In any such series, however, the constant shifting around by a leader may lead some constituents to regard him as irresponsible and be a "cost" to him.

This inability to conduct a precise analysis remains, and the problem becomes even more difficult when we consider several interest groups rather than several political leaders (as individuals) seeking the support of the public. This is so whether or not the group has a leader

1.   who is highly constrained (as in Chapter 14) by the wishes of the members of his or her group and approximates a 100 percent

pure representative, and where the leader and members of the group learn together; or
2. who resorts to simple or stratified random sampling of members of the group because to know their preferences it is less costly to do so than to poll the full membership when it is very large.

These interest groups may in fact be the defense agencies, the presidential office, the environmentalists, and others concerned with taking positions on several (if not many) programs such as the military, the environment, poverty, and transportation (as discussed in Chapter 13). The analysis of the shifting around by each group of its position in reaction to the positions taken by others encounters even greater complexity for quantitative analysis and modeling than when the several behavioral units are individuals motivated by self-interest.

Of course, when we confront the problem (as we do in Chapters 6 and 16) of information research and development for developing not only new technology but new, inventive ideas (procedures) for conflict management, estimation of the probabilities of successful or satisfactory outcomes from diverse combinations of inputs can only be speculative. Here the necessary conditions do not obtain for using the normal distribution for inferring from sampling, although the use of other distributions may be found appropriate.

Finally, before closing this chapter, we may summarize our thinking in terms of a payoff matrix. Among the several actions discussed when we examined the political leader confronting an election were

a_1: do nothing (do not take sample);
a_2: take sample for use in the current election only;
a_3: take sample for use in the current election and in a second election if not already elected; and
a_4: take sample for use in the current election and each of several elections in which he or she may run if not already elected.

Each of these actions corresponds to a row. Among the possible columns that might be perceived by the leader as representing relevant states of the environment (some of which are incompatible with others) are states where

e_1: opponent's behavior and weather are ignored;
e_2: opponent is assumed not to react and weather is ignored;
e_3: one type of reaction of the opponent is assumed possible and weather is ignored;
e_4: a second type of reaction of the opponent is assumed possible and weather is ignored;

e_5:   one type of reaction of the opponent is assumed possible and the weather is good;

e_6:   one type of reaction of the opponent is assumed possible and the weather is bad;

and so on.

A fully rational and informed political leader would consider all these actions and states of the environment and even more – for example, the probability that the opponent will not follow him or her (in reacting) but act simultaneously, the probability that a third candidate will enter the political arena, and so on.

However, the less rational and poorly informed leader might consider only a few actions and a few states of the environment. At the extreme, he (or she) may be precedent oriented, saying that I have never taken a sample before and have been successful in rising in the ranks; why should I now? Or he may have a fix with a Gamson-type package of his culture (as discussed in section 4.3); his taking a sample would be losing face (an indication of a lack of confidence in his ability to win). In such cases, the payoff matrix reduces to one column and the two actions (rows) (1) do not take sample or (2) take a sample, with the cell opposite the first action being perceived to have the higher payoff. Or the leader may be behaving under crisis conditions and perceive only one possible action by his opponent. Or the leader may have limited capacity to handle variables and complicated situations and may be able to consider only actions a_1, a_2, and a_3 and states e_3 and e_4, thus involving six possible payoffs, a situation that fully taxes his mental abilities. And so forth.

7.8   Concluding remarks

We now wish to bring this chapter to a close. This chapter is in one sense the first of several concerned with policy analysis. In this chapter we have focused primarily upon the individual behaving unit, most often the political leader, in his (or her) choice of a set of particular policies, the military effort often being a key policy issue. He was motivated to maximize his payoff (utility) primarily by winning an election. He had in mind the desires (most preferred positions) of the voting population, the limited resources available to implement policies, and other constraints. We considered a series of simplified situations. First we took up a situation of two clusters of voters where the leader is motivated to find a location in policy space that minimizes total patronage costs (broadly defined) for winning an election. We then generalized the analysis to cover many clusters; and with the use of isodapanes we were able to embrace the effect of the possibilities for campaign contributions and other support upon his location in policy space were he to take specific alternative locations that do not minimize total patronage costs.

Possibilities of agglomeration (coalition formation) with other leaders at a particular compromise location in policy space were next considered. This was followed by support area analysis wherein the constituency's most preferred positions are treated as continuously distributed in space but where the analysis is generalizable to handle discrete distributions as well. Competition among two political leaders was introduced, marginal productivity and scale (bandwagon and congestion–pollution-type) effects examined, and then relocation behavior of the Hotelling variety considered. (Next, in Appendix 7.A the analysis is generalized to cover more than two competing political leaders, leading to the study of support areas in ways parallel to those developed by Lösch and Christaller in traditional location theory of economics and regional science and, when differentiated charisma is present, to the von Thünen-type approach.)

In the last section, we dropped the highly unrealistic assumption basic to the preceding analysis that each political leader was fully informed of the distribution (whether discrete or continuous) of the most preferred positions of the voting population. We considered the situations where a political leader had only incomplete information about the distribution of the most preferred positions of the voting population. He or she thus considered the possibility of taking a sample, involving costs. We then investigated in a fairly simplified situation what would be the optimum size of the leader's sample, a zero size (no sampling) being one possibility, for (1) different costs of a unit sample; (2) different perceived payoffs from winning an election; and (3) different degrees of optimism with regard to the probability of his or her winning were the sample mean to deviate from the true mean by no more than some prespecified amount, a parameter that itself can be treated as a variable. Next, we introduced the possibility of winning in a second election if he or she fails in the first and the possibility of additional sampling for the second election. We generalized to more than two elections and introduced a discount factor and an obsolescence (depreciation) rate on sampling information obtained with regard to previous elections in which a leader was unsuccessful. We then considered the investment value of information and the way the question of seeking information through sampling can be viewed in payoff matrix form.

The preceding analyses associated with sampling are operational and to our knowledge represent a significant new advance in policy analysis whether it concerns military (arms control) policy or any other. Clearly, major developments along this line now become possible. It is however beyond the scope of this book to attempt such, particularly when several competing leaders and interest groups are involved in strategic (game-theoretic) behavior.

Finally, we should note that there are many other places at which new, probing analysis is required. Clearly, we should move in the direction of a general equilibrium approach. For example, one serious shortcoming is the implicit assumption that a constituent's most preferred position is unaffected by actions of these leaders.[38] Perhaps this is partially true in our real world, but only partially. Furthermore, we have not made explicit the c-power and other production (or transformation) functions that govern the behavior of at least a fair, if not a large, number of political leaders. In addition, our agglomeration and coalition analysis is most naive, reflecting the relatively underdeveloped (although extensive) state of thinking on this problem. Finally, the entire analysis falls far short of depicting reality because it is essentially static in character and fails to capture the dynamics of the actual world.

Appendixes

7.A   Some further policy space analysis

7.A.1   *Policy space analysis for many political leaders with nonconstant marginal productivity: a parallel to Lösch–Christaller analysis*

When we recognize the existence of bandwagon and congestion effects and hence nonconstant marginal productivity, net price margin lines again become relevant. Take the simplest possible situation, namely, one political leader in isolation. If he or she locates at a point central to a given set of potential constituents, such as A in Figure 7.A.1, and thus serves constituents in both directions from this chosen position, the relevant net price margin line is no longer as depicted in Figure 7.13b but rather as the bold line in Figure 7.A.1. Allow a second political leader to enter the arena. If possible, he or she will choose a noncompetitive location on either side of A, and his or her margin line (e.g., the bold dashed line of Figure 7.A.1) will not intersect A's at any point above the abstinence price level. So likewise with a third, fourth, and so on, to the nth political leader. But if all constituents are to be represented, as in the Lösch location theory model, these margin lines must be compressed together at least to the point where any two neighboring lines intersect at the abstinence price level. This could be imagined to take place. But,

[38] See Stokes (1963), Page (1976), and Norpoth (1979) for a discussion of how the agenda the leaders set and the weights they attach to different issues can influence the voters' most preferred positions.

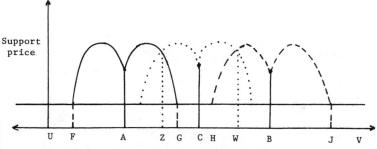

Figure 7.A.1. Competition between political leaders under conditions of nonconstant marginal productivity.

in addition, if existing political leaders are making "surplus" profits (or their equivalent), at some time in this process of appearance of new political leaders, an entering leader C, attracted by these surplus profits, may select a location intermediate between two existing leaders, say, those located at A and B in Figure 7.A.1. This could occur either when the support areas of the two existing leaders are just competitive or before they become competitive. In either case, the new leader competes for the support of the individuals between A and B and is able to do so effectively because he or she can offer a support price that yields a higher net price to individuals at and around C. This then tends to force A and B to shift their locations away from that chosen by the new leader C and hence to become more competitive with the neighbor on their other side. When the line UV extends indefinitely in both directions and when we have complete freedom of entry and exit at zero cost, it may be hypothesized that the equilibrium conditions will be (a) zero "surplus" profits for all political leaders; (b) the same level of support for all political leaders; and (c) the same net support price for the constituents at the margin for all in both directions.[1]

7.A.2 Political leaders with differentiated products and differentiated charisma: a von Thünen approach

Finally, allow three of our initial assumptions (see section 7.5) to be dropped simultaneously; that is, permit

1. three or more political leaders to be in the arena;
2. different support prices to be offered by each leader; and
3. the gradients of the constituent's net price lines to be different for each leader.

[1] For related analysis on the entry of new candidates in an election, see Greenberg and Shepsle (1987) and the literature cited therein.

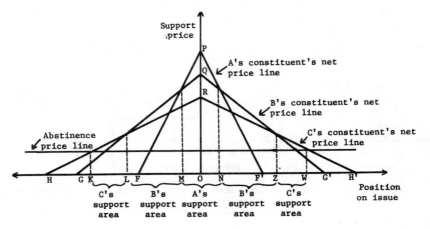

Figure 7.A.2. Support areas of several political leaders located at the same position.

In this situation, an outcome can develop that, at first glance, parallels the von Thünen analysis in conventional location theory.

To show this, suppose there is some factor (historical, previous commitments, psychological, legal, economic, and/or other) that induces several political leaders to choose the same central (or other) position in policy space.[2] Let them have different amounts of political resources at their disposal and different degrees of charismatic appeal to the constituency. As a consequence, different support price offers are made by the leaders (where these offers are determined in large part by the size of the leaders' respective political budgets) and differently sloped constituent's net price lines are realized (in large part because of differences among leaders in charismatic appeal and in the intensity with which the constituents hold to their most preferred position with respect to any leader). Where, say, three leaders are able to remain in the arena, we can have a situation as depicted in Figure 7.A.2. Each constituent will elect to give his or her support to that leader whose support price offer results in the highest net price to the individual (i.e., the largest voter "consumer surplus" at his or her most preferred position). The maximization of this surplus parallels the maximization of economic rent at each loction in physical space.

This type of analysis may be extended to incorporate (1) the effects of scale economies/diseconomies (bandwagon and pollution-type effects) on a political leader's support price offer and hence voter's "consumer surplus" at each position (here net price margin lines would be used in determining support area boundaries); and (2) the effects of product differentiation on a political leader's support price offer (here we may imagine quality differences in the product, promises, and

[2] If we allow a large cluster of voters to concentrate at the center, such would provide additional rationale for this assumption.

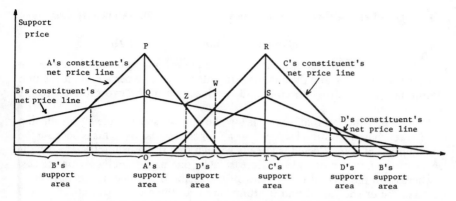

Figure 7.A.3. Support areas of several political leaders located at two different positions.

other "output" of political leaders). Promises, commitments to look after constituents and provide patronage, may be discounted by a factor reflecting the individuals' evaluation of the extent to which a political leader is capable of fulfilling promises and/or meeting commitments. A leader with a proven record of success on this score or with a more coherent and well-thought-out program of action will have a low discount (or even an up-count) factor applied to his or her stated price offer; whereas a leader with a past record of failure to fulfill promises and/or meet commitments or who presents a disorganized and ill-prepared program of action will have a high discount factor applied by potential constituents.

We could also generalize these results to an area in policy space and derive von Thünen-type rings. However, this leads to problems with metrics of the type mentioned in footnote 10. Again, these problems can be avoided if we make additional uniformity assumptions similar to those made by von Thünen (e.g., the plain is evenly endowed with resources, all farmers have the same ability, and factors of production are uniformly distributed). Such additional assumptions would take all leaders and constituents to be alike in the sense that they employ the same metric on any given issue, and these metrics effectively translate to a common unit all sets of issues being considered.

Should there be more than one position at which leaders are located (for the reasons already cited), such as positions 0 and T in Figure 7.A.3, the analysis becomes more complicated. However, the basic analysis does not change. Each individual still elects to support that political leader whose support price offer results in the largest net price (voter "consumer surplus") at his or her most preferred position. It is easy here to introduce the effects of positions especially "productive" for a particular leader. For example, because a leader, say, D, comes from a particular ethnic or minority group, the constituent's net price line associated with his or her support price offer is abruptly elevated at and between those points (say, Z and W in Figure 7.A.3), where the most preferred positions of individuals belonging to this ethnic or minority group are concentrated.

7.B   Further analysis of the election situation and information development

7.B.1   Further discussion of the two-election situation and Table 7.3

In addition to the comments in the text, there are several points of interest in the two-election situation and the outcomes in Table 7.3. These pertain to the relation of optimal sampling (the absolute and relative sizes of the two samples) to the cost of sampling.

We note in Table 7.3 that when c is low the optimal size sample n^{I*} for the first try is lower than the optimal size $n^{I*} + n^{II*}$ for the second try. This is because the probability q of being elected is already so high that if, for example, $n^I = n^{II}$, the leader would find it profitable to decrease n^I by one unit, thereby saving the cost c, whereas on the second try the cost of increasing n^{II} by one unit is only $(1 - q)c$. And he or she would find it profitable to continue to do so until $n^I = 187$ and $n^{II} = 518$ even though the contribution to s is greater for a unit of n^I. However, at a high enough c, the optimal size of the first sample comes to exceed that of the second. This is because the probability of being elected has fallen with lower optimal values of n^{I*} and n^{II*} so that the leader, if he or she starts with $n^I = n^{II}$, cannot afford to forgo shifting units from n^I to n^{II} because now the difference between c and $(1 - q)c$ is no longer greater than the difference in their contribution to $E(\Pi)$ via the difference in their contributions to s. Finally, after a point, the optimal size of the second sample becomes zero.[3] This is because the overall probability of election s has fallen to a very low level as a consequence of a high c so that the leader can afford to shift a unit from n^I to n^{II} even though there is a probability $1 - q$ that it may not be necessary to take that unit in sample n^{II}.

Finally, when comparing the outcomes for $\alpha = 0.4$ with $\alpha = 0.0$, we observe that up to the value of $c = \$500$ the corresponding samples in the former case are always smaller. This is so because the probability for election is always greater for any given size sample when $\alpha = 0.4$; that is, in taking a sample, the marginal-cost-equals-marginal-revenue relation is always reached at a smaller size sample when $\alpha = 0.4$. And accordingly, the values of q, r, s, and $E(\Pi)$ are always higher. Also, up to $c = \$500$, the $E(c)$ when $\alpha = 0.4$ are lower, as can be expected, but at \$2,000 and \$5,000, the $E(c)$ are higher. This is because the probability of election when $\alpha = 0.4$ has become so much higher than that at $\alpha = 0.0$ that it is desirable for n^I to be larger even though the very high c has reduced n^{II*} to zero.

7.B.2   The effects of discounting

To illustrate the effects of the discount rate β, we present in Table 7.B.1 selected outcomes for several rates of discount for the case where $c = \$2,000$, $\alpha = 0.0$, and $\tau = 0.0$. As can be expected, as β increases in Table 7.B.1, the optimal size of the second sample n^{II*} (column 3) decreases (since each unit is of less value) and so does expected gain $E(\Pi)$ (column 7). As a consequence of the decrease in n^{II*}, the probability r (column 5) of election associated with the second try also

---

[3] In Appendix 7.C we demonstrate that when $q \leq 0.5$, $n^{II*} = 0$. In that appendix, we employ the term $(1 - \beta)q$, where β is a discount rate (to be discussed later) that has been set at zero for the present problem.

Table 7.B.1. *Outcomes for selected discount rates*

β	n^{l*}	n^{ll*}	q	r	s	$E(\Pi)$	$E(c)$
0.0	149	311	76.8	96.4	99.2	94.8	4,421
0.1	216	226	85.0	96.1	99.4	93.0	5,000
0.2	266	157	89.0	95.6	99.5	91.7	5,665
0.3	305	95	91.3	95.0	99.57	90.8	6,265
0.4	338	37	92.8	94.2	99.59	90.1	6,813
0.5	364	0	93.8	93.8	99.62	89.5	7,280
0.6	386	0	94.6	94.6	99.71	88.9	7,720
0.7	407	0	95.2	95.2	99.77	88.4	8,140
0.8	426	0	95.7	95.7	99.81	88.0	8,520
0.9	444	0	96.1	96.1	99.85	87.6	8,880

Note: $c = \$20.00$, $\alpha = 0.0$, and $\tau = 0.0$.

decreased up to $\beta = 0.5$. To make up for (counteract) the decrease in n^{ll*}, the optimal size of the first sample n^{l*} increases, as does q (column 4). As a result of the increases in n^{l*} and q and the decreases in n^{ll*} and $1 - q$, the expected cost $E(c)$ (column 8) increases. Finally, the overall probability s (column 6) steadily increases because even though $n^{l*} + n^{ll*}$ decreases, the *effective* size $[n^{l*} + (1 - q)n^{ll*}]$ of the sample (which determines the overall probability s) increases. At $\beta = 0.5$, the discount factor has become so large that it pays to concentrate primarily on sampling for the first try, this sampling however still having value for the second try.

7.C   Technical materials on the value of information

7.C.1   A one-election situation: a one-stage problem

Let V, c, and n be the value of election, the cost of collecting one sample, and the size of the collected sample, respectively. (The leader will be elected and realize the value V if he or she succeeds in capturing more than half of the votes.) If we let

$$y = \text{leader's proposal} (\in R)$$
$$z = \text{opponent's proposal} (\in R) \quad\quad\quad (7.C.1)$$
$$f(x) = \text{density distribution of most preferred proposal}$$
$$\text{positions } x \text{ of voters}$$

and the leader's support area N be

$$N = \{x \in R: |x - y| < |x - z|\} \quad\quad\quad (7.C.2)$$

then his or her expected payoff $E(\Pi)$ is given by

$$E(\Pi) = V \operatorname{pr}\left(\int_{x \in N} f(x)\,dx > 0.5\right) - cn \quad\quad\quad (7.C.3)$$

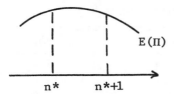

Figure 7.C.1. Two maximizers.

One way to interpret the term pr(·) is that the leader assumes that only if y is "very close" to the true mean μ of the distribution f (i.e., that $|y - \mu| < \bar{\nu}\sigma$, where $\bar{\nu}$ is allowable error in units of the standard deviation) does he (or she) have an opportunity to obtain more than half the votes. The leader, however, may view his opportunities more realistically and assume that if y is not "very close" but still "close" to the true mean (i.e., that $\bar{\nu}\sigma \leq |y - \mu| < \bar{a}\sigma$, where $\bar{a}$ is the second allowable error in units of σ), then he will obtain more than half of voters with probability α. Equation (7.C.3) is then expressed as

$$E(\Pi) = V\left[\text{pr}(|y - \mu| < \bar{\nu}\sigma) + \alpha\,\text{pr}(\bar{\nu}\sigma \leq |y - \mu| < \bar{a}\sigma)\right] - cn \qquad (7.C.4)$$

Finally if we assume that f is the normal function with a mean μ and a standard deviation σ, then by letting the probability density function and cumulative density distribution of the standard normal distribution be $\phi(t)$ and $\Phi(t)$, respectively, that is,

$$\phi(t) = \frac{1}{\sqrt{2\pi}} \exp\left(\frac{-t^2}{2}\right) \qquad (7.C.5)$$

$$\Phi(t) = \int_{-\infty}^{t} \Phi(t)\, dt \qquad (7.C.6)$$

Eq. (7.C.4) can be alternatively written as

$$E(\Pi) = 2V[(1 - \alpha)\Phi(\bar{\nu}\sqrt{n}) + \alpha\Phi(\bar{a}\sqrt{n}) - \tfrac{1}{2}] - cn \qquad (7.C.7)$$

Treating n as a continuous (real) variable, we take the first and second derivatives of $E(\Pi)$ with respect to n to obtain

$$\frac{dE(\Pi)}{dn} = \frac{V}{\sqrt{n}}\left[(1 - \alpha)\bar{\nu}\phi(\bar{\nu}\sqrt{n}) + \alpha\bar{a}\phi(\bar{a}\sqrt{n})\right] - c \qquad (7.C.8)$$

$$\frac{d^2E(\Pi)}{dn^2} = -\frac{V}{2n\sqrt{n}}\left[(1 - \alpha)\bar{\nu}\phi(\bar{\nu}\sqrt{n}) + \alpha\bar{a}\phi(\bar{a}\sqrt{n})\right]$$
$$+ \frac{V}{n}\left[(1 - \alpha)\bar{\nu}^2\phi'(\bar{\nu}\sqrt{n}) + \alpha\bar{a}^2\phi'(\bar{a}\sqrt{n})\right] \qquad (7.C.9)$$

where $\phi'(t) = (d/dt)\phi(t)$. It is evident that the first term on the right side of (7.C.9) is negative. To see the negativity of the second term, notice that $t > 0$ implies

$$\phi'(t) = -\frac{1}{\sqrt{2\pi}} t e^{-t^2/2} < 0 \qquad (7.C.10)$$

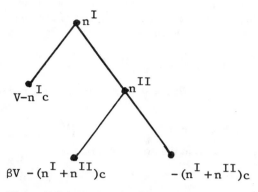

Figure 7.C.2. A two-election tree.

Hence we have $d^2E(\text{II})/dn^2 < 0$ implying that $E(\text{II})$ is strictly concave in n. Since

$$\lim_{n\to\infty} E(\text{II}) \le 2V[(1 - \alpha) + \alpha - \tfrac{1}{2}] - c \lim_{n\to\infty} n < 0 \qquad (7.\text{C}.11)$$

it follows that $E(\text{II})$ has a maximum in the domain Z_+ (a set of nonnegative integers) and it is unique except for a rare event that two consecutive values of n give rise to the same maximal $E(\text{II})$ (see Figure 7.C.1). To sum up:

Proposition 7.C.1: The function $E(\text{II}): Z_+ \rightarrow R$ defined in (7.C.7) has a unique maximizer or two consecutive maximizers.

7.C.2 A two-election situation: a two-stage problem

In this case, the leader has a first opportunity to receive 50+ percent of the vote and be elected (which is worth V); and if he (or she) fails, he has another opportunity to receive 50+ percent of the vote in a second election (which is worth βV, where β is a discounting factor). In seeking the second election, he may make use of the first stage's data and possibly new data (see Figure 7.C.2).

If we let n^i be the number of samples to be collected in the ith round, then the expected profit of the second round given n^I is

$$
\begin{aligned}
E(\text{II}^\text{II} : n^\text{I}) &= \beta V[\text{pr}(|\bar{x}^\text{II} - \mu| \le \bar{\nu}\sigma) + \alpha \, \text{pr}(\bar{\nu}\sigma \le |\bar{x}^\text{II} - \mu| < \bar{a}\alpha)] - c(n^\text{I} + n^\text{II}) \\
&= 2\beta V[(1 - \alpha)\Phi(\bar{\nu}\sqrt{n^\text{I} + n^\text{II}}) + \alpha\Phi(\bar{a}\sqrt{n^\text{I} + n^\text{II}}) - \tfrac{1}{2}] - c(n^\text{I} + n^\text{II})
\end{aligned}
$$
$$(7.\text{C}.12)$$

where $\bar{x}^i$ is the ith round mean of samples (in particular, $\bar{x}^\text{II}$ is the mean of samples collected in both rounds). The leader must maximize $E(\text{II}^\text{II} : n^\text{I})$ as a subproblem of the whole problem. To express the solution of this subproblem in a convenient manner, define a function $e : R_+ \rightarrow R$ by

$$e(n : u) = 2u[(1 - \alpha)\Phi(\bar{\nu}\sqrt{n}) + \alpha\Phi(\bar{a}\sqrt{n}) - \tfrac{1}{2}] - cn \qquad (7.\text{C}.13)$$

Noticing that $e(n : V)$ is identical to $E(\Pi)$ in (7.C.7), we conclude that $e(n : u)$ has a unique maximizer in R_+. Let $n_e(u)$ be the maximizer of $e(n : u)$. Then the solution $n^{II*}(n^I)$ to the preceding subproblem is given by

$$n^{II*}(n^I) = \begin{cases} n_e(\beta V) - n^I, & \text{if } n^I \leq n_e(\beta V) \\ 0, & \text{if } x^I \geq n_e(\beta V) \end{cases} \qquad (7.C.14)$$

Turning back to the first round, the leader is to maximize the expected profit $E(\Pi)$, where

$$E(\Pi) = (V - n^I c)q + e(n^I + n^{II*}(n^I) : \beta V)(1 - q) \qquad (7.C.15)$$

where q is the probability of success in the first round, that is,

$$\begin{aligned} q &= \text{pr}(|\bar{x}^I - \mu| < \bar{\nu}\sigma) + \alpha\,\text{pr}(\bar{\nu}\sigma \leq |\bar{x}^I - \mu| \leq \bar{a}\sigma) \\ &= 2[(1 - \alpha)\Phi(\bar{\nu}\sqrt{n^I}) + \alpha\Phi(\bar{a}\sqrt{n^I}) - \tfrac{1}{2}] \end{aligned} \qquad (7.C.16)$$

As in the problem treated in section 7.C.1, we can then derive:

Proposition 7.C.2: The function $E(\Pi)$: $Z_+ \rightarrow R$ of n^I defined in 7.C.15 has a unique maximizer or two consecutive maximizers.

We are also able to derive:

Proposition 7.C.3: The number of samples in the second round, n^{II*}, is zero iff $\beta q < \tfrac{1}{2}$ at $n^I = n^{I*}$.

For further details see Asami and Isard (forthcoming).

References

Arrow, K. J. (1984) *The Economics of Information.* Cambridge, MA: Harvard University Press.

Asami, Y., and W. Isard, forthcoming, "Uncertainty, Information Costs, and Location Analyses."

Bartels, L. M. (1985) "Expectations and Preferences in Presidential Nominating Campaigns." *American Political Science Review* 79:804–15.

Brady, D. W. (1985) "A Reevaluation of Realignments in American Politics: Evidence from the House of Representatives." *American Political Science Review* 79:28–49.

Christaller, W. (1966) *Central Places in Southern Germany.* Englewood Cliffs, NJ: Prentice-Hall.

Davis, O. A., M. J. Hinich, and P. C. Ordeshook (1970) "An Expository Development of a Mathematical Model of the Electoral Process." *American Political Science Review* 64(June):426–48.

Downs, A. (1957) *An Economic Theory of Democracy.* New York: Harper.

Enelow, J. M. (1984) "A New Theory of Congressional Compromise." *American Political Science Review* 78:708–18.

Fetter, F. (1970) "The Economic Law of Market Areas." In R. Dean, W. Leahy, and D. McKee (eds.), *Spatial Economic Theory.* New York: Free Press, pp. 157–64.

Foster, C. B. (1984) "The Performance of Rational Voter Models in Recent Presidential Elections." *American Political Science Review* 78:678–89.

Greenberg, J., and K. Shepsle (1987) "The Effect of Electoral Rewards in Multiparty Competition with Entry." *American Political Science Review* 81(June):525–37.

Hinich, M. J., J. O. Ledyard, and P. C. Ordeshook (1973) "A Theory of Electoral Equilibrium: A Spatial Analysis Based on the Theory of Games." *Journal of Politics* 35(February):154–93.

Hotelling, H. (1952) "Stability in Competition." In G. J. Stigler and K. E. Boulding (eds.), *Readings in Price Theory*. Chicago: Irwin, pp. 467–84.

Hyson, C., and W. Hyson (1970) "The Economic Law of Market Areas." In R. Dean, W. Leahy, and D. McKee (eds.), *Spatial Economic Theory*. New York: Free Press, pp. 165–9.

Isard, W. (1956) *Location and Space Economy*. Cambridge, MA: MIT Press.

Isard, W., and P. Liossatos (1979) *Spatial Dynamics and Optimal Space-Time Development*. New York: North-Holland.

Isard, W., and C. Smith (1980) "Elementary Locational Analyses in Policy Space." *Papers,* Regional Science Association, Vol. 45, pp. 17–44.

Isard, W., T. E. Smith, P. Isard, T. H. Tung, and M. Dacey (1969) *General Theory: Social, Political, Economic and Regional*. Cambridge, MA: MIT Press.

Lösch, A. (1954) *The Economics of Location*. New Haven, CT: Yale University Press.

MacDonald, S. E., and G. Rabinowitz (1987) "The Dynamics of Structural Realignment," *American Political Science Review* 81(September):775–96.

McKelvey, R. D., and P. C. Ordeshook (1976) "Symmetric Spatial Games without Majority Rule Equilibria." *American Political Science Review* 70(December):1172–84.

Norpoth, H. (1979) "The Parties Come to Order! Dimensions of Preferential Choice in the West German Electorate 1971–1976." *American Political Science Review* 73(September):724–36.

Page, B. (1976) "The Theory of Political Ambiguity." *American Political Science Review* 70(September):742–52.

Page, B. I., and R. Y. Shapiro (1983) "Effects of Public Opinion on Policy." *American Political Science Review* 77:175–90.

Palfrey, T. R., and H. Rosenthall (1985) "Voter Participation and Strategic Uncertainty." *American Political Science Review* 79:62–75.

Poole, K. T., and R. S. Daniels (1985) "Ideology, Party, and Voting in U.S. Congress, 1959–1980." *American Political Science Review* 79:373–99.

Rabinowitz, G. (1978) "On the Nature of Political Issues: Insights from a Spatial Analysis." *American Political Science Review* 72(November):793–817.

Smithies, A. (1941) "Optimal Location in Spatial Competition." *Journal of Political Economy* 49:423–9.

Stiglitz, J. E. (1984) "Information, Screening, and Welfare." In M. Boyer and R. E. Kihlstrom (eds.), *Bayesian Models in Economic Theory*. Amsterdam: Elsevier, pp. 209–39.

Stokes, D. E. (1963) "Spatial Models of Party Competition." *American Political Science Review* 57(June):368–77.

Wittman, D. (1983) "Candidate Motivation: A Synthesis of Alternative Theories." *American Political Science Review* 77:142–57.

Wright, J. R., and A. S. Goldberg (1985) "Risk and Uncertainty as Factors in the Durability of Political Coalitions." *American Political Science Review* 79:704–18.

Zipp, J. F. (1985) "Perceived Representativeness and Voting: An Assessment of the Impact of 'Choices' vs. 'Echoes'." *American Political Science Review* 79:50–61.

CHAPTER 8

National security reasoning: the nature and effectiveness of political argument

Written with James P. Bennett

8.1   Introduction

Although the problem of a leader is often to determine the wishes of a voting population and thereby put forth a platform that corresponds to a modal or other position regarding these wishes, thereby to win an election (as we have discussed in Chapter 7), the problem may also be of a different nature or have other important dimensions. The political leader may represent a sizable cluster of voters and be committed by and large to a platform (set of policies) corresponding to a position with regard to this cluster (subconstituency). His (or her) problem may then be to set forth arguments that persuade voters not in his cluster to support him and his policies (platform) when these voters are unaligned or inclined to support other leaders with different policies. We have in mind arguments that a political leader might make for policies regarding Star Wars or nuclear disarmament, terrorism, ocean resource development, worldwide environmental regulation, protection of domestic industry, and so forth. However, as indicated in the previous chapter, a political leader may not be the only behaving unit actively engaged in policy debate and discussion. Antinuclear groups, a right-wing organization, environmentalists, a steel cartel, or a nation's foreign affairs department may be active, as well as highly motivated individuals or sets of individuals all with varied objectives and objective functions, such as maximizing expected payoff (utility, profits, c-power, etc.) or achieving a satisfactory level of a goal. Often the political leader may be the object of argument.

In any case each (nondictatorial) behavioral unit actively concerned with policy must set forth arguments. Hence we wish to examine in this chapter the nature, structure, and effectiveness of political arguments

This chapter draws heavily upon Bennett (1984b) and Isard and Lewis (1984).

whether we are describing an actual argument or evaluating a possible argument as good, best, or even ideal. We have particular interest in arguments regarding national security. Also, to stay close to reality and to a basic issue of the real world in the early 1980s and to help clarify certain abstract points, we shall examine in detail two of the best political arguments that were set forth in support of a policy of "no first use of nuclear weapons in Europe."

Whereas it is natural to proceed from a discussion of political argument to a discussion of full-blown political debate, which explicitly models two or more parties, we consider the latter to be beyond the scope of this book. We focus on case making rather than on case attacking or case defending, although the boundaries between these activities are blurred.

In section 8.2 we make some general remarks pertaining to political argument, mostly to indicate why formal logic is not generally applicable. Further, we point up some of the difficulties in describing political argument.

In section 8.3 we present the basic elements of a revised Toulmin-type view of political argument involving claims, grounds, warrants, backing, qualifiers, and counterrebuttals. In section 8.4 we indicate how these basic elements have parallels (or are comparable) to elements of decision-making analysis in economics, operations research, and regional science based on an outcome function and payoff matrix.

In section 8.5 we outline two significant political arguments that were set forth for a policy of "no first use of nuclear weapons in Europe" that we use to help clarify points we make about political arguments. Section 8.6 discusses the complex data base requirement of a political argument from both an ideal and a practical standpoint.

In section 8.7 we move on to discuss some major problems in constructing and evaluating more complex political arguments:

1. determining and precisely stating consistent objectives;
2. choosing and defining basic concepts;
3. identifying and relying on presuppositions;
4. defining relevant knowledge and its sources;
5. using historical materials and settling upon pertinent historical interpretation;
6. anticipating rebuttals and countering them;
7. using insiders' or experts' knowledge.

In section 8.8 we study, at a more involved level, justifications based on different kinds of reasoning and consider a hierarchical structure of justifications. Section 8.9 examines the problems in hypothesizing possible worlds, as is necessitated implicitly or explicitly in any complex political argument treating policy, and considers the dynamics and plans that are involved. Concluding remarks are made in section 8.10.

8.2   Some general remarks pertaining to political argument

Many frameworks for argument and reasoning have been set forth over the centuries. Aristotle searched for argumentation that would reveal necessary or probable truth or convincing approaches; and he introduced in parallel both theoretical and practical reasoning, which have since evolved along distinctly separate lines. Much later, from the seventeenth century to the present, most logicians (Leibniz, Descartes, Tarski, Quine, to name a few) researched argument structures designed to maximize the certainty of conclusions and references. They recognized that arguments involving individual beliefs or preferences and departing from the rigor of formal logic lacked the force or certainty of formal proof. Although argument as deduction may be applicable to rigorous science, mathematics, and other areas, it is too limited an understanding of the real world in which politics is central. For example, a formal logic approach that assesses the validity of inferences from premises to conclusions cannot

1. handle the need to investigate, identify, and adopt a reasonable (let alone a most reasonable) compromise position on basic public policy issues and still less so when these issues are emotion laden;
2. effectively confront the effects of practical criticisms and audience reactions and embody them to yield more persuasive argument and reasoning;
3. handle *subjunctive reasoning* defined as reasoning about counterfactual situations or things that might have been true under different conditions or to be reasoning embodying "what if" thinking;
4. embrace reasoning that is
    (a) *tentative* or *provisional,* that is, reasoning that is fully cognizant of the uncertainties of actuality;
    (b) *dialectical,* that is, reasoning that recognizes contradictions and the need to resolve them; and
    (c) *nonmonotonic,* that is, reasoning whose conclusions are sensitive to and changeable with new information (observations, evidence) based on current experience that adds to the inherited stock of information (e.g., sampling observations as discussed in section 7.5).

On the other hand, a formal logic approach can be useful at particular places in a political argument where clear-cut premises are present and deduction is appropriate. It is also useful as a diagnostic tool to unearth implicit premises in an argument and identify incomplete arguments.

Although it is clear that political argument must be viewed as distinct from formal logic, associated argument structures and also rhetoric, there is considerable difficulty in describing political argument. In part this is a consequence of the absence of any generally accepted language for parts of an argument and their relations.[1] Moreover, there exist several perspectives one can take on political argument that parallel the distinction between (1) logic as it is used when verbal and written statements are being made de novo and (2) logic as can be reconstructed from carefully prepared (considered) statements. For instance, one might compare (1) the logical structure of argument in actual, naturally occurring conversations between human beings concerned with explanation[2] and (2) argument in formal settings, particularly as written for a heterogeneous audience. Moreover, in studying political argument, one can focus on "the best case that is made," as we shall be doing when we detail two arguments, or on "the best case that can be made." Legal doctrines of justification typically address the latter.[3] However, it should be recognized that in the extreme, "the best case that can be made" takes us into the construction of "possible worlds" and reasoning about them. Such worlds have been examined by logicians attempting to accommodate subjunctive reasoning and statements of belief (attitudinal propositions) within the orthodoxy of deductive logic.[4]

But, as we shall discuss, there are tremendous difficulties in conducting possible worlds thinking that is appropriate for the policy analyst. This is so because the policy analyst demands that possible worlds be given rich internal structure so that one can evaluate such matters as the feasibility, stability, and impact of policies implemented in those hypothetical worlds. The analyst also demands that the generation of possible worlds from this world be demonstrated in sufficient detail so that one can establish not only that "you can get there from here" but that intermediate steps on the way to more desirable worlds (states of affairs) are them-

---

[1] Compare, for example, the radically different modern schemes of Toulmin (1958, 1972, 1976), Barry (1965), Perelman and Obrechts-Tyteca (1969), and Dubois et al. (1981), with the classic schemes presented in Brandt (1970). Also see Kaplan (1964), Searle (1969, 1979), Robinson (1979), and Searle et al. (1980).

[2] See Goguen, Weiner, and Linde (1983) for further discussion.

[3] See, for example, Wasserstrom (1961), who urges a decision procedure based on a best or proper combination of precedent and individual autonomy and equality. Also see the analysis by Barry (1965), who seeks to understand the best combination of conflicting principles that can be made for particular political institutions.

[4] See, for example, Stalnacker (1968), Lewis (1973), Pollock (1976), and Cresswell (1985).

selves desirable or at least not disqualifying. Further, he or she requires that criteria for evaluation of possible worlds are indeed relevant, that is, make sense for each of the possible worlds under consideration.

8.3   A practical set of basic elements for political argument

Although it would be highly desirable at this time to attempt at least a partial synthesis of the several current views and contributions to the analysis of political argument, such is beyond the scope of this chapter. Instead we shall take one framework, namely, that of Toulmin, Rieke, and Janik (1979) as importantly extended and clarified by Karapin and Alker (1985), and redefine its concepts for our purposes. (We do not consider ourselves sufficiently knowledgeable to select or develop a best framework.) We shall use our revision of this framework to demonstrate the critical importance of political arguments to policy and other analysis in the preceding chapters, thereby hoping to effect useful fusion. We shall of course be particularly interested in arms control policy and any other relating to the management of the arms race.

Toulmin et al. (1979) set forth "six elements that can be found in any wholly explicit argument" (p. 25): claims, grounds, warrants, backing, modal qualifications, and possible rebuttals. We find it useful to hold by and large to his terms but redefine his elements somewhat (as follows), substituting counterrebuttals for rebuttals:

(i) *Claims:* A claim states a conclusion with a goal, in the sense of a destination, in mind. In our political context it may state that a specific policy should be pursued. For example, the claim might be "a policy of *no first use of nuclear weapons* is desirable." Here we view policy broadly; it may be a simple or complex proposal, or a position on an issue, or a simple or complex action, or a plan for a particular point of time, or one that is both spatial and dynamic (over time). A claim may imply one or more objectives or an objective function, if such have not already been explicitly stated, which then are to be made explicit when "grounds" are presented.

Note that when we refer to this concept of a claim, we take it as a central claim or as a motivating focus of an argument. Instrumental or subordinate to this claim may be other claims in an argument such as "a policy of 'no first use' would not lead to World War III."

(ii) *Grounds:* The grounds provide the foundation for the claim. The grounds may provide evidence that the policy (the proposal, position, action, or plan) moves things toward or reaches one or more objectives. The evidence may be quantitative or qualitative. In either case, the evidence may be viewed as data, comprising observations, statistics, outputs of simulations, commonly accepted knowledge, conventions, references, previously validated claims, testimony, and the like. The statement of grounds frequently is marked by such words as "because" or "since."

(iii) *Warrants:* Warrants provide the support, the surface underpinning, and the justification for the connection between the grounds and the claim or for establishing the relevance of the grounds for the claim. A warrant may be a legal precedent, an engineering formula that works, a rule of thumb (e.g., the rank-size rule), a commonly accepted law (the law of supply and demand), or a scientifically established constant (the gravitational constant). At the extreme, it may also be a rule of deduction based on a formal logic.

(iv) *Backing:* Warrants themselves require backing; their trustworthiness or reliability must be established. Such backing may be based on extensive historical experience and theory (as in the case of the law of supply and demand and engineering rules of thumb), or on a set of scientific experiments rigorously conducted (as in the case of the gravitational constant), or on legislation or an amendment of a constitution. Often backing constitutes a general body of information for the specific field of reasoning.

(v) *Qualifiers:* Most arguments can be refuted under exceptional conditions and many under nonexceptional conditions. For example, a sample of public opinion may establish with only 95 percent probability that less than half the constituency supports the Star Wars program; or engineers and scientists may be able to state that due to the unpredictability of weather, a spacecraft launch will be successful only nine out of ten times; or the law of supply and demand only works for achievement-oriented societies. Qualifiers thus make explicit the force, dependability, or certainty to which an explicit claim may be applicable in a particular situation; or they may specify the particular situations to which the claim does not apply. They reveal the probabilistic or presumptive character of the reasoning.

(vi) *Counterrebuttals:* If the argument is not expressed solely with deductive logic (deductive logic can only be rarely employed to treat political arguments in toto), we must recognize that there may be rebuttals – statements that do or could upset the argument. Even if rebuttals are highly unlikely or not immediately apparent, their possibility should be recognized. In certain cases they may be ignored; in other cases they should not only be anticipated but also countered. In the latter cases, counterrebuttals should be part of a strong argument, particularly when rebuttals themselves are questionable, or probabilistic, or based on one of several sets of assumptions.

8.4 Comparability of basic elements in a political argument and in decision-making analysis

Before we present the outlines of two significant political arguments on "no first use of nuclear weapons in Europe," it is useful to compare the basic elements of a political argument with the basic elements of decision-making analysis that we find in economics, operations research, and regional science. This should help clarify the nature of political argument and suggest ways in which further precision in argument may be achieved in particular types of situation. We make this comparison for the first four elements of a political argument discussed in the preceding section:

(i) *Claim:* In a political argument the claim in a statement such as "a policy of 'no first use of nuclear weapons in Europe' is desirable" is comparable to the statement "action a_h is desirable" when, as in Eq. (4.2.16), an outcome function such as

$$o = f(a, e) \tag{8.4.1}$$

is employed. Recall that one can associate a payoff matrix such as Figure 3.1 with such a function, when as in the usual case we consider (1) only a relatively few actions (policy options) by the behaving unit, each corresponding to a row, and (2) only a few combinations of a state of the environment e and the joint response or action $\{a_k\}$ of other behaving units, each combination corresponding to a column. The outcome from the choice of any specific action by the individual and the realization of a combination of an environmental state and joint response is recorded in the cell where the corresponding row and column intersect.

(ii) *Grounds:* The grounds set forth to support the claim that "no first use . . . is desirable" are the data that are presented. In the argument by Gottfried, Kendall, and Lee (1984) to be outlined in what follows, three scenarios are examined:

1. a large-scale preemptive invasion by the Warsaw Pact nations;
2. an inadvertent or spillover war; and
3. a reckless adventure by the USSR, such as the surprise capture of Hamburg or another vulnerable NATO asset.

The outcomes of these scenarios are supplemented by data on the outcome were the status quo to continue. These outcomes are comparable to the outcomes of a payoff matrix that contains

1. only *two* rows [corresponding to (a) the action that would be taken to implement a "no first use" (NFU) policy and (b) the action involved in continuing the status quo], and

2. four columns (one for each of the preceding scenarios and one for a scenario when the Warsaw Pact nations continue with status quo behavior).

(iii) *Warrant:* The warrant in the argument by Gottfried et al. (1984) is that the *outcome* (security) that would result from the adoption of the action corresponding to the implementation of an NFU policy would be larger in every column but one when compared with the outcome from the action that would continue the status quo, and in that one scenario (e.g., reckless adventure by USSR) the outcome (security) would be no less. In the technical jargon of economics and regional science, the warrant is comparable to the statement that for each combination of a state of the environment and feasible joint response by the other behaving units, the outcome o_h from action a_h is as good as, and at least in the case of one combination better than, the outcome from the existing action taken by the given behaving unit or any other action in his or her set of feasible actions $\tilde{A}$.

A weaker assertion might just state that given the probability of each combination of a joint response $\{a_k\}$ of other behaving units and a state of the environment e, the expected outcome $\hat{o}_h$ from action a_h is greater than the expected outcome from any other action. See the discussion in section 4.2. There the states of the environment corresponding to (i)–(iv) should be taken to represent four different combinations of $\{a_k\}$ and e. Note that in these statements o may be considered to be a weighted average (i.e., $\Sigma \ w^J o^J$) of the security outcome o^J for each J, each J being a NATO nation with w^J a prespecified weight attached to its security outcome (where $\Sigma \ w^J = 1$).

(iv) *Backing:* The warrants of Gottfried et al. (1984) are implicitly supported by an assumption that the more secure the NATO nations are from Soviet attack, the better off they are. This is comparable to the statement in economics that the greater the outcome in terms of goods (commodities that are desired), the greater the utility that results.

With regard to the political argument for NFU, there is, however, another essential strand. This is the strand that ultimately provides justification for the set of outcomes used and the implicit claim that they are relevant. This implicit claim is based on the simultaneous use of

1. grounds that lead to the choice of three scenarios in addition to the status quo behavior by the Warsaw Pact and only two actions by NATO; and
2. the warrant, namely, the application of their knowledge that yields the outcomes that Gottlieb et al. (1984) state.

In economics and regional science, the use of the outcome data from a payoff matrix corresponds to an implicit claim that they are relevant. This claim is based on

1. grounds that lead to the choice of the combinations of a state of the environment and joint action of other behaving units that correspond to the columns and of the specific actions that correspond to the rows of this payoff matrix; and
2. the warrant that specifies the particular function $f(a, e)$ that yields the cell outcomes.

The backing for Gottlieb et al.'s warrant to justify the outcome data is the stock of knowledge of distinguished scientists and engineering experts upon which they draw and to which they may have contributed. Some of this knowledge of weapons, defense and attack capabilities, military strategies and the like is presented in the text of their article to be outlined in what follows; other knowledge is presumably contained in a detailed study by a highly respected scientists' group (the Union of Concerned Scientists). In parallel fashion, in economics and regional science the backing for the warrant of a specific production function yielding the outcome data of a payoff matrix is the stock of accumulated knowledge. In economics there are several specific production functions found acceptable for broad classes of situations: the Cobb–Douglas, the Leontief type, the constant elasticity of substitution (CES), and the translog, the last being most popular currently. Each of these functions is based upon an accepted economic theory and an extensive statistical analysis (multiple regression and econometric) of production data. If we employ the first, which has been used for a long time, we have

$$o = \omega K^\eta L^\nu$$

where o is output, ω is a constant, K is capital, L is labor, and η and ν are elasticities of o with respect to K and L, respectively. In one very simple exploration for arms race analyses (Anderton 1986, chap. 29) it has been suggested that

1. o be S_e^J, the nuclear strength of nation J,
2. K be S^J, the stock of nuclear weapons of J, and
3. L be S^L, the stock of nuclear weapons of nation L.

8.5 The outlines of two significant political arguments on no first use of nuclear weapons in the European theater

Now that we have covered the general ground, we can dig more deeply into and examine a number of basic problems in making political arguments. But first, in order to point up effectively the problems we shall examine, let us present the contents of two political arguments, which represent two of the best available. They are in articles by Bundy et al. (1982) and Gottfried et al. (1984), hereafter designated B and G, respectively.

The proposal studied here (as of 1984) is the doctrine of "no first use" (hereafter designated NFU) of nuclear weapons within the European theater. The doctrine was commonly understood to have three parts:

1. a pledge that one will not be the first to use nuclear weapons in the designated theater;
2. preparation for the defense of the theater with conventional weapons and other acceptable means; and
3. suitable reform of NATO's decision-making processes, especially in crises.

The history of NFU in Europe is treated by Weiler (1983). In and up to 1984, the policy of NATO was that nuclear weapons may be used if the conventional forces in Europe or elsewhere are threatened with defeat. It was never the policy of NATO that the use of nuclear weapons would be contingent upon the use or threatened use of such weapons by an opponent. Broadly speaking, the political commitment to forward defense in Germany and the military commitment to first use of nuclear weapons combined to explain much of the 1984 deployment of battlefield and theater nuclear weapons and their integration with NATO forces even in advanced positions.

Because the implications of NFU affected so deeply NATO strategy, force structure, deployments, and possible political underpinnings, the advocate of this policy had somehow to demonstrate that its consequences in an uncertain strategic environment were on balance favorable. All claims of benefit appealed to future possible worlds. The motivation for consideration of NFU, however, was derived from problems imputed to the world of 1984 and, sometimes, from aggravated problems projected from the status quo into the future.

Proponents and opponents of NFU alike were inextricably caught up in "what if" reasoning and argument about hypothetical states of affairs. The styles of such arguments vary.[5] But there is surprisingly little variation in the structure of these arguments when translated, for example, into Toulmin's schema (Toulmin, Rieke, and Janik 1979).

---

[5] Compare the International Commission on Disarmament and Security Issues (1982), Chotiya (1983), Huntington (1983), McNamara (1983), Ravenal (1983), the contributions in Steinbruner and Sigal (1983), and the Union of Concerned Scientists (1983).

There are, of course, differences of scope and focus between the two arguments discussed in what follows. The one by Bundy et al. (B) urges only that a debate on the merits of NFU begin; the other, by Gottfried et al. (G), directly urges that NFU be adopted. However, to convey the plausibility of a doctrine of NFU, B devote most of their argument to establishing the merits of NFU, not to establishing the merits of *debating* NFU. G accompany their argument with graphs to convey schedules of force comparisons after the outbreak of war in Europe; B have no quantitative data in their argument. This contrast reflects stylistic differences in the journals with regard to the selection and use of evidence. (However, as we shall see, B emphasize less easily quantified factors in the definition of the problem with current doctrine.) Finally, the scope for solutions offered by G is somewhat greater, as they view NFU as but one component in the transformation of U.S. defense policies in Europe.

Tables 8.1 and 8.2 contain interpretive summaries of each paragraph of the articles. Where reference to component sentences and phrases is required, these will be given a paragraph number in our text.

Both journals utilize typographical divisions within the text. *Foreign Affairs* (B) uses roman numerals, otherwise unlabeled; *Scientific American* (G) merely highlights the initial letter of occasional paragraphs. In the tables, these divisions are indicated with entries headed by the corresponding roman numeral for B and also by an appropriate roman numeral for G. Description of the corresponding section is then presented in italics. It is important to note that the italicized descriptions are not summaries of paragraphs and derive from attempts to delineate larger-scale structure to the arguments. For several sections in G, no thematic unity is discernible. The highlights may have been done to improve page layout.

Not represented in these tables are the diagrams and figures prominent in G. Much factual information not mentioned in the text is thereby provided to the reader. A footnote to the first page of B gives the offices held by that set of authors.

8.6 The complex data base requirement

Having sketched the detail of two political arguments, of high quality by current standards, we now dig into the basic problems of such arguments. First consider the data base.

A good political argument requires a complex data base. This is so whether the data are narrowly viewed as quantitative-type information (as so often in economics and regional science) or more broadly as equivalent to grounds where it comprises not only specific factual evidence but

Table 8.1. *Summary of paragraphs in "Nuclear Weapons and the Atlantic Alliance"* [a]

Par. Synopsis

I. Introduction and setting
1   Credentials: What follows is the informed judgment of four experts
2   Origins of the doctrine of "first use" (FU)
3   The doctrine of FU remained constant while politics and technology changed
4   FU has been a centerpiece of every U.S. commitment to defend Europe
5   Use of nuclear weapons gives no advantage and could be disastrous, so new doctrine should be explored

II. Problem is alliance disarray under FU
6   NATO is experiencing divisive debates; introduction of American missiles of intermediate range is an instance
7   Arguments in support of deployment of such missiles
8   U.S. sponsorship of modernization is now the issue
9   Neutron bomb is second instance
10   A deeper cause for disputes is excessive nuclear inventories beyond functional justifications
11   Plans for conducting nuclear war in the 1950s and 1960s were kept quiet
12   In the 1970s, U.S. administrations attempting to reinforce deterrence only increased European fears of nuclear war
13   Issues relating to deterrence and doctrine cannot and should not be suppressed
14   There is no reason to believe that usage of nuclear weapons can be kept limited
15   The only important distinction is between use and nonuse: NFU helps maintain this distinction

III. One should not change basis for alliance or erode security guarantee to FRG
16   The major question about NFU should be its impact on deterrence in the central front
17   The role of West Germany is central
18   United States and West Germany share common strategic beliefs and interests
19   Special situation of West Germany: Unlike Britain and France, West Germany is frontline without a national deterrent
20   NFU should not alter security guarantee of United States to West Germany
21   West Germany has a right to voice in U.S. policy debates about European defense

IV. NFU requires changing doctrine and strengthening conventional defenses
22   Preview of conclusions: The study of NFU will recommend it as achievable with increased conventional forces, but political will may be lacking
23   Before adopting NFU, the United States, Britain, France, and West Germany must clarify their resolve to defense of central Europe
24   The governments of these four nations also must examine the use they project for tactical nuclear weapons and the implications of NFU for capabilities in a crisis
25   The professional military may initially be opposed to NFU, but it can be convinced and in any case will accept civilian decisions
26   The contention that NFU indicates less U.S. interest in Europe is false; NFU would emphasize the U.S. commitment through its conventional forces in Europe
27   Realistic examination of the cost of improvements in conventional forces needs to be undertaken; the cost is not too high

266

Table 8.1 (*cont.*)

Par.	Synopsis
28	No one knows what increases would be required, but political will, not economics, is decisive
29	Rapid change is not necessary; it is important to move carefully in the correct direction

V. Steps intermediate to achieving NFU are useful in themselves
30	Examine existing NATO plans for selective and limited use of nuclear weapons
31	A helpful policy short of NFU is "no early first use"
32	NFU as a doctrine is superior to refining nuclear options; it is clearer and simpler

VI. Proposed study of NFU should be done pluralistically, inside and outside of governments
33	Despite the present opposition of the U.S. administration, change in its position is possible
34	Study by private individuals is desirable and popular; it supports the present proposals
35	We urge careful examination of the requirements and benefits of NFU; it is not yet proved, but we emphasize benefits

VII. Benefits of NFU are to simplify deterrence and promote stability
36	NFU simplifies requirements for nuclear capabilities
37	Under NFU one needs only a survivable second strike, so modernization requirements are smaller
38	We do not advocate "minimal deterrence" – the inventories required remain large
39	NFU would diffuse political pressures toward disarmament and Europe-wide nuclear-free zone
40	NFU reduces the risk of aggression by the Soviet Union, which in any case has never been great

VIII. NFU supports desirable U.S. relations with NATO and Soviet Union
41	The problem is political as well as military: Relations with Europe cannot center on roles for nuclear weapons
42	The political coherence of NATO is at least as important as its military strength: We want to reestablish political consensus
43	NFU would not guarantee to the USSR that we would not in fact use nuclear weapons first; ambiguity must remain
44	But NFU is still useful, particularly to the health of NATO
45	NFU can help improve relations with the Soviet Union
46	By reducing pressures for new weapons, NFU might help to achieve arms reductions
47	NFU, if reciprocated by the Soviet Union, would bring "new hope"

IX. This argument should be understood as preliminary
48	The present focus on the central front relates to other NATO and global defense issues
49	We hope for widespread debate of this policy, as has preceded important historical changes in strategy

[a]Bundy et al. (1982) [called B in the text].

267

Table 8.2. *Summary of paragraphs in "'No First Use' of Nuclear Weapons"* [a]

Par.	Synopsis

I. Introduction and setting
1 An FU policy began with the origin of NATO
2 The policy continues despite changes that make it less desirable
3 There have been several calls for change in doctrine
4 The present authors have credentials for the analysis

II. Military situation on central front
5 The military situation finds both sides with nuclear inventories in densely populated areas
6 There are many obstacles to implementing current military doctrine
7 Military and political requirements of NATO conflict
8 War games demonstrate futility of an FU policy
9 Nuclear exchange would cause enormous damage

III. Limited nuclear war in Europe is not viable expectation
10 Keeping nuclear war limited places unrealistic demands upon diplomacy
11 Limited targeting is unrealistic for lack of viable targets
12 No plausible scenario for nuclear exchange avoids likelihood of escalation
13 Under NFU, the function of nuclear weapons is limited to retaliation; the policy has implications for training, planning, and equipping NATO

IV. NFU requires confident conventional defense and would improve crisis management by NATO
14 The belief that the USSR has huge conventional advantage is wrong
15 To make conventional defense practicable, NATO must change force structure and operational plans
16 Warsaw Pact leaders could never be sure that NATO would not use nuclear weapons but would observe conventional changes
17 Potential political paralysis of NATO in a crisis would be averted if the European populace had less expectation of nuclear war

V. NFU is successful in all likely scenarios of WTO aggression
18 Under NFU, forward deployment of nuclear weapons should be changed
19 The contention that NFU weakens the U.S. commitment to defend Europe is false
20 To understand concrete effects of NFU, one must examine scenarios; the first scenario is preemptive full-scale invasion
21 The second scenario is a limited thrust to capture Hamburg
22 The third scenario is a 1914-style dynamic of miscalculation – the most likely
23 On balance, NFU is superior to present doctrine

VI. Miscellaneous and NATO defensive strategy
24 NFU can be generalized to apply to other areas of the globe
25 Related options, such as secret NFU or "no early first use," are inferior to NFU
26 Description of location for a hypothetical conventional weapons WTO attack
27 Objectives of such a WTO attack
28 Military characteristics of such an attack
29 How NATO could meet such an attack
30 NATO's present posture is forward defense

VII. Balance of forces to meet WTO attack is not unfavorable to NATO
31 Total theater forces leave NATO with better than a 1:2 ratio

268

Table 8.2 (*cont.*)

Par.	Synopsis
32	Schedule of relative advantage in combat-ready troops fluctuates indecisively
33	At points of attack, WTO cannot expect overwhelming advantage
34	The balance of air forces follows a similar pattern of fluctuation within bounds of tolerability for NATO
35	Political factors in NATO are important; France would not likely remain neutral
36	The political reliability of some WTO forces is doubtful
37	The conclusion of the WTO enjoying only moderate advantages is robust under variations in the assumptions of this analysis
38	Specific weaknesses in NATO defenses must be addressed to achieve high-confidence nonnuclear defense

VIII. Addressing specific weaknesses in NATO

39	NATO's decisions are now unanimous, making responses slow
40	France should clarify its relations with NATO
41	Deployment and equipment of reinforcements should be changed
42	Readiness can be improved by prepositioning equipment

IX.

43	Fortifications have not been constructed for political reasons
44	Fortifications and prepared positions would assist defense
45	Increasing reserves improves capabilities for protracted conflict
46	NATO leads WTO in certain advanced technologies
47	Smart weapons, with fortifications, assist defense
48	Smart weapons are useful for deep interdiction of offensive
49	Technology is important but not sufficient

X.

50	Military stocks are important and presently inadequate
51	Inexpensive steps can improve survivability of installations in the rear
52	The cost of the above improvements, exclusive of additional reserves, is less than $100 billion over 6 years
53	The cost is less than 2% increase in real terms, below the official target
54	Funds can be found by shifting NATO priorities and diverting funds not used for nuclear procurement

XI. NFU is on balance useful and complemented by other policies

55	Regardless of the policies of the Soviet Union, NFU is desirable; two other critical issues require negotiation
56	Mutual and balanced conventional force reductions would lessen possibility of WTO attack
57	An MBFR (Mutual and Balanced Force Reduction) treaty would avoid conventional weapons race and give NATO leadership indicator of hostile WTO attack
58	A nuclear-free zone, as per the Palme report, would enhance security
59	Sustained support from top political leadership is required to make NFU, MBFR, and NFZ (Nuclear-Weapon-Free Zone) reality
60	NFU would change basis of military strategy and planning, strengthen the cohesion of NATO, and enhance crisis stability, thus lowering the risk of nuclear war

[a]Gottfried et al. (1984) [called G in the text].

any evidence offered in direct support of a claim (Karapin and Alker 1985; Bennett 1984a).

Ideally, the complex data base embodies the perceptions by each relevant actor of his (or her) payoff matrices at every critical point of time when a decision was taken even if it was "do nothing." The numerous possible combinations of a particular action by any actor and an action by every other significant behaving unit together with a state of the environment then constitute the initial conditions for the emergence of a fan of possible worlds as seen by that actor. (Many of these worlds drop out of that actor's consideration because of economic, political, and social infeasibilities.) Thus, the set of these perceptions over all relevant actors (in the past and currently) constitute one major part of the data base.

Another major part of the complex data base, ideally speaking, consists of all objective information on relationships among variables that have existed in the past and are current to the extent that objectivity can be achieved. Moreover, the ideal complex data base has a record of all events that have occurred over time, also organized as chronicles (set of events ordered in time), narratives (which relate events to each other), accounts (which identify at least one agent as causing events), and/or stories (which causally link events at the beginning of a narrative to those at the end), all being operated upon by perspectives (Isard 1981; Bennett 1984a).

Ideally, too, the complex data base should be accompanied by all kinds of frameworks and models to perform diverse simulations and projections into the future for all relevant values of parameters and reasonable sets of assumptions.

Finally, the data base itself is dynamic in the sense that observations occur in time and therefore become data. Subordinate arguments, as they are developed, produce claims that subsequently serve as data. These claims may be revised and retracted so that political argument is not monotonic.

In practice, for any particular political argument, only a tiny fraction of the preceding data base is relevant. For example, there is the invaluable data collection by Singer and his associates on the Correlates of War Project,[6] but for the purposes of B and G such data might be judged to be

---

[6] See, among others, Singer and Small (1969), Singer and Wallace (1970), Singer (1979, 1980), and Small and Singer (1972, 1982). In the last item, e.g., there are presented such critically important empirical materials as quantifying international war by magnitude (nation months), severity (battle-connected deaths), and intensity (fatality ratios); a ranking of wars by these characteristics and relevant frequency distributions reflecting probabilities of observed and expected characteristics; patterns at the systemic level [annual amounts of war begun and under way, secular trends, cycles (periodicity), and seasonal distributions in

much less significant than other data and thus to be ignored given limited resources and time for analysis. On the other hand, the later quantitative analysis in Huth and Russett (1984) involving the study of failures of deterrence would be relevant. At the same time, however, a small if not infinitesimal fraction of the ideal complex data base exists. Further, at any moment of time, a behaving unit, whether an individual, interest group, or some other organization, has

1. limited ability to store, recall, and otherwise retrieve knowledge that is available and conduct analysis, whether in payoff matrix or other form; and
2. limited access to available data because of cultural and other filtering.

However, he or she typically does have some resources for use to seek out, collect, process information, and the like, to develop a relevant political argument. Such then raises a series of problems, as it does for both B and G.

8.7   Some major problems in constructing and evaluating more complex political arguments

8.7.1   Problems in determining and precisely stating consistent objectives

As indicated in our discussion of the two basic elements of claims and grounds, the objectives underlying a political argument must be precisely defined.

Often in a political argument there are at least several levels at which objectives can be involved. A very broad objective of an NFU policy running throughout the two political arguments detailed in the preceding is to maintain the peace, to avert global nuclear war. At a less general level, there is for B the objective to maintain the security of the Atlantic Alliance, to hold to the U.S. commitment to Germany, and to prevent alliance disarray. For G, the objective at a less general level is to deny the Warsaw Treaty Organization (WTO) an easy military victory or to enable NATO to meet Soviet aggression under the three scenarios examined. And so forth. However, one of the major problems in specifying objec-

the incidence of war]; war-proneness of nations; victory, defeat, and battle deaths; and similar types of extensive empirical material on civil wars.

On the more general level, there are extremely valuable collections such as *World Handbook of Political and Social Indicators* (Russett et al. 1964, 1st ed.; Taylor and Jodice 1983, 3rd ed.) for use in the analysis of conflicts in the international system.

tives is to ensure that no inconsistencies or contradictions are involved. On the surface it woud appear, when only a single rather than multiple objectives is specified, that there can be no inconsistency or contradiction; but this is not so. Putting into effect a policy such as NFU would have taken the world of 1984 through a succession of other worlds, one at each of several stages; and clearly the single objective that was aimed at for the last stage would have had to achieve objectives (such as stability, viability, and political feasibility) at intermediate stages. The single final objective would, however, have been inconsistent with such. For example, a shift to NFU policy involving a major shift in weapons production might have under certain circumstances been anticipated to generate major unemployment in certain sectors within the U.S. economy, and hence the policy may have been judged to be politically infeasible. Or, at some stage the implementation of an NFU policy could have generated a type of Soviet reaction that would have undermined such a policy. Note that already the statement of objectives at an early stage of a political argument should desirably be such as to facilitate counter-rebuttals.

B and G do recognize multiple objectives, at least in a hierarchical sense. However, as already indicated, they fail to do so in a thorough, systematic fashion. Yet, given the tremendous gaps in the complex data base available to them, could they have done so, even had considerably more time and effort been devoted to the development of their argument? This point will come up again when we discuss problems in generating possible worlds.

8.7.2   Problems with regard to the choice and definition of basic concepts

Early as well as later in a political argument, major problems in the choice and definition of basic concepts may arise. The concept of "no first use," for example, needs to be defined clearly. Exactly what is involved? Even more difficult may be other more nebulous concepts, such as deterrence. To illustrate, let us briefly examine the latter concept in both B's and G's arguments. Note that although B's motivating concern is alliance disarray, B do assign importance to retaining deterrence. In paragraph 16, B assert that the principal criterion for the desirability of NFU should be its impact upon deterrence in the central front of Europe.

Neither G nor B try to elaborate on the concept of deterrence. This appears to be an important omission because the applicable concept in the proposed world of conventional defense may well differ significantly from the current nuclear-deterrent posture (Huntington 1983). Furthermore, both sets of authors agree that NFU would not remove nuclear deterrence from entering the subsequent decision calculus of either NATO or the WTO.

Is "deterrence" as a doctrine so well understood or consensually understood, at least with respect to its core meaning, that merely to mention the term is adequate in the context of proposing NFU? Alternatively, does the establishment of a contemporary political and military setting (in B, pars. 2–5; in G, pars. 1–3) suffice to inform the reader about this concept? The careful reader of either article will find that he or she will want more information about the role to be assigned to deterrence (nuclear as well as conventional) in the authors' preferred world and about the variety of deterrence doctrine most appropriate to their preferred world with NFU.

Deterrence has a complex internal structure. This is so even when one takes "dissuasion by threat of reprisal" as the core meaning of deterrence, one of the simplest possible meanings. This enormously complicated concept involves all kinds of combinations of the many features of a strategic doctrine (Bennett 1985). For instance, the relationship between contingencies and sanctions in the concept of deterrence if one appeals to "massive retaliation" (one sanction for all contingencies) will look quite different than if one appeals to "flexible response" (a one-to-many relation between contingencies and sanctions).

Further, deep reflective reasoning is required for making a deterrent threat. Clearly, a calculus that goes "three deep" through belief worlds to implement A's attempts to manipulate B's beliefs about A is inadequate if one is concerned with applying deterrence in Europe. One cannot really specify the belief worlds of NATO and the Soviet Union with as few impressionistic assertions as attempted by both B and G.

In brief, from the standpoint of an evaluating analyst, basic concepts need to be defined as rigorously as possible, with the recognition that subjective elements enter in, since the concepts that are considered to be basic evolve out of one's own theories and/or experiences. Yet when the concept is exceedingly complex as deterrence is, should much time and space be given to a discussion of it when the aim of the argument is to be persuasive for an audience that can be turned away by a discussion beyond their limited capacity or motivation to absorb? Would not an oversimplified, incomplete definition of the concept have a greater persuasive force?

8.7.3 Problems with respect to presuppositions and related elements in the development of a political argument

Once we proceed in our analysis beyond claims and grounds and delve into warrants and backing, we run into the use of and the necessity to use presuppositions. Presuppositions represent information (assumed before-hand or taken as given) beyond what is explicitly stated in a text. They can certainly be claimed to be justifiable if in fact such information is implied and shared by the readers (audience). However, if an analyst seeks to model a line of reasoning, he or she may get an unrealistically critical appraisal of the coherence of an argument if important informa-tion – "facts" or "axioms" or relationships – available to the authors is not available to the analyst.[7]

Closely related is the problem of determining knowledge that is implied and shared in conversation (Clark and Marshall 1981). Although the two texts studied here bear little resemblance in planning or format to con-versation, the journals in which they appear (i.e., the characteristics of their readership), the credentials presented by the authors, and dominant modes of thought in contemporary "national security affairs" in the United States all enable the authors to, in some significant sense, mean more than they explicitly say. Most obviously, B are not urging us to adopt NFU; they are merely urging a debate about NFU, but to accom-plish this, they admit to portraying selectively the benefits of a policy of NFU. More subtly, G are not urging France to rejoin the military plan-ning group of NATO; they note only that they think that France would get involved in any general war in Europe (specifically by the fourth day!). But their subsequent computation of force balances and costs as well as their discussion of the defense of likely routes for the invasion of Ger-many all presuppose that the reader has earlier accepted the fact of French involvement and of French coordination with the rest of NATO.

Many presuppositions of a political argument are identifiable. One way to find these is to restate the structure of the argument into some conve-nient logical form; one then seeks presuppositions to provide logical con-nection among the translated parts of the argument.

A second way works from the text. It seeks only presuppositions in the form of references to external material, such as the biographies of the authors in paragraph 1 of B (which, in any case, are conveniently sum-marized in a footnote to the first page).

There are other ways based upon nonstandard formal logics (McCawley 1979; Seuren 1985; Fauconnier 1985); these, however, intro-duce fundamental issues of linguistic pragmatics, which is outside the scope of this chapter.

---

[7] The problems associated with pragmatic presuppositions are complex, and no suggestion that an analyst can deal adequately with them is intended. Nevertheless, three areas of dis-pute seem to divide linguistics on the proper treatment of presuppositions: the relation of presupposition to truth value (Kempson 1975) and indeed the relevance of semantics to presupposition (Gazdar 1979); the proper understanding of the linguistic context in which presuppositions should be sought (Karttunen 1974); and the role of presuppositions in the logical structure of discourse (Hintikka 1969; Katz and Langendoen 1976).

In short, although presuppositions are essential to and legitimate in argument, especially when it is important for the argument to be terse and compact, as is often required in political activity, problems do arise (at least analytically) when in fact the assumption by the proponents of shared knowledge is a poor one. This problem typically arises, for example, when economists and regional scientists use their "accepted" models to derive the outcomes (the o of a payoff matrix) when these models ignore important qualitative political factors, that is, implicitly assume the latter have no effect on outcomes.

8.7.4   Problems with respect to the definition and sources of relevant knowledge

Closely allied with the problems linked to the use of presuppositions are those associated with the definition of relevant knowledge and the determination of sources of such, recognizing, of course, that only an extremely small fraction of the ideal complex data base can be available to and digested by a behaving unit. One traditional definition of knowledge is "true justified belief." Such requires an external, objective standpoint for the attribution "true." It also requires an internal examination of the individual's system of cognition and evaluation to make the attribution "justified." The purpose, of course, of demanding justification of the belief is that we should want to exclude accidentally correct superstition and the like from knowledge. One has to have systematic and appropriate mechanisms for a belief in order that it be counted as knowledge.

How do the policy advocates make claims to knowledge? The most prominent means is their early attempt to establish credentials (par. 1 plus a footnote, in B; par. 4 in G). A second means is by referring to enough information that is shared with the reader to establish a reputation for being well informed. Thus at various points both G and B set down facts to function as setting for more complicated and controversial webs of statement–reason pairs (pars. 1–3 and 9, with accompanying illustrations, in B in Table 8.1; pars. 2–5, 11–12, and 33 in G in Table 8.2, respectively).

The backing used is somewhat different in the two cases, however, in ways that should not surprise us. The four statespeople emphasize the convergence of their beliefs about the proper doctrine for NATO and its impact (pars. 1, 36, 48). They focus upon the collective, process-oriented interpretation of knowledge, reflecting Willard's claim "that knowledge is most often an interpretation that is trusted because of the social comparisons that countenance it" (Willard 1983, p. 5). Agreement among experienced statespeople should, they suggest, strike the reader as evidence in itself that the opinions expressed are reliably true.

The credentials established by G are somewhat different. They are part of a "scientists group" that conducted a serious study of the matter. The study used the judgments of statesmen, but the analysis followed the canons of science (par. 4). Moreover, their argument is accompanied (following the invariant practice of G) by graphically presented quantitative and spatial information. And their journal provides five references, including the article by B.

Many of the apparent differences in claiming sources of knowledge are artifacts of the journal of publication. However, the contrast is unmistakable that B claim to have learned through experience whereas G claim to have required a reliable procedure for drawing inferences from what others have learned.

There are, in effect, social guarantors for the knowledge offered by G, but these have their roots in the community of scientists, not in the convergence of beliefs of experienced statespeople.

But are there other possible sources of knowledge as backing, for example, the knowledge lying behind common law, political ideologies, religious beliefs, and other cultural precedents? And if so, what is the most appropriate use of different sources of knowledge for a political argument? Surely, one should not use just a single source when more than one source exists, especially since knowledge cannot be divorced entirely from subjective elements and the cultural setting.

8.7.5   Problems in using historical materials in particular and settling upon pertinent historical interpretation

B make references to external historical materials at several points in their argument. Table 8.3 lists five principal references, in paragraphs 2, 3, 11, 22, and 49. It is noteworthy that the external materials are utilized in quite different ways.

The first reference appears immediately after the authors establish their own credentials. In highly synoptic form, B manage in paragraph 2 to mention Winston Churchill, Niels Bohr, the Soviet atomic bomb in 1949, the birth of NATO, and communist aggression in Korea. This is less applicable as a summary of the origins of the doctrine of first use than as a way of attaching certain highly reconstructed histories – really a mythical basis for the subsequent political analysis (Alker 1976, 1983) – to gain the reader's acquiescence to a powerful set of beliefs as "shared knowledge." In section III, B argue that perservation of the traditional basis for NATO is important. As early as paragraph 2 they obliquely introduce NATO as both legitimate and effective.

The next paragraph only slightly changes the historical referent: In place of semimythical foundations achieved by colocating NATO among the historical "greats," we are introduced to NATO viewed through the

Table 8.3. *External references in "Nuclear Weapons and the Atlantic Alliance"* [a]

Par.	Reference	Type
1	"We . . . have been concerned over many years. . . . "	Biographies
2	"For 33 years now, the Atlantic Alliance. . . . "	Histories/Myths?
3	"deployments and doctrine have been intended to deter Soviet aggression. . . . "	Histories, Official
6	"the disarray . . . of the Alliance is obvious."	Current events
7	"The arguments . . . by advocates of these deployments contain troubling variations" – only one argument is described	Arguments
11, 12	"This problem is more acute . . . but . . . not new."	Histories
14	"No one has ever succeeded in advancing any persuasive reason to believe that any use of nuclear weapons . . . could . . . remain limited."	Arguments
18	"Both nations believe . . . must be defended . . . must not have nuclear weapons. . . . "	Shared normative beliefs
22	"Evidence [of political war] from the history of the Alliance is mixed."	A history
24, 30, 33, etc.	"existing forces, tactics and general military expectations . . . Administrations . . . revised their thoughts on nuclear weapons policy."	Official policies, operational plans, etc.
28	"literally no one . . . knows what would be needed . . . official and private analyses are static. . . . "	Arguments, policy studies
34	"this cause is argued by such men as. . . . "	Arguments, authorities
36	"The Soviet government is already aware of the awful risk. . . . "	Official statements?/ Personal contacts?
39	"Proposals to make 'all' of Europe . . . a nuclear free zone. . . . "	Arguments?
40	"risk [of conventional aggression] has never been as great as prophets of doom have claimed. . . . "	Arguments?
43, 46	"We would not make that assumption about the Soviet Union, and . . . Soviet leaders could not make it about us."	Model of Soviet Union
49	"widespread consideration . . . helped us . . . toward SALT I . . . Limited Test Ban. . . . "	History

[a]Bundy et al. (1982) [called B in the text].

official institutional memory. The claim, however, is both more direct and more controversial: "Throughout these doctrinal transformations . . . both deployments and doctrines have been intended to deter Soviet aggression and keep the peace by maintaining a credible connection between any large-scale assault . . . and the engagement of the strategic nuclear forces of the United States" (B, p. 74). Surely the authors do not claim that *every* change in deployment or doctrine is to be understood primarily in this fashion. Nor do B, here or elsewhere in the article, claim that historical changes were uniquely required as responses to the changing demands of linkage among the NATO nations to the U.S. deterrent. The argument is rather conveyed in the sense of official history: Historical changes are best understood as sincere attempts to maintain linkage even though specific policies might have been ill-considered (as contended in par. 11). One reads this paragraph as claiming that, despite obscure twists in doctrine, the sincerity of the United States in its purpose of achieving linkage should not be doubted.

On the other hand, reference to historical material in paragraph 22 is employed to ground the contention that political will to achieve military objectives in NATO can be questioned. Can this be the same NATO history of paragraphs 2 and 3? It can, if we integrate it with later historical references in the following way:

> NATO's creation myth shows it to be "good."
> Its members have been sincere in positing security objectives (and the United States has been sincere in attempting strategic linkage).
> But its members have been amiss in their commitment to implementing programs to achieve security objectives.

All this is achieved apparently without effort because the historical "data" cited consists of thoroughly preprocessed, interpretive histories known to the authors and (presumably, because the information is marked as new)[8] shared with the reader. Further, B give the reader little opportunity to find crystallized disagreements with their use of history – to dissent explicitly requires one to argue contentions such as "there was no communist aggression in Korea" (counter par. 2), "doctrinal changes did not respond to changing Western views of Soviet capabilities" (counter par. 3), or "the Alliance has always failed (or succeeded) to meet force goals" (counter par. 22).

Other references to historical materials are more specific. In paragraph 11 are enumerated several instances (or episodes in the continuing story

---

[8] On this point, see Clark and Havilland (1977).

of NATO's evolution) in which plans for the use of nuclear weapons were elusive. Historical precedents for productive outcomes of the debate being urged by B are listed in the closing paragraph 49. In both sets of instances, B urge us to evaluate them as obstacles or diversions from the principal theme of NATO – the quest for security in Europe. A close parallel appears in Propp's treatment of Russian fairy tales (Propp 1977). The grammar of fairy tales enables the hero (here, the United States) to undertake difficult tasks and to suffer temporary setbacks in the course of a larger and ultimately successful quest. Some setbacks are caused by the villain (here, the USSR). Others arise from unwitting acts by the victim (here, Western Europe, especially Germany) or even complicity of the victim. The crucial factor that distinguishes the hero is its unswerving commitment to solving the problem, often by rescue.

The point is not that B are essentially relating policy analysis in the form of a fairy tale, but that historical "facts" as true observations about the past hardly ever enter their argument directly. Instead, B substitute highly sophisticated, interpreted "histories" in support of thematic development. But perhaps they have little choice. To achieve coherence and move between real and counterfactual claims, their account must be somehow prestructured with a framework or template that is at once easily assimilated by the reader and specific about the information that the authors want to be tagged as problematic. A professional historian of Europe evaluating B's article might respond that it was "light" and "exceedingly casual" in its use of history. That is perhaps precisely the effect that B seek to create: Differences of historical interpretation should not be permitted to obstruct policy advocacy.

In short, one must conclude that whereas interpreted histories are often another essential element to help provide warrants and justification, one must still be fully aware of the potential dangers in the excessive (and invalid?) use of such.

8.7.6   Problems in anticipating rebuttals and countering them

B are not bashful about making claims of authority, either to establish their own credentials or to associate their claims with the reputations of others (par. 34 in addition to preceding citations). But they also undertake references to arguments that oppose their own. Three types of counterrebuttal appear in this article: The opposing arguments are self-contradictory; everyone is equally ignorant on this matter; and the opposing views are "strawman" constructions.

In paragraph 7 proponents of the modernization of intermediate-range nuclear forces are identified with contradictory views: Modernization is the cheapest way to meet the threat of Soviet SS-20's in order to retain deterrence, and modernization is needed to guarantee that the escalation of nuclear war in Europe will involve nuclear strikes against the Soviet Union. Of course, not all proponents of force modernization make both claims, as B note. Yet B make no attempt to refute each contention separately.

At two notable points very strong universal claims are made about the absence of an argument. In paragraph 14, in order to dismiss the idea of nuclear war limited to a theater, B state:

> It is time to realize that no one has ever succeeded in advancing any persuasive reason to believe that any use of nuclear weapons, even on the smallest scale, could reliably be expected to remain limited.

We find here three universal qualifiers: "no . . . any . . . any." The rhetorical power derives from liberal use of absolutes. The logical insignificance of this statement derives from the use of one's own private criteria: "succeeded," "persuasive," and "reliably." Subsequent assertions in the same paragraph abandon the private qualifiers but continue to make universal claims. (For example, "There is no way for anyone to have any confidence . . . .") But informally, the scope of the private criteria carried over the entire paragraph. The reader may be excused for not realizing that B's private evaluation perspective in the opening sentence has been dropped in later claims.

Paragraph 28 involves a similarly qualified claim of universal ignorance: "Today there is literally no one who really knows . . . ." The dominating predicate of this sentence is "really" because a syntactic implication is: "There is at least one who wrongly thinks he knows . . . ." To contradict this claim directly places one in the camp of either fools or prophets.

Finally, there are at least two classic strawman presentations of potentially opposing views. The first appears in paragraph 39, where a nuclear-free zone is dismissed. B mention not the most currently influential proposal by the Palme Commission (International Commission 1982) but the far more extreme proposals to make the most of Europe (from Portugal to Poland) such a zone. As G argue, NFU may be quite compatible with the Palme Commission's version of a battlefield nuclear-free zone. The second strawman is the unnamed "prophet of doom" of paragraph 40, predicting Soviet aggression. On the other hand, it is notable that G explicitly consider the Soviet quick strike for limited objectives as plausible enough to bring into their analysis of NFU and to be the only scenario aggravated by adopting an NFU doctrine.

This discussion illustrates that effective advocacy of one's own views is often assisted by unfair characterization of opponents' views. That is, from an analytical standpoint, counterrebuttals may be weak and should be logically or scientifically strong if they are to be used. On the other hand, the proponent may be facing the dilemma be "balanced and unpersuasive" or be "selective and convincing."

8.7.7   Problems with regard to the use of insiders' knowledge

B are careful to avoid claims that they possess secret information about either NATO plans or Soviet decision making. But on occasion they refer to such information in a manner that pragmatically presupposes special knowledge. In paragraphs 24, 30, and 33, NATO policies and operational plans are raised as problematic in contexts where the reader must conclude that the authors possess explicit knowledge. For instance, the conditional voice is used to suggest that the authors are talking not about a hypothetical world but a real one:

> There should also be an examination of the ways in which the concept of early use of nuclear weapons may have been built into existing forces, tactics, and general military expectations . . . There could be a dangerous gap right now.

The claims about knowledge of Soviet views are much weaker and far less important to the argument because the chief virtue of NFU is asserted to be its contribution to NATO unity. Nevertheless, the authors find it useful to assert that the Soviets perceive risks in the use of nuclear weapons (par. 36) and would like to reduce these (which we know because Soviet pronouncements are reasonably informative; par. 46). And neither side could fully trust any pledges of no first use as long as inventories of nuclear weapons remain (par. 43). So we are encouraged to believe that Soviet concerns with nuclear war in Europe are qualitatively similar to our own, and further assignment of motives or plans to the Soviet Union is not relevant to evaluating NFU favorably as an option for NATO.

Clearly insiders' knowledge is relevant and real; however, the reader's (audience's) reliance upon such must be properly qualified.

8.8   Problems in developing justifications (warrants and backing) on a more involved level

In an elaborate and involved political argument, the three elements (i) justifications (warrants and backing), (ii) plans and proposals (as simple or elaborate claims), and (iii) objectives (as associated with claims and grounds) are not wholly separable. The objectives can be conditioned by both justifications and the characteristics of any plan or proposal. Justifications cannot be considered apart from the objectives and the internal structure of a proposal or plan. The plan itself is highly affected by the objectives and justifications. These interconnections are evident in dealing with the highly complicated question of "no first use."

In carefully argued written form, political arguments typically involve justifications of an extended sort, which are often accounts that enumerate one or a few key agents as protagonists linked causally to key events. As we have already mentioned in G's argument, a single reason to find NFU acceptable is the alleged ability of NATO to meet Soviet aggression in three scenarios. Each scenario itself is an account (in the sense of Bennett 1984a); each is not as complex as a story because there is no termination to the listed events that somehow reverses or puts right the initial event that motivated a sequence of actions and reactions. For one scenario at least (par. 21) several possible outcomes are foreseen, each of which leaves unresolved the issue of successful aggression by the Warsaw Pact.

G justify their call for reorganizing NATO's military forces through describing how a Soviet invasion could be executed (pars. 26–28) and how NATO could counter such an attack (pars. 29–30). They justify part of their policy proposal with a reason that itself is another account of a hypothetical sequence of events, the attack on Hamburg, or something similar.

B justify their call for an informed and widespread debate by listing illustrious individuals who support parts of their proposals (par. 34) and also by claiming positive effects of previous debates along these lines (par. 49). In the former case the reason used is roughly "other eminent authorities agree with us"; in the latter it is "this solution worked well previously." Many other types of reasons could be cited, but it is not clear what logical or rhetorical properties they share.

To logicians, a reason is any proposition that forms a step in a completed proof. In political argument, "proof" is too restrictive a concept, and even "proposition" is misleading. People set forth as reasons a variety of statements, such as the following:

> *Relation of necessity:* Characterized by logical "if–then"; assertion of absence of other possibilities (physical determinism); absolute moral requirement; predictive certainty (by an implicit mechanism).

Relation of causation: Characterized by practical sufficiency; statistical, mechanical, or goal-directed causal connection of a direct or indirect sort.

Relation of rationality: Consequence of informed selection or judgment by a sentient behaving unit; characterized by unique perspective; optimal versus satisfactory; predictable versus certain.

Relation of automatic or natural unfolding: Characterized by the consequence of nonintervention; result of the ordinary course of events or development; default outcome; realization of potential of a "natural kind" (Salkever 1983).

Relation of possibility: Consequence of enablement or permission; characterized by an option or variant; exemplified by doubt.

Relation of obligation: Consequence of moral injunction or recognized duty; fulfillment of specifically human potential.

Relation of instance: Example; element or representative membership; illustration or model.

Relation of justification: Characterized by rationale, *ex post* use of any proposition specifically to function as a reason; characterized by claim of blamelessness, good intention, and so on.

Relation of randomness: Characterized by accident, arbitrariness, nonpredictability, and incomprehensibility; mystery.

These kinds of reasons can of course be rearranged and organized in a variety of ways, as they frequently are in a explanation, and thus generating a complex of justifications. Often a complicated political argument may organize justifications in a hierarchical manner. Likewise with claims. For example, we have indicated in section 8.3 that the central claim "a policy of NFU . . . is desirable" is supported by a subsidiary claim (implicit) that the set of outcomes used by G is relevant. This in turn is supported by a still lower order claim, namely, that the set of past data from which the outcome function $f(a, e)$ is derived or on which a body of expert knowledge is based is relevant and so forth. Moreover, a hierarchy of claims (or justifications or both) may be irregular and laterally connected with other hierarchies, regular or irregular.

For an involved political argument there thus exists the problem of the choice of a set of justifications to be used. Although frequently the particular issue, regarding which an argument is being made for a specific policy, will exclude the possibility of using certain kinds of justifications (as a relation of randomness or necessity), there still may be several kinds of justifications that can be used singly or in combination. What would be the most objective, if objectivity could be measured? Or what would be the most persuasive? And so on.

8.9   Problems of dealing with possible worlds, succession of events and dynamics, and plans

Political arguments frequently must involve the consideration of possible worlds – alternative states of affairs that may evolve from the implementation of a given policy. Rules to govern the generation of such worlds are thus required. This need obviously goes well beyond purely formal logic.

Linguistics recognizes a number of verbs and phrases often termed "world-creating predicates" (McCawley 1981). Examples are "dream," "imagine," "hypothesize," and "suppose that." (Other verbs such as "demand," "wish," and sometimes even "seek" can be used to generate counterfactual assertions but not usually entire worlds!) To determine when authors are generating or positing possible worlds, we search for world-creating predicates in the text. Once a particular possible world has been introduced, it is conveniently indexed thereafter with the conditionals "would" and "should" (in the sense of expectation or prediction).

A way to introduce possible worlds is to describe them as "plans," "proposals," or "options." This may be desirable rhetorically in order to downplay their hypothetical or "only possible" nature. It is, in fact, how both B and G introduce the doctrine of NFU implemented as NATO policy.

G's treatment of the military virtues of an NFU policy in paragraph 23 is informative; the text is reduced in what follows to eliminate irrelevant material and simply to label qualifications:

> A no-first-use strategy [introduced as a "new NATO policy" in par. 3 and a "proposal" in par. 5] would be of some value . . . it might increase . . . and it would be distinctly . . . As long as . . . X appears to be quite improbable, and it will become progressively more improbable . . . Although Y cannot be ruled out, it would be.

The remainder of the paragraph describes hypothetical event Y. The conclusion of the paragraph is that "a no-first-use policy significantly increases military stability." Note that the evaluation is not qualified with respect to possible worlds.

The thrust of G's argument here is that

1. we have perturbed the world in which NFU is implemented and find that objections of its desirability are weak; and

2. we have examined (not all possible but) all plausible worlds featuring NFU and find that none is so undesirable as to disqualify the proposal.

However, in considering (let alone generating) plausible worlds, G (as is also true for B) leave much to be desired. The rules for generating alternative future worlds as scenarios are not spelled out. The futures are presented in a very sketchy and selective fashion, so that their internal consistency cannot be examined. For instance, G construct three scenarios about hypothetical military deployments by NATO without introducing Soviet responses in doctrine and deployment. G are not explicit about the political changes within NATO or in the alliance relationships to its member states. In the scenarios, appropriate political adjustments are assumed to be commensurate with the posited military changes.

In any world there are sets of behaving units (individuals, groups, and others) with attributes and relations among them. This conception is very general and therefore is a very powerful one. Further, it places a great burden for the specification of detail upon those who wish to posit hypothetical worlds in the course of political argument. It would be better if the possible worlds could somehow be prespecified, at least to the extent of indicating by some framework what behaving units, properties, and relations are required.

To the extent that worlds worthy of consideration are all very much as the real world, the policy advocate can specify alternative worlds by indicating only those respects in which they differ from the real world. This is adequate for dealing with policies that differ only marginally from the present or for worlds arising in the very near term. Operationally, one might use a framework of the existing world and describe in a top–down fashion the statements about an alternative world that continue to hold after every kind of action by specifying that all states continue to hold except for specific ones, which are deleted.

For possible worlds that differ more than marginally, as would be the case with NFU, or to explore the cumulative long-term consequences of marginal changes, a framework oriented to the existing world is awkward. In particular, it would be a conservative device and could not accommodate the introduction of new actors or the emergence of structurally new relations in alternative worlds. In this connection, see Rescher (1975, 1977).

These rather abstract concerns come down to earth in the texts under examination when one must make claims about the beliefs of other actors in possible worlds. How are we to anticipate reactions by the Soviet Union to a NATO characterized by the doctrine of NFU?

G maintain that NFU brings advantages to NATO regardless of the Soviet reaction. B argue that the Soviets will respond as we would – cautiously at first but probably persuaded over time that doctrine had truly changed. Both B and G appeal to the possible thaw in relations that would follow NATO's adoption of NFU but treat benefits from better relations with the Soviets as bonuses (i.e., not essential to justify moving to NFU).

It is only when B attempt to argue that NFU would not tempt the Soviet Union to adventures that they edge toward stronger claims about knowledge of the Soviet belief subworld in the NFU world. Here they assert the claim without setting forth any reason but follow it with a curious aside that smacks of claims of authority (in consensus):

> The Soviet government is already aware of the awful risk inherent in any use of these weapons, and there is *no* current or prospective Soviet "superiority" that would tempt *anyone* in Moscow toward nuclear adventurism. (*All four of us* are wholly unpersuaded that the Soviet Union could ever *rationally* expect to gain from such a wild effort as a massive first strike on land-based American strategic missiles.) [par. 36, emphasis added]

B do not elaborate on their notion of rationality in the Soviet belief system of the NFU world. Presumably it is carried over intact from this world.

The analysis in neither B nor G is deeply strategic enough to demand much reflective reasoning. Statements of belief, often termed attitudinal propositions in logic, give rise to complications (often resembling intransitivities or opacity) when one wishes to make inferences. B and G limit their claims to, in effect, quoting beliefs of others. They do not attempt to draw inferences from chains of belief, such as "J believes that N believes that J believes that. . . . " But were they, for example, to define fully the concept of deterrence, which as we have pointed out is central to their arguments, they would have to draw such inferences.

In addition to the problems of representing continuity or similarity among worlds and establishing transworld identities, possible-worlds semantics requires statements about the *accessibility* of one world from another.

Accessibility is typically treated as a simple binary relation. World Γ is or is not accessible from world Ω. However, a simple binary relation is not very useful. Important to establishing the feasibility of a proffered policy is the demonstration that one can bring about the desired state of affairs without experiencing unacceptable conditions in the interim, that is, unacceptable in any of the intermediate stages whether the passage through these stages is gradual or by a series of big and small steps. The transformation urged for the real world is usually not only directed, but it is deliberate, with perhaps the rate of change being a constraint (as it is in par. 29 in B).

In political argumentation the function performed by "accessibility" is often replaced by "plan." A policy proposal includes, perhaps in sketchy terms, a plan or plans (often executed in parallel; see par. 55 in G). Treatment of plans is a convenient locus for the introduction of strategic considerations, such as anticipated opposition (par. 25 in B) and counterplanning (no instances in either article!). Yet, counterplanning by the Soviet Union should clearly be considered and be perhaps as closely related to planning as it is to attacks and rebuttals in two-party argumentation (Karapin and Alker 1985; Flowers, McGuire, and Birnbaum 1982).

With respect to accessibility to and other consideration of possible worlds, the arguments of B and G have major inadequacies. Nonetheless we must drastically curtail any temptation for sharp criticism. A plan is an extremely difficult construction. This point is well recognized in the economic and regional planning fields, which, in contrast, are blessed with a much more extensive data base. The most agonizing difficulties in these fields are those associated with anticipating the dynamics that necessarily occur and whose understanding is still well beyond their ken and that of social science in general. Ever since World War II economists have devoted considerable effort to developing satisfactory dynamic models. Very little has been achieved. Hence, in the much more qualitative areas of political argument, one cannot expect very much when dynamics and possible-worlds analysis that embodies, for example, criteria on stability, desirability, and feasibility is undertaken. For a long time, one will need to be content with little progress here.

8.10 Problems associated with learning phenomena, crisis situations, system effects, and multiple-target audiences (interest groups)

A political argument in a complex conflict situation must necessarily be lengthy and involved. This is especially clear when we consider the need, at the time of policy determination, for the recognition of

1. the several policy options available (corresponding to rows, the a, of a perceived payoff matrix);
2. the several relevant combinations of joint actions by other behaving units and possible states of the environment (corresponding to the columns, the $(e, \{a_k\})$, of a perceived payoff matrix; and
3. the fan of first-round intermediate (transitional) worlds generated (corresponding to the outcomes, the o, in the cells of the perceived payoff matrix). (See Isard 1981, 1983a,b.)

Next, one must consider that each first-round intermediate world itself generates a fan of second-round intermediate (transitional) worlds, and so forth, until a final set of relevant possible worlds is conceived. All this takes time and yields experience both in the development of the political argument and its presentation. As a consequence, learning results that should be planned for (anticipated) in the development of the argument. There is the process of learning by the recipients, which must be considered in the presentation. There is as well the learning by those who present the argument – learning from further deliberation, debate, and discussion, feedback on feasibility of intermediate states and other information on outcomes, and so on. This may lead these individuals to set up some new concepts, axioms, and assumptions and advance some new theories and relationships, presuppositions, and so forth. Hence the political argument and its plan, as initially developed and presented, should have considerable flexibility in their specifics since beforehand there is so much uncertainty about how much and what will be learned. But how to ensure such flexibility?

Another set of problems is associated with crisis situations. Although the discussion of feasibility and stability of intermediate worlds takes place, still crisis situations of different intensities will typically arise even when these worlds are feasible and basically stable. The political argument should then be specific on how to cope with them. Moreover, crisis situations often require the production of new information (investment in information R & D) and should be anticipated in an argument. For obvious reasons, explicit recognition should also be given to (a) bureaucratic structures, (b) power and authority relationships in one's own system (nation) and in others that will be reacting, and (c) the way political arguments and behavior takes place in these other systems. In fact, in certain situations the political arguments in several systems (nations) are highly interdependent, the nature and characteristics of argument in one being highly conditioned by the nature and characteristics of argument in the others.

Recognition of the play of bureaucratic structure is easily expanded into the need to consider system effects. The latter may be strong or weak, but they are always there. When strong – as when there is rapidly mounting intensity of hostile actions and reactions in the international or other system or rapid spread of depression and trade restrictions in a world economy – the influence of political argument, whatever its nature, may be negligible and may only serve to exacerbate relationships. So, too, is the case when there is rapid increase in cooperative relationships among systems. Hence, the justification for setting forth a political argument and its very nature may need to be related to system structure, attributes, trends, and effects – another tremendously difficult task that we can only inch forward on at this time given our limited social system knowledge and models.

Lastly, we want to return to problems associated with multiple-target audiences, or interest groups, or clients in the broad sense. As noted earlier, we may consider the outcome o to represent the overall security of an alliance (say, NATO) and to be a weighted average $(\Sigma_J w^J o^J)$ of the security outcome o^J to each nation J $(J = A, B, \ldots, U)$, each having a prespecified weight w^J. But from where do these weights come?

We already observed that B go beyond NATO's security and address that of Germany (par. 17). Much of B's insistence that NFU would in no respect weaken or reduce the U.S. commitment to Germany can be interpreted for German consumption and also Soviet. But B do not discuss elsewhere the implications of an NFU policy for each of the other NATO nations, each of which should be considered to be a target audience.

In general, a political argument should be geared to each of the target audiences (client groups) who are to be the recipients of the argument. It should be stated in terms of the language, knowledge, attitudes, limited abilities at reasoning, learning capacities, perspectives, perceptions (and misperceptions), risk taking, and other psychological, economic, social, and cultural attributes of each of these recipients. However, where target audiences have conflicting aims, desires, modes of reasoning, and so on, the political argument should either be organized differently for each audience or made sufficiently diffuse to appeal to each audience. And in some cases, where there is risk of emotional outbursts that would kill a proposal or plan, the proponents of an argument may justify ignoring certain interest groups or making the argument sufficiently ambiguous so as to avoid such outbursts.

It is at this point, however – where major conflict among interest groups arise because their objectives are diametrically opposed, or because there are major differences among them as to the weights that should be applied to each one's particular objective, or because of other disagreements – that the need for a conflict management procedure becomes urgent. Hence, it may be argued that a well-organized political argument for an equitably structured policy should contain within it an appropriate and acceptable conflict management procedure. We shall discuss the subject of conflict management procedures in Chapter 10.

8.11   Concluding remarks

We conclude that policy analysis and political argument are beset with exceedingly difficult problems. Formal logic has little application. This is so because it cannot handle (1) reasonable compromises, criticism, and reactions that can be constructive (as well as destructive), (2) what if reasoning, (3) the uncertainties and contradictions of real life, and so forth. Yet there is considerable difficulty in and great differences among approaches to describing and defining political argument. To facilitate the discussion of this chapter, we extend and revise one currently used approach, namely, that of Toulmin, and consider the basic elements of claims, grounds, warrants, backing, qualifiers, and counterrebuttals. We then suggest parallels between these elements and the decision-making analysis that is associated with outcome functions and payoff matrices (thereby to stimulate the transfer of knowledge and ways of thinking from one field to the other). We also outline the political arguments in two significant articles in support of an NFU policy to provide a set of concrete illustrations of the more general and abstract points to be made.

The first matter taken up is the complex data base required for any involved political argument. What is available is only an infinitesimal slice of what would be ideal; and further what is available is diminished by the limited ability of any behaving unit to store and retrieve information, let alone nonmisperceived and nondistorted information. Then there are the problems in determining and precisely stating objectives and in choosing and defining basic concepts and variables, neither of which seems to be adequately attacked in any involved political arguments. This is so because of both inadequate theory and data. (Some analysts may hold that an attack on problems relating to objectives, concepts, and variables should precede an attack on the problems related to data. However, despite heated debates on which comes first, this question is still a "chicken and egg" one.) Because of highly inadequate data, limited abilities of policy advocates and the audience, the political culture environment, and other factors, the advocates must rely in their arguments on presuppositions. These are often based on misinformation, misperception, and other invalid elements but are still indispensable for an effective coherent argument. Associated with this problem are the problems linked to

1. the definition and sources of relevant knowledge to be used by the advocate,
2. the making of pertinent interpretations of pertinent historical materials,
3. the development and presentation of counterrebuttals, and
4. the use of insiders' (experts') knowledge and the like.

Perhaps the most serious problems are associated with subjunctive reasoning and with hypotheses about possible worlds – about their structure and about "how we get there from here." Involved political arguments necessarily involve plans that in one way or another imply social–political–economic dynamics. The plans that rely upon major efforts to be explicit on dynamics necessarily are most inadequate. This is because our knowledge of such dynamics is so little and naive.

Policies must be adopted, and sound argument should be set forth in support of any policy. But we must face reality and unhappily conclude that what we can hope to achieve is to avoid bad argument and perhaps cast some limited light on the relative merits of several arguments (each set forth to support a policy). One obvious bad argument is a highly contradictory one based on, say, naive rhetoric. Other bad arguments, particularly on issues that are complex, can often only be exposed by data collection, processing, and generation. Here the use of models can be extremely valuable for generating (projecting) data on outcomes of different policies and scenarios. Hence we must consider such use, as we do in the next chapter.

Nevertheless, despite our unhappy conclusion, we must not give up the effort to at least avoid policies that can only be supported by bad argument. Also, the discussion of the innumerable problems that are rife in political argument has, we hope, suggested some direction in which one can improve a political argument, at least to the extent of making explicit the problems involved. Thus we must go on. We must tackle the next problem that emerges – namely how to resolve conflicting policies set forth by different behaving units (individuals, including political leaders, organizations, interest groups, etc.) when each of the policies can be said to be supported by a nonbad, possibly acceptable political argument. This problem – one of conflict management (coping with conflict) – we attack in Chapter 10, after we examine in the next chapter the use of emerging world models – to add to our stock of knowledge in order to help expose bad arguments and their policy proposals and to help identify the relative merits of different policy proposals.

References

Alker, H. R., Jr. (1976) "Can the End of Power Politics Somehow Be Part of the Very Concepts with which Its Story Is Told?" mimeo. Department of Political Science, MIT, Cambridge, MA.

Alker, H. R., Jr. (1983) "Fairy Tales, Tragedies and World Histories: Towards Interpretive Story Grammars as Possibilistic World Models," mimeo. Department of Political Science, MIT, Cambridge, MA.

Anderton, C. H. (1986) "Arms Race Modeling: Systematic Analysis and Synthesis," Ph.D. diss., Cornell University.

Barry, B. (1965) *Political Argument*. New York: Humanities Press.

Bennett, J. P. (1984a) "Data Stories: Learning about Learning from the U.S. Experience in Vietnam." In D. Sylvan and S. Chan. (eds.), *Foreign Policy Decision Making: Perception, Cognition and Artificial Intelligence*. New York: Praeger.

Bennett, J. P. (1984b) "No Second Thoughts about 'No First Use' – How Can the Policy Analyst Undertake Subjunctive Reasoning in Political Argument?" March, mimeo. Peace Science Unit, University of Pennsylvania, Philadelphia, PA.

Bennett, J. P. (1985) "Pre-Theory for Comparing National Security Policies." May, mimeo. Department of Political Science, Syracuse University, Syracuse, N.Y.

Brandt, W. F. (1970) *The Rhetoric of Argumentation*. New York: Bobbs-Merrill.

Bundy, McG., G. F. Kennan, R. S. McNamara, and G. Smith (1982) "Nuclear Weapons and the Atlantic Alliance." *Foreign Affairs* 60 (Spring):753–68.

Chotiya, P. (1983) "No First Use of Nuclear Weapons." MA thesis, University of Pennsylvania.

Clark, H. H., and S. E. Havilland (1977) "Comprehension and the Given-New Contract." In R. O. Freedle (ed.), *Discourse Production and Comprehension*. Norwood, NJ: Ablex Publishing, pp. 1–40.

Clark, H. R., and C. R. Marshall (1981) "Definite Reference and Mutual Knowledge." In A. K. Joshi, B. L. Webber, and I. A. Sag (eds.), *Elements of Discourse Understanding*. New York: Cambridge University Press, pp. 10–63.

Cresswell, M. J. (1985) *Structured Meanings*. Cambridge, MA: MIT Press.

Dubois, J., et al. (1981) *A General Rhetoric* (trans and ed. P. B. Burrell and E. M. Slotkin). Baltimore: Johns Hopkins University Press.

Faucounnier, G. (1985) *Mental Spaces: Aspects of Meaning Construction in Natural Language*. Cambridge, MA: MIT Press.

Flowers, M., R. McGuire, and L. Birnbaum (1982) "Adversary Arguments and the Logics of Personal Attacks." In W. Lehnert and M. Wingle (eds.), *Strategies for Natural Language Processing*. Hillsdale, NJ: Lawrence Erlbaum, pp. 275–94.

Gazdar, G. (1979) *Pragmatics: Implicature, Presupposition and Logical Form*. New York: Academic Press.

Goguen, J. A., J. L. Weiner, and C. Linde (1983) "Reasoning and Natural Explanation." *International Journal of Man-Machine Studies* 19(6):521–60.

Gottfried, K., H. W. Kendall, and J. M. Lee (1984) "'No First Use' of Nuclear Weapons." *Scientific American* 250(3):33–41.

Hintikka, J. (1969) *Models for Modalities*. Dordrecht: Reidel.

Huntingon, S. P. (1983) "Conventional Deterrence and Conventional Retaliation in Europe." *International Security* 8(3):32–56.

Huth, P., and B. Russett (1984) "What Makes Deterrence Work? Cases from 1900 to 1980." *World Politics* 36:496–576.

Independent Commission on Disarmament and Security Issues (1982) *Common Security: A Blueprint for Survival*. New York: Simon and Schuster.

Isard, W. (1981) "Social System Framework and Causal History: Part I, Learning Processes." *Conflict Management and Peace Science* 6(1):63–94.

Isard, W. (1983a) "Social System Framework and Causal History: Part II, Behavior under Stress and Cognition." *Conflict Management and Peace Science* 6(2):59–93.

Isard, W. (1983b) "Social System Framework and Causal History: Part III, Multi-Role Behavior and Operationality." *Conflict Management and Peace Science* 7(1):87–109.

Isard, W., and B. Lewis (1984) "James P. Bennett on Subjunctive Reasoning, Policy Analysis and Political Argument." *Conflict Management and Peace Science* 8(1, Fall):71–112.

Kaplan, A. (1964) *The Conduct of Inquiry.* San Francisco: Chandler Publishing.

Karapin, R. S., and H. R. Alker, Jr. (1985) "Argument Analysis: A Post-Modern, Dialectical, Graphical Approach," November, mimeo. Department of Political Science, MIT, Cambridge, MA.

Karttunen, L. (1974) "Presupposition and Linguistic Content." *Theoretical Linguistics* 1:181–94.

Katz, J. J., and D. T. Langendoen (1976) "Pragmatics and Presuppositon." *Language* 52:1–17.

Kempson, R. M. (1975) *Presupposition and the Delimitation of Semantics.* New York: Cambridge University Press.

Lewis, D. (1973) *Counterfactuals.* Cambridge, MA: Harvard University Press.

McCawley, J. D. (1979) "Presupposition and Discourse Structure." In C. -K. Oh and D. Dineen (eds.), *Syntax and Semantics,* Vol. 11. New York: Academic, pp. 371–78.

McCawley, J. D. (1981) *Everything That Linguistics Have Always Wanted to Know about Logic but Were Ashamed to Ask.* Chicago: University of Chicago Press.

McNamara, R. S. (1983) "The Military Role of Nuclear Weapons: Perceptions and Misperceptions." *Foreign Affairs* 62:59–80.

Perelman, C., and L. Olbrechts-Tyteca (1969) *The New Rhetoric: A Treatise on Argumentation* (trans. J. Wildinson and P. Weaver). Notre Dame, IN: University of Notre Dame Press.

Pollock, J. L. (1976) *Subjective Reasoning.* Dordrecht: D. Reidel.

Propp, Vladimir (1977) *Morphology of the Folktale* (rev. ed. of 1928 Russian). Austin: University of Texas.

Ravenal, E. C. (1983) "No First Use: a View from the United States." *Bulletin of the Atomic Scientists* April:11–16.

Rescher, N. (1975) *A Theory of Possibility: A Constructivistic and Conceptualistic Account of Possible Individuals and Possible Worlds.* Pittsburgh: University of Pittsburgh Press.

Rescher, N. (1977) *Dialectics: A Controversy-Oriented Approach to the Theory of Knowledge.* Albany: SUNY Press.

Robinson, J. A. (1979) *Logic: Form and Function.* Amsterdam: North-Holland.

Russett, B., H. R. Alker, Jr., K. W. Deutsch, and H. D. Lasswell (1964) *World Handbook of Political and Social Indicators.* New Haven, CT: Yale University Press.

Salkever, S. G. (1983) "Beyond Interpretation: Human Agency and the Slovenly Wilderness." In N. Haan, R. Bellah, P. Rabinow, and W. Sullivan (eds.) *Social Science as Moral Inquiry.* New York: Columbia University Press.

294 I. Basic framework and set of analyses

Searle, J. R. (1969) *Speech Acts, An Essay in the Philosophy of Language.* New York: Cambridge University Press.

Searle, J. R. (ed.) (1979) *Expression and Meaning: Studies in the Theory of Speech Acts.* New York: Cambridge University Press.

Searle, J. R., F. Kiefer, and M. Bierwisch (eds.) (1980). *Speech Act Theory and Pragmatics.* Dordrecht: Reidel.

Seuren, P. A. M. (1985) *Discourse Semantics.* London: Basil Blackwell.

Singer, J. D. (ed.) (1979) *The Correlates of War I: Research Origins and Rationale.* New York: Free Press.

Singer, J. D. (ed.) (1980) *The Correlates of War II: Testing Some Realpolitik Models.* New York: Free Press.

Singer, J. D., and M. Small (1969) "Formal Alliances, 1816–1965: An Extension of the Basic Data." *Journal of Peace Research* 6(3):257–82.

Singer, J. D., and M. Small (1972) *The Wages of War, 1816–1865: A Statistical Handbook.* New York: Wiley.

Singer, J. D., and M. Wallace (1970) "Inter-Governmental Organization in the Global System, 1816–1964: A Quantitative Description." *International Organization* 24(2, Spring):239–87.

Small, M., and J. D. Singer (1982) *Resort to Arms: International and Civil Wars, 1816–1980.* Beverly Hills: Sage Publications.

Stalnacker, R. C. (1968) "A Theory of Conditionals." *American Philosophical Quarterly* Series 2:98–112.

Steinbruner, J. D., and L. V. Sigal (eds.) (1983) *Alliance Security: NATO and the No First Use Question.* Washington DC: Brookings.

Taylor, C. L., and D. A. Jodice (1983) *World Handbook of Political and Social Indicators.* New Haven, CT: Yale University Press.

Toulmin, S. (1958) *The Uses of Argument.* New York: Cambridge University Press.

Toulmin, S. E. (1972) *Human Understanding, Vol. 1: The Collective Use and Evolution of Concepts.* Princeton: Princeton University Press.

Toulmin, S. E. (1976) *Knowing and Acting.* New York: Macmillan.

Toulmin, S. E., R. Rieke, and A. Janik (1979) *An Introduction to Reasoning.* New York: Macmillan.

Union of Concerned Scientists (1983) *No First Use.* Cambridge, MA, February 1.

Wasserstrom, R. A. (1961) *The Judicial Decision: Toward a Theory of Legal Justification.* Stanford, CA: Stanford University Press.

Weiler, L. D. (1983) "No First Use: A History." *Bulletin of the Atomic Scientists* February, pp. 28–34.

Willard, C. A. (1983) *Argumentation and the Social Grounds of Knowledge.* University, AL: University of Alabama Press.

World system models: incorporation of military expenditures and arms trade

Written with William Dean

9.1 Introduction

Having completed the discussion and analysis of political argument as a tool of the political leader or other behaving unit (decision maker) concerned with policy, it would appear desirable (logical) to proceed to consider two political leaders interacting with regard to a conflict. We might imagine each armed with a political argument and each utilizing all available skills of negotiation and resources to obtain a more rather than a less desirable outcome from his or her standpoint. We might next consider conditions under which agreement is possible and in the process discuss effective and ineffective principles of negotiation in diverse conflict situations. Then, we might go on to suggest different conflict management procedures that might be applicable without the presence of a third party. Or, we might consider the introduction of third parties – quasi mediators, mediators, arbitrators, and others – and consider principles or the science of third-party involvement. And so forth. Perhaps these steps would be appropriate for many types of conflict: husband–wife, labor–management in a specific factory, Catholics–Protestants in Northern Ireland, and so forth. However, when we consider major international conflicts – as the U.S.–Soviet confrontation – which are the most important ones from the standpoint of this book, we may need to take still another step prior to suggesting conflict management procedures for use. We may need to examine the whole array of data that is obtainable in support of various political arguments and their underlying policy analysis. We may do this so as to be in a position, at least as objective third-party observers (to the extent that any third party can be objective), to evaluate the data base and validity of the political arguments that might be set forth. In this

Sections 9.5–9.7 and the appendixes to this chapter were written jointly with William Dean.

connection, we need to examine now what "data" and the quality of such that can be generated by models such as world system models. Then we shall be in a position to derive data – as good as is now possible – on the total set of outcomes from the adoption (inputs) of different possible compromise policies (agreements), each corresponding to a joint action (i.e., a combination of a row and a column of a payoff matrix). Then we shall be able to evaluate these possible compromise policies, the political arguments behind them, and the different principles of negotiations employed. In this regard we are in agreement with Raiffa (1982) on the desirability for conducting analysis prior to negotiation, mediation, and/or arbitration. Of course, where there do not exist models, one conducts whatever analysis of the conflict situation that is possible.

Finally, it does not follow that in general the employment of world models or comparable analysis should precede discussion and presentation of available materials to justify the use of a conflict management procedure. Where protagonists and third parties are not sensitive to or flatly reject findings from models and analysis, then it may be more efficient to proceed directly to consideration of the use of principles of mediation and negotiations and their associated conflict management procedures. Once a direct joint action (agreement, or nonagreement when each takes an independent action) has been effected, we may observe the resulting impact and then perhaps project what could have been in evaluating the joint action that was taken.

Many world models have been developed that are based on extensive empirical materials. (We shall not discuss artificial intelligence models that are employed when no empirical materials or only sparse empirical materials are available.) Among others, they are LINK (Klein 1983), the UN (Leontief) Input–Output (Leontief et al. 1977), the OECD Interlink (Llewellyn and Samuelson, 1982), the EEC (COMPACT) (Ranuzzi 1981), Multicountry (MCM) of the Federal Reserve Board (Stevens et al. 1984), and the WDR 4 and 5 [initiated at the World Bank and being extended at Brussels, LaTrobe University, and elsewhere by Meagher (1982), Gunning, Carrin, and Waelbroeck (1982), and others].[1] We shall sketch the major aspects of several. Our task is to analyze exactly how a specific joint action or policy regarding military expenditures enters into and works within each.

---

[1] Still other models are the DRI International; the Wharton Econometrics; the Liverpool (University of Liverpool); the McKibbin/Sacks Simulation (NBER and Harvard University); the Mimmod (International Monetary Fund); the Taylor Simulation (Stanford University) (Taylor 1983); the Deardoff–Stern (1981) World (University of Michigan); the FUGI (Soka University, Japan) (Onishi 1983); the Shishido (University of Tsukuba) (Shishido et al. 1980); DYNAMICO (United Nations) (Costa and Jennergren 1982); and an extended SARUM (Gigengack et al. 1985).

In section 9.2, we sketch the Leontief UN World Input–Output model. We indicate how it incorporates military production and arms imports and exports in its framework and how it can project the impacts of changes in such. In the next section we place the framework within a social accounts data system (matrix), thereby to acquire information on the *distributional* impacts of these changes, that is, impacts on factor earnings, on institutions, and potentially on different income groups and social classes, and also to incorporate other data not ordinarily covered by input–output for analyzing impact.

Section 9.4 briefly comments upon the use of an interregional linear programming model, and section 9.5 discusses the potential of computable general equilibrium (CGE) models. In one aspect these latter models achieve an important advance over input–output, namely, in being able to treat substitution effects and nonlinearities in consumption, production, and trade among world regions. Their ability to project trade flows among regions – a basic channel through which the effects of military expenditures in any one world region are spread throughout the world – is most limited, so in section 9.6 we examine the use of a truncated translog function together with the comparative cost approach for projecting trade flows. In section 9.7 the potential of the gravity model is examined; and in section 9.8 a multimethod approach to trade flow projection is suggested, its usefulness for projecting *arms trade* being considered.

In section 9.9 we examine the extent to which diverse world models – the Computable General Equilibrium, World Econometric (LINK-type), and Programming are able to assist in projecting military expenditures from the interplay of forces able to be captured by (endogenous to) these models. Some preliminary results of such an effort by the LINK model is reported upon. In section 9.10 we examine the potential of the ambitious GLOBUS model and of its fusion with other models and with an integrated multiworld region model.

Section 9.11 presents some concluding remarks, with emphasis on world models as (1) capturing and providing basic data on internal forces that in part operate to influence the level of military expenditures as well as (2) projecting impacts of such expenditures. Both the magnitude of internal forces and these impacts condition and are conditioned by diverse policies on military expenditures and arms control.

9.2   The Leontief World Input–Output (I–O) model

One of the first comprehensive treatments of the interconnections between the various national economies of the world and their military expenditures was undertaken by Leontief and his associates (Leontief et al. 1977; Leontief 1980; Leontief and Duchin 1983). Their pathbreaking work firmly established one method for estimating the *impact,* direct and indirect, of military expenditures upon these interrelated economies. However, they did not attempt any examination of the reverse relationships, namely, the impact of the functioning of these interrelated economies upon levels of their military expenditures – as, for example, is implied by the Richardson model and other models discussed in Chapters 2 and 13.

The Leontief World model covers fifteen world regions:

> *eight developed regions* – Eastern Europe, high-income Asia, North America, Oceania, Soviet Union, South Africa, high-income Western Europe, and medium-income Western Europe;
>
> *three less developed regions with significant resource endowment* – resource-rich Latin America, the Middle East, and African oil-producing nations; and
>
> *four developing regions lacking significant resource endowment* – arid Africa, centrally planned Asia, low-income Asia, and resource-poor Latin America.

The economy of each region is described by a separate standard input–output matrix A given by

$$A = \begin{bmatrix} a_{11} & \cdots & a_{1j} & \cdots & a_{1n} \\ & & & & \\ & & & & \\ & & & & \\ a_{i1} & \cdots & a_{ij} & \cdots & a_{in} \\ & & & & \\ & & & & \\ & & & & \\ a_{n1} & \cdots & a_{nj} & \cdots & a_{nn} \end{bmatrix} \qquad (9.2.1)$$

where each row and corresponding column represents one of the forty-five sectors in the original world model (Leontief et al. 1977), or one of the thirty-four new rows and columns added to the original matrix of each region to study the impact of reduction of military expenditure. These thirty-four new rows account for

> eleven military production sectors,
> eleven sectors for the export of the corresponding military goods,
> eleven sectors for the import of these military goods, and
> the military final demand sector.

In this matrix A, each a_{ij} coefficient, taken to be a constant, indicates the cents' worth of commodity i required per dollar output of sector j (or in physical terms the quantity of input i required per unit output of j). With these constant coefficients we have a linear system, which lends itself to quick (and easy) solutions – and even, too, when certain nonlinear relations are introduced in a proper manner. Elsewhere, the system for an isolated world region has been described, and its virtues and limitations fully discussed (Isard et al. 1960, chap. 8; Miller and Blair 1985, and works cited therein).

In a multiregion Leontief world, where each region has its own input–output set of coefficients, the several regional economies are connected through a trade matrix. The *ideal* trade matrix is one that is fully disaggregated. Each row indicates the export of commodity h ($h = 1, \ldots, l$) from any world region J ($J = A, \ldots, U$) to each region L ($L = A, \ldots, U; L \neq J$).[2] Each column of the trade matrix refers to the import by region L of commodity h from every region J ($J \neq L$). The entries in the cell of some trade matrices may be in physical units; in other trade matrices, they may be in terms of money. A trade matrix may be constructed on the basis of trade data for a given year, in which case it is a reflection of the current state of affairs. However, in the use of a model, we frequently are concerned with projecting the state of affairs for a future (or past) year for which trade matrix data are not available. These data must therefore be estimated explicitly (or implied by estimates of other magnitudes).

Lack of data forces Leontief and his associates to use a simplified scheme for constructing a trade matrix. The imports IM_h^J of a good h by a region J are taken to be a fixed share k_h^J of the region's total domestic consumption D_h^J of that good. That is,

$$\frac{\text{IM}_h^J}{D_H^J} = k_h^J, \qquad J = A, \ldots, K, \qquad h = 1, \ldots, l \tag{9.2.2}$$
$$\text{(importing countries)}$$

Imports come from a world pool of that good, to which pool each exporting region S contributes a fixed percentage $\overline{k}_h^S$. That is,

$$E_h^S = \overline{k}_h^S \sum_S E_h^S, \qquad S = L, \ldots, U \text{ (exporting countries)} \tag{9.2.3}$$

where

$$\sum_J \text{IM}_h^J = \sum_S E_h^S \tag{9.2.4}$$

---

[2] In practice, trade matrices typically aggregate commodities in one way or another.

Thus when consumption in a region of a good h that is imported rises, its total imports rises by the same percentage; and accordingly, each exporting region must supply more to the world pool of that commodity. This requirement corresponds to zero elasticity of substitution ($\sigma = 0$) among the exporting regions in meeting the import need for h of any region. The shortcomings of an approach using a zero elasticity of substitution among export sources are obvious, just as the use of zero elasticity of substitution among factors of production in the Leontief production scheme.[3]

Despite the shortcomings noted in the preceding and others, the Leontief scheme has been invaluable for gaining insight into the impact of a change in military expenditures in one or more regions (countries), particularly in identifying significant indirect impacts. In identifying such, we represent a change in military expenditures in a given region J by the changes in the list of items to be purchased by J's military sector and that when properly ordered may be depicted by the vector ΔM^J. When this vector is specified and is necessarily associated with corresponding offset programs (e.g., change in foreign aid, changes in social welfare programs, reduction of taxes, etc., singly or in combination), we obtain the combined changes in the list of goods. These changes are representable by the vector ΔY^J. If region J were closed (i.e., have no trade with other regions), then the impact on the output of J's sectors (industries) would be given by premultiplying ΔY^J by the familiar Leontief inverse matrix $\overline{A}^J$ (derived from the coefficient matrix A noted before) to yield

$$\Delta X^J = \overline{A}^J \, \Delta Y^J \tag{9.2.5}$$

Here ΔX^J is a listing (in proper order) of the resulting change in the output of each sector in J. For example, the first item in the list might be change in agricultural output; the fifteenth might be change in steel output. For further discussion, see Isard and Schooler (1964) and Leontief and Duchin (1983).

When we record the changes in a greatly enlarged list of items to cover all regions and their associated changes in military expenditures together with their corresponding offset programs, we obtain the vector ΔY, which, if there are U regions, is U times as long as the vector ΔY^J. When we interconnect these regions by the trade matrix discussed in the preceding, we obtain the matrix A, which has U times as many rows and U times as

---

[3] At the other extreme is the case where the elasticity of substitution σ is infinite, as in simplified classical interregional trade theory. Here, when there is more than one region exporting to an importing region necessarily at the same delivered price, any shading of the price by one exporting region leads to its gaining the entire market of the importing region. The "gross" unreality of this approach is also clear.

many columns as A^J. When we multiply ΔY by the inverse of A, we obtain a vector ΔX, which is U times as long as ΔX^J. The vector ΔX then indicates all the direct and indirect impacts on each sector in every region. For example, the first item might be change in agricultural output in the first region; the 230th item, change in steel output in region L; and the last item, change in household income in region U.

With the preceding model, Leontief has derived impacts for several arms limitation *scenarios*. One is where

1. the United States and the USSR reduce military expenditures to a level that is two-thirds of the level that would be reached in the year 2000 if they were to devote the same fraction of their incomes to military expenditures as they did in 1970; and
2. all other regions cut their military expenditures by 40 percent by the year 2000.

Additionally, the developed nations are assumed by year 2000 to allocate 25 percent of the cuts in military expenditures to development (foreign) aid. Under such a scenario, we find, for example, that

1. per capita income of the resource-poor regions would increase from approximately $185 in 1970 to $260 in 2000 (in 1970 dollars)
2. employment in low-income Asia would triple (it would only double under a status quo scenario);
3. world output of food processing would be 3.2 percent higher and that of aircraft 5.7 percent lower in the year 2000 when compared to a status quo scenario;

and so forth. In effect, sector outputs and their employment by region and income, consumption, and investment by region would all be affected.

To sum up, the Leontief model is particularly strong in identifying impacts upon particular, highly disaggregated sectors, upon their demand for and supply of individual commodities and services, and in general in providing information at the microlevel. However, it is subject to certain basic shortcomings.

1. By and large it must assume constant input–output coefficients in production.
2. It must assume constant ratios of a region's imports to its total domestic consumption and constant shares of each exporting nation to a hypothetical world pool of a good.
3. It does not incorporate economic forces that in part determine the level of military expenditures, that is, the military expenditures that are endogenously determined.

In subsequent sections we shall examine to what extent these shortcomings can be overcome by more sophisticated models. However, we first examine a *social accounting framework* that can often be exceedingly useful as a complement to input–output (and vice versa) in providing basic information for policy purposes.

9.3   The social accounting framework

Input–output can provide useful information not only at the microlevel (by sector by region) but also at a more aggregated level – and even at a highly aggregated level. In this connection, it has often been associated with a *social accounts matrix* approach, designated SAM. This approach supplements the input–output coefficients and flow tables with extremely useful tables of aggregate magnitudes. Such a table is presented here as Table 9.1. In this table we follow the outline of a 1973 SAM table for Turkey (Dervis, de Melo, and Robinson 1982, pp. 156, 158) and use its magnitudes. We have, however, provided additional terms to facilitate understanding.[4] Also, we have disaggregated the government sector into two parts, the civilian and the military, and distinguished between civilian and military production activities. We have done so in order to make explicit the government allocation problem between military and nonmilitary programs and the linkage of the military to other sectors of an economy and to have a SAM table that would correspond to Leontief's disaggregated sectors on military goods production and export and

[4] The rows and columns of the SAM table are designated differently than in an input–output table in order to organize data in a way more suitable for social policy purposes. For example, factor income and transfers to household accounts are made explicit to permit more careful analyses of distributional impacts of exogenous changes. A capital account is embodied (although it is simply an aggregation of a Leontief capital flow table) in order to facilitate macrotype Keynesian analysis for fiscal and monetary policy purposes – analysis requiring data on savings and investment. A commodity pool (in large part a dummy) is introduced to see better the operation of markets. However, the SAM table, when fully disaggregated by input–output sector, household type, government program, etc., is simply a rearrangement and reaggregation of the data contained in standard Leontief commodity flow tables. Rows refer in general to value of sales and moneys received, columns to costs of inputs and money payments. For example, receipts of civilian activities are (going across the first row) equal to the value of the output that is transferred to the commodity pool plus subsidies (received from the government) plus export sales. All of this sums to the total value of production. The last is equal to the total cost of production at the bottom of the first column. As another example, money flows of households are (reading down column 6) equal to consumption (in dollar terms) of commodities plus the direct taxes paid for government services plus the savings households place in bank and other capital accounts. Its total money outlays recorded at the bottom of column 6 is equal to the total of household receipts recorded in the total column. For further discussion, see Pyatt and Round (1985) and Thorbecke (1985). We, of course, have specified disaggregations to make the military explicit.
    Finally, the SAM of Table 9.1 is for Turkey, with other nations of the world aggregated into the sector "rest of the world." An interregional SAM would disaggregate this sector by world region and by SAM sector in each region.

import of military goods. Since we do not have actual magnitudes for such sector production and export and import for Turkey for the year 1973, we specify them as unknowns, $x, y, z, \ldots$.

Specifically, we note in the cell of the third column and in the next to the last row that (in millions of dollars) r amount of arms imports (the aggregate of Leontief's eleven import sectors) as well as $\$33.7 - r$ amount of nonarms imports (here always viewed as intermediate goods) go into the pool of various commodities noted at the head of the column. (This pool may be viewed in large part as a dummy account.) Some of these arms imports then enter as part of the inputs x from this pool (row 2) into the military activities (sector) of column 2. Observe also that military activities in the lower part of the first row may produce some goods that are intermediates to other military production, and these goods as well as finished military goods constitute the value y that enters into the commodity pool of column 3. Observe, too, from the lower part of row 1 that the military receives subsidy of v from the government (column 8) and produces goods for export with value t (column 10), this value being the aggregate of Leontief's eleven export sectors.

The second column of the table relates to military production activities (the aggregate of Leontief's eleven military production sectors). Going down that column, we observe that these activities take out of the commodity pool x amount of goods for use as intermediate inputs (as already noted) as well as z amount of labor, w amount of capital services, and s amount of indirect taxes (as payments for government services provided the military sector). Total costs for military production is $x + z + w + s$.

Finally, there are deliveries from the commodity pool (row 2) of u amount of finished goods to the military sector of the government (column 8), the u amount including those *arms* imports that were already finished goods.

There are, of course, many ways to set up a SAM table, the way that it is best for examining one kind of economic problem often being different from that best for examining another kind. But clearly, any way that is appropriate for a system such as the United States, the Soviet Union, and many other countries where military activities constitute a significant fraction of the economy must be explicit about arms imports and exports as well as military production.

We also should note that Table 9.1 is highly aggregated. Column 1 can be disaggregated into as many as 500, if not more, sectors; military production can be disaggregated into many more sectors than Leontief's eleven [as Leontief and Duchin (1983) indicate]. Likewise, with all other columns and rows. In this manner the SAM table can come to include the standard Leontief framework and more, with the macromagnitudes

Table 9.1. *A social accounts table*

Receipts	Inputs into activities Civilian (1)	Military (2)	Inputs into commodity pool (3)	Factor earnings as inputs into household activity (4)	(5)	Households (6)	Government Civilian (7)	Military (8)	Inputs into capital account (9)	Inputs into, remittances from rest of world (10)	Total (11)
Activities												
(a) Civilian	—	—	$463.8 - y$	—	—	—	$1.5 - v$	—	—	$24.5 - t$	$489.8 - (y + v + t)$
(b) Military	—	—	y	—	—	—	—	v	—	t	$y + v + t$
			output values				subsidies			export sales	total value of production output
Commodity pool from outflows	$195.7 - x$	x	—	—	—	224.7	$30.5 - u$	u	58.3	—	509.2
	intermediate inputs					consumption			investment		total value of commodity sales
Factors												
(a) Labor	$138.1 - z$	z	—	—	—	—	—	—	—	—	138.1
	wages										total factor income
(b) Capital	$137.1 - w$	w	—	—	—	—	—	—	—	—	137.1
	rentals										

Institutions	Activities (total costs)	Commodities (total absorption)	Labor income	Capital income	Households	Government	Capital account	Rest of world	Total
(a) Households	—	—	138.1	137.1	—	—	—	19.7 remittances	294.9 household receipts
(b) Government (i) Civilian	18.9 − s (indirect taxes)	11.7 tariffs, for government services	—	—	23.5 direct taxes	—	—	—	54.1 government revenue
(b) Government (ii) Military	s (indirect taxes)	—	—	—	—	—	—	—	
Capital account	—	—	—	—	46.7 private savings	11.6 government savings	—	—	58.3 total savings
Rest of world (a) Nonarms imports	—	33.7 − r (import values)	—	—	—	—	10.5 foreign exchange credits	—	44.2 foreign exchange outflow
Rest of world (b) Arms imports	—	r (import values)	—	—	—	—	—	—	
Total	489.8 − (x + z + w + s); (x + z + w + s) (total costs)	509.2 total absorption	138.1 total factor contributions	137.1	294.9 total outlays (money outflows)	54.1	58.3 capital increase	44.2 foreign exchange inflow	

of Keynesian and econometric studies (to be discussed later) constituting some of the aggregates. For example, see the detailed Table 3 in Leontief et al. (1977).

Finally, we note that the disaggregated SAM table that includes the detail of a Leontief input–output table, Keynesian macromagnitudes, households finely disaggregated by income and other criteria, and government likewise disaggregated by program may be extended to cover much more detail. In particular we have in mind the detail on financial flows. As discussed elsewhere (Isard et al. 1960, chap. 12), an input–output table presenting the actual flows for a given interregional system for a given year and the corresponding interregional SAM are directly obtainable from a more comprehensive table (if it were available) depicting interregional money flows in full. Such a money flow table would cover not only payments each sector receives from its sales and makes for its inputs, but also payments made or received in connection with (1) issuance of stocks, bonds, and short-term loans; (2) profits and interest and rent on assets; (3) change in bank deposits; and (4) insurance, grants, and so on, all disaggregated by world region or other meaningful geographic unit. Moreover, such a money flow table would finely disaggregate the financial sectors of input–output and SAM into several types of bank, savings and loan association, investment institution, and so on. However, whereas from a conceptual standpoint all this is possible, in practice the data are so limited that little progress can be achieved in this direction not only apropos a set of world regions but also a set of regions within a nation such as the United States.

9.4   The interregional linear programming model

At this point we note that another approach, namely, *linear programming,* may be adopted to model the world economic system. This approach has many similarities to input–output. For example, it employs constant-production coefficients and makes extensive use of linear functions to generate solutions. However, unlike input–output, it enables the analyst to consider more than one process for the production of an output and to optimize on some combination of objectives that can be brought together in a single function, linear or nonlinear. Furthermore, it generates shadow prices on scarce resources. Yet, it has major drawbacks. It too often generates complete specialization in production (no crosshauling) and other extreme behavior, which is highly unrealistic. Although ad hoc constraints may be used to preclude such specialization and extreme behavior, these constraints make interpretation of the projected magnitudes more difficult. Nor can the resulting shadow prices be taken to represent market prices. Further, when used in a dynamic context, there are major problems in specifying (as targets) the terminal year capital stocks by sector and their role.

Whereas some analysts may prefer the use of interregional linear programming or an adaptation of it to input–output, by and large it suffers from the same shortcomings. Hence, we choose not to discuss it at the length it warrants.

9.5 Multicountry computable general equilibrium (CGE) models and trade matrix projection

The approaches of input–output and linear programming were inspired by the Walrasian general equilibrium system, first formulated almost a century ago. (See Appendix 9.A for a sketch of an interregional general equilibrium system.) This system was conceived to be largely nonlinear. In view of the hopeless problem of computing a solution to a large nonlinear system, Leontief designed, a half century ago, a linear representation of the system's structure, his input–output framework. This representation made it possible to solve the system, for example, to obtain solutions (values for the unknown sector outputs) when an exogenous or other change was assumed to take place. Now, a half century later, during which there has been a revolution in the development of computer capability, one can reasonably ask: Do we any longer need to linearize the general equilibrium system in order to obtain solutions, thereby to neglect seriously, and to some analysts without warrant, the nonlinearities of reality? The answer is no. To support this answer, we can point to CGE models that have been actively developed in the last decade or so (Ginsburgh and Waelbroeck 1981; Scarf and Shoven 1983; Robinson and Tyson 1983; Shoven and Whalley 1984; Mercenier and Waelbroeck 1984; Ginsburgh and Robinson 1984; Whalley 1985; Chenery, Robinson, and Syrquin 1986).

As noted, linearizing production and trade in a multiregion system amounts to assuming zero degree of substitution between factors in production and between sources of goods in trade. The CGE models explicitly allow for factor and trade substitution in a profit- and utility-maximizing framework. Moreover, they do so within the framework of markets where prices are determined endogenously.[5] Thus these models

---

[5] Recall that input–output operates independently of prices, and so can linear programming when appropriate weights are applied to the variables in the objective function. Further, although there is optimization in linear programming, it is primarily with regard to technical (engineering) efficiency, whereas in CGE models optimization involves not only such efficiency but also efficiency taking into account the reality of price changes.

avoid the first two serious shortcomings of the input–output model listed at the end of section 9.2:

1. the assumption of constant input–output coefficients in production, and
2. the assumption of constant ratios of a region's imports to its total domestic consumption and constant shares of each exporting nation to a hypothetical world pool of a good.

The presentation of the structure of a CGE model involves much more technical materials than input–output. Hence, we have chosen to present these materials in Appendix 9.B and, when desirable, in footnotes. For our purposes, we need to examine in mathematical form only one basic relation to obtain an understanding of the contribution that the CGE model can make and what it cannot do.

Consider a two-variable CGE model where $\tilde{q}_1$ and $\tilde{q}_2$ are the equilibrium quantities of two items – two inputs of a firm such as labor and capital, or imports of a good from two sources such as automobiles from Japan and Korea, or two consumption goods such as food and housing. Let p_1 and p_2 be their prices. Then the basic condition for a price-taking behaving unit (a firm, an importer, or a consumer) to optimize $p_1\tilde{q}_1 + p_2\tilde{q}_2$ (i.e., maximize profits, minimize import costs, or maximize utility, respectively) subject to a constant elasticity of substitution (CES) function[6] is given by[7]

$$\tilde{q}_1/\tilde{q}_2 = \lambda \, (p_2/p_1)^\sigma \qquad (9.5.1)$$

Here, $\lambda = (\rho_1/\rho_2)^\sigma$, with ρ_1 and ρ_2 being share parameters,[8] where σ is a constant $(0 \le \sigma \le \infty)$, being the elasticity of substitution between $\tilde{q}_1$ and $\tilde{q}_2$.

Relation (9.5.1) does allow substitution. Clearly, when p_1 rises, $\tilde{q}_1$ will decline relative to $\tilde{q}_2$. Such a substitution relationship may indeed be appropriate for depicting production and consumption behavior, where the distinction between factors (such as land, labor, and capital) and com-

---

[6] For two variables, the CES function takes the form

$$z = \omega \left[\rho_1 \tilde{q}_1^{\,(\sigma - 1)/\sigma} + \rho_2 \tilde{q}_2^{\,(\sigma - 1)/\sigma} \right]^{\sigma/(\sigma - 1)}$$

where z is the amount of output, or total imports (in effective units), or utility, respectively. For more than two variables, the form is

$$z = \omega \left[\sum \rho_i \tilde{q}_i^{\,(\sigma - 1)/\sigma} \right]^{\sigma/(\sigma - 1)} \qquad \text{for} \quad \sum \rho_i^\sigma = 1, \qquad i = 1, 2, \ldots$$

[7] When we (1) set up the Lagrangian, (2) take the partials of the Lagrangian with respect to both $\tilde{q}_1$ and $\tilde{q}_2$ (which are complex expressions) and set them equal to zero for optimization, and (3) take the ratio of the two partials, we obtain the simple expression (9.5.1).

[8] These parameters indicate the relative importance of $\tilde{q}_1$ and $\tilde{q}_2$ for the realization of z, where $(\rho_2/\rho_1)^\sigma + (\rho_1/\rho_2)^\sigma = 1$.

modities (such as food, clothing, housing, and automobiles) is clear. In this regard, where adequate data are available to estimate σ and other parameters, the CGE model together with a CES function or other relevant nonlinear function to describe the production and consumption processes may be and is frequently used to replace the corresponding linear functions of input–output.

When it comes to using a CGE model with a CES function to replicate trade flows among nations (which frequently is done), serious questions arise. In general, the CES function in a CGE model cannot be said to depict approximately the substitution that characterizes trading behavior among different sources of a given commodity h – for example, between basic steel products from Korea and that from Japan, where the distinction between the two is not nearly as clear as between labor and capital. Nor can the model depict approximately the substitution between any other pair of sources exporting steel products for a given market, or, say, wheat for a particular import market, or many other products for specific import markets – again because the distinction is not nearly as clear as that between labor and capital. Moreover, for any given commodity h, the model often applies the same constant elasticity of substitution σ_h to all those imports from every pair of sources – the same, for example, between Korea and Japan as between Brazil and Belgium in reaching a given import market.[9] Further, it typically ignores (assumes to be zero) transport costs and trade margins. Still more, the use of a CES function in projecting trade flows under cost minimization requires the notion of fictitious, composite commodities with which are necessarily associated fictitious prices.[10] However, these shortcomings in the use of a CES function diminish when broad aggregates of commodities are employed, such as manufactures and agricultural products.[11] In sum, then, there are seri-

---

[9] On occasion, this shortcoming can be tempered by the proper use of nested CES functions.

[10] Such is required in order to have imperfect substitution between any pair of sources of a commodity in meeting an import need – in effect, to have well-behaved, strictly convex isoquants for the corresponding fictitious commodity produced by commodity inputs from two different sources considered thereby as two distinct commodities. These fictitious commodities and their prices, however, do not appear in the basic financial accounts for the importing nation. For further discussion see Armington (1969) and Hickman and Lau (1973).

[11] There has been attention given to the use of a rational-expectations approach in CGE world models. For example, see Taylor (1983). Although the exploration of this approach may provide valuable insights to the investigator, at the current stage of development of CGE models, we judge that the use of such would be premature. From an explanation standpoint, the effects of parameter changes in various scenarios would prove much more difficult to interpret since in an appropriate model they would propagate not only through the current state of affairs but also into future states and then back to the present, at least for several "back and forth" runs. At this stage, simple mental models focusing on a relatively few indicators or proxies and not on the use of the (unachievable) perfect foresight implied in the rational-expectations framework are likely to yield better projections.

ous qualifications to the use of a CES function in projecting the trade flow matrix – a task essential for assessing the spread of effects of military expenditures in one world region to others.

9.6   The translog function, the comparative cost approach, and trade flows

Recently, there have been suggestions that a translog function may be useful for modeling imperfect substitution in trade and thus to replace the zero elasticity of substitution frameworks of input–output. Here any equilibrium export $E_h^{N \to J}$ of a commodity h from a given source N (exporting region) to the importing region J is related to the given total level $\tilde{IM}_h^J$ of J's imports of the fictitious composite commodity[12] and the prices $p_h^{N \to J}$ of commodity h at sources N by a series of first-order and second-order logarithm terms. The standard form when there is constant returns to scale and assuming cost minimization is

$$E_h^{N \to J} = (\tilde{p}_h^J \tilde{IM}_h^J / p_h^{N \to J})(a_h^{N \to J} + \sum_N v_h^{N \to J} \ln p_h^{N \to J}) \tag{9.6.1}$$

where $a_h^{N \to J}$ and $v_h^{N \to J}$ serve as elasticities and where $\tilde{p}_h^J$ is a fictitious price of the composite commodity.

Thus, unlike the CES function, the translog function is not restricted to a single and constant elasticity of substitution. It allows for different elasticities such as the specific $v_h^{N \to J}$ (regarding second-order interactions) and specific $a_h^{N \to J}$ (regarding first-order interactions). On the other hand, the data requirement for estimating these many elasticities is tremendously greater than for estimating the single constant elasticity of the CES function.

This data problem of the translog approach then suggests the use of a *truncated translog* approach, one that can link up with the comparative cost approach of location theory. In the truncated translog approach we cut off consideration of those $p_h^{L \to J}$ whose corresponding export flows $E_h^{L \to J}$ are not significant or promise not to be significant. Thus, in practice, we might consider only three sources, the three most important currently or likely in the future. This is as we do in comparative cost analyses, where because of the possibility of strikes and other disruptions of a trade flow (a supply channel), a profit-maximizing risk-alert behaving unit rarely, if ever, relies 100 percent on one source of a basic commodity

---

[12] Again, if we are to have imperfect substitution, we must necessarily have a smooth, well-behaved (strictly convex) isoquant between any two technically homogeneous commodities such as Japanese steel and Korean steel.

input, or even two, but rather on at least three. In the truncated translog approach we then need to estimate, say, only three $a_h^{N \to J}$ and six $v_h^{N \to J}$ if three sources of supply are generally taken to be adequate and consistent with profit maximizing.[13]

Note, however, that the translog function is only appropriate where we are treating local variation from the cost minimization (equilibrium) situation. This is because it uses a Taylor expansion to estimate the interaction at and around that situation. When there are large changes in the variables and their interactions, the Taylor expansion is inappropriate for use. Thus, over the medium and long run when major changes in output, exports, and imports are anticipated, the use of translog should be avoided. It is over the middle and long run, especially when changes in the σ of a CES function can also be expected, that the use of comparative cost and Leontief approaches becomes more attractive, relatively speaking.

9.7 The potentials of the gravity model

In replacing the zero elasticity of substitution frame of input–output for projecting trade flows, we have not discussed the potential of the gravity model. The appeal of the gravity model for projecting trade flows, which was pointed out long ago (Isard 1954), is that it lays bare two key system variables in operation: (1) mass and (2) resistance to (energy requirement of) movement. It does this without confusion with the many microforces at play, which are generated by the innumerable behaving units of reality. The basic form of the gravity model is

$$I_{ij} = G \mathcal{M}_i \mathcal{M}_j d_{ij}^{-\eta} \tag{9.7.1}$$

where $\mathcal{M}_i$ and $\mathcal{M}_j$ are the masses of the two objects (regions) i and j, and d_{ij} is the intervening distance, G and η being parameters to be estimated. As in Newtonian physics, the greater the product of the masses, the greater the interaction I_{ij}; and the greater the intervening distance, the less the interaction.

There are, of course, many conceptual problems in the use of the gravity model. What are relevant masses? What is the relevant or effective distance? Should the masses be weighted? Should they be raised to a power other than unity? These questions have been discussed elsewhere

---

[13] However, as in the comparative cost approach, we should consider a fourth source if its price is not significantly greater than that of the third cheapest, and also a fifth when its price, too, is not significantly greater than the third.

Also, note that to estimate the v's, one may use observations from different importing firms in J as well as pool data for different years.

(Isard et al. 1960). For our purposes, the relevant masses are the GNPs of countries (or GRPs of world regions). In the simplest case, the relevant distance is transport cost distance, but such may be modified by tariffs, export duties, and the like and by political (partner) biases, cultural, and social affinities, and so on. Volume of trade, in either physical or monetary terms, is the relevant measure of interaction.

Assuming appropriate measures of mass and distance are available as well as sufficient data for estimation purposes, we still confront important conceptual issues. Ideally, the estimation of the G and η parameters from data should involve the full aggregation of all trade flows over any distance interval for some complete set of distance intervals. Such aggregation should be conducted without reference to any specific origin and destination pair. However, in projecting a trade flow matrix, in practice, we must be concerned with both country of origin and country of destination. Hence, some disaggregation is required, although the G and η parameters derived from fully aggregated data may be employed either unmodified or modified by factors relevant to the particular origin–destination pair.[14] [When G is so modified, we replace it in Eq. (9.7.1) with G_{ij}.] Clearly, too, the application for a given origin–destination pair should pertain to total flow between that origin and destination; the application becomes less and less valid as that trade flow is more and more disaggregated by commodity.

The undiluted gravity model does not explicitly deal with prices (in the different countries), factor costs, exchange rates, or many other variables considered by trade theorists. This is so not because the gravity model states that these variables are unimportant but rather because prices, exchange rates, and so on, are among the many variables whose impacts cancel out, especially in the long run, when the system is viewed as a whole. The basic theoretical underpinning of the gravity model, as developed by Isard (1975) and more recently in much more rigorous form by Smith (1978), is that, ceteris paribus, there is a greater probability that a representative behaving unit will undertake a shorter trip or make a shorter shipment – one involving less resistance in terms of energy (physical resource cost) than a longer one. [Note that this hypothesis contains the notion of imperfect substitution. For example, were a new transport link constructed making one node closer to an importing point than a second when the reverse had been true before the construction, export from both nodes would still be realized although the relative size

---

[14] For example, modifying factors may relate to the degree to which the resources of a pair of regions are complementary (competitive) or to the length of the border they may have in common.

(amount) of trade flows would have been reversed.][15] This then suggests that in making long run projections when erratic fluctuations of exchange rates can be ignored and where prices are just cultural symbols, reflecting the interplay of other basic factors, the relevance of the gravity model is greatest; and as the period of projection becomes smaller and smaller and ultimately becomes the immediate short run, the relevance of the gravity model significantly diminishes.[16]

9.8 The multimethod approach for trade projection and arms trade

We now consolidate our discussion on projecting trade flows. At this time, it would seem very desirable to avoid any one particular method for the construction of a trade matrix for some future years or for a year in the past for which data are at best partially available. We favor the construction of a trade matrix, column by column (or even part of a column by part of a column). One column (or part of a column) might be constructed with the use of one method; another by the use of a second; and still another by the use of a third. Available for such construction are the Leontief method, the use of a CES function, the use of a truncated translog function, the use of a comparative cost study, the use of any one of these along with a modified gravity model, the use of a modified gravity model alone, or the use of some other procedure. Clearly, one should not use the CES function for estimating trade in steel ingots and basic steel products. At the same time, one should not use the truncated translog function and comparative cost for any large aggregates of miscellaneous manufactured goods. Moreover, the use of a particular method for estimating any one column is highly dependent on the degree of aggregation of commodities in the trade matrix, the degree of aggregation of

---

[15] Actually, then, when trade in aggregate commodities is being analyzed, the gravity model represents a much more flexible tool than the use of a CES function. One may speculate that the gravity model allows a distribution (e.g., a normal distribution) of such proclivities as to behave irrationally, to achieve diversity (to break a boring routine), to search for (explore) actions that might prove to be more rational, to achieve more security, etc.

[16] In this connection, we might refer to a recent article by Bergstrand (1985). There he obtains rather good results in estimating the parameter for aggregate trade flows for the OECD countries using a gravity model in a proper way. However, being dissatisfied because of an absence of strong theoretical foundations and presumably not being aware of the Smith (1978) development, he introduces price variables to support a "notion that the gravity equation is a reduced form from a partial equilibrium subsystem of a general equilibrium model with nationally differentiated products" (1985, p. 474). However, the results he obtains cannot be judged to be significantly better from a statistical standpoint, and in a very real sense, he loses the main rationale of the gravity model by attempting to derive from trade flows a "microtized" general equilibrium framework.

countries into world regions, the distance into the future or past for which the matrix is to be constructed, data availability, the procedure that a model may require for closure of the trade matrix, and many other factors.

Having now discussed the trade matrix, as typically addressed by the economist, we want to move ahead to examine trade in arms, a most important phenomena for study. We may envisage in a trade flow matrix a column (or set of columns) relating to flows into the military sector of each region J. If the rows of the matrix correspond to the producing sectors j $(j = 1, \ldots, n)$ of each region N $(N = A, \ldots, U)$, including J itself, thereby being Un in number, then the data recorded in the military sector column for J represent the flows into it from all sectors by region in the system. If we then focus upon the flows (imports) from a given region N $(N \neq J)$ and from N's arms-producing sectors, we then have information on arms trade from each originating region N to J.

In projecting such data for any military sector, in general, complex political factors must be presumed to dominate the economic ones. Therefore, lacking reliable quantitative representation of these political factors, we choose to restrict ourselves to examining only incremental changes from the current pattern of arms trade. We thereby assume no basic change in the underlying structure generated by current political, economic, and social forces. Moreover, we confine ourselves to incremental changes resulting only from economic forces since we cannot quantify the political and social.

Clearly, it is not appropriate to use past data for a series of years because of the structural changes that have occurred in recent years. Also, because of secrecy and related factors, reported price data on military items cannot be considered trustworthy. Thus these considerations preclude the use of any translog or CES approach to estimate the data for a column since they rely heavily on the use of past price data. We also must exclude the use of a gravity model approach since we are concerned in arms trade with a fairly small slice of the total trade aggregate, albeit of critical importance. Hence, we are left with the input–output, linear programming, and comparative cost (classical trade theory) approaches.

To project only incremental changes, we suggest starting with the current trade pattern depicted as per Leontief by a set of constants. This gives the ratio of imports of arms by type to domestic production by type for every importing nation and a fixed percentage contribution (share in) the world pool by type for each exporting nation. A major fraction of arms trade is accounted for by sophisticated weapons systems using the latest scientific advances, such as in space and laser technology. There exist major economies of scale in the production of such systems, and those exporting nations (inclusive of Japan) that engage in intense R&D in military systems production are expected to obtain an increasing share of this subpool as these systems become still more sophisticated. Of course, such increasing concentration of production and export may be in part offset by the subcontracting of elements of the production process (coproduction) to nations otherwise excluded from such production. However, it is extremely difficult to anticipate how significant this offset effect will be and how it will be distributed among current importing regions. Hence, the best procedure to project the flows on sophisticated weapons systems is perhaps to use the Leontief constants adjusted to reflect increasing production specialization. The adjustments might be based on relative R&D expenditures across exporting nations. For a relevant discussion of current and recent past R&D expenditures, see Stockholm International Peace Research Institute (1986, chap. 15) and items cited there. Also see Ives (1985) on arms dispersal.

With regard to trade flows in conventional and nonsophisticated weapons systems, there are many factors at play in large part offsetting each other. One, however, namely, a significant shift in the comparative cost position of existing and potential exports, would be major and could suggest clear-cut directions for change of the Leontief constants. Countries such as Korea and Brazil may be able to usurp a major role in certain lines of arms trade, just as Korea and Japan have done in steel and automobile exports. Such an eventuality can be anticipated through the standard comparative cost studies that have, for example, been conducted for steel production. The findings of such studies can be used to help estimate the data in the columns for the appropriate arms items, to be qualified significantly by political factors when appropriate.

9.9 The projection of military expenditures in the CGE, world econometric (LINK-type), and programming models

Hitherto, we have

1. made military expenditures and military production activities explicit in a SAM (social accounting) framework;
2. indicated how the Leontief UN World Input–Output model can provide valuable insights on the impact of changes in military expenditures;
3. suggested a CGE model with a CES or other nonlinear production function to replace the constant production coefficient frame of input–output; and

4. presented a multimethod approach to replace the input–output frame of constant ratios and shares for projecting trade flows and, to whatever extent possible, arms trade.

We now come to the next major problem, which is not attacked by input–output, of projecting military expenditures per se in each world region of a system. As part of this problem, it becomes necessary to project the arms race(s), a task that is exceedingly complex. Yet some insights can be gained from existing knowledge about the economic structure and functioning of the world system.

In projecting military expenditures, the specification of an estimating or behaviorial equation is highly dependent on the particular approach of the model within which the equation is to be embedded. We shall begin the discussion for a CGE-type model and later discuss the problem for world econometric (LINK-type) and programming models.

The vast literature on arms race models surveyed in Chapter 2 identifies numerous relevant factors. However, if the factors specific to any given arms race may be neglected (a very questionable procedure because frequently these specific factors are the dominant ones in a given arms race), only a few general factors capable of quantitative measurement or approximation remain.

One dominant factor in an arms race is clearly the military expenditures or the stock of weapons (as a proxy for military capability) of one's opponent(s) and ally(ies). The stock of weapons, however, may be replaced by a proxy, namely, military expenditures in each of a number of past years (a distributed-lag procedure). [When a world region is an opponent of a given region J, the reaction coefficient multiplying its military expenditures may be taken to be positive; and when an ally, negative (except when J behaves submissively)]. Also, military expenditures may be disaggregated by type of weapon (nuclear, conventional, etc.). Thus when we, for example, consider the arms race between the United States and the Soviet Union, as we shall generally do to provide a concrete illustration when we discuss general points, we have [17]

$$M^U(t) = f(M^S(t), M^S(t - 1), \dots) \qquad (9.9.1)$$

where M^U and M^S are military expenditures of the United States and the Soviet Union, respectively.

However, expenditures for (and thus production of) military goods

---

[17] When this general equation is given a specific form, it will have one or more reaction coefficients. These coefficients might capture a number of friendliness or hostility factors. Such, however, are difficult to quantify and so must be omitted except for a friendliness factor that might be associated with the extent of trade between a specific pair of regions.

takes place at the expense of expenditures for (and thus production of) nonmilitary goods for consumption by final demanders (households and government), by firms requiring intermediate goods for production, and by investors for investment purposes. In a CGE model these demands along with military demands are contained in the demand and supply equations for the output of each sector (adjusted for *net* imports or exports). These equations mediate the competing demands and supplies by determining prices within the constraints imposed by limited resources. Thus prices and resources or some proxies for them must enter into Eq. (9.9.1) to yield

$$M^U(t) = f(M^S(t), M^S(t-1), \ldots, p_m, p_c, R) \qquad (9.9.2)$$

where

p_m = a price index of military goods, a proxy
p_c = a price index of nonmilitary goods, another proxy
R = an index of available resources

Furthermore, the balance of payments, exchange rate, taxes, deficits, and foreign aid[18] – economic factors that arms race scholars have introduced into their models – are all elements that in a CGE framework operate through the market by affecting prices. So they, too, are covered by the price proxies in Eq. (9.9.2) to the extent that the market operates efficiently, as assumed in a purely competitive society.

However, the market in most societies is imperfect, failing to operate properly because public-type goods are involved and because of political and other factors. For example, unemployment in a purely competitive society does not occur, except in the very short run because of diverse frictions. Yet, it is typically a common place phenomenon for most world regions. Thus, for example, if a policy of closing (or partially closing) army bases is proposed on the grounds of increasing GNP, social welfare, and even the military capability of a nation, political leaders representing constituencies in which the bases are located will almost invariably oppose such a policy. In their eyes, such would adversely affect their own welfare, or that of their constituency, or that of other interest groups they represent. Hence, in a CGE model that does not impose full employment by assumption, the level of unemployment acts as a variable that directly affects the level of military expenditures decided upon after political debate and discussion. Likewise, with the deficit (business interests and the political leaders representing them may strongly oppose deficit-creating programs even when such would be judged to be in the interests of

---

[18] Foreign aid may also be included as part of $M^U(t)$ when oriented to military or related foreign policy objectives.

society at large), balance of payments, interest rates, taxes, and so on. So one or more of these factors may enter the estimating equation. If unemployment does, then Eq. (9.9.2) becomes

$$M^U(t) = f(M^S(t), M^S(t-1), \ldots, p_m, p_c, R, \ldots, \text{UN}) \qquad (9.9.3)$$

where UN is the level of unemployment.

Moreover, we should recognize that internal unrest may exist because the basic needs of a fraction of a population are not being met. There may exist an inefficient or grossly unfair distribution system; or the aggregate of consumption goods being produced may be too low; or both. Internal unrest may therefore enter Eq. (9.9.3). So may the international tension level (measured by total world military expenditures, or the aggregate for some grouping of countries) since such may be associated with increasing insecurity. Thus we may obtain

$$M^U(t) = f(M^S(t), M^S(t-1), \ldots, p_m, p_c, R, \ldots, \text{UN, UR}, H) \qquad (9.9.4)$$

where UR and H represent level of internal unrest and level of international tension, respectively.

In practice, however, problems of data and of statistical estimation procedures will severely limit the number and type of variables that we can have in an equation such as (9.9.4).

When a world econometric model such as LINK is employed, a rather different set of variables may be required in an equation to project M^U. This is so because such a model does not have at its core a functioning market. It tends to be a macromodel centering around Keynesian aggregates with micro-Walrasian-type elements entering in a supplementary manner or as an afterthought. This is in contrast with the CGE-type model having hopefully a well-functioning market at its core whose operation is tempered (or constrained) by Keynesian-type relations among macromagnitudes.

To be more concrete, we illustrate with reference to the actual LINK model. This model ties together the ongoing major econometric models being used in each major country or region of the world. No attempt is made to construct at one research institution a standardized model to be applied to each country or region. Rather the model assumes that each model builder knows his (or her) own country (region) best. Each model builder is free to design his model save for equations to link his country (region) to the rest of the world via imports and exports.[19] These equa-

---

[19] That is, except for the linking equations, each model builder selects for his nation a number of key or dependent variables to be projected endogenously within his model. He then identifies for each dependent variable a set of factors that on the basis of theory (i.e., his understanding of behaviorial relationships) are expected to be sufficiently highly correlated with the dependent variable that upon knowing the value of each of these factors (indepen-

tions as well as others associated with trade are designed by an international study group. The methods for constructing trade matrices have already been discussed, and these methods and their variations embrace those considered and used by this study group (Klein 1983, chap. 7).

Our interest at this point concerns the introduction of a military sector and arms trade in each of the country (region) econometric models for which these activities are significant. As in the case of CGE-type models, military expenditures in a nation, say, the United States, should be related to military expenditures of its rival(s) (say, the Soviet Union) and its allies. Thus, Eq. (9.9.1), for the United States versus the Soviet Union, is relevant as a first step.

Since market functioning is not at the core of LINK, we do not have "demand–supply" equations to impose on the transformation function (such as in Figure 2.2) as a constraint between expenditures for military and nonmilitary goods for given resources. Therefore, we must introduce macromagnitudes directly into Eq. (9.9.1). Typically, GNP has been introduced to indicate that, generally speaking, military expenditures vary directly with GNP, ceteris paribus. The greater (smaller) is GNP, the greater (smaller) are military expenditures. Alternatively, other macromagnitudes may be used such as aggregate investment and aggregate consumption. Additionally, since the market is not functioning to treat the employment variable and since the multiplier effect of military expenditures upon employment is often significant for political leaders, unemployment may also be introduced into Eq. (9.9.1). In other situations, the balance-of-trade position, deficits, interest rates, and other variables may be relevant. This is so because the estimating equation for military expenditures may and should differ among the different countries whose cultures and economies differ. For example, military expenditures in both Pakistan and India might well reflect specific variables not present in the U.S. and USSR equations – in particular, because of the proximity of both Pakistan and India to China and their heavy, if not total, reliance on conventional weapons. The Middle East arms race suggests the use of certain variables not present in the estimating equations for other nations, in particular, the intense internal conflicts and sharp social divisions in at least several Middle East countries. Moreover, in certain countries military expenditures are too small an item to justify an estimating equation for them.

This last point suggests that in the further development of the LINK

dent variables) and past statistical relationships between these factors and the dependent variable, we can project the value of the corresponding dependent variable within a pre-specified range of accuracy. Often this model comprises a set of simultaneous equations such that one or more of the independent variables in one equation are dependent variables in other equations.

model (and of many other models seeking to endogenize military expenditures), it is not necessary to introduce at once the military sector for all countries for which that sector is significant. To introduce that sector just for the major powers or for the United States and the Soviet Union alone might constitute a significant advance. At a later time, the introduction of the military sectors for other nations might then be fruitful. Likewise, in treating arms trade. At first, only a significant fraction or aspect of that trade may be made explicit by appropriate disaggregation. At a later time, the projection of an arms trade matrix in full may be attempted. This process of piece-by-piece endogenization of the military sector and the arms trade is an attractive feature of the decentralized LINK model approach. Of course, when each country develops its own estimating equation for military expenditures, it must define and measure any variable that also appears in another country's model in a commonly accepted way, although the reaction parameters of the several countries may reflect different perceptions of that variable.

Despite the particular process of piece-by-piece endogenization just suggested, Klein and his associates in the LINK project have chosen another exploratory path toward endogenization (Klein and Kosaka 1987). It involves four steps:

1. Estimate military expenditures at year t for nation J as a function of current and past military expenditures by allies and adversaries:

$$M^J(t) = f^J(M^A(t), \ldots, M^N(t), \ldots, M^U(t);$$
$$M^A(t-1), \ldots, M^N(t-1), \ldots, M^U(t-\theta)) \qquad (9.9.5)$$
$$N = A, B, \ldots, U$$

2. Recognize that the level of military expenditures of a nation is related to the size of its economy (resource base or productive capacity) as reflected by its GDP (gross domestic product). Hence, estimate the fraction of GDP absorbed by military expenditures as follows:

$$\frac{M^J}{GDP^J}(t) = f^J(\frac{M^A}{GDP^A}(t), \ldots, \frac{M^N}{GDP^N}(t), \ldots, \frac{M^U}{GDP^U}(t);$$
$$\frac{M^A}{GDP^A}(t-1), \ldots, \frac{M^N}{GDP^N}(t-1), \ldots, \frac{M^U}{GDP^U}(t-1)) \qquad (9.9.6)$$

In order to account for strains or slack in an economy and associated nonlinear effects, a price index p^J can be introduced into Eq. (9.9.6), when to do so would be statistically significant.

3. The use of forecasts of GDP^J and p^J of Project LINK over the 1980s would thus allow projections of military expenditures throughout the 1980s. However, this would not allow for feedback from the military to the civilian economy. To accomplish the latter, the LINK researchers

Table 9.2. *Deviation from LINK baseline projections with endogenous defense spending: feedback from shocked arms race model (estimates in percent deviation for 1989)*

	Real GDP	Consumer price index (level)	Interest rate	Unemployment rate	Nominal government spending
France	1.6	−0.3	nil	−0.6	10.3
West Germany	1.5	0.4	0.04	−0.3	1.4
Japan	1.4	0.7	0.03	−0.06	7.9
United Kingdom	1.3	1.1	0.21	−1.7	6.2
United States	2.1	0.2	0.35	−0.2	12.8

estimate public (government) spending $G^J(t)$ as a function (in a marginal sense) of current and past military expenditures as follows:

$$G^J(t) = \phi^J(M^J(t), M^J(t-1), \ldots, M^J(t-\gamma)) \qquad (9.9.7)$$

The preceding reflects the impact upon present public spending of the military system's obligations, procurement, expenditure, and delivery as it is in fact spread over several years.

4. The last step involves using values of $G^J(t)$ derived from Eq. (9.9.7) to resolve the LINK system for new values of $GDP^J(t)$ and $p^J(t)$. Once done, the procedure requires a return to step 1 and subsequent iterations.

Klein and his associates have carried through the preceding operations for Western countries. Some typical findings are recorded in Table 9.2. These findings result from an assumed shock to the world system that involves an increase in defense spending by 10 percent in 1986 and subsequent years in both the United States and the Soviet Union. The table shows percentage deviations for the year 1989 from the LINK projections previously made when the arms race was not incorporated into the model. Thus, for West Germany and the United States for the year 1989 the projections of real GDP are, respectively, 1.5 and 2.1 percent higher when the arms race is incorporated into the model and when the system is subjected to the preceding shock. For these two countries, the consumer price indices for the year 1989 are, respectively, 0.4 and 0.2 higher; and the unemployment rates are, respectively, 0.3 and 0.2 percent lower.

Klein and his associates consider these findings very preliminary. The significance of these data is not in their magnitude but rather in the fact that they represent outcomes of a world model in which the arms race is endogenized. Clearly, Klein and his associates as well as others will be able to come up with more accurate and reliable estimates with further experience and development of the model. It will be these estimates that will be of great value for the analysis of not only the U.S.–Soviet arms control conflict situation but also many others.

We should also note that the LINK model can be easily designed to incorporate into its framework a fully disaggregated input–output structure and thus be able to project impacts of changes in the level of military expenditures. See Isard and Smith (1988).

At this point, we should comment upon the use of a *multiworld region programming model,* which explicitly incorporates the military sector. Such a model may be explored when the data and other problems for a CGE or LINK-type model are considered to be insurmountable. Recall that the objective function and its optimization in a programming model in effect allows one to circumvent the limitation of an input–output model that can provide impact analysis only. Recall also that a programming model can allow for substitution among different processes in producing a good and thus reflect more adequately a region's production possibilities (transformation surface in n dimensions).

In a programming framework, static or dynamic, the input requirements of the military sector can be introduced in each region J when an appropriate set of constants can be determined for approximating that sector's input requirements. In each region, the nonexported output of this sector (we presume that this sector does not produce goods used as intermediates by other sectors) enters directly into the objective function along with the output of finished products by other sectors of the region (and perhaps along with relevant stocks, both military and civilian). Thus, if these outputs can be properly handled in the objective function, desirably in a nonlinear fashion that avoids constant weights, to reflect the best estimate of world social welfare while still leaving the program operational, we shall have endogenized the military sector, albeit in a simplified fashion. In such a programming model, we have, of course, much less freedom in constructing a trade matrix that is not dependent on constant trade coefficients.

9.10   The GLOBUS model and potential developments

Before concluding this chapter, we should look at other world models in which noneconomic variables play a major role – as they do in reality. Here the GLOBUS model (Bremer 1987) is one of the best.[20] In section

---

[20] For a discussion of the problems of modeling the world system in its diverse political and economic aspects, see Deutsch et al. (1977), where some evaluation of the earlier models is also presented. Also see Hughes (1985) and Luterbacher and Allan (1982).

2.11 we sketched this model. It has been made operational, and initial exploratory runs have been performed. It is fully recognized by the GLO-BUS modelers that many of the relations employed are oversimplifications. They are required, however, if the model is to be operational. Hence the value of the model is not in the magnitudes outputted but in the demonstration that progress can be achieved in getting at the interplay of both political and economic variables – progress that can allow further endogenization of military expenditures within a CGE or LINK-type model.

As already noted, Figure 2.7 studies the model within Isard's conceptual framework on Peace Science as a discipline. (Isard's framework is depicted in Figure 1.3 and discussed in section 1.2.) For every nation J ($J = A, \ldots, U$), there are six modules in GLOBUS. Three [DEMO,[21] ECONOMY,[22] and TRADE[23]] fall in Isard's P^J box, the production subsystem of J. A second three modules of GLOBUS [GOV'T,[24] INTERNAL POLITY,[25] and FOREIGN POLICY[26]] fall in Isard's C^J box, the cognitive decision-making subsystem of J. Additionally, GLOBUS has

1. a WORLD MARKET[27] module, which falls in Isard's $\mathcal{R}$ box, the real interaction subsystem dealing with international trade in economic and noneconomic goods; and
2. an INTERNATIONAL ARENA (clearing house) module for hostility and cooperation, which falls in Isard's $\mathcal{J}$ box, the cognitive interaction subsystem dealing with
   (a) the world system's decision making,
   (b) world policy determination, and, in general,
   (c) the international political arena, broadly defined.

We cannot go into details. The important point is that the arms race is embodied in variables considered strategic by diverse arms race modelers – among others, defense expenditures, civilian goods expenditures,

---

[21] DEMO (Demographic subsector) determines changes in a nation's demographic structure, including labor force, school, and retirement age population.
[22] ECONOMY (Domestic Economic subsector) determines changes in a nation's aggregate output, personal consumption, savings, prices, capital stock, interest rates, money supply, etc.
[23] TRADE (Trade Policy subsector) determines changes in a nation's import demand, export prices, and import biases.
[24] GOV'T (Government Budget subsector) determines changes in a government's taxing and spending policies, including defense, education, health, administration, and foreign aid.
[25] INTERNAL POLITY determines changes in a population's support and opposition to the government and the government's reaction to opposition.
[26] FOREIGN POLICY determines changes in a government's reactivity to hostility and cooperation received from others.
[27] WORLD MARKET controls the flow of goods through the international system. It does so by simulating the international marketplace where nations are seen as having import demands, export prices, and a set of import partner preferences.

defense expenditures share, GNP, desired military capacity, actual military capacity, hostility (cooperation), internal violence, imports, and exports. All are contained in the GLOBUS model in association with other key variables of the world system in an interconnected and integrated fashion. For example, from Cusack (1985), we have for the module that covers military expenditures of nation J the following (where the time symbol t is suppressed except for a time lag):

$$\Pi^J = G^{J**} - M^{J*} - GC^{J*} - GK^{J*} \tag{9.10.1}$$

where

G^{J**} = fiscal authorities' aspiration level for maximum total spending
M^{J*} = defense sector's aspiration level for minimum defense spending
GC^{J*} = civilian sector's aspiration level for minimum civilian spending
GK^{J*} = capital sector's aspiration level for minimum capital spending

and where Π^J is thus a "surplus" over which the three sectors just mentioned bargain (fight) for shares as per organizational politics. The *realized* levels are estimated to be

$$G^J = M^{J*} + GC^{J*} + GK^{J*} = \beta_1\Pi^J + u_1 \tag{9.10.2}$$
$$M^J = M^{J*} + \beta_2\Pi^J + u_2 \tag{9.10.3}$$
$$GC^J = GC^{J*} + \beta_3\Pi^J + u_3 \tag{9.10.4}$$
$$GK^J = GK^{J*} + \beta_4\Pi^J + u_4 \tag{9.10.5}$$

where

G^J = total government spending (less debt management payments)
M^J = defense spending
GC^J = exhaustive civilian spending (including purchases of goods and services and transfers)
GK^J = capital spending
β_i = bargaining power of i, $i = 1, 2, 3, 4$

In turn, the preceding four *aspiration* levels are determined by

$$G^{J**} = b_1 GR^J + b_2 STAB^J + u_5 \tag{9.10.6}$$
$$M^{J*} = b_3\alpha'S^Jp^J + b_4 SEC^J + u_6 \tag{9.10.7}$$
$$GC^{J*} = b_5 GC^J(t-1)\left(\frac{CLIENT}{CLIENT\,(t-1)}\right)\left(\frac{IN^J/P^J}{IN^J(t-1)/P^J(t-1)}\right) \tag{9.10.8}$$
$$GK^{J*} = [GK^J(t-1)/IN^J(t-1)]IN^J \tag{9.10.9}$$

where

GR^J = expected government revenues (less debt management payments)

STAB = stabilization policy (rate of unemployment times GR^J for industrialized nations; foreign sector imbalance in the case of developing lands)

α^J = rate of depreciation of J's stock of weapons

S^J = J's stock of military weapons

p^J = cost of a unit of stock

SEC^J = external security of J

CLIENT = principal demographic groups that are serviced by or receive transfers from the government

IN^J = national income of J

P^J = population of J

$b_1, \ldots, b_5$ = appropriate parameters

In addition, the external security of J is defined as

$$SEC^J(ATHREAT\ (t-1) - S^J(t-1)p^J) \qquad (9.10.10)$$

where ATHREAT represents an expected level of military threat directed toward the nation from the multination system. It is a moving average of an annual measure labeled THREAT that incorporates an assessment of the relative hostile intent and capabilities RINTENT of other nations:

$$THREAT\ (\to J) = \sum_N RINTENT\ (N \to J)\ S^N, \qquad (9.10.11)$$

$$N = A, \ldots, U; N \neq J$$

$$RINTENT\ (N \to J) = INTENT\ (N \to J)/\sum_N INTENT\ (N \to J) \qquad (9.10.12)$$

$$INTENT\ (N \to J)$$
$$= HSENT\ (N \to J) \frac{HSENT\ (N \to J)}{HSENT\ (N \to J) + CSENT\ (N \to J)} \qquad (9.10.13)$$

HSENT and CSENT are measures of the annual flow of hostile and cooperative acts, respectively, directed by one nation toward another, where military expenditures of rival nation N are part of HSENT $(N \to J)$. See also Bremer (1987, pp. 360–414).

In brief, the preceding equations and others clearly point up how both economic and political variables can be brought together in one set of equations to yield estimated magnitudes and some preliminary analyses, albeit in an exploratory fashion.

At this point we should also note some ways in which there can be effective fusion of a GLOBUS-type model with models of the world economy, for example, a LINK-type model. Clearly, an extended LINK-type model with an input–output framework embedded in it for impact analysis is much superior in projecting the economic system of the diverse world regions. Hence, to a large extent, we would replace the GLOBUS modules ECONOMY, DEMO, TRADE, and WORLD MARKET (in Figure 2.7) with parts of an extended LINK-type model in such a way that the model feeds, among other items, (1) government revenue into the GOV'T module of GLOBUS, and (2) total population, jobs by type, and personal consumption (by income or other relevant social class) so as to yield for the INTERNAL POLITY module per capita consumption by social class and estimates of class unemployment, elements for evaluating the satisfaction of BASIC NEEDS. Concomitantly, among other items, the extended LINK-type model would receive from the three basic modules GOV'T, INTERNAL POLITY, and INT'L ARENA of GLOBUS

1. civilian expenditures of the government,
2. defense expenditures, and
3. hostility sent (by an actor to a target), cooperation sent, and changes in these two (reflecting in part actual military capability and its changes).

These latter elements come to affect BIAS among trade partners, which then feeds into the WORLD MARKET via the projection of a more realistic trade matrix.[28]

GLOBUS is also able to be fused with an integrated multiregion world economic model in a somewhat similar way to yield even superior projections of military expenditures and other basic variables and the impacts of their changes upon the economy of a nation, its sectors, and its regions. As discussed elsewhere (Isard and Smith 1983), such an integrated multiregion world economic model would comprise a combination of comparative cost–industrial complex, input–output, programming, factor substitution, and econometric modules connected with each other and with an interdependent policy box. The use of such a combination of modules would be consistent with and complement the multimethod approach in the construction of a world trade matrix.

9.11   Concluding remarks

We have covered in this chapter several models of the world system. We tried neither to evaluate these models nor to present a comparative analysis of their relative strengths and weaknesses. Rather we have focused on other matters. One is the need to project a multicountry (world region) trade matrix. Most models are weak in this regard, but such a matrix is essential for capturing spread effects of military expenditures from one country (world region) to another, which as we shall see is important in using conflict management procedures and in negotiations for arms con-

---

[28] For some excellent analysis on how economic trade and hostility (cooperation) and related political variables are interdependent, see Polachek (1980, 1987).

trol and disarmament. Another is to expose as much as possible the arms trade component of that trade matrix and project it since such data and projection can be critical information in negotiation processes. A third is the construction of behavioral equations relating to military expenditures for incorporation into world models. We consider this to be essential for any world model that attempts to illuminate the world economic and political system and the interrelations of its regions and countries. Of course, such construction is essential for the use of any of the CMPs and negotiation processes. We turn to the potentials of such use in the next chapter. Finally, we briefly examined the GLOBUS model, a leading world model in terms of quantifying basic political variables and their interconnections with key economic variables, and briefly considered the possiblity of achieving a superior world model via fusion with other models.

To reiterate, we view world models as a way to provide some of the basic information on outputs (as might be recorded in cells of a payoff matrix) needed for determining wise compromise (conflict management) policy (where each policy taken under consideration may be viewed as a combination of a row and a column of a payoff matrix). Such data not only relate to impacts of different policies on military expenditures and the impacts of military expenditures themselves but also reflect the interplay of internal economic and political forces as they affect the level of military expenditures (and condition policy).

Appendixes: technical materials on multiregion general equilibrium models and use of the multimethod approach for construction of a trade matrix

9.A   The general interregional equilibrium model

An interregional general equilibrium system under conditions of pure competition generally involves U regions ($J, N = A, \ldots, U$), and l commodities ($h = 1, \ldots, l$) with prices p_h^J in each region J. In each region J there are also

1. m consumers ($i = 1, \ldots, m$), each of whom buys $b_{h,i}^J$ amount (in reality often zero) of each good h;
2. n producers ($j = 1, \ldots, n$), each of whom is involved with $y_{h,j}^J$ amount (in reality often zero) of each good h, this amount being negative when h is an input and positive when h is an output; and
3. $\bar{f}$ exporters ($f = 1, \ldots, \bar{f}$), each of whom ships $s_{h,J}^{J \to N}$ amount (in reality often zero) of good h to each region N ($N \neq J$).

The unknowns are

1. the Uml purchases $b_{h,i}^J$,
2. the Unl inputs and outputs $y_{h,j}^J$,

3. the $U(U - 1)\bar{f}l$ unknown shipments $s_{h,f}^{J \rightarrow N}$,
4. the $Ul - 1$ prices p_h^J, and
5. the $U - 1$ balance-of-trade positions of regions.

To determine these unknowns there are:

1. *Uml* budget balance and utility-maximizing conditions for consumers;
2. *Unl* transformation constraints and profit-maximizing conditions for producers;
3. the $U(U - 1)\bar{f}l$ "no profit-from-trade" conditions associated with traders trying to maximize gains from trade;
4. $Ul - 1$ demand-equals-supply conditions; and
5. $U - 1$ balance-of-trade relations.

For detailed discussion, see Isard et al. (1969, chap. 11).

9.B   A computable multiregion general equilibrium model

A representative computable multiregion general equilibrium model is that of Whalley (1985). He considers seven regions and six commodities. Letting X_h^J be the output of good h in region J, V_h^J be the value added (from capital and labor services) in producing h in J, and H_{gh}^J be the use of composite good g in producing h in J, the production functions in Leontief fashion are

$$X_h^J = \min\left(\frac{V_h^J}{a_{vh}^J}, \frac{H_{1h}^J}{a_{1h}^J}, \ldots, \frac{H_{gh}^J}{a_{gh}^J}, \ldots, \frac{H_{lh}^J}{a_{lh}^J}\right) \tag{9.B.1}$$

where a_{vh}^J is the constant value-added requirement per unit of h and $a_{1h}^J, \ldots, a_{lh}^J$ are constant input coefficients for composite goods $1, \ldots, l$. (We assume that one and only one sector, namely, h, produces one and only one good, namely, h.) For value added, we have

$$V_h^J = f_h^J(K_h^J, L_h^J) \tag{9.B.2}$$

K_h^J and L_h^J being capital and labor used in producing h in J. For each composite good g we have

$$H_{gh}^J = H_{gh}^J(H_{gh}^{A \rightarrow J}, \ldots, H_{gh}^{U \rightarrow J}) \tag{9.B.3}$$

where $H_{gh}^{A \rightarrow J}, \ldots, H_{gh}^{U \rightarrow J}$ are the amounts of good g supplied by regions $A, \ldots, U$ to produce h in J. Equations (9.B.2) and (9.B.3) are CES functions of nested form to allow for hierarchical chains of substitution – first between elements within composites and subsequently between composites.

Each agent q ($q = 1, \ldots, \bar{q}$) maximizes utility. Let b_{hq}^J be the amount of h from J demanded by q. His or her demands are then derived from

$$\max u_q (b_{1q}^A, \ldots, b_{lq}^A; b_{1q}^B, \ldots, b_{hq}^J, \ldots, b_{lq}^U) \tag{9.B.4}$$
$$\text{subject to: } \sum_h \sum_J p_h^J b_{hq}^J = \text{IN}_q$$

where p_h^J is the price paid by q for h from region J, being the international price, and IN_q is the income of agent q. When taxes, tariffs, and the like are ignored, as is the case with Whalley, the international price is equal to the local price p_h^J in standard international currency. Four-stage CES and LES- (linear expenditure system) utility functions are employed.

Income IN_q is derived from ownership of factors plus transfers TR_q^J to q from governments of J less direct taxes T_q, that is,

$$\text{IN}_q = \sum_J p_K^J \bar{K}_q^J + p_L^J \bar{L}_q^J + \text{TR}_q^J - T_q \qquad (9.\text{B}.5)$$

where p_K^J and p_L^J are prices of capital and labor, respectively, in J and where $\bar{L}_q^J$ and $\bar{K}_q^J$ are q's ownership of labor used in region J and ownership of capital used in all regions ($J = A, \ldots, U$), respectively.

A general equilibrium is given by a set of goods and factor prices

$$(p_1^A, \ldots, p_I^A, p_1^B, \ldots, p_h^J, \ldots, p_1^U, \ldots, p_I^U)(p_K^A, p_L^A, \ldots, p_K^J, \ldots, p_K^U, p_L^U)$$

such that demand equals supply for all goods and factors in all regions, that is,

$$X_h^J = \sum_N \sum_g H_{hg}^{J \to N} + \sum_q b_{hq}^J, \qquad h = 1, \ldots, I; \ N = A, \ldots, U \quad (9.\text{B}.6)$$

$$\sum_h K_h^J = \sum_J \sum_q \bar{K}_q^J \qquad (9.\text{B}.7)$$

$$\sum_h L_h^J = \sum_J \sum_q \bar{L}_q^J \qquad (9.\text{B}.8)$$

Also, in Whalley's system zero-profit conditions hold for all industries in all regions:

$$p_h^J X_h^J = \sum_g \sum_N p_g^N H_{gh}^{N \to J} + p_K^J K_h^J + p_L^J L_h^J \qquad (9.\text{B}.9)$$

where in producing X_h^J amount of good h, the first, second, and third terms on the right side of Eq. (9.B.9) are, respectively, the costs of intermediate goods, the costs of capital, and the cost of labor.

Finally, in equilibrium for each region J, Whalley requires that the balance of payments (B of P^J) for each region be zero:

$$\sum_{N \neq J} \sum_h p_h^J H_h^{J \to N} - \sum_{N \neq J} \sum_h p_h^N H_h^{N \to J}$$
$$- \sum_{\substack{q \text{ not in } J}} p_K^J \bar{K}_q^J + \sum_{\substack{q \text{ in } J \\ N \neq J}} p_K^N K_q^N = 0 \qquad (9.\text{B}.10)$$

where the four terms of the left side of Eq. (9.B.10) are, respectively, the value of J's exports, the value of J's imports, capital income paid abroad by region J, and capital income received from abroad by region J.

Note that Whalley does not incorporate savings and investment in his model. Savings in the system can be introduced as a constant (or variable) fraction of the income of each agent. These savings can then be apportioned to each goods-producing sector h in each region J as investment needs. The investment demand for any good g by the different producing sectors can then be derived through the use of Leontief capital coefficients, and added on to the other demands in the relevant demand = supply equations.

Note also that implicit in Whalley's Eqs. (9.B.2) and (9.B.7) is a first-order condition for optimization that sets the price of capital in J, namely, p_K^J, equal to its marginal revenue productivity and in Whalley's Eqs. (9.B.2) and (9.B.8) a first-order condition for optimization that sets the price of labor in J, namely, p_L^J, equal to its marginal revenue productivity.

In a count of unknowns and equations, we note that there are, in Eq. (9.B.1), Ul unknown X_h^J, and $U(l+1)l$ unknown V_h^J and H_{gh}^J. Corresponding to these unknowns are Ul Eqs. (9.B.6) defining the X_h^J and $U(l+1)l$ linear Leontief relations contained in Eqs. (9.B.1) establishing the V_h^H and H_{gh}^J as functions of X_h^J. In Eqs. (9.B.2) there are $2Ul$ unknown inputs of capital and labor. These equations are CES equations and so associated with them, given optimization, are $2Ul$ relations determining these inputs of capital and labor. These relations (first-order conditions) are of the form

$$K_h^J = V_h^J(a_{Kh}^J)^{\sigma Jh}(\tilde{p}_{Vh}^J/p_K^J)^{\sigma Jh} \qquad (9.B.11)$$
$$L_h^J = V_h^J(a_{Lh}^J)^{\sigma Jh}(\tilde{p}_{Vh}^J/p_L^J)^{\sigma Jh} \qquad (9.B.12)$$

where $\tilde{p}_{Vh}^J$ is a fictitious price associated with a unit of value added in the production of good h that must be constructed in standard CES manner. In Eqs. (9.B.3) there are $U^2 l^2$ unknown shipments from one region to another (including itself). These equations are CES functions and so associated with them, given optimization, are $U^2 l^2$ relations (first-order conditions) determining these shipments of the form (where superscripts and subscripts are reversed)

$$H_{gh}^{N \to J} = H_{gh}^J (a_{gh}^{N \to J})^{\sigma Jgh}(\tilde{p}_{gh}^J/p_g^{N \to J})^{\sigma Jgh} \qquad (9.B.13)$$

where $\tilde{p}_{gh}^J$ is the fictitious price of the composite good H_{gh}^J that must be constructed in the standard CES manner.

In Eqs. (9.B.4) there are $\bar{q}Ul$ unknown purchases and $\bar{q}$ unknown incomes in the constraint. These equations are CES functions and so associated with them, given optimization, are $\bar{q}(Ul - 1)$ relations (first-order conditions) that together with the $\bar{q}$ income constraints add up to $\bar{q}Ul$ relations that may be compared with the unknown purchases. Equations (9.B.5), which have $2U$ unknown factor prices (Whalley initially sets $TR_q^J = T_q = 0$) provide another $\bar{q}$ equations to be associated with the $\bar{q}$ unknown incomes. The $2U$ unknowns in Eqs. (9.B.5) may be associated with the $2U$ demand-equals-supply Eqs. (9.B.7) and (9.B.8). There are also Ul unknown prices of goods, which may be associated with the Ul no-profit Eqs. (9.B.9) (these equations add no additional unknowns to the system). Finally, there are generally U unknown balance of payments (which in Whalley's model are constrained to be zero). Corresponding to these unknowns are $U - 1$ independent relations in Eqs. (9.B.10) and the equation requiring system closure, namely,

$$\sum_J B \text{ of } P^J = 0 \qquad (9.B.14)$$

9.C   The use of the multimethod approach to trade matrix construction in CGE models

It is pertinent to demonstrate that the proposed multimethod approach to trade matrix construction can be implemented in a manner consistent with the CGE framework. To do so, we refer to the Whalley (1985) model.

The basic requirement with regard to an interregional general equilibrium is that there be as many equations as unknowns (as in Appendix 9.A). In Whalley

(1985) this requirement is met, as discussed in the previous section. However, in Eqs. (9.B.6) our multimethod approach substitutes for his CES function approach in determining the unknown demands $H_{gh}^{N \to J}$ ($N = A, \ldots, U$). His CES function approach derives a relation such as

$$H_{gh}^{N \to J} = H_{gh}^{J}(a_{gh}^{N \to J})^{\sigma^{J}gh}(\tilde{p}_{gh}^{J}/p_{g}^{N \to J})^{\sigma^{J}gh} \tag{9.C.1}$$

to determine the demand $H_{gh}^{N \to J}$, where $p_{g}^{N \to J}$ is N's export price of g. In our multimethod approach we still use this relation when we employ the CES approach to estimate the imports of a good g (say, a broad category such as chemicals) into any region J for production of h or for all production using g. (Note that Whalley's model requires a trade matrix where each column refers not to a single region but rather to each single production sector h of a region J.) When we use the straightforward Leontief approach, as we might when we are projecting imports of arms components when the political structure of the world system is judged to remain stable, we have

$$H_{gh}^{N \to J} = k_{gh}^{N \to J} X_{h}^{J} \tag{9.C.2}$$

Here $k_{gh}^{N \to J}$ is the fraction of good g (arms components) that is imported from N for production of h (weapons) by J, and where X_{h}^{J} is defined by Eqs. (9.B.6). (This fraction corresponds to Isard's interareal production coefficient in the pure interregional model.) In this way we would derive the number to put in the cell in the import column of sector h of J that corresponds to sector g for every region L in the system.

Alternatively, to fill some of the cells in an import column, particularly when the import column represents the needs of all sectors of a region J (and is not for a disaggregated sector h of J), we might employ the gravity model approach when the category of goods imported is large in magnitude, that is, corresponds to an aggregate of many goods (say, miscellaneous manufactures). Then we have

$$H_{g}^{N \to J} = G \frac{\mathcal{M}^{N}\mathcal{M}^{J}}{d_{NJ}^{\eta}} \tag{9.C.3}$$

where $\mathcal{M}^{N}$ and $\mathcal{M}^{J}$ are relevant masses (such as GNP in standard monetary or real terms). The mass $\mathcal{M}^{J}$ may be taken as $\Sigma_{h}p_{h}^{J}X_{h}^{J}$ when properly stated in an international currency, where the p_{h}^{J} and X_{h}^{J} are determined endogenously. Here, d_{NJ} is a relevant distance variable, and η a parameter, both exogenously determined. The mass $\mathcal{M}^{N}$ may similarly be defined.

Where sector g is *highly competitive* (such as steel, automobiles, and wheat) and sector h is *cost sensitive*, a separate cost study of sector g (providing an import of h to J) may be conducted. It would aim to identify for serving the market h in J the three cheapest sources of g and the fractional allocation, namely, the $k_{gh}^{N \to J}$ in Eq. (9.C.2), among them. Then one proceeds as in the Leontief approach.

Use may be had of the somewhat similar truncated translog approach when data are adequate to permit proper estimation of the several elasticities $a_{g}^{N \to J}$ and $v_{g}^{N \to J}$ of Eq. (9.3.2) for at least three suppliers of good g. [In Eq. (9.6.1) the subscript h corresponds to the subscript g used here.] Data are more likely to be adequate for total imports of good g into J as a whole (when J is not disaggregated by using sector h). As with the CES approach, it is necessary to state total imports $\tilde{IM}_{g}^{J}$ of g by J in units of a composite good with fictitious price $\tilde{p}_{g}^{J}$. The true export (international) prices $p^{N \to J}$, as already noted, are endogenously determined.

In sum, the column-by-column multimethod approach for estimating the items in the cells of a trade matrix for a CGE model involves merely the determination of the demands $H_{gh}^{N \to J}$ on the basis of (i) relations and data that would normally be employed in using CES functions alone and (ii) variables that would be endogenously determined, except for the d_{NJ} and η variables of the gravity model. The last two do not impose any formidable obstacle. We should note the possibility of variants of the several methods proposed, particularly through introducing relative prices (and perhaps scale economies) to modify the play of the $k_{gh}^{N \to J}$ in the Leontief and comparative cost approaches and the $\mathcal{M}^J \mathcal{M}^N / d_{NJ}^{\eta}$ term in the gravity model approach. The basic equality of number of unknowns and number of independent relations to determine them is always maintained.

9.D   The use of the multimethod approach to trade matrix construction in the LINK model

In making a projection for a future year, given the base year trade pattern, the LINK approach has each national econometric model estimate its (1) imports and (2) prices on the world market for its exports. It does so on the basis of endogenous variables and on its anticipations of (1) prices it must pay for imports and (2) its exports. Adding over all national models, the estimated imports leads to a total that typically is not equal to the sum of anticipated exports – an inconsistency. Also there typically will be inconsistencies among the set of estimated export prices of the several models, among the set of anticipated import prices, and between these two sets. Such inconsistencies lead under the guidance of the study group to new anticipated import prices and exports that in turn lead to different estimated export prices and imports. A series of iterations typically take place leading to a set of consistent estimates and anticipations, which for each internationally traded good h satisfy the equation

$$E_h^J = \sum_N k_h^{J \to N} \mathrm{IM}_h^N, \qquad J, N = A, \ldots, U; \, J \neq N \qquad (9.D.1)$$

where

E_h^J = region J's exports of h
$k_h^{J \to N}$ = share of N's total imports of h provided by J
IM_h^N = region N's imports

When these equations are expressed in matrix form, we have

$$E = \bar{k} \, \mathrm{IM} \qquad (9.D.2)$$

Note also that LINK employs, as a comparison, the identity in IM:

$$(\mathrm{PE})' k \mathrm{IM} = (\mathrm{PM})' \mathrm{IM} \qquad (9.D.3)$$

where

$(\mathrm{PE})'$ = a row vector of (average) export prices
$(\mathrm{PM})'$ = a row vector of (average) import prices

This states that over all regions, the total value of exports equals the total value of imports.

To incorporate the effects of changing world prices upon anticipated future exports, the study group can specify the various relations (estimating equations) to be used. One relation may specify a CES function approach or a variant of it. Another may simply introduce a change in relevant prices or a specific ratio of prices as basic variables to be used to modify the real trade share coefficients of the base year. Each type of relation (or combination of relations) used leads to a different projection of the trade matrix (pattern) for the future year.

The multimethod approach we propose considers methods that comprise those not directly related to world prices as well as those that are. The gravity model method can be employed in LINK (or any LINK-type econometric model) since it requires measures of mass (such as GNP) that are endogenous in LINK and the same exogenously determined distance variable d_{NJ} and parameter η discussed in section 9.7. The use of comparative cost is also valid since, as in the case of its use in CGE, this approach requires the same studies of highly competitive cost-sensitive sectors, for which only a limited amount of price information is required. The use of the CES approach in LINK, however, could face more obstacles than in the case of CGE. This is so because LINK is not designed, in the development of its core, to collect, process, and otherwise treat past price data to derive relevant elasticities. However, to the extent that such elasticities have already been derived for aggregate trade in general by nations or for key commodities in world trade, these elasticities may be employed to project relevant column entries in a trade matrix.

The use of the fixed-share approach of Leontief is precluded since LINK has at its core world markets and the determination of world prices. Almost necessarily, such directly requires changes in at least some market shares, as already provided for in the various relations proposed for use by the study group.

The use of a truncated translog approach in LINK is fully consistent with LINK's structure since this approach projects trade flows on the basis of prices alone (it is not constrained to use base year Leontief share coefficients). However, its use by LINK faces obstacles in that it requires estimation of many more elasticities than CES and thus the collection and processing of extensive data if such elasticities are not available (as is the current situation) from other studies.

In sum, the multimethod approach, using different methods for projecting the entries in the columns or parts of columns of a trade matrix for a future year, is consistent with the LINK model and is likely to yield better projections of these entries than currently.

References

Armington, P. (1969) "A Theory of Demand for Products Distinguished by Place of Production." *Staff Papers, International Monetary Fund* 16(1, July):159–78.

Bergstrand, J. H. (1985) "The Gravity Equation in International Trade: Some Microeconomic Foundations and Empirical Evidence." *Review of Economics and Statistics* 67:474–81.

Bremer, S. A. (ed.) (1987) *The Globus Model.* Boulder, CO: Westview.

Chenery, H., S. Robinson, and M. Syrquin (1986) *Industrialization and Growth: A Comparative Study.* London: Oxford University Press.

334   I. Basic framework and set of analyses

Costa, A. M., and L. P. Jennergren (1982) "Trade and Development in the World Economy: Methodological Features of Project DYNAMICO." *Journal of Policy Modeling* 4(1):3–22.

Cusack, T. R. (1985) "Contention and Compromise: A Comparative Analysis of Budgetary Politics." International Institute for Comparative Social Research and Global Development, West Berlin.

Deardorff, A. V., and R. M. Stern (1981) "A Disaggregated Model of World Production and Trade: An Estimate of the Impact of the Tokyo Round." *Journal of Policy Modeling* 3(2):127–52.

Dervis, K., J. de Melo, and S. Robinson (1982) *General Equilibrium Models for Development Policy.* New York: Cambridge University Press.

Deutsch, K. W., B. Fritsch, H. Jaguariba, and A. S. Markovits (1977) *Problems of World Modelling: Political and Social Implications.* Cambridge, MA: Ballinger Press.

Gigengack, A. R., H. de Haan, and C. J. Jepma (1985) "Military Expenditure Dynamics and a World Model." Faculty of Economics, University of Groningen, Netherlands.

Ginsburgh, V., and S. Robinson (1984) "Equilibrium and Prices in Multi-sector Models." In M. Syrquin, L. Taylor, and L. E. Westphal (eds.), *Economic Structure and Performance.* New York: Academic Press, pp. 429–50.

Ginsburgh, V., and J. Waelbroeck (1981) *Activity Analysis and General Equilibrium Modelling.* Amsterdam: North-Holland.

Gunning, J. W., G. Carrin, and J. Waelbroeck (1982) *Growth and Trade of Developing Countries: A General Equilibrium Approach.* Discussion Paper 8210, Centre d'Economique Mathematique et d'Econometrie, Universite Libre de Bruxelles.

Hickman, B. G., and L. J. Lau (1973) "Elasticities of Substitution and Export Demands in a World Trade Model." *European Economic Review* 4:347–80.

Hughes, B. B. (1985) *World Futures: A Critical Analysis of Alternatives.* Baltimore: John Hopkins University Press.

Isard, W. (1954) "Location Theory and Trade Theory: Short-Run Analysis." *Quarterly Journal of Economics* 68(May):305–20.

Isard, W. (1975) "A Simple Rationale for Gravity Model Type-Behavior." *Papers Regional Science Association* 34:25–30.

Isard, W., D. F. Bramhall, G. A. P. Carrothers, J. H. Cumberland, L. N. Moses, D. O. Price, and E. W. Schooler (1960) *Methods of Regional Analysis: An Introduction to Regional Science.* Cambridge, MA: MIT Press.

Isard, W., T. E. Smith, P. Isard, T. H. Tung, and M. Dacey (1969) *General Theory: Social, Political, Economic and Regional.* Cambridge, MA: MIT Press.

Isard, W., and E. Schooler (1964) "An Economic Analysis of Local and Regional Impacts of Reduction of Military Expenditures." *Papers Peace Reseach Society (International)* 1:15–44.

Isard, W., and C. Smith (1983) "Linked Integrated Multiregional Models at the International Level." *Papers Regional Science Association* 51:3–19.

Isard, W., and C. Smith (1988) "Alternative World System Models," mimeo. Department of Economics, Cornell University, Ithaca, NY.

Ives, T. (1985) "The Geography of Arms Dispersal." In D. Pepper and A. Jenkins (eds.), *The Geography of Peace and War.* Oxford: Basil Blackwell.

Klein, L. R. (1983) *Lectures in Econometrics*. Amsterdam: North-Holland.
Klein, L. R., and H. Kosaka (1987) "The Arms Race and the Economy." Department of Economics, University of Pennsylvania, Philadelphia, PA.
Leontief, W. (1980) "The Future of the World Economy." *Scientific American* 243(3):207–30.
Leontief, W., and F. Duchin (1983) *Military Spending*. New York: Oxford University Press.
Leontief, W., A. Carter, and P. Petri (1977) *The Future of the World Economy*. New York: Oxford University Press.
Llewellyn, G. E. J., and L. W. Samuelson (1982) "The Analytic Foundation of International Economic Modeling at the OECD." *Journal of Policy Modeling* 4(2):261–73.
Luterbacher, U., and P. Allan (1982) "Modeling Politico-Economic Interactions Within and Between Nations." *International Political Science Review* 3(4):404–33.
Meagher, G. A. (1982) "A Generalized Johansen Formulation of the World Bank WDR4 Global Model." RSA ANZ Section Meetings, Nov. 30–December 2, 1982, mimeo.
Mercenier, J., and J. Waelbroeck (1984) "The Sensitivity of Developing Countries to External Shocks in an Interdependent World." *Journal of Policy Modeling* 6(2):209–35.
Miller, R. E., and P. D. Blair (1985) *Input–Output Analysis*. Englewood Cliffs, NJ: Prentice-Hall.
Onishi, A. (1983) "North-South Relations: Alternative Policy Simulations for the World Economy in the 1980's." *Journal of Policy Modeling* 5(1):55–74.
Polachek, S. W. (1980) "Conflict and Trade." *Journal of Conflict Resolution* 24(1, March):55–78.
Polachek, S. W. (1987) "Nations in Conflict," mimeo. Department of Economics, SUNY Binghamton, Binghamton, NY.
Pyatt, G., and J. I. Round (eds.) (1985) *Social Accounting Matrices: A Basis for Planning*. Washington, D.C.: The World Bank.
Raiffa, H. (1982) *The Art and Science of Negotiation*. Cambridge, MA: Harvard University Press.
Ranuzzi, P. (1981) "The Experience of the EEC Eurolink Project in Modeling Bilateral Trade Linkage Equations." *Journal of Policy Modeling* 3(2):153–73.
Robinson, S. (1986) "Multisectoral Models of Developing Countries: A Survey." Working Paper No. 401, California Agricultural Experiment Station, University of California, April.
Robinson, S., and L. D. Tyson (1983) "Modeling Structural Adjustment: Micro and Macro Elements in a General Equilibrium Framework." In H. Scarf and J. B. Shoven (eds.), *Applied General Equilibrium Analysis*. Cambridge: Cambridge University Press, pp. 243–71.
Scarf, H., and J. B. Shoven (eds.) (1983) *Applied General Equilibrium Analysis*. Cambridge: Cambridge University Press.
Shishido, S., H. Fujwara, A. Kohno, Y. Kurokawa, S. Matsuura, and H. Wago (1980) "A Model for the Coordination of Recovery Policies in the OECD Region." *Journal of Policy Modeling* 2(1):35–55.
Shoven, J. B., and J. Whalley (1984) "Applied General Equilibrium Models of

Taxation and International Trade: An Introduction and Survey." *Journal of Economic Literature* 22(September):1007–51.

Smith, T. E. (1978) "A Cost-Efficiency Principle of Spatial Interaction Behavior." *Regional Science and Urban Economics* 8(4, December):313–38.

Stevens, G. V. G., R. B. Berner, P. B. Clark, E. Hernández-Catá, H. H. Howe, and S. Y. Kwack (1984) "The U.S. Economy in an Interdependent World: A Multicountry Model." Board of Governors of the Federal Reserve System, Washington, D. C.

Stockholm International Peace Research Institute (1986) *SIPRI Yearbook 1986.* New York: Oxford University Press.

Syrquin, M., L. Taylor, and L. E. Westphal (eds.) (1984) *Economic Structure and Performance.* New York: Academic Press.

Taylor, L. (1983) *Structuralist Macroeconomics: Applicable Models for the Third World.* New York: Basic Books.

Thorbecke, E. (1985) "The Social Accounting Matrix and Consistency-Type Planning Models." In G. Pyatt and G. I. Round (eds.), *Social Accounting Matrices: A Basis for Planning.* Washington, D.C.: The World Bank.

Whalley, J. (1985) *Trade Liberalization Among Major World Trading Areas.* Cambridge, MA: MIT Press.

CHAPTER 10

Negotiation/mediation principles and qualitative and quantitative conflict management procedures

Written with Christine Smith

10.1 Introduction

We have now examined world models, the kinds of data they can produce, and the validity of such. In effect, these data are part of the outcome [usually a list (vector) of outcome elements] that might be indicated in a cell of a relevant perceived truncated payoff matrix that each protagonist could construct from his or her particular standpoint, or a third party from his or her standpoint, and so on. Hence with the set of perceived outcomes for each protagonist and third party that might be involved, we can proceed to examine the various conflict management procedures that might be employed to reach some joint action representing an agreement, a compromise policy, nonagreement, and so on. We shall do this having in mind our discussions of the following:

1. the effects on decision making of attitudes, perceptions, propensities, goals (aspirations), motivations, expectations, limited abilities, and so on, of the behaving unit (Chapter 4);
2. the impact of stress and crisis on behavior and the payoff matrix perceived by the unit in view of his (or her) behavioral pathologies (Chapter 5);
3. the way the behaving unit constructs new and/or employs existing mental models of the world, the way he seeks to solve problems using a means–end or other artificial intelligence approach, and the way he goes about investing his resources in the development of information to reduce uncertainties (Chapter 6);
4. the way he might attack the problem of inventing new ideas for conflict management or use his labor and resources to produce new information that helps narrow a conflict (Chapters 15 and 16); or (as in Chapter 14) learn along with other members and

the leader of his group in an iterative way about what a best policy might be for his group;

5. the way he conducts policy analysis if as a political leader he does so (Chapter 7); and
6. the way he sets forth a political argument, utilizing data generated by world system and other models (Chapter 8).

In this chapter, we can imagine that two political or other leaders are involved in a conflict situation, each having conducted his (or her) policy analysis and having set forth an effective political argument that has led to his incumbency (successful election). These two leaders might be, for example, a Gorbachev and a Reagan. They are in major conflict, for example, on an arms control policy. As negotiators or with representatives as negotiators, they are faced, among others, with the question of what principles of negotiation to use. Or if a mediator or other third party is brought into the picture, he is individually faced with the question of what principles of mediation (or, e.g., arbitration) to use. Furthermore, after each leader and third party (if involved) has employed certain principles, they may often find that the conflict is still outstanding and thus confront a second question of what quantitative conflict management procedure to employ to reach an acceptable compromise (agreement).

In this chapter we shall focus on these two and related questions. We shall do so by pulling together into a single operational framework (1) principles of negotiation and mediation as used by practitioners and (2) conflict management procedures (CMPs) as developed by academic scholars. These principles are discussed in such journals as the *Negotiation Journal* and *Journal of Conflict Resolution;* and these CMPs are discussed in such journals as *Conflict Management and Peace Science, Game Theory,* and the *Quarterly Journal of Economics.*

In what follows we develop one of many possible approaches to achieve a compromise joint action or settlement or resolution (partial or complete) of a conflict. Our approach is first to identify relevant key characteristics of a conflict situation and then to consider a set of principles of negotiation or mediation to use to move ahead in achieving a compromise for this situation. Often such will be inadequate so that a further step is required involving the use of one or more quantitative CMPs to achieve the settlement. At this point, the quantitative CMP (together with the associated qualitative CMP) may be evaluated for political and economic feasibility. However, in still another step, models (e.g., world models in the case of some international conflicts) may prove helpful for determining relevant outcomes from the use of these quantitative CMPs.

In this regard they can provide additional information needed by parties to the conflict in order to assess the "acceptability–desirability" of each of the quantitative CMPs proposed for use – thereby to facilitate the selection of the one to implement.

In section 10.2 we define our basic concepts: negotiation, mediation, a principle of negotiation, a principle of mediation, a qualitative CMP, and a quantitative CMP.

In section 10.3 we take the first step, namely, to specify the possible characteristics of a conflict situation so that a negotiator, mediator, analyst, or any other third party can better identify the relevant characteristics of any given conflict situation (as we attempt to do in part in the subsequent chapter with regard to the U.S.–Soviet arms control conflict). The second step is to examine all possible principles of negotiation (section 10.4) and mediation or other third-party intervention (section 10.5) that are or should be applicable or desirable or relevant. These principles are basic for the development of a relevant qualitative CMP given the key and other characteristics of a conflict situation. Then in section 10.6 we cite instances of past applications of the selected principles of negotiations and mediation, and in section 10.7 we discuss several qualitative CMPs set forth by distinguished scholars and professionals.

The third step, discussed in section 10.8, recognizes that a qualitative CMP by itself is often inadequate. It needs to be complemented by a quantitative CMP. Thus in section 10.8, after we generally discuss properties of quantitative CMPs, we list a large number of quantitative CMPs. We then investigate how to identify one or a few that might be relevant, that is, have desirable properties, given the key characteristics of a conflict situation and the qualitative CMP considered relevant. However, a fourth step can be taken. Each quantitative CMP together with its qualitative CMP and direct projection of results can be taken to specify a relevant scenario (an information set) to be inputted into a world system or other appropriate model to provide additional information. We have already indicated in section 9.2 how Leontief and Duchin (1983) inputted several extreme (unrealistic) scenarios into a world system model. Also, we indicated in section 9.9 how a simple scenario involving a shock of a 10 percent increase in U.S. and Soviet defense spending can be put into a LINK world system model. We saw its implications for change in real GDP (gross domestic product), the interest and unemployment rates, and so on.

As just indicated, inputting the information of a scenario into a world system model yields additional information (findings) from that model as outcomes. Such outcomes would reveal whether that scenario meets certain desired ends – whether it guarantees improvement in total (or in each of a series of steps), whether it meets some criteria of national security (e.g., the building up of production potential via investment), whether it satisfies some criteria of stability (e.g., by inducing much greater economic trade among the parties), and so on.

These outcomes of the models together with other information (quantitative and nonquantitative) are taken as a basis for evaluating the desirability of a scenario – in essence, the associated quantitative CMP, given the qualitative CMP and the relevant characteristics of the conflict situation. Elsewhere (Isard and Smith 1982, chap. 9), we have explored a possible crude index of inadequacy (adequacy) for evaluating any given scenario in a quantitative fashion, thus for facilitating the choice of a "best" or acceptable scenario.

The outcomes of the scenarios may also be used as feedbacks allowing for revision of qualitative CMPs if no scenario yields an adequate or acceptable set of outcomes.

In section 10.9 we make a few concluding remarks. Note that in this chapter we do not discuss arbitration or principles of arbitration. Such matters are judged to be beyond the scope of this chapter and book, although many of the principles associated with negotiation and mediation are also applicable to arbitration.

10.2   Basic concepts and definitions

Negotiation is defined as interaction through verbal exchange by one party with his or her opponent(s) in order to come to terms or reach a mutually acceptable agreement or resolution of a conflict. Although negotiation may also be envisaged as verbal exchange via which conflict with one's opponent is waged or escalated without consideration for its impact on the "final" resolution of such conflict, we choose to exclude this type of activity from our definition of negotiation.

Mediation is defined as the process whereby a third party attempts to help conflicting parties reach a voluntary agreement. It is to be distinguished from arbitration where the third party is empowered to make a binding decision to settle a dispute.

A *principle of negotiation* is defined to be a rule of thumb adjudged to be appropriate as a basis for guiding the behavior of a negotiator involved on behalf of a party or personally in typically seeking resolution (partial or complete) of a conflict.

A *principle of mediation* is defined to be a rule of thumb adjudged to be appropriate as a basis for guiding the behavior of a mediator involved with participants in seeking resolution (partial or complete) of a conflict.

A *qualitative CMP* is defined to be a set of mutually compatible[1] (non-contradictory) principles of negotiation, mediation, or other third-party intervention to be used by relevant parties in seeking a mutually agreed upon or imposed resolution (partial or complete) of a conflict.

A *quantitative CMP* is defined to be a means to be used by relevant parties for achieving a mutually agreed upon or imposed resolution (partial or complete) of a conflict that involves the use and processing of data or quantitative information as inputs.

10.3 Conflict situation characteristics: identification of key characteristics for a given situation

We now wish to set down important general characteristics of conflict situations so that their presence or absence may be used to help classify these situations. We do so in Tables 10.1–10.3, which at best only present a partial listing, each section of which should be much further developed by relevant experts. Table 10.1 relates to *structural characteristics of systems,* each participant being associated with some system. These characteristics are under the headings cultural, social psychology, social groups and social organizations, economic system, political system, and other.

Table 10.2 lists *nonsystemic structural characteristics* of conflict situations under the headings nature of disagreement (issues and stakes), participants involved, coalition-related characteristics, reference positions and magnitudes, time-related characteristics, policy options (joint actions) available, fractionation/logrolling possibilities, information-related characteristics, and communication channels available.

Table 10.3 lists relevant *participants' characteristics* under the headings psychological, level of education (sophistication) and knowledge, control of resources, perceptive capabilities, receptive capabilities, learning potentials, and preference structure and statement capabilities.

It is important to note that these characteristics as such may be key elements to the understanding of the conflict and the way negotiators or others attempt to manage the conflict. Equally if not more important in these matters are the differences among participants with regard to these characteristics. For example, if negotiators represent parties from different cultures, the nature of the conflict and attempts to manage it may be much different than when the parties are from the same culture.

---

[1] Mutually compatible principles are loosely conceived here as principles that do not interfere in a major way with each other in the process of reaching an agreement.

Table 10.1. *Systemic structural characteristics*

I. Cultural
   1. Need to have (exercise) power
   2. Need to have identity
   3. Need to achieve
   4. Need to have security
   5. Type of legal system (e.g., Roman, Common, Islamic, Old Testament)
   ⋮

II. Social psychology
   10. Degree of conservativeness (boldness)
   11. Solutions sought via
      • group (bureaucratic) means
      • individualistic action
      • individualistic action subject to group approval
   12. Approach to problem solving
      • calculating (methodical)
      • abstract (logical)
      • intuitive (religiomystic)
      • experimental
      • precedent (tradition) oriented
   ⋮

III. Social groups and social organizations
   20. Degree of division within society
      • regarding public purpose
      • among socioeconomic classes regarding wealth and consumption
      • among political groups regarding influence and power
   21. Status of division within society
      • recently emergent
      • protracted
      • rate of change in (trend)
      • potential for revolution
   ⋮

IV. Economic system
   30. Level and stage of development (developed, developing; established, in take-off)
   31. Growth/decline (stagnation) pattern
   32. Degree of dependence on external relations (trade, foreign aid and investment, military bases, etc.)
   33. Industrial structure and organization (small business, large domestic corporations, multinationals, etc.)
   34. Magnitude and type of structural change
   ⋮

V. Political system
   40. Degree and type of democracy
      • western style
      • military style
      • Soviet-bloc style

342

Table 10.1. (*cont.*)

41.	Position along big power–small power continuum
42.	Stability of incumbent political leaders and political system (party structure)
43.	Internal decision-making (functional) structure
	• centralized
	• decentralized
	• hierarchical

: :

VI. Other
  50. System information (low, medium, high)
  51. Experience with major conflict

: :

Table 10.2. *Nonsystemic structural characteristics*

I. Nature of disagreement: issues and stakes
  100. Qualitative, quantitative, or mixed
  101. Intensity of (major, minor)

: :

II. Participants involved
  110. Number
  111. Presence or absence of
    • negotiators acting on behalf of constituency
    • technical support team
    • third party
    • coalitions among participants
  112. Relations among
    • degree of hostility (friendliness)
    • degree of trust (and mutual respect)

: :

III. Coalition-related characteristics
  120. Type and size of
  121. Stability

: :

343

Table 10.2. *(cont.)*

IV. Reference position and magnitudes
    130. Current situation
    131. Ideal situation
    132. Reservation/fallback position
    133. Worst scenario position
    134. Nature of credible threats/promises
    135. Nature of current demands/offers
    136. Inherent constraints (on actions, outcomes, etc.)
    137. Nonnegotiable issues
    138. Sunk (unrecoverable) costs
                                    ⋮

V. Time-related characteristics
    140. Historical factors
    141. Presence of deadline(s)
    142. Time path of conflict
        • unchanging (static), slowly changing, explosive
        • sharply discontinuous
        • widely fluctuating
                                    ⋮

VI. Policy options (joint actions) available
    150. Number
        • small, many
        • fixed, variable
    151. Component elements
        • one, few, many
    152. Scale of measurement
        • discrete or continuous
        • nominal, ordinal, relative, cardinal
    153. Agenda (sequence of consideration)
        • fixed, variable
                                    ⋮

VII. Fractionation/logrolling possibilities
    160. Regarding issues
    161. Regarding participants (groupings of)
    162. Regarding actions (or elements of actions)
    163. Regarding outcomes (or elements of outcomes)
                                    ⋮

VIII. Information-related characteristics
    170. Quality and quantity regarding structural conflict situation characteristics
        • much or little
        • degree of "accuracy"
        • extent of uncertainty

344

Table 10.2. *(cont.)*

	171.	Quality and quantity regarding participant characteristics
		• as in 170
	172.	Quality and quantity regarding CMPs
		• as in 170
	173.	Models/tools available
		• number, quality, type

                                               ⋮

IX. Communication channels available
    180. Few, many
    181. Formal, informal
    182. Congested, noncongested

Table 10.3. *Participants' characteristics*

I. Psychological
    200. Position along various continua
        • conservative to bold
        • pessimist to optimist
        • risk averse to risk lover
        • competitive to cooperative
        • passive to aggressive
        • myopic to nonmyopic
        • self-interested to altruistic
        • creative to tradition bound
    201. Orientation toward
        • strategies
        • outcomes
        • actions
        • optimization
    202. Pathologies in crisis situations
        • overconfidence in "rightness" of one's proposal
        • insensitivity to objective information questioning "rightness" of one's proposal
        • overvaluation of "rightness" of past proposals that were successful

                                               ⋮

345

Table 10.3. *(cont.)*

II. Level of education (sophistication) and knowledge
    230. General (low, medium, high)
    231. Regarding conflict situations (low, medium, high)
    232. Regarding analytical tools and models (low, medium, high)
    233. Regarding conflict management (low, medium, high)
    234. Nature and extent of misperceptions

                         :
                         :

III. Control of resources
    240. General (economic, political, social, etc.)
    241. Specific to (relevant for) the conflict

                         :
                         :

IV. Perceptive capabilities
    250. Limited or abundant – in noncrisis situations
         • Regarding interdependence
         • Regarding structural conflict situation characteristics
         • Regarding other participants' characteristics
         • Regarding new options and creative approaches
    251. Limited or abundant – in crisis situations
         • as in 250 above

                         :
                         :

V.   Receptive capabilities regarding information
    260. Limited or much (abundant) – in noncrisis situations
         • on interdependence
         • on structural conflict situation characteristics
         • on other participants' characteristics
         • on new options and creative ideas
    261. Limited or abundant – in crisis situations
         • as in 260

                         :
                         :

VI. Learning potentials
    270. Capability (little, much)
    271. Willingness (little, much)

                         :
                         :

VII. Preference structure and statement capabilities
    280. Ordinal
    281. Relative
    282. Cardinal
    283. Interdependent

                         :
                         :

How does a participant identify key characteristics of a given conflict situation? This is a question that each participant must answer. Here, the partial listing of possible characteristics in Tables 10.1–10.3 can be useful to him (or her), but clearly the participant must answer on the basis of his current stock of knowledge, experience, and perceptions, supplemented by learning that he acquires in and out of workshops and other discussion arenas.

What if the negotiators classify as key certain characteristics that involve inconsistencies? For example, one negotiator may insist that the primary issue concerns the perpetuation of a basic religious principle (a qualitative nonnegotiable element) that denies any concern for material welfare, whereas the second insists that economic growth is the primary issue. Such an inconsistency (which is different from conflict over what rate of economic growth should be, say, a nation's goal) may be viewed as a subconflict within the primary conflict and may need to be first resolved, perhaps in the early stages of discussion, or through tactful setting of an agenda by a third party, or in some other manner. In fact, our procedure for managing the primary conflict or others that may be set forth may be employed to reach a settlement (compromise) that eliminates these subconflict inconsistencies.[2]

10.4 Principles of negotiation (for a two-party conflict)

Once negotiators and a third party construct for themselves a mental representation of the conflict and its key characteristics, they are confronted with the questions of what stance to take and what to propose. [Note that we confine ourselves here to a two-party conflict. As indicated in Appendix 3.B and section 7.4, when more than two parties are involved, coalitions become possible. Unfortunately, coalition analysis has little to say for real-life situations, and thus we cannot suggest much with regard to relevant principles of negotiations and later of mediation (when coalitions are possible).] To take a stance or make a proposal, negotiators and a third party must have some rules of thumb, guidelines, cultural norms, ethical standards, or the like that we classify under principles of negotiation and mediation. We now turn to a partial summary of such principles, taking up those discussed by practitioners and scholars in *Negotia-*

---

[2] Of course, inconsistencies regarding characteristics and other inconsistencies discussed elsewhere may persist, and still a partial or full resolution of a conflict may be realized if these inconsistencies are minor and do not bring a process of settlement to a halt.

We note that, as yet, cognitive and other social scientists have little definitive knowledge on the process by which a negotiator (however experienced) identifies within his or her own mind the key characteristics and, later, useful principles of negotiation.

tion Journal and related writings. In presenting this summary, we insist that the reader *constantly keep in mind three caveats:*

1. This partial summary covers only a small fraction of principles advanced over the years by numerous and diverse practitioners.
2. Corresponding to every principle we list, there can be conflict situations in which the opposite of the principle may be claimed to be an effective principle. Hence, we can only claim that the principles we do list can be considered as generally useful, but certainly not for every occasion.
3. These principles are for use by a negotiator in a two-party conflict. Each needs to be reexamined and restated when more than two parties are involved in the conflict.

We find it useful to list our partial summary in Table 10.4 in four sections. Each section corresponds to a phase in the negotiations process; and in this table these phases are ordered in time.[3] The first phase lists principles that may be used by negotiators involved in preparation and analysis prior to their making proposals. Then come principles that may be adopted during the second, proposal-making phase of negotiations. After proposals have been made, there is an interaction phase under which are listed principles that negotiators may employ in an effort to reach agreement on a mutually acceptable "solution" to the conflict. Finally, we list principles that may be employed by negotiators in the last phase in an effort to ensure compliance with and implementation of the agreed-upon "solutions."

However, keep constantly in mind that in any actual set of negotiations this ordering may be reversed and/or modified. In particular, feedback loops, retracing of steps, and the like might reasonably be expected as normal features in a negotiation activity. Moreover, as we shall see from the brief sketches of instances of past negotiations, complexes (combinations) of these principles are almost invariably employed in any given situation. We now discuss each principle in the order in which they are listed in the table.

10.4.1 Principles for the preparation and analysis phase

(a) Understanding enhancement: A negotiator should conduct an analysis to come to understand the interdependent aspects in negotiations, and further,

> the issues and other conflict situation characteristics considered key to him (or her) and his opponent;

---

[3] Of course, for certain situations there need not be as many as four phases; and for other situations, more.

Table 10.4. *Selected principles of negotiation*

1. Preparation and analysis phase
   a. Understanding enhancement
   b. Third-Party intervention
   c. Misinformation spread
   d. Monolithicity attainment

2. Proposal-making phase
   a. Interdependence appreciation
   b. Opponent sensitivity
   c. Pathology awareness
   d. Long run–short run trade-off
   e. Deterrent threat
   f. Unilateral-reward action
   g. Time exploitation
   h. Approximate cost–benefit balance sheet
   i. Monolithicity attainment

3. Interaction phase
   a. Continuous evaluation
   b. Stance–issues separation
   c. Strategic element highlighting and questioning
   d. Trust/respect/knowledge building
   e. Time exploitation
   f. Third-party intervention
   g. Realism in the face of failure

4. Final packaging phase
   a. Enhancement of implementability

possible assumptions about his and his opponent's behavior, that he and his opponent are and might be making in setting forth and responding to proposals and during the interaction phases;

possible proposals and/or negotiation stances that he and his opponent may be making and the points of conflict; and

the logistics of the situation (time and place of interaction, the sequence in which proposals are made, negotiating conventions, etc.).

Moreover, the negotiator should

conduct, when feasible, the preceding analysis with the use of tools and models capable of handling large volumes of data and complex interrelations[4] and

---

[4] This implies (requires) that data sets, computer programs, and/or mathematical models specific to the given conflict situation may need to be assembled and/or developed.

always conduct analysis here (and later on) up to (but not including) the level at which the expected costs of further analysis come to outweigh the expected benefits.[5] [For further discussion of this principle, see Straus (1986).]

(b) Third-party intervention principle: A negotiator should evaluate the conflict situation analysis here (and also later on) to determine whether third-party intervention (in the form of, say, mediation) might prove desirable (in terms of expected costs and benefits) in the proposal-making and/or subsequent phases of negotiation, especially when the parties are deadlocked. [For further discussion, see Fisher (1978), Rubin (1981), and Pruitt and Rubin (1986, chap. 10).]

(c) Misinformation spread principle: A negotiator should spread misinformation (including bluffing, the supression of information, etc.) when, after analysis, he (or she) perceives the situation to be closer to a zero-sum rather than a variable-sum game wherein a competitive rather than an integrative solution would be distinctly to his advantage. (This would be the case where the excess of expected benefits over expected costs was larger from such action than from any other).[6] [For further discussion relating to this principle, see Raiffa (1982, pp. 142–5).]

(d) Monolithicity attainment: A negotiator representing an organization, nation, or other body should, wherever possible, ensure that the body is prepared for negotiation and committed to implement an agreement that might be reached. Such may require that he (or she) conduct an analysis relating to the internal conflicts of that body, thereby to understand how interest groups within the body view the conflict situation and thereby determine how best he can help them reach agreement on priorities and other matters that his behavior is to reflect. Whenever it is to his interest, he should suggest (urge) his opponent to come so positioned. [For some further discussion, see Zartman (1985) and Kelman (1972, 1979).]

10.4.2 *Principles for the proposal-making phase*

(a) Interdependence appreciation: A negotiator should recognize and appreciate the interdependence of the diverse factors and elements in the negotiation process, being particularly alert to the existence (possibility)

---

[5] This assumes that at lower levels expected benefits exceed or equal expected costs.
[6] Or where misinformation spread minimizes the excess of expected costs over expected benefits when every action leads to such an excess.

of common goals. [For further discussion, see Brazerman (1983), Pruitt and Rubin (1986), and Greenhalgh (1987).]

(b) Opponent sensitivity: In selecting and/or presenting his (or her) proposals, a negotiator should recognize and be responsive to his opponent's needs and/or problems. Such needs may cover the need for identity, legitimacy, and a feeling of competence and of being effective. [For further discussion, see Rubin (1983).]

(c) Pathology awareness: In deciding upon a proposal, a negotiator should recognize that he (or she) and his opponent may be suffering from certain decision-making pathologies. Such pathologies may relate to

1. overconfidence in the "rightness" of one's proposal and its probability of being adopted;
2. insensitivity to information critical of the "rightness" of one's proposal; and/or
3. overvaluation of the "rightness" of proposals that were successfully set forth and/or accepted in the past and that led to advantageous outcomes.

[For further discussion, see Janis (1972), Janis and Mann (1977), Jervis (1976), and Lebow (1981).]

(d) Long run–short run trade-off: In setting forth his (or her) proposal, a negotiator should be aware of trade-offs between the immediate short-run gains and possible longer run gains, in particular those possible longer run gains from

1. not precluding future concessions or other changes including fractionation;
2. not precluding future extension of one's alternatives [e.g., via logrolling or mutual pie expansion (bridging) activity];
3. not discouraging or precluding inventiveness by himself, his opponent, or a potential third-party intervenor; and
4. not antagonizing his opponent(s) or casting aspersions on him or her, thereby foregoing future "good" relationships.

The negotiator should conduct expected benefits versus expected costs analysis to help determine how far to proceed down this "flexibility" route. [For further discussion, see Fisher and Ury (1981).]

(e) Deterrent threat: If a negotiator deems it desirable to incorporate threat mechanisms in a proposal, these should in general be deterrent ori-

ented rather than compulsion oriented. [For further discussion of threats, see Schelling (1960).]

(f) Unilateral-reward action: In making a proposal, the negotiator should consider the possibility of a unilateral action that is rewarding to his (or her) opponent but at little cost to the negotiator, thereby to

1. change his opponent's image of him,
2. lead to tension reduction,
3. reduce his opponent's cost of conceding,
4. generate an unstated obligation on the part of his opponent to reciprocate, and
5. help reinforce any tendency toward concession from any or other "good" behavior on his opponent's part. [For further discussion, see Osgood (1962, 1966) and Lindskold (1978).]

(g) Time exploitation: Where possible, a negotiator should exploit the role that time can play in achieving an "advantageous" settlement. He or she should recognize that not all issues may need to be decided at the start. Actions on some issues can be deferred and made contingent upon learning from experiences, especially in view of the uncertainties that no analysis can handle. Hence, the negotiator should consider limiting the proposal to only those issues that need to be addressed at the start. [See Raiffa (1982, pp. 222–5).]

(h) Approximate cost–benefit balance sheet: A negotiator should consider making a proposal consistent with a problem-solving approach, basing it, where possible and appropriate, on a logical step-by-step analysis and the construction of a balance sheet of expected benefits and costs, both to negotiator and opponent. He or she should recognize that intangible elements may be present and that not everything is negotiable. [See Fisher (1978) and Isard and Smith (1982, pp. 343–61).]

(i) Monolithicity attainment: A negotiator should ensure support from the body that he or she may represent for the proposals derived from using the preceding eight principles [(a)–(h)] and others. [Again, see Zartman (1985) and Kelman (1972, 1979).]

10.4.3 Principles for the interaction phase (to reach agreement)

(a) Continuous evaluation: Once initial proposal(s) have been made, a negotiator should continuously evaluate (or reevaluate) the costs and

benefits expected to accrue from each subsequent proposal that he or she may contemplate. This evaluation should be carried out in a manner consistent with the relevant principles outlined in section 10.4.2 using tools and models for analysis wherever possible and relevant. [For further discussion, see Lax and Sebenius (1985).]

(b) Stance–issues separation: A negotiator should evaluate the first and each subsequent proposal of his (or her) opponent in terms of expected net benefits for each party, being careful to separate the opponent's stated position from his underlying basic interest and to assess the effect of his behavioral traits on his negotiating stance (e.g., willingness to concede). [See Fisher and Ury (1981) and Lax and Sebenius (1986).]

(c) Strategic element highlighting and questioning: After each round of proposal making, a negotiator should attempt to both highlight and raise doubts about various elements of the current proposals in an attempt to identify avenues for inventive thinking, concessionary behavior, fractionation, logrolling, and so on, in subsequent rounds. [See Fisher (1978), Raiffa (1982, chap. 4), and Colosi (1983).]

(d) Trust/respect/knowledge building: A negotiator should respond to the emerging dynamics of the conflict resolution process and take actions (including making a proposal) in such a way as to encourage a buildup of mutual understanding-, trust-, and respect-facilitating integrative action. However, he or she should conduct an analysis of expected benefits versus expected costs to help determine how far he should proceed along this "collaborative/conciliatory" path. [Again, see Osgood (1962, 1966) and Lindskold (1978).]

(e) Time exploitation: A negotiator should exploit the role of time. He (or she) should postpone discussion or action on issues too difficult for current resolution, particularly when accumulation of relevant information can be expected. Where possible and appropriate, he should attempt to agree with his opponent on what future joint actions regarding these issues should be adopted if certain events occur. [Again, see Raiffa (1982, pp. 222–5).]

(f) Third-party intervention: A negotiator should periodically evaluate (in terms of expected costs and benefits) whether third-party intervention (in the form of, say, mediation) might prove desirable – perhaps for breaking stalemates, suggesting creative alternatives, and so on. [Again, see Fisher (1978), Rubin (1981), and Pruitt and Rubin (1986, chap. 10).]

(g) Realism in the face of failure: A negotiator should recognize that at times inaction, withdrawal (particularly when loss of face can be avoided), a rigid/inflexible stand, misrepresentation and dishonesty, reneging on commitments (gracefully), and similar behavior may be unavoidable and/or desirable. [See Raiffa (1982).]

10.4.4 Principles for the final packaging phase: enhancement of implementability

When the negotiator represents a body that had not been fully committed to accept an agreement the negotiator is able to work out and when such an agreement has been achieved, the negotiator should

1. develop a political argument that is as sound as possible (as discussed in Chapter 8) and, if necessary, restate the agreement;
2. conduct discussion sessions with their constituencies (bodies); and
3. otherwise engage in activities judged likely to enhance the acceptance and implementation of the agreement. [Again, see Kelman (1972, 1979).]

10.5 Principles of mediation (for a two-party conflict)

Often in conflict situations, participants may agree on the use of a mediator or be required to undertake mediation. For such situations it is relevant to consider principles of mediation. We do so in this section for mediators who have considered the characteristics of the conflict situation as discussed in section 10.3 and have identified or have tried to identify the key characteristics.

We list selected principles of mediation in Table 10.5. They are categorized by three phases: the preparation and analysis phase before mediation and negotiation start, the interaction phase during which mediation and negotiation take place, and the final package phase after an agreement may have been reached. Recall that mediation is a process whereby a third party attempts only to help conflicting parties (the negotiator and opponent of the previous section) to reach a voluntary agreement. The mediator does not have the power of an arbitrator to settle a dispute. The best or strongest mediators may be those whose views have great influence (persuasive power) on how conflicting parties behave; however, these parties do not need to give up any sovereignty over the ultimate choice of a compromise solution (agreement to abide by).

We now consider each principle in the order in which the principles are listed in Table 10.5. However, we should note that the International

Table 10.5. *Selected principles of mediation*

1. Preparation and analysis phase
   a. Own understanding enhancement
   b. Participant understanding enhancement
   c. Monolithicity attainment
   d. Ground rules (agenda) setting

2. Interaction phase
   a. Flexibility in approach
   b. Tread lightly in early rounds
   c. Tension releasing
   d. Impartiality establishment and maintenance
   e. Minimal aim
   f. Single negotiating text
   g. Compromise constraint
   h. Exploitation of fractionation/logrolling/side payment potentialities
   i. Encouragement of inventiveness
   j. Encouragement of analysis by participants
   k. Test for fairness and stability
   l. Time exploitation

3. Final packaging phase
   a. Enhancement of implementability

Mediation Project concluded that the nonmonolithic nature of national interests and the internal battles over national decision making are much more likely to stymie attempts to introduce mediation (the use of third-party intervention) than any of the obstacles the group supposed were the key impediments to the more effective use of mediation (Susskind 1987, p. 4).

10.5.1 Principles for the preparation and analysis phase

(a) Own understanding enhancement: A mediator should conduct such analysis and other forms of preparation to come to understand better the evolving dynamics (the interdependent logistics) of the conflict and

> the issues and other conflict situation characteristics considered critical (and/or emotional) both in an objective sense (as far as possible) and as perceived by the disputant parties;
> the behavioral assumptions that participants may be making when setting forth or responding to proposals during the interaction phase;

the options (alternative actions) available to resolve the conflict both in an objective sense and as perceived by the disputant parties;

the initial proposals and/or "negotiation" stances likely to be brought to the interaction phase by each disputant party and how these initial proposals may differ from actual interests;

the decision-making pathologies to which each disputant party may be subject;

the objectives (targets), absolute minima, reservation prices, and other bounds likely to be imposed by each disputant party;

and, moreover,

engage, when feasible, in the preceding activities through discussions with each disputant in isolation from the other and via the use of tools and models capable of handling large volumes of data and complex interrelations;[7] and

engage in such activities and analysis here (and later on) up to (but not including) the level at which expected costs of further activity and analysis come to outweigh the expected benefits.

[For further discussion, see Carpenter and Kennedy (1985).]

(b) Participant understanding enhancement: A mediator should conduct such activity *prior to interaction* to assist disputing parties to come to understand better the evolving dynamics (logistics) of the conflict, the interdependence of outcomes, and

the critical (emotional) issues and other characteristics of the conflict situation as perceived by all parties – raising doubts where differences in perception are apparent or where perceptions differ from objective reality;

the behavioral assumptions that each party may be making when setting forth or responding to proposals during the interaction phase – raising questions (constructively) where mutually incompatible and/or unrealistic assumptions become apparent;

the options (alternative actions) available to resolve the conflict both in an objective sense and as perceived by each disputant

---

[7] For example, he (or she) should be aware of what insights game theory can provide. See the discussion in Appendix 3.B. Thus while he may recognize that participants may fail to reap the gains from conflict management or resolution because they are uneducated, have misperceptions and are irrational, or possess unfavorable psychological traits and attitudes and the like, they may also fail to do so because being rational and fully cognizant of the possible gains from accepting any position within, say, the core of a game, they are unable to reach a compromise on the division of gains.

party – encouraging each party to discard in the process alternatives misperceived as available and/or unavailable;

the initial proposals and/or "negotiation" stances likely to be brought to the interaction phase by each disputant party – attempting to "modify" these where they appear to be mutually incompatible in the sense of being unlikely to lead to a resolution of the conflict within a reasonable time span;

the decision-making pathologies to which each disputant party may be subject during the interaction phase – encouraging each party to recognize and take into account the problems these pathologies may create during the interaction phase;

the objectives (targets), absolute minima, reservation prices, and other bounds likely to be imposed by each disputant party during the interaction phase – attempting to "modify" these where they appear to be mutually incompatible and/or unreasonable in the sense of placing too great a restriction on the range of possible integrative solutions to the conflict;

and, moreover,

engage, when feasible, in the preceding activities through discussions with each disputant in isolation from the other and via the use of tools and models capable of handling large volumes of data and complex interrelations; and

engage in such activity and analysis here (and later on) up to (but not including) the level at which expected costs of further activity and analysis come to outweigh the expected benefits.

[See Carpenter and Kennedy (1985), among others.]

(c) Monolithicity attainment: Where one or both disputant parties are negotiators representing an organization, nation, or other body constituting more than one interest group, the mediator should attempt (provided expected benefits outweigh expected costs) to ensure that each such negotiator fully represents his (or her) body – in the sense that the leaders of his body have considered the differences among interest groups within the body (in terms of reservation prices, constraints, priorities to be assigned to the various outcome elements, etc.), have informed its negotiator of the acceptable trade-offs between these different stances, and have sufficient confidence in their negotiator's capabilities to be willing to make a prior commitment to implement an agreement that might be reached (see Kelman 1972, 1978, 1979).

(d) Ground rules (agenda) setting: In setting up interaction phase arrangements (agenda, procedural rules, behavioral conventions, etc.) the media-

tor should attempt to acquire, either implicitly or explicitly, as much power regarding control of discussions and final say as is possible without affecting the goodwill, trust, respect, and favorable elements that disputants might contribute positively to the disputant's confidence in him or her as a mediator. [For relevant discussion, see Carnevale (1986a,b), Goldberg (1986), and Murnighan (1986).]

10.5.2 Principles for the interaction phase

In most instances, mediators will be bringing disputants together in a workshop or other similar type of arrangement in an attempt to achieve agreement. The mediator may find the following principles useful during these interaction sessions:

(a) Flexibility in approach: A mediator should bear in mind that there is no best CMP and/or mediation technique for all conflicts. He (or she) should match his characterization of a conflict (grievance) situation (his perception of his role) and his own style (art) to a performance program involving the use of one or more relevant CMPs and other mediation techniques (see Carnevale 1986a).

(b) Tread lightly in early rounds: In early rounds of interactions, a negotiator should

1. foster activity and discussions likely to establish effective communications, building up trust between disputants,
2. encourage the search for universal (common) values and integrative (noncompetitive) solutions, and
3. highlight points of agreement.

[See Kelman (1972, 1979) and Burton (1969, 1972).]

(c) Tension releasing: When relationships among disputants are heavily strained, where tensions are reaching dangerous levels, or where a deadline (or stalemate) impends or exists, a mediator should consider the merits of suggesting a shift to group activities (participatory recreational, social, cultural, etc.) that nurture tension release and mood change (see Raiffa 1982, pp. 4–5).

(d) Impartiality establishment and maintenance: To maintain his or her effectiveness, a mediator should, wherever possible, avoid giving judgmental advice, arguing unnecessarily with disputants, becoming enmeshed in the fighting, accepting one party's definition of the problems, issues, relevant assumptions, and so on, and in other respects estab-

lish and maintain impartiality (see Colosi 1983; Smith 1985; Touval 1985; Haynes 1986).

(e) Minimally acceptable outcome: Where agreement on an integrative or other acceptable solution is not possible, a mediator should at least aim for widespread agreement on a declaration of intent or a statement of general positions (see Azar and Burton 1986, chap. 9).

(f) Single negotiating text: Where protagonists are likely to come to a negotiation session with fixed positions with major differences, the mediator may construct a single negotiating text. This text is to be set forth so that it will be found wanting by both sides and be such as to motivate (provoke) its modification in one or more rounds. In this manner both sides can contribute to the reaching of a single acceptable document that could represent an agreement (see Fisher 1978; Raiffa 1982, chap. 14).

(g) Compromise constraint: A mediator should recognize that not everything is subject to compromise and that some things are subject to more compromise than others (see Isard and Smith 1982, chaps. 11, 12; Azar and Burton 1986, chap. 7).

(h) Exploitation of fractionation/logrolling/side payments potentialities: When the going gets tough, a mediator should consider

> fractionating the problem – to stop mounting distrust or to build up trust from achieving effective compromise on easier issues;
> encouraging logrolling as a mechanism for balancing the effective costs of a participant's concession on one issue with gains from a "reciprocal" concession by the second participant on another issue; and
> encouraging side payments where a party with many resources exchanges some for a desired concession by the second party.

[See Isard and Smith (1982, pp. 361–4); Zartman (1985).]

(i) Encouragement of inventiveness: A mediator should encourage inventiveness by participants when a possible solution is not apparent, being careful not to be too directive and not to place unnecessary restrictions on the use (and/or exercise) of threats in certain situations. He or she should also encourage examination of possibilities for gains and integrative actions from the use (and/or exercise) of rewards, not allow ideas to be automatically dismissed without due consideration of their merits, and, where possible, not allow participants to become too invested in a particular option too early (see Fisher 1978; Fisher and Ury 1981).

(j) Encouragement of analysis by participants: A mediator should encourage participants to use tools, models, data sets, Fisher-type balance sheets, and other techniques to evaluate the impact upon both themselves and their opponent of each proposal under consideration and to evaluate inventive ideas (see Carpenter and Kennedy 1985).

(k) Test for fairness and stability: A mediator should test an evolving agreement for fairness and stability and to ensure that neither party will suffer loss of face, identity, and/or sense of effectiveness (power) as a result of its adoption (see Azar and Burton 1986, chap. 7).

(l) Time exploitation: A mediator should recognize that not all issues may need to be resolved at one and the same time. In particular, he or she should recognize

1. that action on (settlement of) difficult issues may be deferred until a later time after there is learning from experience with the agreement on less difficult issues; and
2. that settlement on issues involving uncertainties about the future may have appeal to participants when the settlement is on what future joint activities participants will adopt if particular events occur.

[Again, see Raiffa (1982, pp. 222–5).]

10.5.3 Principles for the final packaging phase: enhancement of implementability

The mediator should encourage and/or assist participants to

1. develop political arguments that are as sound as possible (as discussed in Chapter 8) and, if necessary, restate the agreement;
2. conduct discussion sessions with their constituencies or bodies; and
3. otherwise engage in activities judged likely to enhance the acceptance and implementation of the agreement by all parties.

[Again, see Kelman (1972, 1978).]

10.6   Instances of past applications of the selected principles of negotiation and mediation

It is instructive at this point to examine very succinctly some instances of past negotiations. One that illustrates well the combined use of many of the preceding principles, though not in the order listed in Table 10.4

Table 10.6. *Some hypothetical importance weights for the United States and Panama[a]*

Issue	Units	Range	Importance weights United States	Panama[b]
U.S. defense rights	Percentage to be given up	10–25	0.22	0.09
U.S. use rights	Number of rights	20–30	0.22	0.15
Land and Water	Percentage U.S. to give up	20–70	0.15	0.15
Duration of treaty	Years	20–50	0.11	0.15
Compensation by U.S.	Millions of dollars	30–75	0.04	0.11
U.S. military rights	Percentage to be given up	10–25	0.02	0.07
Defense role of Panama	Percentage to be given up	10–25	0.02	0.13
Other			0.22	0.15
Total			1.00	1.00

[a]Based upon Raiffa (1982, Table 10, p. 177).
[b]Importance weights for Panama are as perceived by the United States.

and discussed in the previous section, is the Panama Canal negotiations of 1975–6. As summarized by Raiffa (1982, chap. 12), the situation was exceedingly complex, let alone highly emotional. From both sides (the United States and Panama) numerous interest groups were involved, together motivated to achieve diverse objectives. With pressures coming from innumerable directions, both public and private, the U.S. negotiator, Ambassador-at-Large Ellsworth Bunker, spent much time at *own understanding enhancement.* For example, he participated in seminars with these various interest groups in the United States, recognizing that *monolithicity attainment* was not possible at the early stage of negotiations but having in mind the need for moving significantly in the direction of attaining such should a treaty be approved by Congress. In the early stages of the negotiations, Bunker and Panama's foreign minister agreed on general principles to be employed and identified ten basic issues consistent with the principles of *stance–issues separation* and *strategic element highlighting and questioning.* For further *understanding enhancement,* Bunker, with the help of a team of consultants and staff, gave importance weights to each issue for *both* the United States and Panama; some of these issues and their corresponding importance weights are listed in Table 10.6. This table reflects a crude *approximation of a cost–benefit balance sheet.* Once these issues and weights were identified as the core of the conflict, Bunker assigned roles to members of his team and conducted brainstorming type of bargaining sessions to develop a feel for the negotiations coming up – reflecting the use of the principles of *interdependence appreciation* and *opponent sensitivity* as well as the usefulness of analytical frameworks (models), however simple.

Consistent with the use of the principle of *trust/respect/knowledge building,* both negotiators decided to focus initially on those issues that would be easier to resolve, reaching thereby threshold agreements that built up confidence in Panamaneans about the seriousness of the United States in reaching a fair treaty and that considerably eased the problem of final agreement on all issues. Such also pointed up a shifting of priorities of the two sides, reflecting the application of the principle of *continuous evaluation* by both sides.

Another set of negotiations illustrating the use of some of the principles listed in Table 10.4 were those conducted by Ayub (of Pakistan) and Shastri (of India) in the 1965 Indo–Pakistani conflict over Kashmir (Thornton 1985). After a period wherein hostilities had escalated, both came under great pressure from the UN and all outside powers (except China) to enter into negotiations. Recognizing the brink on which they were tottering and the unattractive uncertainties of stepping back, they accepted the invitation of Kosygin (of the Soviet Union) to a meeting at Tashkent. Both saw the need for outside efforts to restore some form of peace – an application of the principle of *third-party intervention.* The participants and Kosygin were not able to reach any agreement on the basic issues (objectives): (1) the demand by Shastri of a "pact of no-war" by Pakistan and India over Kashmir, and (2) the demand by Ayub for "negotiations" on the future status of Kashmir that would lead to a just and honorable settlement. The outcome (agreement) that was realized was a declaration, which in effect restored the status quo ante with regard to territory – a declaration carefully worded so that each leader was able to claim something for his effort. The declaration was an outcome cleverly designed by Kosygin permitting both Ayub and Shastri to save face and at the same time apply the principle of *realism in the face of failure.*

Other important principles of negotiations can be said to have been applied when Sadat undertook his historic visit to Jerusalem in November 1977. Clearly his was a unilateral action aimed at facilitating future negotiations, an application of the principle of *unilateral-reward action.* Although he was fully aware of major short-run costs (the negative reactions of other Arab leaders that would ensue), he surely had in mind the long-run gains that could eventuate – an application of the principle of *long run–short run trade-off.* This visit also reflected his keen recognition of the complex interrelationships that had to be considered in any negotiation between Israel and any of the Arab states and clearly indicated "his willingness to address directly the most deep-seated fear and longing of the Israeli public for genuine acceptance by their neighbors" (Saunders

1987, p. 250) – application of the principles of *interdependence appreciation* and *opponent sensitivity*. In his speech before the Israeli Knesset he referred to the barriers of suspicion, rejection, fear, deception, and hallucination – to the barrier of distorted and eroded interpretation of every event and statement – clearly an application of the principle of *pathology awareness*.

Numerous other instances of use of the preceding and other negotiation principles can easily be found in the literature on international and non-international conflicts.

With regard to instances of the application of the selected principles of *mediation* listed in Table 10.5, we may first refer to the mediation efforts in the Middle East of Henry Kissinger after the October War of 1973 (when the two parties involved were either Israel and Egypt or Israel and Syria) and President Jimmy Carter at Camp David in 1978 (with Israel and Egypt) [see Stein (1985) for a succinct and penetrating analysis]. Both persons had become very well informed beforehand concerning the numerous factors in the conflict, Carter having set up a task force in preparation for his mediation effort, an application of the principle of *understanding enhancement*. Both carefully ordered and controlled the construction of the agenda – an application of the principle of *ground rules (agenda) setting*. Kissinger's tactics were less defined than Carter's; generally he elicited proposals from each side – an application of the *flexibility in approach* principle. In contrast, Carter adopted the principle of a *single negotiating text;* it turned out that the draft of the text on Palestinian autonomy required twenty-three revisions whereas the treaty between Egypt and Israel had to be redrafted eight times. Perhaps it was the principle of *enhancement of implementability* that was most basic to the agreement reached. In both Kissinger's and Carter's mediation, the United States had to

1. guarantee to both sides the *observance* of the agreement (e.g., should the Security Council fail to establish and maintain an international police force, as required by the Camp David treaty, the United States would establish and maintain an acceptable alternative force);
2. provide *insurance against violation* (e.g., Carter committed the United States to monitor the implementation of the limitation of forces arrangement); and
3. furnish *substantial side payments,* for example, Carter's pledge of $3 billion aid to Israel and $2 billion to Egypt.

The role of Algeria in 1980–1 in the U.S.–Iran confrontation regarding the U.S. hostages in Iran also forcefully illustrates the application of several of the principles of mediation listed in Table 10.5. At the start and constantly thereafter, the Algerian mediators had to help the United States to perceive correctly the ideological requirements of the Iranian revolutionaries, to appreciate the factors motivating their behavior, and the like – an application of the principle of *participant understanding enhancement.* At the same time, when the United States was making proposals, these mediators subjected these proposals to careful scrutiny and a stream of questions forcing the United States to present more specific and deeper analyses (reasoning) for its positions and to address more positively certain key points of the Iranians – an application of the principle of *encouragement of analyses by participants.* Also, in the final stage, the Algerian mediators set forth a "declaration" by the government of Algeria, incorporating the points of agreement between the two countries and presumably representing a reasonable solution to the problem – an application of the *test for fairness and stability* principle. Sick (1985, p. 50) concludes:

> The Algerian team was everything one could hope mediators to be: discreet, intelligent, perceptive, persistent, skeptical and inexhaustible. Their careful questioning of the successive U.S. position papers consistently improved and sharpened them. The team was skillful at presenting unpalatable messages to either side when necessary, and with very few exceptions, their judgements proved accurate. When it was necessary to push, they pushed; when discretion called for them to hold back, they showed restraint. In the end they succeeded in improving their stature with both parties.

We can note uses of a number of other principles of mediation. Kosygin's mediation effort in the Indo–Pakistan conflict cited previously clearly involved strict conformance to the principle of *impartiality establishment and maintenance* and the use of the principles of *minimal aim* and *compromise constraints* (in the settlement of minor issues and tactful wording of statements) in order to achieve the reestablishment territorially of the status quo ante in Indo–Pakistan relations. The recommendations of Roger Fisher (1987), an internationally recognized expert on negotiations in what some might consider to be an informally "invited/ assumed" role of mediator in the current (1987) South African conflict, point up the need to apply the principles of *tread lightly in early rounds, tension releasing,* and *encouragement of inventiveness.* Finally, we might mention that in the Lancaster House conference on Rhodesia (1979) Lord Carrington proceeded to divide into three steps the task of settling the three basic issues – namely, those concerned with the draft of a constitution for Zimbabwe, the transitional measures, and the cease-fire – and cumulatively built up vested interests in a final settlement as incremental agreements were reached; his work was an application of the principle of *exploitation of fractionation/logrolling/side payments potentialities* (Zartman 1986).

10.7 Construction and illustration of qualitative conflict management procedures

10.7.1 The construction problem

Given the preceding partial summary of principles of negotiation and mediation, we now proceed to the basic question: How can one use them fruitfully in a conflict? That is, how can one decide on a set of mutually compatible (noncontradictory) principles that can be used in seeking a mutually agreed upon or imposed resolution (partial or complete) of a conflict, each such set being, by our definition in section 10.2, a qualitative conflict management procedure? Again, this question must be answered by any participant who must confront this question. A negotiator may pursue a fixed set of principles out of pure habit, and these principles may be partially contradictory; and he or she may or may not be aware of such. Or the negotiator may be more sophisticated and have in fact the intention to behave in a way consistent with a subset of principles that constitutes a meaningful qualitative conflict management procedure for the given conflict situation.

A mediator may also out of pure habit pursue a fixed set of principles of mediation, again not necessarily noncontradictory; but more likely a mediator that is experienced and qualified will have in mind a subset of principles that constitutes what he or she considers to be an effective qualitative conflict management procedure for the given conflict situation. Likewise, with any other third-party intervenor.

But to repeat, the question of how to decide on a set of principles or what constitutes for a participant a meaningful and useful subset of principles is a question that a participant must decide for himself (or herself) – on the basis of his current stock of knowledge, experience, and perceptions supplemented by learning that he acquires in and out of discussion arenas. The partial summary, involving the presentation of only an incomplete listing of principles, can, however, be of use in this regard.

What if the participants adopt subsets of principles that involve inconsistencies? Suppose one negotiator's subset involves the principle of informal discussion around a round table in a secluded countryside, whereas a second negotiator's subset involves, for example, formal discussion with seating of officials ordered by rank along a long, narrow table in a formal statehouse where on-the-record discussion is governed by protocol. Such an inconsistency may be viewed as a subconflict within the primary conflict, and when it arises before face-to-face interaction takes place, it needs to be resolved – just as with a possible subconflict over key characteristics.[8]

10.7.2 Illustrations of qualitative conflict management procedures

Although we cannot indicate specifically how a negotiator, mediator, or other third party goes about constructing a qualitative conflict management procedure, we can illustrate such procedures that have been described elsewhere and set forth as useful. One such is that of Burton (1969, 1972) as perceived in Isard and Smith (1982), which we now present as a subset of principles that a mediator should follow. In the *preparation and analysis phase* he or she should engage in

(i)   activity to enhance his or her understanding;
(ii)   activity to enhance participant understanding;
(iii) activity to attain monolithicity; and
(iv)   activity to set ground rules (agenda) for interaction.

In the *interaction phase* the mediator should

(i)   tread lightly in early rounds;
(ii)   adopt when necessary tension releasing activities;
(iii) establish and maintain impartiality;
(iv)   recognize constraints on compromises; and
(v)   encourage analysis by participants.

The manner in which these principles are put together in the Burton procedure involves four steps:

1. extension of the number of commodities (commodity space) to include noneconomic goods;
2. recognition that welfare (outcomes) is dependent on the extended set of commodities;
3. recognition that welfare (outcomes) to participants is interdependent; and
4. reassessment of the costs and benefits of alternative joint actions.

As noted in Isard and Smith (1982, pp. 337–8), it is Burton's contention that once these four steps have been taken, the participants will automatically be able to resolve the conflict. This is so because the conflict has been transformed from a "problem" into a "puzzle." The puzzle has

---

[8] When two unsophisticated negotiators have fixed, preset principles that are inconsistent, little if any progress in reaching an agreement may be possible without third-party intervention.

the characteristic that whereas a specific solution may not be automatically identifiable or apparent, it is known that there is a solution and that the application of one or more of the existing quantitative conflict management procedures is adequate for finding this solution. Some of the potentially useful quantitative conflict management procedures will be identified in section 10.8.

Another qualitative conflict management procedure is Fisher's brainstorming session wherein negotiators with one or more third-party intervenors interact. Among others, it involves the following subset of elements:

(i) activities to enhance participants' understanding;
(ii) assessment of third-party intervention;
(iii) approximate calculations of costs and benefits in balance sheet format;[9] and
(iv) activities to enhance implementability.

For a more detailed outline of the actual steps involved in effecting the procedure, see Isard and Smith (1982, p. 359).

Although Fisher suggests a number of quantitative-type tools (parts of quantitative conflict management procedures) for use in these sessions, it may be that none of these tools is used. For example, if the first proposal for resolution that is put forth turns out to be a "yesable" proposition as per Fisher (i.e., acceptable by both parties), then the brainstorming session is over. The conflict is successfully coped with upon implementation of this yesable proposition.

A third qualitative conflict management procedure that also adopts a workshop-type interaction atmosphere for resolving conflict is that of Kelman (1978, 1979). Kelman's approach incorporates diverse principles in a rather complete and flexible manner (see Isard and Smith 1982, pp. 339–43). Kelman's chief contribution centers around the ensuring of political viability (actual implementation of and/or compliance with

---

[9] Fisher's balance sheet format essentially involves posing a potential compromise solution as a question requiring the response yes by all parties if it is to be adopted. An accounting-type balance sheet is constructed for each party with the left-hand side heading "if yes" and the right-hand side heading "if no." Under the if-yes column a party lists first the benefits to be derived from adoption of the proposed compromise and second the costs, where the outputs of the world system and other models could be relevant here. Under the if-no column, a party lists first the costs to be derived from rejection of the proposed compromise and second the benefits. Once a party fills in this table he (or she) then views it in its entirety and comes up with an overall assessment as to whether the proposed compromise is on balance a yesable proposition for him. If each party finds it a yesable proposition, then the proposed compromise represents a solution. If some party does not find the proposed compromise a yesable proposition, then a second proposal must be set forth and new tables filled in.

workshop-identified solutions). Principles listed in Tables 10.4 and 10.5 as relevant in the several phases of the negotiation/mediation figure in Kelman's workshops and all principles identified in each phase can potentially be of use.

10.8   Quantitative conflict management procedures: selection of a best or workable one

Although it may well be that the effective use of a qualitative conflict management procedure by negotiators or by a mediator may *not* require the employment of a quantitative conflict management procedure – as may be the case with Fisher's brainstorming procedure – often this will not be so. Often a quantitative conflict management procedure will be needed with or without the use of tools and models to develop necessary data on outcomes. For example, the participants may be convinced by Burton that important universal values are at stake. Still in the international scene, they may need to solve a problem (Burton's puzzle), perhaps how to allocate the fishing rights in a given ocean area, or how to determine the relative amounts of funds for the control of terrorism, or by what percentages stocks of different weapons are to be reduced. Hence there arises the question: What quantitative procedures are available for use and how can we select one or more for application?

To begin to answer this question, we might present a partial listing of such procedures. But before we do so, it is desirable to consider possible properties of quantitative conflict management procedures so as to obtain insight on how to put together properties in a consistent way to design an effective quantitative CMP, or how to find among the existing quantitative CMPs one that is applicable or conceivably best, in terms of their properties for a given conflict situation and the set of negotiation principles adopted and followed by participants. Hence in Table 10.7 we list desirable properties of quantitative CMPs without implying that any CMP might have all or many of these properties. The listing is only tentative and is subject to significant change. The properties are recorded under the headings information requirements, structural properties, time-related properties, motivating properties, psychological properties, and solution properties. A discussion of this table and many of the listed properties is presented in Isard and Smith (1982, chap. 9).

Some time ago, the authors considered the problem of matching properties of quantitative CMPs with key characteristics of conflict situations where we constructed and discussed for possible use an index of inadequacy (or adequacy) (Isard and Smith 1982, chap. 9).

However, at that time the authors did not set forth a procedure wherein the use of principles of negotiation and mediation, that is, qualitative

Table 10.7. *Selected properties of quantitative conflict management procedures*

A. Information requirements
  1. Regarding own preferences
     • ordinal, cardinal, relative
  2. Regarding others' preferences
     • full, partial, none
  3. Regarding weights and constraints
     • full, partial, none
       ⋮

B. Structural properties
  10. Number of options (alternatives) considered
     • small, large, continuous
     • single, multiple dimensions
  11. Nature of interaction
     • participatory, nonparticipatory
     • face-to-face, non–face-to-face
     • with or without third-party intervention
     • coalition formation (encouraged, discouraged)
  12. Cost
     • in initial phases (high, low, etc.)
     • in later phases (high, low, etc.)
  13. Behavior encouraged/required
     • action oriented
     • outcome oriented
     • objective achievement oriented
     • strategy oriented
  14. Statement capability
     • mathematical (or not)
     • in balance-sheet format (or not)
  15. Context for use
     • when fractionation involved
     • when logrolling involved
     • when side payments involved
       ⋮

C. Time-related properties
  20. Number of rounds (applications)
     • one, many, flexible
  21. Size of steps involved
     • small, large, flexible
  22. Interactive (feedback) effects
     • with learning by participants (or not)
     • with knowledge accumulation (or not)
     • with communication channel enhancement (or not)
     • with misperception reduction (or not)
     • with invention (creative ideas) encouragement (or not)
     • with mechanisms for preference revelation (or not)
     • with bluffing encouragement (or not)

Table 10.7. (*cont.*)

23. Nature of search processes
    - for efficient solutions
    - for satisficing solutions

    ⋮

D. Motivating properties
    30. Focus on improvement
        - guaranteed (or not)
        - overall (strong or weak)
        - on each round (strong or weak)
        - limited commitment (or not)
        - reference point (status quo, bottom line, other)
    31. Focus on concession
        - overall, on each round
        - limited commitment (or not)
        - reference point (ideal point, status quo, other)
    32. Fairness (weighted equity)
        - much, little, none
    33. Permits reformulation of conflict
        - from zero to positive sum game
        - from action to policy oriented
        - from fixed positions (or not)

    ⋮

E. Psychological properties
    40. Security preserving (or not)
    41. Confidence building (or not)
        - overall, on early rounds
    42. Trust building (or not)
        - overall, on early rounds
    43. Change-in-conflict inducing
        - reduction, escalation, none
    44. Reciprocal action induced
        - negative, positive, none
    45. Incentive to think of others (or not)
    46. Leader–follower arrangement (or not)
    47. Strategic potential recognition (or not)

    ⋮

F. Solution properties
    50. Steps involved
        - well defined (or not)
    51. Use of
        - inescapable sanctions (or not)
        - credible threats (or not)
        - veto power (or not)
    52. Preindeterminate (or not)

Table 10.7. (*cont.*)

53.	Unique (or not)
54.	Efficient (or not)
55.	Stable (or not)
56.	Uncertain, risky (or not)
57.	Probabilistic (or not)
58.	Consistent with international law (or not)
59.	Simply stated/clearly understood (or not)
60.	Implementation
	• requires new tools and mechanisms (or not)

CMPs, preceded the use of and in the current context calls for the use of a quantitative CMP. In the current case, the key characteristics of the conflict situation, as derived, modified, and refashioned (redefined) from the use of principles and qualitative CMPs, are the ones to be matched by possible properties of quantitative CMPs. Moreover, the use of principles and a qualitative CMP may have settled on a series of constraints (subagreements, subsettlements) to which a quantitative CMP must adhere if it is to find use – for example, that on one key issue the weight of one of the participants should be twice that of the other, whereas the other should always go first in putting forth a proposal on any round.

We now present in Table 10.8 a partial listing of quantitative CMPs, CMPs that are not too technical and we feel might find practical use. We do not have the space to discuss these procedures except for two to be partially discussed in what follows and the procedure discussed in section 3.3. The reader is referred to Isard and Smith (1982) for a full discussion of these procedures as well as a listing and discussion of some rather technical quantitative CMPs that some sophisticated negotiators, each accompanied by a team of experts, might find occasion for use.

To help differentiate potentially applicable procedures for use in a particular conflict situation, we ask three questions that relate to basic properties of quantitative CMPs:

1. How many actions (options, alternatives, plans, etc.) are possible – a small number or many (continuous)?
2. What kinds of information do participants have concerning their preferences? Can they only rank possible outcomes in order of

Table 10.8. *A partial listing of quantitative conflict management procedures*[a]

1. Compromise over proposed actions (outcomes)
   • in one step *or* a sequence of steps
2. *Min total of:* ranks (highest rank = 1), rank concessions, percentage concessions, percentage goal shortfalls, absolute concessions, *or* absolute goal shortfalls.
3. *Max total of:* rank improvements, percentage improvements, percentage goal achievements, absolute improvements, absolute goal achievements, *or* utility.
4. *Min the difference in:* ranks, rank improvements (concessions), percentage improvements (concessions), percentage goal achievements, absolute improvements (concessions), *or* absolute goal achievements.
5. *Max the min in:* rank improvements, percentage improvements, *or* absolute improvements.
6. *Min the max in:* rank concessions, percentage concessions, *or* absolute concessions.
7. *Max equal:* rank improvements, percentage improvements, absolute improvements, *or* goal achievements.
8. *Min equal:* rank concessions, percentage concessions, absolute concessions, *or* goal shortfalls.
9. Changing actions to "if . . . then . . . " policies.
10. Achievement of minimum requirements (satisficing)
11. Median efficient joint action
12. Concession along efficiency frontier
13. Split the difference in action space or outcome space
    • one step *or* a sequence of steps
14. Weighted average in action space or outcome space
    • one step *or* a sequence of steps
15. Alternating leader–follower
    • in action space or outcome space
16. Leadership principle
    • in action space or outcome space
17. Aggressive follower principle
    • in action space or outcome space
18. GRIT (reciprocated tension-reducing actions, a sequence of)
    • in action space or outcome space
19. Incremax (maximizing in each of a series of small improvement steps) in action space
    • with split the difference
    • with weighted average
    • with alternating leader–follower
    • with GRIT
    • with minimum information
20. Incremax in outcome space
    • with split the difference
    • with weighted average
    • with alternating leader–follower
    • with GRIT

Table 10.8. (*cont.*)

21.	Decremax (maximizing in each of a series of small concession steps) in action space
	• with split the difference
	• with weighted average
	• with alternating leader–follower
	• with GRIT
22.	Decremax in outcome space
	• with split the difference
	• with weighted average
	• with alternating leader–follower
	• with GRIT
23.	Equidistant movement in action space
	• regarding improvement
	• regarding concession
24.	Last offer arbitration (with incentive to think of others)
25.	Hierarchical programming (relaxed or not)
26.	Zeuthen concession (least to lose goes first)
27.	Method of determining group priorities (Saaty)

[a]Procedures 2–8 may or may not involve weights to be assigned to the relevant item of each participant.

preference, or can they do more by stating preferences in *relative terms* (e.g., state that outcome o_1 is valued at one-half that of outcome o_2), or can they do still more by attaching *precise values* to different outcomes (e.g., $o_1 = 50$, $o_2 = 100$, $o_3 = 125$, etc.)?

3. Are the participants concerned with *concessions* from proposed positions that differ, the position of each being that which he or she considers best (or best for the given stage of negotiations), or with *improvements* over the current state of affairs (e.g., one where each is receiving zero gains)?

There are two possible answers to the first question, three to the second question, and two to the third. Altogether, there are twelve possible combinations of answers. Hence, for each combination of answers we can list in a table those procedures that are relevant (applicable), obtaining thereby twelve additional tables. For example, in Table 10.9 we list procedures that may be relevant when the answers to the three questions are

1. a small number of options;
2. participants can *only rank* outcomes in order of preferences; and
3. participants need to focus on improvements over the current state of affairs.

Table 10.9. *Conflict management procedures when (1) there is a small number of options, (2) participants can only rank outcomes, and (3) participants focus on improvements*

2. *Min total* of ranks (highest rank = 1)[a]
3. *Max the total* of rank improvements[a]
4. *Min the difference in* ranks, rank improvements[a]
5. *Max the min* in rank improvements
7. *Max equal* rank improvements
9. Changing actions to "if . . . then . . ." policies
10. Achievement of minimum requirements (satisficing)
24. Last-offer arbitration (with incentive to think of others)
27. Method of determining group priorities (Saaty)[b]

[a]Each of these procedures may or may not involve weights to be assigned to relevant item of each participant.
[b]Isard and Smith (1982, pp. 147–55, 165–8).

The procedures listed in Table 10.9 are procedures that can be used for supplementing the Burton qualitative conflict management procedure.

The first procedure, *min total of ranks (unweighted),* is applicable because it essentially requires each participant to rank the options (alternatives), say, six in number, being considered for adoption – from 1 (most preferred) to 6 (least preferred). Then the mediator (or negotiators) identify that option as the one to be adopted for which the sum of ranks is least. Such a procedure may have considerable appeal to unsophisticated participants who have (or are willing to reveal) only a small amount of information about their preferences.

Another procedure, *max the min rank improvement,* asks each disputant to rank the diverse options including the current state of affairs, thereby to specify for each the improvement by number of ranks of each option over the current state of affairs. Then for each possible option, there will be two numbers, each indicating the number of rank improvements for one of the two participants. One number will be smaller than the other (except when they are the same). This procedure then selects for adoption that option whose smaller number is greater than the smaller number associated with any other option (assuming no ties). It may appeal to participants since it maximizes the number of rank improvements for that participant who realizes the smaller amount of rank improvement – one possible definition (philosophical criteria) of fairness.

But there are other properties noted in Table 10.7 besides those identified in our three questions that a quantitative conflict management procedure might or should possess given the conflict situation. One such property concerns whether or not the outcome from application of the procedure is *preindeterminate*. This property is desirable to help avoid conflict among participants over which procedure to employ when the outcomes of these procedures are predictable, each participant wanting that procedure to be adopted that yields him or her the best outcome. For example, procedures 24 (last offer arbitration) and 27 (method of determining group priorities) in Table 10.9 have this property of preindeterminate outcome. A second property is whether or not a procedure can work if each participant has *little or no information about the other participant's preferences* since frequently this is the case. For example, procedures 9 (changing actions to "if . . . then . . ." policies) and 10 (achievement of minimum requirements) in Table 10.9 have this property. A third property concerns the *cost of application* of the procedure. Obviously, high-cost procedures may be precluded from use when some participants are unable to incur these costs. For example, all of the rank-based procedures (2–5 and 7) in Table 10.9 are low cost.

A fourth property concerns *stability* of the solution from application of a CMP. This property may clearly be desirable for some or all participants, for why bother to adopt a solution that may only be temporary? Only one procedure in Table 10.9 (i.e., changing actions to "if . . . then . . ." policies) has this property when applied in an unconstrained manner. A fifth property concerns whether participants can be *guaranteed improvement* in terms of welfare on each round of application or at least over all rounds combined. Such a property may be essential for conservative-type participants. In Table 10.9 the following have this property: *max the total of rank improvements* (3); *min the difference in rank improvements* (4); *max equal rank improvements* (7); and *max the min in rank improvements* (5).

A sixth property concerns whether participants can hold out for a *limited commitment to change* in actions on each round of application or at least over all rounds combined. This property has obvious appeal once again to conservative-type participants. None of the procedures in Table 10.9 have this property unless appropriate constraints are applied.

A seventh property concerns whether or not application of the procedure will yield a *unique solution* since otherwise we may merely generate another conflict over which solution should be adopted. In Table 10.9 the following procedures are the only ones to have this property in all situations: last offer arbitration (24) and method of determining group priorities (27).

An eighth property concerns whether the procedure encompasses *a mechanism for building up trust* – a property that may be highly desirable in certain types of conflict situation. Only two of the procedures in Table

10.9 can be applied in such a way as to have this property, namely, changing actions to "if . . . then . . ." policies (9) and method of determining group priorities (27). A ninth property concerns whether participants are able to retain a right to reject a final solution that for some reason or other is found unacceptable. This *veto power* has obvious appeal to top dogs as well as others. Such a property could be added to all procedures listed in Table 10.9, except last offer arbitration (24). A tenth property concerns the ability of the procedure to generate a mechanism capable of *discouraging or hopefully eliminating a tendency toward bluffing,* cheating, or otherwise engaging in noncooperative actions. Only one procedure in Table 10.9 has this property, namely, last offer arbitration (24).

For further discussion of these and other properties listed in Table 10.7, see Isard and Smith (1982).

At this point, we need to make explicit the problem of trade-off among properties. That is, if none of the CMPs being considered has all of the properties desired, each having only a different subset of these properties, how should a negotiator or mediator choose among them? The answer to this question can only be made, if at all, in the light of the conflict situation being examined. To illustrate, we might have a situation where the following properties are deemed desirable: veto power, preindeterminacy, low cost, stability, guaranteed improvement, and unique solution. No procedure in Table 10.8 has all these properties. However, if participants are willing to forego veto power and guaranteed improvement, then procedure 24 (last offer arbitration) could be recommended.[10] Alternatively, if participants are willing to forego preindeterminacy and unique solution, then procedures 3–7 could be recommended.[11]

Once a quantitative CMP has been identified as relevant, it together with its qualitative CMP may be viewed as comprising a full CMP, henceforth designated simply as a CMP. If it were to be used for a given conflict situation, each such CMP would generate as a projection a set of results (data or outcomes) that then could be employed to evaluate the economic and political feasibility of that CMP. And comparisons of the results for several CMPs could permit a ranking of their desirability and ease the selection of the most appropriate CMP for the given conflict situation. Such would then end a search.

However, a further step may be taken. The projected results from the

---

[10] However, a constraint would need to be applied when using this procedure in order to achieve stability.
[11] However, constraints would need to be applied in the operation of each of these procedures in order to achieve stability and to permit veto power.

use of a CMP, which together with the CMP may be designated a *scenario,* can be inputted into a world system or other model to yield as additional data further outcomes (e.g., GNP in a nation, employment by region, and per capita income). These outcomes as data together with the data of the scenario can then be what would be tested for economic and political feasibility and soundness. Further, if there are several scenarios, each representing a different CMP (as a combination of a qualitative CMP and a quantitative CMP) to be explored for use, then the several sets of "scenario plus model-generated data" would be what would be compared in the selection of a best or superior CMP. Moreover, the outcomes of the scenarios may also be used as feedback allowing for revision of qualitative CMPs, particularly if no scenario yields an adequate or acceptable set of outcomes.

To be more specific, we may refer back to the three Leontief scenarios discussed in section 9.2. Each one of these represents a set of data that was inputted into the World Input–Output model and yielded additional information in the form of outcomes from the operation of the model. The input plus output data of each scenario then can be examined for relative desirability.

Actually, Leontief did not use any CMP in determining his three scenarios. Each represented what in his mind might be the joint action (policy) that each of the three participants might find optimal (most prefer) for the given state of affairs. In this sense each represented an extreme scenario and one that might well be regarded politically infeasible in the sense that two of the three parties would not find it acceptable. If instead a very simple CMP were to be applied using a split the difference (unweighted average) of the three Leontief scenarios in the search for a politically relevant compromise scenario, then inputting that scenario into the World I–O model would yield outcomes that as data together with the input scenario data would correspond to a set to be tested for political and economic feasibility. Further, if additional compromise scenarios based on the three individually optimal scenarios were derived using other CMPs, such as *min the max* concession on certain key dimensions or the method of determining group priorities, the resulting sets of data (each set comprising both scenario inputs and Input–Output model outputs) could be compared and perhaps all three parties might agree on which was best – or use their rankings of these sets to agree upon a compromise scenario.

In this manner, then, we might be able to investigate more thoroughly the relative desirability of different scenarios for use in managing a conflict.

10.9   Concluding remarks

We have now discussed the basic considerations in the choice of a CMP for use in a conflict situation, the considerations in this chapter utilizing the concepts, analyses, and findings of previous chapters. To reiterate, our approach in this chapter is as follows:

1. A participant should identify relevant key characteristics of a conflict situation; a partial list of characteristics that might qualify as key are presented in Tables 10.1–10.3, relating to systemic structural, nonsystemic structural, and participants' characteristics, respectively.
2. With the set of key characteristics as background, as perceived by a participant, he or she should consider a set of principles (desirably, mutually compatible) for negotiation or mediation to employ to move ahead in reaching a compromise or agreement for this situation, each such set being defined as a qualitative CMP; partial lists of principles of negotiation and mediation are presented in Tables 10.4 and 10.5, respectively.
3. If a participant's qualitative CMP is inadequate or ineffective, which will often be the case, the participant may need to supplement it with a quantitative CMP, having properties appropriate not only for the qualitative CMP but also in view of the key characteristics of the conflict situation; a selected list of properties that a quantitative CMP might possess is in Table 10.7.
4. Each quantitative CMP together with its qualitative CMP and its direct projection of results may be taken to be a scenario to be inputted into a model, thereby to generate additional information for evaluation and for selecting a best or a set of best CMPs for the conflict situation.

This chapter concludes the presentation of the less advanced conceptual materials in this book. In the next chapter we attempt an application.

References

Azar, E. E., and J. W. Burton (eds.) (1986) *International Conflict Resolution: Theory and Practice.* Sussex: Wheatsheaf Books.

Brazerman, M. H. (1983) "Negotiator Judgment." *American Behavioral Scientist* 27 (2, Nov.–Dec.):211–28.

Burton, J. W. (1969) *Conflict and Communication: The Use of Controlled Communication in International Relations.* London: Macmillan.

Burton, J. W. (1972) "Resolution and Conflict." *International Studies Quarterly* 16(1):5–30.

Carnevale, J. D. (1986b) "An Unnecessary Neologism in Two Systems of Mediation." *Negotiation Journal* 2(4):357–61.

Carnevale, P. J. D. (1986a) "Strategic Choice in Mediation." *Negotiation Journal* 2(1, Jan.):41–56.

Carpenter, S., and W. J. D. Kennedy (1985) "Managing Environmental Conflict by Applying Common Sense." *Negotiation Journal* 1(2, April):149–61.

Colosi, T. (1983) "Negotiation in the Public and Private Sectors." *American Behavioral Scientist* 27(2, Nov.–Dec.):229–53.

Fisher, R. (1978) *International Mediation: A Working Guide*. New York: International Peace Academy.

Fisher, R. (1987) "Negotiating South Africa's Future." *Negotiation Journal* 3(3, July):231–3.

Fisher, R., and W. L. Ury (1981) *Getting to Yes*. Boston: Houghton Mifflin.

Goldberg, S. B. (1986) "Meditations of a Mediator." *Negotiation Journal* 2(4):345–50.

Greenhalgh, L. (1987) "Relationships in Negotiations." *Negotiation Journal* 3(3, July):235–43.

Haynes, J. M. (1986) "Avoiding Traps Mediators Set for Themselves." *Negotiation Journal* 2(2):187–94.

Isard, W., and C. Smith (1982) *Conflict Analysis and Practical Conflict Management Procedures*. Cambridge, MA: Ballinger.

Janis, I. (1972) *Victims of Group Think*. Boston: Houghton Mifflin.

Janis, I. L., and L. Mann (1977) *Decision Making*. New York: Free Press.

Jervis, R. (1976) *Perception and Misperception in International Politics*. Princeton: Princeton University Press.

Kelman, H. C. (1972) "The Problem Solving Workshop in Conflict Resolution." In R. L. Merritt (ed.), *Communication and International Conflict*. Urbana: University of Illinois Press, pp. 168–204.

Kelman, H. C. (1978) "Israelis and Palestinians: Psychological Prerequisites for Mutual Acceptance." *International Security* 3:162–86.

Kelman, H. C. (1979) "An International Approach to Conflict Resolution and its Application to Israeli-Palestinian Relations." *International Interactions* 6(2):99–122.

Lax, D. A., and J. K. Sebenius (1985) "The Power of Alternatives or the Limits to Negotiation." *Negotiation Journal* 1(2, April):163–79.

Lax, D. A., and J. K. Sebenius (1986) "Interests: The Measure of Negotiation." *Negotiation Journal* 2(1, Jan.):73–92.

Lebow, R. N. (1981) *Between War and Peace*. Baltimore: Johns Hopkins Press.

Lindskold, S. (1978) "Trust Development, the GRIT Proposal, and the Effects of Conciliatory Acts on Conflict and Cooperation." *Psychological Bulletin* 85:772–93.

Murnigham, J. K. (1986) "The Structure of Mediation and Intravention." *Negotiation Journal* 2(4):351–6.

Osgood, C. E. (1962) *An Alternative to War or Surrender*. Urbana: University of Illinois Press.

Osgood, C. E. (1966) *Perspectives in Foreign Policy,* 2nd ed. Palo Alto, CA: Pacific Books.

Pruitt, D. G., and J. Z. Rubin (1986) *Social Conflict, Escalation, Stalemate and Settlement.* New York: Random House.

Raiffa, H. (1982) *The Art and Science of Negotiation.* Cambridge, MA: Harvard University Press.

Rubin, J. Z. (ed.) (1981) *Dynamics of Third Party Intervention: Kissinger in the Middle East.* New York: Praeger.

Rubin, J. Z. (1983) "Negotiation." *American Behavioral Scientist* 27(2, Nov.–Dec.):135–47.

Saunders, H. H. (1987) "International Relationships – It's Time to Go Beyond We and They," *Negotiation Journal* 3(3, July):245–74.

Schelling, T. C. (1960) *The Strategy of Conflict.* Cambridge, MA: Harvard University Press.

Sick, G. (1985) "The Partial Negotiator: Algeria and the U.S. Hostages in Iran." In S. Touval and I. W. Zartman (eds.), *International Mediation in Theory and Practice.* Boulder, CO: Westview.

Smith, W. P. (1985) "Effectiveness of the Biased Negotiator." *Negotiation Journal* 1(4):363–72.

Stein, J. G. (1985) "Structures, Strategies and Tactics of Mediation: Kissinger and Carter in the Middle East." *Negotiation Journal* 1(4, October):331–47.

Straus, D. B. (1986) "Collaborating to Understand – Without Being a 'Wimp'." *Negotiation Journal* 2(2, April):155–66.

Susskind, L. (1987) "Guidelines for the More Effective Use of Mediation in International Disputes." International Mediation Project Program on Negotiation, Harvard Law School, mimeo.

Thornton, T. P. (1985) "The Indo-Pakistani Conflict: Soviet Mediation at Tashkent, 1966." In S. Touval and I. W. Zartman (eds.), *International Mediation in Theory and Practice.* Boulder, CO: Westview.

Touval, S. (1985) "The Context of Mediation." *Negotiation Journal* 1(4):373–8.

Zartman, I. W. (1985) "Negotiation from Asymmetry: The North–South Stalemate." *Negotiation Journal* 1(2, April):121–38.

Zartman, I. W. (1986) "Practitioners' Theories of International Negotiation." *Negotiation Journal* 2(3):299–307.

CHAPTER 11

Potential for a specific application: the U.S.–Soviet arms control conflict problem

11.1 Introduction

Having treated (1) principles of negotiation and mediation, (2) qualitative and quantitative conflict management procedures, and (3) various aspects of conflicts in general, we now attempt a specific application of the materials covered in this book to the U.S.–Soviet conflict over the arms control problem. We choose this application since

1. many readers are familiar with elements of the U.S.–Soviet arms control problem;
2. it points up well the basic problems involved in coping with conflicts;
3. it is a problem for which the use of analytical tools and sophisticated models is appropriate; and
4. it is such a tremendously important problem that any important insights that might emerge could prove valuable to its future management.

In what we present we do not in any way wish to imply that we have any solution to the problem or an effective approach to the problem. The problem is too complicated and ill-defined for us as outside observers. However, we should recognize that this is in all likelihood so for those negotiators and other government officials who are currently enmeshed in it from both the U.S. and Soviet perspectives. Clearly, a new combined qualitative–quantitative conflict management procedure (CMP) must be tailored (invented) for use on this problem if it is to be managed effectively.

Whereas as this book goes to press a successful initial step in coping with this problem has been achieved by the signing of the INF treaty, it

381

should be borne in mind that this treaty pertains to the elimination of only a very small fraction of the nuclear arsenal, and one of the least important components of that arsenal from the standpoint of U.S. security. The difficult questions relate to control (and reduction) of the stockpile of strategic long-range intercontinental missiles and the ongoing Reagan SDI development that generates escalation – very difficult questions even optimistically assuming the continuance of the much improved psychological background for negotiations currently (mid-1988) existing.

Perhaps the subsequent analysis – which is based largely on the author's extensive reading, experiences, and discussions with knowledgeable scholars and practitioners – can provide one or more valuable insights regarding the essential features of a new CMP.

11.2   Key characteristics of the U.S.–Soviet conflict

In line with the procedure presented in the previous chapter, we now wish to set down key characteristics of the U.S.–Soviet arms control conflict situation. Clearly, among scholars there will be a number of differences as to what these key characteristics are, let alone the complete set of relevant characteristics. However, from observing the conflict as well as reading and critically evaluating much of the accumulated writing and hence knowledge and information relating to the conflict, we judge the following to be key:[1]

1. need for security (both military and economic),
2. high degree of uncertainty,
3. limited or zero reliance on third-party intervention,
4. solutions sought via individualistic action subject to group approval,
5. calculating approach to problem solving,
6. availability of powerful, large-scale models,
7. ability to only rank actions in terms of desirability (ordinal preference structure),
8. fractionation of issues/logrolling possibilities, and
9. need to allow for a high degree of conservativeness.

Others may also be considered key, for example, (1) concern with effects upon and relationships with the "rest of the world" and specific theaters such as the Middle East, and (2) the basic cultural, alliance, and other

[1] These characteristics are associated, respectively, with the following listed in Tables 10.1–10.3: I.4 in Table 10.1, VIII.170 in Table 10.2, II.111 in Table 10.2, II.11 in Table 10.1, II.12 in Table 10.1, VIII.173 in Table 10.2, VII.280 in Table 10.3, VII.160 in Table 10.2, and I.200 in Table 10.3.

asymmetries existing between the Soviet Union and the United States. However, we choose to focus upon the preceding nine items. In what follows we shall elaborate on each of these and discuss the corresponding property of a CMP that is required or highly desirable for that CMP to be effective.

11.3   Key aspects and properties of a CMP for the U.S.–Soviet conflict

It is helpful first to present an overview of some basic points to be discussed in this section. We do so in Table 11.1 wherein we also relate these points to current (1986–7) arms control negotiations. However, this table does not cover complementary aspects of a desirable CMP as discussed in sections 11.3.7 and 11.3.8 and other basic aspects to which a CMP should be sensitive, as discussed in section 11.4.

11.3.1   Security, uncertainty, and restricted veto power

History has bequeathed us with a world containing two big-power nations, each having a set of lesser power nations as allies. Between these two powers there exists much distrust, hostility, grievance, and great differences in political system and ideology. Their leaders and social groups, each with their pet theories and interpretive packages, possess an abundance of misperceptions and misunderstandings and are subject to major decision-making pathologies and highly emotional outbursts and panic-type behavior. We need not go into detail on these aspects, which are well known. At the same time we do possess a stock of analyzable data[2] (however inadequate and misleading), a stock of knowledge, and a stock of productive plant and equipment, all of which can be profitably exploited in the analysis of the current arms control problem.

   Take a first indisputable key characteristic, the need for security. This is a common need that has evolved over the centuries from the competitive urge characterizing social and economic development. An absolute imperative for any conflict management procedure that might be proposed is to ensure that the security of neither of the two parties will be undermined in the solution proposed by the CMP. This need exists

---

[2] For example, see the highly relevant data sets developed by David J. Singer and his associates on the Correlates of War Project (see footnote 6 in Chapter 8) and by others such as Russett et al. (1964), Taylor and Jodice (1983), Merritt and Zinnes (forthcoming), as well as the more restricted subsets of data in the numerous articles in journals such as the *American Political Science Review* and the *Journal of Conflict Resolution* and in such books as Russett (1972) on peace, war, and numbers.

Table 11.1. *Properties of a conflict management procedure for U.S.–Soviet arms control conflict*

Property	Brief statement of rationale	Present in current negotiations?
1. Veto power (restricted when and if desirable)	1. To ensure each party's security	1. Yes
2. Limited reliance on third-party intervention	2. To preserve secrecy on one's own weaponry and internal problems (dissension)	2. Yes
3. Use of models to generate essential economic information	3. To facilitate attainment of concensus (monolithicity) among diverse interest groups in each nation	3. No. If available models have been used at all, they have not nearly been fully exploited. All evidence is that they are not being currently used by U.S. except in a very minor way.
4. Issue fractionation and logrolling for guaranteed improvement	4. To achieve tit-for-tat concessions to effect improvement in security and social welfare	4. Yes
5. Limited commitment on each of a series of steps	5. To recognize conservative nature of one or more of parties and their need to be "sure" about security and welfare improvement on each step	5. Yes
6. Balance-sheet and issue-complex analysis	6. To achieve tit-for-tat concessions on sets of diverse issues to guarantee improvement when step 4 has been exhausted	6. No, except perhaps in a very limited way. The attainment of this property requires a full extensive use of models noted in property 3.
7. Others to be suggested by scholars and further Peace Science research		7. No, since these properties are yet to be designed or invented.

within a world of great uncertainty – not only that associated with normal political and economic development but also that associated with technology and, most unsettling, technological advance in weaponry. Clearly this need must be effectively addressed by any new scenario and conflict management procedure that one might set forth.

Security, however, is a nebulous, complex concept. It has thus far defied any quantitative definition by social scientists. There exists no measure of security that might parallel the concept of GNP as a measure of economic performance or welfare. There is the public's notion and perception of security, that of the incumbent political party, the legislature (Congress), the National Security Council or like body, the trusted associates (Kitchen Cabinet) of the top political leader (the president), the top political leader, and other influential individual groups. Often, in matters of security the focus of certain individuals and groups is on the kinds and significance (weight) of current vulnerabilities of a nation and its adversaries; and the measure of any change in security is directly related to changes in these presumably "more measurable" vulnerabilities. In any case, the diversity of security concepts, often a hodgepodge, within the United States and the existing set within the Soviet Union almost necessarily dictate for any effective CMP the veto power as a property to guarantee at least the current level of security. (We fully recognize that at any point of time the security question may be of a different importance at different places in such a structure, and that such may vary with time.) Possibly, the veto power can be a restricted one – restricted perhaps in the number of times that it can be used, the issues on which it might apply, and even more important the timing of its exercise. In connection with the last restriction, it might be desirable to require that a veto power be exercisable only after there has been extensive discussion (perhaps in a workshop) and effort at mediation on a particular issue.

Also, monitoring and inspection, to be discussed in what follows, is intimately involved with security maintenance.

11.3.2 Limited or zero reliance on third-party intervention

Given the current differences between these two powers, as well as precedence and the dominating concern for immediate security, one cannot expect both nations to be able or willing to agree on an overall impartial third party (mediator) to serve in a general capacity. Further, there is currently too much need for secrecy in the minds of the two nations' leaders. Hence, any CMP that we may propose must be able to function without a third-party intervenor. However, we may expect that on specific and/

or technical issues and perhaps in setting parts of the agenda experts may be brought in. Moreover, each disputant may be expected to brainstorm or otherwise seek the advice of their own "most preferred" conflict analysts at stalemates and other critical points in the negotiations. Hence the principles of mediation listed in Table 10.5, while generally not applicable to the primary conflict, may be used to some extent by conflict analysts when their advice is sought on specific issues. Also, when negotiators assume (often in a covert way) the role of a third party, they may use subsets of these principles of mediation. Finally, the involvement of a third party may be suggested (urged) at certain points, not for any active participation nor to provide advice and ideas to be studied, but rather to be the party upon whom to foist responsibility should the participants fail to reach agreement. Such may encourage participants to be more inventive and bold in their negotiations.

11.3.3 Economic security maintenance and the use of models to generate essential economic information

In the preceding discussion of security we have in mind the traditional notion associated with the prevention of physical violence and political and other forced change that is often occasioned when one nation is conquered by another in a war. But frequently scholars, political leaders, and others speak of other types of security, in particular job and other elements of economic security, security from violation of human rights, and so forth. We feel that any new, effective CMP for the U.S.–Soviet arms control conflict must effectively address the question of economic security, which in effect imposes constraints on the kind of CMP that may be devised as well as the operation of any CMP that might be considered for use. Although many analysts may relegate questions of economic security to the later stages in the U.S.–Soviet negotiations, we judge that such should be considered early on, both in negotiations and in the development of a new CMP. This is so because of the nonmonolithic character of the U.S. political system. (Because of our lack of knowledge and understanding of the Soviet culture and political system comprising diverse nationalities and ethnic groups, we confine the discussion here and often later to the U.S. culture and political system and often our suggestions relate primarily to it.) In the United States, there exists a two-party political system and a legislative body (Congress) that alone has the authority to ratify treaties and similar agreements. This legislative body represents many geographic constituencies within the nation. And any representative is under considerable pressure to oppose any conflict settlement that would lead to a reduction of jobs in the area he or she serves, even when the forces for bipartisanship are strong. Hence, the impacts on diverse areas of any major change in the level and/or composition of military expenditures that would result from the implementation of a new CMP that the United States and Soviet Union might contemplate must be squarely confronted early on and not deferred to discussion at the close of negotiations. Hence, a third basic property of any new CMP should be an ability to use economic models ranging from simple input–output analyses to complex analysis through the use of the much more sophisticated integrated multiregion models in the process of development. Such use would need to identify not only the impact on jobs but also offset programs and other activities required to effect a smooth transition of local economies from military production to civilian activities, often designated the conversion problem.

Also, the early use of models for examining implications of different possible agreements and different steps in these agreements can be extremely fruitful in dispelling much economic uncertainty political leaders have regarding the future states of the economy, thereby to facilitate their taking such steps when economically desirable as well as otherwise.

Let us be more concrete about the use of models. These models are designed to generate data for wise decision making and in our particular case data relating to the political–economic feasibility of each step (round or stage) of negotiations – in terms of both the objectives (goals, criteria, or the like) of the negotiators and the making of sound and political arguments (as discussed in Chapter 8) for taking each step. Having in mind the discussion in Chapter 2 on economic factors considered important by diverse arms race modelers, we must examine the implications of different scenarios with models, where each scenario represents the economic dimensions of a particular relevant step regarding the level/composition of military expenditures. The types of implication to be identified include the impact on

1. employment in each local area (perhaps via a simple regional input–output or econometric model or a sophisticated integrated multiregion model) having in mind possible and likely offset programs and conversion capability, and an acceptable upper bound on unemployment – also thereby identifying and thus being able to defuse beforehand some of the intense opposition by congressional leaders whose constituencies might be adversely affected;
2. the federal government budget deficit (via a national econometric model);

3. interest rates and inflation on the one hand and recession and deflationary tendencies on the other (via diverse models oriented to monetary and fiscal policy analysis);
4. exports, imports, and balance of payments (via world system models such as LINK and GLOBUS and trade matrix projection methods discussed in Chapter 9), with particular reference to any changed competitive position in world markets; and
5. resource costs and GNP growth rates.

Implications for these variables and many more have already been examined for reductions in military spending during the early 1970s in an outstanding comprehensive report sponsored by the U.S. Arms Control and Disarmament Agency (Udis 1970). Such can easily be updated on a continuing basis and extended for constant use for arms control and other problems. [Also see Isard and Schooler (1964) and Isard and Langford (1969) for older literature on offset program analysis.]

In connection with the last item, recall the economic exhaustion-warfare type of analysis presented in Chapter 2. Following the Reykjavik, Iceland, meeting of Gorbachev and Reagan (October 1986), there was much exchange of views on the drain of mounting military expenditures upon the Soviet economy. Some scholars pointed to the possibility that once real consumption per capita was reduced to minimal levels in the Soviet economy, further increases in military expenditures would be at the expense of new investment in productive facilities. Ultimately such could lead to negative net investment (failure to maintain current productive capacity because of insufficient replacement) and thus to an inadequate defense (let alone attack) capability in the future. Alternatively, falling real consumption levels or insufficient increases could lead to uncontrollable internal unrest.

On the more positive side, the data generated by models may point up in concrete ways how decreases in military expenditures and associated offset programs can stimulate very desirable developments, particularly in the Soviet Union where there is a crying need for many highly productive internal developments (infrastructure investments) at many localities. Such provision of data on local and regional development potentials (whether for new Siberian regions or old Ukranian industrial areas or urban redevelopment in the United States) may be quite significant for building up political support for the negotiating political leaders but more significant for facilitating the reaching of agreement on one or more steps given the nonmonolithic structures of both the Soviet and U.S. systems. Indirectly, too, focus on such positive implications tends to counter distrust, hostility, grievance, and other negative-type elements in the conflict.

In brief, the use of models can be extremely valuable in testing for economic and political feasibility of each relevant scenario (which can represent a simple step at one extreme or a complex combined qualitative-quantitative CMP at the other[3]). Each scenario together with a model's output could provide the data and much of the basis for a political argument whether or not the data became available for use by diverse communication groups (newspapers, radio, television, etc.). In addition, comparison of the implications of diverse scenarios that might be inputted into the models provides not only more effective grounds for selecting an appropriate policy (joint action) as noted in Chapter 8, but also can provide the basis for a sound and effective political argument for discarding (eliminating) certain joint actions as undesirable and bad, particularly those that might be set forth by highly charismatic–emotional-type leaders.

11.3.4 Issue fractionation and logrolling for guaranteed improvement

A fourth desirable property of any new CMP is that of guaranteed improvement. The discussion in the previous paragraph has already suggested possibilities for major improvement in the economies (local, regional, and national) of both nations following appropriately formulated disarmament initiatives. More important, however, may be the need to guarantee improvement in terms of "military security." Here, however, we must recognize analytical difficulties because of our inability to quantify such security or key aspects of it. Nonetheless, significant steps can be taken.

In our U.S.-Soviet case, we can expect that the political leaders of each nation have in mind a ranking of diverse weapon portfolios. (A portfolio is defined to be a unique combination of weapons and weapon systems.) The ranking would be in terms of desirability from the standpoint of national security (avoidance of vulnerabilities) and other considerations, one being the relation of a given portfolio to the currently perceived and/or expected portfolios of its opponent. (In economics terminology, the leader may have in mind, most likely unawaringly, a set of indifference curves reflecting his or her judgment concerning the ordinal preference

---

[3] Note that when a CMP calls for a sequence of steps, as in sequential split the difference, it needs to have that kind of flexibility that allows changes in the payoff matrix to be associated with the outputs generated by a model at each step.

structure of the society.)[4] Although theoretically we could imagine that in their negotiations the leaders might consider the use of a veto incremax or decremax procedure to guarantee improvement in their welfare and/ or security, in practice such cannot be realistically expected. This is so because to guarantee that one's proposal is not at the expense of the welfare and/or security of one's opponent (in order for it to be acceptable by the opponent), one would need in this CMP to have some "true information" about the rankings (preferences) of the opponent (except for a special case to be discussed). We cannot expect an opponent to provide such information, that is, to refrain from bluffing that might be to his or her advantage. Hence, we must search for another way for a CMP to guarantee improvement for each party on each round of negotiations (and expected implementation) that might be undertaken.[5]

One possible way employs a step in a CMP that requires a search for issues on which logrolling or an adaptation of it may be pursued – a step that exploits the fractionation principle. In its most effective form, logrolling involves the simultaneous adoption of (a) an action highly desired by (optimal for) one party on an issue that is extremely important for it but of very little, if any, importance to the second party, and (b) an action highly desired by the second party on a second issue extremely important for it but of negligible significance, if any, to the first party. With regard to the U.S.–Soviet conflict problem, some preliminary thinking on the 1987 Reagan–Gorbachev Washington summit suggested that the Soviets might yield significantly on the human rights issue (an issue that appears to be of great significance to the United States and of much less import to the Soviets) in return for relaxation of the restrictions that the United States imposes on trade with the Soviets (an issue considered to be of major significance to the Soviets and of much less import to the United States).[6]

Although we suggest an early exploration of logrolling possibilities in one or more rounds in a CMP for our U.S.–Soviet conflict – and here a CMP may suggest the use of a third party to help identify issues on which logrolling should be considered for use [i.e., issues of equivalent values (importance)] – we may find at a particular point in the negotiations that

[4] Actually, he or she may attach relative and even more precise values to this ranking, but we cannot expect each leader to possess, implicitly or explicitly, a preference structure providing more information than an ordinal one.
[5] These considerations imply that CMPs in categories 16, 17, 19–22, and 25 in Table 10.8 are not applicable to the U.S.–Soviet arms control conflict problem.
[6] Suppose the conflict situation is such that one party's indifference curves (implicit or explicit) approach a set of straight lines with almost zero slope and a second party's approach a set of straight lines with very large slope. In such a situation, it is possible to apply in a logrolling-type manner a veto incremax procedure when each leader possesses only limited information about his or her rival's rankings (ordinal preferences).

simultaneous consideration of two issues may not be possible. In such an eventuality, the CMP should suggest that the leaders, with or without the help of a third party, reorder the issues on the agenda such that an alternating leader–follower arrangement can be effected, particularly when logrolling or an adaptation of it may be possible on more than one occasion. A toss of a coin or other device may be used to determine who should be leader on the first logrolling round.

11.3.5 The need for limited commitment

Logrolling may be possible without the need for limited commitment. The reports on the Reykjavik meeting, for example, suggest that limited commitment was not a prerequisite for effective negotiations. However, it is also clear from reports on previous meetings among Soviet and U.S. delegates that the conservative attitude of the U.S. leadership dictated negotiations through a series of small steps involving careful and well-detailed monitoring and inspection of joint actions regarding weapons production and dismantling. Hence an effective CMP for the U.S.–Soviet conflict must allow for this requirement (constraint) on each round of negotiations.

It should be noted that when the issues pertain to aggregates or large magnitudes such as military expenditures, size of army (in terms of personnel), or number of tanks, which are capable of being treated approximately as continuous variables, there is no problem in defining limited commitment, either absolutely or percentagewise. However, when an issue concerns items that are few in number and where units are complex and sophisticated entities composed of many finely articulated elements, there can be serious difficulties in specifying limited commitment.

11.3.6 Balance-sheet and "issue-complex" analysis

Suppose that it were to turn out that logrolling (fractionation) of the conflict on two specific issues, with or without limited commitment, has proceeded (if at all) as far as it can, and a stalemate on further negotiations has been reached. At such a point, a CMP might then suggest the use of a modified Fisher balance-sheet approach.[7]

A modified Fisher balance-sheet approach essentially relies on specifying for each party a plus (an advantage or gain), a minus (a disadvantage or loss), or a zero (no advantage or disadvantage) for each important or relevant item of a proposed joint action. Such a joint action might

---

[7] For a brief description of this approach, see footnote 9, Chapter 10.

involve, of course, offers, promises, demands, threats, and the like. By using these symbols (or a more elaborate set such as "$++$," "$+++$," "$--$," and "$---$" to depict a finer representation of gains and losses), the Fisher balance sheet can be geared to trade off analysis where not all considerations can be set down in a precise, quantitative manner. In particular, this approach can be very effective in identifying possible trade-offs between the two parties on sets of issues (issue complexes). One set (issue complex) may be more important to one party than a second set, whereas the reverse might hold for the second set. Thus an effective CMP should dictate a search for such sets and the use of the Fisher approach if such sets are identified.[8]

For example, at Reykjavik one might argue that there was some attempt at logrolling on issue complexes, with Fisher balance-sheet analysis at least implicitly undertaken by each party. At least this would appear to be so to an outsider not present at the meetings who had access to accounts published by those present (Adelman 1986; Petrovsky 1986) and the numerous statements and interpretations appearing in the media. On the issue regarding the number of years before any Strategic Defense Initiative (SDI) deployment, the United States was willing to yield, accepting an increase in this number from $7\frac{1}{2}$ to 10. This was a small give (a minus) for the United States since there was little confidence in the U.S. scientific community that the United States would be ready for any such deployment by year $7\frac{1}{2}$. In contrast, such was a major gain (a major plus) for the Soviet Union since it would give the Soviets another $2\frac{1}{2}$ years to catch up to U.S. technology. On the other hand, the willingness of the Soviets regarding medium-range missiles to return to the original U.S. option of completely eliminating U.S. and Soviet missiles in Europe, *leaving aside the French and British nuclear capabilities,* represented a major step forward on a second issue of presumably great importance (a major plus) to the United States but presumably of much less importance to the Soviets as a concession (a minus) because of the major advantage it has regarding conventional weapons in Europe. The willingness to consider confining the Soviet warheads and intermediate-range nuclear forces to 100 in Asia (where in 1986 they had over 500) with a right for the United States to have 100 warheads in its continental area in an almost total disarmament package was another issue (a third one) of perhaps greater relevance to the Soviets (and would appear to be a "plus" for the Soviets) while of little significance to the United States. All the preceding was coupled with the willingness of both sides in two five-year

[8] In one sense, such implies a search for indifference curves over possible issue complexes wherein a combination of limited commitment and guaranteed improvement, with perhaps the imposition of additional constraints, is achievable in an involved incremax manner.

periods to eliminate all strategic nuclear arms – bombers, air-launched cruise missiles, intercontinental ballistic missiles, submarine-launched ballistic missiles and the weapons they carry (Adelman 1986, p. 4) – what would appear to be for both sides a combination on net of major plusses – provided in the eyes of the Soviet Union the United States would have agreed to confine all SDI research and testing to the laboratory.

Undoubtedly this assessment of the trade-off on the preceding issues that was almost reached is incorrect in one or more aspects and, more seriously, oversimplifies the highly involved character of the negotiations. Nevertheless, this particular experience at negotiations where each party in a partial way had defined for itself that issue complex of major significance to it helps illustrate the process of logrolling on issue complexes. A full discussion of the formation and structure of issue complexes is beyond the scope of this chapter.[9]

11.3.7   Other useful aspects

When the Fisher balance-sheet approach has been applied as fully as possible (if at all), there are other procedural elements that might be attempted on different issues and at different points in the negotiations process.

On certain issues, particularly when they are small and when parties can only think of improvements and concessions in terms of ranking the desirability of joint actions, an effective CMP should permit (encourage) the use of

1.   the principle of min the difference in rank improvements or concessions,
2.   the principle of max the min in rank improvements,
3.   the principle of min the max in rank concessions,

or any of the other principles associated with the first eight categories of CMPs listed in Table 10.8. Even at times, equidistant movement in action space, last-offer arbitration, and method of determining group priorities (categories 23, 24, and 27 in Table 10.8) might be used on specific issues and so should be allowable in an effective CMP. For example, at Reykjavik the willingness of the parties to settle upon a ten-year postponement before any deployment of SDI – a $33\frac{1}{3}$ percent increase from $7\frac{1}{2}$ to 10 by Reagan and a $33\frac{1}{3}$ percent decrease from the lower limit of 15 to 10 by Gorbachev – can be viewed as an instance of "equidistant move-

---

[9] An issue complex has certain similarities to an industrial complex, an urban complex, and an activity–industrial complex. For a discussion of these, see respectively, Isard, Schooler, and Vietorisz (1959), Isard et al. (1960), and Isard (1974).

ment in action space," although as already indicated, these one-third percentage changes were probably not of equal significance.[10] See Isard and Smith (1982) for further discussion of these principles. Always, as already noted, an effective CMP should permit and encourage unilateral concessions and reward actions – the basic force in the use of GRIT (reciprocated tension-reducing actions), category 18 of Table 10.8.[11]

11.3.8   Use of the time exploitation principle

A very last step in a CMP for the U.S.–Soviet conflict would fall back upon the principle of time exploitation. This might occur after brainstorming in the Fisher manner has failed to break the impasse when negotiations have bogged down. There are very likely to be issues over which differences cannot be resolved at this stage. Some are too emotional and must allow for time during which the participants can "cool down" – and perhaps gain further understanding of their own and their opponent's perception of those issues. Other issues strike at basic cultural differences that may never be resolvable and therefore should be put on a back burner (i.e., shelved), perhaps never to be removed from that burner.

Another basis for the use of this principle recognizes the great amount of uncertainty that exists about all kinds of objects and relations at given points of time, in particular, the nature and effectiveness of weapon systems currently existing, being constructed, and likely to be produced in the future. Here, compromise and decisions may be achieved not on a joint action to be taken now, but on a joint action to be taken in the future with respect to each state of the environment and in particular each state of weapon technology that might be realized – in one sense contingency planning.

11.4   Other basic aspects to which a CMP should be sensitive

11.4.1   Monitoring and inspection

Although we have not specifically dealt with monitoring and inspection in this chapter, it is obviously a key issue that must be addressed con-

---

[10] See Adelman (1986) and Petrovsky (1986). However, Adelman suggests that the Soviet Union did not make it explicit that at the end of ten years either side could be free to deploy its strategic defence system (p. 7). That is, perhaps only some acceptance of deployment was in the minds of the Soviets.
[11] Note that the principles involving: (a) changing actions to "if . . . then . . ." policies, (b) achievement of minimum requirements (satisficing), (c) split the difference in action or outcome space, (d) weighted average in action or outcome space, and (e) alternating leader–follower (associated with categories 9, 10, and 13–15 of Table 10.8) have already been suggested for use in one way or another in the previous discussion in the text.

stantly. This issue clearly calls for advice by technical experts on both sides and is beyond the competence of social scientists per se. Thus, it is not discussed in this chapter. However, it must be in the forefront in the discussions in each of the preceding sections on the use of the veto power (section 11.3.1); the limited, if any, reliance on third-party intervention (11.3.2); the use of models in setting relevant constraints and to generate essential economic information (11.3.3); issue fractionation and log rolling for guaranteed improvement (11.3.4); the need for limited commitment (11.3.5); balance-sheet analysis (11.3.6); other useful aspects (11.3.7); and the use of the time exploitation principle (11.3.8).

Monitoring and inspection is not a simple task, the very concept of such being extremely elusive. It touches upon the use of classified information; the activities of the Central Intelligence Agency (CIA), the KGB, and other governmental agencies; trade policy; and numerous other elements. Most relate to secrecy; and even though there has been much discussion about the desirability of encouraging trade and information exchange to lead the United States and Soviet Union to possess portfolios of weapon systems that are more alike, thereby reducing uncertainty as to the capability of each other's weaponry, it is inconceivable in the minds of the parties that secrecy will not be sought by one's opponent and will not come to exist in one form or another. Thus the issue of monitoring and inspection must be squarely confronted and dealt with in as best a way as possible by any effective CMP. We note that the current (mid-1988) implementation of the INF treaty represents a significant step forward in dealing with this issue, but monitoring and inspection regarding intercontinental missiles and on-going SDI-type developments can be exceedingly much more difficult.

11.4.2 Understanding enhancement and knowledge accumulation

Consistent with the discussion of principles of negotiation, the application of any effective CMP for the U.S.–Soviet conflict should be accompanied by continuous efforts at understanding enhancement and knowledge accumulation. Such might take place at times in preworkshops, workshops, seminars, brainstorming sessions, and the like, often involving face-to-face interaction of the negotiators but at other times indirect interaction via third parties. There should be constant attempts at improving communications, developing common language, focusing on universal values and goals (such as the desire to decrease, if not eliminate, the probability of an all-out nuclear war), enlarging perspectives, correcting misperceptions and misunderstandings, and exposing misrepresentations and decision-making pathologies. Concomitantly, there should be efforts:

1. to reduce excessive emotional involvements (and perhaps defer highly emotional issues) and avoid undue reliance on precedents;
2. to eliminate fixed positions and stances and tendencies to bluff;
3. to foster flexibility in the use of guiding principles in the making of proposals;
4. to attenuate grievances and hostility;
5. to build up trust and confidence via unilateral concessions and reward-type actions; and
6. to increase the sensitivity of the negotiators to the trade-offs between the long run and short run.

11.4.3 Recognition of the play of personality and sociocultural factors

Regardless of how well a CMP is structured and carefully thought out with reference to a given conflict situation, the play and interplay of the leaders' personalities is unavoidable. Such, together with their moods generated by the particular configuration of events and circumstances at particular decision points of time, is at best only partially predictable and thus can only be partially reckoned with (incorporated) within a well-designed CMP. Hence, the course of negotiations can well proceed in unpredictable and undesirable directions. Put in a stronger way, from the standpoint of conflict management, each personality has idiosyncracies and deficiencies. The leaders' attitudes and moods are often subject to whimsical and other random change; and although positive and appropriate at certain times, they can be negative, noncooperative, and defeating at other times. Moreover, the leaders' drive for power, their desire for respect and prestige, and so on, can vary over time in intensity as well as their risk aversion, risk capability, and effort at optimization.

Additionally, each leader belongs to groups of different sorts. The views and attitudes of his (or her) cadre of immediate friends and close advisors (his kitchen cabinet) can shift back and forth and thus its influence upon his behavior via groupthink and the like. During the negotiations the leader and these individuals have experiences and learn, and this too comes to influence the leader's behavior directly and indirectly through changes in the group's set of schemata and interpretive packages. Furthermore, pressure groups and others are constantly hounding or indirectly affecting the thinking of the leader and the particular aspects of his personality that are active. Still more, there is the influence of public opinion – about which we shall say more later – which often can take sudden, unpredictable turns.

Consequently, the leaders' dominating personality traits, emotional states, perceptions, attitudes, and thus behavior are unpredictable in many respects at any decision time point. Any effective CMP must be sensitive to this and allow for contingencies and specifically for the use of the time exploitation principle to put off a decision when one or more of these elements suggest a negative outcome.

11.4.4 Continuous information research and development

As both U.S. and Soviet officials learn from experience in negotiations, they can be expected to become simultaneously more sophisticated in their strategies. They see what works and what does not; they come to understand better the complexities involved; they come to know better how to use models and computer-oriented analysis. This means that a CMP that may be currently effective today may not be so tomorrow when more sophisticated negotiators are interacting. Moreover, society continues to become more and more complex. This means that scenarios emanating from an effective CMP for inputting into a model must reflect this greater complexity in order to be relevant.

Additionally, there is the current inadequacy of our existing CMPs. Thus, on the basis of our existing stock of CMPs and knowledge, any CMP that we currently design as the most effective (or one of the most effective) should foster the need for continuous information research and development – to explore new means–end heuristics and other artificial intelligence probes into problem solving; to learn more about mental representations and the use of intra- and interdomain analogies in their formation; to develop new and more appropriate models to capture not only the existing but also the growing complexity of interdependence among nations and their parts; to invent new concepts, new methods of interaction, and new ways to construct payoff matrices to portray more efficiently and extensively the decision situation; and in general to nurture fresh attacks on the problem of conflict management, covering not only piecemeal improvements but also highly creative, drastically different (nonorthodox) sets of steps.

11.4.5 Exploitation of the force of public opinion

Though supported by a cadre of close associates and intimate friends and also by interest groups that are sympathetic to and/or gain much from current policy, leaders must nonetheless confront the public, perhaps not in the immediate short run but surely in the middle and long run. Public opinion (including world opinion and that of those nations that are actual or potential or even nonpotential constituents to which a leader is sensitive) can alter the leader's [and his (or her) group's] attitude and choice of action. This is because

1. he may have a strong drive to stay in power or for his party to stay in power; or
2. he may obtain much personal satisfaction (utility) from widespread public support; or
3. he may be the type of person who is guided by "high" principles and wishes to be a true representative of his constituency.

He may also be pragmatic and recognize the need to form coalitions (as per the discussion in Appendix 3.B and section 7.4) with other leaders and groups and thereby the need to change his proposals to garner the support of their constituents. On the other hand, he may possess charisma, know how to arouse public support through appeal to national interest and pride, be able to intensify feelings of insecurity in the public in order to gain its backing for large increases in the defense budget, and in general be capable of manipulating public opinion and exploiting the "sheepishness" and gullibility of the public. In any case, an effective CMP must recognize and be able to cope with such interdependence and potential interaction.

11.5   Stability: an achievable property?

Stability is often considered by scholars to be an essential property of a CMP. Some analysts might also consider this property to be key for an effective CMP for the U.S.–Soviet problem. However, unlike deterrence capability, which often is considered to be a credible and strong inescapable sanction to nuclear warfare, especially if there could be in place safeguards against accidental and terroristic nuclear attacks, there is nothing of a similar nature in the U.S.–Soviet arms control conflict problem that can serve as a strong stabilizing element. Monitoring and inspection that would reveal the failure of a power to comply with an agreement when coupled with the consequent (hopefully strong) negative reaction of the world constituency and one's own public represents one stability element that can be significant. Another might be whatever sanctions the United Nations might be able to impose. Economic pressures in one's own nation from any increase in military expenditures can be still another. Increase in the volume of and specialization in trade among the two powers is one more. Likewise is a leader's conscience. But unfortunately, there is no strong inescapable sanction such as deterrence capability regarding nuclear attack that can keep the two big powers from breaking a deescalating agreement and from initiating a reescalation of the military effort. In sum, all that an effective CMP can hope for, given our current stock of knowledge, is a state of semirestful stability, achievable via a set of diverse but relatively weak stability elements.

11.6   Some nonbasic factors

The U.S.–Soviet arms control conflict problem is unique. It does not require certain properties of a CMP that other conflict problems might often find critical. Pointing up some of these properties may be useful in the sense that should they be incorporated in a CMP under consideration, they may be considered for elimination (shedding) when to do so might strengthen the effectiveness of other key properties and of the CMP as a whole.

One of these relatively unnecessary properties for a U.S.–Soviet conflict management procedure is *efficiency.*[12] [Many CMPs have been designed to have this property (see Isard and Smith 1982).] In this conflict, what is highly desirable are steps *forward* in the sense of reduction in military expenditures and in the stocks of weaponry. To insist upon (require) that an efficient and only an efficient level of disarmament (in the sense of reaching the economist's efficiency frontier) be achieved is not only unrealistic but would most probably forestall progress. Negotiations at any point of time should be viewed as highly successful if they clearly reverse the escalation of arms production and development and if they achieve just a reasonable level of disarmament and weaponry stock reduction.

Low cost is another property that is inessential to negotiations in the U.S.–Soviet arms control conflict. Both nations have large resources, and the cost of steady continuous negotiations with whatever large staffs they consider desirable can be at most an insignificant fraction of GNP, whereas the potential savings of lives can easily be judged to be of infinite value. Of course, negotiation teams and staff should not be so large that they encumber and inordinately delay negotiations. Time is an important factor in negotiations and should be carefully used.

A third property considered important for CMPs in general is *preindeterminacy.* There already exist in the U.S.–Soviet conflict problem so many uncertainties and so much unpredictability concerning personality traits that will come to the fore, and concerning the state of affairs and summary cues that will exist at each point in time during a negotiations process, that preindeterminacy of outcomes is assured. Therefore, because it is assured, the need for such a property in an effective CMP for this conflict does not exist and need not be designed for.

There are still other properties that are inessential, such as a requirement that there be a *unique outcome* (often considered desirable by econ-

---

[12] Such implies that efficiency-oriented categories 11, 12, and 26 of CMPs listed in Table 10.8 are not relevant.

omists and applied mathematicians). The reader may refer to Isard and Smith (1982, chap. 12) for further discussion of properties.

11.7   Concluding remarks

We have now considered both key and unnecessary properties of an effective CMP for the U.S.–Soviet arms control conflict situation. We did so having in mind that if this situation is ever to be managed (let alone resolved) before a nuclear war occurs, it will require the "invention" of an as yet unknown, to-be-developed procedure. On this matter, one must not be lulled into a sleep by the signing of the INF treaty and the much improved psychological background for current (mid-1988) negotiations. Given the ongoing SDI-type developments both in the United States and the Soviet Union, any sudden adverse change in this psychological background (which history teaches us often occurs) may lead to an arms control problem even more (perhaps much more) serious than immediately after the breakdown of the Reykjavik meetings.

While as yet an unknown procedure awaits discovery, we judged it worthwhile to examine what we could say about an effective CMP that might be somewhat useful, fully recognizing that there will be among scholars differences about what should be key and inessential properties of an effective CMP for this situation whose dynamics are so unpredictable.

One key property now appears to be a veto power, perhaps only a restricted veto power, in a negotiations process that is not dependent upon (but open to) the use of third-party intervention. Coupled with this is the need, given the nonmonolithicity of the U.S. Congress and the Kremlin, for the use of models to help ensure that there will be developed a set of complementary (offset) programs to counter unemployment and other negative impacts upon local and national economies, so that agreements on arms reduction and management can obtain the required amount of support for ratification.

Clearly each step or set of steps in the negotiations process should guarantee nondeterioration and, desirably, improvement in the security position of each nation and the productivity of its economy. Some form of logrolling on issues with or without limited commitment is one device that can be attempted and should be possible in an effective CMP. Perhaps only logrolling on sets of issues may be possible, and here a balance-sheet approach may be utilizable. One of many other devices such as unilateral concessions might also be fruitful at one or more points in the negotiations process and be associated with a property of an effective CMP; and clearly the time exploitation principle should be incorporated.

However, efficiency, low cost, preindeterminacy, and solution uniqueness as properties are not essential, though such may be present. Finally, at this time we know of no way to assure both short-run and long-run stability within an effective CMP, no matter how desirable such a property would be.

With these remarks we close this chapter. We would have liked to have reached a stronger set of statements but unfortunately cannot. Nonetheless, we consider our probe useful in (1) exposing the tremendous complexity of the problem, and (2) offering another approach that we hope provides some useful insights through the way we have developed materials and synthesized them.

References

Adelman, K. L. (1986) "What Happened at Reykjavik." *Disarmament* 9(3, Autumn):1–14.

Isard, W. (1974) "Activity-Industrial Complex Analysis and Environmental Management." *Papers Regional Science Association* 33:127–40.

Isard, W., and T. Langford (1969) "Impact of Vietnam War Expenditures on the Philadelphia Economy." *Papers Regional Science Association* 23:217–65.

Isard, W., and E. Schooler (1964) "An Economic Analysis of Local and Regional Impacts of Reduction of Military Expenditures." *Papers Peace Research Society (International)* 1:15–44.

Isard, W., and C. Smith (1982) *Conflict Analysis and Practical Conflict Management Procedures.* Cambridge, MA: Ballinger.

Isard, W., E. Schooler, and T. Vietorisz (1959) *Industrial Complex Analysis and Regional Development.* New York: Wiley and MIT Press.

Isard, W., D. F. Bramhall, G. A. P. Carrothers, J. H. Cumberland, L. N. Moses, D. O. Price, and E. W. Schooler (1960) *Methods of Regional Analysis.* New York: Wiley and MIT Press.

Merritt, R. L., and D. A. Zinnes, *Data Development in International Research,* forthcoming.

Petrovsky, V. F. (1986) "What Happened at Reykjavik." *Disarmament* 9(3, Autumn):15–26.

Russett, B. (ed.) (1972) *Peace, War and Numbers.* Beverly Hills: Sage Publications.

Russett, B., H. R. Alker, Jr., K. W. Deutsch, and H. D. Lasswell (1964) *World Handbook of Political and Social Indicators.* New Haven, CT: Yale University Press.

Taylor, C. L., and D. A. Jodice (1983) *World Handbook of Political and Social Indicators,* 3rd ed. New Haven, CT: Yale University Press.

Udis, B. (ed.) (1970) *Adjustment of the U.S. Economy to Reduction in Military Spending.* U.S. Arms Control and Disarmament Agency, Washington, D.C. (December), Document ACDA/E-156, reproduced in revised and reduced form as B. Udis (ed.) (1973) *The Economic Consequences of Reduced Military Spending.* Lexington, MA: Lexington Books.

CHAPTER 12

Summary of Part I and conclusions

It is now time to summarize Part I, provide some perspective on the chapters in Part II involving more advanced (technical) analysis, and set forth some conclusions:

Recall the purposes of this book. One is to provide a sound structure for study in the Peace Science field. We do not profess to have covered all the areas that need to be examined and investigated. There are a number that other scholars would add and judge essential. Yet, we do feel that we cover a significant range of areas and do adequately indicate how they are interconnected so as to yield a unified, coherent structure. The chapters that have already been developed establish a significant breadth in terms of a set of interrelated areas that can constitute a meaningful whole. However, in these chapters we have tried to avoid materials that are fairly technical and that would interfere with obtaining the overall view by readers less versed in technical materials. So we have confined such materials to footnotes, Appendixes, and the chapters in Part II. These chapters are essential, however, for not only do they present materials of considerable importance to the conceptual framework of Peace Science, but, more significant, they establish the fact that Peace Science must and does have depth equal to that in other social science disciplines.

A second purpose of this book is to demonstrate the applicability of the methods and approach of Peace Science, particularly with regard to a major international conflict. We have tried to do so in the preceding chapter dealing with the U.S.–Soviet arms control conflict situation. While we are not out there, involved in the negotiations, we believe we have demonstrated how the materials presented in Chapters 2–10 relate forcefully to this conflict situation and how they can be profitably employed in connection with this conflict and even perhaps state complexities in a more lucid and analyzable manner and provide some insights that the negotiators might find enlightening.

The preceding points can perhaps be made more forcefully and clearly with a figure. We attempt to do so with Figure 12.1. At the top of this figure, in box 1, we indicate the class of conflict situations with which analysis may be concerned or to which belongs a particular conflict situation with which we are concerned. For this book, arms races and arms control conflict situations is the class in which we have been interested. Further, we are concerned with controlling and managing these conflicts, that is, to temper or eliminate any escalation and, desirably, to set in place a process of deescalation. There are many different kinds of equation that can be employed to depict an escalation–deescalation process. We illustrate with the classic Richardson equation, for which the major problem is to change ρ^J, c^J, and g^J, the reaction, cost, and grievance parameters, respectively. Again, see box 1.[1] We shall say more about this later.

The next step that we take in this book, and one that is generally to be recommended, is to survey the literature on the class of conflict situations of concern, especially the literature that might bear directly on the particular conflict situation being confronted. This is to be done in order to identify the characteristics and relationships that scholars consider key (see box 2). In Chapter 2 we surveyed the literature on arms race models, much of which is oriented to big-power arms races, and discussed scholarly thinking on key factors. (A synthesis of these factors is presented at a fairly technical level in Chapter 13.) Although the basic relationships in an escalation–deescalation process may be depicted in a highly, aggregative macromanner, such as in the classic Richardson model, behind these macro- (aggregative-) type relationships are numerous behaving units, individuals, and groups interacting with each other. The behavior of each of these units, especially the key political figures and influential groups, must be understood. Hence in Chapter 3 we probe into such. Attitudes are discussed and, with the use of the concept of a payoff matrix, how they affect the choice of an action. The various elements of interdependent decision making, and particularly the role of guiding principles, are presented as well as a brief look at how such a principle embodied in a CMP (conflict management procedure) may be used in reaching joint actions to manage a conflict. We also looked at behavior from the stand-

[1] Recall that in this equation M^J = military expenditures of country J at time t; $\dot{M}^J$ = change in those expenditures at t; M^L = military expenditures of its rival nation L at t; ρ^J = a reaction coefficient indicating J's reaction in terms of military expenditures to a unit of L's military expenditures; c^J = a coefficient representing the cost (expense burden) to J per unit of its military expenditures; and g^J = the grievance J holds against L.

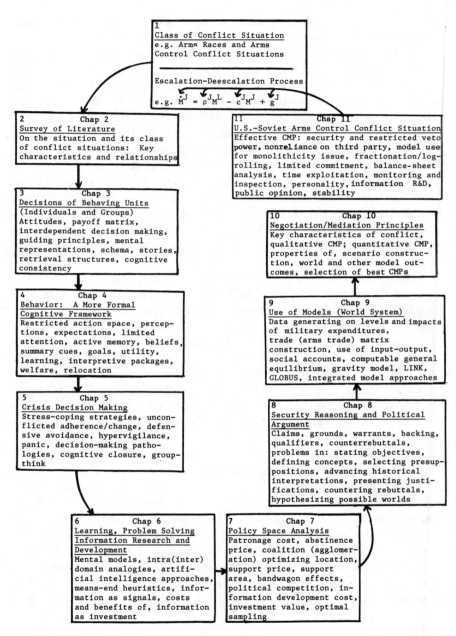

1
Class of Conflict Situation
e.g. Arms Races and Arms
Control Conflict Situations
_____

Escalation-Deescalation Process
e.g. $\dot{M}^J = \rho^J M^L - c^J M^J + g^J$

2 Chap 2
Survey of Literature
On the situation and its class
of conflict situations: Key
characteristics and relationships

11 Chap 11
U.S.-Soviet Arms Control Conflict Situation
Effective CMP: security and restricted veto
power, nonreliance on third party, model use
for monolithicity issue, fractionation/log-
rolling, limited commitment, balance-sheet
analysis, time exploitation, monitoring and
inspection, personality, information R&D,
public opinion, stability

3 Chap 3
Decisions of Behaving Units
(Individuals and Groups)
Attitudes, payoff matrix,
interdependent decision making,
guiding principles, mental
representations, schema, stories,
retrieval structures, cognitive
consistency

10 Chap 10
Negotiation/Mediation Principles
Key characteristics of conflict,
qualitative CMP; quantitative CMP,
properties of, scenario construction, world and other model outcomes, selection of best CMPs

4 Chap 4
Behavior: A More Formal
Cognitive Framework
Restricted action space, perceptions, expectations, limited
attention, active memory, beliefs,
summary cues, goals, utility,
learning, interpretive packages,
welfare, relocation

9 Chap 9
Use of Models (World System)
Data generating on levels and impacts
of military expenditures,
trade (arms trade) matrix
construction, use of input-output,
social accounts, computable general
equilibrium, gravity model, LINK,
GLOBUS, integrated model approaches

5 Chap 5
Crisis Decision Making
Stress-coping strategies, unconflicted adherence/change, defensive avoidance, hypervigilance,
panic, decision-making pathologies, cognitive closure, groupthink

8 Chap 8
Security Reasoning and Political
Argument
Claims, grounds, warrants, backing,
qualifiers, counterrebuttals,
problems in: stating objectives,
defining concepts, selecting presuppositions, advancing historical
interpretations, presenting justifications, countering rebuttals,
hypothesizing possible worlds

6 Chap 6
Learning, Problem Solving
Information Research and
Development
Mental models, intra(inter)
domain analogies, artifi-
cial intelligence approaches,
means-end heuristics, information as signals, costs
and benefits of, information
as investment

7 Chap 7
Policy Space Analysis
Patronage cost, abstinence
price, coalition (agglomeration) optimizing location,
support price, support
area, bandwagon effects,
political competition, information development cost,
investment value, optimal
sampling.

Figure 12.1. The circular flow of analysis.

point of cognitive scientists concerned with mental representations, schema, stories, retrieval structures, cognitive consistency, and the like (see box 3).

However, the approaches of economics, regional science and operations research, and cognitive science and their listing of significant factors need to be examined in a deeper and more interconnected fashion. For noncrisis situations, we developed a more formal, but still a conceptual, framework of interdependent decision making. We looked at the restricted action space, perceptions, expectations, the limited number of things a behaving unit can attend to, active memory, relevant beliefs, summary cues, goals, utility, learning, interpretive packages, welfare, the shifting of individuals from group to group, the relocation of groups in policy space, and other related elements (see box 4). For crisis decision situations and again in a conceptual but formal integrated fashion, we paid attention to stress-coping strategies such as unconflicted adherence, unconflicted change, defensive avoidance, and hypervigilance, taking into consideration decision-making pathologies such as cognitive closure, groupthink, and other associated factors (see box 5).

As noted in Chapter 4, learning is a basic phenomenon, and for many conflict situations that learning associated with creative problem solving and information research and development is required. Frequently, existing conflict management procedures and problem-solving methods are inadequate. New ones must be designed (invented). Hence in Chapter 6 we explore how better mental models of a problem can be constructed, exploiting fully the possibility for solutions through intradomain and interdomain analogies. We examine artificial intelligence approaches (e.g., means–end heuristics) and from an economics standpoint consider the kind and extent of information that should be sought (produced) as an investment, taking into account diverse costs and benefits (see box 6). In Chapters 14–16, respectively, we present at a more advanced (technical) level

14. a model of learning by a group and its members;
15. a model of information production (and investment in information) by participants and a mediator to facilitate the management of a conflict; and
16. an exploratory model relating the demand for and supply of creative ideas and information for invention and innovation of new conflict management procedures.

Although the interaction of a multitude of individuals and groups must be recognized and taken into account in the study of any class of conflict situations, and often too in a particular conflict, certain individuals and groups have more importance than others. Therefore their behavior must be probed at greater depth. In the class of arms races and arms control conflict situations, it is the political leaders (and their groups) who are most influential. Thus, we must conduct policy space analysis, as in Chapter 7, wherein expenditures on the military is one basic policy issue. There we consider a political leader proposing a platform or a set of policies (a location in policy space) in competition with others in order to be in power. With his (or her) limited resources, he must take into account the distribution of voters' most preferred positions in this space, their abstinence price, patronage costs, required support prices, support area, bandwagon effects, the need to be part of a coalition, and other factors in order to identify his optimal location (set of policies). In doing so, he may also incur costs in sampling a voting population to obtain valuable information on the distribution of voters' preferences, which information may have an investment value; and so forth (see box 7).

However, a political leader (or other individual or group) very often needs to be persuasive. He (or she) may need to set forth an effective political argument, as is discussed in Chapter 8. He may need to state his claims, the grounds for them, warrants, and scientific and experimental backing and qualifications and be prepared to counter rebuttals. Desirably, he should state consistent objectives, clearly define concepts, carefully select presuppositions, properly use historical materials, develop sound justifications, and set forth plans and realistic versions of possible worlds that "one can get to from here" (see box 8). We illustrated these considerations with regard to the "no first use of nuclear weapons in Europe" arguments.

Political arguments require data for supporting claims and for achieving widespread support for policies. Here models can be extremely useful in generating required data, even if they are simply best projections. In Chapter 9 we focus upon generating data relating to levels of military expenditures and the impacts of these expenditures on trade (via trade matrix construction) and other key magnitudes, paying special attention to arms trade. We consider the use of input–output, social accounting, programming, computable general equilibrium, gravity, econometric (LINK), and GLOBUS models and frameworks and suggest multimethod and integrated model approaches (see box 9).

Given all the survey findings, analyses, and generated data of Chapters 2–9, we consider in Chapter 10 principles of negotiation and mediation. After all, political leaders (and other relevant figures), even when fully armed with much data and effective arguments and solid public support, must come together (face to face or otherwise) to iron out their differences, in whole or part, in a conflict. Hence we must examine

1. principles of negotiation and mediation that might be used;
2. how qualitative CMPs (built upon these principles) relate to the key characteristics of and relations in a conflict situation;
3. how quantitative CMPs with desirable properties may be required and developed; and
4. how scenarios (based on qualitative and quantitative CMPs) may be constructed to be inputted into world system and other models to generate outcomes that serve as additional data.

Such data together with the scenarios then provide a framework for evaluating the political and economic feasibility of a scenario and for comparing the desirability of different CMPs (see box 10).

Finally, in Chapter 11 we take up the U.S.–Soviet arms control conflict situation to illustrate in a more concrete way the applicability of much (but not necessarily all) of the material and analyses in the preceding chapters. For this conflict, in which national (military) security is of paramount importance, we judge that

1. a veto power, perhaps a restricted one, is essential for an effective CMP;
2. such a CMP should rely on only limited, if any, third-party intervention;
3. the use of models should be strongly encouraged in order to achieve as much monolithicity (consensus among different interest groups and legislators represented by a leader) as is possible;
4. issue fractionation and logrolling should be explored to guarantee improvement;
5. limited commitment should be possible;
6. balance-sheet analysis should be able to be conducted when appropriate; and
7. the principle of time exploitation should be used.

Problems exist in the following areas:

1. monitoring and inspection;
2. precluding the interjection of negative personality elements;
3. encouraging continuously understanding enhancement and knowledge accumulation and the conduct of research and development for the invention of new ideas and CMPs;
4. effectively using public opinion; and
5. achieving stability (see box 11).

We close the circle in Figure 12.1 by referring back to the initial conflict situation with which we are concerned – the U.S.–Soviet arms control conflict situation – and the relevant escalation–deescalation equation

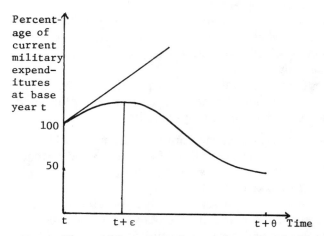

Figure 12.2. An agreed-upon time path of military expenditures.

such as might be the one at the base of box 1 in Figure 12.1. If an effective CMP coming out of box 11 is identified and implemented, there are at least four possible types of impact. First, it might lead to immediate simultaneous reductions in military expenditures, namely, in M^J and M^L. Second, the CMP might help reduce the ρ^J reaction coefficient, namely, the tendency for J to increase military expenditures given its rival (L's) expenditures (and anticipated changes in them). Third, it might affect the c^J cost coefficient, most likely decreasing it. Fourth, it might help reduce the g^J parameter because J's grievance toward L may be tempered, its distrust of as well as hostility toward L reduced, and its ambition curbed. To be even more concrete, we may imagine an agreement may have been reached that directly affects the ρ^J coefficient for each nation, fully recognizing the need for a smooth conversion of plant and labor from military production to civilian (in the economies of the nation and its regions and their diverse sectors) and the associated need for legislative and other support. It would call for a gradual slowing down of the *rate* of growth of military expenditures with time, eventually to become zero, say, at time $t + \epsilon$ (at which time military expenditures would be larger than at time t), thereafter to become negative and to decrease steadily for a while and then smoothly to begin to increase and become zero – so that a much lower level of military expenditures is attained at, say, time $t + \theta$ ($\theta > \epsilon$) (see Figure 12.2).[2] We may imagine that Soviet and U.S. math-

---

[2] In Figure 12.2 we measure percentage of military expenditures along the vertical and time along the horizontal. The rate of increase of military expenditures over time at base year t is given by the slope of the line drawn up and to the right from the 100 mark on the vertical.

ematicians together with their political leaders might develop equations to depict variation over time in ρ^J to accomplish this end, with c^J and g^J constant. However, other equations might be developed to recognize that c^J and g^J would likely change over this time period.

This completes our summary and Part I of this book. We trust that new understanding is now possible and that new insights have been gained. As already mentioned, the subsequent chapters on advanced analysis probe more deeply at key points in the field of Peace Science and illustrate the more sophisticated analysis that scholars in the field may be motivated to pursue and that some should pursue.

PART II

Some advanced analyses

CHAPTER 13

Synthesis of arms race models

13.1   Introduction

In this chapter, we turn to a synthesis of arms race models. Chapter 2 surveyed the existing models, and subsequent chapters examined diverse forces related to arms races and arms control. Yet, in no way have we covered more than a small fraction of the tremendous amount of complex interdependencies (direct and indirect) of the almost infinite number of factors at play in the current world system. However, given the limited space within which to write about such, we first must break the circle of interdependencies at some critical point and then examine them from this vantage point, aiming to have some reference to a significant part of the total picture under constant change.

For our synthesis, we begin with the insatiable needs of humans and the limited resources available to meet them. This gives rise to (1) cooperation where joint efforts and use of the different specialized know-how and knowledge of individuals and groups are required and (2) competition. Competition gives rise to conflict, the evolution of laws and other ways to control resources and their use, the emergence of the intangible concept of power and physical means to exercise power, and thus, at a given point of time t, the allocation of funds $M^J(t)$ for use in the production of weaponry (a current flow) and its accumulation and maintenance as stock, $S^J(t)$. The actual production, however, involves a command or order, which in turn involves a decision. This may have been the outcome of a conflict situation with respect to different interest groups (with different objectives) or even the different subpersonalities of an individual. The decision, however, may have involved a choice among two or more options that may have been associated, perhaps unawaringly by the behaving unit or group of behaving units, with a payoff matrix. This

413

matrix may have been truncated because not all options and states of the environment may have been perceived and may be fictitious in the sense that certain options and environmental states may have been assumed to exist or be possible that in fact may not have been feasible or possible. The perception of such a payoff matrix may have resulted from previous experience and learning. And so forth in unending fashion.

This general discussion then suggests that we conduct this synthesis within the $\mathcal{MJR}$ paradigm for Peace Science suggested by Figure 1.3 and developed in Isard (1979, 1980) and Isard and Smith (1982, chaps. 14 and 15). As depicted in Figure 1.3, the world system $\mathcal{S}$ consists of three main subsystems: the *information* subsystem $\mathcal{M}$, the *cognitive decision-making* subsystem C, and the *production–consumption–trade* subsystem P. Recall that within the last is a national component for each nation J designated P^J, $J = A, \ldots, U$, and an $\mathcal{R}$ component that interconnects the several national production systems as well as provides interface inputs to each. The $\mathcal{R}$ component was taken to represent the world market broadly conceived.

The $\mathcal{R}$ and the P^J components are also interconnected with the C subsystem and all its parts. These latter cover for each nation J a decision-making (policy formation) component C^J, $J = A, \ldots, U$, and an $\mathcal{J}$ component that interconnects these national components and provides interface inputs to each. The component $\mathcal{J}$ was taken to represent the international political arena.

Finally, the P, C, P^J, C^J, $\mathcal{R}$, and $\mathcal{J}$ are also interconnected with the information $\mathcal{M}$ subsystem in obvious ways. Therein lies the knowledge base including know-how (technology) of the total system, though all parts of the system have only incomplete access to it.

13.2   Synthesis: the Richardson side of the coin

Given this framework as background, we can now proceed with our synthesis more effectively. Without question, a basic element must be an action–reaction relation. Hence, where M^J and M^L represent military expenditures of nations J and L, respectively, and S^J and S^L their weapons stocks, we have in its simplest form

$$\dot{M}^J(t) = \rho^J M^L(t) + \cdots \tag{13.2.1}$$
$$M^J(t) = \rho^J M^L(t) + \cdots \tag{13.2.2}$$
$$\dot{M}^J(t) = \rho^J S^L(t) + \cdots \tag{13.2.3}$$

or

$$M^J(t) = \rho^J S^L(t) + \cdots \tag{13.2.4}$$

where ρ' is a reaction coefficient. Or as discussed in section 2.2, since

$$\frac{M'(t)}{p'(t)} = \dot{S}^J(t) + \alpha S^J(t)$$

where $p'(t)$ is the unit cost or price (taken as given) of an average piece of weaponry and α is a depreciation (obsolescence) rate of weapons stocks, we can have

$$\dot{S}^J(t) = -\alpha S^J(t) + \rho' S^L(t) + \cdots \qquad (13.2.5)$$

Bearing in mind that units of ρ' and other parameters and variables will be different from one formulation to another of the action–reaction process, we can state the preceding relations in the more general form

$$\chi^J(t) = \rho' \chi^L(t) + \cdots \qquad (13.2.6)$$

where χ can be taken to represent M, $\dot{M}$, S, or $\dot{S}$, and where the relation can be stated differently for J and L.[1] Actually, J may react to both M^L and S^L, in which case we might have

$$\rho' \chi^L(t) = {}^1\rho^J {}^1 M^L(t) + {}^2\rho^J {}^2 S^L(t) \qquad (13.2.7)$$

Alternatively, differences in, or ratios of, or sums of relevant magnitudes may be pertinent for particular arms races and even a submissiveness coefficient. And so forth.

Nation J's reaction, however, may be related not only to the current but also to past values of χ^L; in such a case, a cumulative memory factor is involved. So we may have

$$\chi^J(t) = \int_{t_0}^{t} \rho^J e^{-r(t-\tau)} \chi^L(\tau) \, d\tau + \cdots \qquad (13.2.8)$$

where $\tau = t_0, \ldots, t - 1, t$ and where t_0 is the earliest year of memory for J, the parameter r being a "forgetting" (or discount) rate. Moreover, J may react to expected future values of χ^L. In doing so, to play safe, it may overreact. Thus the parameter ρ' may be greater for a year in the future than for a year in the past. Further, r, although a "forgetting" rate for past years, may be either an upcount or a different discount rate for future years. Hence letting both ρ' and r vary with τ, we obtain

$$\chi^J(t) = \int_{t_0}^{t_1} \rho^J(\tau) e^{-r(\tau)(t-\tau)} \chi^L(\tau) \, d\tau + \cdots \qquad (13.2.9)$$

---

[1] Recall that M^J is a given for year $t - 1$, so that both Eqs. (13.2.2) and (13.2.4) are in effect laws of change, crudely speaking.

where $t_1 = t + \theta$, the year $t + \theta$ being the last year to which J's foresight extends [or to which it compresses (cumulates) all future activities of L beyond t_1]. Because data available for hypothesis-testing purposes are by units of time, it is fruitful at this point to restate Eq. (13.2.9) into a relation over discrete units of time. We have

$$\chi^J(t) = \sum_{t_0}^{t_1} \rho^J(\tau)[1 + \bar{r}(\tau)]^{\tau-t} {}^\prime\chi^L(\tau) + \cdots,$$

$$\tau = t_0, t_0 + 1, \ldots, t, \ldots, t_1 \tag{13.2.10}$$

where $\bar{r}(\tau)$ is typically positive for past time, zero for the current, and either negative or positive for future time.

A next step is to recognize that reactions of J (as summarized in its military outlays) differ according to the weaponry of L. So letting Λ, $\Lambda = 1, \ldots, \bar{\Lambda}$, represent different types of weaponry, that is, $\Lambda_1 = $ conventional weapons, $\Lambda_2 = $ strategic weapons, and so on, we have

$$\chi^J(t) = \sum_{\Lambda,\tau} {}^\Lambda\rho^J(\tau)[1 + \bar{r}(\tau)]^{\tau-t} {}^\Lambda\chi^L(\tau) + \cdots,$$

$$\Lambda = 1, \ldots, \bar{\Lambda} \tag{13.2.11}$$

Here, also, a distinction between threatening and nonthreatening weapons or weapons categories characterized by different negative effects (externalities) upon the security of a rival may be of key importance. Moreover, the magnitudes may be adjusted to take into account technological change (e.g., in accuracy) and thereby become qualitative–quantitative indices. Here an investigator may wish to view $\chi^J(t)$ as the sum $\Sigma_\Lambda {}^\Lambda\chi^J(t)$ of expenditures on different types of weapon or expenditures resulting from different types of reaction.[2]

Additionally, we may wish to embrace a U-nation framework. Accordingly, Eq. (13.2.11) becomes

$$\chi^J(t) = \sum_{\Lambda,\tau,L} {}^{\Lambda,L}\rho^J(\tau)[1 + \bar{r}(\tau)]^{\tau-t} {}^\Lambda\chi^L(\tau) + \cdots,$$

$$\Lambda = 1, \ldots, \bar{\Lambda}, \quad L = A, \ldots, U; L \neq J \tag{13.2.12}$$

where ${}^{\Lambda,L}\rho^J(\tau)$ may be negative when L is an ally, zero or negligible when L is neutral, and positive when L is a rival or allied to a rival.

---

[2] Implicit in Eq. (13.2.11) is the assumption that each type of weaponry contributes to security or to utility in an independent and additive way when security is taken as a function of military outlays. The last dollar spent on (the marginal cost of) each type of weaponry adds an equal amount to security or utility. This assumption of independence is a strong one and cannot be said to characterize reality since the presence of different amounts of one type of weapon clearly affects the marginal contribution to security that another type can make. This formulation avoids the problem of defining equivalence classes of weapons.

If we now let $\bar{\rho}^J(\tau)$ be a $(U-1)\bar{A}$ row vector and $\chi^L(\tau)$ the corresponding $(U-1)\bar{A}$ column vector where

$$\chi^L = {}^1\chi^A, {}^2\chi^A, \ldots, {}^{\bar{A}}\chi^A; \ldots, {}^A\chi^N, \ldots; {}^1\chi^U, \ldots, {}^{\bar{A}}\chi^U, \quad \chi^L \neq {}^1\chi^J, \ldots, {}^{\bar{A}}\chi^J$$

and let $\tau = t$ and only t for reasons to be discussed, Eq. (13.2.12) becomes

$$\chi^J(t) = \bar{\rho}^J(t)\chi^L(t) + \cdots \tag{13.2.13}$$

These two terms are recorded in the bold rectangle in the C^J box of Figure 13.1 with the bold arrow indicating the flow of information concerning $\chi^L (= \chi^L(t-1) + \dot{\chi}^L(t-1))$. The boxes C^L and P^L should be considered to be depicted $U-1$ times, once for each nation $L, L = A, \ldots, U; L \neq J$.

Now consider in a general fashion the play of Richardson's fatigue, burden, cost, or equivalent factor. As in Eq. (2.2.1), Richardson and his followers introduce this factor by adding on a second term.[3] One can also introduce it in a multiplicative or other fashion, but since there seems to be no better rationale for doing so and since it is easier to treat an additive relationship, we continue the Richardson tradition. Accordingly, a generalization is immediate when we add to Eq. (13.2.12) the term $-\Sigma_i c_i^J M^J$, $i = 1, \ldots, n$, where from one possible standpoint

c_1^J = J's cost burden (in the narrow sense) per unit M^J, taking into account the rate of growth of GNP;

c_2^J = the positive effect per unit M^J upon public opinion and the economy through creating new jobs when a state of unemployment exists (here $c_2^J < 0$);

c_3^J = the positive effect per unit M^J through the expansionary stimulus that a unit has upon J's economy when it is in a period of depression or recession, for example, when idle resources exist and the utilization of productive capacity is below some upper bound, say 85 percent (here $c_3^J < 0$) – note that c_2^J and c_3^J may be combined into a single parameter;

c_4^J = the negative effect per unit M^J when a unit of M^J increases the deficit DE^J when $DE^J \geq B$ where B is a lower bound below which the deficit does not constitute a drain on J's economy;

c_5^J = the negative or positive effect per unit M^J when public opinion, respectively, disapproves or approves of military expenditures or when public concern and public support are manifest in these respective ways;

[3] Note that if we were to let L equal J in Eq. (13.2.12) and in $\rho^J(\tau)\chi^J(\tau)$ let $\rho^J(\tau) = -c^J$ and let $\tau = t$ and otherwise zero, the simple Richardson fatigue factor would be covered by Eq. (13.2.13).

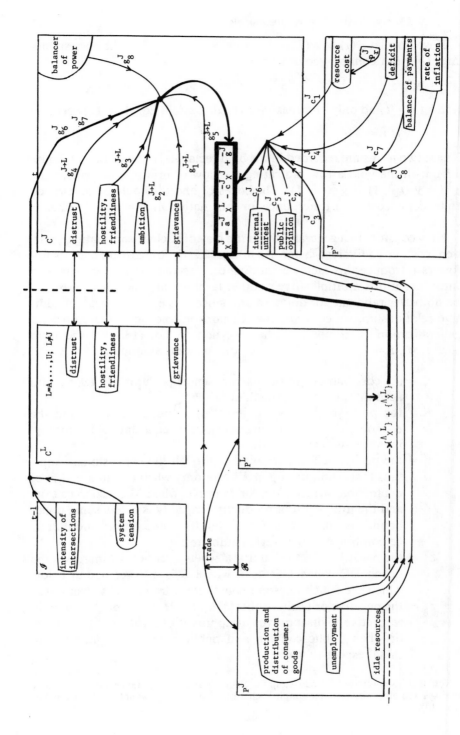

Figure 13.1. The generalized Richardson model in the $\mathcal{MIR}$ framework.

c_6^J = the negative effect per unit M^J upon internal unrest (when per capita income for a certain sizable fraction of the population falls below the poverty level, i.e., when basic needs of this fraction are not met);

c_7^J = the negative or positive effect per unit M^J when unfavorable or favorable balance of payments, respectively, exist;

c_8^J = the negative or positive effect per unit M^J when the rate of inflation is above some general acceptable level or below some other level;

$c_9^J, \ldots$ = parameters employed to treat diverse dummy variables as say Rep., which takes the value 1 when the Republican party is in office and otherwise zero, or to recognize the electoral cycle, the economic planning cycle, or the need for technological leadership, and so on.

The preceding set of "burden factors," negative and positive, attempts to be specific on various *internal* factors singled out by arms race scholars and commented upon in previous sections. However, since these factors are not 100 percent independent of each other, an analyst may wish to combine certain economic factors into one or more aggregates, and likewise with some of the noneconomic factors. Or he or she may wish to form other sets or combinations of factors.

When considering a generalized burden term for nation J, we may also need to consider magnitudes for time other than t. For example, suppose J assumes that L always reacts to J by increasing its military expenditures at the same rate that J does. Suppose also at time t that, without reference to future military expenditures, J's optimal response involved a substantial rate of increase in military expenditures. However, if this were to lead L, via the mutual stimulation effect, to respond at the same rate and possibly force J in the subsequent time period to follow with another high rate of increase, in turn leading L to respond with the same high rate, and so on, such a sequence of reactions might lead to a situation where J's resources are so tied up with weapon production that it may not have adequate civilian goods left over to meet its replacement needs (depreciation) on nonmilitary investments. This process, as per Wolfson (1985), could result in a deterioration of J's productive capacity at an increasing rate. Having this possible outcome in mind, J may then significantly lower its otherwise optimal rate of growth of military expenditures for time t.[4] Hence, we add to Eq. (13.2.12) the more embracive term

---

[4] Were J to have abundant resources while L has limited resources, J may increase its otherwise optimal rate of growth of military expenditures in an attempt to bankrupt L's economy if such were deemed a desirable objective.

$-\Sigma_i \Sigma_\tau c_i^J(\tau)M^J(\tau)$ to cover the effect of expected future military expenditures of J, multiplied by appropriate parameters where the parameters themselves may be time dependent.

This change is also appropriate when J considers the impact of current military expenditures on unemployment, not only today's but also tomorrow's, and the deficit, not only today's but also tomorrow's, since weapon programs once initiated take several years to complete. Likewise with internal unrest, public opinion, and other variables. Note that the time-dependent parameters $c_i^J(\tau)$ allow for different effects upon military expenditures at time t of one dollar of expected military expenditures in the different future time periods.

If we now let $\bar{c}^J = \Sigma_i c_i^J$ and again let $\tau = t$ and only t for reasons to be discussed, the general term $-\bar{c}^J(t)\chi^J(t)$ can be taken to replace $-\Sigma_i \Sigma_\tau c_i^J(\tau)M^J(\tau)$ where we take $\chi^J(t) \equiv M^J(t)$. We have therefore added $-\bar{c}^J\chi^J$ to the rectangle in the C^J box in Figure 13.1 for time t. Via lines and arrows we have also indicated there the several specific c_i^J factors that sum to $\bar{c}^J$.

We now turn to a generalized concept of grievance. In Eq. (2.2.1) the Richardson model specifies a grievance factor g^J (with appropriate units) that is sometimes viewed as ambition with regard to position in the international system or associated with such factors as hostility and the state of international tension. To generalize in one way, let

$g_1^{J \to N}$ = the grievance that nation J holds against its major rival nation N.

The grievance may have accumulated over a number of time periods, so that for year t we have

$$\sum_{t_0}^{t} [1 + \bar{r}(\tau)]^{\tau-t} g^{J \to N}(\tau), \qquad \tau = t_0, \ldots, t \qquad (13.2.14)$$

Further, J may have grievances vis-à-vis (1) each other nation or (2) each of several blocks $\mathcal{C}$ ($\mathcal{C} = A, B, \ldots$) of nations where at one extreme a bloc can consist of one nation only. In the case of the former we obtain

$$\sum_{L}\sum_{t_0}^{t} [1 + \bar{r}^L(\tau)]^{\tau-t} g_1^{J \to L}(\tau),$$
$$L = A, \ldots, U; L \neq J \qquad (13.2.15)$$

In the case of the latter, we obtain the same term when $\mathcal{C}$ replaces L and excludes any bloc to which J belongs. For the case where J's grievance is regarding the rest of the world (the rest of the world constituting one bloc), g_1^J should replace $g_1^{J \to N}$ in term (13.2.14):

$g_2^{J \to N}$ = the ambition that nation J has for dominating its rival nation N.

Similar to $g_1^{J \to N}$, this factor may be more properly represented as an accumulation over time and may be relevant with regard to J dominating one or more nations other than N, or the rest of the world, or to J's bloc dominating other blocs. Hence it can be treated in the same more general way as $g_1^{J \to N}$:

$g_3^{J \to N}$ = the hostility (friendliness when negative) that nation J has with
       regard to nation N;
$g_4^{J \to N}$ = J's distrust (trust when negative) of nation N.

Again as with $g_1^{J \to N}$, these two factors may each be more properly represented as an accumulation over time and may be relevant with regard to one or more nations other than N, or to blocs of nations other than J's, or to the rest of the world. Hence, each can be treated in the same more general way as $g_1^{J \to N}$. Also some analysts may define the reaction coefficient ρ^J of Eq. (13.2.10) so as to embrace the hostility and distrust factor, either in whole or part. These factors, too, along with ρ^J may be associated with the diplomatic climate between J and N at time t and with a change in diplomatic time T (discussed in section 2.7) and the associated $(dE/dT)(dT/dt)$, particularly in crisis situations:

$g_5^{J \to N}$ = an appropriate index of the extent of trade of J with N.

Again, as with $g_1^{J \to N}$ this factor may be more properly represented as an accumulation over time but in this case over expected magnitudes for future years, properly discounted or upcounted, as well as for past years. Hence, for this factor $\tau = t_0, \ldots, t, \ldots, t_1$. As with $g_1^{J \to N}$ this factor may be relevant with regard to one or more nations other than N, or to blocs of nations other than J's, or to the rest of the world. Hence it can be treated in the same more general way, with some adjustments, as $g_1^{J \to N}$. Also, some analysts may define the reaction coefficient ρ^J of Eq. (13.2.10) and the hostility (friendliness) factor $g_3^{J \to N}$ so as to embrace the trade factor, either in whole or part:

g_6^J = the level of international tension as perceived by J, a factor that
       may have already been covered in part or in whole in those discussed previously or may be better depicted by sums of military expenditures or weaponry stocks or other systemwide magnitudes;

$g_7^J, g_8^J, \ldots$ = parameters to treat other factors that are of significance and not already included by an analyst in those already discussed, such as (1) the intensity of intersections with other nations as a whole or with some nation N (in which case the superscript $\rightarrow N$ needs to be added), (2) the need for J to serve in a balancer-of-power capacity, or (3) the existence or nonexistence of a state of war mobilization in one or more nations.

Hence, a generalized "grievance–hostility" term for Richardson-type model might be stated as

$$\sum_{i,\tau,\mathcal{C}} [1 + \bar{r}_i(\tau)]^{(\tau-t)} g_i^{J\rightarrow\mathcal{C}}(\tau) \qquad (13.2.16)$$

where $i = 1, 2, \ldots$ represents the component factors; $\tau = t_0, t_0 + 1,$ $\ldots, t_1$; $\bar{r}_i(\tau)$ represents a discount or upcount factor varying with both i and τ, often taking a value of zero; $g_i^{J\rightarrow\mathcal{C}}(\tau)$ often takes the value zero; and where $\mathcal{C} = A, B, \ldots$ refers to blocs of nations, which at one extreme can be single nations such as N or at the other extreme the rest of the world but does not include J or the bloc to which J belongs.

The preceding set of grievance–hostility factors, negative and positive, attempts to be specific on various external factors singled out by arms race scholars and commented upon in Chapter 2. However, since these factors are not 100 percent independent of each other, an analyst may wish to combine certain of these factors into two or more aggregates.

If we now let $\bar{g}^J = \Sigma_{i,\mathcal{C}}\, g_i^{J\rightarrow\mathcal{C}}$ and let $\tau = t$ and only t for reasons to be discussed, we can add it to the other terms in the bold rectangle of the C^J box in Figure 13.1 for time t. This yields the basic equation

$$\chi^J(t) = \bar{\rho}^J(t)\chi^{\bar{L}}(t) - \bar{c}^J\chi^J + \bar{g}^J \qquad (13.2.17)$$

which when we take $\chi(t) = M(t)$ and have as given $M^J(t-1)$ leads to the familiar form of the Richardson equation [see Eq. (2.2.1)]

$$\dot{M}^J = \bar{\rho}^J M^{\bar{L}} - \bar{c}^J M^J + \bar{g}^J \qquad (13.2.18)$$

Underlying Eq. (13.2.18), however, is a broad range of effects that are more fully covered if we allow τ to vary from t_0 to t_1 and take into account both "memory" and the past and "anticipations" and the future.

Although Eq. (13.2.18) may be relevant for J and other nations, we must recognize the various asymmetries that can exist among nations. They may relate not only to differences in the nature of the reaction function (e.g., nonadditive for one nation and additive for another), reflecting differences in psychophysical and attitudinal responses and environmental situations, but also to the relevance and weighting of different factors (security, growth, factor endowment, ambition, basic needs, etc.).

Also, we should bear in mind that sudden jumps (of the Thom catastrophe type) may appear in the time path of M^J as a result of a number of factors, for example, a small change over time in the reaction coefficient ρ^J (Isard and Liossatos 1978) or in R&D outlays that lead to a sudden major technological advance in weaponry or in the vote pattern that brings into office a political party with a drastically different foreign policy, and so on.

13.3   Synthesis: the optimization side of the coin

Having generalized the several terms of the Richardson equation, we move ahead to incorporate the optimization process implied by practically all arms race models. Though the Richardson model, in its simplest form and as widely used, does not explicitly introduce any payoff, utility, welfare, or other objective to be optimized, optimization, however crude, is present. At the least, it is implied by a thinking behavioral unit, strategy oriented or not, who chooses one level of military expenditures (action or option) rather than another. Even a satisficing behavioral unit optimizes on leisure or time for other pursuits once a satisficing level of military expenditures is identified.

In arms race models, security S_e^J (as a function of S^J and other magnitudes) is a desirable goal, commodity, or whatever one defines it to be. When the problem and thus objective function (implicit or explicit) is narrowly defined to focus on security and security alone, a reaction corresponds to a choice of an action that is best from some standpoint. Hence, we might have a simple objective function, for example, a utility function such as

$$u^J(t) = u^J(S_e^J(t)) \tag{13.3.1}$$

and the problem is to choose a level of military expenditures $M^J(t)$, of which $S_e^J(t)$ is a monotonically increasing function, to maximize that utility. (As noted in Chapter 2, an adequate measure of social utility or social welfare or an appropriate way to proceed from individual preferences to social preferences has as yet to be developed. However, public opinion polls can give some indication of social preferences.)

However, a Richardson-type model typically has a "burden," "fatigue," or "cost" element where this element almost invariably, if not invariably, relates to the economy. When $M^J(t)$ rises, so does this element under the assumption of a full (or near-full) employment economy.

Clearly, if there were unlimited resources available, the price of all resources would be zero, and there would not be a burden, fatigue, or cost factor. So since a burden is assumed to exist, limited resources are implied. Furthermore, since at full (or near-full) employment this burden rises as $M^J(t)$ rises, this means that there is a trade-off at a rate frequently unjustifiably assumed to be constant. Hence, there is implied a transformation function[5]

$$f(C^J(t), M^J(t))/p^J(t), R^J(t)) = 0 \qquad (13.3.2)$$

defining the efficient production plans possible given the current technology and available resources (productive capacity) $R^J(t)$, defined in physical (nonmonetary) terms, where p^J is the unit cost (or price) of an average piece or composite unit of weaponry. Thus, the choice problem associated with the function in Eq. (13.3.1) is not a valid one. Rather J must choose that level of $M^J(t)$ that maximizes on its objective, again let us say utility, given by

$$u^J(t) = u^J(C^J(t), S_e^J(t)) \qquad (13.3.3)$$

subject to the transformation function of Eq. (13.3.2), where

$$S_e^J(t) = f(S^J(t), S^L(t), \dots) \qquad (13.3.4)$$
$$S^J(t) = S^J(t-1) + \dot{S}^J(t) \qquad (13.3.5)$$

and where

$$\dot{S}^J(t) = M^J(t)/p^J(t) - \alpha S(t-1) \qquad (13.3.6)$$

$p^J(t)$, α, and $S^J(t-1)$ being given.

An alternative approach would have J maximize (1) its security or utility from security given a prior determination of a fixed amount of resources to be devoted to civilian goods production, or (2) production of civilian goods or utility from civilian goods given a prior determination of a fixed amount of resources to be devoted to military goods production. However, this approach, more suited for programming models, is still forced to confront the problem (implicit or explicit) of trade-off. This is so because a prior determination of a fixed amount of resources devoted to either civilian or military goods production always implies

---

[5] The transformation function of Eq. (13.3.2) yields a two-dimensional transformation curve for given $R^J(t)$, such as in Figure 2.2. However, one may wish to disaggregate C^J into different good-using categories (and where prices are given, different spending categories) such as household consumption C_H^J, private investment I_P^J, government consumption regarding civilian programs C_G^J, government investment regarding civilian programs I_G^J, etc. In this case, $C^J(t)$ in Eq. (13.3.2) is replaced by these several variables, and we obtain a general n-dimensional transformation function.

that the choice of that fixed amount, and not a smaller or larger amount, is optimal and can only be optimal in view of what resources remain for military or civilian goods production, respectively.

At this point note that the security variable S_e^J may be disaggregated into several types of security need. Thus,

$$u^J(t) = u^J(C^J(t), {}_aS_e^J(t), {}_aS_e^J(t), {}_sS_e^J(t)) \qquad (13.3.7)$$

where ${}_aS_e^J(t)$, ${}_aS_e^J(t)$, and ${}_sS_e^J(t)$ might be defined, respectively, as security associated with a deterrence weaponry (capability), security associated with an attack weaponry (capability, sometimes associated with the commodity c-power),[6] and security associated with political and economic spheres of influence (e.g., number and strength of allies and/or friendly nations as affected by military and other related foreign aid provided by J). In this situation, a number of weapons may contribute to both deterrence and attack capability. We assume that military and other related foreign aid along with expenditures by weapon type are covered by $M^J(t)$ and $\dot{M}^J(t)$ and are always associated with an optimal choice of ${}_aS_e^J(t)$, ${}_aS_e^J(t)$, and ${}_sS_e^J(t)$, the trade-off between expenditures on new and existing types of weapon reflecting the need for technological leadership and the probability of cost overruns, particularly on new weapons.

Recall that when we speak of deterrence and attack capabilities, such can be defined only with regard to a fictitious missile war, a war that is describable by Eqs. (2.5.1)–(2.5.5) and (2.5.9)–(2.5.12) and the associated discussion. Accordingly, each level of ${}_aS_e^J(t)$ and ${}_aS_e^J(t)$ is associated with values of J's control variables that maximize the payoff from a missile war.

Also, when we state the optimization process, we must include in $M^J(t)$ or otherwise embody expenditures on those activities associated with both acquiring intelligence regarding the rival's weapon stock and capabilities (and reducing uncertainties in general) and those leading to secrecy regarding one's own. These activities absorb resources [designated N in the resource constraint Eq. (2.7.8)]. They also change the variable $S_e^J(t)$ since it is related to estimated levels of $S^L(t)$, $L = A$, ..., U, $L \neq J$, and other magnitudes. Moreover, we must also recognize that security, particularly as it is perceived by nonmilitary interest groups and individual behaving units, is based on considerable information provided by military and intelligence agencies, and it may be that such agencies of several rival nations collude by generating misinformation to further their own interests (when measured, say, by size of military budget).

---

[6] See Isard et al. (1969, pp. 584–5) for a definition of c-power.

The optimization problem, as thus far stated, is still inadequate. It fails to capture certain dynamic elements that can be conceptually specified. The very production of civilian goods C^J at any given time τ implies an allocation of such goods for both current consumption purposes $C_0^J(\tau)$ and gross investment $I^J(\tau)$. (Recall the discussion in section 2.5.) Gross investment then changes production capacity, increasing or decreasing it according to whether gross investment exceeds or falls short of investment required for replacement purposes (to offset depreciation and obsolescence of current productive capacity). Production capacity in turn is an effective index of the resources of a nation, which we have represented by $R^J(t)$ in Eq. (2.7.8), Eq. (13.3.2), and others. Thus in the choice of any level $M^J(t)$ in Eq. (13.3.2), one must consider the associated civilian goods production that results from the efficient operation of the economic system and the consequent investment. This investment (if nonzero on net) changes $R^J(t)$ in future years $\tau = t + 1, t + 2, \ldots$ and in turn the $M^J(\tau)$, $S_e^J(\tau)$, and $u^J(\tau)$ in these years. Hence, the problem for the nation (its political leader or a beneficent dictator) may be viewed as the choice of a level of military expenditures $M^J(t)$ to

$$\max \ W^J = \int_t^{t_1} e^{-r(\tau - t)} u(C_0^J(\tau), S_e^J(\tau)) \ d\tau \tag{13.3.8}$$

$$\text{s.t.} \quad f^J(C^J(\tau), M^J(\tau)/p^J(\tau), R^J(\tau)) = 0 \tag{13.3.9}$$

where

$$C_0^J(\tau) = C^J(\tau) - I^J(\tau) \tag{13.3.10}$$
$$I^J(\tau) = \phi^J(C^J(\tau)) \tag{13.3.11}$$
$$\dot{R}(\tau) = I^J(\tau) - \bar{\alpha}R^J(\tau) \tag{13.3.12}$$

$\bar{\alpha}$ being a rate of depreciation or using up of resources, and for the initial condition

$$R^J(t) = R_t^J \tag{13.3.13}$$

R_t^J being the given resource base at year t.

Also we have

$$S_e^J(\tau) = \psi^J(S^J(\tau); S^L(\tau), \ldots) \tag{13.3.14}$$

for given $S^L(\tau), \ldots; L = A, \ldots, U; L \neq J$.

This formulation of the optimization problem is still inadequate since an appropriate statement of the dynamics of the problem should require the behaving unit to select a time path of military expenditures so that we could specify the equation

$$\dot{S}^J(\tau) = M^J(\tau)/p^J(\tau) - \alpha S^J(\tau - 1) \tag{13.3.15}$$

for the initial condition

$$S^J(t - 1) = S^J_{t-1} \tag{13.3.16}$$

S^J_{t-1} being the given weaponry stock at year $t - 1$, and where $p^J(\tau)$ is given and α is a constant. However, in the very short run of organizational politics, which is the political process that always determines military expenditures for a given year (time point), the political leader or the interest groups or legislature, which we discuss in what follows, behaves very much more as organizational person rather than economic person. Hence, we shall assume that the behaving unit, although it may be long-sighted with respect to resources and the need to maintain and increase productive capacity, is extremely short-sighted when it comes to military expenditures. It concentrates upon the level of current-year expenditures $M^J(t)$ and disregards entirely the issue of military expenditures in subsequent time points, confident that that issue will be properly handled when the time (the short run) for a decision on that issue comes around.

Several additional points need to be discussed. First, the Richardson-type behavior such as in Eq. (13.2.18) is already embodied in this utility formulation. This is so because the condition for maximization requires, in n-dimensional space, tangency between the transformation surface of Eq. (13.3.9) with an appropriate indifference surface. For any given level of investment, this indifference surface reflects the interplay of the $\bar{p}^J$, $\bar{c}^J$, and $\bar{g}^J$ parameters appropriate to the behaving unit, that is, this surface gives the response $M^J(t)$ to the values of all the appropriate variables contained in Eq. (13.2.18). This response is consistent with maximization of W^J of Eq. (13.3.8).

Another problem concerns the relation of $S^J_e(t)$ to $M^J(t)$. It is clear that the military expenditures in any time period are not all embodied as new weapons in the stock of that period but to a stream of additions to the new stocks in future time periods. Correspondingly, $\dot{S}^J(t)$ is a result of weapons maturing at time t from a series of military expenditures over several time periods in the past.

Next, we cannot assume that J knows the $S^L(\tau)$, $L = A, \ldots, U; L \neq J$, of any other nation for all future time periods. Typically, J recognizes that at least one other nation is interested in optimization and can conduct strategic analysis, and this would come to affect its choice of $M^J(t)$. According to rigorous differential game theory, J would precalculate how its armament expenditures should depend on the weapons stocks of all nations for all future time periods (see Simaan and Cruz 1975a,b). However, the logical refinements of differential game analysis cannot be said to characterize many aspects of reality. Decision makers employ cruder methods for determining (identifying) optimal behavior. Put in another way, even the simple straightforward utility function of Eq. (13.3.7) (let alone the theoretically more appropriate social welfare function W^J) to be maximized subject to constraints plays down the immensely more complicated strategic framework from which stems the objective function of reality. This function, as is widely recognized, evolves out of the politics of organizational person (already referred to) as it takes place in many nations. To the materialization of this objective function we now turn. We do so against the background of Majeski's organizational politics model discussed in section 2.8.

In an organizational politics model, there typically exists a finite number of interest groups. Although these groups may all make a proposal simultaneously, typically some one interest group makes a first proposal on one or more key magnitudes, military expenditures being a basic one in our study. The group clearly has in mind, however crude, some welfare index, payoff, utility, or something similar that it wishes to maximize. Let us say utility. Whereas in making a proposal on the level of military expenditures, it is not essential that national security S_e^J be one of the key variables in the utility function, generally we expect this to be the case. [We recognize that S_e^J, as defined by Eq. (13.3.4), is not an objectively measured variable, being perceived differently from one interest group to another; as many other perceived variables, we take it to have a precise definition.] We also expect there to be other key variables (associated with diverse objectives) of significance to one or more interest groups. One class of these variables pertains to noneconomic commodities such as c-power (measured by, say, size of military budget), c-rectitude, c-solidarity, c-respect, and c-prestige (measured by public opinion polls) or some index or weighted average of these, which we designate ξ_i^J for interest group i, $i = 1, 2, \ldots, n$. Another class of variables concerns magnitudes such as investment, expenditures on programs (environmental, low-income housing, health, etc.), deficits, tax rates, balance of payments, and interest rates or some index or weighted average of these, which we shall treat in terms of percentage rates of change designated γ_i^J for interest group i. Thus the general utility (welfare) function for any group i is

$$u_i^J = u_i^J(S_e^J, \gamma_i^J, \xi_i^J) \tag{13.3.17}$$

Moreover, there is frequently the need (or desirability) of being viewed by the public or others as responsible. We assume that the less responsible is one's proposal, the less weight it will carry in public, legislative, and other discussions. This need then sets bounds on proposals, the bounds being subjectively determined, often fuzzily. For example, for an interest group i (say, the Defense Services Agencies) whose proposal $\overline{M}_i^J$ for, say, military expenditures is well in excess of some reference level M^J_{Ref} (say, last year's military expenditures), we may have regarding its weight v_i

$$\frac{\partial v_i}{\partial(\overline{M}^J_i - M^J_{\text{Ref}})} \begin{cases} = 0 & \text{for } \overline{M}^J_i - M^J_{\text{Ref}} \leq B_i \\ < 0 & \text{for } \overline{M}^J_i - M^J_{\text{Ref}} > B_i \end{cases} \tag{13.3.18}$$

where B_i is an upper bound. Similarly, a relevant lower bound may exist for another interest group (say, an environmental lobby) whose proposal $\overline{M}^J_i$ is well below M^J_{Ref}. Together the upper and lower bounds define the responsibility set $\overline{MR}^J_i$.

In connection with proposals of expenditures on other programs (activities) there are also upper and lower bounds. If we let these bounds pertain to growth rates γ^J_i, then for the upper bound we may have:

$$\frac{\partial v_i}{\partial(\overline{\gamma}^J_i - \gamma^J_{i\text{Ref}})} \begin{cases} = 0 & \text{for } \overline{\gamma}^J_i - \gamma^J_{i\text{Ref}} \leq \overline{B}_i \\ < 0 & \text{for } \overline{\gamma}^J_i - \gamma^J_{i\text{Ref}} > \overline{B}_i \end{cases} \tag{13.3.19}$$

which together with a lower bound specified in parallel fashion defines the responsibility set $\overline{\Gamma}^J_i$.

No standard procedure exists by which to bring together the various proposals of interest groups (the behaving units in the organizational politics literature) to adopt a compromise proposal on an item. One of the simplest ways is to take an average of proposals, equally or unequally weighted, with weights being subject to change when a proposal is considered to be irresponsible. But in actuality such a simple procedure is not common. As discussed in Chapter 10, many different procedures can be used ranging from rank-oriented concessions and improvements to last-offer arbitration, incremax and decremax, priority determining, hierarchical programming, and so forth. In the use of a procedure, coalitions may be formed (such as the military–industrial complex), disrupted, and reformed in unending fashion; legal restrictions may be in force; and in general diverse cultural factors may stimulate and constrain behavior, processes, and outcomes. All this has been discussed elsewhere (Isard and Smith 1982). For our purposes, we assume a legislature (or an equivalent body) that determines (sets) the compromise proposal, let us say by use of a weighted average in a coalitionless framework. See the equation at the top of the C^J box at the right in Figure 13.2. When i makes responsible proposals, the weight v_i is identical to the w_i weight taken to be inherent in the social system of a nation. When i's proposals are not fully responsible, $v_i < w_i$, in accord with Eqs. (13.3.18) and (13.3.19). See the second equation in the C^J box.

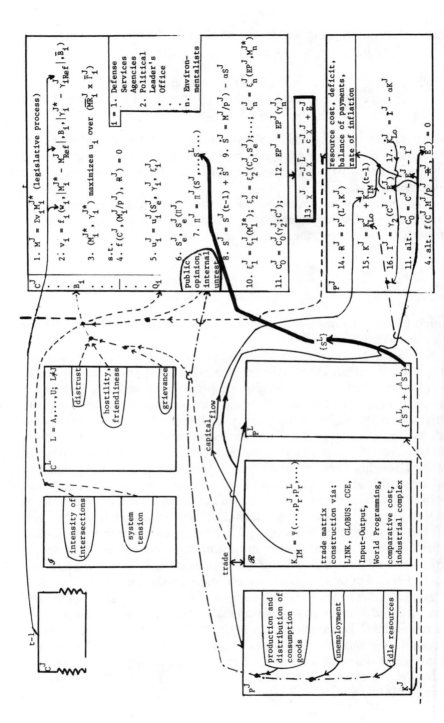

Figure 13.2. The optimization side of the coin in the $\mathcal{MJR}$ framework.

Now consider specific interest groups. Following Majeski, the administrative units of the military sector, taken to be the Defense Services Agencies (as is so for the United States), make the first budget proposal (request) for year t. Via their expectations of the political leader's (president's) proposal, they propose a level of military expenditures $M_1^{J*}(t)$ based on

1. their last year's proposal $M_1^{J*}(t-1)$,
2. the leader's last year's proposals $M_2^{J*}(t-1)$, to which, in the case of the United States, we have added,
3. last year's increase in Soviet military expenditures $\dot{M}^{L*}(t-1)$ [compare Eqs. (2.8.1) and (2.8.2)]. The level $M_1^{J*}(t)$, by implication, maximizes their utility function, given the need for responsibility and desire for commodities (e.g., c-power and national security) associated with one or more of their "subobjectives."

Theoretically, for dynamical analysis, we should require the Defense Services Agencies to look beyond the current year and do sophisticated analysis of the effects of its proposed military expenditures upon future productive capacity, stocks of weapons, c-power and security, and welfare in general. With certain modifications, its welfare function might look similar to that for the nation depicted by Eq. (13.3.8), and its problem might be viewed somewhat as the nation's depicted by Eqs. (13.3.8)–(13.3.16). Actually, appropriate analysis of such a problem is beyond the capacity of these agencies and hardly what in practice the agencies do. In view of uncertainties, limited time for research and decision making, and their own limited capabilities, they almost invariably eschew such sophisticated analysis even though aware of some of the potentials of such. They are fully cognizant of bureaucratic momentum and precedent decision making. They therefore judge that in the future adequate productive capacity, adequate rates of investment, adequate security, and so on, will be reasonably ensured provided at least a *certain* rate of increase in investment, say, γ', is obtained in year t. Since

$$\gamma'(t) = \frac{I'(t) - I'(t-1)}{I'(t-1)} \tag{13.3.20}$$

the choice of a specific $\gamma'(t)$ then determines the level $I'(t)$ of investment and thus $C_0'(t)$ once $C'(t)$ is determined by the choice of $M_1'(t)$.

Alternatively, the agencies may look upon γ' as a variable. Again, because of bureaucratic momentum and precedent decision making, they judge that once an appropriate (and responsible) level is secured for the current year t, this will ensure future-year rates adequate to meet the needs for national security and c-power. In this more general case, the utility function of these agencies (where $i = 1$) becomes

$$u_1^J(t) = u_1^J(S_e^J(t), \gamma_1^J(t), \xi_1^J(t))$$ (13.3.21)

which is the fifth statement in the C^J box of Figure 13.2.

At this point, observe that the rate γ_1^J may, in a more generalized fashion, be taken to be the weighted average $\Sigma w_1^{h,J} \gamma_1^{h,J}$ of several rates $\gamma_1^{h,J}$, $h = 1, 2, \ldots$, where $\gamma_1^{h,J}$ is the rate of growth in investment (or expenditures) in the hth sector, activity, or other relevant category.

As before, $S_e^J(t)$ [or each type of security $_aS_e^J(t)$, $_aS_e^J(t)$, $_sS_e^J(t)$] may be taken as a function of $S^J(t)$, $S^L(t)$, $\ldots$, that is, of the stocks of weapons (or stocks of types of weapon) held by various nations. See Eq. (13.3.14) and Eqs. (13.3.15) and (13.3.16), where S^J and $\dot{S}^J$, respectively, are defined for given α, p^J, and S^L, $L = A, \ldots, U$, $L \neq J$. However, for an organization associated with the defense sector, we might have

$$S_e^J(t) = S_e^J(\Pi^J)$$ (13.3.22)

where Π^J is the payoff from a hypothetical missile war as defined by Eq. (2.5.8).

In the calculation (estimation) of the payoff, the attitude (e.g., degree of conservatism) of the Defense Services Agencies as well as the calculation (estimation) of the numbers of surviving missiles are critical factors.

In Eq. (13.3.21), relevant for the Defense Service Agencies and others associated with the military sector, ξ_1^J might be c-power and only c-power, or a weighted average of noneconomic commodities, or an index of such. We take $\xi_1^J(t)$ to be given by

$$\xi_1^J(t) = \xi_1^J(M_1^{J*}(t))$$ (13.3.23)

that is, a function of military expenditures and only military expenditures. See the tenth statement in the C^J box of Figure 13.2.

In this framework, the Defense Services Agencies, when more rather than less sophisticated, select $\{M_1^{J*}(t), \gamma_1^{J*}(t)\}$, which is that combination within the responsibility product set $\overline{MR}_1^J \times \overline{\Gamma}_1^J$ that maximizes its utility subject to the transformation function of Eq. (13.3.9). See the third and fourth statements in the C^J box of Figure 13.2. At the other extreme, when narrow and less sophisticated, the agencies simply select $M_1^{J*}(t)$, the level of military expenditures within the responsibility set $\overline{MR}_1^J$ that maximizes its utility. In between these two extremes, the agencies may feel that the legislature and political leader (president), individually or jointly, can be relied upon to allocate the $C^J(t)$ so as to ensure an adequate level of investment and growth in productive capacity. For them, γ_1^J may still not be a relevant variable, or it may be such that for all γ_1^J or for all $\gamma_1^J \geq \overline{\gamma}_1^J$, where $\overline{\gamma}_1^J$ is a rate certainly assured by legislative and executive action, $\partial u_1^J / \partial \gamma_1^J < \epsilon$, some very small value.

Also, the agencies (and the interest groups discussed in what follows) may in fact be sophisticated enough to recognize the differential game aspects of the conflict situation; but we assume that they are not capable of and do not possess sufficient information for developing appropriate strategy (behavior). We assume they take as given S^L, $L = A, \ldots, U;$ $L \neq J$, and behave myopically regarding the behavior of other interest groups and ignore the feedback of the legislative decision regarding $M^J(t)$ upon security $S_e^J(t)$ and their c-power $\xi_1^J(t)$.

When we consider a typical nonmilitary organization, a somewhat different approach may be followed in setting forth a budget request (proposal). Take the office of the primary political leader, for example, the prime minister's office in the case of Britain and the presidential office in the United States. As a component of the vector of expenditures on diverse programs that maximizes the political leader's utility, his (or her) most desired level M_2^{J**} of military expenditures may be considered too "idealistic," say, too high, as in the case of the current (1988) president of the United States. In that sense it may be said to lack responsibility. To achieve full responsibility, which requires recognizing the needs and objectives of the several interest groups involved, the political leader proposes something less than $M_2^{J**}(t)$, namely, $M_2^{J*}(t)$. Of the various combinations of program expenditures in (or close by) his set of responsible combinations $\overline{MR}_2^J$, the one that maximizes his utility is one that involves $M_2^{J*}(t)$ as the level of military expenditures. His utility u_2^J is given by

$$u_2^J(t) = u_2^J(S_e^J(t), \gamma_2^J, \xi_2^J(t)) \tag{13.3.24}$$

where $\xi_2^J(t)$ is a relevant noneconomic commodity such as c-respect, or some other commodity perhaps related to an index of public opinion, or some index or aggregate of noneconomic commodities. We take ξ_2^J to be given by

$$\xi_2^J(t) = \xi_2^J(C_0^J(t), S_e^J(t)) \tag{13.3.25}$$

See the tenth statement in the C^J box of Figure 13.2. Here $C_0^J(t)$ is household consumption and may be taken to represent the extent to which the basic needs (food, housing, health, etc.) of the leader's constituency are currently met.

We assume that the political leader, as the Defense Services Agencies, compresses all the future into a variable γ_2^J whose value he (or she) selects. For a sophisticated political leader surrounded by expert economists, this variable may be the growth rate of GNP in the current year, obtainable from an efficient allocation of civilian goods production $C^J(t)$ to household consumption $C_0^J(t)$ and investment $I^J(t)$ or to a more disaggregated set of categories. For other political leaders, $\gamma_2^J(t)$ may be a weighted average of rates of growth (or decline) of investment (or expenditures) in several sectors, activities, or relevant categories. A satisfactory $\gamma_2^J(t)$ [where $\gamma_2^J(t)$ is adjusted to take into account the current business cycle situation] is such as to ensure, on the basis of sociopolitical–economic momentum, satisfactory rates of growth of GNP (or sectors or activities) in the future – and thus satisfactory rates of growth of productive capacity and of the potential for meeting basic needs of the constituency and mounting military expenditures necessary to achieve security. Given the utility function of Eq. (13.3.24), the political leader then selects the optimal combination of $M_2^{J*}(t)$ [which then via Eqs. (13.3.9) and (13.3.14)–(13.3.16) yields $S_e^J(t)$ and $C^J(t)$] and $\gamma_2^{J*}(t)$ [which then leads to the allocation of C^J between $I^J(t)$ and $C_0^J(t)$]. Once $C_0^J(t)$ and $S_e^J(t)$ are determined, the level of ξ_2^J is determined by Eq. (13.3.25). This optimal choice may be said to be reflected in Majeski's finding that $M_2^{J*}(t)$ for the president of the United States for the period 1953–76 is related to several reference magnitudes: (1) the president's last year's request, (2) the current Defense Services Agencies request, and (3) the expected federal deficit. See Eqs. (2.8.3) and (2.8.4).

At least one more type of interest group should be discussed, namely, a nonmilitary interest group with one or a relatively few narrowly defined objectives. Take a group, the environmentalists, primarily concerned with environmental quality and its improvement. Ideally, it would like to select a very low level $M_3^{J**}(t)$ of military expenditures because not only is the military sector a heavy environmental polluter, but also its expenditures are at the expense of other social welfare programs. However, to avoid being considered irresponsible, it chooses a higher level $M_3^{J*}(t)$. This higher level is consistent with a vector of program expenditures that is in (or close by) the set of responsible vectors and maximizes the environmentalist's utility $u_3^J(t)$ given by

$$u_3^J(t) = u_3^J(S_e^J(t), \gamma_3^J(t), \xi_3^J(t)) \qquad (13.3.26)$$

Here, $\xi_3^J(t)$ may correspond to the noneconomic commodity c-rectitude (a measure of achievement of the moral principles attached to the preservation and enhancement of the environment). We take $\xi_3^J(t)$ to (1) depend primarily on and to vary directly with the level of expenditures $EP^J(t)$ on environmental protection programs and (2) vary inversely with the level of military expenditures. That is,

$$\xi_3^J(t) = \xi_3^J(EP^J(t), M_3^J(t)) \qquad (13.3.27)$$

See the tenth statement in the C^J box of Figure 13.2. The variable ξ_3^J could also be an index or weighted average of noneconomic commodities.

In Eq. (13.3.26) the variable $\gamma_3^j(t)$ is taken to be the rate of growth of expenditures on environmental protection programs. Hence

$$\gamma_3^j(t) = \frac{\mathrm{EP}^j(t) - \mathrm{EP}^j(t-1)}{\mathrm{EP}^j(t-1)} \tag{13.3.28}$$

The variable $\gamma_3^j(t)$ could be constructed to be related to the growth rate of expenditures on several related programs.

Once again, the interest group compresses all the future into the variable $\gamma_3^j(t)$. Because of bureaucratic momentum and precedent decision making, a satisfactory $\gamma_3^j(t)$ is taken to be such as to ensure satisfactory rates of growth in environmental protection expenditures and related programs in future years. Also in the utility function of Eq. (13.3.26) we have included the security variable $S_e^j(t)$ in order to have the same general utility function Eq. (13.3.17) for each interest group i. However, in the case of the environmentalists, its utility may be highly insensitive to large changes in $S_e^j(t)$, ceteris paribus.

Given its utility (welfare) function [Eq. (13.3.26)], the environmental group then selects the optimal combination of $M_3^{j*}(t)$ [which via Eqs. (13.3.9) and (13.3.14)–(13.3.16) yields $S_e^j(t)$ and $C^j(t)$] and $\gamma_3^{j*}(t)$ [which via Eq. (13.3.28) determines the amount $C^j(t) - \mathrm{EP}^j(t)$ to be allocated by the competitive market to investment, household consumption, and other nonmilitary and nonenvironmental activities and programs].

At this point, note that we have digressed from the Majeski approach. Once the president has chosen $M_2^{j*}(t)$, Majeski has Congress identifying its $M_4^{j**}(t)$ and selecting its optimal responsible level $M_4^{j*}(t)$ and later making a supplemental appropriation so that the Department of Defense achieves its $M_3^{j*}(t)$, the actual level of military expenditures, at a responsible level lower than its ideal level $M_5^{j**}(t)$. As already indicated, we prefer to view the nation's legislature as an implicit mediator of the wishes and demands of different interest groups of the nation. We have the legislature hear the proposals of all and be sensitive to their relative importance, that is, attach weights to these proposals, which weights derive in part from the C^j cognitive decision-making system. It reaches a compromise level $M^j(t)$ using one of the simplest of many possible conflict management procedures.[7]

---

[7] In a pure abstract sense, we can also imagine that the legislature serves as a competitive political market. Each of the several legislators represents a number of interest groups so that many interest groups can be said to be involved. Each interest group sets forth its proposal on military expenditures M_i^j, growth rates γ_i^j for one or more sectors or programs, etc. Its representative brings these proposals to the political market, which takes place when the legislature meets. Through the operation of the market, which can be simulated as the economic market employing a fictitious participant who controls prices (the implicit price of tax money in the case of the political market), the diverse demands of the many interest groups can be mediated and an equilibrium vector of growth rates and expenditures by type and program can be derived (see Isard et al. 1969, pp. 669–77, 750–7).

This model and Majeski's are just two of many possible organizational political models oriented to the U.S. social system, which differs greatly from the social systems of other nations. Hence, they can be viewed only as very special cases of the general utility framework that we have set forth. Realism, responsibility, recognition of interdependence, precedence, and other factors come to constrain proposals that utility-maximizing behaving units make. Through institutional processes, typically involving the use of a conflict management procedure, formally or informally, the units' proposals lead to a decision, whether joint or not, by default or not, on the level of military expenditures.

Before closing, we wish to indicate more explicitly how arms race phenomena connect with other basic processes taking place within the world system. Figure 2.7, pertaining to the GLOBUS model within the $\mathcal{MJR}$ paridigm of Peace Science, is particularly instructive in this regard and should be constantly referred to in the following discussion. We show in Figure 13.2 flow of capital from the $\mathcal{R}$ box (relating to the world economic and financial markets) to the P^J box, the production subsystem of nation J. As indicated in the $\mathcal{R}$ box, this flow is a function of the prices of capital services (interest rates on capital) in the several nations of the world. These prices, of course, are interconnected with and generated by the savings (negative and positive), investment, financial, and other behavior of diverse sectors of each national economy and by the linkages among these national economies. Such behavior and linkages are explicitly examined in world system models such as LINK, GLOBUS, the United Nations World Input–Output model, the Novosibirsk World Programming Model, and comparative cost and industrial complex models, discussed in Chapter 9 and in Isard and Smith (1982, 1983).

In addition to prices, the flow of capital is greatly influenced by political stability, expectations of inflation rates and foreign exchange rates, and other factors. In Figure 13.2 the capital flow of the previous time period from the $\mathcal{R}$ box then enters into statement 15 in the P^J box as $K_{IM}^J(t-1)$ (capital imports), which supplements K_{LO}^J (the local stock of capital[8]) to yield the capital K^J, which together with the labor force L^J are taken to be the main determinants of $\mathcal{R}^J$ (J's resources or productive capacity). See statement 14. This capital flow can be a very significant factor in that it can affect in a major way $\mathcal{R}^J$, which enters into the transformation function (statement 4) and frequently constitutes a binding constraint.

---

[8] We define K_{LO}^J broadly to cover capital investments in mineral resource development and the accompanying value of these resources. Investment in human resources is embodied in L^J.

A second critical connection with the world economic system $\mathcal{R}$ and the production systems P^L, $L = A, \ldots, U; L \neq J$, of other nations is via trade, that is, commodity flows (exports and imports). Again, the projection of such has been examined in Chapter 9. Such flows of civilian goods[9] enter into P^J, the production system of J, in statement 16 as E^J. When E^J is negative (representing net imports), it supplements the current output C^J of civilian goods, and this permits larger investment I^J, or larger household consumption C_0^J, or both. When E^J is positive, it reduces the allocation of current output to one or more of these items. In this sense, commodity imports (exports) relieve (increase) pressures on current productive capacity to meet various demands placed on it, and this comes to affect directly and indirectly the resulting level of military and other expenditures. Note that E^J and K_{IM}^J have impact on the balance of payments, rate of inflation, and so on, as indicated by relevant arrows. Note also from statement 17 that via its effect on gross investment I^J, trade has impact on $\dot{K}_{LO}^J$, the net change in capital stock of J. (In statement 17, α represents a depreciation coefficient, and the term αK^J roughly represents replacement needs.) The capital stock $K^J(t - 1)$ of the previous period plus $\dot{K}_{LO}^J(t)$ yields $K_{LO}^J(t)$.

Last, when exports (and imports) are taken into account, the transformation function of statement 4 in Figure 13.2 must be replaced by the statement 4 alt. at the bottom of the P^J box and statement 11 must be replaced by statement 11 alt. Note that in allowing E^J to enter into statements 4 alt., 16, and 11 alt., we are assuming that actual magnitudes of net exports (imports) are known at the decision point of time during time period t, when in fact during that part of this time period subsequent to the decision point, net exports (imports) can only be estimated. This is, of course, a common problem in a dynamics-type model when discrete units of time are prescribed by available data and other factors. The same type of problem arises where the net change in $\dot{K}_{LO}(t)$ is taken to enter into $\mathcal{R}^J$ (productive capacity) when actually only that part realized before the decision point of time is known.

13.4 Concluding remarks

In drawing this chapter to a close, we reiterate that what we have attempted is to pull together and synthesize where possible the various

---

[9] Flows of military goods, which are largely associated with foreign military assistance, are taken to be embodied in the M^J/p^J magnitude, as associated with the variable $_sS_e^J$, security from spheres of influence. To avoid complexity, we assume that there exists no trade in strictly military goods for the purpose of profit.

key factors and relationships found in the extensive literature on arms race models. In part we have been motivated to do so in order to provide a background that can make clearer the differences and similarities among the diverse arms race models and to make explicit what each one does and does not do. In part we have been motivated to effect the synthesis of elements of diverse models in order to increase our understanding of arms race phenomena and also lay the groundwork for the construction of superior arms race models by scholars in the future. The generalized reaction, burden, and grievance-type coefficients, for example, represent what we consider to be one significant direction of synthesis and allow a scholar more effectively to design a model consistent with his or her theories and experience.

Further, we have found that the diverse arms race models, in their different emphasis and foci, may be viewed as falling on one of the two sides of the same coin. Those following the Richardson tradition with emphasis on reaction, burden, and grievance factors imply utility maximization or the equivalent. Those that focus on some payoff, utility, or other objective function and its optimization imply the Richardson-type of reaction, burden, and grievance factors. These two different emphases are depicted somewhat summarily in Figures 13.1 and 13.2, where we have placed selected symbols and relationships in the relevant boxes of the $\mathcal{MJR}$ paradigm for the field of Peace Science. These figures allow us to see more clearly how the arms race processes fit into the set of processes characterizing the functioning of the world system and the role that arms race phenomena must play in world system models.

More concretely, the synthesis pursued in this chapter hopefully enables us to put into (develop for) world system models, such as LINK, World Input–Output, and GLOBUS, behavioral equations on military expenditures, and scenarios on arms escalation–deescalation significantly better than the crude ones reported upon in Chapter 9, which we are currently forced to use. Moreover, this synthesis should enable us to treat more effectively the direct and indirect impact of escalation–deescalation processes and military expenditures upon the world system as well as the direct and indirect influence of the functioning of the world system upon these processes and expenditures.

References

See those listed in Chapters 2 and 9.

CHAPTER 14

Learning by a group, its leader, and its individual members

14.1   Introduction

In Chapter 6 we probed into the analysis of learning that comes from search for new information and in general research and development aimed at reaching a solution (or a more satisfactory one) to a problem that cannot be attacked routinely, as is certainly the case with the U.S.–Soviet arms control problem. We presented three approaches: (1) cognitive science, (2) artificial intelligence, and (3) economics. Admittedly, all three approaches and others require major development since the effective analysis by each of learning for problem solving has only been recent. Moreover, such analysis is exceedingly complex, involving uncertainty and the interrelated play of a host of factors because the desired learning requires creativity. Hence, we find it fruitful to attempt to probe further into this subject area with the use of mathematics. As can be expected, where we can conduct rigorous mathematical analysis, as in this chapter where we model one type of learning by a group (its leader) and its members, we admittedly have little to say about creative information research and development. This is because of the very strong assumptions about behavior we must make in order to achieve rigorous analysis. As with many of the models developed by economists, regional scientists, game theorists, and operational researchers, models involving such strong assumptions cannot be said to depict reality (e.g., see Killingsworth 1982) and hence are primarily useful, as in the study of problem solving, for providing key insights, however few, into the actual processes of inven-

This chapter draws very heavily upon and reproduces considerable materials in Isard et al. (1969, chap. 15), in whose development Tony Smith was involved as a joint author. Also, the author is grateful to Kai Michaelis for invaluable help in developing the Appendix materials. The shortcomings of this chapter, however, are solely those of the author.

439

tion and research and development and what motivates behaving units to engage in such.

In Chapter 15 we shall pursue less rigorous mathematical analysis, and accordingly we perhaps have more to say. There we examine the decision to engage in information research and development as an investment decision, in particular in an attempt to manage (resolve) a conflict. We draw upon relevant dynamical systems analysis in economics and regional science, but our analysis is meant to be only suggestive and not rigorous.

Finally, in Chapter 16 we enter into some exploratory analysis; and in order to avert any sharp criticism by rigorous analysts, we designate this activity as purely speculative, based on nonrigorous intuitive probes. That chapter attempts to analyze the invention and innovation process with regard to new creative ideas for problem solving, as is surely and sorely required for developing U.S.–Soviet arms control policy. In that chapter, we find it very helpful to use mathematical symbols and analogues (in particular, a two-equation-of-motion system) from physics and from regional science as they relate to spatial dynamics. Though what we present is pure speculation, we sometimes cannot but help feel that it constitutes a more fruitful and insightful probe than those in Chapters 14 and 15 and in many other works of a much more rigorous character.

In the present chapter we develop in section 14.2 a qualitative model of the learning process by a group and its members as a first extension of learning via research activity by the individual and group, as discussed in sections 4.2.6 and 4.3.6, respectively. In section 14.3 we move on to a quantitative approach with members only learning. Next, in section 14.4 we explore a quantitative approach with both the leader and members learning. Section 14.5 concludes with a discussion on generalizations for a hierarchical social system. The Appendix examines the technical question of convergence to a solution.

14.2   A qualitative approach

To begin to probe into a group's learning process where members' learning is also involved, we first construct a simple macro–micro model. Although we view this model as applicable to sequential decision processes within groups in general, we develop it for a political group confronting some issue (such as a platform or policy statement) and where it must choose among alternatives.[1]

---

[1] This political group may be a national political party, each member being a leader of a state group; or the state political group, each member being a leader of a substate group; or a city ward unit, each member being a voter.

To start, we suppose that certain group "orientations," beliefs, and so on, within the group constrain the set of perceived alternatives to be considered for debate and discussion. Typically, differences of opinion will arise among members as to which of these alternatives is "best" for the group as a whole. Hence, we assume that with the aid of some well-established decision procedure (such as a majority rule), the group is always able to resolve its differences and choose a unique alternative. Nevertheless, after observing the outcome of the alternative chosen (say, that of a public opinion poll conducted by telephone immediately after the choice of the alternative), certain members of the group may change their opinions concerning the relative merits of the alternatives. In fact, the group's beliefs as a whole may change. If these changes are sufficiently great, the members of the group may then be motivated to reconsider the decision. Hence, if the choice of an alternative by the group is retractable (at negligible cost), we may imagine a learning process for the political group in which a sequence of trial-and-error decisions leads it eventually to a choice of some "equilibrium" action for its given situation.

In modeling this learning process, we develop a macro–micro model of the political group, incorporating the interrelated elements just outlined. We then treat sequences of group decisions as an equilibrating adjustment process, as in the cobweb model of economics and the Simon–Homans model in sociology (Simon 1957, chap. 6).

We begin by formulating a background model in purely qualitative terms. Rather than employing specific "variables" that can be precisely defined and measured, we speak more generally of those group properties that constitute the relevant "elements" of the model. That is, instead of defining specific "functional" relationships among variables, we define looser relationships among elements that we here call "determinental" relationships, such as "element v is a determinant of element η."[2]

The first group property that constitutes an element of our model might be designated the orientation (or disposition or style) of beliefs. The part of the *orientation belief system B* relevant to the particular issue discussed is designated $\overset{\iota}{B}$. This system is taken to be a reflection of the group's general political outlook, be it liberal, conservative, or otherwise; and as per Gamson (1981), it is also taken to include its "packages" involving beliefs regarding causal relations and other items.

To be more specific, we postulate that $\overset{\iota}{B}$ depends on two relevant elements. The first is the set of physical and cultural factors the group has inherited from its environment. We designate this element of influence

---

[2] We drop this distinction in the next part, where we develop a quantitative model with specific functional relationships, and show how this model can yield a precise solution under certain conditions.

as the *heredity H* of the political group and assume that it remains constant over time. It includes, among other factors, the set of institutional characteristics, procedures, symbolism, goals, roles, and other customs inherited from the past as well as certain age, sex, race, nationality, and other relevant characteristics of its members. The second is the present state of the group's *active memory* $\overset{a}{Me}_m$ (active knowledge) about its environment, which over time has been accumulated and organized in terms of what it perceives to be meaningful relations.[3]

Thus, using the symbol d to denote a determinental relation, we have the following relationship at any point (designated as move m) in the group's decision process:

$$\overset{r}{B}_m = d_1(\overset{a}{Me}_m; H) \tag{14.2.1}$$

This relationship may be read as "the element $\overset{a}{Me}_m$ and H are the determinants of $\overset{r}{B}_m$." See the upper left-hand side of Figure 14.1.

We take $\mathcal{P}(A)$ as the *perceived set of alternative action choices a* that may be taken on that issue. However, typically, only a small number of such alternatives can be placed upon the floor for deliberation, debate, and discussion by the group. We designate this reduced set as the group's *perceived restricted action* space $\mathcal{P}(\tilde{A})$ and on any move m take it to be influenced by the group's active memory $\overset{a}{Me}_m$ as well as its relevant orientation and beliefs $\overset{r}{B}_m$.[4] That is, we have

$$\mathcal{P}(\tilde{A}_m) = d_2(\overset{a}{Me}_m, \overset{r}{B}_m, \mathcal{P}(A)) \tag{14.2.2}$$

(See the upper left-hand side of Figure 14.1.)

Given the perceived restricted action space $\mathcal{P}(\tilde{A}_m)$ on any move m, the key element of the group decision process on that move is its action choice a_m from $\mathcal{P}(\tilde{A}_m)$. The factors determining this action choice are as follows.[5]

First, the participants must be able to anticipate (expect) the outcome $\hat{o}_m$ from each possible action choice a_m. Hence we assume that for the decision process of the political group, there exists an outcome function θ that associates with every possible action choice $a_m \in \tilde{A}_m$ on each move m a unique outcome o_m. (To avoid complexity, we assume that this function is constant over time.) That is, we have the determinental relationship

$$o_m = d_3(a_m; \theta) \tag{14.2.3}$$

(See the middle right-hand side of Figure 14.1.)

---

[3] This is an extension of part of Equation (4.3.2) already noted, namely, $\overset{r}{B}_m \subset \overset{a}{Me}_m$.
[4] Such memory and orientation may be assumed, e.g., to be fully reflected in the views and attitudes of the group's leader, who is taken as a strictly average (100% representative) member of the group.
[5] However, see the somewhat different discussion of these factors in section 4.2.5.

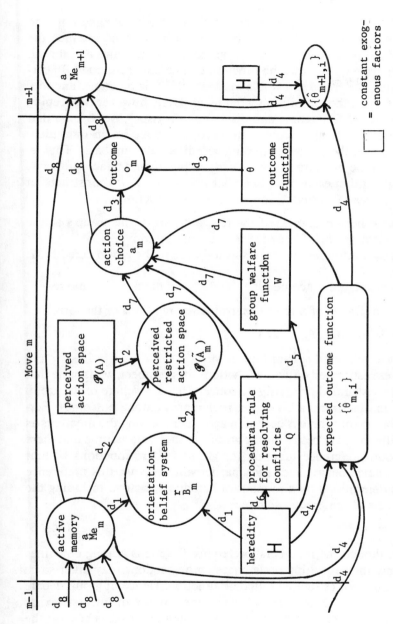

Figure 14.1. Flow diagram of the qualitative macro–micro (learning) model.

Now if the group were knowledgeable of this actual outcome function θ, there would be no need for a sequential decision process since the members could presumably decide on an action choice once and for all. In reality, however, the outcome function can be only estimated. In certain situations, the group as a whole may estimate this outcome function, for example, with the aid of a research team. Here, however, in keeping with the notion of full debate and discussion on issues, we assume that at least some aspects of outcome estimation are done on an individual basis by each member rather than on a coordinated group basis. That is, we view outcome estimation as a micro rather than a macroproperty. Hence, we posit that each group member i $(i = 1, \ldots, n)$ constructs an *estimated outcome function* $\hat{\theta}_{m,i}$ on move m as a function of

1. his (or her) awareness of the relevant part of the group's active memory (stock of knowledge) $\overset{a}{M}e_m$ on that move;
2. his own attitudes and biases as reflected in the group heredity H; and
3. his estimated outcome function $\hat{\theta}_{m-1,i}$ on the previous move.

That is, we have a set of n microdeterminental relations of the form[6]

$$\hat{\theta}_{m,i} = d_{4,i}(\overset{a}{M}e_m, \hat{\theta}_{m-1,i}; H) \qquad (14.2.4)$$

(See the lower left-hand side of Figure 14.1.)

Given these estimated outcome functions for members, we assume that each member is guided primarily by concern for the welfare of the group as a whole in determining his or her preferences among outcomes. Further, we assume that there is common agreement among the members as to which outcomes are better for the group. In short, we assume that there exists a group preference function (or group welfare function) W that guides the choice behavior of each participant. Because this preference function is determined by a number of hereditary factors, including the inherited goals of the group, we have

$$W = d_5(H) \qquad (14.2.5)$$

But even though the members' preference functions among outcomes are the same, their resulting preferences among actions may differ since each has a different estimated outcome function. Hence, if group debate and discussion on the issue reveal that some conflict of interests exists among the members as to which action each member feels is best for the

---

[6] If we were to postulate a more rational individual as per economics, we would have an estimate of a prospect (a probability distribution over outcomes). See Isard et al. (1969, p. 167).

group on move m, we may define a mixed-motive game situation for the members on that move. We then assume that among the properties the group inherits is a procedural rule Q (such as a majority voting rule or the use of a simple weighted average) for resolving conflicts of interest. Thus we have

$$Q = d_6(H) \tag{14.2.6}$$

In sum, each action choice a_m for the group is determined as a function of the perceived restricted action space $\mathcal{P}(\tilde{A}_m)$, the group welfare function W, and procedural rule Q together with the set $\{\hat{\theta}_{m,i}\}$ of n estimated outcome functions of its members.[7] That is,

$$a_m = d_7(\mathcal{P}(\tilde{A}_m), \{\hat{\theta}_{m,i}\}; W, Q) \tag{14.2.7}$$

(See the center of Figure 14.1.)

Given this action choice by the group, a unique outcome o_m then results from the determinental relationship given in Eq. (14.2.3). This outcome in turn constitutes new information and changes the group's active memory (knowledge) according to the macrodeterminental relation

$$\overset{a}{M}e_{m+1} = d_8(a_m, o_m, \overset{a}{M}e_m) \tag{14.2.8}$$

This change in active memory (shown in the upper part of Figure 14.1) may then be regarded as *learning L* by the group. That is, on move m we have

$$L_m = d_9(\overset{a}{M}e_{m+1}, \overset{a}{M}e_m) \tag{14.2.9}$$

Nevertheless, the preceding change in information and hence active memory will, in general, lead the group to reconsider its present decision (i.e., action choice). For example, on the macrolevel, the change in active memory (knowledge) may lead the group to change its orientation belief system $\hat{B}$ [as in (14.2.1)] as well as redefine its perceived set of relevant alternatives $\mathcal{P}(\tilde{A})$ [as in (14.2.2)]. This is so because the true outcome function θ, which is not known, can now be better estimated with the additional observation (unless the outcome was exactly as expected by the group as a whole.)[8] On the microlevel the change in active memory (knowledge) of the group implies change in the active memory of each member i. This is so because the expected outcome function $\hat{\theta}_{m,i}$ of i at move m is by Eq. (14.2.4) based upon at least part of the active memory

---

[7] In using this notation, we let $\theta_{m,i}$ denote a representative element of this set. Also, in Eq. (14.2.7) we assume elements W and Q are constant.
[8] The total stock of knowledge Me also changes so that alternative forms of the learning function (14.2.9) are possible.

$\overset{a}{Me}_m$ of the group. So if $\overset{a}{Me}_m$ changes to $\overset{a}{Me}_{m+1}$, the $\hat{\theta}_{m,i}$ will also change to $\hat{\theta}_{m+1,i}$.[9] The new function $\hat{\theta}_{m+1,i}$ will then lead to new outcome estimates for each action and, in general, to new preferences among action choices by the members. Together with the new $\mathcal{P}(\tilde{A}_{m+1})$ these changes in preferences will motivate a new round of group decision making.

In Figure 14.1 we have summarized this general model in graphic terms. The arrows between elements depict the determinental relationships hypothesized and are labeled in accord with the determinental expressions discussed in the preceding. The figure clearly shows that it is the change in $\overset{a}{Me}_m$ (stemming from the realized outcome o_m associated with the action choice a_m and implicit expected outcomes), which constitutes the major linkage between moves. This change initiates a group-learning process by which information is continually fed back and reevaluated by the members of the group. Moreover, the figure shows that the direct effects of this learning process (i.e., the changes in $\overset{a}{Me}_m$, $\overset{b}{B}_m$, $\mathcal{P}(\tilde{A}_m)$, and $\{\hat{\theta}_{m,i}\}$) may lead to a change in the group's action choice from a_m to a_{m+1}. This process continues until at some round $m + h$, an action a_{m+h} is taken for which the resulting changes in $\overset{a}{Me}_{m+h-1}$ are so small that two things occur: (a) the group as a whole is not motivated to change $\mathcal{P}(\tilde{A}_{m+h})$; and (b) each member i is no longer motivated to change $\hat{\theta}_{m+h,i}$. If such an action can be achieved by the group, we shall say that it has reached a state of equilibrium, for clearly the adjustment process must then come to a halt.

We now conclude our brief presentation of a model based on "determinental" relationships. Although this approach has helped to illustrate some of the major factors that may influence political decision behavior, the model itself is, of course, too qualitative. It provides us with no detail on the adjustment process, nor does it permit us to examine equilibrium properties. Hence, we are now motivated to consider ways of "operationalizing" this qualitative model in order to gain deeper insights into the behavior of political groups.

14.3   Toward a quantitative approach with members only learning

We attempt in this part to quantify the macro–micro political model by replacing determinental relations among general elements with functional relations among specific variables. We do not attempt to preserve

---

[9] This in turn points up the expectation factor embodied (implicitly) in the variable $\overset{a}{Me}_m$ in Eq. (14.2.8) and hence in the learning Eq. (14.2.9). Such then is consistent with the explicit expectation variable $Exp^i(t - 1)$ discussed in section 4.3.3.

all the elements of the qualitative model already developed but instead concentrate on those elements that seem the most important. Finally, it should be emphasized that the variables and functional relations used here to "operationalize" the macro–micro model are designed primarily as illustrations of the ways in which such a model might be constructed. Our aim is to reflect the major elements of the model within as simple an analytic framework as possible.

To begin, consider the specific problem of a platform committee of a national political party, henceforth designated the *party*, which must decide on the level of foreign aid for military purposes that it should advocate. Imagine that the national foreign aid bill could never realistically exceed \$10 billion. Measuring foreign aid in billion dollars units, we may characterize *actions* a for the party as a scalar variable with range $0 \leq a \leq 10$. Finally, as we designate the highest possible level of foreign aid in A by the parameter $\bar{a}$ (which equals 10 in our case), we may define A in terms of the parameter $\bar{a}$ as

$$A = \{a \mid 0 \leq a \leq \bar{a}\} \tag{14.3.1}$$

In this way, the element A of the qualitative macro–micro model may now be replaced by the scalar parameter $\bar{a}$.[10]

Given this characterization of the party's action space, we now consider the elements of the decision process that will lead the party to the choice of an action a on each move. To begin, the members of the program committee (e.g., political representatives of each state), henceforth designated *members* of the party, must be able to associate outcomes with each possible action. Imagine for simplicity that given any policy statement $a \in A$ on foreign aid, the members of the party perceive only one relevant property of the associated outcome, namely, the public support accruing to the party from that statement. If this support is measurable in terms of the percentage of support (favorable response) the party receives in an objectively conducted public opinion poll, we may characterize *outcomes* o for the party as a scalar variable with (normalized) percentage range $0 \leq o \leq 1$.

Next assume that given any policy statement a_m at move m, there exists a unique percentage support o_m that the party will receive. This

---

[10] Observe that this representation is made possible only by assuming that the left-end point of A is always zero. More generally, we might represent the left-end and right-end points by $\bar{a}_1$ and $\bar{a}_2$, respectively. Even more generally, we could define A as a union of disjoint intervals rather than a single interval. Further, we could extend A to multidimensional intervals. However, the essential ideas of the model are all exhibited in the simple case, to which we restrict our analysis.

may be characterized by the following functional relation (we use f to denote *functional* relations):

$$o_m = f_1(a_m), \qquad 0 \le a_m \le \bar{a}, \qquad 0 \le o_m \le 1 \qquad (14.3.2)$$

The function f_1 here corresponds to the outcome function θ in the qualitative macro–micro model. We have depicted such an outcome function f_1 in Figure 14.2. Here f_1 is shown as a *unimodal* ("single-peaked") curve with a unique maximum level of support (70 percent) corresponding to a policy statement advocating \$4 billion in foreign aid.[11]

If the party members were fully aware of this outcome function f_1, presumably they could settle on a final policy statement (probably in the vicinity of \$4 billion if f_1 has the form of Figure 14.2). However, many forces constrain the party. Most notable is the fact that the members are not fully informed of f_1. As in the qualitative model, then, we assume that the members $i = 1, \ldots, n$ attempt to estimate this outcome function on each move m. But here we make certain simplifying assumptions as to the nature of these estimates. First, we assume the numbers represent a continuous unimodal function.[12] Each member acts on the hypothesis that there is some unique policy statement $a^* \in A$ that would yield the party maximum public support and that that support falls off monotonically for policy statements on either side of a^*. Since the maximum support level at a^* defines the *mode* of this hypothesized outcome function, we designate a^* as the *modal policy* in A. Thus, in estimating this outcome function, we assume that on every $m = 1, 2, \ldots$

1. each party member i constructs an estimated modal policy $\hat{a}^*_{m,i} \in A$, and
2. each member i assumes that for any policy statement $a \in A$ with

---

[11] In general, however, we need only assume that this actual outcome function f_1 for the party is continuous and not necessarily unimodal. But we do make the important assumption that f_1 is constant over time regardless of how many times the party changes its policy. As in the qualitative model, then, we assume here that the party's policy decisions are *retractable without cost*. This simplification allows us to focus on a representative move m in the sequential decision process without paying attention to the previous history of the process.

In a more realistic model one might introduce the estimation of change in f_1 from move to move. Although we avoid this added complexity, it is of interest to note that probable decreases in party support resulting from numerous policy changes could signficantly affect the equilibrium properties of the model. For example, it might be reasonable to assume that members would be more and more reluctant to change policies on each successive round, thereby strengthening the equilibrium tendencies of the process.

[12] Technically, we need not even require continuity, but we assume all functions continuous for sake of simplicity.

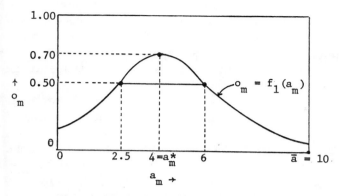

Figure 14.2. Outcome function.

$a \neq \hat{a}^*_{m,i}$, all policy statements between a and $\hat{a}^*_{m,i}$ will yield higher support levels than a.[13]

These two assumptions enable us to characterize each member i's estimated outcome function on move m by the single scalar variable $\hat{a}^*_{m,i}$.[14] For the moment, we postpone the question of how these estimates are constructed and assume that a set of estimated modal policies $\{a^*_{m,i}\}$, $i = 1, \ldots, n$, exist on move m.

Given their estimated outcome functions, the members must be able to state preferences among outcomes. Recall from the qualitative model that at the macrolevel a *group welfare function* W is assumed to exist and to be correctly perceived by each member of the group. We now assume at the microlevel that

3. each member $i = 1, \ldots, n$ perceives the group welfare function W to be a monotonically increasing function of outcomes (levels of support) o, and
4. each member i is motivated to achieve that outcome o that maximizes the group's welfare $W(o)$.

[13] More formally, if $a \in A(a \neq \hat{a}^*_{m,i})$ yields the outcome o, then for any $a' = \lambda a + (1 - \lambda)\hat{a}^*_{m,i}$ with $0 \leq \lambda \leq 1$ whose associated outcome is o', member i assumes, on move m, that $o' > o$.

[14] Observe that $\hat{a}^*_{m,i}$ does not characterize a unique outcome function but rather a class of outcome functions, namely, the class of continuous functions f from A to the unit interval $[0, 1]$, for which (i) f is strictly increasing on $[0, \hat{a}^*_{m,i}]$; and (ii) f is strictly decreasing on $[\hat{a}^*_{m,i}, \bar{a}]$. Since these are the only properties of member i's estimated outcome function required for our analysis and since each value of $\hat{a}^*_{m,i}$ uniquely defines such a class, we need only identify i's estimate as a member of the class corresponding to some particular value of $\hat{a}^*_{m,i}$.

Assumptions 1–4 thus imply that each member i will be motivated to propose his or her estimated modal policy $\hat{a}_{m,i}^*$ as the optimal course of action for the group. Hence we assume that in the initial round of informal discussion and exchange of information among the members prior to any group decision, these estimated modal policies emerge as the respective positions, or stands, of each member.

Following this initial period of discussion and information exchange on any move, a set or agenda of relevant alternatives must be constructed for formal debate and discussion. Assume that the leader of the group is responsible for this task. His (or her) objectives are taken to be twofold. First, he wishes to center debate and discussion on a restricted, but reasonable range of alternatives. In our example, he may decide that the largest proposal for foreign aid should not exceed the smallest by more than $2 billion. We denote the size of this range (interval) as the *maximum spread s* of alternatives.[15] The parameter s thus constitutes a control variable for the leader. Second, the leader wishes to locate this spread of alternatives within the action space in a manner that in part represents the thinking of the various members and that thus may be said to reflect the overall "orientation" b of the party. Although many factors interplay in a complex manner to determine party orientation, we assume that the leader perceives the range of possible party orientations as a one-dimensional continuum extending from a very strong interventionist, anticommunistic aggressive position (high advocated level of foreign military aid) to a noninterventionist, low-concern-with-foreign-power-politics position. Furthermore, we assume that he perceives the advocated position of each party member within this action space continuum as reflecting that member's relative political orientation, that is, the leader defines member i's *orientation* $b_{m,i}$ on move m as

$$b_{m,i} = \frac{\hat{a}_{m,i}}{\bar{a}}, \qquad 0 \le \hat{a}_{m,i} \le \bar{a} \tag{14.3.3}$$

where $b_{m,i} = 0$ represents extreme noninterventionism and $b_{m,i} = 1$ extreme interventionism. Finally, the leader defines the *party orientation* b_m on move m as a simple weighted average of these member orientations. That is,

$$b_m = \sum_i w_i b_{m,i} \tag{14.3.4}$$

where the weight w_i for each member i satisfies $0 \le w_i \le 1$ and where

---

[15] We assume in general that $s < \bar{a}$.

$\Sigma_i\, w_i = 1$. The set of weights $\{w_i\}$ constitute another set of control variables for the leader. By these weights he reflects his own perception of the relative influence of each member on the overall orientation of the party. If, for example, he judges that all members are equally influential, he sets $w_i = 1/n$, $i = 1, \ldots, n$. By substituting Eq. (14.3.3) into Eq. (14.3.4), we obtain

$$\overset{b}{b}_m = \frac{1}{\bar{a}} \sum_i w_i \hat{a}^*_{m,i} \tag{14.3.5}$$

or, more generally,

$$\overset{b}{b}_m = f_2(\{\hat{a}^*_{m,i}\};\, \bar{a},\, \{w_i\}) \tag{14.3.6}$$

Next, to reflect the orientation of the party in the spread of alternatives chosen on each move m, the leader defines the party's *orientation position* $\tilde{a}_m$ in the joint action space as

$$\tilde{a}_m = \bar{a}\overset{b}{b}_m \tag{14.3.7}$$

or, more generally,

$$\tilde{a}_m = f_3(\overset{b}{b}_m;\, \bar{a}) \tag{14.3.8}$$

We assume he takes this orientation position $\tilde{a}_m$ as the center for the maximum spread of alternatives.[16] Hence, given the parameters s and $\bar{a}$, the value of $\tilde{a}_m$ now defines the *restricted action space* $\tilde{A}_m$ for the party on move m. In general, $\tilde{A}_m$ will simply be the interval of actions between $\tilde{a}_m - \frac{1}{2}s$ and $\tilde{a}_m + \frac{1}{2}s$. However, we also require that $\tilde{A}_m$ always be a subset of A. Hence we assume that when $\tilde{a}_m$ is very close to the endpoints of A, the political leader simply excludes that part of the spread of alternatives not in A by defining

$$\tilde{A}_m = \{a \in A \,|\, \max(0,\, \tilde{a}_m - \tfrac{1}{2}s) \leqq a \leqq \min(\bar{a},\, \tilde{a}_m + \tfrac{1}{2}s)\} \tag{14.3.9}$$

In this manner we characterize $\tilde{A}_m$ as an interval in A whose endpoints are continuous functions of a single scalar variable $\tilde{a}_m$ together with the parameters s and $\bar{a}$.[17]

---

[16] Observe that $\tilde{A}_m$ always contains a spread of alternatives at least of length $\frac{1}{2}s$ and hence is never empty.

Since $\tilde{a}_m$ is a convex combination of elements in A, $\tilde{a}_m$ always lies in A. Hence, assuming $s < \bar{a}$, no more than half the maximum spread of alternatives can ever lie outside A.

[17] Observe that by combining Eqs. (14.3.5) and (14.3.7), we can write $\tilde{a}_m$ directly as $\tilde{a}_m = \Sigma_i\, w_i \hat{a}^*_{m,i}$. In this sense the group orientation $\overset{b}{b}_m$ may be regarded as a formal "redundancy" in the model. However, in keeping with the general qualitative model, we choose to retain some concept of "group orientation" in the quantitative model, even though it plays only an incidental role.

Having defined $\tilde{A}_m$, we assume that the leader opens formal debate and discussion. Each member i makes a *proposal* $a_{m,i}$ within $\tilde{A}_m$. By our assumptions, i always proposes that policy from $\tilde{A}_m$ that he or she believes will maximize the party's overall welfare W, namely, the policy in $\tilde{A}_m$ that is "closest" to the estimated modal policy $\hat{a}^*_{m,i}$. This policy will be $\hat{a}^*_{m,i}$ if $\hat{a}^*_{m,i}$ lies in $\tilde{A}_m$; otherwise, it will be the policy represented by that endpoint of $\tilde{A}_m$ closest to $\hat{a}^*_{m,i}$. Hence we may define $a_{m,i}$ by the implicit functional relation

$$|a_{m,i} - \hat{a}^*_{m,i}| = \min_{a \in \tilde{A}_m} |a - \hat{a}^*_{m,i}| \qquad (14.3.10)$$

where $\tilde{A}_m$ is defined by (14.3.9) and the vertical bars denote absolute value. For each value of $\hat{a}^*_{m,i}$ and $\tilde{a}_m$ together with the parameter values of s and $\bar{a}$, this relation defines a unique value of $a_{m,i}$ that we now write as

$$a_{m,i} = f_{4,i}(\hat{a}^*_{m,i}, \tilde{a}_m; s, \bar{a}) \qquad (14.3.11)$$

In general, the proposal $a_{m,i}$ will not be identical for each member i; that is, a conflict of interests (views) will arise as to which policy is "best" for the party. As in the qualitative model, we now assume that there exists some decision procedure for the group by which members may always resolve such conflicts of interests. For simplicity, we assume this procedure consists of some weighted averaging of the set of proposals $\{a_{m,i}\}$. More specifically, we assume that each member i possess some *decision weight* $q_i \geq 0$ (which may be a vote or some measure of status, seniority, etc., in the party). Then defining $q = \Sigma_i\, q_i$ as the *total decision weight* for the party, we assume that the group decision procedure always yields that *party policy a_m* defined by

$$a_m = \frac{1}{q} \sum_i q_i a_{m,i} \qquad (14.3.12)$$

or, more generally,

$$a_m = f_5(\{a_{m,i}\}; \{q_i\}) \qquad (14.3.13)$$

This party policy is then adopted on move m and announced to the public. Through the "outcome function" f_1 postulated in Eq. (14.3.2), the policy a_m generates some level of public support o_m. Depending on the attitudes, state of knowledge, and so on, of the members, this outcome o_m may cause the members to alter their estimates $\hat{a}^*_{m,i}$ of the modal policy a^* and thus lead to a new round of decision making. Hence it is this feedback of information that completes the decision "cycle" and provides the crucial link between moves. This linkage embodies the *group learning* *process* of the qualitative model and clearly shapes the whole dynamics of our sequential decision process. Hence we now wish to focus on this learning process and to consider several possible approaches to modeling it. Before doing so, however, we summarize in Figure 14.3 the results thus far obtained. Here we replace the elements of the qualitative model with variables and the determinental relations with functional relations. The linkages corresponding to the functional relations $f_1, \ldots, f_5$ are depicted as solid lines.

Note that all the elements of Figure 14.1 (with the exception of hereditary factors H) are reflected either explicitly or implicitly by the variables and parameters in Figure 14.3. Orientation $\hat{B}_m$ corresponds here to $\hat{b}_m$, and the estimated outcome functions $\{\hat{\theta}_{m,i}\}$ are characterized here by the estimated modal policies $\{\hat{a}^*_{m,i}\}$. Similarly, the perceived action space $\mathcal{P}(A)$ is represented by $\bar{a}$, and the perceived restricted action space $\mathcal{P}(\tilde{A}_m)$ is represented by relative orientation position $\tilde{a}_m$ together with the maximum-spread parameter s and the action space parameter $\bar{a}$. The procedure Q is represented by the decision weights $\{q_i\}$. Since the welfare function W is instrumental both in the identification of the estimated modal policies $\{\hat{a}^*_{m,i}\}$ as the advocated policies (and hence orientations) of the members and in the determination of the proposals $\{a_{m,i}\}$ within the restricted action space, it is reflected implicitly in the functional relations f_2 and $f_{4,i}$ of Figure 14.3. The adopted party policy a_m and the resulting outcome o_m correspond identically in the two figures, and the outcome function θ corresponds to f_1. The final element of Figure 14.1, namely, the group's knowledge $\overset{a}{M}e_m$ is embodied in the key functional relation $f_{6,i}$ (indicated by dashed lines in Figure 14.3). This function, which corresponds to the group learning process, is designated as the *learning function* in the macro–micro model. We now turn to the consideration of this function.

Observe first that there is an important difference between the learning processes postulated in the qualitative and quantitative macro–micro models, respectively. In the qualitative model, the group learning process was assumed to embody *both* micro- and macroelements. Recall from Figure 14.1 that $\overset{a}{M}e_m$ directly influences the estimated outcome functions $\{\hat{\theta}_{m,i}\}$ on the microlevel and both orientation $\hat{B}_m$ and (indirectly) the restricted action space $\tilde{A}_m$ on the macrolevel. In the quantitative model, however, the learning function $f_{6,i}$ is a purely microrelation. Hence in Figure 14.3, the only direct change from move to move is in the set of estimated modal policies $\{\hat{a}^*_{m,i}\}$. These new policies in turn determine both a new party orientation $\hat{b}_{m+1}$ and the restricted action space $\tilde{A}_{m+1}$ by way of functions f_2 and f_3, respectively. Hence, the group learning process is here viewed solely as a microphenomenon; only the members as separate indi-

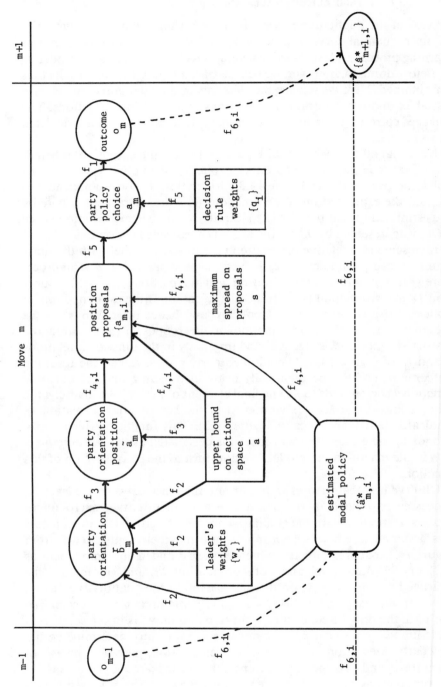

Figure 14.3. Flow diagram of the general quantitative macro–micro (learning) model.

viduals directly respond to changes in information. The question remains, however, as to whether it is meaningful to speak of a group learning process at the *macro*level. To this question we shall return after developing a very simple approach to the microlearning process.

Consider the following type of response behavior for each party member i. Suppose i's level of satisfaction with the party policy a_m adopted on move m varies directly with the resulting level of popular support o_m for that policy. The lower o_m is, the less satisfied he (or she) is with a_m. Further, suppose that whenever i is dissatisfied with a_m, he is motivated to change his estimated model policy $\hat{a}^*_{m,i}$. In changing his estimate, we may imagine that there is some fixed policy toward which he always tends. This policy, which we designate as i's natural or *inherent position* a^{**}_i on the given issue, might be taken to reflect his own personal conviction or disposition on the issue, in contrast to the position he thinks is best for the party. (In the case of foreign military aid, for example, i may be against such altogether, but he may still recognize that it is better for the party in the long run to support some aid.) Hence we imagine that this inherent position for i (of which he may not even be consciously aware) comes to influence his views as to what is best for the party. The more dissatisfied he is with present party policy, the stronger this influence becomes. This pattern of responses to new information may be described in terms of classical learning theory as an instance of the "reinforcement hypothesis." Here the reinforcement is "negative" in the sense that whenever he is dissatisfied with party policy, his own personal conviction on the issue is reinforced. We might characterize this behavior by the following simple learning model:

$$\hat{a}^*_{m+1,i} = \lambda_i a^{**}_i + (1 - \lambda_i)\hat{a}^*_{m,i}, \qquad 0 < \lambda_i < 1 \qquad (14.3.14)$$

Whenever he is dissatisfied with party policy, he shifts his estimated modal policy $\hat{a}^*_{m,i}$ toward his inherent position a^{**}_i by an amount that depends on some "intensity parameter" λ_i. Nevertheless, this model is not complete, for we have not yet specified what we mean by "dissatisfied." Unlike the simple dichotomous outcomes of "reward" or "punishment" in a simple learning model, we have here a continuum of outcomes ranging from, say, "i is completely satisifed" (when $o_m = 1$) to "i is completely dissatisfied" (when $o_m = 0$). As one approach to this continuous problem, we may hypothesize that the more dissatisfied i is (i.e., the lower o_m), the more rapid his movement toward a^{**}_i. In other words, suppose we now let the parameter λ_i depend on the level of o_m observed. We then require that as o_m falls, the rapidity of movement toward a^{**}_i rises, that is, that λ_i be a *monotone decreasing* function of o_m. If we require further that i will never move when he is completely satisfied (i.e., that λ_i

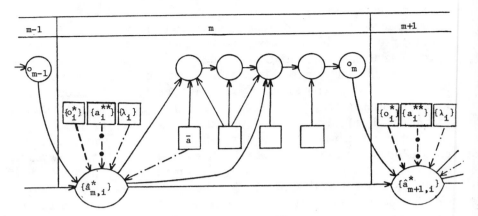

Figure 14.4. Flow diagram of learning models.

$= 0$ when $o_m = 1$) and that he will shift all the way to a_i^{**} whenever he is completely dissatisfied (i.e., that $\lambda_i = 1$ when $o_m = 0$), the simplest possible functional relation satisfying these conditions is seen to be

$$\lambda_i = 1 - o_m \qquad (14.3.15)$$

As a first possible learning function, we thus have from (14.3.14) and (14.3.15)

$$\hat{a}_{m+1,i}^* = (1 - o_m)a_i^{**} + o_m\hat{a}_{m,i}^* \qquad (14.3.16)$$

or, more generally,

$$\hat{a}_{m+1,i}^* = f_{6,i}(\hat{a}_{m,i}^*, o_m; a_i^{**}) \qquad (14.3.17)$$

This function provides one possible way to complete the macro–micro model, as shown by the heavy solid lines in Figure 14.4.

To gain insight into the dynamic properties of this completed model, we must examine the learning function of Eq. (14.3.16) in more detail. In Figure 14.5 we have plotted four representative "learning curves" from this function, each corresponding to a different value of o_m (for the particular case $a_i^{**} = \frac{3}{4}\bar{a}$). Each curve assigns a unique value of $\hat{a}_{m+1,i}^*$ to every possible value of $\hat{a}_{m,i}^*$. First consider the curve defined by $o_m = 1$. In this case, $\hat{a}_{m+1,i}^* = \hat{a}_{m,i}^*$ for all possible values of $\hat{a}_{m,i}^*$. Hence we may conclude that whenever a party policy achieves 100 percent support, the decision process will come to a halt, and the party will have achieved a state of equilibrium. Next, consider $o_m = 0$. In this case $\hat{a}_{m+1,i}^* = a_i^{**}$ for all values of $\hat{a}_{m,i}^*$ (i.e., each member i fully adopts his (or her) inherent position a_i^{**} on move $m + 1$). But having once adopted this position, i's estimated

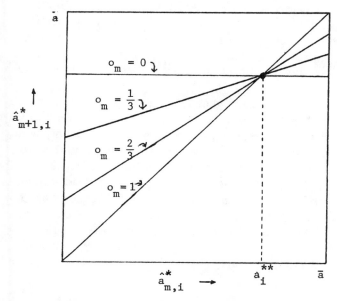

Figure 14.5. A linear learning model.

modal policy will remain at a_i^{**} whatever the value of o on any subsequent move since all curves intersect the 45° line at a_i^{**}.[18] Hence the decision process again comes to a halt. Between these two extreme values of o_m, however, each member i always shifts $\hat{a}_{m,i}^*$ toward a_i^{**}. In this middle range, the decision process converges uniformly to an equilibrium position in which each member i ultimately adopts his inherent policy a_i^{**}. Observe that in this equilibrium state for the party, i's equilibrium proposal will always be that position in the party's restricted action space that is closest to his inherent position a_i^{**}. Also, the equilibrium party policy is obtained from the application of each member i's decision weight q_i to his equilibrium proposal.

In short, we see that the convergence properties of this learning function are so strong that we can say much about the equilibrium states for the entire model by simply examining this function. Of course, the existence of policies a_m that yield outcomes of $o_m = 0$ or $o_m = 1$ depends on the nature of the actual outcome function f_1 that we postulate. Further-

[18] In other words, a_i^{**} is a fixed point of the function $f_{6,i}$ in Eq. (14.3.17) for all values of o_m. Such a fixed point may be criticized as one of the least realistic features of this type of model, in the sense that i can never be made dissatisfied enough to move from this point – even for $o_m = 0$.

more, although we can assert that a unique equilibrium exists for all values of o_m in the middle range $0 < o_m < 1$, the equilibrium policy itself will depend on the values of the parameters $\bar{a}$, s, $\{w_i\}$, $\{q_i\}$, $\{a_i^{**}\}$. We could write a complex expression for this equilibrium policy in terms of the parameter values, but it suffices to observe that it is uniquely defined.

Although this linear model is analytically quite simple, it leaves much to be desired as a description of actual behavior. However, several modifications are possible that generalize its applicability considerably without altering the analysis significantly. First, we can easily relax the assumption that the members will be content with their positions *only* if 100 percent support is achieved by some party policy. Instead, suppose member i will be satisfied with any party policy that yields a level of support equal to or greater than some level o_i^* (such as 51 percent). Then we may imagine that he or she will continually shift position toward a_i^{**} whenever $0 \leq o_m < o_i^*$ and stop whenever $o_i^* \leq o_m \leq 1$. As a simple generalization of Eqs. (14.3.16) and (14.3.17), we then have

$$a_{m+1,i}^* = \begin{cases} (1 - o_m/o_i^*)a_i^{**} + (o_m/o_i^*)\hat{a}_{m,i}^*, & \text{for} \quad 0 \leq o_m < o_i^* \\ \\ \hat{a}_{m,i}^*, & \text{for} \quad o_i^* \leq o_m \leq 1 \end{cases}$$

$$(14.3.18)$$

or, more generally,

$$\hat{a}_{m+1,i}^* = f_{6,i}(\hat{a}_{m,i}^*, o_m; a_i^{**}, o_i^*) \tag{14.3.19}$$

This function may be depicted graphically by simply substituting o_m/o_i^* for o_m in Figure 14.5. By so doing, we have "collapsed" to the 45° line all those learning curves that correspond to values of o_m ranging from o_i^* to 1, that is, for which $o_m/o_i^* \geq 1$.

This more general learning function can be incorporated into the macro–micro model by simply adding the new set of parameters $\{o_i^*\}$, as shown by the heavy dashed line in Figure 14.4. As one might suspect, the possibilities for rapid convergence to equilibrium are in general much greater for this new model. In particular, if we define $o^* = \max (o_1^*, \ldots, o_n^*)$, then any policy yielding an outcome $o_m \geq o^*$ will leave all members satisfied with their present positions and hence will yield equilibrium for the party.

14.4 Toward a quantitative approach with leader and members learning

Having just developed a rather simple learning model in which the leader does not learn, we now develop one in which he or she does learn and where such learning comes to affect both the members' and group learning. A more involved feedback effect is thus involved. To ease the presentation, assume that for the first two moves the new model has the same form as the previous one (or any other that leads to policy choices on the first two moves). On the third move, the leader assumes a more aggressive role. There has been experience (policy choices made and outcomes observed), and the leader uses this as a guide in determining a new policy. Each member, too, is influenced by this experience when making policy proposals.

More specifically, let each member i on any move $m + 1$ give some attention (weight) to the change in the leader's specification of a policy for the party, that is, to $a_{m+1} - a_m$. That is, we alter Eq. (14.3.18) to read

$$\hat{a}^*_{m+1,i} = \begin{cases} (1 - o_m/o^*_i)a^{**}_i + (o_m/o^*_i)\,\hat{a}^*_{m,i} + \epsilon_i(a_{m+1} - a_m), \\ \qquad\qquad \text{for} \quad 0 \le o_m < o_i \qquad (14.4.1) \\ \\ \hat{a}^*_{m,i}, \qquad\qquad\qquad \text{for} \quad o^*_i \le o_m \le 1 \end{cases}$$

or, more generally,

$$\hat{a}^*_{m+1,i} = f_{33,i}(\hat{a}^*_{m,i},\, o_m,\, a^{**}_i,\, o^*_i,\, \epsilon_i,\, a_{m+1},\, a_m) \qquad (14.4.2)$$

where ϵ_i is a constant reflecting member i's sensitivity to changes in the leader's choice of a party policy position.[19]

These facts, of course, imply that the leader first specifies the party's policy position a_{m+1}. In setting a_{m+1}, we assume that the leader considers two basic elements.

1. He (or she) must ask whether the shift from a_{m-1} to a_m on the previous move was in the "right" direction, that is, led to an improvement in outcome such that $o_m > o_{m-1}$. If this is the case, then the direction of shift in the party policy position should be retained. That is, if $a_m > a_{m-1}$,

---

[19] Thus after the third move of this model, the individual i is no longer restricted to make a proposal within an interval (agenda) set by the leader. That is, we no longer have relations (14.3.6) (i.e., f_2 in Figure 14.3) and (14.3.8) (i.e., f_3 in Figure 14.3). In this situation, the individual is only restricted (if at all) by the initial bounds 0 and $\bar{a}$. Hence, the relation (14.3.11) (i.e., $f_{4,i}$ in Figure 14.3) is replaced by $\{\hat{a}^*_{m,i}\} \equiv \{a_{m,i}\}$. That is, the individual's policy proposal is now identical to his estimated modal policy, where the latter is now determined by (14.4.2) (i.e., $f_{33,i}$ in Figure 14.6) rather than (14.3.17) (i.e., $f_{6,i}$).

then a_{m+1} should also be chosen so that $a_{m+1} > a_m$; and if $a_m < a_{m-1}$, then the leader should ensure that $a_{m+1} < a_m$. However, if the shift on the previous move was in the "wrong direction," that is, led to a deterioration in outcome such that $o_m < o_{m-1}$, then the direction of shift should be reversed. In other words, if $a_m > a_{m-1}$, then the leader should choose a new party policy position a_{m+1} such that $a_{m+1} < a_m$, and if $a_m < a_{m-1}$, then he should ensure that $a_{m+1} > a_m$. If it so happened that $o_m = o_{m-1}$, then this first element should not have any effect on the leader's choice of a_{m+1}. Mathematically, this directional change phenomenon is reflected in the Δ term in the following decision rule for the leader[20]:

$$a_{m+1} - a_m = \xi_m(o_m - o_{m-1})\Delta \quad \text{for} \quad \Delta = \begin{cases} +1 & \text{if} \quad a_m \geq a_{m-1} \\ -1 & \text{if} \quad a_m < a_{m-1} \end{cases}$$

$$(14.4.3)$$

or, more generally,

$$a_{m+1} = f_{35}(\xi_m, a_m, o_m, o_{m-1}, \Delta) \tag{14.4.4}$$

where ξ_m is a parameter reflecting the importance the leader attributes to the difference $o_m - o_{m-1}$ in choosing a_{m+1}.[21]

2. He must also be sensitive to changes in the proposals $\{\hat{a}^*_{m,i}\}$ of party members – weighted in terms of their relative influence $\{w_i\}$ on the party's policy position. That is, he must respond to the element

$$\sum_i w_i \frac{\hat{a}^*_{m,i} - \hat{a}^*_{m-1,i}}{\bar{a}}$$

when choosing a_{m+1}. So we change Eq. (14.4.3) to read[22]

$$(a_{m+1} - a_m) = \xi_m(o_m - o_{m-1})\Delta + \mu_m \sum_i w_i \frac{\hat{a}^*_{m,i} - \hat{a}^*_{m-1,i}}{\bar{a}} \tag{14.4.5}$$

---

[20] The rationale for this Δ term is the following. If $o_m - o_{m-1} > 0$ and if it had been that $a_m > a_{m-1}$, then we want $a_{m+1} > a_m$; hence in (14.4.3), Δ should be $+1$. If $o_m - o_{m-1} < 0$ and if it had been that $a_m > a_{m-1}$, then we want $a_{m+1} < a_m$; hence in (14.4.3), Δ should be $+1$. On the other hand, if $o_m - o_{m-1} > 0$ and if it had been that $a_m < a_{m-1}$, then we want $a_{m+1} < a_m$; hence in (14.4.3), Δ should be -1. Finally if $o_m - o_{m-1} < 0$ and if it had been that $a_m < a_{m-1}$, then we want $a_{m+1} > a_m$: hence in (14.4.3), Δ should be -1.
[21] In the Appendix, ξ_m may also be taken as a variable set by the leader, subject to certain constraints.
[22] Thus, after the third move of this model, the relations governing the leader's behavior have also changed. In addition to the elimination of relations (14.3.6) (i.e., f_2 in Figure 14.3) and (14.3.8) (i.e., f_3 in Figure 14.3) mentioned in footnote 19, we now also eliminate relation (14.3.13) (i.e., f_5 in Figure 14.3) and its associated decision rule weights $\{q_i\}$. This latter relation is the effect replaced by (14.4.6) (i.e., f_{35} in Figure 14.6).

or, more generally,

$$a_{m+1} = f_{35}(\xi_m, a_m, o_m, o_{m-1}, \Delta, \{\hat{a}^*_{m,i}\}, \{\hat{a}^*_{m-1,i}\}; \bar{a}, \{w_i\}, \mu_m) \quad (14.4.6)$$

where μ_m is a parameter that, given ξ_m, reflects the importance the leader attaches to this second element. In that case it must be assumed to be set such that the second term is never allowed to dominate the first, that is,

$$\left| \xi_m(o_m - o_{m-1})\Delta \right| > \left| \mu_m \sum_i w_i \frac{(\hat{a}^*_{m,i} - \hat{a}^*_{m-1,i})}{\bar{a}} \right| \quad (14.4.7)$$

The corresponding flow diagram is Figure 14.6. There we see how i's proposal $\hat{a}^*_{m+1,i}$ at move $m + 1$ is related to the several variables and parameters. These relations are indicated by dashed lines and are organized so that the elements determining each of the three terms on the right-hand side of Eq. 14.4.1 converge on one of two points, with an arrow going from each of these two points to the $\hat{a}^*_{m+1,i}$ ellipse. For example, the three elements o_m, o^*_i, and a^{**}_i involved in the first term converge on one of these points.

Figure 14.6 also indicates how the leader's determination of the party's policy position a_{m+1} at move $m + 1$ is related to the several relevant variables and parameters. These relations are indicated by the solid lines and again are organized so that the elements determining each of the two terms on the right-hand side of Eq. (14.4.5) converge on a single point.

Finally, the cross-hatched line in Figure 14.6 indicates that the relation f_1 linking outcomes to action (policy choices) remains unchanged from previous models.

Figure 14.6 clearly depicts the more complex feedbacks at work in situations where we allow both the leader and party members to learn over a sequence of moves. However, it can be proved, as we do in the Appendix, that under a set of very reasonable conditions the model depicted in Figure 14.6 can (after a series of feedbacks) lead the system to converge to an equilibrium position. In our context, this equilibrium position is a Nash equilibrium, that is, a position where neither the leader nor any member is motivated to change his or her action.

14.5 Generalization to the hierarchical social system

Now we are ready for generalization with regard to the hierarchical structure of our social system. The program committee of the political party in our example can be replaced by the members of any group and the leader of the committee by the leader of that group. The members of a group can each in turn be a leader of a next lower group (a subgroup).

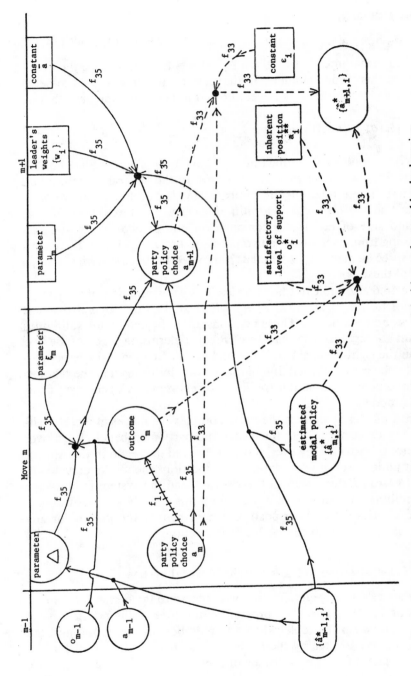

Figure 14.6. Flow diagram of quantitative (learning) model with members and leader learning.

For example, each member of a program committee can be a leader of the political party in his (or her) state. Recall that the position that any member i adopts in the program committee (say, group 1) reflects a natural inherent position a_i^{**}. However, as a leader and representative of his constituents, each member's a_i^{**} typically (ideally) reflects his own wishes and those of his constituents and, in particular, can correspond to an equilibrium response by his subgroup (his constituents as well as himself) to its external environment, including group I. Thus after the higher group I reaches an equilibrium position, which we now designate a_I^{**} (involving a process wherein each $i \in I$ made a proposal $\hat{a}_{m,i}^*$ on each move m and wherein his a_i^{**} remained constant), the subgroup of which i is a leader may reconsider its situation. In particular, it might do so if a_I^{**} is different from either group I's previous position or from the position the subgroup had anticipated. For the subgroup, its environment has changed; and accordingly, after a series of interactions among the subgroup's members during the next unit of time, the subgroup's inherent position (or equilibrium response) may change from a_i^{**} to $\tilde{a}_i^{**}$.

In turn, we envisage the higher group as an individual member (represented by its leader) of a still higher group II. (For example, the leader of the program committee can be a member of an executive committee of which a presidential nominee may be the top man.) Thus, the higher group's equilibrium response a_I^{**} changes to $\tilde{a}_I^{**}$ to be consistent with the equilibrium solution a_{II}^{**} of the still higher group, and in turn the equilibrium solution for the lower group (subgroup of which i is leader) becomes $\tilde{a}_i^{**}$.

In the preceding sense, we then envisage an overall equilibrium solution for a hierarchical structure within which learning takes place at every node and for each group within that structure. Each group consists of a leader and members. Except for the very top group, the leader is an individual member of the next higher order group thereby serving as a linking pin. Except for a lowest level group (e.g., a family), each member is a leader of a subgroup, thereby also serving as a linking pin. However, to ensure convergence to an overall equilibrium position, conditions in addition to those discussed in the Appendix would need to be met.

14.6   Concluding remarks

In this chapter we have developed, in step-by-step fashion, a model wherein members as well as a leader of a group learn. We have, moreover, suggested how it relates to the hierarchical structure, however irregular, of decision making in advanced, industrialized nations such as the United States, the Soviet Union, Britain, and so on. The discussion in the last section clearly demonstrates its partial applicability to decision making in such structures – that it can furnish some important scaffolding, if not new insights, to help think about how key political figures such as Reagan and Gorbachev are locked (trapped) into hierarchical structures in making basic decisions and in struggling to learn more about the needs and wishes of their hierarchically ordered (however irregular) constituents and how better to be sensitive to them.

Yet, many important aspects of the learning process have not been attacked in this chapter and have been purposely avoided by the construction in this chapter of a conflict situation to motivate the development of the model. One is learning that builds up the stock of knowledge and thus is associated with the generation of information having an investment value. Another is learning that does not involve the orderly processes depicted in this chapter but rather involves highly creative, unpredictable piecing together of bits of knowledge and experience. To these two aspects, we turn in Chapters 15 and 16, respectively.

Appendix: proof of "reasonable" convergence in model with leader and members learning

Let us state the following three conditions:

1. The outcome function $o(a)$ is strictly quasi-concave and everywhere either strictly increasing or strictly decreasing except at the optimal point (such as in Figure 14.2).
2. No infinite sequences of infinitesimal small adjustments are allowed.
3. The adjustments are not "too large" (to be defined in what follows in connection with the ϵ_m parameter).

If these are met, then the group policy choice decision will converge to the optimal policy choice decision, unique in the sense of assumption 2 (i.e., the decision will lie within an area that may be characterized as comprised of points infinitesimally close to the "true" optimum).

We first prove convergence for the case when the group's action is determined by (14.4.3). The proof proceeds in two steps. It is first shown that the group action a_{m+1} will always be chosen from an interval containing the optimal action. We then prove that after a finite number of adjustments, the interval width will decrease. Together, these two steps ensure convergence.

Initially, the group action space $A = [0, \bar{a}]$, and we assume that a^*, the optimal action, lies strictly between lower and upper bounds (designated l and u, respectively). That is, $0 < a^* < \bar{a}$. In the first two moves, the group has chosen two actions, a_0 and a_1. We assume without any loss of generality that $0 < a_0 < a_1 < \bar{a}$. Let $I = [l, u] = [0, \bar{a}]$ be the current interval that contains a^*. The group can use the information already obtained from the adoption of a_0 and a_1 to adjust I. Suppose that $o_0 < o_1$. Then the outcome function $o(a)$ is decreasing between a_1 and a_0; and the optimal action a^* cannot be less than a_0. Hence $a^* \in [a_0, \bar{a}]$ and an updated interval I with $l = a_0$ and u unchanged at $\bar{a}$ has been determined. Similarly, if $o_1 < o_0$, then $a^* \in [0, a_1]$, and a new upper bound $u = a_1$ can be set. In the next move, $m + 1$, the group chooses its action according to (14.4.3).

We now make more precise assumption 3, namely, that the adjustment may not be "too large." Let the parameter ξ_m be a scaling factor that reflects some of the information contained in knowing the interval I. In particular, we assume that

$$\xi_m = \begin{cases} \tfrac{1}{2}(u - a_m) & \text{if } \Delta(o_m - o_{m-1}) > 0 \\ \tfrac{1}{2}(a_m - l) & \text{if } \Delta(o_m - o_{m-1}) < 0 \end{cases} \tag{14.A.1}$$

This will ensure that

$$a_{m+1} = \begin{cases} \xi_m (a_m, u) & \text{if } \Delta(o_m - o_{m-1}) > 0 \\ \xi_m (l, a_m) & \text{if } \Delta(o_m - o_{m-1}) < 0 \end{cases} \tag{14.A.2}$$

So if $a_m \in I$, then $a_{m+1} \in I$. Hence the group chooses an action from an interval I containing the optimal action a^*. It now remains to show that after a finite number of adjustments, the width of I will be reduced or that otherwise convergence is assured.

Consider the case when $a_m > a_{m-1}$. Hence from (14.4.3), $\Delta = +1$. Suppose $o_m < o_{m-1}$. Then the outcome function $o(a)$ was decreasing between a_{m-1} and a_m. Hence the optimal action $a^* < a_m$. So a new upper bound for future actions is a_m. The new interval $[l, a_m]$ will contain the optimal solution, and its width is strictly smaller than that of $[l, u]$ since $a_m < u$. Similarly, if $a_m < a_{m-1}$ and $o_m < o_{m-1}$, the optimal action $a^* > a_m$, which therefore constitutes a new lower bound. Since $a_m > l$, $[a_m, u]$ is strictly smaller than $[l, u]$.

In either case, changing the direction of shift leads to an improved (better) bound for the value of the optimal action. In a similar way it can be shown that two successive shifts in the same direction also leads to an improved bound.

Finally, either the group will change its direction of shift or not. In either case, the interval containing the optimal action is shrunk. Hence, it will converge to the optimal action a^* given assumption 2. This completes the convergence proof for adjustments according to (14.4.3).

We next prove convergence for the case when the group's actions is determined by (14.4.5). Recall (14.A.1). Selecting ξ_m ensured that the adjustment due to the $\xi_m(o_m - o_{m-1})\Delta$ term is at most half the length of the permissible maximum adjustment. By (14.4.7), the combined adjustment in Eq. (14.4.5) will lead to a permissible outcome, that is, an action $a_{m+1} \in I$. The remainder of the proof of convergence according to (14.4.5) is essentially the same as that for (14.4.3).

Note that although this proof assumes mechanical behavior, it holds also for any behavior of a leader who is given the unrestricted authority to set a parameter $\bar{\xi}_m$ and who does so on each move, provided that $0 < \bar{\xi}_m < \xi_m$ as defined previously and subject to the revised condition

$$\left| \bar{\xi}_m(o_m - o_{m-1})\Delta \right| > \left| \mu_m \sum_i w_i \frac{a^*_{m,i} - a^*_{m-1,i}}{\bar{a}} \right| \tag{14.A.3}$$

Hence, although the optimal action a^* is predictable, the movements toward it may take a great variety of paths dependent on both the cultural factors and the group rules of reality, which impose additional constraints on steps that may be taken by a leader and members of a group, provided they are consistent with the ones already specified.

In one sense, the leader who sets $\bar{\xi}_m$ on any move has full control of the movements toward equilibrium subject to the restriction (14.A.3). In this regard the leader may be sensitive to members' proposals and choose a time path of actions (proposals) and reactions (i.e., movement toward the equilibrium point) that has appeal to the members of his or her group. Yet on the other hand the cultural factors and group rules may be such as to make the leader a purely mechanical reactor (responder). For example, suppose a group rule requires the leader to choose $\bar{\xi}_m$ such that

$$\left| \bar{\xi}_m(o_m - o_{m-1})\Delta \right| = \rho \left| \sum_i w_i \frac{(a^*_{m,i} - a^*_{m-1,i})}{\bar{a}} \right| \qquad (14.A.4)$$

with $0 < \bar{\xi}_m < \xi_m$ and where $\rho = 1.1$ whenever possible and is always the maximum possible value when ρ must be less than 1.1. This situation would force the leader into a passive-type role quite similar to that of a fictitious market participant or fictitious political participant (see Isard et al. 1969).

References

Anselin, L., and W. Isard (1979). "On Alonso's General Theory of Movement." *Man, Environment, Space, and Time* 1(1):52–63.

Gamson, W. (1981). "The Political Culture of Arab-Israel Conflict." *Journal of Peace Science* 5(2):79–94.

Isard, W., T. E. Smith, P. Isard, T. H. Tung, and M. Dacey (1969) *General Theory: Social, Political, Economic, and Regional.* Cambridge, MA: MIT Press.

Killingsworth, M. R. (1982) "'Learning by Doing' and 'Investment in Training' Synthesis of Two 'Rival' Models of the Life Cycle." *Review of Economic Studies* 49:263–71.

Simon, H. A. (1957) *Models of Man.* New York: Wiley.

Webster's Third New International Dictionary (1961). Springfield, MA: Merriam.

CHAPTER 15

Information research and development from a dynamical system viewpoint

Written with Christine Smith

15.1 Introduction

In the previous chapter we presented a rigorous model for group and individual learning. However, to prove the existence and convergence to an equilibrium position, strong and unrealistic assumptions were involved. Here we present a purely conceptual model, one designed to capture some of the investment aspects of information development discussed in Chapter 6. As pointed out in Chapter 11, such information development is urgently needed for inventing new ideas and creatively designing a new effective conflict management procedure for handling the U.S.–Soviet arms control conflict situation. No formal rigorous analysis is attempted. We want to focus on a particular participant in a conflict situation and also on a mediator (third party). We want to explore whatever potential exists for a dynamical systems type of analysis, particularly for replicating or simulating learning within workshops or brainstorming sessions (as briefly discussed in Chapter 10) designed to achieve conflict management.[1] We also have in mind to explore the extent to which such analysis can be used to select among conflict management procedures and identify new, superior procedures. Clearly the state of dynamical systems analysis is too primitive to deal with the dynamics of reality, and yet it is worthwhile to see what we can learn from its use. In the following presentation

The valuable assistance of Kai Michaelis in presenting the mathematics is gratefully acknowledged; however, the authors alone are responsible for any errors. This chapter draws very heavily upon materials in Isard and Smith (1983).

[1] See Isard and Smith (1982, chap. 10) for a general discussion of the workshop as a tool for conflict management and the learning process that goes on therein. This chapter follows the definition of concepts presented there.

we shall concentrate upon the stock of information as the basic state variable that is undergoing change over time – a variable that many would agree is key in workshop and interactive sessions. Because of the difficulties of dynamical systems analysis we shall not consider changes in any other key variable.

In our dynamical systems analysis, we posit that at the start each behaving unit (participant, mediator, and others) possesses a stock of knowledge. Each then utilizes this stock plus the labor and other stocks and resources that the person commands to maximize satisfaction (utility, payoff, profit) over a time period perceived as relevant. This time period may be considered a planning horizon. In allocating resources among diverse activities to maximize satisfaction, the individual considers the utility from use of resources for (1) current consumption, (2) the production of other goods for current and possibly future consumption, and (3) the production of new information to serve as capital, thereby to make the future use of resources in production much more effective.

To keep things simple, we shall assume only two participants J and L and a mediator Z (J could be the United States, L the Soviet Union, and Z a team of UN personnel or a highly respected figure in the background). We may imagine that the participants are attempting to inch their way forward. Our first model is constructed for pedagogical purposes alone. It is a static-type model that makes the highly unrealistic assumption that participants do not learn (i.e., add to their knowledge stock from one time period to the next); it is designed to familiarize the reader with notation and to present the problem more sharply. A second model posits a situation wherein both the participants J and L are passive, that is, do not learn from interaction; the mediator, however, does. A third model posits a situation wherein one participant, say, J, does learn; the mediator and L are passive and do not learn.

15.2   A background static-type model

For the first model we employ Figure 15.1. We associate with each participant J and L a box C^J and C^L, respectively, which covers the cognitive decision-making activities of that participant. The contents of this box as well as the $\mathcal{J}$ box to be mentioned in what follows immediately are fully sketched in Figure 1.3 and the associated discussion and described in Isard (1979, 1980) and Isard and Smith (1982). Associated with the mediator Z is the $\mathcal{J}$ box, which corresponds to the political arena in which debate, discussion, and interaction take place. For our purposes here, however, we may also view the upper part of this box as the C^Z box.

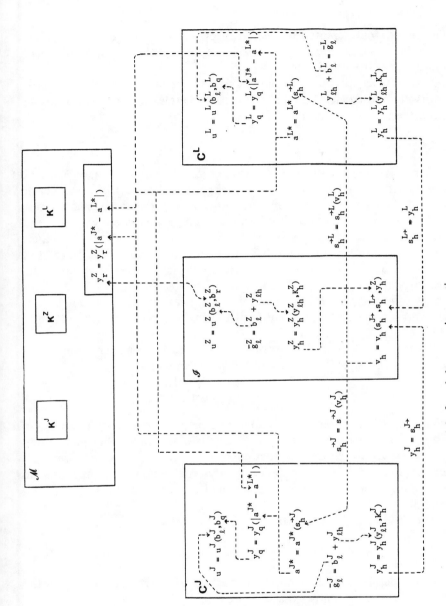

Figure 15.1. Static model of workshop-type interactions.

The $\mathcal{M}$ box corresponds to system information, and again its contents and relationships to the other boxes are fully presented in Isard (1979, 1980) and Isard and Smith (1982).

Associated with each participant and the mediator is a "two-goods" utility function as indicated at the top of the relevant box. For example, for J, the utility function is

$$u^J = u^J(b_l^J, b_q^J) \tag{15.2.1}$$

Here b_l^J represents the consumption of leisure (nonuse of labor) and all other goods obtainable through exchange for labor or from production generated by the direct use of labor. Also, b_q^J is taken to be consumption of the noneconomic good or commodity, c-security (where we place "c-" before the word security and later other words to indicate that we are thinking in terms of a commodity in an economic sense). [See Isard et al. (1969, chap. 12).] The reader, however, may wish to view b_q^J as consumption of some composite of noneconomic goods. In Eq. (15.2.1), u^L (the utility of participant L) is excluded as a relevant variable, although Burton and other workshop analysts would include it (see Isard and Smith 1982, chap. 10).

We take J to be a self-interested participant. He (or she) is motivated to maximize his utility subject to his labor constraint:

$$\bar{g}_l^J = b_l^J + y_{lh}^J \tag{15.2.2}$$

where $\bar{g}_l^J$ is his currently available amount (say, twenty-four hours) of labor; y_{lh}^J is the amount of his currently available labor that he explicitly decides to use in the production of information (good h); and b_l^J is the amount of this labor devoted to normal economic pursuits and leisure and may be viewed as a residual once the amount y_{lh}^J is determined.

The production function for J is, in its simplest form,

$$y_h^J = y_h^J(y_{lh}^J, K_h^J) \tag{15.2.3}$$

which is depicted in the lower part of the C^J box. In this version of the model J's stock of knowledge, K_h^J, is assumed constant.

The second good b_q^J entering J's utility function is the amount of c-security he (or she) comes to possess and currently consume [c-security is a good that cannot be diminished by consumption (see Isard and Smith 1982, chap. 10)]. The amount of c-security y_q^J produced, which, as we have already noted, becomes available for immediate consumption, is a function of (inversely related to) the absolute difference ($|a^{l*} - a^{L*}|$)

between the most preferred joint actions of both participants. That is, as indicted in the C^J box[2]:

$$y_q^J = y_q^J(|a^{J*} - a^{L*}|) \tag{15.2.4}$$

The most preferred proposal of a participant, say, J, is dependent upon the information $s_h^{\rightarrow J}$ he or she obtains from debate, discussion, and interaction within the political arena. That is, as indicated in the C^J box,

$$a^{J*} = a^{J*}(s_h^{\rightarrow J}) \tag{15.2.7}$$

and symmetrically for L, we have

$$a^{L*} = a^{L*}(s_h^{\rightarrow L}) \tag{15.2.8}$$

The information $s_h^{\rightarrow J}$ and $s_h^{\rightarrow L}$ received by J and L, respectively, is a function of the total interaction v_h in the political arena. That is, as indicated in Figure 15.1 between the $\mathcal{J}$ and C^J and the $\mathcal{J}$ and C^L boxes, respectively,[3]

$$s_h^{\rightarrow J} = s_h^{\rightarrow J}(v_h) \tag{15.2.9}$$
$$s_h^{\rightarrow L} = s_h^{\rightarrow L}(v_h) \tag{15.2.10}$$

---

[2] Our measure of difference, which is here a distance, requires that if there are two or more dimensions relevant for defining a joint action, then there exists a constant with appropriate units that transforms (equates) one unit of distance on any one dimension to a unit on any other second dimension. Although a general Minkowski metric could be employed to measure $|a^{J*} - a^{L*}|$, the reader may find it more convenient to think in terms of the more familiar Euclidean metric. An alternative, $(a^{J*} - a^{L*})^2$, would result in a relation that has nicer mathematical properties.

Note that when there are more than two participants, we need to specify differently Eqs. (15.2.4) and (15.2.24), which show how the noneconomic commodities c-security and c-respect, respectively, are produced. For example, when we refer to L and c-security, among possible specifications are

$$y_q^L = y_q^L\left(\max_{Q, Q'} |a^{Q*} - a^{Q'*}|\right), \qquad Q, Q' = L, J, J', J'' \cdots \tag{15.2.5}$$

and

$$y_q^L = y_q^L\left(\sum_{Q, Q'} |a^{Q*} - a^{Q'*}|\right), \qquad Q, Q' = L, J, J', J'' \cdots \tag{15.2.6}$$

The former focuses on the range, paying no attention to the differences between proposal pairs within that range. The latter focuses on a simple summation of differences, without paying attention to the size distribution of these differences. Still other specifications might associate weights with the proposals of each pair of participants, and so forth.

[3] We make the strong assumption that all information produced by any mediator or participant is "good" information in that it leads to more good debate, discussion, and interaction, which in turn enables participants to narrow down their differences. Thus the partial derivatives obtainable from Eqs. (15.2.9)–(15.2.11) are all positive, and we assume that other partials to be noted in what follows have the sign implied by this assumption. When this is not the case, interaction may lead to escalation rather than resolution of the conflict.

In turn this interaction, as indicated in the $\mathcal{J}$ box, is a function of information $s_h^{J\to}$, $s_h^{L\to}$, and y_h^Z provided (transmitted) by participants J, L, and the mediator Z, respectively, namely,[4]

$$\nu_h = \nu_h(s_h^{J\to}, s_h^{L\to}, y_h^Z) \tag{15.2.11}$$

Note that as indicated in Figure 15.1 we are assuming that all the information y_h^J and y_h^L produced, respectively, by J and L is transmitted to the political arena. That is,

$$s_h^{J\to} \equiv y_h^J \tag{15.2.12}$$
$$s_h^{L\to} \equiv y_h^L \tag{15.2.13}$$

The y_h^J and y_h^L, as we have already noted, are produced in the C^J and C^L boxes, respectively, and we have taken them to be a function of the inputs of labor y_{lh}^J and y_{lh}^L, respectively. This then brings us back to the basic decision that the individual J must face: Given his (or her) labor constraint, how much labor should be put into current production in order indirectly to produce and consume c-security, namely, b_q^J, and thus how much to consume in leisure and other uses, namely, b_l^J? Formally speaking, the answer to this question when all functions are well behaved is given by the first-order condition for maximization of his utility associated with his single control variable y_{lh}^J (or b_l^J). To derive it [bearing in mind that the amount b_q^J of c-security realized depends not only on J's input of labor for producing information, but also on the inputs of L and Z and using the constraint (15.2.2)], assuming an interior maximum,[5] our problem is

$$\max u^J = u^J[(\bar{g}_l^J - y_{lh}^J), b_q^J(y_{lh}^J, y_{lh}^L, y_{lh}^Z)] \tag{15.2.18}$$

for which, given y_{lh}^L, y_{lh}^Z, we set

$$\frac{du^J}{dy_{lh}^J} = 0$$

---

[4] We assume here and subsequently that there is no transmission (transport) cost in or resistance (lack of receptivity) to the flow of information. Also both here and later we must reiterate that what is important for J is not an actual magnitude (state) of a variable (whether quantitative or qualitative) but rather his or her perception of that magnitude. To conduct a dynamical systems analysis, however, it is necessary to ignore the perception factor or, where possible, embody it in a mathematical function.

Additionally, with regard to Eq. (15.2.9) [or (15.2.10)] we could make explicit a process whereby J (or L) inputs labor to filter out relevant information ν_h generated by the interaction. Such filtering or similar processes such as scanning may also occur elsewhere within the system to which we will henceforth not refer.

[5] When this assumption is relaxed, we set up the Lagrangian

$$\mathcal{L}^J = u^J[(\bar{g}_l^J - y_{lh}^J), b_q^J(y_{lh}^J(y_{lh}^J, y_{lh}^L, y_{lh}^Z)] - \lambda^J(\bar{g}_l^J - y_{lh}^J), - \mu^J(-y_{lh}^J) \tag{15.2.14}$$

which implies

$$\frac{\delta u^J}{\delta(\bar{g}_l^J - y_{lh}^J)}\frac{\delta(\bar{g}_l^J - y_{lh}^J)}{\delta y_{lh}^J} + \frac{\delta u^J}{\delta b_q^J}\frac{\delta b_q^J}{\delta y_{lh}^J} = 0 \qquad (15.2.19)$$

Since

$$\frac{\delta u^J}{\delta b_l^J} = \frac{\delta u^J}{\delta(\bar{g}_l^J - y_{lh}^J)}$$

and

$$\frac{\delta(\bar{g}_l^J - y_{lh}^J)}{\delta y_{lh}^J} = -1$$

we obtain[6]

$$\frac{\delta u^J}{\delta b_l^J} = \frac{\delta u^J}{\delta b_q^J}\frac{\delta b_q^J}{\delta y_{lh}^J} \qquad (15.2.20)$$

From Eq. (15.2.20) we see that to maximize his (or her) utility, J should allocate his labor between leisure and production of c-security in such a way that the marginal utility of labor in leisure and other uses (i.e., $\delta u^J/\delta b_l^J$) comes to equal the utility of that c-security derivable from his marginal unit of labor engaged in the production of information [i.e., $(\delta u^J/\delta b_q^J)(\delta b_q^J/\delta y_{lh}^J)$].[7]

which leads to the following first-order conditions:

$$\frac{d\mathcal{L}^J}{dy_{lh}^J} = 0 = -\frac{\delta u^J}{\delta(\bar{g}_l^J - y_{lh}^J)}\frac{\delta(\bar{g}_l^J - y_{lh}^J)}{\delta y_{lh}^J} + \frac{\delta u^J \delta b_q^J}{\delta b_l^J \delta y_{lh}^J} + \lambda^J + \mu^J \qquad (15.2.15)$$

$$\lambda^J(\bar{g}_l^J - y_{lh}^J) = 0; \qquad \bar{g}_l^J - y_{lh}^J \geq 0; \qquad \lambda^J \geq 0 \qquad (15.2.16)$$

$$\mu^J(-y_{lh}^J) = 0; \qquad y_{lh}^J \geq 0; \qquad \mu^J \geq 0 \qquad (15.2.17)$$

Note that it is not possible for both λ^J and μ^J to be greater than zero; λ^J can be greater than zero only if $\bar{g}_l^J - y_{lh}^J = 0$; and μ^J can be greater than zero only if $y_{lh}^J = 0$. In Eq. (15.2.14), λ^J represents the welfare (shadow price) to J were he to have another unit in his initial stock of labor; and μ^J represents the welfare (shadow price) to J were he able to go into debt for one unit of labor input.

[6] In longhand form, the right-hand side of the equation may be written as

$$\frac{\delta u^J \delta b_q^J}{\delta b_q^J \delta y_q^J}\frac{\delta y_q^J}{\delta |a^{J*} - a^{L*}|}\left[\frac{\delta(|a^{J*} - a^{L*}|)}{\delta a^{J*}}\frac{\delta a^{J*}}{\delta s_h^{-J}}\frac{\delta s_h^{-J}}{\delta v_h}\frac{\delta v_h}{\delta s_h^{J-}}\frac{\delta s_h^{J-}}{\delta y_h^J}\frac{\delta y_h^J}{\delta y_{lh}^J} \right.$$
$$\left. + \frac{\delta(|a^{J*} - a^{L*}|)}{\delta a^{L*}}\frac{\delta a^{L*}}{\delta s_h^{-L}}\frac{\delta s_h^{-L}}{\delta v_h}\frac{\delta v_h}{\delta s_h^{J-}}\frac{\delta s_h^{J-}}{\delta y_h^J}\frac{\delta y_h^J}{\delta y_{lh}^J}\right] \qquad (15.2.21)$$

[7] It does not necessarily follow that at all points of time the individual does input his labor to produce information. At some, if not many or all, points of time, the marginal utility of labor in leisure and other uses may exceed whatever utility may result for J from the information he may produce with any labor.

Note that in this model, the variable K_h^J, J's stock of information, does not enter since this stock as well as L's and the mediator's does not change. This is a basic assumption of our static model that must be relaxed when we proceed to the next models involving dynamic elements.

For the second participant, L, the exact same type of analysis pertains. For the mediator Z however, we have a slightly different problem. Mediator Z's utility function is related not to the consumption of c-security but the consumption of c-respect, namely, b_r^Z. That is, as noted in the upper part of the $\mathcal{J}$ box,

$$u^Z = u^Z(b_l^Z, b_r^Z) \qquad (15.2.22)$$

Z, too, is subject to a labor constraint, namely,

$$\bar{g}_l^Z = b_l^Z + y_{lh}^Z \qquad (15.2.23)$$

He (or she) faces the problem of how to allocate his current available amount $\bar{g}_l^Z$ of labor for consumption in leisure and other uses b_l^Z and as an input y_{lh}^Z in the production of information that ultimately will yield his c-respect for current consumption.

The production of this c-respect is a function of the difference between the most preferred joint actions of J and L, that is,[8]

$$y_r^Z = y_r^Z(|a^{J*} - a^{L*}|) \qquad (15.2.24)$$

The production of this c-respect represents the bestowal by the world community of c-respect upon Z according to the degree of success he or she achieves in reducing the difference between these most preferred joint actions. Therefore, the production of c-respect is indicated in Figure 15.1 as taking place within the $\mathcal{M}$ box and c-respect flows from this box to the mediator's utility function. As already noted, a^{J*} and a^{L*} are given by Eqs. (15.2.7) and (15.2.8), which are related to s_h^{-J} and s_h^{-L}, respectively. These information flows in turn derive from the debate, discussion, and interaction, namely, ν_h, which is given by Eq. (15.2.11). Note that in that equation the information y_h^Z produced by Z enters as a basic input that thus comes to influence the difference ($|a^{J*} - a^{L*}|$). The amount of y_h^Z

---

[8] Whereas in Eq. (15.2.4) we visualize J and L each obtaining more and more c-security for current consumption as the difference $|a^{J*} - a^{L*}|$ becomes smaller and smaller, the reader may hesitate to accept the notion that Z obtains more and more c-respect as that same distance becomes smaller and smaller. He or she may hesitate to do so because in certain real conflict situations only a negligible amount of c-respect is accorded the mediator until a compromise solution is actually achieved, for example, until a treaty is signed. Analytically this would cause problems with our formulation involving well-behaved, continuous functions. We can avoid the problem, however, by employing a function such as

$$y_r^Z = 1 - (|a^{J*} - a^{L*}|)^{1/10,000} + c \qquad (15.2.25)$$

produced, however, is a function of the labor input y_{lh}^Z that Z makes and the fixed capital stock K_h^Z of information. As indicated in the $\mathcal{I}$ box,

$$y_h^Z = y_h^Z(y_{lh}^Z, K_h^Z) \tag{15.2.26}$$

Hence, to repeat, the mediator, as with each participant, faces the labor allocation problem, namely, how much labor to provide as an input to produce information [which ultimately determines in part how much c-respect (he or she) consumes] and how much residually to consume in leisure and other uses. Formally speaking, the answer to this question when all functions are well behaved is given by the first-order conditions for maximization of his utility associated with his single control variable y_{lh}^Z (or b_l^Z). To derive it (bearing in mind that the amount b_r^Z of c-respect to be realized depends not only on his input of labor for producing information but also on those of J and L) and using the constraint (15.2.23), assuming an interior maximum,[9] our problem is

$$\max u^Z = u^Z[(\bar{g}_l^Z - y_{lh}^Z), b_r^Z(y_{lh}^J, y_{lh}^L, y_{lh}^Z)] \tag{15.2.27}$$

for which, given y_{lh}^J, y_{lh}^L and paralleling the discussion immediately after Eq. (15.2.18), we obtain as a first-order condition[10]

$$\frac{\delta u^Z}{\delta b_l^Z} = \frac{\delta u^Z}{\delta b_r^Z}\frac{\delta b_r^Z}{\delta y_{lh}^Z} \tag{15.2.28}$$

From Eq. (15.2.28) we see that to maximize utility, Z should allocate his labor between production of c-respect and consumption in leisure and other uses in such a way that marginal utility of leisure (i.e., $\delta u^Z/\delta b_l^Z$) comes to equal his utility of that c-respect derivable from his marginal unit of labor engaged in the production of information [i.e., $(\delta u^Z/\delta b_r^Z)$ $(\delta b_r^Z/\delta y_{lh}^Z)$].[11]

The preceding model does not guarantee the compatibility of the necessary conditions for equilibrium of the three behaving units J, L, and Z. To ensure compatibility, certain very strong assumptions must be made

---

where c is a constant depending upon the maximum distance between a^{J*} and a^{L*}. Specifically, we set

$$c = \max{(|a^{J*} - a^{L*}|)^{1/10,000}} - 1$$

[9] When this assumption is relaxed, we must set up a Lagrangian, and first-order conditions must be stated in a fashion parallel to that indicated in footnote 5.
[10] The longhand form of the right-hand side of this equation is of the same form as Eq. (15.2.21) and is presented in Isard and Smith (1983, p. 21).
[11] Note that this formulation of the problem does not imply that complete resolution of the conflict is always achieved. In many situations, particularly when $|a^{J*} - a^{L*}| \to 0$, the marginal utility of leisure and other uses, so foregone because more labor is required by J and L to reduce this difference any further, comes to exceed the utility gains from additional c-security that may be generated.

about the utility functions of these units. These restrictions are formally stated in Isard and Smith (1983), in particular in Lemma 1 of the Appendix of their manuscript, which contains the proof of compatibility under these restrictions.

15.3   A dynamical systems learning model for the mediator

Having now presented the framework of a static model, we take up a first dynamic model for which Figure 15.2 pertains. In this figure we only indicate those aspects that are different than in Figure 15.1. In the first model only the mediator learns. He (or she) learns in the sense that he builds up a stock of relevant knowledge so as to be able to take "more informed" actions, make "more informed" suggestions, and reach "more informed" decisions. Participants J and L do not learn. Hence at any point of time t, when the latter make a decision as to how to allocate their labor, they have completely forgotten about the knowledge both (1) produced in all previous time periods (whether they or others produced the knowledge), and (2) acquired, for example, regarding the a^{J*} and a^{L*}, during the debate, discussion, and interaction in previous time periods.

Only Z does not forget. Although this assumption is extremely strong, it does permit us to chip away at the problem.

Since J and L do not learn, both their situation and behavior are as depicted in the static model. Equation (15.2.20) is the first-order condition for J's maximization of his or her utility; and when L replaces J in these equations and J replaces L, it is the first-order condition for L's maximization of utility.

As already indicated, we consider Z's learning as equivalent to building up his or her stock K_h^Z of information. One of the simplest ways to treat such learning then is to assume that of the information $v_h(t')$ produced at time t' [see Eq. (15.2.11)], only a fraction of it comes to be added to the mediator's stock of knowledge – the stock of knowledge at the initial point of time t_0 being K_{h0}^Z. That is, setting

$$s_h^{\rightarrow Z}(t') = v_h(t') \tag{15.3.1}$$

we have the highly simplified learning equation[12]

$$\dot{K}_h^Z = \zeta^Z(s_h^{\rightarrow Z}(t')), \qquad \text{where } 0 < \frac{\delta \dot{K}_h^Z}{\delta s_h^{\rightarrow Z}} < 1 \tag{15.3.2}$$

---

[12] A more realistic learning equation would include a decay factor in order to preclude unlimited exponential growth in the stock of knowledge. Thus Eq. (15.3.2) might be replaced by

$$\dot{K}_h^Z(t') = s_h^{\rightarrow Z}(t') - \alpha(K_h^Z(t'))^\eta \qquad \text{with} \quad \alpha > 0 \quad \text{and} \quad \eta > 1$$

where the term $\alpha(K_h^Z(t'))^\eta$ represents "forgetting" and other factors leading to a decrease in

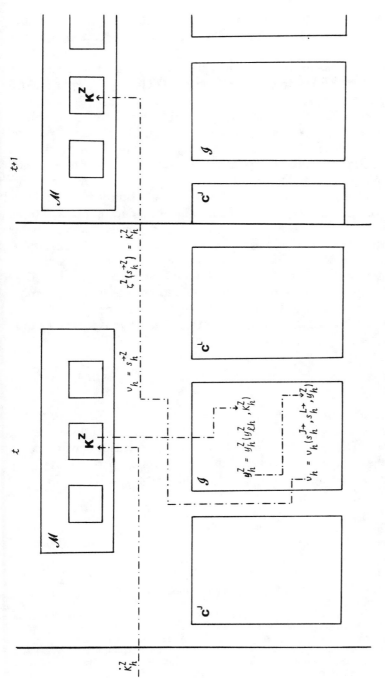

Figure 15.2. Dynamical systems learning model for a mediator Z.

See Figure 15.2, which shows how the $s_h^{\rightarrow Z}(t)$ enters at time $t + 1$ into Z's production function (15.2.26). The subsequent increase in ν_h yields $s_h^{\rightarrow Z}(t + 1)$.

Since the increase in the mediator's stock of knowledge at t' makes it possible for him (or her) to produce knowledge at later points of time still more effectively than possible without such an increase, the mediator now associates with an increase in a unit of his labor in producing knowledge at t' not only the value of that knowledge at t', but also, its value as an addition to his capital stock of knowledge – making more productive his labor at producing knowledge at all subsequent points of time, which in turn leads to still greater additions to the stock of knowledge. This enhanced value is then to be compared with the utility from the consumption of leisure and other goods foregone at the current point of time.

Note, however, that because the mediator must now consider the value of currently produced information for use in generating additional information at succeeding points of time, the mediator must necessarily be concerned with the stream of utility flows over all these points of time and with the maximization of this stream and no longer with the maximimization of his or her utility at the current point of time.[13]

In brief, leaving out the time argument t, the problem is to select a time path for $y_{lh}^Z \equiv g_l^Z - b_l^Z$ so as to

$$\max \int_{t_0}^{t_1} u^Z \left[(\bar{g}_l^Z - y_{lh}^Z),\, b_r^Z(y_{lh}^Z, y_{lh}^J, y_{lh}^L) \right] dt' + f^Z(K_h^Z(t_1)) \qquad (15.3.4)$$

for the relevant time horizon or planning period $t_0, \ldots, t_1$, where t_1 may in some cases correspond to the time when the mediation process ends, and where $f^Z(K_h^Z(t_1))$ corresponds to the value, often designated scrap value, of the stock of knowledge at the end of planning period t_1. At every point of time t' the mediator is subject to the learning Eq. (15.3.2).[14]

Z's stock of knowledge at time t'. To illustrate, let $s_h^{\rightarrow Z} = \omega K_h^Z$ with $\omega > 0$, a term that leads to exponential growth of K_h^Z. We then have

$$\frac{\delta \dot{K}_h^Z}{\delta K_h^Z} = \omega - \alpha\eta(K_h^Z)^{\eta-1} \qquad (15.3.3)$$

For $K_h^Z < 1$, we have steadily increased K_h^Z when $\omega > \alpha\eta$. Also when $\omega = \alpha\eta$, K_h^Z reaches a maximum when $K_h^Z = 1$ and then starts decreasing, reaching a value of zero (a steady state) for large enough values of K_h^Z. More generally, when $\omega > \alpha\eta$, K_h^Z reaches a maximum for some $K_h^Z > 1$; and when $\omega < \alpha\eta$, K_h^Z reaches a maximum for some $K_h^Z < 1$.

For background materials on dynamical system models see Isard and Liossatos (1979).

[13] In the usual problem, utility at a future point of time is appropriately discounted (upcounted). However, here we avoid such complication and the associated additional notation by assuming a zero discount rate.

[14] And, of course, an initial condition where $K_h^Z(t_0) = K_{h0}^Z$, where K_{h0}^Z is Z's initial stock of knowledge at the initial point of time t_0.

To obtain first-order conditions for the mediator to maximize his or her utility in this new, learning situation, we set up the current Hamiltonian[15]

$$\mathcal{H}^Z = u^Z[(\bar{g}_I^Z - y_{Ih}^Z), b_r^Z(y_{Ih}^Z, y_{Ih}^I, y_{Ih}^L)] + \beta_h^Z[\zeta^Z(s_h^{-Z})] \tag{15.3.5}$$

Assuming that the preceding function attains an interior maximum,[16] the maximum principle with respect to the control variable y_{Ih}^Z, given y_{Ih}^I and y_{Ih}^L, is $d\mathcal{H}^Z/dy_{Ih}^Z = 0$, which, in accord with the discussion associated with Eq. (15.2.15)–(15.2.20) and (15.2.28) yields[17]

$$\frac{du^Z}{db_I^Z} = \frac{\delta u^Z}{\delta b_r^Z} \frac{\delta b_r^Z}{\delta y_{Ih}^Z} + \beta_h^Z \left[\frac{\delta \zeta^Z}{\delta s_h^{-Z}} \frac{\delta s_h^{-Z}}{\delta v_h} \frac{\delta v_h}{\delta y_h^Z} \frac{\delta y_h^Z}{\delta y_{Ih}^Z} \right] \tag{15.3.6}$$

and the canonical equation

$$\frac{\delta \mathcal{H}^Z}{\delta K_h^Z} = -\dot{\beta}_h^Z$$

yields[18]

$$\dot{\beta}_h^Z = - \frac{\delta u^Z}{\delta b_r^Z} \frac{\delta b_r^Z}{\delta K_h^Z} - \beta_h^Z \left[\frac{\delta \zeta^Z}{\delta s_h^{-Z}} \frac{\delta s_h^{-Z}}{\delta v_h} \frac{\delta v_h}{\delta y_h^Z} \frac{\delta y_h^Z}{\delta K_h^Z} \right] \tag{15.3.7}$$

We know from Eq. (15.3.7) that β_h^Z is the value generated by an additional unit of capital stock of information.[19] This value is the sum of three

---

[15] Strictly speaking, the utility function u^Z should include K_h^Z as an argument. Following conventional practice, however, we assume that Z derives no utility directly from holding a capital stock.

[16] When this assumption is relaxed, we need to maximize the Hamiltonian using a Lagrangian formulation similar to that discussed in footnote 5.

[17] The longhand expression for $(\delta u^Z/\delta b_r^Z)/(\delta b_r^Z/\delta y_{Ih}^Z)$ is of the same form as Eq. (15.2.21) and is presented in Isard and Smith (1983, p. 21).

[18] The longhand expression for $(\delta y^Z/\delta b_r^Z)/(\delta b_r^Z/\delta K_h^Z)$ is of the same form as Eq. (15.2.21) and is presented in Isard and Smith (1983, p. 25). Strictly speaking, we should add to the two conditions (15.3.6) and (15.3.7) the following

$$\frac{\delta \mathcal{H}^Z}{\delta \beta_h^Z} = \dot{K}_h^Z = \zeta^Z(s_h^{-Z}) \tag{15.3.8}$$

$$K_h^Z(t_0) = K_{h0}^Z \tag{15.3.9}$$

$$\beta_h^Z(t_1) = \frac{\delta f^Z(K_h^Z(t_1))}{\delta K_h^Z}$$

[19] For any t, this is seen by multiplying both sides by dt' and integrating to obtain

$$\int_t^{t_1} \dot{\beta}_h^Z(t') \, dt' = - \int_t^{t_1} \left(\frac{\delta u^Z}{\delta b_r^Z} \frac{\delta b_r^Z}{\delta K_h^Z} \right) dt' - \int_t^{t_1} \beta_h^Z \left(\frac{\delta \zeta^Z}{\delta s_h^{-Z}} \frac{\delta s_h^{-Z}}{\delta v_h} \frac{\delta v_h}{\delta y_h^Z} \frac{\delta y_h^Z}{\delta K_h^Z} \right) dt' \tag{15.3.10}$$

so that performing the integration on the right-hand side and other operations, we get

$$\beta_h^Z(t) = \int_t^{t_1} \left(\frac{\delta u^Z}{\delta b_r^Z} \frac{\delta b_r^Z}{\delta K_h^Z} \right) dt' + \int_t^{t_1} \beta_h^Z \left(\frac{\delta \zeta^Z}{\delta s_h^{-Z}} \frac{\delta s_h^{-Z}}{\delta v_h} \frac{\delta v_h}{\delta y_h^Z} \frac{\delta y_h^Z}{\delta K_h^Z} \right) dt' + \beta_h^Z(t_1) \tag{15.3.11}$$

parts. The first two parts represent values stemming from the presence of that additional unit of capital stock in the production function of Eq. (15.2.26). As a result, the output of information (y_h^Z) is increased currently and at each subsequent point of time and leads to increased utility from the resulting greater output of c-respect (b_r^Z) currently and at each subsequent point of time. This is indicated in the first term of Eq. (15.3.11) and constitutes the first part of the value of β_h^Z. The second part results from the fact that the preceding increase in output of information (y_h^Z) currently and at each subsequent point of time leads to increase in s_h^{-Z} and thus Z's stock of knowledge currently and at each subsequent point of time. Each unit of this additional stock has a value $\beta_h^Z(t')$. The third part constitutes a scrap value of a unit of K_h^Z at time t_1.

Thus, as anticipated, Eq. (15.3.6) equates the marginal utility of leisure with the utility from c-respect directly derived from the value of the marginal unit of labor in producing c-respect [the first term on the right-hand side of Eq. (15.3.6)] plus the value β_h^Z of a unit of capital (stock of information) times the number of units of capital (i.e., s_h^{-Z} or ν_h) produced by the marginal unit of labor, a fraction of which by Eqs. (15.3.1) and (15.3.2) is automatically added to Z's capital stock.

15.4   A dynamical systems learning model for a participant

A third model, again a dynamical systems model, but one that is as simplified as the previous one, allows only one participant, say, L, and not the mediator Z, to learn. It is easily seen that the format and conditions of the model are exactly the same as the previous model except that L's stock of knowledge K_h^L changes whereas Z's stock K_h^Z does not.[20]

Again, however, we must be explicit about our assumptions. We are assuming that J and Z do not learn, a very strong assumption, as we already noted.

In this third model, both J's and Z's situation and behavior is as depicted in the static model. Equation (15.2.20) is the first-order condition for J's maximization of his or her utility, and Eq. (15.2.28) is the same for Z's maximization of utility. For L, the problem is different than in the static model since now L must associate with any increase in a unit of labor in producing knowledge at t' not only the value of that knowledge at t', but also its value as an addition to the stock of knowledge (capital) in making labor more productive at all subsequent points of time. This

---

[20] A figure very similar to Figure 15.2 can be constructed to depict the changes in the stock of knowledge of L.

enhanced value is then to be compared with the utility from the unit of leisure foregone at the current point of time.

In brief, L must consider the stream of utility flows over all points of time from t to t_1 and thus the maximization of this stream. The problem is then to

$$\max \int_t^{t_1} u^L[(\overline{g}_l^L - y_{lh}^L), b_q^L(y_{lh}^J, y_{lh}^L, y_{lh}^Z)] \, dt' + f^L(K_h^L(t_1)), \qquad t < t' < t_1$$

(15.4.1)

and where in our simplified fashion we postulate

$$\dot{K}_h^L(t') = \zeta^L(s_h^{\rightarrow L}(t')), \qquad \text{where } \frac{\delta \dot{K}_h^L}{\delta s_h^{\rightarrow L}} < 1$$

(15.4.2)

That is, L's increase in the stock of knowledge at t' depends on flow of information received from debate, discussion, and interaction in the workshop.

Paralleling Eq. (15.3.5), we set up the current Hamiltonian

$$\mathcal{H}^L = u^L[(\overline{g}_l^L - y_{lh}^L), b_q^L(y_{lh}^J, y_{lh}^L, y_{lh}^Z)] + \beta_h^L[\zeta^L(s_h^{\rightarrow L})] \quad (15.4.3)$$

Assuming that this function attains an interior maximum,[21] the maximum principle with respect to the control variable y_{lh}^L yields[22]

$$\frac{du^L}{db_l^L} = \frac{\delta u^L}{\delta b_q^L} \frac{\delta b_q^L}{\delta y_{lh}^L} + \beta_h^L \left[\frac{\delta \zeta^L}{\delta s_h^{\rightarrow L}} \frac{\delta s_h^{\rightarrow L}}{\delta v_h} \frac{\delta v_h}{\delta s_h^{L \rightarrow}} \frac{\delta s_h^{L \rightarrow}}{\delta y_h^L} \frac{\delta y_h^L}{\delta y_{lh}^L} \right]$$

(15.4.4)

The canonical equation yields[23]

$$\dot{\beta}_h^L = -\frac{\delta u^L}{\delta b_q^L} \frac{\delta b_q^L}{\delta K_h^L} - \beta_h^L \left[\frac{\delta \zeta^L}{\delta s_h^{\rightarrow L}} \frac{\delta s_h^{\rightarrow L}}{\delta v_h} \frac{\delta v_h}{\delta s_h^{L \rightarrow}} \frac{\delta s_h^{L \rightarrow}}{\delta y_h^L} \frac{\delta y_h^L}{\delta K_h^L} \right]$$

(15.4.5)

---

[21] When this assumption is relaxed, we need to maximize the Hamiltonian using a Lagrangian formulation similar to that discussed in footnote 5.

[22] The longhand expression for $(\delta u^L/\delta b_q^L)(\delta b_q^L/\delta y_{lh}^L)$ is as given in Eq. (15.2.21) once the symbol L replaces J and vice versa.

[23] The longhand expression for $(\delta u^L/\delta b_q^L)(\delta b_q^L/\delta K_h^L)$ is of the same form as Eq. (15.2.21) and is presented in Isard and Smith (1983, p. 28). Strictly speaking, we should add the following to the two conditions (15.4.4) and (15.4.5):

$$\frac{\delta \mathcal{H}^L}{\delta \beta_h^L} = \dot{K}_h^L = \zeta^L(s_h^{\rightarrow L})$$

(15.4.6)

$$K_h^L(t_0) = K_{h0}^L$$

(15.4.7)

$$\beta_h^L(t_1) = \frac{\delta f^L(K_h^L(t_1))}{\delta K_h^L}$$

(15.4.8)

The interpretations of these two equations are similar to those of Eq. (15.3.6) and (15.3.7) in the previous model.

15.5   Concluding remarks

This chapter has made a start at employing dynamical systems analysis to replicate the learning process, particularly as it goes on in workshops and brainstorming sessions concerned with conflict management in non-crisis situations. From a practical standpoint, little is gained from this exercise. Moreover, to avoid excessively extended mathematical statements, we have allowed only one participant or mediator to learn. Where more than one learn, their interactions over time involve many effects of different orders of indirectness.

Despite this lack of reality, the effort clearly reveals the need to account for knowledge accumulation and "decumulation" processes in workshops and other negotiation-type situations. Unfortunately, it is also extremely difficult to model these processes because

1. the participants involved have limited stocks of information and capacity to learn;
2. they frequently misperceive outcomes, actions of others, the state of the environment, and so on;
3. they usually possess rather fixed (inflexible) belief patterns; and
4. for other reasons already stated in earlier chapters.

Also the production of information typically is by discrete units, and at times new information may have negative as well as positive effects on the outcome of the conflict–resolution process. Nevertheless, this chapter gives some inklings of how to proceed to do more realistic dynamic modeling of these, even though much more work needs to be done; for example, the group equilibrium solution of a Nash-type must be replaced by an interaction mechanism over time that allows for a more accurate specification of conditions under which participants will achieve mutually acceptable and stable outcomes.

References

Isard, W. (1979) "A Definition of Peace Science, the Queen of the Social Sciences, Part I." *Journal of Peace Science* 4(1):1–47.

Isard, W. (1980) "A Definition of Peace Science, the Queen of the Social Sciences, Part II." *Journal of Peace Science* 4(2):97–132.

Isard, W., and P. Liossatos (1979) *Spatial Dynamics and Optimal Space-Time Development.* Amsterdam: North Holland.

Isard, W., and C. Smith (1982) *Conflict Analysis and Practical Conflict Management Procedures.* Cambridge, MA: Ballinger.

Isard, W., and C. Smith (1983) "A Dynamical Systems Approach to Learning Processes in Conflict Mediation and Interaction." In W. Isard and Y. Nagao (eds), *International and Regional Conflict.* Cambridge, MA: Ballinger.

Isard, W., T. E. Smith, P. Isard, T. H. Tung, and M. Dacey (1969) *General Theory: Social, Political, Economic and Regional.* Cambridge, MA: MIT Press.

CHAPTER 16

Invention and innovation in information research and development for problem solving: an exploratory view

Written with Bruce Burton

16.1 Introduction and general remarks

As already stated, the rigorous materials in Chapter 14 on the model of learning by a group and its individual members has little to say about creative information research and development, an activity urgently needed to break the decades-old U.S.–Soviet stalemate on major arms control. Nor do the less rigorous analyses in Chapter 15 using dynamical systems analysis. At the present moment, clearly what is required is some relatively "wild" type of analysis, highly imaginative and unorthodox, perhaps paying no attention to canons of scientific rigor, to suggest insights along entirely new directions. It is in this spirit that we develop the exploratory materials of this chapter. The materials, however, are designed for attacking in general the set of conflict situations that require inventive ideas and then innovation; only some of the materials are directly applicable to the U.S.–Soviet arms control conflict.

Also, we should once again stress the strategy dynamics of reality, which partly justifies the little regard in this chapter for scientific rigor and orthodoxy (e.g., we do not hesitate to contemplate violation of the law of conservation). In particular, as we keep on pointing out, participants frequently (if not constantly) learn and accumulate knowledge from experience in negotiations and from research if such is conducted. For example, foreign affairs (state) departments of nations grow in size, employing more and more specialists, involving more and more collec-

This chapter, as first written for presentation at the North American Conference of the Peace Science Society (International), University of Illinois (Urbana), 1983, was subsequently rewritten with Bruce Burton with major improvements to present its ideas in a form more appropriate for attacking regional development problems. See Isard and Burton (1986). However, the author alone is responsible for any shortcomings of the analysis that follows.

tion, processing, and interpretation of data, using computers more and more extensively, and so on. While participants learn, they develop more and more sophisticated strategies. Typically, these strategies result in deadlock, and then it becomes the task of the mediator (conflict analyst or peace scientist) or society in general to develop (construct, invent) new discussion frameworks, new environmental settings, new communication channels, new educational programs, and in general new conflict management procedures. Such is necessary in order to make possible, in a recognizable way, feasible joint concessions (decremax processes), or joint improvements (incremax processes), and so forth. In a sense we confront a never-ending task of invention and innovation – that is, research and development in a broad sense. Here invention and innovation is with respect to ideas, in contrast to the invention and innovation with respect to new technologies when we are involved with national and regional development problems.

Although there exist many definitions of invention and innovation, in what follows we formally define invention as *devising new ways of attaining given ends* – in our context the effective management of a conflict problem. (See Kennedy and Thirwell 1972.) As such, invention embraces both the creation of ideas previously nonexistent, using either new or existing knowledge, and the rediscovery of ideas that have previously existed but had not been judged worthwhile. We define innovation as the *effective application of inventions in a conflict situation for the first time.* Innovation typically raises the level (state of the art) of conflict management practice.

For us, five categories of factors define the process of invention and innovation of conflict management procedures (qualitative, quantitative, and combinations of qualitative and quantitative):

1. *Needs and demands* (the $\check{K}$ factor, as discussed in section 16.3);
2. *Communication* (presentation) *of need or demand* (the ξ factor, as discussed in section 16.4);
3. *Invention, the production of knowledge* (basic research), *and know-how* (applied research or potential innovation) (the $\acute{K}$ factor, as discussed in section 16.5);
4. *Communication* (transmission and diffusion) *of invention* (scientific knowledge and potential innovation) *to nodes* (locations) *of possible use* (the first part of the *l* factor, as discussed in section 16.6); and
5. *Adoption and implementation* (the second part of the *l* factor, as discussed in section 16.7).

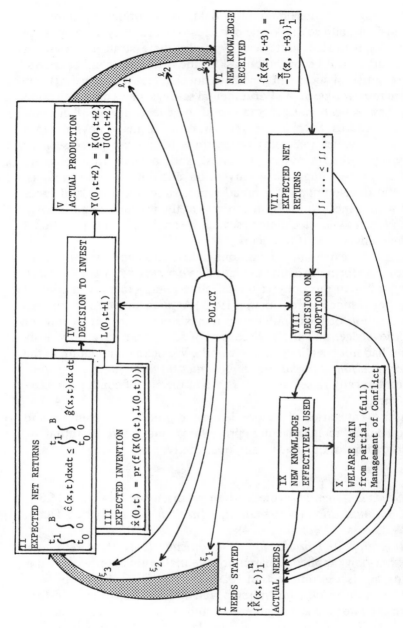

Figure 16.1. Process of invention and research and development: the generation and implementation of creative ideas.

The discussion of these factors follows a physical system framework that is illustrated in Figure 16.1. We consider that such an approach helps to ensure that resulting analysis will have greater consistency and balance than might otherwise be the case. In the development of our thought, we are also influenced by the writings of Schumpeter (1939), Hagerstrand (1953), and Usher (1954).

16.2 Basic variables and parameters in a two-equation (laws of change) model

In developing a conceptual framework for invention and innovation with respect to ideas, we draw analogies with physical systems discussed elsewhere (Isard and Liossatos 1975, 1979, chap. 6) and that from the standpoint of economics and regional science have appeal for defining optimal space–time development. There a one-commodity model was constructed having the production relation

$$Y(x, t) = f(K(x, t), L(x, t)) \qquad (16.2.1)$$

where

$Y(x, t)$ = the amount of the commodity produced at location x at time t per unit of distance;

$K(x, t)$ = the stock of the capital at location x at time t, the stock being a density (a magnitude per unit distance); and

$L(x, t)$ = the amount of resources (labor and others) applied at location x at time t per unit of time per unit of distance

and the following two equations of motion:

$$\dot{K}(x, t) = f(K(x, t), L(x, t)) - C(x, t) - \overset{\circ}{U}(x, t) \qquad (16.2.2)$$
$$l\dot{U}(x, t) = \xi \overset{x}{K}(x, t) - \nu U(x, t) \qquad (16.2.3)$$

where

$\dot{K}(x, t)$ = the addition of stock at (x, t) per unit of time, a time rate of change;

$C(x, t)$ = consumption at location x at time t per unit of time per unit of distance;

$U(x, t)$ = amount of flow through x at time t per unit of time per unit of distance;

$\dot{U}(x, t)$ = the addition to flow at (x, t) per unit of time, or time rate of change;

$\overset{\circ}{U}(x, t)$ = spatial rate of change of $U(x, t)$;

$\overset{x}{K}(x, t)$ = spatial rate of change of $K(x, t)$; and

l, ξ, ν = parameters to be discussed in what follows.

[Equation (16.2.2) is derived from the production relation (16.2.1) and the conservation equation

$$\dot{K}(x, t) = Y(x, t) - C(x, t) - \overset{x}{U}(x, t)] \qquad (16.2.4)$$

We now adapt this model to the problem at hand.

1. We take the one commodity to be information and assume that it all becomes effective as knowledge and know-how.

2. To avoid complicating mathematical statements, we do not include in Eq. (16.2.2) a term $-\alpha K(x, t)$ that would correspond to the depreciation of a stock per unit of time, α being a rate.[1]

3. Although at times information, as a commodity, may be physically consumable, by and large it is not. We therefore treat it as a public good whose use (consumption) by one unit does not diminish the stock that is available for use (consumption) by any other unit. By this convention, $C(x, t)$ in Eq. (16.2.2) is always zero. We are also assuming that addition of information at any time or place does not contribute to loss of knowledge and know-how at any time or place.

4. For simplicity we assume that all production of information takes place at a single location that for convenience we designate $x = 0$. It may be a single basic research center consisting of many or as few as one inventor. The many may be working in teams or individually. The location $x = 0$ may also be viewed as an aggregate of all locations at which inventive research is being conducted. Thus from Eq. (16.2.1)

$$Y(0, t) = f(K(0, t), L(0, t)) \geq 0 \qquad (16.2.5)$$
$$Y(\bar{x}, t) = f(K(\bar{x}, t), L(\bar{x}, t)) = 0 \qquad \text{for all } \bar{x} \neq 0$$

5. The distance between $x = 0$ and any using location $\bar{x}$, $\bar{x} = x_1, x_2, x_3, \ldots$, is defined by the number of behaving units (agencies and the like including those at other using locations) through which messages and information must flow. To ease exposition, we assume that no two behaving units are situated at the same location and that the distance between any two neighboring units is always Δx. Thus the distance between $x = 0$ and $x = \bar{x}$ is $(n + 1) \Delta x$, where n is the number of intervening units. For any using location $\bar{x}$, the locations of intervening units in order are $x_1, x_2, \ldots, x_n$, all to the right of $x = 0$ in the positive x direction. Distance may be not only physical distance, but also economic, psychological, political, social, ideological, and other.

---

[1] Such would correspond to the term $-(G/C)\rho(x, t)$ in the system for an electric transmission line discussed in Isard and Liossatos (1979, p. 153). This latter term corresponds to a loss of charge density, G/C being the loss coefficient and $\rho(x, t)$ the charge density. The reader can refer to Isard and Liossatos (1979, pp. 72–84) for discussion pertaining to the inclusion of depreciation.

6. From the standpoint of any using location $\bar{x}$, all information $U(x', t)$ arriving at an intervening location x' passes through it subject to the normal delays and losses defined by the parameters of the system. However, from the standpoint of x' all information received is available for use and becomes an addition to its capital stock; none is lost through export. Likewise, for $\bar{x}$ Thus, by statements 3 and 4, Eq. (16.2.2) becomes

$$\dot{K}(\bar{x}, t) = -\overset{x}{U}(\bar{x}, t) \qquad \text{for all } \bar{x} \neq 0 \tag{16.2.6}$$

where $-\overset{x}{U}(\bar{x}, t)$ is gross imports. This convention, characteristic of many public goods and of information in particular, violates the law of conservation so often employed in physics, economics, and regional science.

7. Since all information is taken to flow in the positive x direction, location $x = 0$ receives no inflow (all locations are at or to the right of $x = 0$ by convention).[2] Hence $\overset{x}{U}(0, t) = 0$. So by this convention and statement 2, Eq. (16.2.2) becomes, for $x = 0$,

$$\dot{K}(0, t) = f(K(0, t), L(0, t)) \tag{16.2.7}$$

8. We now consider the $-\xi\overset{x}{K}(x, t)$ term in Eq. (16.2.3), the second equation of motion. Let $D(\bar{x}, t)$ be the demand (need) for new information at time t at location $\bar{x}$, which represents the difference between a desired (aspired for) stock of knowledge $K^*(\bar{x}, t)$ and an existing stock $K(\bar{x}, t)$. That is,

$$D(\bar{x}, t) = K^*(\bar{x}, t) - K(\bar{x}, t) \tag{16.2.8}$$

9. Suppose the level of information desired by $\bar{x}$ is attained by $x = 0$. That is, suppose after sufficient resources are applied to production,

$$K(0, t) = K^*(\bar{x}, t) \tag{16.2.9}$$

Then, using the calculus formulation to ease exposition and assuming for convenience that the number n of intervening units (one at each unit of distance) is infinitely large, we may set $\bar{x}/n = dx$. Hence

$$\frac{D(\bar{x}, t)}{n} = \frac{K(0, t) - K(\bar{x}, t)}{n} = \overset{x}{K}(x, t) \qquad \text{for } x = 0, x_1, x_2, \ldots, \bar{x} \tag{16.2.10}$$

That is, the $K(x, t)$ function over x as we have defined the x dimension in nonphysical space is a straight line with negative slope $-[D(\bar{x}, t)/n]$

---

[2] This point follows also from our assumption that all locations of invention are assumed to be aggregated at the location $x = 0$. This assumption can be weakened if we assume that any using location $\bar{x}$ is connected, institutionally or otherwise, to one and only one source of new information.

10. Take the parameter ξ to represent a velocity. In some physical systems, it corresponds to an elasticity coefficient. In our model it is the speed at which the message on the local demand (need) at $\bar{x}$ reaches $x = 0$, the location of invention (production of new information). When there are n intervening units between $x = 0$ and $x = \bar{x}$, ξ may be viewed as the average speed at which the message passes through these points, that is, through the units of distance corresponding to these n units ($\frac{1}{2} \Delta x$ being to the left and $\frac{1}{2} \Delta x$ to the right of each unit). The transmission speed in some cases may be retarded and in others accelerated.

11. In Eq. (16.2.3) we take $\dot{U}(0, t)$ to represent the production of new information, that is, $\dot{U}(0, t) = \dot{K}(0, t) = Y(0, t)$. We may consider for a problem on hand that the existing flow of relevant information $U(0, t)$ is zero; or if some actually exists, we may arbitrarily set the level at zero.

12. Accordingly, the l parameter may be viewed as an inertial coefficient, the inverse of a velocity, or the time it takes for a flow to cover a unit of distance. Or Eq. (16.2.3) may be rewritten as

$$\dot{U}(x, t) = - \frac{\xi}{l} \overset{x}{\dot{K}}(x, t) - \frac{\nu}{l} U(x, t) \qquad (16.2.11)$$

Then the $1/l$ parameter may be viewed as a velocity, giving the average speed at which new information produced at $x = 0$ is transmitted to the using location $x = \bar{x}$.[3]

13. In Eq. (16.2.3) the term $-\nu U(x, t)$ corresponds to a loss of newly produced information in passing through location x (the unit of distance centering around x) due to resistance. It is a frictional force that may be said to reduce the force associated with the term $-\xi \overset{x}{\dot{K}}(x, t)$. Or, if $\dot{U}(x, t)$ is the information that must be received at $\bar{x}$ for the realization of a new effective conflict management procedure, then $-(\nu/l)[U(x, t)]$ must be added to $\dot{U}(x, t)$ to give the total information that must be produced at $x = 0$ or transmitted when x is an intervening location, so that the demand $\dot{K}(\bar{x}, t)$ is met.

---

[3] Were the ν factor zero, the ratio ξ/l might be interpreted as measuring the rate of progress in the adoption of an inventive idea or procedure, as it is made applicable, that is embodied in a potential innovation. The larger it is, the greater the rate of progress. This follows since at any receiving location $\bar{x}$, $\dot{K}(\bar{x}, t) = - \dot{U}(\bar{x}, t)$, that is, the realized increase in know-how (which we take to be know-how implementable in terms of a realizable innovation) is equal to the realized "flow in." But such a flow in $- \dot{U}(\bar{x}, t)$, is also dependent on (1) the "flow out" $\xi \overset{x}{\dot{K}}(\bar{x}, t)$ of the demand message from $\bar{x}$ to its neighbor on the way to the location of inventive action ($x = 0$) and hence is directly proportional to the ξ coefficient; and (2) the resulting flow out $l\dot{U}$ of requested (needed) new information (invention) from $x = 0$ and hence is inversely proportional to the l coefficient.

As a mathematical statement of the process of invention (innovation) or of the production and diffusion of new information within the information subsystem $\mathcal{M}$ (see Figure 1.3), the preceding abounds with deficiencies. First, it needs to be restated as a set of difference equations with time lags. Second, it is questionable from the very start, for the violation of the law of conservation for processes within the information subsystem makes it illegitimate to draw analogies from physical systems. Third, it is inadequate in the sense that while it explicitly recognizes the resistance to the flow of newly produced information with the $\nu U(x, t)$ term, it fails to make explicit the resistance to the flow of the message from $\bar{x}$ to $x = 0$. Nonetheless, we have presented the preceding statements in this section for two reasons:

1. We hope, because of its many obvious deficiencies, that it will prod others to put forth more adequate statements.
2. We find it extremely useful in suggesting *categories* of factors to develop in the verbal presentation that follows and for helping depict the process with the use of Figure 16.1.

16.3 Need and demand for invention (new conflict management procedures, discussion frameworks, and so on): the $\overset{x}{K}$ factor

Start with the "needs stated" box, box I, at the extreme left of Figure 16.1. In a conflict situation, especially one that has not been immediately managed through existing procedures, framework, and so on, almost by definition there is a need and demand for invention.[4] The demand may be considered to be of two types. One is the demand associated with the need for a once-for-all solution to a normal, nonprotracted explicit conflict. The other is a steady, persistent demand that is associated with protracted social conflicts and the like. There always are protracted conflicts, between the "in" groups and the "out" groups, between developing and developed nations, among religious groups, among minorities, and so on. Northern Ireland and Lebanon are cases in point. Hence there is always a latent demand for invention, and it is a constant latent demand since these conflicts always keep changing in character and scope.

For the moment, concentrate on this type of demand. For much, if r ot most, of the time, it is covered up (has not surfaced) and is implicitlike.

---

[4] Note that the demand $\overset{x}{k}$ may be disaggregated by type of knowledge, where each type is specific to a subconflict of the total conflict situation or by another meaningful set of categories so that $\overset{x}{k}$ becomes a vector, that is, $\overset{x}{k} = (\overset{x}{k}_1, \overset{x}{k}_2, \ldots)$.

It needs to be made explicit and recognizable. To do so, the participants need to make statements, express the issues that are involved (reflecting of course their perceptions and misperceptions), and give vent to their emotions in the process. This is not an easy task especially if different cultures and languages are involved. In any case the demand is there. It needs to be identified and properly stated so that it can be translated into a common language. For protracted social conflicts this constitutes the $\overset{\vee}{K}$ factor. Since more than one behaving unit (group, individual i, $i = 1, \ldots, n$) may have a need and demand for new creative ideas, we have designated such by $\{\overset{\vee}{K}(\overline{x}, t)\}_1^n$.

Note that many of these protracted social conflicts represent a gradual shifting of influence, power, and control of resources (including the vote) from one group to another. A typical case is when one ethnic or religious group grows in numbers whereas another declines. Here the dynamics of the situation, as it complicates the issues, must be explicitly recognized and if possible anticipated so that a transition can be effected through a sequence of arrangements (compromises) recognizing the changing relative influence (resources, numbers) of the groups in conflict.

Another category of conflict is that which exists in a crisis. Here the time for statement, transmission of messages to locations for invention and innovation, diffusion of ideas, decision, and implementation is very short. Nonetheless, the first stage must be squarely confronted. The issues must be stated before any of the later stages can be entered into. Because of the shortage of time, the statement of the issues may be incomplete, inaccurate, and misleading, involve misperceptions, and in other ways be incorrect. Such tends to impede the management of the conflict. An intense demand (need) for new creative ideas, the $\overset{\vee}{K}$ at location $\overline{x}$ at time t, may warrant the allocation of a large amount of resources to the task.

The current U.S.–Soviet arms control conflict (1988) can be viewed as a nonprotracted explicit conflict; yet it contains many elements of a protracted nature.

16.4   Communication (presentation) of need or demand: the ξ factor

Although actual needs and demands may be identified, estimated, or otherwise specified, there exists the problem of making them known in their true nature at the locations (points of potential information supply) of the third party (mediator) or other behavioral units whose role is to invent, that is, carry on research and development of ideas. This is indicated by the shaded arrow in the upper left of Figure 16.1 going from the "needs stated" box to the "expected net returns" box, box II, and is embodied in the ξ factor.[5]

First there is the problem of apathy, the lack of motivation to take the effort to state needs and demands. It may not be worth the effort in the view of the affected parties, particularly those who have been underdogs in protracted social conflicts and have had their voices stifled. Second, there is the problem of translation. The people at $\bar{x}$ need to put their demands and needs into the language of the receiver; accurate translation may be in fact impossible because of cultural differences that have led to nontranslatable concepts and values. There may be difficulties in doing this even when the same language presumably exists between a sending behavioral unit (location) and a receiving one. For example, a sender may not have the proper vocabulary and/or grammar. Third, in political systems such as those that characterize the United States the needs and demands are to be made explicit and set forth by the political representatives (leaders) of a constituency (say, a minority). All too often, however, a representative fails to do so, perhaps because he (or she) is not a 100 percent true representative (e.g., he may feel compelled to state the needs and demand of only a subgroup of his constituency), or fails to perceive these needs and demands accurately, or is interested to some degree or entirely in his own welfare and that of his immediate associates. His statements thus distort these needs and demands and thus at least in part delays the transmittal of the true needs.[6]

All of the preceding may be taken to be problems of initiating the transmission of a message from $\bar{x}$. Once a message is initiated at $\bar{x}$, it must be transmitted to the behavioral unit at location $x = 0$ for the creation of new ideas and know-how. The transmission may be direct as when only a mediator or other third party is involved and assumes the role of an inventor.[7] However, the transmission may be indirect in that a message

---

[5] This problem exists not only at some point of time that corresponds to the beginning point for the development of invention and effective innovation, but also at any subsequent point of time when *feedback* of information on difficulties in implementation of a potential innovation and on changes in $\check{k}$ or other elements resulting from an innovation is desirable for evaluation and refinement purposes.

[6] There are of course differences among behavioral units in ability to perceive needs, ranging from the poverty-stricken unit that is almost fully isolated in a society with a primitive educational system, and thus knowing little about what is possible, to the advanced highly educated, sophisticated but conservative unit that fails to perceive the steady decline actually taking place or imminent in its influence since currently and in the past it has been a strong bulwark of the existing order.

[7] Even when only a mediator or third party is involved, there is intervening distance, psychological, social, ideological, etc., since at the minimum the role of the mediator is different from that of the participant.

must go through one or more intervening behavioral units, as when the Secretary General of the United Nations or his or her delegate is involved, or the International Court of Justice, or the International Monetary Fund. Hence, there may be a series of obstacles along the way, for example, one at every stage (node) through which the message is passed.

In transmission a first problem may be that the actual channel for transmission may not exist or may be blocked, as is frequently the case for minority groups – cultural, political, and social.[8] Further, society may judge that the cost of providing channel infrastructure may not be warranted by potential gains to society. Next at each of the bureaucratic agencies, regional divisions, levels of a religious hierarchy, and so on, to which the message must go, there may be a problem of both reception (recognition) and retranslation for further transmission. The problem of reception is again one of language understanding, whereas the problem of retransmission is in part the ability to retranslate the message for receipt at the next node along the channel. Moreover, the actual channel from any one obstacle point to the next may not exist, or may be congested with part or all of the message lost, or may be completely blocked.

In essence, then, the message, however adequately stated at the initial point of propagation, may be subject to a series of losses and distortions before it is finally received and digested at the location $x = 0$ where invention is to take place. All these losses and distortions are associated with resistance factors that are included in the ξ parameter. However, the analyst may wish to remove some, if not all, these resistance factors from the ξ parameter and treat them separately with a new parameter, μ.

Recall that it takes time to cover a unit of distance, including time to put the message into appropriate symbols, to understand (unravel or decode) a received message, and to translate the message for receipt for understanding by the next behavioral unit. Hence, the velocity parameter ξ may be disaggregated into $\xi_1, \xi_2, \xi_3, \ldots$ parameters, as indicated in Figure 16.1.[9]

In the case of the current U.S.–Soviet arms control conflict situation (1988), there is no explicit mediator or third-party intervenor, although there is a host of pressures from the World Community outside these two powers – in some sense acting as a set of third-party intervenors. On the other hand, there exists the constant requirement for the effective needs and demands of one power to be translated into the language of the other,

---

[8] Frequently, violent discontent of a minority group reflects such blockage.
[9] Also, if a problem requires that $\check{k}$ be disaggregated, then corresponding to each $\check{k}_i$, $i = 1$, $2, \ldots$, there would be a relevant ξ_i ($i = \alpha, \beta, \ldots$) and perhaps a μ_i.

at least to the extent that this is possible (we constantly are aware of the misunderstandings arising from the nontranslatability of concepts and symbols). Here sensitive third parties functioning as more than mere professional translators are constantly required. Again, although it does not seem likely that the two big powers will ever consent to have a third party act as a mediator, or one to whom to state their views of the problem and related matters so that the third party might design (invent) workable conflict management procedures, there are nonetheless agencies such as the United Nations and scholars (e.g., peace scientists) who are in effect informally at work in designing (inventing) new procedures and setting them forth as if they were at location $x = 0$. A main difficulty that these intervenors confront is that of obtaining accurate information on each power's needs and demands because appropriate transmission channels do not exist, are congested or blocked, involve numerous intermediate bureaucratic agencies, and the like and because on certain matters the powers may be employing a principle of misinformation in their current or for their planned negotiations. The ξ factor is very much at work.

16.5 Invention, the production of creative ideas and scientific knowledge (basic research) and know-how (applied research or potential innovation): the $\acute{K}$ factor

Following economics, we conceive of a production function for creative ideas and scientific knowledge as involving all kinds of inputs – labor, capital, energy, materials – and the existing stock of knowledge K at the points of production.[10] The decision to produce new creative ideas and information is an investment decision since, once produced, the new ideas and information are added to the stock of knowledge K that generates valuable services over a time period. Hence, as for any investment the volume of investment, whether by private enterprise (profit motivated) or by a public body (social welfare motivated) or a consortium of both, is determined by an appropriate expected benefit–cost relation over an appropriate period of time and set of locations.[11]

---

[10] The stock of knowledge K is a density per unit area; and current services from this stock are what constitute the inputs when we enter K into a production function. Recall that for the purposes of this chapter, we assume the knowledge stock is never diminished when services from it are employed in production and never depreciates (diminishes) over time.
[11] See Chapter 15 for an attempt to make explicit in mathematical form the stream of benefits over time from new knowledge (invention) that is produced and to pin down the investment problem in terms of marginal (first-order) conditions.

Ignoring discounting over time, taking the planning horizon to extend from time t_0 to t_1, and using locations for $x = 0$ to $x = B$, we may in an oversimplified fashion state the relation as

$$\int_{t_0}^{t_1} \int_0^B \hat{c}(x, t) \, dx \, dt \le \int_{t_0}^{t_1} \int_0^B \hat{g}(x, t) \, dx \, dt \qquad (16.5.1)$$

In estimating any such relation, opportunity costs must be explicitly considered where $\hat{c}(x, t)$ is expected costs at location x at time t and $\hat{g}(x, t)$ is expected gains (benefits) at location x at time t. [Clearly, marginal (first-order) conditions should also be stated as well as others and, in addition, numerous constraints imposed.] See box II, on expected net returns, at the top of Figure 16.1.

However, unlike most production functions, there exists a highly stochastic element in invention; the creation of a novelty or synthesis is largely unpredictable. Hence the relations (16.2.1) and (16.2.4) must be restated to yield output $Y(0, t)$ and thus $\dot{K}(0, t)$ as a prospect or a probability distribution, where admittedly output itself is exceedingly difficult to measure. In box III, on expected invention, at the top of Figure 16.1 we have indicated this by placing a "hat" ($\hat{\ }$) on top of $Y(0, t)$ in the production function noted there and a pr with brackets on the right-hand side.

Note, however, that although from an R&D policy standpoint this benefit–cost (economic) approach may be appropriate for "motivating" invention (a supply of new knowledge, in actuality), much invention takes place *autonomously* by creative and curious minds concerned with "pure understanding" only and motivated to "unravel the mysteries of the universe."

Once calculations are made during time t and if they yield positive expected net returns, a decision to invest $L(0, t + 1)$ labor and other resources is made in time $t + 1$, and actual output $Y(0, t + 2)$ is realized in time $t + 2$. See boxes IV and V at the top of Figure 16.1.

It may be useful to note briefly several types of conflict situation for which invention is required.

1. As already noted, we may be dealing with highly sophisticated participants, for example, strategy experts who are right-hand persons of key political leaders who from experience and research may possess a large stock of analytical information regarding strategic behavior. They may have reached a deadlock in making proposals for handling the conflict, for example, because each miscalculated the others' actions and took a fixed position, which together with the others' fixed positions is infeasible. Here, new

information must be produced by attacking the problem at a deeper level, or with a different focus, and so on.

2. Alternatively, two political leaders may view the conflict situation as a zero-sum game and cannot agree to a 50–50 split or any other. Here, as per Burton an invention is required that
   (a) effectively brings universal values into the situation,
   (b) in the minds of the participants converts the game into a positive-sum game, and
   (c) persuades or leads them or otherwise promises to bring them to an acceptable compromise.

3. Alternatively, the participants may come from quite different cultures; one may represent an industrialized society, whereas the other may represent a culture, highly mystical (religious), that has hardly been impacted (if at all) by modern scientific advances and tradition. Here, the invention must concentrate on the development of perceptions of equivalent values. Specifically, if there is a give and take on the part of two or more participants, the give and take must be perceived as equivalent by each participant.

4. Alternatively, two political leaders may come from cultures with diametrically opposed values. Here invention must take probably its most creative form, once some common language has been developed and skill in translation achieved, since penetrating understanding of perceptions and misperceptions and how these may be altered is required.[12]

The production of creative ideas and scientific knowledge for mediation purposes and for conflict management can often be disaggregated into two main parts: (1) generation of *basic* creative ideas and knowledge and (2) generation of *applied* knowledge, that is, the invention as it is embodied in a potential innovation (conflict management procedure)

---

[12] Idea invention has all the characteristics that a problem of technological invention has. According to Usher (1954), a leading scholar on the process of invention, a cumulative synthesis (Gestalt-type) approach must be employed in explaining invention. The transcendentalist approach (the unpredicted occurrence of a brilliant idea) and the mechanistic process theory (necessity is the mother of invention) are each inadequate in basic aspects for this task. See Ruttan (1959). Usher focuses on four basic steps: (1) the perception of the problem (an incomplete or unsatisfactory method of satisfying a want); (2) the setting of the stage (the bringing together of the data or elements through some particular configuration of events or thought); (3) the act of insight (where large elements of uncertainty are present); and (4) critical revision (for full understanding and effective operation). Although in this chapter we assume that the insight may come only from a mediator or a third party or other individuals than the participants, as Fisher and Ury (1978, 1981) note, the participants themselves may assist in the invention and thus to some extent play the role of an inventor.

with all bugs removed. Whereas for the purposes of this chapter we take the production of both to occur at and only at the aggregate location $x = 0$, there is often reason for the production of applied knowledge (removal of the last bugs and adaptation of the creative idea and invention to local conditions and the specific conflict) to be decentralized and even to take place at the locations (national capitals) of the participants. One reason for such is a need for some ongoing applied research at any $\bar{x}$ in order to have available locally skills and know-how to implement an innovation (e.g., a new conflict management procedure) when such needs to be done.

With regard to the U.S.–Soviet arms control issue, the very "production" of invention confronts serious obstacles and distortions. In the case of the United States after World War II the invention/innovation function was assigned, at least in part, to the newly created Arms Control and Disarmament Agency. But this agency has in effect become a tool of the presidential office. Further, the more recently created U.S. Peace Institute has already been significantly infused with myopic national interest concerns. Similar statements can be made with regard to the Soviet units formally assigned the "noble" invention/innovation generation mission.

Moreover, a more subtle set of obstacles are at play, certainly in the United States. There exist foundations with noble purposes, but these most often turn out to be noble purposes with regard to national interest only. They allocate large funds for basic research on international security and arms control. But they tend to be administered by those scholars who have been successful in traditional disciplines and are highly perceptive and informed with regard to national problems or by personnel influenced by such scholars. Their funds operate to lure away creative minds from the nontraditional paths from which stem most basic inventions of the sort required to break the impasses in the U.S.–Soviet negotiations on arms control. They rarely support the desired research of unorthodox, "nonsafe," highly internationally oriented creative minds; and if they support research of these minds, it is by and large research that has been redirected to national interests and/or along more traditional disciplinary lines.

16.6   Communication (transmission and diffusion) of creative ideas and scientific knowledge and potential innovation to locations of possible use: the l factor

Once an invention has been created and worked over so that it corresponds to a potential innovation, we reach the problem of communication (transmission and diffusion), the issue that has perhaps been most extensively discussed in the literature on invention and innovation.

The issue breaks down into several subproblems. The first is the actual statement of the invention and advance in scientific knowledge. Here, there may be inertia (part of the l factor) on the part of those who have achieved the invention and advance, reflecting an excessive conservatism (risk avoidance) that may delay a report on an advance until there is 100 percent certainty about it – for example, a formal mathematical proof that a procedure will yield a unique solution and some pilot testing with an "experimental" group. Or the inventor or scientist may be simply indifferent to reporting it – may lack concern for application and use. More important is the need to translate a technical paper or an advance into a form that is understandable (recognizable) by participants (potential users) in the sense that they come to recognize clearly the different actions that are feasible. There may be one or more bureaucratic or organizational divisions through which the report must go, each involving a retranslation or restatement. Furthermore, at one or more points the advance may need to be worked upon to remove the bugs in the application of it as an innovation. At these points, applied research may be required as well as a reporting of findings in an appropriate language for later receivers. At each of these points there may be delays, inertia, and obstacles. Still more it takes time for an innovation to be demonstrated successfully and, where space (distance) intervenes, for the message to be passed on by word of mouth from one person to another, from one point in space to another, and so on. Hence, there results further reduction in the speed of diffusion, that is, an increase in the time it takes the invention ultimately to reach the location of the potential users (participants). Another aspect of the communication problem is one associated with the hierarchical structure of communication. Frequently a message must proceed from the point of invention to a primary node (e.g., a capital city). Then it must spread to a second-order node, then on to a third-order node, and so forth. This may be so because of the existence along the way of formal or informal transmission channels.[13]

In brief, numerous delays and resistances are encountered as embodied in the l parameter. See the shaded arrow at the right of Figure 16.1. Ultimately, the new knowledge created at $x = 0$, namely, $\dot{U}(0, t + 2)$, is

---

[13] In a more general sense, the diffusion process [as Pred (1977a) observes] may take place via diverse communication modes over a diffusion network via the spatial–temporal overlay of many individual diffusion processes (face-to-face contacts, agency-to-agency links, agency-to-individual or to other behavioral unit connections, etc.). Also, we must recognize that there may be differences among the several receiving units (participants in a conflict) in their access (in terms of social, ideological, or other distance) to the locations of new invention – in terms of the single mediator or set of intervening units – differences in face-to-face contacts, institutional ties, receptivity and cultural resistances, etc. Also see Arrow (1962), Domanski (1977), Brown (1980), and Binswanger et al. (1978).

received at a location $\bar{x}$ of potential users as new knowledge $\dot{K}(\bar{x}, t + 3)$ at time $t + 3$. See box VI. As with the ξ parameter, the l parameter may be disaggregated into several factors or sets of factors, namely, l_1, l_2, l_3, as indicated in Figure 16.1.

When we examine the U.S.–Soviet arms control issue, we find many transmission difficulties. For example, there exists the major problem of transmitting an inventive idea up to the top where the political leaders and their associates interact. Suppose a creative scholar were to develop a framework that makes explicit workable ways to capture the universal values at stake in effective arms control, or indicates ways to obtain clearer perceptions of equivalent values, or develops a new set of definitions that would be more acceptable to both powers, or sets forth new concepts or models that eliminate insurmountable disagreement on relevant variables and the like, or involves some combination of these elements. This framework and its elements must still be taken up the bureaucratic ladder and be subject to time delays and other obstacles imposed by a bureaucratic hierarchy containing administrative and research personnel who are by and large behind the times regarding analytical techniques, that is, usually have little appreciation for the most recent analytical tools and concepts developed. [For example, they may be well versed in the use of input–output in identifying impacts of military expenditures that they learned while graduate students but not at all aware of the strengths and weaknesses of CGE (computable general equilibrium) models.] Too often, they are narrow-minded and myopic regarding international problems. Even at the top, where there may be brilliant minds that had digested all new ideas in their respective fields (economics, political science, sociology, law, etc.) some thirty to forty years ago, there is considerable resistance to new creative ideas. Those at the top are no longer fully informed on recent developments in their fields. They are certainly less receptive to new ideas than they once were.

16.7   Adoption and implementation

The actual possession of information about a new potentially applicable communication mode, discussion framework, educational program, environmental setting, or conflict management procedure in part or in its entirety by participants at the local level does not ensure that the potential innovation will in fact be adopted and implemented. A number of obstacles must be overcome. First there is the inertia about doing anything, even if one has knowledge. The attitude "new ideas have always failed in the past" or "things just cannot get better" may stand in the way.[14] (This is especially so when, e.g., participants have been in office for a long time and lack the exploratory urge of youth.) Moreover, if the adoption of a new idea, process, and so on, threatens the position of an "in-group," it may have the effect of stimulating that group to meet the competition of the new innovation by strengthening its fixed position, particularly if a drastic reorganization of the structure (political, economic, and social) upon which it sits is implied.[15] Then, if significant resources are needed to put into effect the potential innovation (the reorganization of a governmental agency, imposition of new regulations, education of a legislature or constitutency, etc.), there is the problem of obtaining these resources.

Still another problem may arise from the existence of many different interest groups (subconstituencies) at the local level with conflicting objectives. In order to implement the innovation, a participant (political leader) may need to reach a compromise among these interest groups, presumably through the use of a different or even the same conflict management procedure.

Finally, we should keep in mind that many *institutional* innovations must be effected if the potential innovation in conflict management is to be implemented. Here is where knowledge in the social sciences and related professions such as law can be essential; and here research may be required to obtain this knowledge.

In Figure 16.1 we have indicated in box VII that new knowledge (creative ideas) received at using location $\bar{x}$ is evaluated in terms of expected net returns and at time $t + 4$ may be effectively used (box IX), leading presumably to a welfare gain from partial or full management of a conflict (box X). However, whether or not the new knowledge is effectively used, there is *feedback* in the sense that, for example, actual needs may have changed as a result of this process or require restatement, as indicated by the arrows that lead into the *actual needs* box (box I). Although the process may stop at this point, more likely it will continue, and most certainly in the case of a protracted conflict (as in Lebanon) or in a Big Power conflict, which because of the dynamics of the international scene never becomes fully managed. In these cases, we may imagine the process often

---

[14] Moreover, as we have earlier noted, if the new creative idea (invention) is not along lines that had been expected by a participant, it may often be dismissed as inapplicable or ignored. To ensure the adoption of new applicable ideas, there must often be a learning process.
[15] As per Kaniss (1977), this is akin to the problem of taking power away from the élite and transferring it to the exiles and of making a community more receptive to the new ideas of exiles.

to be iterative and ongoing in repetitive fashion and with one or more stages in continuous operation but with fluctuating intensity.

The adoption and implementation of new procedures and ways of thinking is extremely difficult in the case of the U.S.–Soviet arms control problem. One major difficulty, already alluded to, is pointed up by the failure of the U.S. Congress (which alone has the power to ratify treaties) to go along with the Salt II agreement. The very democratic ways of the United States run counter to the principle of monolithicity in negotiations. The president and his associates rarely if ever can count beforehand on sufficient support of Congress to ensure the passage of proposed treaties and like agreements with the Soviets, particularly those that may evolve from the use of highly inventive and innovative ideas. These proposed treaties and agreements too often run counter to at least several of the interpretive packages by which members of Congress representing different constituencies operate. Soviet leaders undoubtedly have similar problems of eliciting support within the Kremlin.

16.8   The role of policy

In the center of Figure 16.1 we have constructed a policy circle. At every point in the process discussed in this chapter, policy may and often does enter. Policy exists at the start of the process through encouraging and helping participants (localities, nations) to state their needs in a conflict situation, whether ongoing, protracted, or new. Through provision for monitoring communication channels, policy affects the speed and ease by which the message is communicated. The very decision of whether or not to invest in the production of invention is a policy issue. The dissemination (diffusion) of new basic knowledge and its transformation into applied knowledge ready for innovation is a function of policies in force. Adoption and implementation are, as already suggested, affected by numerous types of policy. See Ewers and Wetteman (1980) and Goddard (1980).

16.9   Conclusions

We have tried to discuss in a balanced fashion various forces at work in the invention–innovation problem for conflict management. This problem will always exist since at least some strategists may always be expected to have absorbed the full stock of existing knowledge regarding conflict management. When two or more such strategists confront each other in a conflict, a deadlock may frequently occur. At this point, invention (new knowledge) is absolutely essential.

In this chapter, we have found it useful in section 16.2 to make analogies to the forces at play in a typical physical system. Such does suggest useful categories of forces. Such also suggests, because of its major inadequacies for our conflict management problem, where at least some new insights on relevant categories are required. We have found five categories of factors useful:

1. the need and demand for inventive ideas, inclusive of their statement for transmission to a relevant receiving unit in a language understandable by the latter;
2. the actual transmission of the message, its retranslation as often as is required, and the overcoming of obstacles to reach the location of invention;
3. the production of inventive ideas, new discussion frameworks, new environmental settings, new communication channels, and in general new conflict management procedures;
4. the spread of invention and know-how (as potential innovation) to using locations inclusive of translations and retranslations as required to be understandable by relevant receiving units and including the overcoming of apathy and resistances along the way; and
5. the implementation and effective use of potential innovations.

We now close this chapter with explicit recognition of the many important variables (factors) already discussed that we have not confronted. Among others, these comprise the whole range of cognitive variables that govern the behavior of diverse units: the inadequate ability of these units to absorb the knowledge concerning an invention; their limited knowledge (memory), truncated perceptions, and misperceptions; their apathy and lack of interest in the conflict problem; their inefficiency in production and their willingness to be satisfied with "far-from-optimal" solutions; and the like. Moreover, the process discussed here largely pertains to noncrisis situations. Invention is also relevant for crisis situations, and the process of invention in such situations must undoubtedly be significantly different in some respects.

Last, our discussion of invention has been divorced from the unique characteristics of any specific conflict situation and from the needed properties of a conflict management procedure to cope with these characteristics. Clearly, in part, these characteristics and properties define the vector of needs and demand, that is, the $\check{K}$, so that there is a unique vector associated with each conflict situation. And as a consequence, the desired invention may not relate to a conflict management procedure as a whole but rather to the addition of desirable properties to one or more specific conflict management procedures, or to the elimination of undesirable properties in them, or to new syntheses (fusion) or complexes of properties from two or more existing procedures.

Finally, with regard to the U.S.–Soviet arms control problem, we have noted, at each of the five stages discussed, one or two of the various difficulties in the invention (designing) and implementation of new conflict management procedures (quantitative, qualitative, or a combination of both).

References

Arrow, K. (1962) "The Economic Implications of Learning by Doing," *Review of Economic Studies* 29(3):155–73.

Brown, L. A. (1980) *Innovation Diffusion: A New Perspective*. London: Methuen.

Binswanger, H. P., V. W. Ruttan, and U. Ben-Zion (1978) *Induced Innovation*. Baltimore: Johns Hopkins.

Domanski, R. (1977) "The Diffusion of Technology and Innovation on the International Level." In *Peace and the Sciences*. Vienna: International Institute for Peace.

Ewers, H. J., and R. W. Wettemann (1980) "Innovation-Oriented Regional Policy." *Regional Studies* 14:161–79.

Fisher, R., and W. Ury (1978) *International Mediation: A Working Guide*. New York: International Peace Academy.

Fisher, R., and W. Ury (1981) *Getting to Yes*. Boston: Houghton Mifflin.

Goddard, J. B. (1980) "Industrial Innovation and Regional Economic Development in Britain." Discussion Paper No. 32, Centre for Urban and Regional Development Studies, University of Newcastle-upon-Tyne.

Hagerstrand, T. (1953) *Innovations forloppet ur Korologisk Synpunkt,* Gleerup (trans. by A. Pred as *Innovation Diffusion as a Spatial Process*). Chicago: University of Chicago Press, 1967.

Isard, W., and B. Burton (1986) "Regional Research and Development Revisited." In J. H. P. Paelinck (ed.), *Human Behaviour in Geographical Space*. London: Gower, pp. 27–44.

Isard, W., and P. Liossatos (1975) "Parallels from Physics for Space-Time Development Models: Part I." *Regional Science and Urban Economics* V(1):1–34.

Isard, W., and P. Liossatos (1979) *Spatial Dynamics and Optimal Space-Time Development*. New York: North Holland.

Kaniss, P. (1977) *Evolutionary Change in Hierarchical Systems: A General Theory*. Regional Science Studies Series, Cornell University.

Kennedy, C., and A. P. Thirwell (1972) "Surveys in Applied Economics: Technical Progress." *The Economic Journal* 82(325):11–72.

Pred, A. R. (1977a) "The Location of Economic Activity Since the Early Nineteenth Century: A City-systems Perspective." In B. Ohlin, P. O. Hesselborn, and P. M. Wijkman (eds.), *The International Allocation of Economic Activity*. Great Britain: Macmillan, pp. 127–47.

Pred, A. R. (1977b) *City Systems in Advanced Economies: Past Growth, Present Processes and Future Development Options.* New York: Halstead.

Ruttan, V. W. (1959) "Usher and Schumpeter on Invention, Innovation and Technological Change." *Quarterly Journal of Economics* 73(November): 596–606.

Schumpeter, J. A. (1939) *Business Cycles.* New York: McGraw-Hill.

Usher, A. P. (1954) *A History of Mechanical Inventions,* 2nd ed. Cambridge, MA: Harvard University Press.

Notation

Where a symbol has several meanings, the relevant meaning is clearly evident from the text.

Script

$\mathcal{C}$ coalition, bloc of nations, challenge
$\mathcal{H}$ Hamiltonian
$\mathcal{I}$ cognitive interaction (international arena)
$\mathcal{L}$ Lagrangian
$\mathcal{M}$ information stock, information subsystem
$\mathcal{P}$ perception of ( ), perceived item, element, magnitude
$\mathcal{R}$ real interaction (world market)
$\mathcal{S}$ social system

Roman/italic

a action, proposal, position in policy space, allowable error, a magnitude
a_{ij} input–output coefficient
$\{a_k\}$ joint action of other behaving units
$\{\bar{a}^K\}$ joint action of other groups
A action space, matrix of input–output coefficients
$\tilde{A}$ restricted action space
$\bar{A}$ inverse matrix
AP   appropriations
AT   attitude
Att   things to which a unit can attend
b item (purchase) for consumption, consumed item, amount of civilian goods, a parameter
$\flat$ overall orientation of group
B boundary, beliefs, belief system
$\bar{B}$ lower bound

506

b relevant beliefs, belief system

BP   bargaining power

B of P   balance of payments

c cost, amount of security produced

c-   prefix to indicate that value element that follows is viewed as commodity

C consumption, output of civilian goods, civilian casualties

C_0 consumption of civilian goods

d input of security as a good

d_i determinental relation ($i = 1, 2, \ldots$)

d as subscript or superscript to mean desired

d_{ij}, d^{IJ} distance between i and j or L and J, respectively

D demand, defense index, defense index function, difficulty (ease) of exit, domestic consumption

DC   diplomatic climate

DE   deficit

e state of environment, equilibrium point, compromise joint action, ratio of magnitudes, base of natural logarithms

E set of possible states of environment, exports, conflictual behavior events

$E(\ )$ expected value or magnitude of item contained in parentheses

Exp   expectations

EP   environmental program expenditures

f function, general symbol for exporter, destructive effectiveness

F filtering activity

g gain, grievance

$\bar{g}$ stock of commodity

G goals, government spending, gravitational constant

GDP   gross domestic product

GNP   gross national product

GRP   gross regional product

h general symbol for a commodity or informatiom

H hostility, international tension, heredity

H^J_{gh} input of composite good g in producing h in region J

i general symbol for an individual behaving unit or object

I general symbol for a group, investment, an interval, or interaction

IM   imports

IN   income

IV   investment value

j general symbol for a firm, producer, or economic sector (industry)

J general symbol for a nation, region, participant, or behaving unit

k general symbol to represent other behaving units, a coefficient, a fraction, or a fractional share

K stock of capital, knowledge

$\dot{k}$ rate of flow (over space) of knowledge

l commodity, labor input of an individual, labor as a commodity, a lower bound, an inertial coefficient

L general symbol for a nation, region, participant, or behaving unit; learning, labor, labor and other resources (in an aggregate sense)

m move, general symbol for a consumer

mc marginal cost

mr marginal revenue

mu marginal utility

M military (defense or arms) expenditures, migration

$\overline{M}$ responsibility set of military expenditure proposals

$\tilde{M}$ military expenditure proposal

Me memory

$\mathring{M}e$ active memory

MM millions

MMM billions (American)

n size of sample, general symbol for a firm or economic sector (industry)

N general symbol for a nation, region, participant, or behaving unit, leader's support area, resources absorbed (expenditures) by intelligence activities

o outcome, outcome function

p price, unit cost (purchase price), psychological sensation

$\tilde{p}$ fictitious price

pr probability

P production–consumption–trade subsystem

POP population

q decision weight, probability, commodity c-security, general symbol for agents

$\tilde{q}$ constant elasticity of substitution function magnitude representing amount of output, total inputs, utility

Q nation, region, or other participant; procedural rule for resolving conflicts; age; combined quantitative–qualitative index of capability of weaponry stock

r regret, revenue, probability, discount rate, forgetting rate, commodity c-respect

R resources (monetary), resolve, resistance (congestion) to entrance into a group

$\mathcal{R}$ resources (real)

$R\&D$ research and development

s saving ratio, stimulus, probability, shipment of a good, range (maximum spread) of alternatives, flow of information (at microlevel)

S stock of weaponry, nuclear missiles, state of system, general symbol of exporting nations

$\mathcal{S}$ minimum (maximizing) number of surviving missiles

Se security

SC summary cues

SG subgoal

t time point, a year

t_0 initial point of time

t_1 terminal point of time

$t + \theta$	a year θ years in the future
t.c.	transport cost
T	diplomatic time, a set, taxes
TR	transfers
u	utility, utility function
$\mathring{u}$	lower bound on utility
$\bar{u}$	upper bound
U	general symbol for nation or region, flow of information (on macrolevel)
$\mathring{U}$	spatial rate of change of U
UN	unemployment
UR	unrest
v	foreign aid expenditures, effectiveness in terms of civilian casualties, index of unattractive (push-out) features, a weight.
V	value added, value of winning
w	weight or index of attractive features
W	welfare, welfare function
x	location, position
$\bar{x}$	mean of samples
X	output (input–output model)
y	output (when positive) or input (when negative) in production plan (at microlevel), leader's proposal
Y	final demand in input–output model, output (at macrolevel)
z	object, item, relation, position, dummy variable
Z	political leader, mediator, actor
z_+	set of nonnegative integers

Greek

α	rate of depreciation, rate of decay, rate of forgetting, speed of adjustment
$\bar{\alpha}$	rate of retaliation, rate of launching
β	rate of discount, parameter, costate variable, ability at information processing, value of unit of capital
$\bar{\beta}$	firing rate
γ	rate of growth, depreciation factor, ability to handle multiplicity of variables
Γ	transition function, hypothetical world, responsibility set of growth rates
Δ	small change in, parameter
ϵ	a parameter, a constant, scaling factor, very small value
η	elasticity coefficient, exponent, element
θ	time period, aggression parameter, outcome function
θ_s	obstacles to search
λ	parameter, costate variable
Λ	type of weaponry
μ	true mean or value, costate variable, parameter
ν	elasticity coefficient, coefficient of friction, a magnitude
$\bar{\nu}$	prespecified satisficing level, allowable error in units of standard deviation

ν_h interaction in political arena

ξ ability at finding new information, index (or weighted average) of non-economic commodities received, velocity factor, a parameter

π payoff, net gain, revenue surplus

ρ reaction coefficient, share parameter, charge density

$\boldsymbol{\rho}$ matrix of reaction coefficients

σ standard deviation, elasticity of substitution

τ point of time, year, time period, probability

υ fraction of available resources, an element

ϕ mapping, function, probability density distribution

Φ cumulative density distribution

χ general variable representing military expenditures, change in military expenditures, stock of weaponry, change in stock of weaponry

Ψ time interval, mapping, function

ω reaction factor, coefficient, constant

Ω hypothetical world

$\digamma$ function

Selected mathematical symbols

$*, **$ optimal, most desired, equilibrium value

$\hat{\ }$ expected

$\subset$ contained in

$\gtrsim$ significantly greater than

$|\ |$ absolute value

$\#$ payoff matrix

$\exists$ there exists

$\in$ an element of

$\notin$ not an element of

$\cup$ union over all individuals

Author index

Subject index